Historism

By the same author

Machiavellism (1957)
(*Die Idee der Staatsräson in der neueren Geschichte*)

Historism

The Rise of a New Historical Outlook

Friedrich Meinecke

HERDER AND HERDER

1972
HERDER AND HERDER NEW YORK
232 Madison Avenue, New York 10016

Translated by J. E. Anderson
from the German edition,
Die Entstehung des Historismus,
published 1959
(R. Oldenbourg, Munich)

This edition first published 1972
by Routledge & Kegan Paul Ltd., London
No part of this book may be reproduced
in any form without permission from
the publisher, except for the quotation of
brief passages in criticism

ISBN 0 665 0049 9
Library of Congress Catalog Card Number: 73–186993
© this edition Routledge & Kegan Paul 1972
Printed in Great Britain

Dedicated to the memory of the University of Strasburg
in the days before the war

Have I not already written to you, 'Individuum est ineffabile', from which I derive a whole world?

(Goethe to Lavater, 1780)

Contents

Contents

Book two: The German Movement

Foreword

The transformation of the writing of history in the nineteenth century is to a large degree the work of the great German masters from Niebuhr and Boeckh to Mommsen and Burckhardt, from Savigny and Ranke to Max Weber and Troeltsch. Ideas are not born of ideas by parthenogenesis. The process which led to the new historical vision, and even more to its dominant influence over much of the political and intellectual life of the West, has its roots in great social and cultural changes which go back to the Renaissance and the Reformation, if not beyond. The rise in historical consciousness, the best known and most notorious outgrowths of which are the ideologies of nationalism and power politics, responded to the need at once to explain and to justify the open struggles of nations and classes in its day. Its beginnings can be traced to many lands, but it first found systematic expression among German thinkers and was historically connected with the rise of the national German State. Radical political developments are often preceded by a ferment in the realm of ideas, and it is in the German-speaking lands that the new sense of historical development developed into a powerful and influential current of ideas. Individual thinkers, and, after them, wider groups—academic, political, artistic, religious—began to conceive of all human activities as elements in unified, 'organic' social wholes, not static institutional structures, but dynamic processes of development of nations, cultures, classes—social 'organisms' held together by impalpable and complex relationships which characterised living social wholes, quasi-biological entities which defied analysis by the exact quantitative methods of chemistry or physics. Such forms of life, it was held, could be felt, or intuited, or understood by a species of direct acquaintance; they could not be taken to pieces and reassembled, even in thought, like a mechanism compounded of isolable parts,

obedient to universal and unaltering causal laws. The thinkers who
revolted against the central classical and Christian concept of a
world governed by a single, static Natural Law, in any one of its
many forms, stoic or Aristotelian, or Thomist, or the causal-mech-
anistic patterns of the French Enlightenment, were seldom unworldly
philosophers. They were, for the most part, deeply involved with the
political societies and nations to which they belonged; and they saw
their intellectual activity as bound up with the rise of a new order of
things in which the German peoples played a leading part. They were
acutely conscious of their own German roots in the Reformation, in
Pietism and the mystical and visionary movements that preceded it, in the localised, provincial, tradition-bound social,
political and religious life of German cities and principalities.
Above all, they were acutely aware of the differences between their
world and the universalism and scientific rationalism deeply embedded in the outlook of the civilisations west of the Rhine. As
scholars, critics, historians, they investigated, collected, described,
analysed, explained; as men and citizens they were caught up in the
social and political questions and struggles of their society. Whatever
their convictions, they did not isolate these functions from one
another: in varying degrees they were identified with the activities of
parties and movements, and were often linked by direct personal
relationships with their leaders. This gave particular life and force,
as well as, at times, considerable public influence to the points of
view that they were held to represent. It was the political commitment
of some of the major figures of the new historical school that (despite
the earnest efforts of some of them to preserve a degree of detachment) communicates to their historical works a sense of moral and
political direction, whether they are dealing with their own times or
with remote cultures and situations. While this may have been equally
true of historians in other countries—Macaulay and Grote, Michelet
and Guizot cannot be described as politically neutral writers—in
Germany this acquired the status of an almost official national philosophy of history. This applies, for all their differences, as much to
Niebuhr and Mommsen, Droysen and Max Weber as to such violently partisan writers as Treitschke or Sombart; and it is, in a
measure, no less true, for all his agonised desire to rise above immediate and ephemeral considerations, of the last great representative of this tradition, Friedrich Meinecke.

In his three celebrated masterpieces,[1] he addressed himself to some
of the central issues of his own time, and traced their origins and
development. In particular he described with exact and unassailable

[1] The two volumes that preceded the present work are *Weltbürgertum und
Nationalstaat* published in 1907 (in its English version, *Cosmopolitanism and*

learning the gradual waning of an older European outlook dominated by the notion of a timeless, unaltering Natural Law (disobeyed
by wilful rulers, individual or collective, only at a fearful cost) and
its supersession by the concept of the nation, conscious of its unique
individuality and its overriding claims, and answerable only to itself.
He gave a classical account of the tensions which this brought to
light between, on the one hand, commonly accepted universal human
values, the rights of individuals or groups and the general moral principles that governed human conduct, and, on the other, the claims of the
State which, in moments of crisis, comes into violent conflict with
the rules of common human morality—claims the satisfaction of
which alone, at whatever price, will ensure the security, the power
and the greatness of the nation to which statesmen owe their
primary allegiance. His discussion of this issue is throughout dominated by his awareness of the unresolved problem of the relationship
of what Savigny had called 'silently operating forces' which, in the
end, determine the direction of a society and of the development of
its members, to what he recognises as the freedom of action, within
historically determined limits, on the part of human beings, and,
consequently, of the corresponding degree of historical responsibility which must be attributed, or denied, to this or that individual
or group or policy. But the *idée maîtresse* that obsesses him, as it
obsessed his forerunners, is of the properties of those—for him the only
genuine—associations of men which possess each its own individual
laws of growth, its own unique 'organic' character—social wholes
which develop like plants, obedient each to its own specific nature,
and which can, therefore, neither be explained, nor understood, nor
maintained in the light of laws or principles which falsely assimilate
them to some generalised pattern that ignores their own peculiar
essence, the individual goals in terms of which they live and act,
values incommensurable with those of other societies or periods, in
terms of which alone all that they are and do can be explained or
justified. Inevitably he came to be profoundly troubled by the evident
irreconcilability of the moral relativism to which this seemed to lead,
and the allied notion that success alone—at times mere power—is the
sole arbiter of what truly counts and is worth living (and, it may be,
dying) for, with the need for something more than such subjectivism;
something more than values revealed to the capricious individual
intuition of an individual thinker or poet or statesman—the need for
common ground between men, a common purpose which, even if not
universally accepted, is at any rate valid for many men for long stretches

the *National State*, trs. Robert B. Kimber, with an Introduction by Felix Gilbert
(1970)), and *Die Idee der Staatsräson* published in 1924 (in its English version
Machiavellism, trs. Douglas Scott, Introduction by Dr W. Stark (London, 1957)).

of history, and can provide some approach to objectivity in determining basic values—greatness and littleness, good and evil, progress and retrogression. Meinecke saw the rise of the notion of individuality and variety of paths of development on the part of States—independent social organisms—as the greatest break in the continuity of European thought since the Reformation. And indeed, viewed in retrospect, it can scarcely be denied that the great movements by which the last two centuries have been violently swayed—traditionalism and pluralism, romanticism and the Promethean conception of man, anarchism as well as nationalism, individualist self-realisation no less than imperialism, racism, and all kinds of social and political irrationalism, all stem in varying degree from this vast revolt against what Meinecke calls 'the generalising view'—belief in scientific uniformities, or the sway of Natural Law, as well as the varieties of positivism, utilitarianism, rationalism, but above all the great monistic conception of the Universe as a single, unvarying system, intelligible in the light of reason to all men—if only they have eyes to see—at all times, in all conditions, everywhere.

In the volume devoted to the origins of the new historical consciousness, Meinecke sets himself to trace the new outlook from Leibniz and Voltaire, Montesquieu, Vico, and Burke to its final triumph in the works of the great German founders of the new historical method. Meinecke was a man of vast and disciplined erudition, with a degree of intellectual scruple and sensitiveness to the finest nuances of ideology and outlook uncommon even among his great predecessors: his essays on his three heroes, Möser, Herder, and especially Goethe, which form the greater part of the last panel of the great triptych, distinguished as they are by a delicate interweaving of description, ideas and historical circumstance, of the personal temperament of individual thinkers with the quality of life of the society in and for and about which they wrote, demand a good deal more of the reader than the sweeping generalisations of bolder and often more superficial historians of ideas. His style, like the subject matter, is complex and, at times, opaque (Mr Anderson's translation is a heroic achievement), the method, at times, unfocused and impressionistic. Meinecke is intensely anxious not to fall into the errors he castigates in the hated Natural Law, mechanistic, all-levelling, eighteenth-century Encyclopaedist tradition. He is fearful of oversimplifying, of concepts that cut into the living flesh of social or individual sentiment or ideology which calls for all the powers of the most responsive 'individualising observation' (to use his phrase)—of vivisecting it with the surgical knife of some dogmatic theory or ideology. He is anxious to convey what Möser called 'the total impression', which cannot be obtained by mere analysis of the parts, still less by the application of some Procrustean historical pattern, which fails to convey the tone, the unique colour, what the German historicist thinkers referred to as the *Zeitstil* or *Volksstil* which permeates all the activities of an individual or a society, its sciences as much as its arts, Richelieu's dispatches as much as his love letters—he wishes to avoid constricting and distorting formulas, fanatical faith in laws that social change must obey, into which all the facts must be compressed, no matter how much the subject matter may resist such schematism. Meinecke draws his portraits with an infinity of tiny strokes; and even though the main lines emerge, those who are accustomed to histories of ideas composed by analytic thinkers who operate with sharp definitions of terms, divisions into types, lines of ideological descent boldly and vividly presented, may occasionally be lost in this great forest, even though the general shape traced by the author need never, in fact, be lost sight of. Those who are prepared to follow Meinecke's carefully qualified, but never prolix or repetitive, prose will be handsomely rewarded. What this method serves to keep alive is an unbroken sense of reality—of the flow of social, political, artistic, religious, personal life and its complex patterns as it affects, and is affected by, beliefs, ideals, their vision of themselves and their past by individuals and communities—a sense of the concrete, many-faceted, changing, never completed, life of societies.

No doubt the view of history as the development of social, political and moral organisms—of Aristotelian entelechies the interplay of which constitutes the growth of the human spirit—a neo-Platonic-Hegelian vision—is only one of many conceptions of what men live by, and likely to be found wanting by those who demand stricter methods of verification by the application of empirical or scientific tests, even if the results so obtained do not answer all our questions, or do not answer them at a sufficiently profound level of imaginative enquiry. Nevertheless, there is no doubt that, apart from its historical and political influence and its transforming impact on general ways of thought and feeling in the West, this approach (whatever its metaphysical shortcomings) did more to enlarge the horizon and perspectives of historians than the positivist doctrines against which it reacted so strongly. Meinecke was brought up in the faith of this movement, and used its own canons, like Dilthey (by whom he was profoundly impressed) and Max Weber and Rickert, to describe and resurrect its origins for scientifically minded generations which had begun to be exceedingly sceptical about its validity.

What gives extraordinary vitality to Meinecke's account of the revolution of the historical consciousness in the beginning of the last century is the fact that he himself was no less deeply agonised by the problems that he treated than those who first addressed themselves to them. He grew up, as Professor Hinrichs in his most revealing Introduction tells us, in the heyday of Prussian nationalism by which he was deeply affected. Such problems as the relation of values (both of historians and of men in general) to objectively established facts and to the conclusions of the natural sciences; the relativity of different outlooks and of the values that they embody; the conflict between the claims of the national and international order, of the State as against those of other associations, or of individual rights; the justification of the use of force, in particular of war; the apparent incompatibility between the methods of the natural sciences and those of humane studies, and the implications of this for political and individual morality; all these problems arose for him not merely as a historian or as a student of historical method, but as a German and a human being; he was tormented by them all his life. His conscience on these matters is never wholly clear: he does not try to evade painful issues: he patiently searches for solutions; he hopes to find some man of genius who will solve or resolve these problems of theory and practice to which he does not pretend to have found a final answer. The time at which he wrote this book was one of crisis, which consciously or unconsciously offered a parallel to that earlier critical turning point in German history, when the German *Geist* was hemmed in on one side by the levelling spirit of French revolutionary and Napoleonic centralisation and rational organisation, contemptuous of tradition and of the individuality of different societies—together with the complementary influence of British industrialism and its destruction of ancient ties, and on the other, threatened by the menacing barbarous great power in the East. If the German 'spirit' won this war on two fronts, and established the great unified German state, it had done so at what might be thought by some to have been a fearful cost in moral values. After 1918, with Bolshevism in the East, and once again what he regarded as a shallow liberal universalism in the West, Meinecke put all his hopes in a mysterious synthesis of the claims of individual liberty and morality with the needs and values of public life in the majestic historical march of the great organic whole—the national state. For him it represented the central educative, spiritualising agency which shaped men and alone made possible the development of all that they lived for—moral goals and feelings, art, personal relationships, the conquest of brute nature within and without. He spoke about the Western civilisation; but what he cared for most was, of course, Germany, her culture and her survival: he feared equally the Scylla of timeless, abstract principles that took no account of life and change, and the Charybdis of relativism that destroyed morality or reduced its goals to matters, in the end, of subjective temperament or inclination. This conflict shaped itself in his mind as the tension between men and historically evolving institutions that are the same men conceived in social and historical terms. *Historismus* is the conception that with passionate, but at times painfully uncertain, hope he looked to as the solution ; as it was in 1815 and 1848, so it must be in 1918 and 1932. This is the vision that communicates an almost religious fervour to his entire conception of history, and infects his prose style; it derives from Herder and Ranke, rather than his idolised master, the calm, unhistorical Goethe. For a time he seemed to believe that Hegel had managed to heal the wound that Machiavelli had inflicted upon the body politic of Europe by demonstrating the irreconcilability of personal and political morality; he almost managed to persuade himself that the great metaphysician had somehow succeeded in satisfying the claims of political and personal—human—morality in a sublime synthesis; or if Hegel did not succeed, then this was achieved, in his own intuitive, unsystematic, but concrete and miraculous fashion of which only a man of genius is capable, by the incomparable Goethe. He worshipped Bismarck, whose policies seemed to him—as to so many German academics of the time—to have created conditions in which alone the German nation could realise its character and destiny. In 1914 he was among those who looked with mounting hope to the fulfilment of the great Prussian dream. 1918 brought home the consequences of such views. Cautious and conservative by temper, he was not a chauvinist; he accepted the Weimar Republic and supported it loyally to the end. He was a patriot and a nationalist, but he was not prepared for inhumanity. State authority had its limits; a very old man, he did not bow before Hitler or Hitlerism. His bitter reflections after the final débacle is a sad and depressing document. Read objectively, it is a statement of the bankruptcy of much of what he and his generation of German scholars had stood for. Meinecke was an unswervingly honest man, and although the prejudices of his time and class shine through, his unerring—sometimes painful—consciousness of where the true moral centre of gravity of a given social or moral situation lies, seldom fails him. This together with his prodigious learning and feeling for the complex web of ideas, movements, institutions, events and personalities of the principal actors, makes his account of the rise of German historical thought a still unsuperseded classic. In the dark days that followed the German defeat in 1918, he plainly found relief in returning to the finest hour of German cultural life and the new vision of history which is its heart. His task, in theory, was only to describe, only to record, the achievements and aspirations of others; but in fact they were his own. The story is told by a participant, not by a mere observer. The paean to Goethe, even the excuses Meinecke offers for the declared distaste for history and the distinct lack of veneration for the authority of the State on the part of that otherwise almost perfect being, seem to spring from a pathetic wish to save what he can from the shipwreck of the German culture in which he was brought up, to return to the heritage of poets and scholars, the degradation of which sends him back to a scrutiny of its beginnings in happier and better times. The period of which he writes is the springtime of the great development which, by the time he completed his three great treatises, had ended in darkness and an unimaginable disaster. In the period with which this volume is concerned the romantic German dream is still distant from the terrible nightmare into which it would later turn: hence the fresh and glowing colours with which he paints the pioneers of genius in whose society he delights to move, founders of the school of which he was, and probably knew himself to be, the last authentic master.

Isaiah Berlin

Introduction

Friedrich Meinecke once confessed with reference to his last work, *Die Entstehung des Historismus*, that the questions discussed in it had been his preoccupation for some decades, not only in his professional capacity, but also 'as a guiding principle of life in the highest sense of that expression'.[1] For, in dealing with the historical method and the modern historical outlook, we are concerned, he maintained, not only with a scientific principle and its application, but also with a guiding principle of life, a view of human life as a whole, from which that scientific principle arose in the first place'.[2] For 'scientific history only uses what has first been at work as a principle and guide, as a means of knowledge and an attitude, in the inner life of modern man, and as such goes on producing an effect that extends far beyond the merely professional scientific sphere'.[3]

The question of the growth of historism thus involves an intellectual and spiritual revolution of the most universal nature, and deals with the development of ways of thinking and feeling previously quite unknown. These were a prelude to the growth of the historical sense and modern scientific history, and they formed its necessary historical basis—and a basis for other developments as well. This historical fact of new definite guiding principles of life breaking through an older and contrasting level of human thought and feeling which had up till then been accepted as absolutely true—this again presented Meinecke (to repeat his own words) with 'a problem of life in the highest sense'. In other words, his early and lifelong concern with this problem was closely interwoven with his personal thought

[1] On the subject of the history of the rise of historism, and Schleiermacher's idea of individuality see: *Vom geschichtlichen Sinn und vom Sinn der Geschichte* (2nd ed., 1939), p. 95.
[2] *Ibid.*, p. 96. [3] *Ibid.*, p. 95.

and the problems of his own time. This raises the further question of the biographical foundations of *Die Entstehung des Historismus*; and the question is at once seen to be wider when we consider Meinecke's own repeated indications that his three great books on the history of thought—*Weltbürgertum und Nationalstaat, Die Idee der Staatsräson in der neueren Geschichte* (English translation (1957), *Machiavellism*) and *Die Entstehung des Historismus*—all had their origin in a common source. During his work on *The Historical Method* in 1932, Meinecke celebrated his seventieth birthday, and friends presented him with an original painting by Hans Thomas, depicting 'the smooth-flowing Upper Rhine near Säckingen, where it passes through broad meadows with thickly-wooded banks'. In his speech of thanks,[1] Meinecke said:

> It was by the Upper Rhine that I first faced all those historical questions to which my whole subsequent life's work has been devoted. I do not know if I shall be able to leave behind me in anything but a fragmentary form the attempt I am now making to find an answer to the last and most difficult of these questions, but the one that lies closest to my heart.

The same thoughts are expressed in the second volume of his reminiscences concerning his time at Strasburg (1901–6).

> The roots of the three works dealing with the history of thought, which I was able to publish in the three decades between 1907 and 1936, go back into the ideas that passed through my mind in this place. They were partly leading thoughts already firmly rooted in my mind, and partly indicated a shift of interest towards new and enticing phenomena of the historical world to which I had hitherto been a complete stranger.[2]

It was at Strasburg that he conceived the idea embodied in his first book, *Weltbürgertum und Nationalstaat*. It contains a sentence—to which we shall return—in which Meinecke subsequently saw the germ of his *Entstehung des Historismus*.[3] It was in that happy year 1905, when he visited Florence at Easter time, that he was seized by the thought of Machiavelli and 'the oppressive problem of power

[1] Printed circular letter, Berlin–Dahlem, end November 1932.

[2] *Strassburg, Freiburg, Berlin 1901–1919. Erinnerungen* (1949), p. 40. Similarly in *Die Entstehung des Historismus*, see below, p. lxi: 'Everything that is common to the three books goes back to the first conceptions of my happy years at Strasburg a generation ago. I dedicate my book to these memories, and the few survivors of that period to whom I send my greetings will know how important for our lives was the intellectual constellation gathered together in those days in the cultural life of the Upper Rhineland'.

[3] *Strassburg, Freiburg, Berlin*, p. 191.

politics in the midst of a world so full of beauty'. It was this journey, too, that formed a starting-point for his later *Idee der Staatsräson*.[1] In this same year, 1905, his *Zeitalter der deutschen Erhebung* became linked[2] with the idea (already in its formative stage) behind *Weltbürgertum und Nationalstaat;* and it was in this year that he apparently began the first direct approach to the great problems dealt with in *Die Entstehung des Historismus*. Meinecke arranged in his seminar a small celebration of the hundred-and-first anniversary of Schiller's death, in which he took for his subject Schiller's inaugural address at Jena on the nature of universal history.

> The spirit of Schiller was very close to us that day at every point. The progressive and enlightened optimism with which he looked out on world history could no longer be reduced to the same denominator as our historical realism. . . . Since then I have been turning over in my mind the things that separate us from, and those that unite us with him in our present-day historical outlook.[3]

It is clear, then, that behind the *Entstehung des Historismus* there was in Meinecke's thought 'a problem of life in the highest sense'. Furthermore, it is clear that the *Entstehung des Historismus* had grown from the same intellectual roots as his previous two works on the history of ideas; and in all three works the theme is that of new, concrete, individual ways of thought in conflict with the older abstract and absolute approach. We are therefore led to enquire whether there was some dominating problem of life in Meinecke's thought as a whole, of which these three great books depict different, yet essentially related, aspects. But this question, again, can only be answered along historical lines, by an enquiry into Meinecke's own inner development. In the course of this we shall see that the source of this basic problem—even where his book on historism is concerned—is shown by the details given in his autobiography to lie further back in the past than his years on the Upper Rhine.

Meinecke once spoke of a process of loosening that went on throughout his life in respect of his inner relationship to the world of his North German and Prussian homeland.[4] Of all the various, but closely connected, components in the circle of his parents' house and home—orthodox piety, a conservatism that was very loyal to the throne, and a Christian-Socialist outlook—the religious support was

[1] *Ibid.*, p. 43.
[2] See the reference to *Das Zeitalter der deutschen Erhebung* in *Weltbürgertum und Nationalstaat* (3rd ed., 1915), p. 20, note 1.
[3] *Strassburg, Freiburg, Berlin*, pp. 46 ff.
[4] *Erlebtes 1862–1901* (1941), p. 95.

the first to give way. Meinecke tells us of the struggle which took place about the time of his confirmation (1878) to find a philosophy of life, and subsequently of that with his father, who was much concerned with his son's spiritual welfare and sought by every possible means to indoctrinate him with the orthodox piety which was his own source of inspiration and happiness.[1] Here, as has so often been the case, an excess of 'churchiness' had precisely the opposite effect to what was intended. The religious links with his home were broken for ever,[2] whilst the Prussian–conservative–royalist foundations and the sense of social responsibility aroused by the Christian-Socialist Party socialism stood the test over a long period, if not for the whole of his career.

But what kind of an intellectual world did this young man look out upon in the late 1870s, after he had turned away from the orthodox ecclesiastical standpoint? The foreground of the intellectual stage had been occupied since the middle of the century by a materialistic, positivist or pantheistic natural science, which had 'enclosed the universe within the brazen fetters of a mechanistic causality'.[3] Meinecke as a young man first met this spirit of what was then an up-to-date scientific doctrine in the field of poetry, especially in the poems of Wilhelm Jensen and Wilhelm Jordan, two thoroughly derivative writers, of whom Jordan more especially stood for the plea that poetry of the mythological age should be superseded by a modern 'poetry of scientific knowledge'. The product of this trend was a kind of didactic poetry, combining materialist and Darwinian thought with a nationalistic Niebelungen romantic background to form a kind of 'German Faith' that was antagonistic to Christianity. These men acted on the youthful Meinecke merely as an intellectual catalyst, 'like a spark falling into gunpowder':[4] they awakened in him a philosophical sense in place of the Christian religious outlook which had failed to develop.[5] From them he drew a 'very confused and immature pantheism';[6] but he did not acquiesce in their demands— echoed also by genuine poets such as G. Keller and Theodor Storm—that the human soul should bow before the god of Natural Law which now occupied the Almighty's throne. The youthful Meinecke had indeed lost his belief in the God of the Bible who is a personal worker of miracles and therefore interferes with the normal course of nature and history; but he still kept his belief in a divine background to the world disclosed in 'the world of ideals'.[7] This first speculative beginning led him on through Preger's *Geschichte der deutschen Mystik im Mittelalter* to historical phenomena 'which

[1] *Ibid.*, p. 74. [2] *Ibid.*, p. 80. [3] *Ibid.*, p. 75.
[4] *Ibid.* [5] *Ibid.*, p. 76. [6] *Ibid.*, p. 75.
[7] *Ibid.*, p. 76.

appeared to be related in content';[1] and thence to the pantheistic sects of the Middle Ages, and on to the Gnostics and their connection with Neo-Platonic philosophy.[2] Clearly, then, he had a deep and twofold experience: on the one hand, there was the iron framework of strict causality taught by the natural sciences and materialism; on the other, a spark of what he felt to be divine in his own breast, proceeding from the same divine underlying basis of the world, from which springs the realm of ideals; yet in his thinking, the natural and the spiritual were still linked with one another by a somewhat vague pantheism. Meinecke left school a freethinker, but 'feeling a need to interpret the world along idealist lines'; yet somewhat defiant, and proud of his right to a freedom of conscience which gave him such a stern sense of personal responsibility—the latter an inheritance from his Protestant background, bequeathed to him by his father in spite of all the well-meant pressure that he had put upon him in his upbringing.[3]

The next stage was ushered in by a course of lectures given by Droysen, on 'The methodological and encyclopedic approach to history', which the young student attended. In these, the famous teacher awoke in the pupil on two occasions something that was already dormant but had not yet taken clear shape.[4] The first time this happened was when Droysen was holding forth as follows:

> If we call everything that a single person is and has and produces A, this consists of $a + x$, where a includes all that comes to him from outward circumstances (his country, his race, his period and so on), and the minute x his own contribution, the work of his own freewill. But however small (almost to vanishing point) this x may be, it is of infinite value, and from the moral and human point of view, the only thing of value. The colours, brush and canvas used by Raphael were made of materials that he had not created, and he had learnt how to use them for drawing and painting from such and such masters; the idea of the Virgin, saints and angels had been taken over from the Church's tradition; and such and such a convent engaged him to paint a picture for a particular sum of money. But the fact that such an occasion, such materials and technical conditions, such traditional models were used to create the marvels of the Sistine Chapel, shows the infinite worth of the infinitesimal x in the formula $A = a + x$.[5]

---

[1] *Ibid.*   [2] *Ibid.*, pp. 76 ff.   [3] *Ibid.*, p. 81.
[4] *Ibid.*, pp. 86 ff.
[5] J. G. Droysen, *Historik: Vorlesungen über Enzyklopädie und Methodologie der Geschichte*, ed. R. Hübner (2nd ed., 1943), pp. 397 ff.

'That's it!' wrote Meinecke in his reminiscences; and he was over-
joyed at that period to discover 'this secret of personality, which
forms the basis of all historical achievement'.[1] This was the first
upsurge of the idea of individuality as the key to historical thinking
in Meinecke's mind, which was subsequently to carry it far beyond
Droysen's concept of individuality, conceived as it was in rather more
ethical terms. The other point in Droysen's lectures which kindled a
flame in the mind of the youthful Meinecke was its conclusion,

> that we are not like the natural scientists, who have all the
> means for carrying out experiments; we can only search, and
> go on searching. Then it follows that even the most thorough
> research can only reveal the most fragmentary glimpse of the
> past, and that history and our knowledge of it are poles apart. . . .
> It would discourage us, but for one fact—we can at any rate
> follow the development of *thought* in history, even in spite of
> the fragmentary nature of our material. . . . Thus we do not
> arrive at a picture of the past as such, but only our interpreta-
> tion and intellectual reconstruction of it.[2]

Droysen sees in history a coherent whole made up of the acts of will
proceeding from ethical individuals, but considers that it does not
come into existence except through the decisions of the historian,
who adopts a consciously moral standpoint. But the youthful
Meinecke, in a very fortunate misunderstanding of these words of
Droysen's, took them as a recognition of history as essentially the
history of thought and of ideas; for as an old man he was to confess
that his inclination towards the history of thought was a kind of
inborn 'original sin'.[3] And lastly, this history of thought was conceived as a history of problems—an insight that was also due to the
inspiration derived from Droysen, which proved a permanent
driving-force in all his scientific work: 'this longing to tackle the
pressing and torturing problem that demanded an answer'.[4] The real
historical question (so Droysen had taught)

> has a far wider content than anything I have learnt; it is a kind
> of presentiment that comes to me out of the sum total of all
> that I have inwardly lived through and experienced. That is
> why I have to ask these questions, and why I put them in this
> way.

[1] *Erlebtes 1862–1901*, p. 87.
[2] J. G. Droysen, *op. cit.*, p. 316. The version of this passage printed in Hübner's edition of the *Historik* was taken from Meinecke's college note-book.
[3] *Erlebtes 1862–1901*, p. 77.   [4] *Ibid.*, p. 88.

This is where the inner connection between the personal and the contemporary problems of the historian, and the problems of history that press upon him and demand to be dealt with (pointed out in this passage by Droysen) became so significant for Meinecke. It is therefore quite understandable that the short outline of the historian's craft which Droysen put before his audience remained for Meinecke 'a treasure-chest' which constantly accompanied him, along with the poems of his beloved Mörike.[1]

Again, according to what Meinecke tells us, Droysen's lectures reflected a last bright glow of the German idealism belonging to the great era of the Wars of Liberation, and shone on a professional activity that was 'in danger of becoming colourless'[2] by reason of the positivist outlook prevailing at that time. This dominant contemporary climate, 'seeking to give the humanities a highly exact and empirically certain character', was also partly responsible for the choice of Meinecke's line of study.[3]

> The idea of the creative spirit individualised in the manifold marvels of history and human life was still admittedly marginal among the various influences then at work upon me: it did not vitally penetrate all the teaching I received. True, the spark that the aged Droysen had kindled in me still burnt on in my quiet hours, but was obscured by the demands of study.[4]

Dilthey, who would have been the best man to feed this flame and lead the way through the study of Kant on to post-Kantian metaphysics, was left on one side as far as Meinecke was concerned, because 'at that time he was generally considered rather abstruse and unintelligible'.[5]

Another short period of crisis was needed to produce a further clarification of the basic idealist position. This came during the time that Meinecke was teaching in the household of the Pomeranian landowner von Oertzen, in whom he saw visibly embodied 'the Christianity he had experienced at home but had hitherto decisively rejected', and saw it afresh as 'a wonderful power for making it possible to lead a godly life', so much so that it turned his thoughts for a brief moment towards a possible switch round of his studies to theology.[6] After a day or two this thought of a complete change was put aside, and Meinecke's 'free idealism' emerged victorious from this last confrontation with dogmatic Christianity. It was a struggle that clarified his thought and also enabled him to take up a new position. He 'cast off his original pantheistic shell' by deciding that

[1] *Ibid.*, p. 91.   [2] *Ibid.*, p. 87.   [3] *Ibid.*, p. 119.   [4] *Ibid.*
[5] *Ibid.*   [6] *Ibid.*, p. 129.

there was no simple answer to the question of the manner in which the divine principle is active in the world, and came to the conclusion that although it existed, it was not recognisable in its actual connection with the world, which could not be thought of as a directly divine creation, but only as having some relationship to the divine.[1] And here we are confronted with a root problem for Meinecke's thought: how could it be that the free intellect in all its spontaneity, moral consciousness and creativity was so interwoven and intertwined with the biological and mechanistic causality of the total world-framework? It is the problem of the dualistic appearance of a transcendental unity, the question of the more detailed relationship between a and x in the historical individuality that creates culture. This is the problem which the mature Meinecke of the year 1925 could still express as follows:

> Culture and nature—we can even say God and nature—are no doubt a unity, but a unity in which there is division. God wrestles His way up out of nature with sighing and groaning and laden with sin, and is therefore in danger at any moment of sinking back into nature. That would seem to be the last word for the ruthless and for the honest observer; but it cannot be altogether the last word. Only a faith that has become more and more universal in its content and is ready to go on wrestling with doubt can win through to the assurance that there is a transcendental solution for this problem of life and culture that appears to us so insoluble. But we have lost the belief that any philosopher has provided, or can provide, this transcendental solution.[2]

But pure history was not as yet to be the field in which the youthful Meinecke was to solve this problem, in the ultimate analysis the problem of what was eternal in his own personality and in this transitory world. In his own professional province he was a specialist in the history of Brandenburg and Prussia, whose views were still naturally those of Prussian academic patriotism, though he was already inclining to shift his scientific emphasis from the age of absolutism as seen through the eyes of Droysen and Koser, to the age of liberation and the German Christian circle and Frederick William IV. In Droysen's interpretation, with its reduction of all actions to something extremely material, Meinecke could find no room for the deeper psychological insight into the souls of individual statesmen;[3] but what Frederick William IV had stood for had still

---

[1] *Ibid.*

[2] 'Kausalitäten und Werte in der Geschichte' (1925), in *Schaffender Spiegel: Studien zur deutschen Geschichtsschreibung und Geschichtsauffassung* (1948), p. 82.

[3] *Erlebtes 1862–1901*, p. 69.

been a spiritual force in the world of his family home. It was in connection with a current intellectual problem of the time that Meinecke as a young man first tried to clarify his own position. The question at issue was the contemporary dispute between the historical and the natural science interpretations of the world and the meaning of life. In the words of Wilhelm Windelband,

> the controversy was at its hottest where it came to the point of finally deciding to what extent an individual person owed the essential worth of his life to his own self, or to the overriding circumstances of his environment. Universalism and Individualism again came into violent conflict, as in the Renaissance.[1]

This opposition culminates in the question 'in what sense and within what limits the *life of the soul* can be subject to the methods of cognition belonging to the natural sciences; for this is the first point at which the claim of these methods of thought to have sole philosophical validity must be decided.' The materialist and positivist thinkers were making great efforts 'to consider even man's social life, historical development and the general circumstances of intellectual existence from the point of view of natural science'. The thesis for Meinecke's State university examination in 1887,[2] probably set by Dilthey, but at Meinecke's own request, was as follows: 'A comparison between the methods in the natural sciences and in the humanities'. Ever since the days of Droysen's lectures, this problem had confronted the youthful Meinecke.[3] He accordingly introduced his theme by examining whether the methods of natural science were also valid for the exploration of the mental life of man with material drawn from 'the movements of the day'; but it is clear that for him there was at the back of all this a central problem of his life, for he remarks that 'the deepest questions of human life are often broached by the apparently most innocent and innocuous controversies'. To Meinecke, the heart of the problem seems to be the freedom of the will, for if the network of strict causality in the sense maintained by natural science is to extend without a break over the field of history, then all spontaneous happenings must be ruled out. Even if one admits that the world of morality and history are partly subject to the laws of strict causality,

[1] Wilhelm Windelband, *Lehrbuch der Geschichte der Philosophie*, quoted here in the 9th and 10th eds (1921), p. 528.

[2] Friedrich Meinecke's literary remains in the Berlin *Hauptarchiv*. Reproduced in shorter and revised form in the *Vossische Zeitung* (1887), Sunday supplements, nos 48 and 49 to nos 555 and 567 of 27 Nov. and 4 Dec. In the 5th volume of this present edition, which will contain Meinecke's essay on the philosophy of history, Eberhard Kessel will publish this work for the first time, with some consideration of the newspaper version as well.

[3] *Erlebtes 1862–1901*, p. 132.

one is straight away brought up against the difficult question 'whether there also exists, along with this sum-total of conditions that influence our actions, a small—it may be infinitely small—x of personal and genuinely spontaneous activity that directs what we do'. And Meinecke, falling back upon Droysen and quoting his illustration of the Sistine Chapel, affirms this so to be 'of immeasurable force', for it would include the entire moral worth of man, his unique value as a whole. In Meinecke's view, the ground for assuming the existence of such a spontaneous x is the existence of a moral consciousness.

> It is a mysterious sensation. The scene below surveyed from the watchtower of our observing mind is the world of causality. Only up here in its lofty seat is our self-consciousness, whence all perception and all thought proceeds—the very negation of that law, which determines everything below. . . . That claim of our immediate feeling does not come under the jurisdiction of reason. There is no question of a plaintiff or defendant standing before a judge, but of two parties confronting one another, each of whom has an equal right to plead its claim to life. . . . They are two unequal sons of one mother; both of them are rooted in the mental life of man. Feeling and moral conscience stand confronting the web of causality, in which reason must needs operate by the pursuit of strict logical processes.

These are sentences of great importance, not only because they are part of the earliest expression of Meinecke's theory of history, which runs through in a direct line to his final essays 'Kausalitäten und Werte in der Geschichte' (1925) and 'Geschichte und Gegenwart' (1933), but also because they are a direct pointer to Meinecke's own problems concerning life and the intellect. The mental life of man is the common mother of two unequal, mutually hostile sons, who yet stand on a footing of equal rights. On the one hand the intellect, on the other direct feeling and moral consciousness. The former takes its stand upon the universal reign of law; the latter on freedom, spontaneity and individuality. This strongly stressed and strongly felt dualism in human nature between the law-making intellectual powers and the individualising and intuitive powers of the soul is probably also traceable to Meinecke's own personal predisposition, shaped as it was both by his rationalistic inheritance and the Romantic or Late-Romantic inclinations of his character and disposition.[1] Meinecke's early conception of individuality is thus still strongly ethical, under the influence of Droysen and Kant; but we shall have to follow up the gradual change in his outlook, and the broadening

[1] *Ibid.*, pp. 12, 44, 77.

and deepening that took place. The central problem for Meinecke was to be the contrast between universal law and individual spontaneity. Here, it first presented itself to him as a problem of freewill, of freedom and necessity, and assumed the garb of a scientific controversy between two methods conditioned by the methodological issues of his time. This problem was to assume the most varied forms, and was destined to find its highest and most universal expression in the contrast between nature and culture.

While he was working on his first treatise on a theory of history Meinecke read the first volume of Wilhelm Dilthey's *Einleitung in die Geisteswissenschaften*, and in so doing gained permanent access to the great philosopher of the cultural and intellectual world. One can well understand that Meinecke should have attributed the inspiration of his first theoretical work to both Droysen and Dilthey[1] when one is confronted in the *Einleitung in die Geisteswissenschaften* by sentences such as these, which proved so formative in Meinecke's thought:[2]

For the motive force behind the customary view of these intellectual disciplines as a unity clearly marked off from those of the natural sciences is a pointer to the depth and totality of human selfconsciousness. Man, as yet unaffected by any examination of the origins of the world of thought, already finds in his self-conciousness the sovereignty of the will, responsibility for his actions, a power to subject everything to the process of thought and to offer spiritual resistance as lord of the free castle of his personality which distinguish him from nature as a whole. Within this realm of nature he sees himself, to borrow a phrase from Spinoza, as an *imperium in imperio*. And as the only firmly existing fact, as far as he is concerned, is that of consciousness, this independence of the mental world operative within him constitutes the sole worth and purpose of his life; each of his actions aims at the creation of autonomous mental facts. Thus he separates from the kingdom of nature a realm of history, where, in the midst of the network of objective necessity that constitutes nature, freedom flashes forth at innumerable places throughout the whole. It is here that the actions of the will stand in contrast to the mechanical sequence of natural changes, which already contains from the beginning all that develops throughout its course. The will is able to exert a force and make sacrifices which the individual appreciates even in his present experience; and these acts of will do really produce results, and do really bring about developments in the person

[1] *Ibid.*, p. 132.   [2] *Ibid.*, p. 6.

and in humanity. They go far beyond the empty and barren recurrence of natural sequences in the human consciousness, which seems to be the ideal of historical progress worshipped by the idolaters of a purely mechanical development of intellect.

But over and above this basic attitude Meinecke was to discover in Dilthey two other elements that proved of great importance in the development of his thought. In the first place, there was the enlargement of the concept of individuality from Droysen's predominantly moral interpretation to a broader conception of a psycho-physical whole representing an infinite world which 'in the ultimate analysis contains within itself the boundless realm of nature',[1] and constitutes a symbiosis of biological, mechanical and mental causality.[2] It was probably in this connection that Meinecke was first confronted with Dilthey's dictum *individuum est ineffabile*[3]—Dilthey speaks here of the 'unique quality of each of these separate individuals who are active at any and every point in the boundless cosmos of the mind'.[4] This strengthening and deepening of the concept of individuality was one element that Dilthey managed to communicate to Meinecke as a young man. The other element was no less important. It was the 'natural system' of the humanities, which first appears in this book of Dilthey's. In this work he shows how in recent times the mediaeval metaphysical interpretation of the course of history and the doctrine of the State and of society was replaced by the 'natural system' based upon the concept of Natural Law; and that this change took place after men had become aware of the contradiction between the old metaphysics and the methods of the new natural sciences.[5] As interpreted by Dilthey at that time the 'natural system' did not as yet take account of the formative influence of Neo-Stoicism, but simply arose through the transference of the mechanistic concept of causality in the natural sciences to the human individual and to his psychological, social and political life.

> The method (says Dilthey) by which the 'natural system' dealt with religion, law, morality and the State was an incomplete method. It was predominantly based upon the mathematical procedures that had proved so extraordinarily successful in the world of mechanical explanation. . . . The basis of these procedures was an *abstract scheme of human nature*, which sought to explain the facts of this historical life of man in terms of few and rather general psychic components. . . .[6]

---

[1] *Ibid*. p. 29. [2] Especially pp. 14, 17, 19. [3] *Ibid*., p. 29.
[4] *Ibid*. [5] *Ibid*. pp. 373 ff.
[6] *Ibid*. p. 379. The italics are Dilthey's.

In this conception of a 'natural system' governing the history of thought introduced to Meinecke by Dilthey, he was confronted with another scheme of thought alongside the mechanistic–naturalistic network of strict causality. Though it was connected with the latter, it contrasted strongly with the individualising scheme of thought that he had already adopted. This was the concept of Natural Law, of which Dilthey wrote: 'The fundamental mistake made by the old school of thinkers concerned with the Natural Law was to isolate individuals in this fashion and then to put them together in a mechanical manner so as to constitute society'.[1] The contrasted elements of natural science and the humanities, causality and spontaneity, nature and culture, became even further emphasised in this opposition between the concept of Natural Law and an individualising scheme within the humanities themselves.

And there is a further side to this contrast which we must now examine. We must begin by once more recalling Windelband's words pointing out that the conflict between a natural-scientific and a historical outlook on the world broke out most violently at the point where it was a question of

> finally deciding to what extent an individual person owed
> the essential worth of his life to his own self, or to the over-
> riding circumstances of his environment. Universalism and In-
> dividualism again came into violent conflict, as in the Renais-
> sance.

This question of the supremacy of the individual over, or his subordination to, the universality of law was also a form of the opposition that so powerfully obsessed Meinecke between individual powers and supra-individual conformity with unvarying law. Up till now it was as metaphysician, historical theorist and historian that Meinecke had been involved: now this question challenged him more particularly as a historian and a politician. For Meinecke did not want to be a mere professional scholar, but an individual in the fullest sense, with a many-sided and well-developed humanity. With this end in view, he needed also to work out a relationship to the State and to be active in the State as a part of his own personal development. It was 'the ethos of an interconnection between all the values in life ... and in the final analysis a religious outlook on culture', as Meinecke himself expressed it in his reminiscences.[2]

The first fruits of his thinking under the influence of Droysen and Dilthey, and in controversy with friends of his youth, Otto Hintze and Otto Krauske, were represented by the first volume of the *Leben des*

---

[1] p. 31.   [2] *Erlebtes 1862–1901*, p. 154.

Generalfeldmarschalls Hermann von Boyen, which appeared in 1895, and marked a stage in Meinecke's intellectual development. In the foreword, Meinecke at once shows what a lofty and all-embracing position he assigns to the science of history in the cultural realm as a whole. He was attracted by the possibility of 'depicting the constant inner connection of all Boyen's military thought with the general intellectual and political life of the nation', and he suggested that the best service

> that scientific history can render to the several fields of our culture is to strengthen the consciousness of such links. It can do so by showing that all specialisation and all technical excellence are by themselves useless unless they are constantly revitalised by the forces of general spiritual and moral impulses.[1]

Meinecke's *Boyen* lies on the watershed between old and new, and it takes its place in the transitional phase of Meinecke's thought from Idealism to Romanticism. It is a work that can put forward quite modern demands, and yet can defend them by arguments drawn from the old moribund world of thought.[2] Such a position, occupying a half-way house between two different ages, between Rationalism, Idealism and Romanticism, between Universalism, Individualism and Nationalism, and illuminated by them all, must have proved extremely attractive to Meinecke and must have given him an opportunity to make his own fundamental standpoint more obvious.

Thus in Meinecke's *Boyen* we do indeed meet with a deepening and refining of his thoughts about individuality. This is achieved by his taking for the first time as his opponents not the old scheme of strict scientific causality, but rationalism and the ideas based on Natural Law. His thought on the subject of individuality has thereby taken on a 'historical' dress, and now appears as the product of a historical development and historical controversy. Kant is here regarded as the expression and climax of the Age of Enlightenment,[3] and his idealism of moral freedom, whose influence was evident in Droysen's ethically conceived notion of individuality, is felt to be the boundary provided by Natural Law for the modern concept of individuality. His verdict on Kant's categorical imperative runs as follows:

> But such compelling and powerful principles are seldom without a splendid onesidedness, a certain violence done to the finer aspects of the inner life. Thus Kant too did violence to many a 'tender shoot' among the human plants with his ruthless eradication of all empirical elements from the moral law. For in the

---

[1] *Boyen*, I, p. v.   [2] *Ibid.*, p. 122.   [3] *Ibid.*, p. 83.

realm of experience there is an endless variety of individual feelings, and a vast range of them, that go to the making of an action—worthy and unworthy, noble and reprehensible—because after all there resides in each one of us a specific voice that shows him his own proper way to act, a way that is often a much steeper path and more beset with renunciations than would be the course laid down by the general moral law. In his anxiety to arrive at a unified and necessary principle for moral action, Kant looked down on this whole realm of the empirical as something random and unstable, and sacrificed the inner unity of man because he could not find the detailed link between the inclinations and feelings on the one hand and the formal moral law on the other. . . .[1] Just as Kant fails to discover the way to the inner organic unity of human impulses, so does the conception of the nation as an organic unity remain beyond the rationalistic interpretation of the State. In the same way that enlightened despotism so often simply suppressed the apparently irrational customs and views of the people, and sought to regulate their lives as much as possible by rational standards, Kant also strove to discover such rational principles of a strictly necessary kind. To no small degree, then, this ruthless banishing of anything 'given' in human experience from the moral law, which is at first sight an action of singular boldness, was to a considerable extent the result of a movement that sought to force the wayward movements of the feelings and the imagination under the control of enlightened reason. . . .[2]

In *Boyen* Meinecke was already talking of the

outlook of contemporaries who thought in terms of natural law, and were confident that the reasonable and enlightened administration of the Prussian State would win an easy victory over the forces of national tension (between the Germans and the Poles). But Boyen was already to some extent aware of their importance, and their roots which went down into the soul of the people. . . .[3]

As an 'antidote' to rationalism, Meinecke pointed to

the jubilant awakening of a new spirit that is also deeply rooted in the national soul as seen in the poems of Goethe and the thought of Herder . . . there was a fervent enthusiasm for all that was free and natural in what poured forth from his pen . . . . Goethe, Herder and their fellow protagonists rediscovered the

[1] *Boyen*, I, p. 82.   [2] *Ibid.*, p. 83.   [3] *Ibid.*, p. 57.

roots linking men to nature by seeing man as only the highest expression of a creative power that was active throughout the universe. There thus evolved the idea of a free organic development, passing on its fruitfulness from one generation to another, but requiring particularly at this present stage the unfettered growth of individuality.

In this context, Meinecke speaks plainly of 'the newly released forces of individuality' over against nationalism and the ideas of Natural Law.[1] Here too he is indebted to Dilthey, in particular to his chapter on Shaftesbury and Spinoza in his *Leben Schleiermachers*, which he quotes at this point. Meinecke owed the conception of man as the highest product of a creative power that is at work everywhere in the universe to the knowledge of Shaftesbury he had derived through Dilthey. As mediated by Dilthey, the pronouncements of the Stoic and Roman moralists on the subject of man's moral autonomy are raised to a level of principle which leads directly on to Rousseau, Kant, Herder and Schiller, and to Goethe's essay, '*Nature*'.

There is a constructive power in human nature; there is no division between its moral and its artistic capacities; it finds its ultimate meaning in the teleological character of human instincts so that the single human being is as a part of the universe naturally drawn towards the whole. . . . The law of nature by which the individual gravitates towards the whole demonstrates in personal experience the relationship whereby the inner force and immanent purpose of the part is linked with the entire universe. The creative power within me, which directs my life towards an ideal, is linked by the universality of feeling to the spirit that is the mind and life of the universe. . . . Our knowledge has as its object the unified mechanisms of nature. In the time of Newton, these were principally conceived in terms of the mutual relationship of the heavenly bodies as governed by the laws of gravity. But we must also look upon every organism as a system in which the parts are subordinated to the whole by a corporate unity of purpose. This organic world shows a creative power in action in the plant and in the animal, in the growth of organisms from the germ-cell, and in the instincts by which nature taught us long before there was any conscious education. And so the recognisable unity that runs all through the machinery of nature is an indication of an indwelling creative power that works with consummate art.[2]

[1] *Boyen*, I, p. 89.
[2] W. Dilthey, *Das Leben Schleiermachers*, 2nd ed. (1922), vol. 1, pp. 178 ff.

Shaftesbury's view of the individual as a purposive unity organised by a creative power, in which the same plastic forces are at work as in the world as a whole, was destined to serve as a key for Meinecke to the conception of individuality put forward by the German movement, though he did not in the end adopt the monism and pantheism to which Shaftesbury subscribed. More especially, however, along with the idea of purposive individuality, Meinecke adopted that of organic development, which he describes for the first time in the first volume of his *Boyen* as 'passing on its fruitfulness from one generation to another'. In the discussion with Lamprecht contained in the first and second volumes of *Boyen* on the collective and individualistic conceptions of history (1896), Meinecke made it clear that he conceived individuality and its mental world as being formed and shaped by an organising and creative mental power, indissolubly present in the germ-plasm which fused all other causalities and influences into a specific and particular synthesis:

> Lamprecht does indeed speak of the nucleus of individuality which we know by experience, but his understanding of this is different from our own. He is clearly of the opinion that it would be in principle, though not in fact, possible to dissolve it. But in our view it is plainly by its very nature an indissoluble unity. It is the inner sanctuary in which the whole philosophy of life is rooted. Its separate elements may have come together from all manner of different sources; but the fact and the manner of their union is to a large extent due to the spontaneous action of the a priori x in the man.[1]

In the second volume of the *Boyen* (1899), it is noteworthy that for the first time there becomes apparent the historical problem of a gradual change over from an outlook based upon the concept of Natural Law to one essentially based upon history. Boyen's education as a young man was rooted in rationalism; but partly through Kant's influence, and partly through 'his own inner disposition', he worked his way up to

> a strong autonomous inner life. And this indeed came about as a matter of fact more through the steady warmth of his inner life than through any deliberate overcoming of the rationalist theories that would reduce the personality to one single level.[2]

A new personality is achieved not by theoretical conquests, but by a change in the whole attitude to life. For as Meinecke remarks:

> Even the attitude to life, this most direct and apparently indissoluble and most original expression of the inner man, is subject

[1] *Hist. Zeitschrift*, 77 (1896), p. 165.   [2] *Boyen*, II, p. 406.

to the changes and chances of history. Though it may in essence be the same in all its various stages, we nevertheless only see it in its changing forms. Its development from the 18th to the 19th century has been marked by three, if not four, great stages. It has passed from rationalism, through the idealist philosophy of the Classical period, to the historical and inductive outlook of recent decades, which must soon come to terms with a pure naturalism.[1]

Changes in the conception of the world are also shown by Meinecke to go back to more general changes in the total 'outlook on life', and such a change was responsible for the growth of a 'historical and inductive view of the world'. In another passage, Meinecke attempts to explain how the experiences of that period had led to the conversion of the concept of progress based upon Natural Law into the idea of historical development. He says of Boyen:[2]

He wished to arouse a moral and patriotic way of life in the State and in society by an education directed from above, in forms prescribed by the enlightened legislator. This was an unconscious after-effect of his rationalistic view that there existed a *lex naturae*, an objective, rational ideal for life. But it was already somewhat illogically yet powerfully linked with a new and important principle. The outlook based on Natural Law had quite early on incorporated the notion of progress and a steady development of the world towards fulfilment. This was an idea that Boyen had eagerly taken over from Kraus's utterances in Königsberg. It was not a very long way from this point to the recognition of historical development, whose successive steps followed closely upon one another, though each had its own particular cause and connection. The great experiences of contemporary history were in fact driving men's minds in that direction. Changeableness and development on all sides, development and improvement of the individual person, of society and the State, a struggle between the old and the new, movements of thought that swept on, conscious of victorious power in spite of all suppression—all these constituted the strongest fertilising agents for the idea of evolutionary history that can possibly be imagined.

According to Meinecke, Boyen's mental world combined the technological and the developmental outlook,[3] the conception of Natural Law and historical modes of thought.[4]

---

[1] *Ibid.*   [2] *Ibid.*, pp. 410 ff.   [3] *Ibid.*, p. 411.
[4] *Ibid.*, p. 412.

Reason (says Boyen) provides the legislator with his goal; the prevailing culture, the particular qualities of the people, the length of the course, existing rights and even prejudices condition the various stages of progress and the forms that it must take.[1]

States, races, rulers—all these have their appointed historical purposes and their particular life-tasks, which they can either fulfil or miss. But when Boyen attempts to demonstrate the realisation or failure of such purposes in the actual events of history, his ideas are a combination of rationalistic teleology and historical thought.[2]

As we saw in Boyen [Meinecke continues][3] there was a combination of concepts of Natural Law and historical thought which, in spite of all the contradictions and divergences between these two principles, could produce valuable scientific results in combination and lead to true and important insights which passed over into and were absorbed by subsequent generations, though their partial origination in the concept of Natural Law has been almost forgotten. His rationalistic, teleological thinking has contributed not a little to the clear working out of the concept of a nation and a national State. . . .[4] Add to this Boyen's actual political experiences, and a strongly individual inner life, and it becomes clear that here was all the capacity for seeing past history in a particularly clear and vivid light.

For the development of the notion of nationality from its roots in Natural Law, political empiricism and the concept of the individual both come in at this point to explain Boyen's sense of history. We can hear the three themes of Meinecke's three great works on the history of thought sounding from afar to make up a single harmony. But the second volume of his *Boyen* gives evidence of a further transition from the concept of Natural Law to historism, in the course of which there emerges from the combination and tension between Natural Law and historical thinking a habit of historical thought-forms which is finally and permanently victorious. Meinecke shows that in Boyen's mind

the teleological viewpoint attempted to trace out the historical realisation of ideas, and in so doing could no longer be blind to

---

[1] *Boyen*, II, p. 411.   [2] *Ibid.*, pp. 411, 413.   [3] *Ibid.*, pp. 412 ff.
[4] At this point Meinecke quotes in elucidation of the sequence of thought from a fragment by Boyen, *Über den Entwicklungsgang der Völker*: 'It is a peculiarity of our power of thought that it assumes a purpose in all objects that are recognised as independent, and seeks to discover this purpose, as well as the laws by which it is accomplished.'

the manifold contradictions between idea and actuality. It was therefore compelled to adopt a more historical conception of reality.

In becoming aware of the power of contemporary circumstances, which dim the pristine brightness of ideas, Boyen had to admit that there could not be any absolute standard of judgment in these matters, but that each age must be understood in the light of its own specific and peculiar qualities.

> The more energetically and inductively this type of teleological thinking sought to master history as a realm of rational purpose, the more speedily it so to speak undermined its own foundations and opened the way to a more empirical and objective interpretation.[1]

So Boyen seems to confront us as the first example of a dialogue between the concept of Natural Law and historical thinking in one and the same human mind, and points forward to the march of similarly disposed personalities in the *Entstehung des Historismus*. But all this is only incidental to the broad trend of the narrative, and must not be exaggerated by treating it in isolation. Meinecke himself has said that his *Boyen* betrays a certain inclination towards a history of thought, which here comes into contact with other tendencies that were now beginning to blossom forth in him. But the author sees in his *Boyen* too much respect as yet for the material events; for in his own judgment he had not yet assumed a standpoint sufficiently raised above the drama of history, so as to give a certain freedom of outlook.[2] He did not fully achieve this freedom, and with it a breakthrough to a pure history of thought, until his period of teaching at Strasburg. This is not the place to go into the genesis of *Weltbürgertum und Nationalstaat* (1907). Here, it is only of importance to indicate the significance of this book for the development of Meinecke's thought on the problem of historism.

This brings us to the decisive years in Meinecke's creative activity. His setting is 'the cultural province of the upper Rhine', that south-west German cultural unity consisting of Alsace and Baden, with Strassburg and Freiburg on the right and left banks of the Rhine.

> At that period [wrote Meinecke] it was a smiling countryside as it lay there bathed in sunshine. We looked upon it as a single region, and it was felt to be so by our reason, our hearts, our historical, political and cultural inclinations, and our emotions. It was a region of inexhaustible historical wealth and it was

---

[1] *Boyen*, II, p. 415. [2] *Erlebtes 1862–1901*, p. 221.

infused on all sides with the fresh life of new intellectual movements.[1]

In his reference to the latter, which were of the greatest help to him personally, Meinecke is thinking more especially of the 'south-west German philosophy group' led by Wilhelm Windelband and Heinrich Rickert, as well as 'the two mighty men of Heidelberg', who 'worked at acquiring a deeper grasp of historical problems, particularly at the unprejudiced exploration of historical backgrounds'— men such as Max Weber and Ernst Troeltsch.[2] Meinecke was directly led to Windelband and Rickert by the dualistic problem that had presented itself in his professional studies—the question of the relationship between the natural and the historical sciences. In his Rectorial address at Strasburg in 1894 on 'History and Natural Science',[3] Windelband had attempted to distinguish between these two disciplines according to the difference in their methods. On the one hand there was the individualising and ideographical method, on the other the law-deriving method; and this difference was transferred to the researcher as a subject in search of knowledge, who in the capacity of natural scientist thinks 'without regard to values', and as a historian 'in terms of values', the values of culture and civilisation. Rickert then took up this distinction between the generalising scientific method that ignores values, and the individualising method of cultural science with its emphasis on values, and developed it into a self-contained system of the theory of knowledge in his two books *Kulturwissenschaft und Naturwissenschaft* (1899) and *Grenzen der naturwissenschaftlichen Begriffsbildung* (1902). In particular, Meinecke adopted Rickert's philosophy of values into his theory of history, though he later introduced certain modifications into it. Values meant to Meinecke 'Culture in the highest sense of the word . . . that is to say, new awakenings, revelations of the intellectual and spiritual within the causal network of nature.'[4] He agrees with Rickert that 'the small selection of what we consider worthy of research from among the vast mass of past events is made in accordance with its relationship to cultural values.'[5] On the other hand, he did not accept Rickert's demand that the historian should only be concerned to search into and depict facts that are related to values, but should not himself assess their value; for Meinecke points out that the very selection of facts in terms of value is not possible without a process of evaluation. Moreover, Meinecke maintains, the values to which

[1] *Strassburg, Freiburg, Berlin 1901–1919*, p. 55.   [2] *Ibid.*, p. 51.
[3] Wilhelm Windelband, *Präludien, Aufsätze und Reden zur Philosophie und ihrer Geschichte*, 9th ed. (1924), vol. 2, pp. 136 ff.
[4] 'Kausalitäten und Werte in der Geschichte', in *Schaffender Spiegel*, p. 66.
[5] *Ibid.*

historical facts are related do not, as Rickert suggests, fall into such general categories as religion, state, law and so on; the historian already interprets the individual concrete content of such categories as more or less worthwhile—that is to say, he evaluates it. 'The description and illustration of facts of cultural worth is not possible without a lively feeling for them in terms of the values they disclose'.[1] It is in these values that Meinecke sees a revelation of the divine in history; and in the historian's attention to them he discerns the possibility of the historian's finding God in history. Above all, however, Meinecke developed his own system of cultural values, in which he distinguishes between 'intentionally' produced ideas and pictures of a religious, philosophical, artistic, scientific, political and social kind, and those which blossom forth by the way, without being intended from the start—cultural values, in fact, which arise from the concrete necessities of practical life.[2] In the first case, man attempts the straightest and steepest ascent from nature to culture; in the second, he remains on the plane of nature, but looks up to the towering peaks of values which seek to lead him on. The State is thus pre-eminently the sphere in which values come to birth, often from very obscure and lowly origins, as it were by a shifting of the axis from nature towards culture. And lastly, a further element that comes in here is the problem of the relativity of values that so profoundly exercised Meinecke, to which we shall return in a later connection.

Starting out from Rickert's position, Max Weber, in his essays on the logic of the cultural sciences[3] published since 1903, wrestles with problems similar to those of Meinecke. These essays deal with the sphere of the social sciences, and are likewise concerned with actions lying on the boundary between the natural and the spiritual. In contrast to Meinecke, he makes a sharp distinction between the 'value-relationship', by which any phenomenon can be recognised as worthy of research, and the practical 'value judgment', in which the researcher's personal interest or inclination towards a particular ideal comes into play and is liable to cloud the objective truth of the findings. In this recognition of the contemplative value and the rejection of the value judgment, Max Weber also proclaimed the 'value-detachment' of the cultural sciences—a course in which he was not followed by Meinecke, who moreover was of the opinion that Max Weber's temperament did in fact give colour and liveliness to his splendid historical researches and descriptions as a result of the unconscious value-judgments at work in them.[4] And lastly, Meinecke

---

[1] *Ibid.*, pp. 66 ff.   [2] *Ibid.*, p. 83.
[3] Max Weber, *Gesammelte Aufsätze zur Wissenschaftslehre* (1922).
[4] *Schaffender Spiegel*, p. 230, note 4.

did not believe in such 'value-detachment' in the science of history because he would not and could not exclude the religious, history being for him an organ for the recognition of God: 'A man wants to find confirmation in the revealed history of the world for what he feels to be the goal of his own spiritual life.'[1] In spite of this difference of outlook, Max Weber, when he visited Meinecke at Freiburg, could confirm Meinecke's hope that 'although our approach and technique are very different, we are both pulling on the same rope'.[2] During his work on *Weltbürgertum und Nationalstaat*, Meinecke had in fact in front of him Weber's researches into the connection between Capitalism and Calvinism.[3]

During Meinecke's years on the Upper Rhine, Ernst Troeltsch published in the *Archiv für Sozialwissenschaft und Sozialpolitik* the material that formed the greater part of his *Soziallehren der christlichen Kirchen und Gruppen*, which appeared in 1911. He also began from 1918 onwards to publish separate portions of his second (and as far as Meinecke was concerned, even more important) book *Der Historismus und seine Probleme* (1922). In the personality of Ernst Troeltsch, Meinecke was confronted with the problems of the historical outlook in a powerful individual embodiment. He observes that

> his main positive themes and aims are often somewhat out of relation to the phenomenal richness of his sublimated historical views, so that his powerful utterance often fails to arrive at any clear and unambiguous personal conclusions at the end of a magnificent resumé of the life and thought of other nations.[4]

But this observation really belongs to the years they both spent in Berlin from 1915 onwards. So does the problem raised in essence by Troeltsch during these war years and deeply wrestled with by Meinecke as well—the problem of the contrast between the German mind and that of Western Europe. But there was already a scientific problem bound up with this, which Troeltsch had brought to Meinecke's notice as early as the Upper Rhine period, and which linked up with the opposition he was already feeling between thought based on Natural Law and the individualising historical outlook. Meinecke became concerned with the concept of Natural Law which had bound the European peoples together right down to the eighteenth century, and its subsequent transformation from the Christian concept of a Natural Law taken over from the ethics of Stoicism into

---

[1] 'Kausalitäten und Werte in der Geschichte', p. 67.
[2] *Strassburg, Freiburg, Berlin 1901–1919*, p. 102.   [3] *Ibid.*
[4] 'Ernst Troeltsch und das Problem des Historismus' (1923), in *Schaffender Spiegel*, p. 212.

the modern profane concept of Natural Law.[1] These ideas of Troeltsch carry Dilthey's approach to the ideas of Natural Law a stage further, and are at once discernible in Meinecke's *Idee der Staatsräson* and in *Die Entstehung des Historismus*.

The deviation of the development of German thought from this common European basis of Natural Law is a theme that had already been broached in *Weltbürgertum und Nationalstaat*. This was Meinecke's first great book on the history of ideas. It is the first to use his typical method of walking on a mountain ridge in dealing with the history of thought—the illumination of the history of certain ideas by monographs on particular representative thinkers. It is devoted to the German variety of the process of building a nation, considered as a product of modern individualism. And under the influence of Troeltsch, or at any rate in agreement with him, Meinecke sees this modern individualism as divided from the outset into two branches. One branch derives from Natural Law and looks towards democracy; the other, which he here again calls 'aristocratic in the spiritual and intellectual sense', is concerned with 'the liberation and increase of all that is best in man'.[2] He is referring here to the individualising ideas of the German Movement, with its emphasis on the fulfilment of personality. In this passage he refers in a note to Troeltsch's distinction between rational and irrational individualism put forward in an essay on *Das Wesen des modernen Geistes* (*The Essence of the Modern Spirit*). Although the liberal and democratic branch is kept in view when dealing with the idea of a German nation-State (especially in the second book) the centre of gravity is placed in the conservative-romantic branch. Meinecke traces the development from, and the coming to terms with, thought based upon Natural Law, and the far-reaching effects of a fusing of the process of nation-building with the growth of modern historical thought, arising from a new concept of individuality in Germany based upon ideas of Natural Law. Meinecke speaks in this book of 'the voyage of discovery which the German spirit undertook with such zealous enthusiasm in the realm of the individual', and which 'has begun to reveal individuality in everything that unites individuals to human beings'.[3] There is also a connection here with the arguments presumably referred to by Meinecke when he says in his reminiscences that *Weltbürgertum und Nationalstaat* contains sentences in which he now sees the germ of his much later book, *Die Entstehung des Historismus*:

[1] Ernst Troeltsch, *Die Soziallehren der christlichen Kirchen und Gruppen* (1911), *passim*; and by the same author, 'Das stoisch-christliche Naturrecht und das moderne profane Naturrecht', *Hist. Zeitschrift* (1911), 106.
[2] *Weltbürgertum und Nationalstaat*, quoted here from the 3rd ed. (1915), p. 9.
[3] *Ibid.*, p. 295.

What is the general origin of our historical and political thought-forms, and our sense of individuality even in the supra-individual groupings? It is surely clear that it is essentially derived from an individualism that has in the course of centuries deepened its originally superficial view of the essence of an individual until it has got down to the root-levels, and so revealed the links that bind the specific single life to the specific life of the higher human groupings and orders. There is individuality, spontaneity, an urge towards self-determination and extension of power observable on every hand, and not least in the State and the nation.[1]

The concluding phrase leads on to *Die Idee der Staatsräson*, which develops the thought of the State as an organic and individual structure with its own specific vital ideas which 'can only maintain its full strength if it is able somehow or other to achieve further growth'.[2] But the clearest indication of the root connection between Meinecke's three great books on the history of thought is given by a chapter in *Weltbürgertum und Nationalstaat*, where the subject is Adam Müller in the years 1808–13, and the author is discussing Burke. Burke [says Meinecke]

administered the first decisive shock to the interpretations of the State current in the 18th century, and added elements to all thought about the State that have never since been eradicated. He taught men to have a deeper veneration and understanding for all the irrational constituents in the life of the State—the power of tradition, of custom and of instinct, and the subconscious impulses of feeling. It cannot be said that he precisely discovered them, for every practical politician in recent centuries from Machiavelli onwards has known of them and used them. Up till now, they had not appeared to the practical man to be more than human weaknesses, to be taken advantage of or spared according to convenience; whilst to the theorist they had seemed rather to be something to be ashamed of. If a thinker recognised these elements at all, he did so only by renouncing the true ideal of reason. This was so with Montesquieu, and, as we have seen, with Wilhelm von Humboldt. But this purely negative approach to historical thought, which was reached by the most perspicuous (one might even say the most enlightened) of the 18th century enlighteners, was lacking in the real joy the study of history should produce, nor did it command the heart's allegiance. Whoever was the first to acquire such an outlook

[1] *Ibid.*, pp. 190 ff.   [2] *Works*, vol. 1, p. 1.

would be the discoverer of the true values in history. In the sphere of political and social institutions, Möser was perhaps the first to open up this new source of delight. But Burke surpassed him in depth of political understanding and in the breadth of his effects, for Burke had the good fortune to write at a favourable moment, when the spectacle of the collapse of pure reason in France proved so useful to his case. . . .[1]

But it is not only the contrast between the outlook based upon Natural Law and the thinking based upon individuality, between 'the historical and absolutist pattern of thought' (as Meinecke already puts it),[2] not only this theme that runs all through *Weltbürgertum und Nationalstaat*. It also already contains the idea of development in the historical outlook, as distinct from the concept of progress or the merely evolutionary concept. This distinction is justified by the richer measure of spontaneity and the greater capacity for plastic change[3] which a truly historical approach embraces. On the very first pages Meinecke shows himself to be in conscious possession of this idea of historical development which distinguishes him from other thinkers. He explains that nations and national States have, like all historical structures, a highly specific character.

They are singular, not indeed in the sense that a view of history influenced by the Romantic outlook has long maintained—namely, that everything specially characteristic of a particular nation is to be ascribed exclusively to its 'national spirit'—but in the sense that a nation's essential character, as in a single individual, is due to contact and exchange with its neighbours. Thus, the mutual contacts between nations and nation States may have the profoundest effect on their development. And so even a single historical moment, a single great event in the lives of peoples and national States as they affect one another, may lead the individual life of the particular nation or national State along paths that could not have been foreseen with any certainty from the trend of their previous development. It is quite possible that there are limits to these outside influences, dependent on the particular characteristics of the individual nation concerned; and it may well be that only a nation already possessing these qualities as it were in a latent form can bring them to full fruition and convert them to its own pattern of life. But even then it may be doubted whether these latent possibilities are specific to all nations, or only to those in which they develop;

---

[1] *Weltbürgertum und Nationalstaat*, pp. 132 ff.

[2] *Ibid.*, p. 143. [3] *Die Entstehung des Historismus*, p. 5.

in other words, whether there are categories of qualities, or only peculiar qualities attaching to individual nations. Yet one fact remains beyond dispute: influences coming from outside can notably determine the course of development in a single nation or nation-State.[1]

But *Weltbürgertum und Nationalstaat* not only points ahead to *Die Entstehung des Historismus*, it goes beyond it, inasmuch as it extends the line of the Romantics—Novalis, Friedrich Schlegel, Fichte and Adam Müller—to include Ranke, and arrives at important insights into Ranke's connections with Fichte and the Romantics, which others have since dealt with more fully.[2] Thus, in many respects *Weltbürgertum und Nationalstaat* reads like an anticipatory continuation of *Die Entstehung des Historismus*.

As to the *Idee der Staatsräson*, we know that it was planned from the start as a work dealing with the antecedents of modern historism and was to have been called *Staatskunst und Geschichtsauffassung*.[3] In his reminiscences as well as in the book on the *Staatsräson*,[4] Meinecke put forward the following view: the doctrine concerning the interests of the State developed by the theorists of modern statecraft since the time of Machiavelli elaborates and focuses the individual aspects of particular States. As Meinecke had recognised very early in his career, the individual aspect is the 'taproot' of the modern historical sense.[5] But the 'cataclysm' of the First World War[6] brought about a shift in the view of this problem, such as we shall also be able to observe in his *Historismus*. Meinecke also applies his conception of development to his *Staatsräson*, when he says: 'A tree can be excused if its exposure to the weather causes it to be distorted somewhat from its original direction of growth. I hope this book may also be excused in so far as it shows signs of having grown rather than been ready made'.[7] The shift of perspective in viewing this problem

---

[1] *Weltbürgertum und Nationalstaat*, pp. 15 ff.

[2] Cf. Carl Hinrichs, *Ranke und die Geschichtstheologie der Goethezeit* (1954). This book is by no means simply an exposition of Meinecke's subject-matter with added material, as has been suggested in some quarters, but deals with the theological aspect of the rise of historical thinking, which Meinecke leaves on one side. That is to say, it deals with the conflict between it and the absolute claims of the Christian revelation, whilst in Meinecke the principal 'antagonist' to historism is the absolute Natural Law which is placed in the foreground. Moreover, this book relates Ranke to certain fundamental ideas of an idealistic and romantic theology of history, and in so doing reveals the influence of Neo-Platonic thought in a quite concrete manner, whereas Meinecke only hints at it rather mistily.

[3] *Strassburg, Freiburg, Berlin 1901–1919*, p. 191.

[4] *Works*, vol. I, pp. 25 ff.

[5] *Strassburg, Freiburg, Berlin 1901–1919*, p. 191.

[6] *Works*, vol. I, p. 482.   [7] *Ibid.*, p. 26.

had taken place because 'the shock of national collapse . . . had brought the really basic problem of state interest before my eyes in all its fearfulness'.[1] Thus there came in, in advance and alongside of the observation of a connection between politics and history, between the idea of reasons of State and the idea of historism, the relationship of politics to morals, of 'Kratos' to 'Ethos', which was now seen to be the real problem concerning the interest of the State. Nevertheless, the new insights linking *Die Idee der Staatsräson* with the essential ideas involved in the development of historism are of great importance. They show that *Die Entstehung des Historismus* may to some extent be viewed as the crowning of a life's work, which had had to struggle into being through wrestling with the problems of the previous books.

We may at this point attempt to indicate shortly the most important elements in Meinecke's *Die Idee der Staatsräson* as regards the further development of the problems connected with historism. First, there is a close verbal agreement with the initial sentences of *Die Entstehung des Historismus*, in which the author points out that the growth of a new historical outlook followed upon and was connected with a secular transformation of human thought in general which the West experienced at this period:

This was perhaps the greatest revolution of thought the West had ever experienced. For it brought a shattering of hitherto prevailing belief in the comprehensible unity and uniformity of reason, and so of its universal validity and the pronouncements based upon it. This belief was dissolved by the recognition that reason could not provide general precepts for life, but only an infinite variety of forms of an evidently individual character; and that their ultimate unity was only to be found in an invisible, metaphysical and universal ground of being. All history now began to take on a different aspect. It no longer looked to be on one simple flat level that could easily be surveyed; it was seen to be a matter of perspective, and to possess infinite depths of background. No longer could men go on believing, as they had so far done, in a never-ending recurrence of the same pattern of events; they were now confronted with an eternally new birth of the specific and unique. This more mature and deeper picture of the world created by the growing German historism required a certain pliability of thought and a language capable of handling ideas of a more complicated, imaginative and mystical kind . . .[2] This new feeling for the individual was like a fire which not all at once, but gradually, took hold on every depart-

[1] *Ibid.*   [2] *Ibid.*, pp. 425 ff.

ment of life. To start with, it was mostly the lighter and more inflammable material (the individual personal life, the world of art and poetry) and then the heavier materials, and especially the life of the State . . .[1]

And this from an earlier passage:

From the deepening individualism of the single personality there now began to be formed on all sides in Germany, now in one way, now in another, a new and more vital image of the State, and, what was more, a new outlook on the world, which was now seen to be full of individuality. In every individuality, whether personal or supra-personal, a specific and peculiar law of life was seen to be at work, and nature and history together came to be viewed as 'an abyss of individuality' (to quote the words of Friedrich Schlegel).[2] For all individuality was held to proceed from the one maternal bosom of a divine Nature. Individuality on all sides, and an identity between the natural and the spiritual, and through this identity a strong but invisible bond knitting together the abundant wealth of constituents that go to make up an individual and prevent them from flying apart—these were the powerful new ideas that now burst forth in Germany in one form or another.[3]

Meinecke puts forward as the second of the great leading concepts of the period, along with the concept of individuality, the idea of identity,[4] particularly as embodied in Hegel. In his writings, by virtue of the concept of identity everything individual serves to realise the one and only reason 'which knows the art of making good and evil, the elemental and the spiritual, subservient to its purposes'.[5] 'This doctrine of the skilful cunning of reason was only the logical result flowing from the philosophy of identity, which needed a means for demonstrating the unity and reasonableness of the whole world fabric.'[6] Meinecke sees the earlier historism as still dominated by the philosophy of identity and the concept of natural law, which, though intrinsically outmoded, nevertheless continued to exercise an effect. 'Both of them, although in different ways, had satisfied the deep human need for absolute values, for some kind of clamp to hold together the elements in life that would otherwise fly apart.'[7] After the monistic identity philosophy had been finally dissolved (though not without some ominous after-effects), thus removing the last

---

[1] *Ibid.*, p. 426.
[2] This expression already occurs in *Weltbürgertum und Nationalstaat*, p. 250, cf. *ibid.*, p. 143.
[3] *Works*, vol. I, p. 425.   [4] *Ibid.*, p. 427.   [5] *Ibid.*
[6] *Ibid.*, p. 432.   [7] *Ibid.*, p. 443.

containing bonds of the individual, there remained (in Meinecke's view) the historical concept of individuality, which continued to prove its indispensable value as a key to the understanding of psychological phenomena.[1] Not till this point do we reach the pure and mature historism in Meinecke's sense of the term. It rests upon the two corresponding ideas of individuality and development; and it is the origins and growth of this as part of intellectual history that *Die Entstehung des Historismus* goes on to expound. This brings us, however, to the difficult internal problems of historism, which were fully faced by Meinecke for the first time in *Die Idee der Staatsräson*. Here, too, the First World War caused a shift in perspective of these problems compared with *Weltbürgertum und Nationalstaat*.

Here, in his first work on the history of ideas, Meinecke had stated that concepts of world citizenship and universal ideas were, as far as their content was concerned, both ethical and religious concepts.[2] But he maintained that there was in general an individual, as well as a universal side to the moral concept, and from this side even the apparent amorality of national power politics could be morally justified. . . . 'For that which proceeds from the depths of an individual nature of a being cannot be immoral.'[3] These astonishing sentences show in the first place that Meinecke's idea of reasons of State was deeply rooted in the concept of individuality; and second, that in the nationalistic mood of his Upper Rhine period, when his views on culture were highly optimistic, he still completely affirmed the notion of reasons of State as an individual law of life for each State. Third, they show that in the background there was a completely thoroughgoing affirmation of the concept of individuality which appeared to go even to the point of recognising an individual morality. In his *Staatsräson*, however, this recognition assumed a 'sphinx-like aspect'[4] and is to be numbered among the 'only too many things in which God and the devil seem to have become intermingled'. And Meinecke steered equally clear of giving an absolute and positive value to the concept of individuality. In *Die Idee der Staatsräson*, Meinecke not only speaks of the dangers of the identity concept, but also of the dangers of the concept of individuality. As construed by Hegel, the danger in the former was that the actual 'which appears to be wrong was somehow transfigured into the reasonable'; and the doctrine of the wise dispensation of reason which enabled it to bring good out of evil caused the purely natural and darker side of reasons of State and 'the excesses of power politics' to be lightly excused.[5] Meinecke now saw that this danger also lurked in the new doctrine of individuality. Instead of the inter-

---

[1] *Ibid.*, p. 501.   [2] *Weltbürgertum und Nationalstaat*, p. 89.
[3] *Ibid.*   [4] *Works*, vol. I, p. 510.   [5] *Ibid.*, pp. 432 ff.

pretation that nothing can be immoral which proceeds from the deepest individual levels of any being's nature, the view now becomes as follows:

> It [the new doctrine of individuality] could easily act as a temptation to the morality of a single person if the right of individuality to express itself to the full was held to be unlimited, and was set up as a higher morality over against the general moral code. If applied to the supra-individual State, it could be used to legitimise all its excesses in the way of power politics as unavoidable by-products, organic to its essential being . . . In this way both the identity and the individuality concepts, two of the loftiest and most fruitful ideas of the German mind at that period, showed the tragically double-edged quality of all great historical ideas and forces.[1]

These doubts, however, also served to open up the problem of relativism which was closely connected with historism. In *Weltbürgertum und Nationalstaat* there was still talk of the *delight* in history: historism was a 'source of delight' which Möser had been the first to reveal in Germany in one particular sphere. The new attitude, and the source from which it sprang, first came to the fore a year before the appearance of the *Staatsräson*, in an essay published in 1923 on *Ernst Troeltsch and the Problem of Historism*.[2] In this essay, Meinecke stated that 'even our pride in the peculiar German concept of the State, with which we went to war and stood against the world' was closely connected with the doctrine of individuality.

> It was precisely this desire to be different from the rest of the progressive modern world which was bound to be taken amiss by a way of thought that believed in a general, but not in an individual, reason in things. But our desire to be different turned into a national tragedy. And whereas up till now our historism which individualised everything had lured us on with a happy outlook on the world, full indeed of struggle, but thoroughly creative struggle, we now began to sense profoundly tragic problems even in this prospect, and our picture of the world began to look much more sombre. This was not so much on account of the spiritual isolation in which we now found ourselves—for that was something we could bear, as long as historism continued to give us an inner feeling of superiority and a firm anchorage for facing all the basic problems of life. It has lavishly endowed us with intellectual treasure and taught us to understand the past and all its greatness, to love it and

[1] *Ibid.*, p. 433. [2] In *Schaffender Spiegel*, pp. 211 ff.

imitate its way of life, in a manner that produces a fabulous and fairylike atmosphere. But, to link up now with the observations we took up at the beginning, it is precisely this pluralism of individual values, which we discover on every hand, that may throw us into confusion and perplexity, particularly now in our state of clouded vision. Everything has individuality and is a law to itself, everything has its law of life, everything is relative and in a state of flux: then give me something, man cried out, on which I can stand firm. How can we emerge from this anarchy of values? How can one get back from a purely historical outlook to a doctrine of values?[1]

And the *Idee der Staatsräson* goes on:

this new principle of individuality, as it stretched out further and further, striding from one discovery to another, tracing out an individual law and an individual movement on all sides, threatened in the end to run off into a relativism that would no longer recognise anything solid or absolute in history, but was tolerant of any intellectual movement and any individual trend. It understood everything and forgave everything, and so (to quote Dilthey's words) ended up in 'an anarchy of convictions'.[2]

And yet Meinecke wrote his account of the origins and growth of historism 'with an affirmative intention'.[3] As he had already said about the idea of historical individuality in *Die Idee der Staatsräson*, 'we cannot and must not renounce this idea'.[4] In view of Meinecke's recognition 'that there is certainly a corrosive poison in a historical outlook which sees everything in relative terms',[5] this is at first sight a surprising fact; but this position was made possible by Meinecke's previous essays, in which he wrestled with the obscure problems of the historical approach with a boldness that reached the furthest limits of knowledge, and in so doing managed to secure a firm foothold for his own convictions. The standpoint Meinecke achieved provided no simple, facile and generally illuminating or revolutionary solutions, it was no patent medicine, but rather a somewhat wavering outlook, a mixture of resignation and faith, very nearly bordering on 'an honourable agnosticism',[6] yet not content to stay there. It was an outlook representative of the best in the German attitude to history, with Ranke and Droysen as its godfathers. We can also note here a

[1] *Ibid.*, pp. 223 f.   [2] *Works*, vol. I, pp. 442 f.
[3] See below, p. liv.   [4] p. 501.
[5] 'Geschichte und Gegenwart' (1933), in *Vom geschichtlichen Sinn und vom Sinn der Geschichte*, p. 13.
[6] An interpretation of a Rankean term in *Aphorismen und Skizzen zur Geschichte* (1942), p. 157.

growing closeness to Goethe, which reached its climax in *Die Entstehung des Historismus*.

The manner of Meinecke's answer can be read in the first of the three explanatory essays, the one on Troeltsch, published in 1923, in which he characterises his own method:

It belongs, however, to the inmost essence of an individualising historism that although it does not make any metaphysical presuppositions, it is nevertheless forced to arrive at metaphysical conclusions. An unprejudiced observation of individual living entities, and the conviction that they cannot be understood along purely causal lines, compels the historian to assume a metaphysical background. And he believes that this approach is a more scientific one than that of his positivist opponents. But just because historism must always remain within the bounds of the scientific and never leave the field of experience, the historian is reluctant to entrench himself in metaphysics and is content to put out suggestions and hints of a general kind. That which represents its scientific strength, however, is from the ethical and practical point of view a weakness. The historian is not in a position to say anything decisive and definite, and more particularly anything of general validity and attractiveness for the masses, on the subject of the highest values in life . . . his metaphysical words of comfort about the world as a whole are reserved for a highly cultured élite . . .'[1]

In the second of his two explanatory essays entitled *Causality and values in history*, published in 1925, his theme is 'that only weak and faithless souls will lose heart and faint under the burden of such a relativist historical approach. It cannot shake the belief in an unknown absolute. But to demand that this unknown absolute should reveal itself in tangible form is a remnant of an anthropomorphic conception of God.'[2] In this interpretation of history, Meinecke is, as we have already noted, indebted to Troeltsch as well as to Rickert. From the former he took over the idea of relative values, which he had contrasted with an out-and-out relativism:

Relative values are not the same as a general relativism, which ends in anarchy, mere chance and sheer caprice; they stand for the interweaving of the factual and the ideal aspiration, which is always in a state of flux and always freshly creative, and can therefore never be defined in timeless and universal terms.[3]

[1] *Schaffender Spiegel*, p. 120.   [2] *Ibid.*, p. 233.
[3] Ernst Troeltsch, *Der Historismus und seine Probleme*, 1922, p. 211.

Or (to quote Meinecke's words):

> A relativity of values is nothing but individuality in the historical sense; it is the always specific and essentially valuable expression of an unknown absolute; for this is what faith believes in as the creative ground of all values. And this absolute stands in contrast to all that is merely relative and conditioned by the temporal and the natural.[1]

The basis of relativism is the fact that the spontaneity of personality, which creates all the intellectual and moral values by whose virtue nature is transformed into culture, and which arises from the creative ground of the absolute, is closely connected with causality of a biological and mechanical kind, in a mysterious manner not at all clearly understood by the historian. The mind, the eternal, has to wrestle with nature, with the transitory, in individual ways that are constantly changing; and it is from this struggle that the totality of values, the intellectual and spiritual culture of mankind, are born. Thus, historical individualities are no more than phenomena exhibiting certain tendencies towards the good, the true and the beautiful, that is to say, the imperishable; but as such they have meaning and value for us. In the individual expressions of the values the historian catches a glimpse of the absolute, the divine, the eternal in the midst of the transitory world of history. 'In history, we do not see God, we only sense his presence in the clouds that surround him'; so wrote Meinecke even on the final page of *Die Idee der Staatsräson*,[2] where he certainly also stated that the absolute revealed itself to modern man without disguise at two particular points: 'on the one hand, in the pure moral law; on the other, in the highest achievements of art.'

At this point there is an obvious connection with the third of the essays under discussion entitled *Geschichte und Gegenwart* (*History in Relation to the Present*), published in 1933.[3] Once again, Meinecke conjures up the delights and the dangers of the historism 'which has opened up for us the marvellous worlds of new historical understanding in respect of everything that wears a human look', but has also 'gradually undermined all the firm ground of definite and absolute ideals on which humanity had up till now reckoned to have a solid foothold';[4] and he then goes on to ask: 'Has . . . historism, and the relativism that is its special product, the power by itself to heal the wounds inflicted by it?'[5] Meinecke distinguishes between three

---

[1] *Schaffender Spiegel*, pp. 84 ff.   [2] *Works*, vol. I, p. 510.
[3] *Vom geschichtlichen Sinn und vom Sinn der Geschichte*, pp. 7 ff.
[4] *Ibid.*, pp. 10 ff.   [5] *Ibid.*, p. 13.

attempts to find an 'antidote to the poison of relativism'.[1] First, the Romantic attempt to lay down as its canon a particular period in the past. But this attempt 'to hold up certain stages of the past as a norm and standard for the present and for all the processes of history' was bound 'to break down at once under the corrosive criticism of relativism'. Then came the flight into the future: it was not in the past, but in the future, that men were to seek the aim and purpose that alone could give meaning to the senseless flux of mere becoming. But this concept of progress and perfectionism is overclouded by the 'shadows of the problems connected with modern civilisation'.[2] The stream of becoming which makes everything relative has this same effect on the two attempts at a solution put forward by the Romantics and the optimists of progress. 'They both have this inherent weakness, that whether they swim with it or against it, they both plunge into this stream.' They are both to some extent horizontal solutions. But the question needs to be looked at *vertically*, and this is what the third solution (Meinecke's) undertakes to do. Along with Goethe and Ranke, Meinecke surveys each epoch from above, and sees every individual form in connection with a higher world, 'in immediate relationship with God'. According to Meinecke, historical individuality (that is to say one that creates values) must have an urge to 'look for and find the eternal in the momentary, in the individual constellation of life'.[3] Here, the guiding star must be conscience, which must be taken into account even by a theory of history, 'because an interpretation of history without a firm ethical foundation is merely at the mercy of the waves'.[4] At this point, Meinecke is blending Ranke's concept of the immediate relationship of historical phenomena to God with Droysen's ethical individualism of the conscience. From the latter's treatise on history he quotes these words: 'Only a man's conscience is an absolute certainty to him: it is his truth and the centre of his world'; and he coins a phrase that is reminiscent of Droysen: 'In the last resort, all the eternal values of history arise from the ethical decisions of men in action.'[5] Meinecke's last word on the problem of relativism is 'that in the voice of conscience . . . all that is fluid and relative in form suddenly becomes firm and absolute'.[6] 'In the conscience, individuality blends with the absolute, and the historical with the present.' Conscience is 'the faculty most closely related to God in us', and the significance that history can have for us is 'to understand the revelation of that which is God-related in our humanity, and to take it into ourselves and live by it'. Its absolute significance, however, in the sum-total of the

---

[1] *Ibid.*, pp. 14 ff. [2] *Ibid.*, p. 17. [3] *Ibid.*, p. 19.
[4] *Ibid.*, p. 20. [5] *Ibid.*, p. 21. [6] *Ibid.*, p. 20.

universe is something we do not know.[1] Finally, Meinecke's doctrine of history, and the place of conscience in it, are amplified and deepened by what he adds in something he wrote after the *Entstehung des Historismus*, entitled *Deutung eines Rankewortes*—probably the profoundest of his contributions to the theory of history. There, he also sees in conscience the possibility of transcending the contradiction between divine immanence and transcendence that had engaged him all his life.

> The human conscience tells us about what is good and evil. It also plays a part (though not such a direct one) in bringing to birth and sustaining all the other higher values. And in conscience we see all at once a power which we can call both immanent and transcendent. It is within us, and yet it can also tell us that there is something there which is both outside us and above us, on the far side of the universal interplay of forces, which can never by themselves adequately explain it . . .[2]

Through conscience we come to 'postulate and surmise a certain divinity in the world. And even the historian must subject the phenomena of history to the verdict of the conscience as the human organ of this divinity'.[3]

We must conclude our study at this point, without exhausting the whole content of Meinecke's historical and theological legacy to the world in his last years. Our purpose has been to show how he fortified himself in the face of the dark problems of the historical and the relativist approaches before and during the time he was writing his last work, *Die Entstehung des Historismus*. Of all his works, therefore, this book comes before us as the least burdened with the general issues of his time. It can thus devote itself entirely to the scholarly and scientific problem suggested by its subject. His arduous spiritual wrestling had won through to a conviction of the ultimately positive character of one of the greatest revolutions in Western thinking, the second great achievement of the German mind subsequent to the Reformation. He could now write a large part of the history of this intellectual revolution 'in an affirmative mood', wholly concentrated on the problem of how the new world-outlook would shape, fascinated by the intellectual and spiritual drama that unfolded before him, and no longer needing to take those torturing looks down into its possible abysses; for he had already gazed into them with open eyes, and had tried to build some bridges to span them.

We cannot attempt the further task of analysing Meinecke's great

[1] *Ibid.*, pp. 21 f.
[2] *Aphorismen und Skizzen zur Geschichte*, p. 154.
[3] *Ibid.*, p. 157.

work on the history of ideas. The purpose of this introduction was to show the way into it, and to indicate how it arose from his studies as a whole, and the position it occupies in the total picture. It carries us as far as the threshold of mature historism, which finds further and fuller expression in the memorial address on Leopold von Ranke of 23 January 1936, given in the Preussische Akademie der Wissenschaften. But we also know that he had already laid a foundation in *Weltbürgertum und Nationalstaat* and *Die Idee der Staatsräson* for both the further development of the historical outlook and the study of the Romantics in the person of Adam Müller, Fichte, Stein, Wilhelm von Humboldt, Hegel and Ranke.[1] In the *Idee der Staatsräson* dealing with the earlier history of his outlook, Meinecke, in developing his doctrine of interests, was in fact only dealing with a side-shoot, though at first he had mistakenly considered it to be the main stem. Here, the growth of the historical outlook still appeared as a kind of reflex called forth by the peculiar development of Europe itself, with its intricate pattern of free and independent States, among people of intellectual importance, and producing in them the doctrine of State interests, with its feeling for the individuality of the separate States.[2] In *Die Entstehung des Historismus* this movement is shown to be the outcome of genuinely independent and revolutionary processes of experience and thought, particularly on the part of political thinkers; and this movement is traced from its 'precursors'—Shaftesbury, Leibniz, Gottfried Arnold, Vico and Lafitau—on through the history of the English and French Enlightenment and the English Pre-Romantics, as far as the German movement and its crowning figures Möser, Herder and Goethe, who were of such decisive importance for the growth of historism.

Carl Hinrichs

[1] As Parerga and Paralipomena to *Die Entstehung des Historismus* we should particularly mention in addition the following: the essays on 'Klassizismus, Romantizismus und historisches Denken im 18. Jahrhundert', 'Zur Entstehungsgeschichte des Historismus und des Schleiermacherschen Individualitätsgedankens', in *Vom geschichtlichen Sinn und vom Sinn der Geschichte*, p. 46 f., p. 95 f.; 'Schiller und der Individualitätsgedanke. Eine Studie zur Entstehungsgeschichte des Historismus', in *Wissenschaft und Zeitgeist*, 8, 1937, partly reproduced in the *Frankfurter Zeitung*, nos. 581–2 of 14 November 1937; also the 'Aphorismen und Skizzen zur Entstehungsgeschichte des Historismus', in *Vom geschichtlichen Sinn und vom Sinn der Geschichte*, pp. 120 ff., and in *Aphorismen und Skizzen zur Geschichte*. For the many items and problems published by Meinecke while working at the *Historismus* in the proceedings of the Prussian Academy and in the *Historische Zeitschrift*, which were incorporated into the book, see the Friedrich Meinecke Bibliography drawn up by Anne-Marie Reinold (1952), p. 157.

[2] *Works*, vol. I, p. 287.

Preliminary Remarks

It might seem somewhat presumptuous to write an account of the origins and growth of historism that adopts an affirmative attitude, seeing that for years the cry has been sounding that historism must be transcended. But intellectual revolutions that have once taken place cannot be treated as though they had not happened, and deprived of further effect. Each of these revolutions continues to work deep down, even though superseded by a new one, as we see happening today. And, as we shall see in this book, the rise of historism was one of the greatest intellectual revolutions that has ever taken place in Western thought.

Anyone who has read my book will probably recognise the fact of this revolution. But people do not take kindly to the word historism as a term denoting the content of this revolution, for it is a recent word, really a century later than the origins of what it purports to describe. And it very soon acquired a pejorative sense, suggestive of exaggerations or distortions. I have come across its earliest use—without any derogatory meaning—in K. Werner's book on Vico (1879), which speaks of 'Vico's philosophical historism' (pp. xi and 283). It then occurs (though with a derogatory meaning) in Carl Menger's controversial reply to Schmoller: *Die Irrtümer des Historismus in der deutschen Nationalökonomie*, published in 1884. The author understood by this word the exaggerated importance ascribed to history in the national economy, of which he thinks Schmoller is guilty. Anyone wishing for further information about the history of this word can consult Karl Heussi's *Die Krisis des Historismus* (1932). So it came about that the very odium which was as a rule attached to this word in its earliest uses brought about a certain consciousness that there lay concealed beneath the culpable excesses and weaknesses associated with it a great and powerful phenomenon of intellectual history that needed a name, but as yet had none. It came to be recognised that what was being combated and considered harmful had in fact grown from the same soil that had nourished all the humanities which had flourished anew since the beginning of the nineteenth century. Abusive words sometimes turn into complimentary labels when the person criticised adopts them because he somehow senses that what they criticise is closely connected with the best that he has to give. He must pay good heed to justifiable criticism, but stand by all that is best in him. This was what happened to Ernst Troeltsch. In the year 1897 he was still agreeing with the general regret that there had now appeared in the learned world a 'historism' which 'saw its appointed task in the understanding rather than in the reshaping of reality' (*Schriften*, 4, 374). In 1922, shortly before his death, he published his great work on historism and its problems, in which he combined an honest criticism of its weaknesses with a deep justification of its inner necessity and its fruitfulness.

In the first place, it must be said that historism is nothing else but the application to the historical world of the new life-governing principles achieved by the great German movement extending from Leibniz to the death of Goethe. This movement is the continuation of a general Western movement, but its culmination is to be sought in the great German thinkers. This was their second great achievement, to be ranked along with their first, the Reformation. But as there was a discovery of quite new life-governing principles, 'historism' stands for more than simply the application of scientific methods of thought. The world and all its life take on a new aspect and present a profounder background once one has become used to looking at them along these new lines. It will be enough at this point to indicate briefly the essential matters to be dealt with in detail in the rest of this book. The essence of historism is the substitution of a process of *individualising* observation for a *generalising* view of human forces in history. This does not mean that the historical method excludes altogether any attempt to find general laws and types in human life. It has to make use of this approach and blend it with a feeling for the individual; and this sense of individuality was something new that it created. This does not mean that up till then the individual elements in mankind and the social and cultural structures created by man had been totally ignored. But it was precisely the deepest-moving forces of history, the human mind and soul, that had been held captive by a judgement that confined itself to general terms. Man, it was maintained, with his reason and his passions, his virtues and his vices, had remained basically the same in all periods of which we have any knowledge. This opinion was right enough at heart, but did not grasp the profound changes and the variety of forms undergone by the spiritual and intellectual life of individual men and human communities, in spite of the existence of a permanent foundation of basic human qualities. In particular, it was the prevailing concept of Natural Law, handed down from antiquity, which confirmed this belief in the stability of human nature and above all of human reason. Accordingly, it was held that the pronouncements of reason, though they could certainly be obscured by passions and by ignorance, did nevertheless, wherever they could free themselves from these hindrances, speak with the same voice and utter the same timeless and absolutely valid truths, which were in harmony with those prevailing in the universe as a whole.

This belief in Natural Law was able to combine with Christianity through the adaptations revealed by Ernst Troeltsch. We can hardly imagine what this concept of Natural Law has meant for Western man for almost the last two thousand years, whether in its Christian form, or in the secular form that has emerged again since the Renaissance. It was a fixed Polestar in the midst of all the storms of the world's history. It gave thoughtful men an absolute anchorage in life, all the stronger if it was crowned by the Christian belief in revelation. It could be applied to the most varied ideologies, even those that were strongly conflicting. Human reason, taken to be eternal and timeless, was held to justify them all, without its being noticed that in the process reason itself lost its timeless character and showed what it really was—a power that was as mutable as history and constantly took on new and individual forms. If one were inclined to indulge in romantic leanings, it would be possible to envy this illusory outlook and characterise it as the happy and creative naivety of youth. For it was connected with the much envied certainty about the correct manners and modes of life and the unlimited capacity for belief belonging to earlier centuries. It may perhaps be objected that religion had more to do with this than Natural Law. But the two had in fact been blended together for a long time, and in practice they exercised a common effect on people. We are only concerned at this point with the particular stage of Natural Law which immediately preceded historism. We are not concerned with solving the problem whether, and to what extent, Natural Law does, in spite of all objections, contain a kernel of appeal that is constantly springing into new life because it answers to certain timeless human needs. There is general recognition that it did continue to exercise power— and still does today—as a historical idea, both at the same time as and after the rise of the new method of historical thinking. Thus the nineteenth century was really a crucible for the intermixing of these two ways of thought. And to a greater extent still the history of the genesis of historism in the second half of the eighteenth century, which we are setting out to describe, resulted in mixtures and refractions, with a deposit of the old alongside the emergence of the new.

Since that time, historism has assuredly become such a standing ingredient of modern thought that an alert mind can trace its effects in almost any important judgment on human structures. For there is nearly always (more or less clearly expressed and accompanying this standpoint) an idea that the specific nature of this structure depends not only on external conditions but also on conditions within the individual. But only in a very few large-scale phenomena has historism so far succeeded in developing its full depth and power. The dangers confronting it up to the present day have been that it would lose its depth and be adulterated by the infiltration of coarser elements into its world of thought. This might lead to the opinion that it was on the way to becoming an unrestrained relativism and might paralyse the creative powers of mankind. We know that historism only finds a hearing with the few and does not appeal to the multitude. But we can discern in it the highest stage so far reached in the understanding of human affairs, and are confident that it will be able to develop sufficiently to tackle the problems of human history that still confront us. We believe that it has the power to heal the wounds it has caused by the relativising of all values, provided that it can find the men to convert this '-ism' into the terms of authentic life.

It is, therefore, our intention to describe the course of events that led to the rise of historism and to show that it was a stage in the development of Western thought. For there is an intimate connection between evolutionary and individualising thought-forms. It belongs to the essence of individuality (that of the single man no less than the collective structures of the ideal and the practical world) that it is revealed only by a process of development. There are indeed different conceptions of development: Rickert once distinguished no less than seven. And it will be shown that in the genesis of historism several different views were at strife with one another. We are not anticipating, but merely noting by way of approach, that for the purposes of purely historical observation a necessary distinction must be made. There is a difference between the evolutionary conception of historism with its greater degree of spontaneity, plastic flexibility and incalculability, and the much narrower idea of a mere unfolding of an existing bud, which also differs from the perfectionist ideas of the Enlightenment, later transformed into the popular, or the more refined, conception of progress.

The idea of development superseded the method of dealing with historical changes prevailing hitherto, which is known as pragmatism. It was closely connected with the concept of Natural Law, and since it was based upon an assumption of an invariable human nature, it treated history as a useful collection of examples for pedagogical purposes, and explained historical changes in terms of superficial causes, either of a personal or a material kind. A distinction can therefore be made between a personalistic and a materialistic pragmatism. Here, too, it will be left to the subsequent exposition in the text to make this question clear. For at all points it is a question not only of grasping the chief features in this new outlook in conceptual terms and ranging them summarily under certain '-isms', but also of realising that we are dealing with a living whole, with spiritual entities made up of individuals, such as communities and generations, as historism has come to recognise.

It was this recognition that also decided what form the exposition should take, and how the material should be selected and arranged. There seemed to be two possible ways. Either one could put the problems amenable to general ideological treatment in the foreground, and weave the contributions of the several thinkers into a pure history of problems and ideas. This is a method particularly attractive to thinkers who are philosophers, or who approach the matter from the direction of individual and systematic scientific disciplines. It does indeed throw direct light on the connections between the ideas; but it fails to make clear the connection of these ideas with their individual living background and underlying basis, and is in danger of turning living history into conceptual hypostases. Thus the pure historian finds some justification for his own method, which is to concentrate on living human beings and use them as material for the study of changing ideas. He then has to choose whether he will bring as many or as few as possible actors on to the stage. The intellectual changes (especially those of the eighteenth century) can be followed in a countless number of smaller figures, whose participation in these changes must not be under-estimated. They would provide material for useful monographs. But if the aim is to establish an explicit connection between the general course of development and the individual contributions to its origins and progress, the only practicable plan is to undertake a kind of mountain journey along the ridges, attempting to get across from one high peak to the next, in the course of which it will also be possible to get glimpses of mountains and valleys that cannot actually be visited. I have in the present book followed this same method, which I also employed in my earlier works on the history of thought.

The choice of material, therefore, was centred round the three great German thinkers in whom the earlier historical approach of the eighteenth century blossomed into full flower, and who then prepared the ground for its further growth. These men above all needed to be studied in their individual thought structures; and in order to understand them, it was necessary to trace the most important stages leading up to them from the early eighteenth century onwards—again as far as possible in individual pictures. At the same time it was important not to lose sight of the general connections with the history of thought as a whole, often going back into antiquity, and to give at least some indication of them. The Natural Law, Neo-Platonism, Christianity, Protestantism, pietism, Natural Science, the seventeenth and eighteenth century thirst for travel and discovery, the first stirrings of freedom and a feeling of nationality among the peoples—all these needed to be taken into account. Last but not least, there was the new poetical movement of the eighteenth century; and this and all the other forces needed to be related to their social and political background. It was the combined operation of all these in the souls of highly gifted men that gave rise to historism; and it is these that will be reviewed in this present work, though only in the effects and transformations that are attributable to their creators and their predecessors in this line of thought.

There would be no difficulty in increasing the number of forerunners to the three thinkers selected, but this would hardly increase the amount of essential and indispensable material. Along with the great historians of the Enlightenment in France and England, we have also included the Pre-Romantic movements in both countries as preliminary stages, particularly because of their importance for Herder, not excluding Burke, although they only became significant in the later development of historism that followed these three thinkers.

My original purpose had been to include this too, and to end with the story of the youthful Ranke's development. I can now only add as a supplement to this book my address in memory of Ranke, given on 23 January 1936 at the King Frederick Anniversary of the Prussian Academy of Sciences. My years begin to make themselves felt, and I can now only hope to pick one or two threads out of the mighty fabric of the earlier nineteenth-century German history, but not to cover the whole. I am confident that younger hands will take up and complete this task.

In this earlier nineteenth-century, the only figure to come into my book is Goethe, in the period of his maturity. I am well aware that the consummation of his historical thought, as I attempt to portray it, took place in the atmosphere of the early nineteenth century. I recognise that a contribution was also made by the rising Romantic movement, the impetus of German idealism, with its philosophy of history most profoundly represented by Hegel, and above all the impressive historical events of these years. For Goethe seems to have had a unique power of imbibing those influences of his time in a way which suited his genius. But the tree that now bore this fruit was rooted in the world of the eighteenth century. The historical thought of its period developed more profoundly and comprehensively than in the earlier and middle years, though it was not essentially different; and it must therefore be reckoned as the highest achievement of the eighteenth century in this sphere. The ruling spirits of particular centuries, and their specific achievements, have a way of overlapping one another, rather as high projecting bow-windows and balconies in narrow streets almost touch from either side and can easily be joined together. And so Goethe's projection into the nineteenth century can suitably be included in a scheme that otherwise only embraces the eighteenth century.

The theme I have chosen has never before been dealt with as a unity. Dilthey's splendid sketch of the eighteenth century and the world of history (*Schriften*, vol. 3) was indeed the most important previous work on which to base my own. But it stops before Herder, which means that it does not attempt any direct account of the origins and rise of historism, but only describes the achievements of the Enlightenment which preceded it. I do not deal with the history of historical writing, such as Fueter and Moriz Ritter have recently given us, but only with the history of the standards of value and formative principles in general lying at the back of all historical thought. Something of the kind is also being attempted by two valuable and very recent works, which largely correspond in their choice of eighteenth-century thinkers with the selection made by myself. I refer to Trude Benz's Bonn dissertation of 1932 on anthropology in the historical writings of the eighteenth century, and Kurt Breysig's book, *Die Meister der entwickelnden Geschichtsforschung* (1936), which appeared shortly after I had finished my own book. But the special questions they pose are from the start very different from my own approach. In particular, Breysig's scholarly ideal is that of a refined positivism, and this is the standard by which he judges the great historians of the eighteenth century—a standard, I should add, that is very different from those of historism applied by himself.

But there were a number of separate earlier works that I took into consideration, monographs on individual historical writers and thinkers, as well as those that have examined the changing interpretations of particular historical objects and problems and explain them in terms of the history of thought, thus coming up against the same problems with which I am myself concerned. There is a masterly treatment by Spranger of the history of the cyclic theory of culture and the problem of cultural decay (Sitzungsberichte d. Preuss. Akad. d. Wiss., 1926). This same problem of decay and changing interpretations is dealt with in Walter Rehm's *Der Untergang Roms im abend-*

ländischen Denken (1930). Stadelmann, to whom we are already indebted for an excellent monograph on Herder's sense of history (1928), has also produced 'Die Grundformen der Mittelalterauffassung von Herder bis Ranke' (*Deutsche Vierteljahrsschr. f. Literaturwiss. etc.*, 1931). Bertha Moeller, 'Die Wiederendeckung des Mittelalters' (Cologne thesis, 1932) took up the same theme, and so did Giorgio Falco in *La polemica sul medio evo* (I, 1933), and W. Schieblich in *Die Auffassung des mittelalterlichen Kaisertums in der deutschen Geschichtschreibung von Leibniz bis Giesebrecht* (1932). I have proved the usefulness of such special studies and detailed cross-sections of history over twenty years, and have myself dealt with Germanic and Romance thought in the changing interpretations of German history (*Hist. Zeitschr.*, 115; 'Preussen und Deutschland im 19. und 20. Jahrhundert', 1918); and at my instigation Erwin Hölzle followed the matter up in *Die Idee einer altgermanischen Freiheit vor Montesquieu* (1925). I had now only to consider how far I should make use of this kind of enquiry in my present undertaking. I decided in the end neither to neglect them entirely, nor to let them so dominate the scene as to have a decisive influence in my choice and arrangement of material. For my purpose is to go down to the deeper levels of intellectual and spiritual life, from which the changes in thought about the individual problems of history arise. And this is only to be attained by immersing oneself in the lives of the great individual personalities. My business was to seek out men, and not particular historical questions, however wide in scope they might be. And so any discoveries that I made had to be worked into my picture of the mental structure belonging to these individual thinkers.

Finally, I should like to refer the reader, for a fuller treatment of many points that have only been touched upon here, to my earlier books *Weltbürgertum und Nationalstaat* (1908; 7th impression 1928) and *Idee der Staatsräson in der neueren Geschichte* (1924; 3rd impression 1929), both of which contain my present theme in an implicit form. Everything that is common to these three books goes back to the early ideas of the happy years I spent a generation ago in the university of Strassburg. I dedicate this book to the memory of those days; and the few survivors from that period, to whom I extend my greetings, know what a wealth of intellectual talent there was in that cultural circle of the Upper Rhine.

I have undertaken this third and final pilgrimage through the high peaks with the resignation of old age, which recognises much better the many difficulties of the task and therefore puts a higher value on its demands. Yet I am only too conscious that I have not been able to give more than a fragment of that ideal solution of the problem which has stood so alluringly before my eyes.

Book one

The Early Stages and Historical Writing in the Period of Enlightenment

Chapter one

The Forerunners

An attempt will be made to give the salient points in the origin of historism. The whole process depended on breaking down the rigid ways of thought attached to the concepts of Natural Law and its belief in the invariability of the highest human ideals and an unchanging human nature that was held to be constant for all ages. The first step in this direction was a general change in philosophical thought already discernible in the seventeenth century, and notable in the philosophy of Descartes. Up till then, in the naive conviction that human reason was supreme, the aim had been to use it as a means of comprehending the objective content of the world. Now, the question that came to the fore concerned the cognizing subject and the basis of its authority by reason of its own inherent laws. This swing towards the problems of subjectivity is the first preliminary sign of the coming revolution in thought that we are about to delineate. But it often happens in the antecedents of revolutions that those very changes which are being prepared in the secret depths have to start with, and for a long time to come, the very opposite effect, and positively strengthen the existing state of affairs. The cognizing subject of Descartes and the subsequent French Enlightenment working under his influence, was not yet the individual subject in all its manifold historical forms, but a generalised subject, the abstract man of Natural Law. And the universal laws discovered in him therefore only served at first to confirm the upholders of Natural Law in their dogmatic certainty that it held the key to the understanding of human affairs. This key seemed to be a process of thought, now raised to a level of mathematical clarity and cogency, in the forefront of which was the strict application of causality. The epoch-making discoveries of the natural sciences confirmed this supposition to an undreamt-of extent and even extended their influence into the sphere of history. Thus,

3

the changes occurring in the field of history were now also brought under the strict control of mechanical causality to such a degree that even the internal changes in human nature appeared to be no more than rearrangements, under the influence of strict causality, of the same everlastingly recurring pattern of basic material. But to those who were striving to achieve mathematical certainty for thought, reason, conceived as the organ for proclaiming ideals, remained just as stable as it had appeared to the thinkers of old whose framework was Natural Law. Thus, as far as the French Enlightenment prevailed, there was no weakening, but a positive strengthening of the concepts centred in Natural Law, which, as we have suggested, already had latent within them the germs of decay, as will be seen in the history of the French Enlightenment.

There was more to be hoped for, as a means of loosening up the historical world, from English empiricism and sensualism after Locke had shattered the belief in innate ideas. The belief in the absolute character of the truths revealed by reason now went into the melting-pot. The desire was aroused to study human phenomena and the historical changes they had undergone in a calm and unprejudiced way. In the course of this study, men came to a more exact knowledge and better appreciation of the world of irrational mental forces, the feelings, urges and passions which Natural Law, so proudly entrenched in reason, had hitherto neglected. The causal significance, and sometimes also their usefulness for human purposes, also began to be more truly evaluated. But in this process the mind became a *tabula rasa,* which was at once filled by the experience imported by the senses, and so lost its activity and spontaneity. The new method, moreover, was more fitted for revealing the separate faculties of the soul than the principle of its inner coherence. For in this examination, too, men were still in bondage to a mechanical causality, which now proceeded to transfer its triumphant advance from the field of natural sciences to that of the humanities. Alongside the old Natural Law, which was really nothing but the law of reason and a belief in reason, there now appeared a new naturalism bound up with a series of inconsistent compromises. This, too, will be evident as the story of the English Enlightenment unfolds.

Only by a deeper understanding of the human soul could the old Natural Law and the new naturalism be transcended and a new sense of history be achieved. The man who first opened the way to this deeper understanding was not himself immediately in a position, nor did he feel called upon, to apply it thoroughly to the historical field. Changes in intellectual outlook do not take place as rapidly as this, especially when it was a question of bursting through a crust that had been built up over the millennia and went back into the world of antiquity. But it is a remarkable fact that it was just at the turn of the seventeenth and eighteenth centuries, when the great movement of Enlightenment starting in England was about to pursue its victorious advance, that there grew up simultaneously in England and Germany, and soon afterwards in Italy, new movements of thought containing the potentiality to transcend this Enlightenment, whether represented by the English empiricists or by the French rationalists. And this was the work of Leibniz, Shaftesbury and Vico, who worked quite independently of one another, each from his own particular presuppositions and in his own individual environment. But the inner unity of Western culture was shown by the fact of their almost simultaneous appearance. Shaftesbury (1671–1713) died in the same city of Naples in which his contemporary Vico (1668–1744) lived, and it may be presumed that the two men met (cf. Nicolini, *La Giovinezza di G.B.Vico*, 1932, p. 92). And Leibniz (1646–1716), who was Shaftesbury's senior, made intellectual contact with his younger contemporary in their lifetime. Leibniz was delighted to read Shaftesbury's *Moralists*, which was published in 1709, and found that it contained almost the whole of his *Theodicy*, which came out in 1710. Vico's work remained almost unnoticed among the endeavours we are about to describe. We shall also insert one earlier German contemporary of lesser importance, Gottfried Arnold, who deserves to be ranked with the forerunners as a representative of the circles who were being stirred to new spiritual and intellectual activity. But Leibniz and Shaftesbury stand out as the pre-eminent intellectual forces, whose work bore fruit half a century later in the new German movement period following the Seven Years War. They were like a Castor and Pollux in the heavens, far outshining the great stars of the French Enlightenment which had meanwhile risen in the firmament. Perhaps Shaftesbury's influence on them was more immediate and closely related than that of Leibniz because he was the less intellectual of the two. He was rather an enthusiast, and an aesthetic, imaginative man of feeling, who made an immediate appeal to the human soul in its entirety.[1] We shall therefore turn our attention to him in the first place.

I Shaftesbury

Alongside English practical experience and sobriety of outlook which are such a predominant feature, there has sounded from time

---

[1] In an acknowledgment both of Leibniz and of Shaftesbury, Herder wrote in 1770 to Merk (*Lebensbild*, 3, 1, p. 110) about Shaftesbury, that he 'was the first to present a philosophy of optimism in such a way that it spoke to the heart, whereas Leibniz presented it only to the intellect'.

to time a note of refined and tender melody and lively beauty, together with a certain need for aesthetic and romantic expression, at once recognisable in the plastic arts and in lyrical poetry. The racial theorist would trace this back, with very uncertain justification, to the Celtic element in the English national inheritance. Shaftesbury was a representative of this type. He was an aristocrat by birth and culture, with freedom to shape his own life; and he grew up at a time when his nation and State had secured their own internal freedom, and were now beginning to make their influence felt with increasing self-assurance in Europe and in the world as a whole. Weiser, in his book *Shaftesbury und das deutsche Geistesleben* (1916), rightly calls attention to an inner connection between this lord's ideals of political freedom and the open-hearted universal joy and piety of the thinker. He could only conceive of a high level of intellectual culture of a stable and durable kind in a free political State, and saw the rise and fall of art and science as dependent on the waxing and waning of internal political freedom. *Liberty and letters* gave the foremost, though not as yet the profoundest, of his solutions to this problem. A thought that had already been at work in the ancient world, in the early days of the Empire (especially in Pseudo-Longinus Περὶ ὕψους, c. 44), thus awoke to new life through his influence in the English atmosphere of the Glorious Revolution, and was to be constantly recurrent throughout the eighteenth century.

There is another connection that must be kept in mind for the history of thought and especially for the rise of historism, and one of even greater significance. It, too, takes us back into the ancient world, for it was from this world that there arose not only the concept of Natural Law, which so limited any deeper research into the human soul because of its predominant intellectualism and rationalism, but also the world of Platonic and Neo-Platonic thought, which drew more deeply on the inner life, and which had already been taken up by the Cambridge school of philosophers who preceded Shaftesbury. It was probably from them and from the Renaissance philosophy of Giordano Bruno that Shaftesbury received the golden vessel containing the Neo-Platonic ideas, which were linked together down the centuries by a chain of mystically or pantheistically inclined thinkers from Dionysius the Areopagite onwards in such a way that new forms and applications of these ideas, produced by individuals and conditioned by particular periods, were constantly being created. Even where there was no complete remodelling of these ideas, their application to particular spheres of life often had a tremendously vitalising and creative effect. To adopt a favourite Neo-Platonic image, one might compare them to a beam of light which, though itself invisible, has the power to illuminate a wall some distance

6

away. We need not therefore be concerned with the whole of Shaftesbury's philosophy, which ultimately issued in a fusion of ethics and aesthetics. It will be enough to pick out the features that will recur in an obvious and demonstrable form in the earliest pioneers of historism.

It was intentionally stated above that Platonic and Neo-Platonic thought drew more deeply from the inner man, and not that it had a deeper insight into the soul, than the concept of Natural Law. The more intensive preoccupation with the obscurer depths and mysteries of the soul did not suit the strongly intellectual cast of ancient thought, which was much more interested in the objective world. But the Platonic Eros, which was striving to rise to the true essence of the world, to the realm of archetypes and ideas, had its origins in the unconscious depths of the soul. Christianity and the human mood in the closing years of the ancient world strengthened the inclination of the soul to open itself more fully and fervently to the divine. This tendency was also at work in the philosophy of Plotinus. The principal relationship was between the human soul and God, and not between the human soul and history; and it was within the Platonic–Neo-Platonic movement that those elements were developed which reached out beyond the understanding and the reason. Then men began to look out from this once realised basic relationship between God and the soul to the world as a whole, with all its variegated content, and perceived everywhere, as they had within themselves emanations from the original divine source, reflections and broken gleams from the original divine light, and a coherence of all the separate parts to form a living and moving whole, though as much as ever in a supratemporal and really unhistorical sense. The dominating ideas, however, in the historical sphere were duration within change, the permanent core and the ever-recurring types in all world events, the eternal reaffirmation of the one nexus between God and the world, the emanation of all the manifold variety of things from the one divine and original power which embraced them all and vitalised them all, a power superior to the world and beyond the scope of thought. These ideas were held to give mastery over the bewildering variety of the world's course and the world's phenomena, but only in the sense that they could well be left to themselves, without anybody troubling to penetrate the secret places of their transformation into actual history. Incidentally, the doctrines of the Stoics and the Natural Law about the supra-temporal invariability of human nature, and the timeless and absolute ideals of a humanity broadly based upon reason, could still be included in this outlook, for they, too, confirmed the concept of duration in the midst of change. So it came about that the ideas based upon Natural Law (essentially

7

unhistorical and static in outlook) and the Neo-Platonic ideas (essentially dynamic, but not as yet displaying any deeper interest in history) could still continue to exist side by side.

If our judgment is correct, it would seem that Shaftesbury too belonged to this mixed type, although his inclination was preponderantly towards Neo-Platonism. His ideas of virtue, representing the climax of his ethics, were just as absolute, supra-temporal and independent of external ordinances, changing opinions or customs, just as firmly based upon the nature of the universe, as the Stoics' concept of Natural Law. He believed in the 'natural rule of honesty and worth' (*Misc. Refl.*, V, 3). He even ventured to say the same about virtue as the reviver of Natural Law, Grotius, had said about law—namely, that it was even independent of God Himself (*Moralists*, II, 3), because God must necessarily be good.[1] It was not on this, but on the Neo-Platonic elements in his thought, that the power of his intellect rested, a power that was to have a progressive effect and in the end influence even the historical world. The decisive element was his trustful confidence in the derivation of all things from God. He was sure that we too are indwelt by the primaeval soul of all things; and this was not in his case due to any mystical urge for union of the soul with God or any isolated dialogue between himself and the Almighty, but to the observation of all the living processes in action around him, in a spirit of openness to the whole universe and with a thirst for all its beauty. This clear and sanguine outlook on life, unrestricted by any dogmatic Christian imagery, brought him near to the outlook of the Enlightenment and made him sympathetic towards its views. The particular point that separated him from this school was his aesthetical sense, which remained unstunted by any intellectualist thought. Everything in the world, as far as he was concerned, pointed to coherence, unity and wholeness, in great things no less than in small; everywhere there was evidence of a living relationship and sympathy between all the parts, and a common purpose uniting them. It seemed impossible to him that matter could, through mechanical self-action, produce the plants and trees and animals, and man himself. The unity and identity of our own personalities, he maintained, could not reside in material that was exhausted after a number of years, but in a formative inner spirit, the 'inward form'. *Inward form and structure, inward constitution, inward order, inward character, inward worth and liberty, inward sentiments and principles*—these were his favourite expressions. In the beginning,

---

[1] His judgement is based entirely upon Natural Law when he says that the follower of a religion which considers cats, crocodiles, and such harmful or low animals to be holy, is morally at fault when it treats opponents of its religion as enemies on the strength of this belief. *An Inquiry Concerning Virtue or Merit*, I, 3.

spirit rules over matter, and not matter over spirit. Spirit alone gives form. Beauty never lies in the material, but in the form, the formative power, the idea. The creative centre of his teaching was this energy that he equated with spirit, form and formative power, and which he tried to identify as the inward and active nucleus of every living creature; and it was this teaching that was to work later on in Germany with such illumination and kindling of enthusiasm in a younger generation. Shaftesbury's view was thoroughly Platonic, in that he placed the creative power positively higher than the creature and distinguished the realm of structures shaped by man or nature, but not self-acting (which he called 'dead forms') from the 'formative forms', which went back to the origin and source of all beauty and goodness, the primaeval soul behind all things. It was a delightful picture of the cosmos that Shaftesbury drew, based upon a step-by-step structure, unity and manifold variety, and culminating in an entire harmony. As Dilthey has shown (*Schriften*, 2, 400), his hymn to Nature in *The Moralists* is re-echoed in the essay on Nature of 1782, under the inspiration of Goethe, and was the subject of a poem by Herder (*Works*, 27, 397).

The most important feature, however, for our problems is that Shaftesbury's teaching also contained the first recognition of the principle of individuality. All particular forms, he held, although ultimately one by reason of a common unifying principle, yet always possess their own peculiar and indwelling 'genius'. This reveals itself only in action, life and practical effort, which alone display its beauty. The picture that confronted him, then, was that of an unresting creative movement, pervading all things, taking on an endless variety of forms, and constantly fashioning new life out of death. Though this movement seemed restless, it was nevertheless derived from an ultimate power that was at rest in the eternal regions, whose highest laws were regular, invariable and enduring. Yet the individual who became fully aware of this splendid picture of the universe and absorbed it into the depths of his being could thereby become possessed of a very special source of power. Whether the individual was engaged in practical affairs, or seeking to probe some theoretical aspect of life, he must everywhere feel called to some specific activity peculiar to himself, and yet feel his dependence upon a higher power and know himself to be an organ for the service of the divinity in freedom; and this knowledge should make him both proud and humble. And everything a man created or saw created bore a certain shape or form, and as such was not merely material, but continued to constitute an active power capable of creating other forms. These were thoughts that could one day lead to a deeper understanding of history. Everywhere there was this interlocking of freedom and

9

necessity and a constantly self-reproducing wealth of specific forms that grew from some inner centre and were shaped by some formative idea. In this way the normative thought-forms of Natural Law (although Shaftesbury's teaching preserved their essential features) were transcended in a manner that was not so much revolutionary as almost naively simple.

But was there not a danger in this teaching that life and the world itself might dissolve into a splendid and ingenious pageant of appearances? Shaftesbury would not and could not pass over the problem of a theodicy, the question of the origin, existence and activity of evil in the world, and of the world's incompleteness, in spite of its derivation from God Himself. It is not our business here to go into the philosophical weaknesses or merits of his answer, but only to enquire whether it had anything to contribute to the future of historical thought.

It had indeed something to contribute, and that along two main lines of thought. One of them was generally Christian and Neo-Platonic, though Shaftesbury added deep and original feeling to it, and this must never be forgotten by the historian; the other, originating in Shaftesbury's own peculiar aesthetic talents, though in harmony with the Neo-Platonic view of the world, opened up fresh possibilities even to the historical outlook.

In *The Moralists*, Shaftesbury makes Philocles say: 'Viewing things through a kind of magical glass, I am to see the worst of ills transformed to good, and admire equally whatever comes from one and the same perfect Hand'. To which Theocles replies: 'In an infinity of things, mutually relative, a mind which sees not infinitely can see nothing fully, and must therefore frequently see that as imperfect which in itself is really perfect'. And in another passage:[1]

> Do not let yourself be depressed by the spectacle of misfortune and suffering in history and by the catastrophes that take place, but remember 'how vain and ridiculous the thing is itself, considering the vastness of time and substance, the abyss before and after, the fleeting generations of men and other beings, waves of the sea, leaves of grass, the perpetual change and conversion of things one into another. That this was necessary, from causes necessary, and (whether Providence or atoms) could be thus only, and could not have been otherwise. That this is not only what was necessary but what was best, since the mind or reason of the universe cannot act against itself; and what is best for itself, itself surely best knows.' You are perhaps afraid that the

_____

[1] The essay on 'Necessity' in Rand, *The Life, etc., of Shaftesbury* (1900), pp. 90 ff.; cf. Weiser, *loc. cit.*, p. 362.

swiftly growing power of France will lead to a universal monarchy? May it not in fact be the best means of preventing this?

This leads on to the second consoling thought, which takes us from this glimpse into the eternal, with its demand for religious faith, into the finite world, with its mixture of enigma and clear proof. Pleasure and pain, beauty and ugliness seem (writes Shaftesbury in *The Moralists*) to be everywhere interwoven as in a many-coloured carpet of irregular workmanship, yet beautiful in its total effect. The beauty of the world is altogether based upon contrasts, so that a general harmony may come forth from the interaction of manifold and contradictory principles. Even the deserts and waste places, although they are fearful and arouse our horror, have their own peculiar beauty and mysterious charm. Even the serpents and wild animals, although repellent to us, are in themselves most beautiful. Poisons may have their beneficent uses. Deceitfulness and religious zeal may exist together in one and the same character, as has often been the case, producing on balance more innocent delusion than intentional deception in this world of ours.

One more thoughtful example may be quoted from another work. In his *Essay on the Freedom of Wit and Humour*, Shaftesbury says that heroism and philanthropy are almost the same thing. But through a slight misapplication of these emotions, the hero and liberator can easily become an oppressor and destroyer.

Here it is clear that his thought is beginning to touch the world of history, and it is pointing to possible ways of interpreting it that are different from those of the rationalistic Enlightenment. In its eyes, deception and honest religion, heroism and tyranny, appeared to be generally irreconcilable, because there was so much purely intellectualist prejudice and such fixed ideas of Natural Law, that its upholders were unable to imagine that what is logically and morally distinguishable may nevertheless be inextricably interwoven in actual life. Even Shaftesbury, when moving in exclusively ethical realms of thought, did not steer entirely clear of this intellectualism (as for example in his *Inquiry Concerning Virtue or Merit*). But when he surveyed the world and its life as a whole, he sensed that life could not be spiritually mastered by the intellect and rational ideas alone. Thus his aesthetical sense, riding easily on the wings of the harmonious picture of the universe presented by Neo-Platonic metaphysics, created the means for the new recognition of history. Whilst everywhere teaching respect for the concepts of wholeness, form, shape, inward centre and active power in reference to living things, Shaftesbury was also able to come to terms with the oppositions and contradictions existing not only between them, but in the very living things themselves. It was not in spite of, but precisely because of, these contradictions that they seemed to him good and beautiful, for in his eyes everything, great and small, was part of the one overarching harmony of the universe.

There was one final point indispensable for a deeper insight and understanding of historical events, and that was enthusiasm; it was, Shaftesbury's works taught us, a motive power for the observer, in addition to the aesthetic sense and the metaphysical urge. The author wrote in *Moralists* that all genuine love and admiration is enthusiastic, and so are pure scholarship, the travels of explorers, gallantry, war and heroism; they are all based upon enthusiasm! To the rationalist who based his thinking on Natural Law, enthusiasm was a flame that needed careful observation and measures of protection, though here and there it might be usefully harnessed to action. For many contemporaries, enthusiasm was synonymous with fanaticism, which a man might well be proud of having avoided. This difficulty also found an echo in Shaftesbury's open and enquiring mind. In *A Letter Concerning Enthusiasm* he remarks that never in our nation was there a time in which folly and extravagance of all sorts were more sharply observed and wittily ridiculed than they are today. Where was the dividing-line between healthy and overbearing enthusiasm? And how was one to judge between its various effects in the sphere of history? Shaftesbury's answer to this problem, although in many respects limited by the outlook of that age, nevertheless opened the way to a deeper understanding of irrational phenomena in history. He remarks with reference to Epicurus that in spite of all his inclinations towards the miraculous and the supernatural, he showed an innate and a profoundly human mental disposition; and whether the events dealt with were false or true, the symptoms of their appearance would in any case be the same. In his view, then, the fanatic and the true prophet could not be distinguished from one another by any external evidence. Only by controlling and understanding ourselves with 'good-humour' could we find an antidote to enthusiasm that runs riot. He remarks incidentally, however, in a mood of reflection that only God knows whether something of this kind of enthusiasm did not after all help us to throw off the papal yoke.

His teaching that enthusiasm was the necessary atmosphere for all higher mental and moral life threatened to shake the walls of partition which prevented men from getting a glimpse of spiritual life and history as a whole. But Shaftesbury was not yet in a position to pull them down altogether and to apply his new outlook to the historical world as a matter of principle and on a larger scale. For the time with its own specific tasks was not yet ripe for this. It was in the process of working through from the shackles of dogma and ecclesiasticism to a freer and more interior view of life, and this involved a battle. During battles it is not easy to be just to your opponents, or to discover on the enemy side too, as Shaftesbury's theory really demanded, active and formative powers at work, and harmonies born of opposites. Behind this dogmatic and ecclesiastical spirit from which release was sought, its opponents could always sense as its specific upholders the caste of priests, whose thirst for power and intolerance could be directly felt; and it was on them that the pragmatic method now laid the chief blame. And so Shaftesbury came out in more or less open combat against the zealot-like clerisy of the English High Church party. He was freer and less prejudiced in his approach to the Roman Catholic Church, which he had seen in Italy, with its veneer of ancient and splendid culture. He saw that it not only worked by the usual outward means on the superstition of the masses, but also taught its proselytes the 'inward way of contemplation and divine love'; and his judgment was that the astonished observer in Rome would either return with the most terrible revulsion against the whole race of priests, or with admiration and a desire to be reunited with Rome (*Misc. Refl.*, II, 2). That did not represent a full historical understanding of the situation, but only a preliminary stage towards it. But however deeply he was convinced of the original religious disposition of the human soul, and however profoundly sensitive he himself was to the element of religious veneration in all exaltation of the spirit, and even in the transition from veneration to fear and awe (*Misc. Refl.*, II, 1), the 'spirit of bigotry' remained for him, and for all the other leaders of the Enlightenment, a basically evil constituent of Western man. And his most noteworthy attempt to explain this in historical terms was introduced by a treatment of religious history along Enlightened lines. In other words, it was pragmatic in character. He went back to the Egyptian priestly caste, with its hereditary character and land-owning wealth, though he did not forget to give some of the incidental reasons for superstition, such as those arising from the climate and so on; but his main conclusion was 'that dominion must naturally follow property' (*Misc. Refl.*, II, 1), and quietly reflected on the power still wielded by the English High Church party through its ownership of land. And he held it to be a principle of political arithmetic that in each nation the quantity of superstition was in almost direct proportion to the number of priests, soothsayers and so on. He then boldly affirmed that the apparatus of Egyptian religion had been 'metamorphosed' into a 'spirit of bigotry' which continued to be active in the latter days of the ancient world and down into Christian times (*Misc. Refl.*, II, 2).

It is remarkable that in his reflections upon the State there is a touch of genius in his handling of the historical roots of any structure. He drew more upon a deeper knowledge of the soul than upon historical experience, but then went on in the typical spirit of the Enlightenment to pronounce the subsequent forms of these structures to be normative for the future. He ridiculed the prevailing mechanical doctrine of the origin of the State in a contract. For then the State would become a kind of invention or artificial product (though with typical English sensibility he called this 'civil government and society'), whilst in reality the social bonds between men and all their ethical leanings in this direction were something original and given by nature. At this point he discussed the contemporary States in the spirit of the thinkers of the Enlightenment, and put forward a theme which was to be variously applied during the whole of the eighteenth century, namely that the really natural and healthy States were the small ones. 'Vast empires are in many respects unnatural' he says in his *Essay on the Freedom of Wit and Humour*.

Finally, it must be acknowledged that Shaftesbury was not able to win a complete victory in the field of human activity closest to his heart, where the thought-forms based upon Natural Law still held the upper hand. In Greece and what Rome had learnt from Greece, and in what some of the master-figures of the Renaissance had learnt from both of them, Shaftesbury saw eternal and timelessly valid 'right models of perfection' for art and scholarship (*Soliloquy, passim*). In the *Querelle des anciens et des modernes*, which was then exercising men's minds in France, he was therefore on the side of the Classical ideology.[1] In his praise of 'the refined manners and accurate simplicity of the ancients' (*Misc. Refl.*, V, 2) we can discern the forerunner of Winckelmann. Looked at from this point of view, all the taste for the Gothic and the Mediaeval seemed to him to be of a piece with the exotic Indian and Japanese influence which he saw stirring in the England of his day; and he pronounced them both to be thoroughly unnatural. He thus found it impossible to grasp the greatness of Shakespeare. Shaftesbury's judgments on him in his *Soliloquy*, which fix upon points of detail and contain more regrets than praise, show a lack of discernment for the real centre in a man's life and outlook, which was to make his own philosophy so rich in content for coming ages.

But the deepest source of this feeling is not to be found in a passionate search for individuality in general, but rather in an overmastering aesthetic search for harmony, proportion and symmetry, amounting to a positive religion, in every single organic structure.

[1] Cf. on this subject Weisbach in the *Deutsche Vierteljahrsschrift für Literaturwissenschaft* . . ., XI, 4.

He was well aware that nature herself distinguishes everything she creates from every other thing by giving to each a specific and original character. But he required the artist working from nature to smooth off the edges and corners, the 'singularities', in order to avoid the appearance of caprice (*Essay on the Freedom of Wit and Humour*). He was thus more interested in the typical in art than in the purely individual. It could also be said that at this point he was correcting his own idea of nature (which was really more true, but seemed to him too empirical) by a higher concept of nature which brought all elements into harmony with one another. For to him nature was essentially harmonious, and the heart of harmony was nature.[1] This new Natural Law, constructed along Neo-Platonic lines, was incomparably deeper in meaning than the old pattern constructed on an intellectual and moral basis, because it was sensitive to the more delicate and the less obvious notes of the subjective life. But it still sought for eternally valid principles, just as the old Natural Law had done.

In the early stages, the development of artistic taste obviously started everywhere from the astonishing, the wonderful and the tremendous (as it clearly does with children) but when it reached the stage of the natural and the simple, and the true imitation of nature, as in Greece, it was henceforth precluded from reaching any higher or different development ascending to a new scale of values (*Soliloquy*, IV, 2). Thus even this stirring of the evolutionary concept was halted by the wall of the absolute ideal.

Far from reproaching him with this limitation, one must see this as inner necessity for the history of thought. For all his freedom of spirit, Shaftesbury was a thoroughly positive man to whom any kind of disruptive scepticism was abhorrent. He wanted only to replace the old absolute values by new and deeper ones; and in order to satisfy him, these needed to be as absolutely valid as the old. This was part of the continuity of development, which could only free itself slowly and step by step from the old ways of thought. Even what was new and powerful in his circle of ideas could not be taken up and formed into a new category of thought till another fifty years had gone by, and in a new period and against a new national background.

II Leibniz

Shaftesbury's late impact on European thought shared this fate with

---

[1] I cannot therefore agree with Weiser (*loc. cit.*, p. 58) that the classicist element in Shaftesbury was 'inorganic'.

Leibniz's philosophy. It depends on the particular time and circumstances as to whether certain thoughts expressed by great thinkers bear their full fruit; if so, they then usually exercise an influence going far beyond their author's original intention and so help to create something new. The basic ideas of Leibniz's philosophy as far as they had seen the light up to his death in 1716 also produced within the earlier German Enlightenment a type of philosophy distinguishable from both the English and the French movements by a greater understanding of the autonomy of spirit. But it was not yet able to loosen the rigid thought-forms of an intellectualism steeped in the concepts of Natural Law. Yet in 1765, when his *Nouveaux Essais sur l'entendement humain* became known, not only did a more complete interpretation of his system give his thought a new and powerful glow, but above all and even more so the very different intellectual attitude of a new generation. It may probably be said that he was now better understood than half a century earlier. But it is more doubtful whether he himself would have admitted this to be so. For the mathematical and rationalistic side of his system, which was now somewhat eclipsed, may well have been as close to his heart as the dynamic–individualistic side which shone forth with such fresh clarity. Be that as it may, we can for the purposes of our enquiry allow ourselves, as we did with Shaftesbury, to dwell for a while on a part of his philosophy, though we shall be able to see it through the eyes of the later and not the earlier historism.

Leibniz is a good example of the truth that both the loosening up of dogmatic and ecclesiastical thought after the end of the Wars of Religion, and the development of the natural sciences in the later part of the seventeenth century, were prerequisites for the rise of historism. This eirenic thinker and mediator between the different confessions saw the one Christian truth, which he still accepted as such with dogmatic conviction, nevertheless existing as a matter of actual fact in different individual forms, which could not simply be condemned. The natural light of reason, far from being in contradiction to the faith, confirmed him in the belief that the fundamental truths of Christianity were essentially at one with it. His dearest and deepest wish was to use the aid of reason to bring the confessional varieties of belief back to this oneness: 'the spirit who loves unity in diversity' is one of the most characteristic phrases in his *Nouveaux Essais*. As yet, however, he would not have been able to affirm the opposite (the love of diversity in unity) with the full force of his sensitiveness to the worth of the individual. But it is abundantly clear that he gave full recognition to diversity in general, and heard in it the harmonies that go to make up unity; and he expounded this relationship in a highly creative manner.

The same picture of unity and diversity was presented to him by the new vision of the universe seen through the eyes of natural science. Here he felt a thorough modern, equipped with new insights over against the world of antiquity. Unity and a regular framework of coherent law were now seen to be combined with a richness of content that was quite unknown to those of antiquity. They had not yet (as he tells us in his *Theodicy*) seen the new prospect of a universe containing innumerable worlds with the same possibility of being inhabited by rational beings—although they need not necessarily be men. Our earth was thus only an appendage to one particular sun; but the whole vast realm of space might well be full of benediction and felicity. He conjectured, then, that there was rational life everywhere in the universe, but in a countless variety of forms, though all the one coherent work of a 'supra-mundane intelligence', God.

Here, however, just as in Shaftesbury, we catch a glimpse of the Neo-Platonic view of the world coming through from antiquity, according to which all separate beings have received their own specific nature from one sole supreme and universal first cause, on which it is all dependent. In the preface to his *Theodicy* he stated that all beauty was but a reflection of the light that streamed forth from God. Yet his conception of God was not only more essentially theistic and Christian, but (it may be said) more pragmatic and more in line with the intellectualism of his period than the mystical and supra-logical outlook of Neo-Platonism. It was no use his undertaking to avoid anthropomorphism in his picture of God. His God who has called this world into being as the best of all possible worlds, in spite of its imperfections, in a supreme wisdom that has taken full account of all possible consequences, is after all nothing other than the most completely conceived human being, raised to an infinite degree and endowed (as even he himself admits in the *Theodicy*) with the qualities of the supreme monarch or the greatest of all architects. Pictures of God often contain an element of definite historical thinking, a view we shall find confirmed in the case of Leibniz. As he was a mathematician of genius, whose new methods went far beyond those of mere geometry, so his system of 'pre-established harmony' with its complete equivalence of secondary and final causes, its strict mechanical interpretation of the whole world of bodily motion, and yet the non-mechanical activity of monads fitting in harmoniously with it, its principle of continuity that links everything closely together, both great and small—all this was first and foremost a kind of tremendous mathematical world-formula attempting to effect the most intimate possible union between spirit and nature, the determined and the determining, freedom and necessity. This inclusive notion is mostly considered today to have been exploded; but it is of

17

particular importance for us to note that it contained a germ capable of epoch-making development, going far beyond all thought tied to Natural Law, and destined later on to bear fruit in historism. This was the idea of specific individuality, spontaneously operating and developing according to its own particular laws, which is yet the offshoot of a single law-abiding universe. The resulting picture of the universe was of such a kind that it was bound in the end to shatter the mathematical character of the formula applied to the universe. By going back to the fundamental Neo-Platonic idea, it envisaged an endless multiplicity of active and closely interconnected forces proceeding from a final and supreme source and origin. The problem of unity and multiplicity posed to him by the religious and scientific situation of his time thus received a metaphysical solution, which was yet not purely metaphysical, but was destined to be confirmed in the future by the direct testimony of historical experience.

In order to understand the rise of the concept of individuality in Leibniz's mind, it will be as well to go behind the incentives given him by the religious and scientific situation of his period to the personal element in his own character, for the central ideas of a philosopher are always rooted in the depths of his original cast of mind and nature. To be sure, we must not ascribe to Leibniz the stirrings of a modern subjectivity. For he was, like the rest of his contemporaries, still permeated by the sense of man's duty to fit in with the law-abiding framework of life and the universe. But it is worth noting that in the year 1663, as a young man of sixteen, he touched upon this problem in a disputation at Leipzig, *de principio individui* (pub. by Guhrauer 1837 and in the *Philos. Schriften*, pub. by Gerhardt, 4, 15 ff.). In this, he showed himself to be still tied to the methods and approach of the Scholastics; but there is a certain sentence which holds out rich promise for the future: *pono igitur, omne individuum sua tota Entitate individuatur*—the individual becomes an individual through the whole of his nature. Moreover, it was a peculiar characteristic of the man that he was very ready to be influenced by other men's opinions, and to admit all that was good in them. 'Strange as it may sound,' he said (Dilthey, *Schriften*, 3, 25), 'I approve of most of what I read'. And so although one may well speak of an innate individualistic trait in Leibniz, it was a generous individualism that was quick to recognise and give validity to another man's thoughts, but was also intent upon bringing unity and harmony into their various elements.

His idea of individuality led him to formulate his doctrine of monads. At the back of bodies, but inseparable from them, he held, there are simple substances of an individual kind, not extended in space, which act as vital forces and shape the bodily form, which he

18

called monads; and amongst these he counted the human soul. The compelling part of his system, which did not appear to be able in any other way to arrive at a pre-established harmony of all things, was that, after conceding to the Cartesians, perhaps over-generously, that the world of bodies was subject to purely mechanical laws, it could nevertheless deny that mental and spiritual actions were conditioned by external events. Rather (as he explained) was the soul dependent solely upon God and upon itself. Deeper reflection would show that everything, including even images and passions, arose completely spontaneously from their own causes. The thought of an unconditioned and direct relationship between God and the soul suggested a background of Christian and Protestant sympathy. His cast of mind led him to pursue this idea by purely mathematical methods, which then made him base his notion of the individual upon God. He was persuaded that the infinite God revealed Himself in the infinite variety of individuals. In the *Nouveaux Essais* (III, 3) he says that the individual contains infinity within itself; and only he who is in a position to grasp the infinite can recognise the principle of individuation illustrated in this or that object, which is a consequence of the mutual interdependence of everything in the universe.

A further relativist conclusion that he drew from his doctrines was of immense importance for historical thought in the days to come. Since each monad, as he emphasised with a touch of Neo-Platonism, was a living mirror of the universe, there existed an infinite number of different pictures of the world which, through the various viewpoints of each monad, only represented the perspectives of a single universe (*Monadology*, §§ 56 & 57). This kind of relativism was in keeping, as we have already seen, with his own personal disposition.

In Leibniz's view, it was on this rock of individuality that every attempt to explain the world in terms of the mechanical motion of atoms was bound to come to grief. He accordingly confined the mechanical principle to the world of material bodies, though even here he saw individuation at work, for he even ascribed 'soul' (or as he preferred to call it in this case, entelechy) to the plants, and saw in them too a force that worked formatively from within. And so, if we rightly interpret the account in his *Nouveaux Essais* (II, 27), the little 'period' scene that was enacted in the Charlottenburg park was of considerable importance in the history of thought. He relates how a high-ranking princess of great intelligence (he probably had Sophia Charlotte in mind) once observed in the course of a walk that she did not believe there was such a thing as two completely identical leaves. Thereupon a spirited nobleman expressed the opinion that it would be easy to find such a pair; but in spite of a thorough search in the gardens, he had been unable to produce them. Leibniz was right in saying that observation of this kind had been neglected up till then, with the result that philosophy had moved away from the most natural ideas. In this outlook, Leibniz showed himself to be well ahead of his age; he was a man who already descried the outlines of a new continent.

But, as we have already hinted, Leibniz set up a further pointer in that direction as he became aware of the process of development necessarily implicit in individuality and in the monad. In his teaching, monads and the universe, individuality and infinity, were terms that belonged together. Thus each monad and each single soul, although not open to physical influences, was a mirror of the whole universe; never with complete clarity, but with varying degrees of clarity, from the confused and imperceptible little acts of 'perception', present within us at any moment in countless number, up to the insights of reason, attained by 'apperception' and reflection. It followed, then, that the soul could have something within it without being clearly aware of it, and a sharp dividing line between the world of the imperceptible and the actions of clear consciousness would indeed be something extraordinary. This picture was probably still seen in a strongly intellectual light. It only made a distinction between lesser and greater degrees of clarity in perception, while failing to notice the part played and the development undergone by the sum-total of the interior powers, and more especially the imagination (cf. Croce, *Vico's Philosophy*, p. 52). In spite of this limitation, Leibniz's was an epoch-making advance, for it opened up the sphere of the soul's unconscious life to scientific observation and evaluation, and built a bridge between it and understanding and reason. It rescued the latter from the isolated position they had occupied in the thought-forms shaped upon Natural Law, and showed that the inner life of the soul was an arena of dynamic development from the lower to the higher stages. It may be remembered that Plotinus (*Enn.*, IV, 4) had ascribed to the human soul the capacity to be in possession of faculties of which it was not conscious. Leibniz goes on to explain that we discover innate truths not only through the *lumen naturale* of reason, but also through instinct, in particular those of a moral kind. Our taste, too, depends upon the small imperceptible acts of perception, as well as observed pictures that are clear as a whole, yet confused in detail. Later on, in considering Möser's historically fruitful doctrine of 'total impression', we shall see a sudden recrudescence of this idea, which we have already met in Shaftesbury, though used in a different way. By virtue of the small perceptions, Leibniz tells us in the introduction to his *Nouveaux Essais*, as his thought ranges far afield and ascends to lofty peaks, 'the present is big with the child of the future, and filled with the life of the past. By virtue of these everything fits in together—σύμπνοια πάντα, as Hippocrates remarked.'[1] This word about the breath of the universal life, inspiring all individuality and linking the ages together, was also destined to inspire the youthful Herder in days to come.

But it is necessary at this point, as with the related ideas of Shaftesbury, to recall the limitations of Leibniz's outlook. For it happened almost by an accidental application of his doctrine, one might say, that he burst the bonds of the concepts based upon Natural Law from below without realising it, while consciously maintaining its top layer of dogma, and so did not manage to carry through his new insights to their logical conclusion. The process of development within the soul which he discovered was directed by him in such a way as to produce, as the highest result of mental and spiritual evolution, not the products of individual thought, but normative truths of absolute validity. Basing his thought upon Natural Law, he maintained that there were certain necessary, eternal and innate truths which, although partly arising along with the instincts, were yet ultimately only to be classified by the light of reason. True, he was well aware, and often emphasised, that even the possible perception of these eternal truths by this human light of reason was anything but complete and decisive. There were spiritual realms above us capable of a higher knowledge, though the highest was only accessible to deity. But even the incomplete possession of the higher truths attainable by man still has an absolute character, and a certain fixed and static nature such as belonged to the truths of Natural Law. To be sure, Leibniz could justifiably maintain the existence of timelessly valid truths in logic and mathematics; but what was the position in the world of moral ideas and the so-called natural theology? These, he maintained, were derived from axioms by the light of eternal reason, axioms whose complete certainty was only vouched for by this same reason.

Thus the development in the human soul discovered by Leibniz, leading up from the obscure and confused perceptions into the clear apperceptions of reason, and to the normative regularity of eternal truths, was more a process of completion than of genuine historical evolution, which must at every stage produce individual forms, even though these might be to some extent blended with the typical and the general. 'Everything strives for perfection', says Leibniz in his *Système nouveau de la nature*, 'not only as regards the universe in general, but also as regards the creatures in particular'. It will be important for all our subsequent studies to take a firm grasp of this essential difference between the idea of development in the historical

---

[1] Hippocrates did in fact speak of a σύμπνοια μία as is demonstrated by Boutroux in his edition of the *Monadologie*, p. 177.

sense, and the thought of perfection as embodied in the outlook of the Enlightenment. As we saw, even Shaftesbury's concept of development became arrested in this view of perfection.

Within Leibniz's system of thought there was another limitation to the idea of development. The single monad was considered by him to be both indestructible and eternal. True, these monads could over the course of time take on successive lower or higher forms of existence, and so to this extent participate in an upward development. But they had no power to bring about transformations in other monads, for although a monad might remain permanently linked with the universe as an imperfect mirror of its activities, it could only live exclusively according to its own laws given to it by God. The effect of this was to exalt the concept of individuality at the expense of the notion of development. For it is of the essence of historical development that the active individual forces should operate upon one another from within, so as to be fruitful in the production of new forms. To adopt Shaftesbury's language, we might say that they must be 'formative forms'. It may be objected that Leibniz's doctrine of monads might be valid for the transcendental sphere, but would not apply without further consideration to the empirical world of history. Yet it may be said to have erected inner walls of partition within the deepest active forces in history, for the monads now appeared to be a bundle of countless single threads only tied together at the ends that were held by God. The thought laboured under a certain mathematical compulsiveness derived from Leibniz's view of the universe, according to which the problem of unity and multiplicity could be solved in this way and in no other. But its effect on the nascent idea of historical development might well be to give it a certain monadological exclusiveness, and narrow it down to a bare concept of evolution. We shall also be further concerned with this line of thought in subsequent pages.

The greatness of Leibniz, however, lay in the fact that he was able to be a torchbearer both to the German movement of Enlightenment that followed after him, and to the German idealism and historical outlook which were its offspring. He was enabled to do this by his most original philosophical ideas, and not by his ideas of history or by his own historical writings. Those philosophical ideas are scattered through the inexhaustible material of his writings and letters, and were never collected into a corporate body of doctrine. Only a part of them have ever seen the light of day. And his *Annales imperii occidentis Brunswicenses*, covering the years 768 to 1005, were never completed, and were only published in the nineteenth century, by Pertz (1843 ff.), long after the moment when they would have been important for scholarship. The Frenchman Davillé has worked on this collected material with devoted and exemplary industry and great enthusiasm, though he is not always completely reliable in the use of his sources. He has attempted to put together a picture of the historical Leibniz in his *Leibniz historien* (1909, 798 pp.), representing him as one of the greatest historians of all time. But we cannot ourselves agree with this verdict. 'Leibniz', says Dilthey (*Schriften*, 3, 36), 'no longer attempted to integrate the world of history into his philosophical system'. This is true in the main, but we are still left curious to see how this gigantic confusion of philosophical and historical material looked, and to know whether it may not provide links here and there between these two worlds. And in fact, this eminent thinker does provide not only typical features of the stage in the development of historical thinking that had been reached at that time, but also the preliminary revolt of an innate genius against the limitations inherent in himself and in the mind of his age. Both of these, the typical as well as the original in Leibniz's thought, belong to any picture of the antecedent stages in the rise of historism.

Leibniz's ascription of a utilitarian and moral purpose to historical knowledge is typical of his outlook. In his *Theodicy* (II, 148) he says plainly that the foremost aim of history, like that of poetry, is to teach prudence and virtue by means of examples, and to portray vice in such a way as to call forth abhorrence for it. Here, it is possible that the ethical and religious tendencies of his work made him go beyond what was suggested by his own inner inclinations. For his programme of historical research put forward in the preface to his *Accessiones historicae* (1700) mentions other motives and aims, such as the direct satisfaction to be gained from *res singulares*, and the tracing back of present events to their original causes. We shall see how important this intention became. At bottom, it was perhaps Leibniz's strongest motive; but at the conscious level, the utilitarian moralism was predominant.

Again, it was typical of the period that in the midst of the gradual secularisation of the European outlook and the attention given to new ideas, purely ecclesiastical and theological aims should no longer hold the entire field. There was a newly awakened and insatiable interest in the historical material of all ages, as yet mostly centred in the absolute values of Christianity, but hungry for all available aspects of the historical world. The antiquarian urge, which had at all times been exemplified by specific and particularly gifted individuals, had now become a fashion of the period. The increase of weighty historical literature and monumental encyclopedias in the second half of the seventeenth century, and such a work as Pierre Bayle's *Dictionnaire*, with its clear evidence of bursting through theological assumptions, show that historical interest was on the increase.

And thirdly, we can cite as typical of the period round about 1700 the new and growing urge to treat with greater accuracy and better critical sense all the material that had been collected with a bearing upon the past. True, the beginnings of the critical method in handling documents from the past go back a good deal earlier, to the labours of the great Dutch and French philologists and latter-day humanists, and even to the early humanists. The historical past now became generally more interesting to an ever-widening circle, and the natural sciences set a great example by showing that a more accurate picture of reality could only be obtained by more rigorously precise methods. Confronted by this example, scholars began to feel an obligation to follow along the same lines. The Benedictine monk Mabillon was a pioneer in this adventure, with his epoch-making criticism of documents. The Jesuit Papebroch sought to go one better in an unrestricted scepticism that was, however, confined to the documentary sphere. But now there arose along with this antiquarian interest a scepticism in religion and philosophy, represented in Bayle's *Dictionnaire*, from which an exaggerated claim has been advanced that he was the real creator of historical precision (Cassirer, *Philosophie der Aufklärung*, p. 276). At the same time Leibniz was doing his best in all his historical works to satisfy the new critical standards,[1] though he was probably more sensitive than Bayle to the difficulty of using incomplete and confused source-material in order to establish the true facts of the case. Even at that period, men began to feel the need to add factual criticism to the criticism of sources. However, the pragmatic tendency of the time towards hasty explanation of the unintelligible in terms of what could be easily grasped soon made itself strongly felt. But Leibniz had a significant premonition that there would have to be a digging down to even deeper levels in order to exhaust the theme *de fide historica* (*Nouv. Ess.*, IV, 16). We cannot here do more than give these indications, for the development of the critical method, although always connected with the development of the historical sense, really requires special treatment. Not till a full breakthrough of the sense for individuality and a classification of the theory of knowledge offered by Kant's philosophy could the critical method be given an inner assurance that would protect it against the arbitrary imaginations of pragmatism.

That period has been called the age of polyhistory; but it has been rightly observed of Leibniz that he was not so much a polyhistorian as a panhistorian. For his ultimate aim was to find some intellectual link which would unite his whole antiquarian knowledge with his philosophy, though he was never indeed successful in this quest. 'The

---

[1] On the subject of his recognition of Mabillon and Papebroch, cf. E. Seeberg, *Gottfried Arnold*, p. 339.

people who rely upon philosophy and argument', he wrote in 1700 to Burnet (Davillé, p. 355, n. 4; *Philos. Schriften*, pub. by Gerhardt, 3, 270), 'usually despise all researches into antiquity, and the antiquarians on their part ridicule what they call the philosophers' dreams. But it is right to seek to do justice to the merits of both'. His words show, however, that he still saw these two worlds as alongside one another, not involved in one another. The world of 'eternal truths' still ranked higher in his estimation than the world of 'factual truths'.

But there was no lack of slight connecting-links between these two worlds. There was, for example, the basic idea in his philosophy of a principle of continuity, which called attention to small causes with big effects; and we are even reminded of his doctrine of individuality, which bore fruit in his innate urge to push his antiquarian researches in every possible direction. He eagerly followed all the tracks left by men of all times and in all places, from the prehistoric barrows, urns and skeletons discovered in his own Lower Saxony, the Etruscan and Roman inscriptions of Italy, to the new marvels being revealed in China by the Catholic missionaries at this period and the memoirs of the seventeenth-century statesmen among whom he had grown up. His *Protogaea* (published in 1749; first rough sketch in *Acta Eruditorum*, 1693) was intended as an introduction to his Annals, and dealt with geography, geology, and the oldest human remains in Lower Saxony. It was, in a smaller and more concrete setting, a kind of prelude to Herder's later attempt to deduce the history of humanity from cosmic and terrestrial presuppositions. There can scarcely be any modern historical and empirical science that does not in some way or other have Leibniz as its forerunner.

The knowledge he sought for was to be causally linked together; and it is this that often gives his interests such a modern tinge. He says of geography that one can use it to determine the true interests of every people and every government (Davillé, 436). This is, moreover, an idea that had already cropped up in the doctrine of the State's interests during the early seventeenth century (*Idee der Staatsräson*, p. 196). As historiographer of the Guelphs, he had already had to pursue intensive genealogical studies, and he saw their importance, because they threw light on the *connection naturelle des hommes*, and so belonged to the nerves and sinews of history (Davillé, 441). At this point the demand for continuity and causal connection becomes a demand for a genetic causal link; and this was to be more splendidly demonstrated in his famous efforts towards a science of linguistics with the aim of establishing the relationship between the various languages and getting nearer to the original speech of man. For he saw the different languages as 'the oldest monuments of the human race' (*Nouv. Ess.*, III, 2; Davillé, 403), the witnesses to the origin of the inter-relationship and the migrations of the peoples, the mirror of their intelligence and their character; they stood in the same relation to these as the moon does to the sea. In order to have a right understanding of this question of the primitive language and the earliest civilisation from the point of view of the history of thought, it must be borne in mind that it may well have already arisen in the minds of inquisitive readers of the Bible. Leibniz himself is reminiscent of this approach when he supposes that the German language has preserved a particularly large quantity of original elements—Adamitic elements, as Jakob Böhme called them (*Nouv. Ess., loc. cit.*). And there were very daring hypotheses about the family relationship between widely separated peoples current among the seventeenth-century antiquarian scholars, often linked with biblical material. Yet even these interests were already having a fresh and brilliant light thrown upon them from the new illumination produced by his doctrine of individuality. For Leibniz maintained that a study of all the languages in the universe would not only elucidate material things and the origin of the various peoples, but also help to bring new knowledge about our own mind and the marvellous variety of its accomplishments. The example of the Greeks and Romans and the modern French, and the sad contrast with his own German people, impressed vividly upon him the truth that nations and their languages always flourish together.

> I do not believe that such a thing could happen by chance.
> I believe that just as there is a connection between the moon and the sea, so there is a relationship between the rise and fall of peoples and their languages.[1]

He had a delicate individual feeling for the untranslatable quality of such words as the Greek 'ostracism' and the Latin 'proscription', and deduced from the dual existence of literary languages and popular languages among the Greeks and Romans, and still more among modern nations, certain consequences that were full of ingenious suggestiveness (*Nouv. Ess.*, III, 9). His studies of the changes in the meaning of certain words already strike an evolutionary note.

All these interests arose from a general movement, from the hunger for material felt by that century, and developed in Leibniz's mind into actual problems for historical research in the future. His glance swept with the far-ranging eye of an eagle over the whole world of history. It is striking to see what sureness of judgement he showed in

---

[1] *Ermahnung an die Teutsche, ihren Verstand und Sprache besser zu üben*, ed. P. Pietsch, pp. 307 ff. I am indebted to the editor of Leibniz's works, Prof. Paul Ritter, for these and other valuable observations.

his appreciation of the great turning-points in whole epochs, of what Ranke called the 'historic moment'. He was superior to his successor Voltaire in his feeling for the essentials in the destinies of the nations. This is clearly shown by his masterly *Brevis Synopsis historiae Guelficae* (Pertz, *L.s. gesammelte Werke*, 1, Series 4, 277 ff.), with its sketch of early mediaeval development. The old division of world history into four world empires was rejected by Leibniz, who divided it as it then became usual into ancient history, the Middle Ages, and Modern times. His horizon of interest stretched from the primitive beginnings of the human race to the peoples of the Far East and the Cabinet secrets of his own day, and he deliberately wished to adorn his history of Brunswick with historical discoveries *qui tireront sur l'universel quoy qu'elles naissent de nostre histoire particulière* (Davillé, 558, *Works*, ed. Klopp, 6, 371). But it was precisely these annals that showed how hybrid and unfinished in form was the historical writing of the time to which Leibniz had to have recourse. The annals' form was like an enormous prison in which he had to house a mighty complement of knowledge (more than 2,000 closely-printed pages), but could only divide it up in a very rough and superficial fashion. As an official State history, the work had to give preference to personal history, State events and chronicles of war, as well as ecclesiastical history, but these were seldom connected by any interior thread; they were mostly set down in purely chronological order. Yet the great thinker revealed himself here in many flashes of insight, in detached judgments of universal significance, in the raising of important problems worthy of further research, in numerous retrospective glances or peeps into the future. He would tenderly bring out anything that threw light on mental and spiritual culture, so that now and again there is a real touch of genuine, mediaeval colour. But the work as a whole remained within the conventions of learned historical writing, and belongs rather to a history of research on the Middle Ages, or of the critical method in history, than to a history of the origins and rise of historism.

Attempts have also been made to describe Leibniz as a forerunner of what Western Europeans have been pleased to call 'the history of civilisation', which first came to fruition in Voltaire's historical writings. But here, too, considerable reservations must be made, and we must not overlook what was individual and at the same time restricted by the historical conceptions of his period. All the later historical writing dealing with culture and civilisation, with its deliberate suppression of all local politics and military events, was rooted in the self-consciousness of a self-emancipating middle class. But in Leibniz's historical efforts there is as yet no trace of this tendency. He was the servant of both prince and state, the good

Christian and the great scholar and thinker of the time around 1700, and the Germany of 1700, a Germany which (as he himself once pensively remarked) did not possess great capital cities like England and France. The servant of princes was at heart already inclining to withdraw in favour of wider German and humanitarian sympathies; yet there were limits to what a German servant of princes and imperial patriot, a far-sighted Protestant and a scholar in 1700, could hope to achieve in the way of useful and worthwhile human tasks. And these limits controlled the choice of what may be called his sphere of interests in the history of culture, if one may judge by the various observations scattered throughout his work. And so this included besides politics, law and military affairs also economics, interpreted along mercantilist lines as a part of politics. Not only ecclesiastical history in the narrower sense, but everything that had proceeded from the bosom of Christianity in the way of rites, uses, sects and popular beliefs—all this attracted his attention. First and foremost, one can descry in what he called *Historia litteraria*, and recommended for study, a prelude to the future historical treatment of culture. For this study was intended to show the origins and progress of the various sciences and inventions (not forgetting sports and games, as an expression of the human spirit) from the oldest times up to the present day. It was to thank the inventor and encourage his successors; and as in the history of philosophy, so here also, he required the emphasis to be placed not so much on the personal and biographical, as had hitherto been the custom, but on the material and factual, and the advance of knowledge (Davillé, 348 ff.). Once again, then, he was the first to dig deeper into the layers of human history, and to add new brilliance to the optimistic belief in progress cherished by the thinkers of the Enlightenment. But here, too (as we have already seen in his doctrine of the inner life) the concept of development was still somewhat shackled by the idea of perfection.

All the same, it is wonderful to observe how this great mind, with all its conscientious research-work, and almost pedantic devotion to the typical interests of the seventeenth-century princes' world, even down to details of ceremonial, could also have such a free and wide-ranging conception of humanity as a whole. He became conscious of the oneness of the human task in its progress through growing knowledge; and this formed the central idea of the Enlightenment. In contrast to the broad national currents of the Western European Enlightenment, the specifically German task was to carry on a dual life of the narrowest involvement in apparent trivialities of small principalities combined with a free and universal outlook. It was precisely this tension, however, that enabled the mind to rise to higher flights than could be attained by the purely national cultures of the West. Leibniz believed that the whole human race was destined to rise to a higher plane of perfection. But this was where his thought took on such great and dynamic proportions, in keeping with the concept of endless movement embodied in his philosophy. He envisaged this human progress not as tending towards some paradisial final state, but as an endless process. *Nec proinde unquam ad terminum progressus perveniri* (Davillé, 709; *Philos. Schriften*, pub. by Gerhardt, 7, 308). In the year of his death (1716) he wrote that the universe was ever changing and moving towards new perfections, although it lost some of the old ones (Davillé, 709; *Philos. Schriften*, pub. by Gerhardt, 3, 589). In this prospect of an everlasting metamorphosis and a continuous rise and fall of changing factors, Leibniz for once passed beyond the limitations of his own perfectionist outlook.[1] He did not allow himself to be led astray by the premonition vouchsafed to him by his genius of a great revolution impending upon the eighteenth century, which he prophesied as the effect of the spread of selfish and destructive opinions, to the detriment of the fatherland and the common weal (*Nouv. Ess.*, IV, 16). Looking at the new secular belief in progress through the eyes of a Christian and theistic faith in Providence, he was able to blend the two, and console himself with the thought that this same Providence would help the human race in and through this revolution. And although in this thought something of his pragmatic conception of God once again crops up, he yet managed to weave the pragmatism that overvalued the purposeful activities of the individual, but was so much in keeping with the customs of an absolutist age, into the texture of his concept of progress. For he expected marvellous things to happen in the upward movement of the human race, perhaps even in quite a few years, through the agency of some great prince who would have a long reign of absolute peace and be concerned to make men happier, more peaceful in outlook and more able to control the forces of nature (*Nouv. Ess.*, IV, 3, and conclusion).

Any consideration of his historical thinking and his philosophy reminds us simultaneously of the years 1700 and 1800 in the history of German thought. He was never able to complete the greatest task he had undertaken, namely the full working out of the concept of individuality; this was something he had to hand on to the coming century. His path was barred by the old Christian framework of

[1] These limitations are still visible, however, in another passage: *Universum est ad instar plantae aut animalis hactenus ut ad maturitatem tendet. Sed hoc interest, quod nunquam ad summum pervenit maturitatis gradum, nunquam etiam regreditur aut senescit.* Bodemann, *Die Leibnizhandschriften der K. öff. Bibl. zu Hannover*, p. 121.

Natural Law and by the new requirement put forward by natural science, that human affairs must also be amenable to timeless law. Thus his understanding of the primacy of the eternal truths over the factual, empirical truths was, as we have seen, still conceived in terms of Natural Law. In his *Theodicy* he indulges in frequent polemics against the jejune scepticism of Bayle, and is led to speak of the course of human life and the effects of misfortune and sin. But he viewed this always in the light of universal principles, and did not regard the individual as a law to himself in each and all of his actions. He glanced in passing at the primitive races, and praised the strength of spirit shown by the Red Indians in sorrow and misfortune (III, 256). Yet he judged them, not by the underlying assumptions of their own way of life, but by the normative ideal of the rational man. Yet, as we have seen, his sense of the individual was already active in the wealth of his historical interests. Although he was not able to deal logically with the whole range of human life, the vital power latent in his doctrine of monads led him, at any rate in principle, to knowledge that was to prove of the greatest significance. The determinist feature in this doctrine of monads enabled him to take a look into the depths of the individual human destiny. 'The idea (*la notion*) of an individual substance', he wrote in his *Discours de métaphysique* (*Philos. Schriften*, pub. by Gerhardt, 4, 436; Davillé, 696), 'embraces definitely all that it will ever experience'. Alexander the Great's and Caesar's destinies were laid down in their natures, for 'all that ever happens to us is only the result of our essential being' (*loc. cit.*, pp. 433, 438, 439). This line of thought leads on to Goethe's 'imprinted form that evolves in the course of life'.

Leibniz's great ideas, in preparing the way for historism, did not as yet produce any stirring experience that saw all things human in a new light, as did the later 'Sturm und Drang' period. But they were more than the product of a keen and adventurous mind that could combine mathematical ideas and progressive thought with a touch of genius. Leibniz, like Shaftesbury, can only be understood in the framework of the secular Neo-Platonic tradition, which saw each single life as a reflection of the divine, and man as a microcosm of the macrocosm. Leibniz took up this thought with the deep devotion of a German Protestant believer, quietly deepened and widened it, but covered it with the resplendent mantle of an intellectualism that was still characteristic of this period.

III Gottfried Arnold

Was it possible in the age of Leibniz, and if so, to what degree, to burst the bonds of thought-forms based upon Natural Law by an avowed battle against intellectualism? The answer is given by Gott-fried Arnold's *Unparteiische Kirchen- und Ketzerhistorie* (1699–1700; the references here are to the edition of 1729 in two volumes).

Arnold (1666–1714) carried on a battle against the 'over-acute and clever reason' not only of his contemporaries, but of all the preceding centuries, and was inspired by a genuine passion. But he could only conduct this struggle on the basis of a radical and mystical spiritual-ism, to which he had gravitated from a previous pietism. He remained deeply attached to this spiritualism when, about the turn of the century, he reverted to pietism and took up ecclesiastical office. His book was produced before this last development, and represents a radical attitude. But even this pietism, which was then in the ascen-dant in Germany, drew on the mystical inheritance, and has been called a kind of tame ecclesiastical or sectarian mysticism. The pietists, the mystics and the spiritualists as a whole, however, repre-sented a continuation of the Neo-Platonic spiritual chain of in-fluence. They did this in their own way, which was different from Shaftesbury's approach. Their attitude was not (like his) aesthetically open-minded and universalist in outlook, but rather subjectively pious and yearning for a sense of divinity. This Neo-Platonic line of thought, beginning with Dionysius the Areopagite, had become blended with Christianity, and since the Renaissance, the humanist movement and the Reformation had been taken up not only by whole sects, but, more important still, by detached and original thinkers. Arnold's great historical work served as a collecting-point for their ideas, as Erich Seeberg has shown in his study of Arnold (1923),[1] a work of great intensity, deep thought, and wide scholar-ship. Our purpose here will not be to enquire what were the intricate roots of his interpretation of history as they extended back into the past, but rather, looking ahead, to ask what significance his views may have when considered as a possible root for the coming of his-torism, and to see what they could, and what they could not, con-tribute to it. As his influence upon the century, great though it was, cannot be compared with that of Shaftesbury and Leibniz, it will be enough to appreciate his thought in summary form.

We shall have to note in Arnold, as we did in both Shaftesbury and Leibniz, the appearance of the same phenomenon, one that we shall encounter a good many times in the future. The thinking based upon Natural Law was loosened up by a spiritual process which neverthe-less still bore specific signs of this same bondage. The heart of this

[1] A summarising essay, 'G. Arnold's view of history', *Zeitschr. f. Kirchengesch.*, vol. 38, had been published earlier. Seeberg also edited *Selections from G. Arnold's Works* (1934).

thinking based upon Natural Law had been from the ancient world onwards an intellectualism that trusted in the power of reason, interpreted as intellect, to arrive at truth. This confidence in reason was so great that the truth revealed was held to be universally valid and timeless, and was treated as uniform and absolute. This way of thinking, as we have already noted, could only be broken down from the direction of the inner man, from a rising consciousness that reason interpreted as intellect was not sufficient to discover the decisive and vital truths on which historical thinking also depended. But to begin with, this revolution of the irrational against the rational itself remained under the spell of the rational, in that it ascribed to the spiritual values it discovered just as absolute, timeless and uniform a character as belonged to the truths attained by the thought-processes derived from Natural Law. Just as in Shaftesbury we were able to speak of a new Natural Law constructed along Neo-Platonic lines, so to an even greater degree was Gottfried Arnold's universal and historical outlook, looked at as a framework of thought, a kind of 'Natural Law of the soul'.

According to Arnold, there is one fundamental, timeless and ever-recurring spiritual process fulfilling itself in the life and history of mankind, from Adam to the point of time which he thought to be imminent, the ἀποκατάστασις πάντων in which 'all creatures will be brought back into that original and most blessed oneness . . . as into a fathomless sea of eternal love' (1, 1202). This fundamental process is an 'either–or' of good and evil, a choice between the world, selfishness and sin, 'the sinfulness of men and the old Adam', and a flight from the world, a rejection of selfishness, an opening of the soul to God, an illumination by Him, a becoming one with Him, a mystical state. History has only one lesson, namely that over against the overwhelming mass of worldly and sinful events of life, there stands the spiritual life of the few genuine believers—who existed even before Christianity, and are still to be found outside the Christian fold. We can leave on one side the theological question of how Arnold could combine this religious universalism, and a fervent Christian faith in God's revelation through the Word, with the spiritualistic concept of an illumination of the pious through the ever-renewed direct action of the Holy Spirit. But it is decisive for our purposes that, starting from his principles, there was no new and direct way to the understanding of world history, beyond the interpretation in the pragmatic terms of Natural Law which had hitherto prevailed. Any such approach was considered worthless in the main, if not positively pernicious, 'since human mistakes, follies and sins permanently constitute the greater part of the human story' (1, 453). He could therefore only set out ecclesiastical history at such tremendous length because it served to warn men off from evil. For he dated the decline of the Church and the appearance of a wicked clerisy within her at the very beginning of the post-apostolic age. He traced the corruption on through the Middle Ages, now in growing and now in static form, as far as the forerunners of the Reformation and the young Luther, in whom the Eternal Light shone somewhat more brightly; but saw in Luther's later disputations and intolerant Schoolmen's theology, and that of Lutheranism in general, a new descent into corruption. Yet even in the worst times, he maintained, there had been pious individuals in the Church itself and in the sects, which he held to have been often wrongly declared heretical, though he did not love the sectarian world and could draw distinctions between one heretic and another. The worst heretics of all, in his view, were the heresy-makers of the official Church.

His view, then, was a peculiar combination of a very ancient idea of history as a whole (the scheme of a Golden Age, followed by degeneration, with the hope of a future world renewal) and the dualistic and unhistorical idea of a constantly repeated pattern of much darkness and little light existing side by side in this world. There were incidentally mystic grounds of consolation for the small numbers of the sons of light. But in this scheme the historical world was to meet a fate analogous to that to which the Enlightenment looked forward. Just as the latter exaggerated the place of Natural Law and set up reason as an absolute standard of value for history and for its whole course, which was predominantly irrational, though now and again showing signs of reasonable development; so did Arnold's spiritualism make the absolute worth of the soul enlightened by God the corner-stone of the world's history. But here, as we have seen, the familiar process repeated itself: for in Arnold's eyes, human nature was just as fundamentally unchanging as it had always been for the thinking based upon Natural Law. 'There is only one kind of tragedy and comedy being played on earth; the only difference is that diverse persons take up the characters' (in Seeberg, p. 143). Accordingly he derived the historical events themselves entirely as pragmatism did from the same unvarying stock of qualities possessed by the agent —and in his eyes these were mostly bad. All this shows that there was no stirring at all of any notion of development in Arnold's thought. Even the decline noted by him at the end of the apostolic age was not due to any development, but simply to the irruption of the principle of evil that was always close at hand; though he could on the other hand also speak of a passing 'irruption of the good principle in the early days of the Reformation' (1, 494).

But it was quite simply that (as Seeberg rightly points out on p. 147) he was the first historian to move the human soul into the centre of history. However monotonous the soul's decisions for good or evil sound in his historical narrative, he does still conceive them as a totality conditioned not by the understanding and the reason, but by the will—that is, by the basic direction of the soul. According to one of his main theses, a man becomes a heretic not through false opinions, but through a corrupted will, 'which at once drew the understanding on to its side' (1, 38). For his mystical requirements, the actions of the understanding and the 'acute power of reason' were mostly evil. Therefore, he cried, let men cut loose from letters, from ideas, from scholastic theology and from Aristotle, and let them go to the innermost source of the soul's life in God. Moreover, as we have already discovered, it was the single lonely seekers after God whom he sought for and saluted in the pages of history. Is there already some inkling here of individualism in the sense of the concept of individuality upheld by historism? Or at any rate a step on the way to it?

Starting out from the individuality of the human soul and the human forms and communities created by man's individuality, this line of thought sees all these forms, however much of a type they may seem to be, as still individual creations, and regards each single man as surrounded by these forms and higher communities and in constant mutual interaction with them. Arnold was lacking in this sense of the individual embedded in a common life that was itself an individual structure. As Seeberg himself (p. 146) quite rightly says: 'As in the historiography of the Enlightenment, the single person remains isolated, without any inner connection with the society in which he lives'.

On the other hand, is at least the separate human soul conceived in individual terms by Arnold? The deepening and inward turning of the soul which he preached in order to make it a mirror of the divine light had little differentiation about it. According to him, the experience of rebirth was really the same everywhere—if we are to follow Seeberg's estimate of his views (p. 218). And Arnold held that this rebirth was to have such an ascetic effect on practical life that it would kill all those movements which disturbed mystical union with God; it would in effect lead to a positive enmity against the world of culture. Arnold took offence at Luther's delight in joyful singing and dancing (1, 505), and at Melanchthon's enthusiasm for Homer (1, 563 f.); and found that the Antichrist had made use of the organ-pipes in churches. All this immediately reminds us of the tight-laced restrictions placed upon individuality by pietism, intended to ensure that the life of the soul, though narrower and poorer in content, should on the other hand be more deeply receptive to the one influence that really mattered. Mere 'selfhood', however, was suspect as a root of evil. Arnold (Seeberg, p. 174) wrote the following couplet:

> Geh aus dir selbst und deiner Eigenheit,
> So bist du in der Welt von Welt befreit.[1]

But this brings us up against one of the strangest and most important phenomena in the history of German thought in the eighteenth century. For pietism, which we can take Arnold to represent at this point, sought to place restrictions upon individuality and yet at the same time powerfully stirred up its deepest recesses in the soul. In so doing, it brought about an inner tension of forces which ultimately favoured the awakening of individuality. In spite of the absolutising and regularising of the spiritual values that pietism and mysticism had created, they must be numbered among the most active forerunners of the new individualism, which in its turn became the seedbed for historism. Thus a main line (though not the only line) of development leads from pietism through the 'Sturm und Drang' movement to historism. That German pietism was a psychologically necessary preliminary to the 'Sturm und Drang' movement, and helped finally to mobilise all the forces of the spirit, is accepted today as one of the assured results in the history of thought.[2] Indeed, it is even in danger of being too formally emphasised at the expense of the whole wealth of motives active in the eighteenth century. But it was pietism, and the moderated mysticism surviving in it, that was the first force in Germany to draw a small section of men of all social ranks out of the dull acceptance of conditions as they were, and accustom them to combine a quiet and peaceful exterior existence with an exaltation of the inner life. They learnt the secret of rising above the prosaic dullness of everyday life, and of raising the joys and pains experienced in small things on to a level of greatness. They found how to listen to their inner feelings and discern their worth or worthlessness, how to discover secrets within themselves, and so to become even more fully aware of the 'selfhood' which they intended to suppress. It is not our purpose here to speak of the specifically religious content and value of pietism, but only to note the fact that religious values can often be converted and fruitfully transferred to quite different spheres of life. The new German poetry from Klopstock's time onwards was to be the first to experience this. Its very vocabulary and imagery, as Burdach has shown, are evidence of the

---

[1] Forsake thyself and thy identity;
    So wilt thou stay in the world—yet from the world be free.
[2] Cf. Burdach, Faust and Moses in the *Reports of Proceedings of the Berlin Academy*, 1912; Unger, *Hamann und die Aufklärung*, 1925; Korff, *Geist der Goethezeit*, I, 1923; Koppel S. Pinson, *Pietism as a Factor in the Rise of German Nationalism*, 1934 (reviewed by me in *Hist. Zeitschrift*, 151, 116).

pietistic influence and the mysticism that preceded it. We shall be confronted with it once again in the youthful period of Herder and Goethe.

Goethe, too, provides important evidence of the special influence of Gottfried Arnold's *Ecclesiastical History and History of Heresies*,[1] and of their connection with our theme. He read them in his years of youthful ferment after 1768, when he had come back from Leipzig to Frankfurt, and was collecting material for a new intimate life (*Dicht. u. Wahrh.*, vol. 2, bk 8). 'This man is not merely a reflective historian: he is also pious and sensitive.' He accordingly noted that Arnold, with his new organ of knowledge, the soul, was advancing beyond the bounds hitherto set by pragmatism to the confines of genuine history. And with this realisation may have come a suspicion that history contains within itself not only pragmatically explicable facts, but also spiritual material. Further, Goethe was to experience through Arnold one of those unintended effects of pietism and mysticism in his own person. Arnold had unintentionally provided a collection of portraits of religious individualities, especially from the later years of the Reformation onwards, by presenting a moving variety of remarkable individuals, solitary seekers after God who had come into collision with the ruling theology of their time; and he had often quoted their own words. He did not mean to show their more peculiar and individual traits, but those which constantly recurred. He intended to illustrate by their example the one fundamental mystical experience, and not infrequently he read his own ideals of total piety into the lives of these peaceful revolutionaries. But in the youthful Goethe this gallery of portraits aroused 'the spirit of contradiction and the delight in paradox'. Arnold's bold revolt against ruling conventions, to take up his own words (1, 638), against the '*präjudicium autoritatis* and especially *pluralitatis*', pleased Goethe. 'I diligently studied the various opinions, and as I had often heard it said that in the end every man has his own religion, it seemed to me perfectly natural that I too should form my own.' And then follows the account of the fanciful religion of his youth with its strong Neo-Platonic colouring, which he conjured up at that period, certain basic elements of which became permanently fused with his inmost self.

And so Arnold's Christian mysticism leads back at this point to its own source in Neo-Platonism and this in turn, in company with

[1] Further testimony on this point is in Seeberg, *loc. cit.* Also some further details on Arnold's relations with Thomasius and the Enlightenment, which can be left out as far as we are concerned. In my copy of Arnold, there is the following handwritten observation from the eighteenth century: 'Forster relates, in the history of Halle University, p. 87, that Thomasius was always wont to say that whoever had two coats should sell one and buy this book of Arnold'. Cf. Arnold, 2, 1363.

other elements drawn from this century, was able to prepare new channels for historical thinking. But even the basic notion of Christian mysticism and pietism (the direct intercourse of the single soul with God, in the face of which the external world sinks to nothingness) was potent enough to produce new individual life and so the prerequisites for a new insight into humanity and the world of history. Incidentally, it must not be forgotten that this basic idea was the deepest artery of Protestantism and especially of German Lutheranism, though it has often been hidden from view. Shaftesbury, Leibniz and Arnold all lived and thought in an atmosphere of spiritual independence from worldly authority, and faithful dependence on the Almighty. This, in the ultimate analysis, was the secret of their preparation for the coming of historism. And now, in turning to Vico, we shall see what could be done for historism in the more restricted conditions of the Catholic world.

IV Vico/Lafitau

It is no mere chance that the thinkers who proved capable in the first thirty years of the eighteenth century of preparing the way for a new type of historical thought able to overcome the Enlightenment that was just rising to full power, should have come from Germany, England and Italy. For in spite of all the divergencies of spirit that have been deepened by divisions of religious belief, these nations are bound together by a certain affinity, a greater capacity than that of the French to overcome the restrictions of intellectualism, to think from within and with the use of all the inward powers, and so to build up spiritually rich individuality. In the Renaissance, Italy showed the way. The Counter-Reformation and foreign rule then narrowed down the path of development, but was never quite able to close it. The scientific life of Southern Italy in particular had withered into a dry and abstract scholasticism which could not be revivified even by the fresh winds of Cartesian philosophy and mechanistic thought. At this point there appeared, like the vision of some miraculous oasis, Giambattista Vico (1668–1744), a manifestation of the most original and inexhaustible spiritual and intellectual power. This modest man, outwardly rather unfortunate in his circumstances, and ignored by his contemporaries, was Professor of Rhetoric at the University of Naples. All on his own, he took up the battle against Cartesianism and Mechanism, as well as against the prejudices of the great seventeenth-century teachers of Natural Law; and in his *Scienza Nuova* (in the three editions of 1725,

1730 and 1744), he created an entirely new organ for historical thought.[1]

Here, there was no question of a slow and tranquil liberation from Natural Law, as with Shaftesbury and Leibniz, but an irresistible irruption, the irruption of a definite type of thinker with great imaginative gifts and intuitive propensities, possessed indeed of greater logical powers, but whose thought proceeded from the very depths of his soul, piercing the barriers of intellectualism, and finally arriving at its own true character and so at the acquisition of new knowledge and insight. There had again and again been such irruptions in men of genius ever since Plato, Plotinus and Augustine, but they had never been able to alter the entire intellectual climate, nor even effect a complete breakthrough as far as they personally were concerned. Vico, too, was unable to achieve either of these goals, and, as we shall show, he remained in one essential respect behind Shaftesbury and Leibniz, although in another he went far beyond them. On the other hand, it was granted to these two men to be the first links in a chain and teachers of the successful generation that was to follow them. Vico, however, left only the very slightest traces of influence on the thinkers we shall be considering, and must be regarded as a solitary and unrecognised outsider in the intellectual life of the eighteenth century. Montesquieu possessed his book, but did not apparently make use of it.[2] Hamann obtained it in 1777, but was disappointed that he did not find precisely what he hoped it would contain for the purposes of the economic studies he was pursuing at the time, and so put it on one side (*Schriften*, 5, 267). Herder, who is otherwise almost extravagant in giving details of the authors who interest him, did not make any reference to him till quite late on in the *Humanitätsbriefe* (*Works*, 18, 246), where there

---

[1] There is a critical edition of the *Scienza Nuova* based on the text of 1744, with the variants of 1730 etc., by Nicolini (3 vols), Bari 1911–16. Cf. also Benedetto Croce, *Bibliografia Vichiana*, 1904 and *La Filosofia di G. Vico*, 1911, used here in the German edition of Auerbach–Lücke, *Die Philosophie G. Vicos*, 1928. Further literary references are in the helpful book by R. Peters, *Der Aufbau der Weltgeschichte bei G. Vico*, 1929. There is an older rather literal translation of the *Scienza Nuova* by W. E. Weber, 1822; and a good and more recent one (though considerably abbreviated) by E. Auerbach (n.d.) [1924]. There are some valuable observations on Vico in Spranger, 'Die Kulturzyklentheorie und das Problem des Kulturverfalls', in the *Proceedings of the Preuss. akad. d. Wiss.*, open meeting of 28 January 1926. Cf. also O. Frhr. v. Gemmingen, 'Vico, Hamann und Herder' (thesis, Munich, 1919); E. Auerbach, *Vico und Herder*, Deutsche Vierteljahrsschrift f. Literaturwiss. und Geistesgesch., vol. 10 (1932); G. Mayer, 'Die Geschichte bei Vico und bei Montesquieu, in the *Festschrift f. Fr. Oppenheimer*; Nicolini, *La Giovinezza di G. B. Vico*, 1932.

[2] Cf. Croce, p. 243. A slight trace of a possible effect of Vico's doctrine of the cycle will be mentioned later on, in the section on Montesquieu.

is a page of warm appreciation; and there is no indication that he knew of Vico's work in the years of his own great output. Goethe had his attention directed to Vico during his Italian journey, and sensed the breath of genius; but he apparently looked upon him more as a pointer to the future than an interpreter of the past, and never returned to study him further.

It may well be that even in the eighteenth century there were free borrowings from Vico without mention of his name. But up till now there has been no completely convincing evidence of this.[1] Where it is a question of contacts with Vico's thought, they are not (with few exceptions) of such a marked character as to be most probably traceable to him, but might equally well be spontaneous independent creations. This is especially true of his new attitude to primitive times, primitive poetry and Homer, which, as we shall see, is in tune with a good deal in the English Pre-Romantics. But some, though not all, of his great and novel thoughts were able before long to bear fruit elsewhere even while his published work remained so neglected; and this is a sign that a more general intellectual need for them was now pressing upon the world of thought. Other ideas of his did not come into their own, or at least provoke astonishment, until the nineteenth century, when their author received greater, though by no means full, recognition. It was really not till the early twentieth century that Benedetto Croce gave the lead in recovering the treasures of Vico's thought at an ever-increasing depth. Perhaps this was all part of the obscurity of his wrestling and groping spirit, ever searching but never coming to the end; or (to adopt Croce's language) part of his inspired confusion or confused inspiration by the unfathomable, which could show each generation a new aspect. In his works, it is as though one wandered over great piles of fantastic and random ideas, and yet everywhere saw the glint of gold beneath them.

We must perforce pass over many of the problems and obscurities of his thought in order to pick out in simplified form those ideas which show some connection (whether by way of anticipation or kinship, or by contrast) with the coming historism. His theory of knowledge and his metaphysical philosophy, with which Croce deals so thoroughly, must at any rate be briefly suggested. His type of mind destined him to become a Platonist in the broader sense, just as he had in youth eagerly digested the Neo-Platonists of the Italian Renaissance (Nicolini, *La Giovinezza di G.B. Vico*, p. 103). He assimilated his contemporary surroundings as naturally and deeply as a

---

[1] Robertson, *Studies in the Genesis of Romantic Theories in the 18th Century*, 1923, assumes on pp. 287 ff. that there was a fairly strong influence by Vico upon the German movement, and especially Herder; but he does not adduce any proof.

plant takes up the constituents of the soil. The result was that he did not lose the consciousness of a strict Catholic faith even where his new thoughts seemed to be leading insensibly away from the divine transcendence that he had so strongly emphasised, and threatened to centre upon the divine immanence in the world. The Neo-Platonic picture of the world is still evident in his doctrine of the 'metaphysical points', that is to say, interior forces of an immaterial kind through which God calls life and movement into being, where the mechanistic framework of cause and effect only represents the outer surface of things. In spite of some permanent differences we are reminded here of Shaftesbury's *inward form* and Leibniz's doctrine of monads. But Vico's deeper basic principle, already distantly reminiscent of Kant, was that one could only have knowledge of that which one had created. This principle, combined with the anti-mechanistic trend of his imaginative conception of nature and with his distaste for modern mechanistic science and Cartesianism, led him on to a great conviction that was far ahead of his time. He saw that the sphere which man was best able to have knowledge of was not physical nature, which God had created and was therefore alone able to know in full, but that of history, the 'world of nations' created by men. In this sphere, although the full truth of things was still reserved for God, man could nevertheless arrive at the probable. Subjectively, as his work of discovery proceeded and as he burnt his way deeper and deeper into the heart of things, he raised his expectations still higher and believed that he could achieve full certainty about divine providence with the help of history.

And now let us look at the basic ideas in his view of history.

He begins with a remarkable and problematical compromise between Christian doctrine and a newly achieved historical insight. Humanity was created good by God, endowed with free will, sinned through its own fault, then was punished by the Flood and almost annihilated. The survivors became divided into the chosen people, the Jews, who received the divine revelation and under divine leadership entered upon an exceptional way of life, and the ancestors of the heathen peoples. They had sunk to an almost animal condition, and from this they only slowly reascended. These were the fantastically depicted 'giants'. Religion, albeit of a misty sort, originating in the most primitive mentality, in the fear of a higher power that revealed itself in lightning and thunder, then becomes the means of rehumanising the giant race and of gradually leading to the rise of social institutions and finally to the racial groupings. Then follow for each of the peoples considered separately, successive divine, heroic and human epochs. The divine or Golden Age is not here understood in the old idealising sense, but as the age when the first gold of the world (that is, its first corn) was sown, and in the imagination of primitive men the gods walked upon earth. All peoples (with the exception of the Jews) go through the same evolution as does the single person, the analogy with whom is constantly borne in mind, from the most primitive stage of existence to the mature state of a rational humanity, which constitutes true human nature. Here, the most important idea was that the spiritual and mental make-up of man had constantly varied down the ages. At first it too had been on the animal level; then step by step it had become more human; and it was these changing human states that had produced the corresponding level of morality and social and political institutions for each particular stage, from the stateless solitary existence of the giants up to the people's republic and complete monarchy. But as the power of creative imagination loses strength, reflection and abstraction take its place. Justice and natural equality, the reasonable nature of man, 'which alone is the true human nature', win their way and prevail. But human weakness does not ever allow perfection to be reached or maintained. When the consummation is near, the people are over-taken by inner moral decay and sink back into their earlier bar-barous state, whence the whole process begins anew—*corso e ricorso*.

Thus this doctrine looks in the first place like a grandiose renewal at a deeper level of the Ancient World's view that history was cyclical, which had been revived during the Renaissance. According to the teaching of Polybius, not only did the constitutional forms follow one another in a definite cycle, but also the mental make-up of the peoples responsible for producing them. It is not only the *virtù* of the peoples (as Machiavelli had already added to make the doctrine more profound) that rises and falls and shows incidental migrations from one people to another; instead of the migration of a single mental power, he posits the regular transfer of whole complexes of powers within the same people, where each of these systems has its own particular capacities as well as its special virtues and defects. And so out of this step-by-step development of the human mind and soul there arise the ups and downs of fortune experienced by the various peoples.

There had never been such an all-embracing account given of the history of the peoples into which humanity is divided, nor one that probed so searchingly to the very root of events. But revolutionary and fruitful as this picture appears, it does not exhaust the important material or the depth of ideas that Vico's work contains. Here, too, we are presented no doubt with traditional material, but transformed into something new and original, which was then, whether under Vico's influence or not, to become the basis of modern historical thought.

41

In particular, it is Vico's notion of providence that presents us with a number of profound problems. He shared with all Christian philosophers of history from St Augustine to Bossuet the firm belief that God rules the world according to His purposes, and orders the destinies of peoples according to His will. But how does He rule? And how, when, and where does He make known His will to the peoples? Up till then the prevalent view concerning human suffering (which was to persist long after Vico's day in Christian circles) had been the anthropopathic conception of a God whose angry punishment or healing grace was directly perceptible in the fortunes or misfortunes of races and peoples. Where possible, this God was even thought to intervene through miracles or marvellous acts. But there is no hint of all this in Vico's thinking. He took the decisive turn whereby Christianity could to a certain degree be reconciled with a philosophy of immanence. God could be thought of as acting through nature, through the human nature He had himself created, in the world of history—always excepting the chosen people, the Jews. It is the nature of man only to think of his own personal advantage. The Divine Spirit allows human passions free play, for He has given man once and for all the gift of freedom; but at the same time God from His position of superior wisdom so directs the course of things that out of it develop civic order, the gradual conquest of barbarism, and, finally, humanity. To quote Vico's own words, 'God has made these limited human aims subservient to His own higher aims, and has constantly directed them so as to maintain the human race upon this earth'. This reminds us of Hegel's 'List der Vernunft' (cunning reason) and Wundt's doctrine of the heterogeneity of purposes. Later on, when we come to Herder at a later stage in the development of historism which we have undertaken to describe, we shall return to this problem. It had always been a Christian conception that God also uses the wicked as instruments of His will; but as a rule this had been thought of in personal terms, as applied to individual cases. Vico went right down into the depths and saw the whole life of history as the natural outcome of human passions with their inevitable limitations which, nevertheless, issued in meaningful and valuable results because a higher reason over-ruled the unreason of men. He withdrew the divine hand, as it were, to a greater distance from history, though without weakening its control, and gave history its natural freedom of movement. It was a decisive act in the direction of a secularised history, which is the basis of all modern historical thinking; and Vico took this step, not (like the thinkers of the Enlightenment) as a sceptic, but as a believer. He only made a beginning, for history, as he viewed it *sub specie aeterni*, still seemed to be subject to the direct will of God. But in his new way of looking at things there lay, all unknown to him, an impelling urge to interpret history purely as the outcome of immanent forces and laws. Critics have even ascribed to him, though perhaps too sweepingly, a growing tendency, as the work proceeded from the first to the second *Scienza*, to lay increasing stress upon the immanental, as opposed to the transcendental, principle in God's dealings with the world (Peters, p. 18 and *passim*). At all events, his conscious will was certainly not moving in this direction. This is shown by the great importance attached by him to religion as the chief means for gradually humanising primitive humanity. Even though it was a misty and false religion, it had originally been kindled in the crude brains of the giants by the lightning God revealed to them in the thunderstorm, and by the fear He thus aroused in them. 'Only through their religions', he concludes, 'have the peoples been led to do good deeds moved by sensual impulses'. This judgement embraces even the heathen religions as the instruments of God, which was another step towards the secularisation of history; for up till then, Christian thinkers had only been willing to concede them a debased and distorted character as vehicles of revelation. But Vico now saw religion in general as the most valuable force in history.

Vico's view that men themselves did not know what they were doing when they created civic order and culture, but were only following their narrow, selfish, sensual interests of the moment, had a further liberating influence on historical thought. It cut the ground from under the doctrine based on Natural Law, according to which the State had come into being through a rational contract made by men among themselves. And in a wider context, it cut at the root of pragmatism in general, the widely prevailing habit that would far outlast Vico's day of assuming conscious purpose everywhere, and thus of seeing in the great historical institutions the deliberate design of individuals. To the pronouncement of rational metaphysics, *homo intelligendo fit omnia*, he opposed the pronouncement of an imaginative metaphysics, *homo non intelligendo fit omnia*. It was a mistake he explained, to suppose that Minos, Theseus, Lycurgus, Romulus and the other Roman kings had issued general laws. The insight that emboldened him to throw over the Classical tradition at this point went back, however, to something deeper in his make-up, something that had not only been empirically explored and recognised, but had been known through the experience of twenty years of harassing work, often achieved with a heavy heart and throbbing pulses. He had come to an experience of primitive man, primitive times and primitive poetry—the poetical, imaginative and emotional thinking of this primitive man who was horrible and grossly cruel, yet also large-hearted, inventive and creative. He was a creature of whom modern man could hardly form any conception. In his youth he had read Lucretius' didactic poem *de rerum natura*, and its powerful picture of primitive times had a lasting effect on him in several specific particulars (Nicolini, *La Giovinezza di G.B. Vico*, pp. 121 ff.). But he added new and original sources and methods of knowledge. He sank himself in the human world of Homer, with its ethics the exact opposite of all modern ideas; in the earlier Roman Law with its rigidity and cruelty; in Tacitus' *Germania*; and he penetrated (as far as it concerned wishful and compulsive thinking) into the mind of the child. Then, primed with all this knowledge, he turned his attention to the behaviour and customs of his own countrymen from the lower classes; and finally made felicitous use of what was as yet a scanty knowledge of the mental constitution of the primitive American peoples. Combining all these sources with a touch of genius, he came to see that man must once upon a time have been very different indeed from the picture drawn by the later Schoolmen's philosophy and poetry, and even from the idea held by the great modern exponents of Natural Law. For these latter thinkers had never got beyond pictures of the human race in its natural condition, before there was any State, of a much too schematic character, and too much modelled on the normal human being.[1]

This new insight involved a decisive breach in the belief in the uniformity of human nature, as it had come down from the Ancient World, with its background of Natural Law. It seems likely that it was this that gave him the urge to rethink the inherited Christian doctrine of providence and to give it the new direction indicated above. For somehow or other it must be part of the divine will that man had once upon a time been so completely different from what he is at present, and that modern man could have evolved without any conscious intention, by a blind and yet in fact creative process of unreason.

The way was now clear for the concept of historical development, in a strict and logical form which had never previously been applied to it. But before we can evaluate its essence and its limitations, we must take a quick glance at some particular consequences of this new discovery as a whole. Vico was proud of having opened up by its means a new access to the real Homer. The ideas that had already emerged in antiquity had obscured the real Homer and made him out to be a teacher of secret wisdom and the creator of Greek customs and civilisation. Vico removed this veneer and saw Homer as the poetically splendid mirror of a magnificent barbarism. He did not

[1] Cf. Jellinek, *Adam in der Staatslehre* (selected writings and speeches, 2, 40): 'Primitive man in the conception of Natural Law was endowed with a fully developed reason'.

look at him in personal terms but as the reflection of a whole people, who were really the authors of this poetry insofar as it represented their history celebrated in song. All the thought and speech of primitive man was poetic and imaginative through and through. The myths represented, in his view, nothing but poetic historical narrative presented through different categories of imaginative ideas arising from the vast store of human fancy. Hercules, for example, was not a real person, but genuine historical life was mirrored in him as representing 'the heroic character of the founders of the peoples viewed from the standpoint of effort and exertion'. The myths and the languages, the most genuine remains of those days, became in his eyes the real source of historical knowledge, and the accounts of later historians and philosophers, distorted by prejudices of their own period, ceased to be of value. Although he himself often fell victim to the spirit of these primitive times and interpreted their myths in a wildly fantastic fashion, this was a psychologically necessary accompaniment to his exploring vision. He was possessed by an almost demonic passion to escape from the fallacious categories of our own insipid reflective thought conditioned by this present age, and plunge into the horror of the primitive world as it really was. He showed not the slightest trace of the Romantic longing or idealisation that were often to be directed towards primitive times and early man in the course of the increasingly sentimental outlook of the century. In his case, admiration for their poetic power was always tempered by horror for their inhumanity. If anything, he had inherited some touch of the attitude adopted by the most distinguished men of the Baroque period, something of the contradictory and sensual mixture of admiration and horror with which Boccalini had gazed a century before into the abyss of *raison d'état*. But Vico did to some extent manage to achieve the ideal expressed later on by Ranke, the ideal of a complete eclipse of self in order to become a vehicle for the overpowering might of historical phenomena.

Vico's feeling for the truly and genuinely antique enabled him to restore to Roman history, and especially the ancient laws, which he studied intensively, something of their original complexion. He recognised the peculiar combination of formal stiffness and sensual poetic power characteristic of primitive law, and the politically formative importance of the class struggle between Patricians and Plebeians and the class struggle in general;[1] the intermixture of continuity and change in the history of the constitution and Roman institutions; and amid a medley of daring ideas he intuitively hit upon the causes which flow with such powerful effect from the natural interests of

[1] Perhaps Machiavelli's *Discorsi* had an influence on him at this point. Cf. Nicolini, *La Giovinezza di G. B. Vico*, p. 107.

society. There as elsewhere, his sense of stratification was important, the survival of remnants of ancient constitutions and customs embedded in more recent material—what was later called *survivals*, which are to the historian what leading fossils are to the geologist. Vico was apt to compare them, in a splendid picture he repeatedly used, to sweet water brought down with such a mighty current that the impetus carries it on far out to sea. He saw nothing as static, but as developing from something and evolving into something further. 'The nature of things is nothing but their rise (*nascimento*) at particular times and under particular circumstances.'

This brings us to the limitations in his conception of development. In his newly-achieved picture of the evolution of the Roman State and people, no significant part is played by either leading personalities or external wars and struggles for power. It has rightly been said that he allowed the pendulum to swing violently in the direction of collectivism (Peters, p. 19). True, he thereby overcame the personalist trend of pragmatism, but he could not abolish the instinct that recognised the power of personality in history, of which pragmatism was a somewhat perverse and shortsighted expression—a power which, though firmly rooted in history, can nevertheless impart new direction and new impetus to its course. Nor can the concept of historical development and the destinies of States and peoples altogether dispense with war and power politics as determining factors even for their inner life, and as incalculable elements in their rise and fall. It is the leading personalities and the wars that most obviously give the course of events its peculiar and incalculable character, and ensure that it can never be brought under hard and fast laws. But Vico was so swept away by his new discoveries that he insisted on reading general laws into the whole of this *storia ideal' eterna*, as he was never tired of calling it. 'It had to be so, it is bound to be so, and it is destined to be so in the future', was the prophetic cry that in his almost unfeeling enthusiasm he launched against the past and the future history of the world. For he was persuaded (as we have already seen) that all peoples must necessarily go through precisely the same course of evolution in their mentality, customs and constitutional forms as were exemplified above all by the Romans. The notorious exceptions to this scheme, whether it was the Carthaginians or the primitive peoples in America, were declared by him to be due to accidental causes. But he treated the Romans (as Croce pertinently remarks) not as Romans, but as a sample or general model of a people. And in the same way it is no good looking for world history in Vico's writings, for he ignored the inter-connections between the peoples on a world scale, as they come about more particularly through wars and the transference of cultures. One of his main theses was that each people spontaneously produces from within itself the same stages of evolution. He had worked this out for himself, for in an earlier piece of writing (cf. Croce, p. 169) he still considered the Romans as pupils of older Italian and Greek peoples. He was not wholly mistaken, for modern research also allows for the tendency towards analogous and comparable stages of development in the ascent from the primitive to the cultured level. Everywhere, however, the typical is blended with the entirely individual, whereas Vico showed interest only in the typical and not at all in the individual. He probably saw that some individual forces must be at work, through the climate and other local factors, but he set these aside as quite unimportant.

Indeed, he probably preferred the Greeks, Romans and other peoples who had arisen in the West since the ancient world, not only because he knew incomparably more about them than about the peoples of the Far East and the New World, who were in principle included in the same category, but also because he felt his own destiny much more strongly and instinctively bound up with them, and because his pulse beat more in sympathy, we may say more individually, with theirs. But the deep individual characteristics acquired by each people through its racial connections and its special historical experiences escaped him altogether. His peoples were certainly not endowed with any specific individual *Volksgeist* (national spirit).

The history of the world was represented as a bundle of similar developments of peoples, as a ripe bunch of grapes in which each grape appears to be much like any other. He taught the development of the type, the characteristic specimen of a people, but without the development of individuality. This conception of development was therefore strictly limited to the idea of mere evolution. He was the forerunner of the modern positivism and collectivism, but only of historism to the extent that it, too, in its richer and more complicated picture of development, allows for the development of the typical as well. Vico's common legacy to historism and to positivism was his universal extension of the sphere of history to all the peoples of the world, and the inductive method of enquiry which he pursued, somewhat arbitrarily in detail, but splendidly on the broad scale of principle. Insofar as his methods did not remain inductive but presumed to indulge in the most daring deductions, he certainly overstepped, metaphysically speaking, the limits of both historism and positivism. He boldly claimed, for example, that the laws he had discovered were equally valid for the imaginary case of other worlds that might have come into being. The same can be said with even greater justification about his exemption of God's people, the Jews, which was dictated by his belief in divine revelation.

E   47

Goethe was to be the first to acquire some deeper understanding of the relationship between the type and the individual, that mysterious problem of historical life that can never receive an entirely logical solution. The human mind produces an abundance of recurring structures in state, society, religion, economics, and even in the human character; and these types partake of the essence of individuality to the extent that they, too, only reveal themselves through development. They do not remain static, but are constantly changing, either advancing or decaying. A man like Vico, who showed such power to break through the static thought based upon Natural Law and displayed such a deep and intensive grasp of the genesis, growth and decay of a type, clearly also had the necessary background and capacities for understanding the individual in history. Why did he never give his talents full play in this direction?

Croce gives an ingenious answer (pp. 126 ff. and 183). He sees in the remarkable exemption of the Jews from the general laws of development a deliberate 'turning of the blind eye', such as occurs with many cultured and scholarly believers. And if Vico had penetrated into the separate individual lives of nations, he would either have had to follow the unscientific example of Bossuet, and trace the hand of God at every step, or secularise history in its entirety. He was not willing to do the former, and he dared not do the latter; and so the only course open to him was to look at the facts from a standpoint that his philosophy allowed him, and to see history as an eternal process of the spirit which embraced only the general, but not the individual.

It may perhaps be objected that the later examples of Herder and Ranke show the possibility of combining the idea of divine providence in history with a full sense of the individual. But these examples arose in a changed mental climate. Vico, on the other hand, was the first to escape from the bondage of Natural Law, and his thinking bears the marks of this breakthrough. We will therefore try to draw out Croce's line of thought. It would seem as though this was a parting of the ways in the mental history of Vico, not only as between the thinker and the Christian believer, but also in the sense that a surviving remnant of his static thinking based upon Natural Law was at variance with his new dynamic concept of development. He still showed traces of the synthesising spirit of the great system-builders of the seventeenth century, but as yet none of the joy of the Enlightenment in analysing and decomposing facts, which, combined with a boundless curiosity for the manifold and colourful variety of historical life, we shall also find to be one of the preliminary stages in the individualising outlook on the world. More still did he lack the element of subjectivity, the concern for the needs and problems of the individual soul, through which a growing consciousness of a man's own individuality was later destined to lead to an appreciation of individual personalities in history. He was absorbed in humanity as a whole, but not interested in men as individuals. This, however, had always been the attitude of Natural Law, a position from which he only differed by virtue of his deeper and more absorbed preoccupation with the subject of humanity. The Natural Law of the seventeenth century sought for eternal, timeless and simple laws for humanity, and Vico sought them too. Only there was this great difference—that he discovered not only permanent laws of being, but also laws of development. Instead of the proposition that the essence of human nature recurs and is basically unalterable, he introduced the proposition that the universally valid forms for determining the changes in human nature were recurrent and basically unchanging. He put a dynamic content into a static vessel, thus furnishing one of the greatest examples of the continuity of development in the history of thought, by virtue of which the defeated cause somehow or other lives on in the cause that triumphs. As far as he was concerned, however, the containing vessel may have seemed of greater value than the contents.

But our picture of the vessel and the content must not be interpreted in a too static and external fashion. The strangest mixture of fixity and movement in this thought is shown by the most daring of his doctrines, that of the *ricorso* which necessarily follows upon the *corso* of a people's history, and once more leads up from barbarism to the human level. The sample of actual history that confronted him was the rise of the Western peoples from the low levels of the derelict Roman Empire and barbarian migrations. He calls this piece of history a *ricorso* and in so doing was guilty of a *quid pro quo*. For the new Western peoples, as he himself recognised, were not purely and simply identical with the debased peoples, not even the Italian people. Properly speaking, then, they were now beginning a *corso*, not a *ricorso*. As regards the other peoples he dealt with or touched upon, he did not even attempt to show that there had been a *ricorso*. And yet he was led on by a great awareness of the deep gulf between the end of the ancient world and the revival of Western culture, and of the continuity of history that nevertheless linked them together in the story of the world. Even if it was not the selfsame peoples who rose again, they did so in any case as heirs of the cultural riches and traditions of the ancient world. And however wild Vico's reconstructions may have seemed in detail, it was nevertheless a great and fruitful act of perception that discerned analogies between the social development of Rome and that of the Western Middle Ages. In both cases, the central point was the development of land ownership and all that flowed from it. It was a deep piece of insight, too, to discern that the barbarism of the *ricorso* arising from the moral breakdown of the age of reflective humanity was worse than the primitive barbarism of the *corso*. He did not indeed claim that the *corso* and *ricorso* of the peoples were in this respect absolutely identical, for Christianity, coming into the presumptive *ricorso* of the West in place of the heathen religions, brought with it a new character, even though (if we correctly interpret his thought) a higher humanity was displayed by it than in the *corso* of the Ancient World. But these are all questions that Vico himself did not finally solve, for there is no lack of contradictions and obscurities here, and there is a certain veil of obscurity over the doctrine of the *corso* and *ricorso* in general. It was prophecy on a vast scale, and as such differed in essence from the knowledge of primitive times arrived at by inductive and intuitive methods.

Again, it was a great feature in this teaching that he rose superior to the contradiction between cultural optimism and cultural pessimism. It is remarkable how rapidly he passes over the age of humanity in his outline of the epochs, which should (according to what he maintained) have brought the unfolding of the true human nature. Although he praised it, he saw it as doomed to perish tragically on account of the ineradicable weakness of human nature. Yet from this downfall and through the worst periods of barbarism it would emerge phoenix-like from its ashes and climb again to new heights. As a believing Catholic he saw this rhythm of growth, decay and renewal as God's way of preserving the human race. The mechanical notion of mere decay, which threatened to rob history of all meaning, was thus transcended by the higher idea of an inexhaustible regeneration which belongs to humanity as a whole, though not to the individual: 'The eternal sea of birth and grave'. Later on, a rightly understood historism, though no longer able to use Vico's rigid cyclical scheme of thought, revived the rhythm of 'death and rebirth' which he had sensed.

How different then were the ways that led to historism from Shaftesbury and Leibniz on the one hand, and from Vico on the other. The former, combining Neo-Platonic and Protestant thought, managed to approach the concept of individuality, but were stopped short on the way to the idea of development by the ideal of perfection, which was still to be largely dominant in the eighteenth century. Vico, with his Baroque and Catholic approach, was able to accomplish a miracle in the history of thought in profoundly understanding a strange human mentality without being captured by the idea of individuality. He taught the doctrine of development, and not of individuality, so that even the idea of development became restricted to mere evolution; but he then gave it a much more profound dimension by the idea of regeneration, and the significance and unique value of each stage of development. Even Leibniz, as we may remind ourselves, with his notion of endless progress that would not be disturbed, but rather advanced, by the prospect of a revolution, was not very far from the conceptions of Vico's macroscopy. His bundle of monads that were dependent upon God is strangely similar to Vico's bundle of peoples dependent upon God. The interest displayed by both of them in the primitive and early history of mankind was destined, as we shall see, to bear fruit in the eighteenth century as a movement towards the transformation of historical thought. With Vico, this interest rose to a genuine deeply-felt sense for primitive times: but Leibniz's colder, scholarly scrutiny could only discern the importance, but not the deeper implications, of this new subject of history. The same is perhaps true of the exploration undertaken by both in the field of languages as an expression and a source of historical life. All Vico's work has more feeling and psychical depth, and is at the same time intrinsically blended with the human spirit in its totality.

In order to appreciate the greatness of Vico's contribution towards exploring the spirit of primitive times and towards divining its laws of development, we can set alongside him by way of comparison another contemporary writer. A year before the publication of Vico's first *Scienza*, the Jesuit Lafitau published his great work, *Mœurs Sauvages Amériquains comparées aux mœurs des premiers temps* (2 vols, Paris 1724). In it he attempted, on the basis of first-hand knowledge of the primitive American peoples, to compare their religious ideas, customs and general institutions with the accounts given by the authors of Classical times of primitive conditions among the population of Greece and Asia Minor. He had lived for five years as a missionary among the Iroquois and Hurons of Canada; and attentive observation of all their life had convinced him that their cultural level was by no means as low as it was generally thought to be in Europe. He was struck by the similarities with much that Herodotus relates about the barbarians of Thrace and Asia Minor, and primitive customs in general and in the Bible. And in particular the religion of the Red Indians, debased as it was, seemed to contain traces of a belief in God that had once upon a time been purer in form. Before Lafitau's time, there had often been much puzzling about the origins of the primitive American inhabitants. To him, it seemed most likely that they had migrated from the north-east of Asia, which must have taken place gradually soon after the Flood. His zeal for knowledge combined with his religious enthusiasm in the bold hypothesis that the American Indians were blood-relations of the barbarians occupying Greece before the Hellenes and colonising Asia Minor, and had preserved remnants of a purer faith as the heritage from the one-time original revelation of God to the earliest men. That was an argument which he thought would disarm the atheists.

This strikes us in the first place as only one of those over-bold genealogical hypotheses used by the antiquaries of the seventeenth century (often on the score of very superficial evidence) to link up often widely scattered peoples. Even Grotius had ventured to derive the Yucatan Indians from the Christian Abyssinians (Lafitau, 1 412). But Lafitau was far superior to his predecessors in a very accurate knowledge of the real conditions and thought-moulds of the primitive peoples that is still of value today. He also had a keen eye for the institutional element in peoples in general. Perhaps he was the first to discover the widespread existence of matriarchal law (which he called *ginécocratie*) in all parts of the known world, traceable as far off as Africa and even in the law of inheritance among the Basques today. He even went so far as to advance rather tentatively the bold suggestion that his Iroquois and Huron Indians were connected with the peoples of Lycia.

Lafitau shared with Vico the capacity for daring ideas. But Vico's intuitive genius discovered real development and analogous developmental tendencies among all the peoples, whereas Lafitau tried to explain the similarities between primitive cultural stages solely through the mechanical expediency of hypothetical genealogies conceived according to the Biblical pattern. He interpreted what he saw in front of his eyes not in terms of development, but simply as traditions that had suffered from debasement. The ideas, customs and general institutions among these primitive peoples were described by him with the eye of a skilful and intellectually trained observer, who understood human nature and was balanced in his judgments. Vico, on the other hand, could feel deep down in himself something of the awful primitive darkness, and used creative imagination to link up the inner life of primitive men with their institutions. But these two thinkers were at one in a large and fruitful underlying hypothesis— namely, that religion was the most powerful ferment in the existence of primitive peoples, pervading and influencing the whole of their life. *La religion influoit autrefois dans tout ce que faisoient les hommes*, wrote Lafitau (1, 453). We even find him attempting something like a comparative history of religion; though his dogmatic assumptions and the tendency to think in terms of Natural Law meant that he fell back upon the ideas of tradition and debasement, and the permanent and unchanging deposit of good and bad qualities in human nature (cf. 1, 484).

His attempt to disarm atheism by showing how widespread were the traces of a primitive divine revelation could cut both ways. It was not difficult for the naturalists and deists of the eighteenth century to turn this round into an indication of universally present traces of natural religion. But his work, which was often used, was of still greater service to the growing needs of the century for a more accurate knowledge of mankind as it had once been in its natural state, discerned by sympathetic inner alignment with the primitive spirit. Lafitau did not, like Rousseau later on, sketch a lost paradise: he was too objective and sober for that. But through his writings natural man rose in popular estimation and appeared to be possessed of peculiar virtues that had been weakened through the humanising of Europe (2, 281). And zeal for comparing the characters and general human institutions among peoples was rescued by him from the primitive stage of random ideas and, in spite of some relics of this tendency, raised to the higher stage of seeing the prior need for the preliminary collection of ample empirical material. In this way the Jesuit's book was of service both to the historical writers of the Enlightenment and to the coming historism. It needed only some blending with imagination and feeling to light up the picture drawn by him and give it real power. Herder valued the book, and called it 'a compendium of ethics and poetics of untamed man' (*Works*, 9, 542; cf. also 5, 167). For in it he found well-attested knowledge of peoples in their natural condition, and especially an understanding picture of the intensively religious character and charming power of their songs and dances. Herder, too, was attracted by Lafitau's suggestion of traces of a primitive revelation among all peoples.

And so in a certain way Lafitau came to take the place that Vico, had he not remained unknown, might have occupied in the eighteenth century, though he was not of the same calibre, albeit by no means an unimportant figure. The four prominent thinkers we have dealt with from the early eighteenth century (Shaftesbury, Leibniz, Arnold and Vico) together represent the basic elements on which the coming historism was to be built. These were Neo-Platonism, pietism and Protestantism; a new aesthetic sensibility; new and deeper feeling of the need for contact with primitive humanity; and at the back of all these the stirring of a new spiritual and mental life. And so when the historical thinking of the century concerned itself in the first place with conquering the world of history and infusing new life into it by the methods of the Enlightenment that were at first of a very different kind, this was no detour, but an inner enrichment of the line of development through a series of tensions that were in the end to prove most fruitful.

Chapter two

Voltaire

The first and crowning achievement of the Enlightenment in the historical sphere is to be seen in the work of Voltaire. In many respects, it is true, the historical achievements of Hume, Robertson and Gibbon may be ranked higher than Voltaire's; but no one occupies such a broad and obvious and above all effective position within the whole development of historical thought. Even to contemporaries, he ranked as the pioneer of a new line when his *Essai sur les mœurs et l'esprit des nations*, begun in 1740, first saw the light. It was published in parts in 1745 and 1750, and again in 1753–4, 1756 and 1769. Here, he offered a universal history from the times of Charlemagne onwards, and in summary form (from 1756 onwards) even of the beginnings of human civilisation as a whole; and in so doing opened up quite new horizons. His *Siècle de Louis XIV* was begun in 1735, the first two chapters appearing in 1739, and the book as a whole in 1751, with a final edition in 1766. It showed how it was possible to write the history of a limited period using new tools and including new material.[1] But now the world was to witness the tremendously exciting spectacle of an event which took place in Germany not long after, and which was destined to surpass these new achieve-

[1] Our analysis can principally be confined to these two works, since they contain everything essential and influential in Voltaire's interpretation of history. For the textual history and use of sources, cf. the edition of the *Siècle* by E. Bourgeois; G. Lanson, *Voltaire*, and 'Notes sur le siècle de Louis XIV', in *Mélanges Ch. Andler*, 1924 and Voltaire, *Œuvres inédites p. p. F. Caussy*, I, 1914. It has sometimes been maintained that Bolingbroke's *Letters on the Study and Use of History*, 1735, had a significant influence upon Voltaire, but I can find no evidence for this view. Bolingbroke wrote in the first place with an eye to the education of enlightened politicians. For the differences between Voltaire's and Bolingbroke's handling of history, cf. W. Ludwig, *Lord Bolingbroke und die Aufklärung* (1928), p. 35 f.

ments in historical thought, namely the production in this neighbouring country of ideas that were even more epoch-making. In the same year 1769 in which Voltaire's *Essai* appeared in definitive form, Herder wrote down in the diary of his journey to Riga the new and revolutionary thoughts that were subsequently to burst forth in the 'Sturm und Drang' movement. They were destined to work like yeast on the whole mental and spiritual life, with poetry, art and philosophy in the forefront, and not least to transform the whole of historical thinking. The Enlightenment receded into the background, and the day of historism dawned. But even in Herder's interpretation of history, however sharply it differed in many respects from the Enlightenment, there were traces of continuing influences from Voltaire. The constantly recurring and inexhaustibly enticing problem of the relationship between what seem to be mutually opposed intellectual movements crops up again at this point. Such movements apparently conflict, and then win the ascendancy over one another; and yet all the while there is an inner continuity between them. In this case we have to look not only forwards, but also backwards, in order to get a full grasp of Voltaire's historical achievement, for Voltaire's historical writings, like the whole of the Enlightenment, were the fruit of much earlier thinking. Voltaire's work needs to be seen both as an original creation, and as a wave in the stream of inherited thought.

Indeed, the new and original elements in it are inseparably connected with the historical situation produced by the flux of events in France and Western Europe. And Voltaire's work can claim to be the clearest intellectual mirror of this situation. The political, social and intellectual factors of the time are reflected in it with the circumscribed clarity beloved by that age. And this incomparably steely neutrality, which yet displayed great elasticity, was able to subject the whole historical scene to its own standards with a sovereign certainty of touch. Never had there been an age that looked back on the past with such an autonomous attitude and with such complete self-assurance.

There are three particular trends that characterise the historical situation and the leading ideas of Voltaire that were conditioned by it. The first and probably the most important was the new feeling of satisfaction with this present life that had been aroused in the French bourgeoisie, and which rapidly increased during the decades following the War of the Spanish Succession. True, there was at the same time a strong political unrest, an uneasiness about absolutism and about the frightful slaughter of the wars that it had supported. But Louis XIV also left behind him a heritage of glory and of increased national self-confidence. And this was perhaps more vividly appreciated than the heritage of financial decay from which the State was suffering, though it did not really affect the private individual. The economic crises of the Regency period were more a symptom than a material check on the urge felt by the citizen to increase his wealth as rapidly as possible. These crises were caused by various oversea enterprises. Yet these had widened the mental field of vision and had brought a new curiosity in its train along with the material interests. But prosperity and wealth were in the first place utilised to refine the standard of life. Commercial calculation and speculation were already there in abundance, but had not yet acquired the absorbing and breathless intensity of modern capitalism. The principal thing (and here one can recall Voltaire's own practice in the matter) was the spirited and tasteful enjoyment of what had often been somewhat dubiously acquired. The fine flower of enjoyment, however, was to be found in society, in the salon, the theatre, and relationships with women—all the brilliant and luxurious adventures with which we are so familiar from the story of Voltaire's youth. Voltaire himself says of the *liberté de table* (*L'Ingénu*, c. 19), that it was reckoned in France to be the most precious of all the freedoms one can enjoy on earth. Those were then the *douceurs de la vie*, the *douceurs de la société*, which flowed from the *art de vivre*, and the *culture de l'esprit*, of which Voltaire speaks again and again with personal satisfaction. In his time, he reckoned, Paris surpassed Rome and Athens in their most brilliant period. Why, he asks in his *Essai* (c. 50), do Orientals not have good taste? Because they have never lived in female society and have not had the same opportunities as the Greeks and the Romans to cultivate their minds. The essay was originally conceived in order to satisfy the requirements of his friend, the Marquise du Châtelet, with whom he was living at Cirey. It was not purely a thirst for historical knowledge that caused the gifted lady to express a wish for a book on the history of the world since the time of Charlemagne which should be as instructive as Bossuet's sketch of universal history up to that period. But she wanted to have the historical material served up with a certain selectivity and form in order to help her overcome the 'dégoût' she had hitherto felt for modern history. Voltaire interpreted her wishes[1] as a desire for history in philosophical form. He took it that she would not want to read about everything that had happened, but only to learn useful truths; she would want a general idea of the peoples who had inhabited and devastated the earth, and of the outlook, manners and customs of the principal nations, with only a skeleton of the essential facts. It would be necessary to know the great deeds of those rulers who had improved the lot of their peoples. But there was no need to study the details of the many struggles for power and contending interests that had no significance for the present age.

[1] 'Introduction' or 'Avant-propos' to the *Essai*, and the 'Remarques' at the end.

Thus, it was as a philosopher that he approached history; his intention was to offer 'a philosophy of history', an expression that he was the first to coin, which he then gave as a title for the introduction to his *Essai* when it was published in 1756. This happily-coined new term became the parent of new intellectual creations of which Voltaire could as yet have no idea. It became a challenge to the future to fill it with a content that he would never have understood. The philosophy of history written by this great figure of the Enlightenment did not attempt to scale the heights that a real philosopher would have aspired to; neither did it plunge as deeply into the material of history as the historical writer had up till then been accustomed to do. Voltaire's intention was to keep close to life throughout in order to master the ways of practical living. For him, then, the philosophy of history meant nothing else but the drawing out of 'useful truths' from the events of the past.

If his plan is compared with its execution in these two works, and if one asks what ultimate, central and simple purpose underlay his efforts, the answer can only be that he wanted to write the universal prehistory of the French bourgeoisie, that civilised, refined, intelligent, industrious and comfortable class in which he took such delight. Their intellectual position and their way of life formed his basis of comparison for all historical phenomena. He constantly noted all that corresponded, or did not correspond, with them. It was on this balance that he weighed the destinies, mental outlook, manners and customs of the peoples whose life he was investigating; and as a result the scales rapidly rose in favour of the conditions of his own time that he himself knew in their full development. But even these he considered to be not yet quite complete, for they were not yet fully protected against the forces of a barbarous past that were still at work in the world. It might almost be said that he took all these disturbances of the life of enjoyment as a riotous liver might take the pressure put upon him by impatient creditors—either with anger, or, as in his novel *Candide*, with Gallic humour and resignation. He reserved his full combativeness, sustained by a genuine and personal hatred, for the fanaticism and superstition that he felt to be supported by the powers of religion and the Church. As the years went on, it became increasingly his life-purpose to fight against them under the battle-cry *écrasez l'infâme*, as it was also the special purpose of his historical writings. But this purpose alone would hardly provide a sufficient reason for the inexpressible trouble that he took to reveal the barbarity, misery and misfortunes of humanity in the past. There was a certain contradiction, for instance, between his declaration that the contemptible struggles for power engaged in by princes were not worth a philosopher's attention, and his narration of them (although accompanied by exclamations of reluctance) with a detail that almost equalled the traditional historiographers. But this devotion to the seamy details of historical life enabled him to savour with a peculiar personal relish the feeling of good fortune that it was his lot to belong to a better and more perfect world.

This sense of good fortune was supplemented by a second factor which determined his historical thinking, namely a tremendous impression made by the discoveries of the natural sciences and mathematics during the half century immediately before his time, and particularly by Newton's theory of gravitation. It would be an exaggeration to derive his thought-forms and those of the whole Enlightenment from this alone. For long before these discoveries there had been a movement of free thought, a revolt of the men whose whole thought was sensuous and naturalistic against the straitjacket imposed by the Christian Church. But now there was triumphant proof that this straitjacket was an artificial construct and that the universe obeyed laws totally different from those taught by the Church. It was like a sudden glimpse into the depths of the universe when men learnt that the motions of the heavenly bodies as a whole followed clearly demonstrable mathematical laws. And hence it was concluded that this must everywhere be so. 'It is obvious', wrote Voltaire (Art. 'Idée', in *Dict. philos.*) 'that a universal mathematics controls the whole of nature and brings about all its effects'. The world, it appeared, was a machine, constructed by the eternal geometer; everything was the necessary effect of eternal and unalterable laws (*Essai,* Remarques IX). All the events of the universe are necessarily linked together (*Essai,* c. 124). There can be no miracles, no exceptions to these laws of nature. God is the slave of His own laws. The miraculous edifice of revealed Christianity therefore collapsed in fragments. True, under the pressure of those in power, Voltaire did not as yet dare to deny or ignore Christianity altogether, but avenged himself for the formal obedience he felt bound to offer from time to time to the ecclesiastic authorities by the scornful irony and the sparkling wit that he showered upon them. He breathed an internal sigh of relief at the feeling of release from their bondage, and saw in the ascendancy of mathematical laws, to which he now gave his allegiance, the only true freedom. He therefore concluded with strict logic that these laws also governed the moral life. *Le physique gouverne toujours le moral*[1] (Art. 'Femme', in *Dict. philos.*).

But we must ask a further question. Why was the assumption of a

---

[1] G. Merten in 'das Problem der Willensfreiheit bei Voltaire', thesis, Jena, 1901, shows that this strict determinism only developed between 1740 and 1755. Cf. also Bach, 'Entwicklung der französischen Geschichtsauffassung im 18. Jahrhundert', thesis, Freiburg, 1932, p. 52.

deity enthroned above the universe any longer necessary at all, if he was no more than the slave of his own laws? Why not make the laws themselves the lord and creator of all things, and so pass over from a transcendental to an immanental view of the universe, a conception of strict mechanical causality? Why not replace deism by an uncompromising atheism? Other thinkers of the Enlightenment had dared to take this step, but not so Voltaire. He was prevented from doing so by the age-old thought-pattern which could only conceive of a meaningful whole as the work of a conscious reason, and could not imagine a machine, such as the universe now appeared to be, without an engineer who had constructed it. And at this point we pass over to the third of the influences that affected Voltaire's historical thinking—his moralism.[1] In speaking of Voltaire's moralism, we should not think in the first place of his own private morals, for in his own life he showed himself a creature of naked impulse, with an often ridiculous blend of natural kindness, emotional fits of justice, and all manner of wickedness and sordid unscrupulousness. But he felt the need for a certain quantum of general morality as a basis for society, and more particularly as a security and a necessary condition of that more refined society in which he felt at home. An enjoyment of this was what he prized most highly of all. But this enjoyment (as he saw with civic and commercial shrewdness) was not secure without the general acceptance of the most simple and natural of the moral commandments, which he traced back to the two basic feelings of pity and justice (*Essai*, Introd.). Interpreting them still in a self-centred and utilitarian spirit, he would often derive them from the precept: 'Treat other people as you yourself wish to be treated' (*Essai*, Remarques XVIII; Art. 'Athée', in *Dict. philos.*, etc.). A later and equally utilitarian positivism sought to derive morality from the natural impulses inherent in life towards self-preservation and adaptation. But in Voltaire's view, this would have been too insecure a basis, and too difficult for the average understanding. He would hardly have understood the concept that in the course of development, the immanent factors in life might produce something new, something that had not been in nature from the beginning. His thought was more inclined to be rooted in the old tradition of Natural Law, which knew nothing of the development of truths revealed by reason, but ascribed to them a timeless and absolute character. His new mechanical view of the universe reinforced this sense and required that the moral law, too, should have something

---

[1] For the further nuances and motifs in his thought, which led him to the verge of pantheism, cf. Sakmann, *Voltaires Geistesart und Gedankenwelt*, pp. 152 ff. Here and throughout this book we must confine ourselves to those parts of his thought that were of importance for his treatment of history.

of the character of a mechanical law. He effected this by making it the indispensable bond of society and declaring it to be 'a fundamental and unalterable law'. 'There exists but one morality as there exists but one geometry' (*Dict. philos.*, Art. 'Morale'). But that was not enough to give it the highest authority and dignity. Recourse must be had to the Christian concept of God as the giver of the moral law, which at once led back to Voltaire's idea of an 'author of nature' who was responsible for the whole fabric of the universe. Thus the old theism was transformed into deism by this mechanistic thinking. But the impelling motive for bringing thought to rest at this level was the practical indispensability of the idea of God. 'If God did not exist', so runs a notorious saying by Voltaire, 'it would be necessary to invent him.'[1] His God was the God of middle-class security.

The institution of the Deity was not the only thing Voltaire was forced to borrow from his hated Christianity. He had borrowed the idea of God with calculated deliberation, but quite unconsciously his whole picture of life and of the universe owed its being to the secular tradition not only of Natural Law, but also of Christian thought, even if it was in some respects only an inverted Christianity, a profane theology, as Benedetto Croce has called it.[2] Voltaire believed in an eternal *raison universelle*, just as the orthodox Christian believes in an eternally valid dogma revealed by a supernatural reason. The battle between heaven and hell was replaced by the battle between reason and unreason. This new dogmatic dualism, which now penetrated his historical thinking down to the deepest levels, was basically more lacking in unity than the old Christian dualism. For the latter pointed to the obvious limitations of all human wisdom and reason, and so was able without any breach of logic to awaken belief in a suprahuman wisdom. Voltaire's appeal to the limitless sovereignty of human reason, on the other hand, was bound to lead directly and positively to the conviction that the laws of mechanistic causality were absolutely valid. A strictly mechanistic habit of thought cannot, however, end in a dualistic, but only in a monistic, picture of the universe. Only a logical break could turn it into the former; and we have seen the inner motive that brought this about.

This was an inwardly incoherent view of the world, then, patched together from two essentially different basic outlooks. The gulf between mechanism and moralism could only be filled at a pinch by morals

---

[1] Goethe remarks in his *Geschichte der Farbenlehre* (Jubilee ed., 40, 279): 'He must be suspected of everywhere proclaiming his deism with such vigour merely to free himself from all suspicion of atheism'. Goethe's suspicion is perhaps a shade too strong.

[2] *Zur Theorie und Geschichte der Historiographie*, pp. 204, 214.

becoming mechanised. Voltaire repeatedly taught that the moral law remained the same at all times and among all peoples, and could never be torn out of the human heart. One cannot but recognise the human warmth with which he sought it and pointed out its traces everywhere in the life of history. But incomparably more often he had to point to its infringement. He noted that of all laws, this was the one that had been least obeyed.

> Yet it rises up against him who disobeys it: it seems as though God had implanted it in human beings to counteract the law of the strongest and to prevent the human race from compassing its own destruction through warfare, chicanery and scholastic theology (*Essai*, Remarques XVIII).

Thus the world of history now gave the appearance of a dualistic juxtaposition and opposition of reason and unreason. On the side of reason were to be found not only the stable and eternal moral law implanted in the human breast, but also the purified power of judgement that led the way to the true, the useful and the beautiful, so creating all the good things of life that delighted Voltaire's heart. But it, too, had to contend with the power of unreason and suffer at its hands, with the result that the older nations in particular represented a mixture of 'extreme folly and a little wisdom' (*Essai*, Intro.). And for the same reasons their pronouncements on what was true or useful or beautiful would have the same identical content, provided that they were fully cleansed from the contamination of unreason. Reason was the gold that was to be had at small price; unreason the combined mass of all the other earthly materials God had given to men along with the gold; and from these men had now to cleanse themselves step by step. In this work of purification man was left to his own resources and, as we have already seen, could not expect any further direct assistance from God. For the machine once created by God now had to pursue its own serene course according to the laws controlling it. Why God the Engineer constructed the world machinery in that particular way and had made human life so full of suffering and evil was a question that Voltaire considered to be past human understanding. As the whole of his philosophy was lacking in spiritual depth, it came to rest at this point with a shrug of the shoulders in a comfortable agnosticism.

We will leave on one side the other incongruities and uncertainties in his thought upon these matters, in particular those that were caused by the influence of a Lockean sensualism. It was enough for Voltaire that his picture of the universe based upon a mechanistic morality and a rationalist outlook afforded him all the help and the standards that he had practical need of in order to forge from his understanding of history a weapon to fight for the shaping of his cultural ideals. The decisive motive behind all his historical writing was to put the whole of the world's history at the service of the Enlightenment on behalf of the human race, and to show how the Enlightenment had its roots in history.

Here was a new, magnificent and epoch-making enterprise. Not absolutely new, to be sure, but new as far as that age was concerned. If we enquire what distant forerunners he had had in this attempt to support a universal philosophy of culture by showing its bases in universal history, we should have to go back to the authors of late antiquity and mediaeval Christianity, to Eusebius, Augustine, Otto von Freising and all their successors. They had been the first to introduce the idea of a unified and universal history held together by one universal idea.[1] And just as Voltaire took over from the world of Christian thought the dualistic principle which he then proceeded to secularise, so also did he take over the need to support it by a universal history. Bossuet had undertaken to write such a history; and it was from him and his *Discours sur l'histoire universelle* (1681) that Voltaire received the impulse to invert and secularise the picture of Christian history.

The new element in Voltaire's historical writing, then, was its content and the aggressive propaganda presented in the spirit of a conqueror with which he sought to change men's outlook. True, the historians of the Renaissance period and of humanism, Machiavelli and Guicciardini in particular, had introduced new intellectual material, but this had happened with a naive matter-of-courseness and had not involved any particular polemics against tradition. There had indeed been individual approaches as well that went further and deliberately used history as a basis for specific ideals of life (such as the works of Sebastian Franck and Gottfried Arnold); but this had not caused any general revolution in method. But Voltaire's attempt to base a new universal cultural ideal on a fresh interpretation of universal history marked the beginning of an altogether new era of the Western mind. For it involved violently withdrawing the historical world from the relatively peaceful atmosphere in which it had hitherto existed and plunging it into the stream of the present. This meant that history was set permanently on the move and given new topicality. Henceforward, the battle about the interpretation of universal history in the past would always go hand in hand with all the controversies about the shape of things to come, and the one could not be carried on without the other. Voltaire's service to the world of history was thus to give the people of the West a conviction that every great new ideal needs to be broadly based upon history; only in this

[1] Cf. *ibid.*, p. 163.

way could the opponents of the new and the upholders of the old ideals be compelled for the first time to justify their views at the bar of history. In the controversies that from now onwards were conducted with historical weapons between the various ideologies, there was a constant danger that historical truth would be obscured through the tendentious thinking engendered by these ideologies. Yet even historical truth could console itself with the fact that it found a resting-place with certain independent spirits, and was actually advanced by the critical discussions and disputes that took place between successive schools of historical interpretation. But Voltaire was the writer who first opened up this new arena of conflict about the history of the world. However critically one may judge the incompleteness of his historical thinking, there was about him a driving-power which by its inherent dialectic could not but blaze the trail into a land of new intellectual discovery.

But it is the constant consolation and justification of historical thought to be always catching sight of something creative amongst the incomplete phenomena of historical life. Although Voltaire was restricted by his world outlook in seeing the creative elements of history, yet there are signs here and there of a movement towards a more living approach. Above all, one cannot fail to be filled with admiration for the factually and objectively creative effects that were produced by his work as a historian.

The greatest achievement that his intellectual equipment enabled him to produce was the structurisation of the historical world according to his own carefully conceived plan. In so doing, he displayed the sovereignty of historical judgment and a complete freedom from convention. This was the crowning achievement of his mind, of which Goethe said (in a letter to Frau von Stein of 7 June 1784) that it was not merely a lofty standpoint, but, as it were, the prospect seen from a balloon floating high above everything. Never before (with the exception of the approaches mentioned above) had there been such a deliberate and determined effort to distinguish between the valuable and the valueless in the broad mass of historical events. Up till then, historical writers had been in the grip of a naive realism. They had been largely under the spell of the material handed down to them and had felt compelled to reproduce large tracts of this in a passive manner, without subjecting it to any inward appraisal. This was particularly true of the material furthest in point of time from their own age. The nearer the particular theme came in time and in content to their own world, the more readily they were able, insofar as they had the power, to infuse it with their own spirit. Probably the most successful writer in his ability to appraise material in the more distant past, and to produce a tasteful arrangement of what he held to be characteristic and important, was Bossuet, in the third part of his *Discours sur l'histoire universelle*. But despite his already growing sense of the causal interconnection between all historical events, of the *enchaînement de l'univers* (III, c. 2), he had in the end confined his material for a universal history to what was of importance for the destinies of the people of God and the life of the Church. But Voltaire consciously and vigorously broke through this restriction. He rejected the principle which confined selection to the Jewish and Christian world, and opened up the entire historical life of mankind to the searching and incisive judgment of the historian. He generated the courage among mankind to become its own architect on every side and to shape the historical cosmos after its own design.

Looked at against the whole background of the history of ideas, this was probably a premature breakthrough of subjectivity into a sphere where up till now only a naive realism had prevailed. People had been of the opinion that the historian, insofar as he could keep free of passion and bias and was a lover of the truth, could hope to become a clear mirror for truth and actuality. Men were not yet aware that historical truth is not something given from the start, which has only to be freed from certain accidental veils, but is something that has to be newly created by constant fresh attempts on the part of the researching mind, whose subjectivity is quite as often a source of power as it is a hindrance in the acquisition of knowledge. Kant's criticism was the first to prepare the way for the recognition of this complicated process, though it did not become clear all at once.[1] In Voltaire, however, subjectivity was as yet without an awareness of its limitations and sources of possible error, and rejoiced in the naive belief that it was the organ of a universally valid and impeccable reason; and in this belief it proceeded to shape the world of history according to its own requirements. It was thus in a fair way to making great discoveries, but also in a fair way to falling into serious mistakes.

All these three ingredients in Voltaire's historical thought (the mechanistic, the moralistic, and the sense of civilised satisfaction) combined to produce this effect. They all played a part in the universal broadening of the historical interest and the enlargement of its horizons, which constitutes a further important title to fame for Voltaire as historian. The mechanistic element was to some extent the pioneer and accomplished the preliminary heavy labour. By its own essential weight it drove through to a universal comprehension of all times and all peoples, all that bore the human likeness, in what, by an extension and a surpassing of Bossuet's work, he called 'the

[1] Cf. Unger, 'Zur Entwicklung des Problems der Objektivität bis Hegel', in *Aufsätze zur Prinzipienlehre und Literaturgeschichte*, 1929.

necessary interlinking between all the events of the universe'. Likewise, and without more ado, he shattered to fragments all the Christian dogmatic components of the historical picture as so far received, and in particular the divisions that had been set up between the Christian and non-Christian peoples, thus secularising the whole of history. Everything was now on the same level, worthy of the same interest and open to the same criticism. It was criticism in particular that had been entirely lacking in Bossuet. However superficially and over-hastily this criticism may often have been handled, it was yet a step fraught with immense consequences that a universally applicable method of criticism should have been practised at all. The obvious imperfections of this method would then impel men to replace it by better and more delicate tools of knowledge. It was factual criticism that Voltaire used, and his procedure was extremely summary, based as it was on what a mechanical interpretation of the laws of nature and of life experience seemed to him to render probable. Even his many attempts at source-criticism were as a rule no more than factual reasoning of this kind. Taken as a whole, however, Voltaire's work proved a powerful incentive towards basing criticism upon a strictly causal and reliably supported understanding of the course of historical events.[1]

In particular, interest was aroused in looking for the causes at work in the beginnings of human culture and the life of primitive man. True, this was not due to Voltaire alone. We have already seen it stirring in Leibniz, Vico and Lafitau. In 1750 and 1754 Rousseau published his two famous *Discours*, which held up an idealised picture of the innocent natural man with his few wants and contrasted it with the civilisation of his own day, which he declared to be contrary to nature. But in England, as we shall see, about the middle of the century or even a little earlier, a new and more general interest was being aroused, no longer of a purely antiquarian kind, in primitive times and the natural conditions of early humanity. In this there were two chief motives at work, the thirst for knowledge on the part of thinkers in the Enlightenment, and the desire for mental participation and empathy. It will be evident later on what powerful revolutions in historical thought were brought about by these two motives; but even the former, which could alone influence a Voltaire, proved thoroughly fruitful in the realm of knowledge.

However much ridicule Voltaire poured upon Rousseau's theme,

[1] As it is outside our present purpose to trace the detailed development of critical methods of research, we may refer the reader for further information on Voltaire to: Sakmann, *Hist. Zeitschrift*, 97, pp. 366 ff.; Black, *The Art of History*, pp. 51 ff.; and Ritter, *Entwicklung der Geschichtswissenschaft*, pp. 248 ff. Ritter is quite correct in pointing out that earlier and contemporary learned research (Mabillon, Beaufort, etc.) was considerably superior to Voltaire's.

it nevertheless became clear from a thesis put forward in the *Discours* of 1754 that the dating hitherto applied to primitive times must be pushed considerably further back, and that it was a question of reckoning in millennia where up till now men had reckoned in centuries. When he wrote the introduction to his *Essai*, it may well be that the stimulus had come from Rousseau, or that he had reached these conclusions independently. In any case this new suggestion proved very fruitful in assessing the older cultures. For example, what was known of the cultural achievements of the Chaldeans and of the earliest political conditions in China clearly pointed to extremely long preparatory stages. 'The progress of the intellect is so slow, the illusions to which our eyes are subject are so powerful, the tyranny of inherited ideas is so potent', Voltaire wrote, that it was impossible to think of putting the Chaldeans only some 1900 years before our era. In so saying, he anticipated what the recent wonderful results of Mesopotamian and Indian excavations have fully substantiated. The information about the high level of Chaldean culture on which Voltaire based this judgment was distinctly dubious. But his methodical insight into the natural conditions and the necessary age-long preparation for the first basic achievements of culture was nothing less than epoch-making.

Modern theories of descent and prehistoric research have brought an even deeper understanding of the slow pace of the early stages in cultural advance. At any rate Voltaire had the courage to recognise and proclaim the outstanding truth that man occupied the first place among the animals who lived a group or herd life, and had originally lived in a condition not unlike that of the animals. He was in sound agreement with the heart of Aristotelian teaching about ζῷον πολιτικόν and stressed the social nature of early man, in contradistinction to Rousseau's erroneous opinion that the solitary life was man's true condition before he had been spoilt by civilisation of any kind.

The mechanistic thought that had contributed to these conclusions was in Voltaire's eyes a means to an end, and not an end in itself. He used it, but it did not satisfy his intellectual appetite. He was too great a connoisseur of pleasure to have any desire for pure and strict knowledge for knowledge's sake. True to the mood of an unsatisfied pleasure-seeker, he could often enough draw from the mechanical character of all events the disgusted conclusion that blind chance rules over all. But it would be a mistake to see this idea as the ruling motif in his interpretation of history. History offered him more than the meaningless interaction of blind forces. His heart rose wherever he discerned in the world even the rudiments of likenesses or parallels to his own enlightened culture, and so was able to justify it in terms of universal history. And because his moralistic and civilising cultural ideals were blended with the bitterest resentment against its Christian opponents, he was delighted to reveal the cultural achievements of the pagan world that had so far been kept in the dark, and to consign the chosen people, the Jews, with their special revelation, to the category of barbarians, and generally castigate them. He found no difficulty in doing this by dint of choosing one-sided examples from the Old Testament, which he was constantly searching for suitable material. From this he would turn with all the greater enthusiasm to the culture of China. Since the middle of the seventeenth century the accounts given by the Jesuits had caught the attention of the West, and even Leibniz had taken a burning interest in acquiring more detailed information about China.[1] The old notion, based on Natural Law, that human nature was the same everywhere, was now destined to move forward to a new stage as these cultured nations from outside the European circle came into view. Efforts then had to be made to discern beneath the foreign veil (which was explained along mechanistic lines as due to natural conditions) the self-same human being whom people had always believed in, and to demonstrate that here too he bore the marks of the same natural reason. The Enlightenment now saw in China one of its most powerful pieces of evidence. For here there had been in existence since the time of Confucius, long before Christianity, a clear and simple religion of reason and a highly developed system of morality, marked by excellent laws and gentle manners and customs. Confucius, as Voltaire delighted to proclaim, declared no mysteries, but was content simply to preach virtue. He taught that God had Himself implanted virtue in the human heart, that man was not born evil, and only becomes so as a result of his mistakes (*Essai*, Introd.). Voltaire's cool critical sense prevented him from too warmly idealising this exemplary notion; and it was constantly active, along with his sympathetic understanding. He even saw among the Chinese a confirmation of the fact that the common people needed the coarser food of superstition, whilst the enlightened authorities could not help accommodating themselves to circumstances and tolerating superstitious sects. Furthermore, his critical reflection concerned itself with the remarkable fact that the Chinese were indeed far in advance of all other nations in morality, that 'first of all the sciences', and had reached a mature stage even in very early times. On the other hand, in other branches of knowledge, skills, artistic taste and so on, they had remained at a stage of arrested development. The explanation that he

[1] O. Franke, 'China als Kulturmacht' or 'Leibniz und China', *Zeitschrift der Deutschen Morgenländ. Gesellschaft*, vols 2 and 7; Reichwein, *China und Europa*, 1923; W. Engemann, 'Voltaire und China', thesis, Leipzig, 1932.

offered did not probe very deeply. The problem presented to the thinkers of the Enlightenment by a foreign and relatively highly developed culture of a quite different kind could not as yet be solved by them, because they were only able to make mechanical comparisons between isolated parts and features of these cultures on the basis of the unsatisfactory standard of their own culture. Yet even Voltaire could voice a suspicion that in order to understand a foreign intellectual and spiritual culture, one would have to immerse oneself thoroughly in its environment. It is characteristic that the apologetic interest of the Enlightenment was needed to bring this insight within his purview. He was concerned at this point to refute the Christian reproach that had been levelled, now at the alleged atheism, and now at the seeming idolatry, of the Chinese regime which he so much admired. 'The greatest misunderstandings about the rites of China have come about because we have judged their usages in the light of our own; for we shall carry with us to the end of time the prejudices born of our contentious spirit' (*Essai*, c. 2). And in the chapter of the *Essai* (c. 6) devoted to Mahomet, he also says that we must guard against the habit of judging everything in the light of our own customs.[1]

It is important for the history of ideas to realise that it was quite possible to recognise these hindrances to the understanding of foreign individualities, and yet not enter into a real comprehension of them. In this respect Voltaire had few equals in his exploration of strange and foreign worlds and the things they contained.[2] He gave a brilliantly colourful description of the Eastern world, and his account of the strange and attractive Japanese culture was an artistic masterpiece, which already had some air of individuality about it (*Essai*, c. 142). In his narrative of Western history, too, he often paused in astonishment at phenomena that seemed to combine the most contradictory features, and yet formed a very effective whole. He wrote, for instance, about French behaviour at the time of the Massacre of St Bartholomew: 'This mixture of gallantry and fury, of lust and slaughter, forms the strangest picture that has ever portrayed the contradictions of the human spirit' (*Essai*, c. 171). And again, in France's more recent past, he wrote of Mme de Maintenon, with her 'mixture of religion and gallantry, of dignity and weakness, which is so often found in the human heart, and existed in Louis XIV' (*Siècle*, c. 27). Again, he was fascinated by the picture of Dutch life, which

[1] Cf. also Sakmann, 'Universalgeschichte in Voltaires Beleuchtung', *Zeitschrift f. franz. Sprache und Literatur*, 30, 3. Also *Voltaires Geistesart und Gedankenwelt*, p. 106.

[2] Apart from his *Essai*, we must also remember his many separate historical articles in his *Dictionnaire philosophique*, with their wealth of reference to antiquity—mostly, it must be admitted, in order to refute Christianity.

foreigners were never tired of admiring in its peculiar blend of sea, city and landscape that constantly confronted them (*Essai*, c. 187). 'But', he continues, 'evil is always mixed with good, and men so often depart from their principles, that when this Republic oppressed the Arminians it came near to destroying the freedom for which it had fought'. His admiration for England and her constitution are well known; and in an article for the *Dictionnaire Philosophique* ('Gouvernement'), he concluded that in comparison, Plato's Republic was only a ridiculous dream. Yet he noted that out of this wonderful constitution had come appalling abuses which made human nature shudder. He referred to the Cromwellian period, when a grotesque fanaticism had swept like a raging fire through this great and beautiful house, unfortunately built of wood. Then in William of Orange's time the house was rebuilt in stone, and would now endure for as long as anything human can endure. The following observation is particularly instructive as to his manner of thought. Although he based the excellencies of the English Constitution on a peculiar 'mixture of contrary qualities' due to England's insular situation, he concluded not only with a wish that it could be transplanted, but with a belief that this was perfectly possible. Incidentally, he asked himself the enticing question why coconuts should ripen in India, yet should not succeed in doing so in Rome. But he comforts himself with the playful answer that even in England the coconuts of wise legislation do not always ripen, and in any case they have only been cultivated for a short while.

And yet on another occasion he could say, in perfect accord with the positivist environmental theory: 'Everything depends on the time and the place at which one was born, and the circumstances in which one lives' (*Dict. philos.*, Art. 'Grégoire VII'). And so there was a perpetual struggle going on in him between the mechanistic and the moral standpoint for the interpretation of historical phenomena. But he was not aware of a struggle, and was inclined to hand himself over with naive assurance first to one, and then to the other. In his eyes, the moral law itself did indeed possess the characteristic of mechanical stability. Thus in the ultimate analysis the whole vast tableau of periods and peoples, with all its strange mixtures and varieties, lay spread out before his eyes in an astonishing simplicity and clarity. Along with climate and soil, human nature, compounded of the various passions plus a quantum of 'universal reason', was one of the principal factors, and habit (which he rather strangely distinguished from the propensities of human nature) was the other.

Everything intimately connected with human nature is alike, from one end of the universe to the other; everything dependent upon habit is different, and it is a mere accident if it turns out to be alike. The realm of habit is very much wider than that of nature: it covers all manners and customs, and spreads variety over the universal scene. Human nature, however, extends over it a certain unity, for it sets up everywhere a small number of immutable principles . . . Nature has placed passions in the human heart . . . Habit brings it about that the evil passions cause different forms in different places (*Essai*, c. 197, cf. also c. 143).

Montesquieu had seen climate as the most powerful cause of the differences in the human race, and in so doing had entered upon the dubious and misleading course of attempting to understand the life of history first and foremost in terms of its physical conditions. Voltaire's easier approach did not involve any such purely causal restrictions; and looking out from the vantage-point of the Enlightenment, he could see other factors whose influence on history was even stronger. 'Climate', he observes (in his article, 'Climat', in *Dict. philos.* where he is arguing against Montesquieu), 'has some power, but the government has a hundred times as much, and religion combined with government has more power still'. This judgement that the state and religion are the strongest causal factors in history commands respectful attention. We have still to show how it worked out in the details of Voltaire's interpretation of history. At this stage when we are still concerned with its general characteristics, it will be enough simply to note that it does not contradict his opinion quoted above about the power of custom to produce all manner of variety. For in his view, even the state and religion, as far as they took on various historical forms and did not follow the normative patterns of pure reason, also belonged to the vast realm of custom.

With regard to the immeasurable wealth of variety to be found in this realm, Voltaire, the enlightened thinker, was able to make use of what may be called relativism, the view that develops with the growth of historism into a respect for the specific individual life of the historical structure. True, the relativism of the Enlightenment could only operate in an external fashion, from a mechanistic causal standpoint, and not from within. A relativism with interior foundations would have contradicted the current belief based upon Natural Law that there were certain timeless and invariable norms of life. But the equally strong urge of the Enlightenment towards universal enquiry, the impulse to capture humanity in all its manifestations, was now also likely to lead to a relativist outlook because of the sheer vastness of the variety it revealed. In this way the Enlightenment's historical curiosity was without doubt a preparation for a deeper historical relativism. In the main, however, Voltaire's was the genial man of the world's respect for the strange variety of beliefs and customs. He looked down on them with a reflective eye because he thought he knew, at least in a general way, how they had come into being. To his mind, they would all have been the calculable products of partly stable and partly variable factors, provided always that one had all the necessary data to hand. True, he was of the opinion that in fact only a very small number of reliable data were available to throw light upon the causal interlinking of all things. He could therefore never put history on the level of the mathematical certainty that was possible in the natural sciences (Art. 'Histoire', in *Dict. philos.* and *Annales de l'Empire*, cf. Henry I). So it remained open to a historian such as Voltaire to view all historical variety, in the first place, like the constantly changing pictures of a kaleidoscope where it is perfectly clear that the general sequence is purely mechanical, though it is not possible to predict or control the changes in each picture individually. Voltaire could only have adopted the expression *individuum est ineffabile* in the sense that it was in fact, though not in principle, impossible to treat the composition of an individual as a calculable entity.

Passions are passions, vices remain vices, and reason is reason. It was on this sober circumscription of the separate psychological elements and the interaction between them instituted by nature, that Voltaire's historical psychology was based. And yet in the course of his tireless excursions through the gallery of historical characters he received impressions that were hard to reconcile with this one-track interpretation of the fundamental psychological forces within the human being. For instance, there was Calvin, with his appallingly hard and unmerciful outlook, and yet a man of the greatest selflessness (*Essai*, c. 134). There was the monastic life, which had 'done both so much good and so much evil' (*Essai*, c. 139); there were the Conquistadores, with so much heroic courage, and so much horrible savagery: 'from the same source, namely acquisitiveness, come so much good and so much evil'. We are astonished and appalled, he wrote, by this mixture of greatness and cruelty (*Essai*, c. 148 f.). In another passage he goes rather deeper, when he writes that the vices of men are often bound up with their virtues (*Essai*, c. 134). But he cannot get further than the simple noting of these remarkable connections between good and evil, now with a shrug of the shoulders, now in a moralising vein—connections that lie deep down in the human soul. 'It is a characteristic of human nature to contain within itself the best and the worst' (*Essai*, c. 147). The irrational depths of the soul remained a sealed book to him.

But Voltaire would not have been Voltaire if he had for ever remained content simply to exhibit the kaleidoscope of periods, human beings and peoples. The very mechanistic basis of his thinking prompted him to go beyond a mocking, disgusted, deeply moved or astonished contemplation, as the case might be, of individual phenomena. He was impelled to search for at least some larger parts of that 'eternal chain' of causality which binds together past, present and future. This impulse would have been more effective still, and might well have led him to work out a strictly positivist line of developmental thought, had not the sensualist side of him been stronger than the spirit of enquiry. But the spirit of enquiry was certainly present, and was able here and there to establish fairly extensive causal connections between events. It must be set down to his credit that he was not content merely to disgust his contemporaries with lurid pictures of the Middle Ages, but sought for the fundamental causal relationships that presided over its confused material. Thus he says (*Pyrrhonisme de l'histoire*, c. 25) that he found 'the thread leading through the great labyrinth' of the period between Charlemagne and Charles V in the struggle for Rome carried on between the Emperors and the Popes. In this verdict he was taking the first step towards an understanding of the Middle Ages in terms of universal history.

After his death, he was rightly held in honour for his ability to grasp the intellectual transformations within a nation in terms that were almost those of modern history. By diligent study of the Old Testament, Voltaire found how to disentangle the various layers of tradition and so distinguish, at any rate in a broad way, between the various stages of Israelite religion.[1] He also made fruitful enquiries into the influence of foreign religions (Egyptian, Persian and Greek) upon the Jewish faith, though they were not unmixed with one-sided accusations, for his main purpose throughout was to destroy the nimbus that surrounded the Chosen People. There was as yet no inner urge to understand the gradual growth and development of nations. He was quite content merely to display to the faithful with scornful laughter the *disjecta membra* of the old Judaism, and demonstrate that they could never have constituted a unified corpus of divine revelation. Thus he showed how narrow the boundaries are within which hatred can open up new historical vistas.

In order to see the point at which his ideas come closest to a concept of development, we must go back to the treatment of the earliest stages in human culture. The important insight, that the building up of the early cultures must have required much longer periods of time

[1] Sakmann, *Voltaires Geistesart usw.*, pp. 235 ff. We may again recall the various articles in the *Dictionnaire philosophique* in which Voltaire handles the history of Christian dogmas and institutions in such a way as to show the manifold variations and contradictions they contain.

than had hitherto been allowed for, was indeed reached in the first instance along mechanistic and empirical lines. A comparison between culture and barbarism, and consideration of the weaknesses inherent in human nature, made it seem impossible to him to believe the naive accounts of tradition. Behind this, however, there immediately arose the question how man had ever been able to make the transition from the animal-like state of the primitives to the first beginnings of culture. At this point the rigid psychology of the Enlightenment, the dualism of reason and unreason which he had elsewhere applied with such thoroughness to the world of history, clearly became inadequate. It seemed to him inappropriate and hazardous to speak of the 'reason' of the primitives. And so, taking an analogy from the animal world, he declared that instinct had been humanity's earliest guide, and defined instinct as 'an arrangement of the organs so that their interaction develops in course of time'. Nature, he went on to remark (*Essai*, Introd.), inspires us with useful ideas which are the precursors of all our reflections. Thus there is, as it were, a kind of pre-reason. The way would now have been clear for a conception of historical life less in terms of conscious reason and more concerned with the prior and parallel developments in man— more able, in short, to discover the important historical forces at work on the irrational side of life. English sensualism and empiricism, as expounded by Hume, were to advance further along this path. It may be assumed that Voltaire too was led by English influence to move in this direction. But it was only a tentative gesture, made in order to gain some understanding of the original condition of humanity. At this point he, too, could speak of the organs 'unfolding' (*se déployer, se développer*). But for everything else that man proceeds to do in history with the help of a reflective reason that has now become self-conscious, and for all that lies ahead of him, Voltaire repeatedly uses the watchwords *perfection* and *perfectionner*. Morality is 'perfected' by the Chinese; the fine arts, sometimes with more emphasis on the plastic, sometimes on the verbal, were 'perfected' in the four golden ages of humanity which he so greatly admired, those of Pericles and Alexander, of Augustus, the Medici and the age of Louis XIV. But to Voltaire, to attain perfection always meant to approximate to a definite, unchanging and timeless ideal set up on the basis of an inner necessity by the purified reason of mankind. There is (he held) only one very simple and universally valid morality, and only one standard of good taste in the world, which serves as the yardstick for the artistic achievements of all the nations.[1] And so the Chinese, whom he awarded an A mark for morality,

[1] Cf. *Dict. philos.*, Art. 'Goût'. For Voltaire's abortive attempts to show the relativity of taste, cf. Sakmann, *Voltaires Geistesart und Gedankenwelt*, pp. 118 ff.,

had to be content, as we saw, with a C or D mark for art. It is enough here just to remind ourselves of the intolerance and arrogance of his aesthetic judgement. He reproached Shakespeare for barbarism, although he had himself in days gone past pointed the way to him with a mixture of honest amazement and reluctance; he preferred Tasso to the Iliad and Ariosto's *Orlando* to the *Odyssey* (*Essai*, c. 121)—to quote only a few of countless similar judgements.

For mechanism had even invaded his aesthetics, and the whole concept of perfection was thoroughly mechanical. This was the framework in which everything in his picture of history operated that was beyond the category of merely kaleidoscopic change. Even the beginnings of a biological interpretation of human nature, which we noted in his teaching on the subject of reason, bore a mechanistic character. He taught that a law is given by nature to every species of being, a law which is invariably obeyed. The bird builds its nest; the stars go on their appointed course; man is created for society, and is perfectible within the limits that nature herself has laid down for his perfection (*Essai*, Introd.). There are probably solid and impassable barriers to man's upward progress; but who would venture to give them static shape? But Voltaire, with yardstick and chalk in hand, was prepared to say where the goals and limits of perfection lay in any particular period. And the pitiful contentment with which he exalted the specific perfection of a particular cultural milieu as the *non plus ultra* was equally unfortunate. It is almost superfluous to add that these were always and everywhere the cultural ideals of his own French environment, in which he saw the peak and the limits of perfection for the history of the whole world. Voltaire says in his *Siècle de Louis XIV* (c. 34) that men achieved more illumination in the preceding century than in all the previous span of time.

Sometimes, instead of the word 'perfection', Voltaire would use the expression 'the progress of the human spirit'. But it would be a grave misconception to credit him with an optimistic belief in progress such as his predecessor, the Abbé Saint Pierre, had held and the later thinkers of the Enlightenment and European liberalism in general had amplified.[1] This was no *progressus in infinitum* in Leibniz's sense, latent in the very essence of history, but only an approximation to the ideals of reason and civilisation belonging to his own time; it was only another word for 'perfection'. Since, according to Voltaire, the constituents of human nature, reason and unreason, always remained the same, the conflict between them could only be a

and Merian-Genast, 'Voltaire und die Entwicklung der Idee der Weltliteratur', *Roman. Forsch.*, 40. 1.

[1] Cf. what is said in Chapter 4 about Turgot and Condorcet, and Delvaille, *Hist. de l'idée de progrès* (1910).

constantly fluctuating one and could never issue in a decisive result. Periods of progress and perfection could well be followed by reversions to barbarism. Yet even this idea bore a mechanistic rather than an evolutionary character. This is why Voltaire was not capable of the full-blooded optimism and faith in the future held by the later Enlightenment. The sense of sober reality belonging to the end of the seventeenth century was still too powerful an element in his outlook. Moreover, his ideal of enlightenment was too selfish and too much bound up with the interests of the higher levels of society in France and Europe, to produce that necessary universal impetus which was to lead to the later belief in an all-conquering human progress. Sceptical realism and joy in the Enlightenment were very closely connected in his make-up, though they never succeeded in ousting one another. It was precisely their violent collision that produced the daily and hourly sparkle of his wit, the inimitable *esprit Voltairien*, which could contemplate even the hour of death with a grimace and a caper. In such an attitude to life, the enjoyment of the present moment was the supreme good. Voltaire enhanced this personal pleasure by justifying it at the bar of universal history. But neither the experiences of universal history, nor his own desire for comfort, were enough to make belief in the continuance or even increase of all the joys of the Enlightenment in the more distant future appear at all probable. 'The time will come when savages will be performing operas, and we shall have reverted to the Red Indian dances (*danse du calumet*).'[1] In such an atmosphere, there could, at times, arise a rather shallow feeling of resignation at the tragic transience of all human cultural values; but there could hardly be any kind of appreciation for the idea of development in any shape or form. The world and its history remained in the end only a kaleidoscopic succession of bright and sombre pictures.[2]

Genuine historical development can never be 'finished': it flows on, and takes incalculable new forms within the limitations set by human nature. History cannot, so to speak, be boarded up at either end. But Voltaire did presume to nail up boards of this kind. To be sure, even he did not think that in the France of his day perfection had already been reached at every point. The power of the *infâme*, of superstition and fanaticism, was still far too great for that. But in his eyes the moral, cultural, social and political ideals of the Enlightenment were absolutely perfect and unsurpassable; and they were in a

---

[1] *Mélanges littéraires*; Delvaille, *loc. cit.*, p. 311.

[2] Sakmann (*Voltaires Geistesart usw.*, p. 309 and 'Universalgesch. in Voltaires Beleuchtung', *Zeitschrift. f. franz. Sprache und Literatur*, 30, 15), takes what is on the whole a correct view of Voltaire's attitude to progress, and von Martin, *Hist. Zeitschrift*, 118, 12, is wrong in holding forth against his view. Cf. also Delvaille, *loc. cit.*, p. 323. Bach is rather uncertain on this question, *loc. cit.*, p. 54.

fair way to occupy the throne. And, as is particularly significant for his pattern of thought, it was precisely in those spheres in which he personally exercised his talents that he regarded the height of perfection as already attained, and so boarded up the world at that point. He held that the Epic, the Tragic, and High Comedy (*Siècle*, c. 32) all had their definite and limited possibilities, which eventually became exhausted. Abbé Dubos did indeed maintain that men of genius could devise a number of new types,[1] always provided that nature created them. Once the truths of morality and the representations of human misfortunes, weaknesses and so on had been shaped by skilful hands, Voltaire maintained, nothing remained but to imitate them, or to stray from the right path. 'Thus genius only has *one* century; after that, it must inevitably degenerate.'

On the question of genius, the epochs of historical thinking were later on to be divided. Voltaire asked whether genius was fundamentally anything more than talent? And was talent anything else than the disposition to succeed in an art? (Article on 'Génie' in *Dict. philos.*). In Abbé Dubos, however, who was criticised by Voltaire, the new concept of genius was already being proclaimed. He saw genius as something inexhaustible and incalculable, and subsequently, ranging over the whole field of history, he also discerned in this something inexhaustible and incalculable, and in this way could, as it were, overhear the roaring of the torrent of genuine development.

There can be no doubt in this connection that Voltaire himself possessed a streak of genius. This was not poetical genius, but rather a powerful and original vitality. His mental life as a whole was more touched with genius, more inexhaustible and incalculable than his theories. Incidentally, this was why he could now and again (but not very often) freely admit that there was something of the numinous and the international about the character of art.[2] But even the greatest geniuses of the Enlightenment, including Rousseau himself, were condemned to remain the slaves of a theory that could only express their genius incompletely, or even not at all.

And so on the whole, Voltaire only recognised the perfectibility of certain given elements and dispositions in man up to a specific and calculable degree. When this point had been reached, man could remain at this level, if fortune smiled upon him, or could once again degenerate and sink back to his former state. In principle, then, human ascent from the primitive stage of instinctive activity, on

---

[1] Dubos, *Réflexions critiques sur la poésie et la peinture*, 1719 (ed. of 1740, II, 55).

[2] Brandes, *Voltaire*, 2, 49; Gerbi, *La Politica del Settecento*, pp. 54 ff.; *Dict. philos.*, Art. 'Enthousiasme'.

through the *raison commencée* to the *raison cultivée*, follows a geo-metrical straight line; though in the history of the world as it actually is, this line is constantly being disturbed and distorted by the power of the unreason which is part and parcel of the human inheritance. But in this mechanically and mathematically conceived picture of history there lurked an inevitable inner contradiction. Man was thought of as a piece of clock-work, provided by nature with certain specific wheels and springs, partly good and partly bad, and then wound up; after which, he was left to himself. And now a remarkable thing was to take place: this clock was to become its own clock-maker and itself undertake the necessary improvements to its mechanism until it reached the stage of perfection for which it was designed. Quite unconsciously, Voltaire was here making a great concession to the creative qualities of historical man in respect of new developments. But he was not in a position to recognise this creative power himself.[1] All the possibilities of history were circumscribed and strictly limited in his eyes because his contentment with his own civilisation and the spell of mechanistic thought made it impossible for him to look beyond his own historical stage, and robbed him of any desire to do so. And so the spirit of the ages, which Voltaire undertook to lay hold upon, could not in fact rise above the spirit of its interpreter—Voltaire himself.

The spirit of the times, the spirit of the nations, the spirit behind historical forms in general—these are a constant theme in Voltaire's writing. It is part of his basic procedure as a historian to reduce the individual features that particularly strike him in a given period, or people, or historical form, to a common denominator, which he called its *esprit* (or sometimes *génie*). The title of his *Essai* announces as its theme *les mœurs et l'esprit des nations*, and he even went as far as to call his work as a whole a *histoire de l'esprit humain*.[2] History so interpreted seemed to him to be the really philosophical way of writing history. This was a powerful and epoch-making conception, which loses none of its historical importance because of the lack of adequate execution we have already alluded to. Nor is its significance in any way diminished by the fact that long before his time men were in a fair way to select from the wealth of historical detail certain subordinate historical units that could be illuminated by some specific principle, and speak of their *spiritus*, genius or *ingenium*, their soul. There were roots stretching far back into antiquity, to Plato, to the

---

[1] The words uttered in old age, in a letter of 1773 (Brandes, *Voltaire*, 2, 49): 'Il faut avouer que, dans les arts de génie, tout est ouvrage de l'instinct', can probably be taken as a late concession to modern ways of thought and not as a piece of self-acquired wisdom in old age.

[2] Von Martin, *Hist. Zeitschrift*, 118, 25.

Stoa, and to Neo-Platonism, which would need separate individual treatment.[1] At any rate in the late seventeenth and early eighteenth century there was a growing tendency to speak of the spirit of peoples and States and other entities. It is in Bossuet, whose *Discours sur l'histoire universelle* served as the model which Voltaire aspired to imitate and surpass, that this expression *esprit* (only rarely *génie*) occurs. Bossuet also attempted to sketch national character on several occasions, and he even spoke of the *caractère des âges* in one passage (II, c. 27). The Venetian diplomats of the seventeenth century were already speaking of a *genio della nazione* in their political reports.[2] In Saint-Évremond, Leibniz, Shaftesbury, Boulainvilliers and Abbé Dubos, it became increasingly common to speak of a spirit (*esprit* and *génie*) of the nations, and sometimes of the ages. In the introductory address given by Abbé Dubos at the Paris Academy in 1720, he dealt with a theme that was pregnant with meaning for the future, the spirit (*génie*) of languages, and pointed out that the character of each nation was perceptible in the expressions and even the words of its language.[3] It is remarkable that the Enlightenment increased the urge to get at the 'spirit' of human creations, a something that could not be accurately described in rational terms, as the operative force, where previously writers would have preferred as far as possible to ascribe this to mechanical laws of motion. But this was indeed an impossibility; and so the position represented by this doctrine of the 'spirit' behind human creations showed that the Enlightenment was already almost outgrowing its rationalising and mechanistic ways of thought and being directed into a new and supra-rational realm. Movements of this kind are particularly significant in the history of ideas, because they reveal the germ of what is to come in the previous only just nascent period, and so demonstrate the deep continuity of all development.

To begin with, it is true, this 'spirit' of human things was understood in a somewhat external way. Voltaire, in his *Dictionnaire philosophique*, writes under the heading 'Esprit':

> One speaks of the spirit of a corporation, or a society, in order to express its habits, its manner of speech or behaviour, its

[1] Stenzel's essays on the concept of the spirit in Greek Philosophy and elsewhere (*Die Antike*, I. II. IV.) might be quoted in support. Von Moeller, *Entstehung des Dogmas von dem Ursprung des Rechts aus dem Volksgeist*, Mitt. d. Inst. f. österr. Gesch.–Forsch., p. 30, contains very little on this point. There is also a probable link with the Christian doctrine of the Holy Spirit and the Pneuma. Cf. also Weiser, *Shaftesbury etc.*, pp. 210 ff. and especially the article 'Geist' by Hildebrand in *Grimm's Dictionary*.

[2] Von Schleinitz, 'Staatsauffassung ... der Venezianer in den Relationen des 17. Jahrhunderts', unpublished thesis, Rostock, 1921.

[3] Morel, *Étude sur l'Abbé Dubos* (1850), p. 102.

prejudices; one speaks of the spirit of a law in order to distinguish its intention; of the spirit of a work, in order to make its character and aim intelligible. One could speak of an *esprit de vengeance, de faction etc.*, but not of an *esprit de politesse*, because *politesse* is not a passion controlled by a powerful leading motive that could metaphorically be called *esprit*.

Sometimes, however, he adds, *esprit* denotes the most subtle part of matter, that which has never been seen yet gives life and movement. In this Voltaire was reviving the ideas of the Ancient World, which held the essence of the soul to be no more than the finest and most invisible matter. But it is also clear that as with moralism, so here with *esprit*, there was a tendency to mechanise and schematise it. Equally inadequate was his definition in the article 'Génie' of *génie d'une nation* as what distinguished it in character from other nations —its customs, chief talents, and even vices. He also makes the interesting observation that no nation has made as free a use of the word *spiritus* as the French. Voltaire and Montesquieu between them certainly gave a strong impetus to reflection upon the essence of the 'spirit' in human creations.

On the subject of the *esprit* and *génie* of nations, Voltaire says at one point in the *Essai* that on the whole it is of an enduring nature, and shows little change; moreover, it is always to be found in the small number of those who govern the masses and set them to work. This second judgment, with its pragmatic colouring, although not without a certain element of truth, shows how little he could do justice to the constituents of a national spirit which arose from the deeper levels of the national life. This pragmatism also prevented him from working out the further implications of a national spirit in deliberate and lively detail.[1] He was more original and fertile in his teaching about the *esprit* of the ages. Here too, as we have already seen, he had had occasional forerunners. But no one, with the possible exception of Leibniz, had ventured to speak in such vigorous terms of the definitely characteristic spirit of an age. 'My aim', he wrote, 'is always to observe the spirit of the age, for this is what directs the great events of the world'. (*Essai*, c. 80). His *Siècle de Louis XIV* opens with the famous words that he is not concerned to depict for posterity the deeds of a single man, but 'the spirit of men in the most enlightened century that has ever existed'. Although the execution of this purpose fell short of the author's intention, and although in the political parts of the work the narrative often descends to a mere enumeration of actions and events, it had a far-reaching and generally fertilising effect. It gave historical writers a

---

[1] Cf. M. Ritter, *Entwicklung der Geschichtswissenschaft*, p. 242.

distaste for mere stories of 'heroes, States and the lives of men', and aroused an ambition to grasp the connections that knit together all the phenomena of an age, and show how all single lives and separate events are dependent upon them. 'Every man', (we read in the *Essai*, c. 82) 'is shaped by his own century; very few men rise above the manners and customs of their age'. If one enquires, however, into the ultimate motives at the back of Voltaire's programme, the limitations of his historical thought at once become apparent. His desire to recognise the spirit of the age was not primarily a desire for knowledge, but rather a desire to enjoy. The civilised cultural ideal in which he delighted needed the contrast of darker ages to bring out its full taste. It has already been pointed out, and need not be elaborated, that the *Essai* tends throughout to depict the Middle Ages as a time of rough manners and darkest superstition. 'A comparison of these centuries with our own, whatever the perversities and misfortunes we have to put up with, must bring home to us our own good fortune in spite of our almost insuperable tendency to praise the past at the expense of the present' (*Essai*, c. 82). And so, in the end, the spirit of the ages as depicted by him in its successive manifestations was nothing but the assessment of its balance-sheet in terms of reason and unreason according to the currency valid at the time of the Enlightenment. This can be most clearly seen in the pictures of Asian cultures which Voltaire's resentment against Christianity made him delight to sketch, from the dark portrait of the Middle Ages, on through the more enlightened days of the Renaissance and the renewed darkness of the Wars of Religion, to the sunrise of modern Western European civilisation. Voltaire might be styled the historical banker of the Enlightenment, who calculated and administered on its behalf the funds of universal history.

Nevertheless, as we have repeatedly seen, there are signs that his vital and ever-moving spirit, though failing to break through the barriers of his rigid theories, was able to effect a certain loosening. We have seen his amazement at the mysterious 'mixture' in history, which might well arouse in the minds of more sensitive readers new ideas leading far beyond his own limitations. In general, his capacity to be astonished at the wonders of history, at the profound changes in men, and finally at the 'mystery of the universe' (*Essai*, Résumé), sometimes notably breached the wall erected by the proud self-satisfaction of the Enlightenment and the self-assurance with which its judgments were pronounced. It was all of a piece with the consciousness of human solidarity which was perhaps almost the highest achievement of the Enlightenment, and with a sense of humanity's involvement in a destiny that transcended all limitations of nationality and religion. We are concerned at this point, says Voltaire (*Essai*,

c. 83), with the fate of mankind, and not with mere dynastic revolutions. Every writer of history, he held, should have said *homo sum*; yet most of them did nothing but describe battles.

And so although Voltaire was not always successful, he did at any rate manage to paint pictures of the spirit of the age which possessed some historical dynamic power, at least in those places where his enlightened ideals hit upon phenomena that were inwardly related to them, and yet were interwoven with foreign material. The short Chapter 118 in the *Essai*, entitled 'Idée générale du seizième siècle', opens the lists in historiography for the countless attempts that have since been made to gather together the amazing ensemble of this period, with its struggles for power, its extraordinary men, its intellectual revolutions, its discoveries and disturbances, and wealth and industry, and survey it from a universal point of view. Luther, indeed, was disdainfully and anonymously disposed of in passing with a side-glance at religious quarrels, and even in the following chapters only depicted in caricature. But then in the chapters dealing with the Huguenot wars and Henry IV (Voltaire's favourite) he recovers something of the genuine atmosphere of the period. We see how he represents the actions of men as directly conditioned by the contemporary atmosphere, but also how strongly he brings out the power of a personality in the figure of Henry IV. Voltaire puts forward the antithesis that the century of Louis XIV was much greater than that of Henry IV, but that Henry IV was a greater man than Louis XIV. Thus in spite of all the justifiable objections of modern criticism, the *Siècle de Louis XIV* retains its imperishable charm through its inner attraction towards all that was in sympathy with its ideals, through the brilliance of its portrayal, the lively interest which makes it take note of even those things of which it disapproves, and by the breadth and fullness of the account it gives of the customs, conditions and thoughts of the period. Even today it is not possible to understand the age of Louis XIV to the full if one forgets the effect that it had on Voltaire, its own historian, who had grown up in its midst.

It has often been the custom to represent Voltaire's chief contribution to the writing of history as his success in getting away from the sheer mass of material that used to pass as cultural history. Not infrequently in the past, social history had not meant much more than a variegated picture-book of social customs and arrangements, technical inventions and progress, and material factors in the external life of men, even down to the details of food and drink. In actual fact, this so to speak lower middle-class interest in history was decidedly stimulated by Voltaire. He did this as an upper middle-class French citizen, fully conscious of all that the bourgeoisie had achieved in the intellectual, economic and technical fields since the decline of feudalism and chivalry. He gave a higher status to the first French upper middle-class citizen to stand out in history, Jacques Cœur, the fifteenth-century financier, than he did to the Maid of Orleans. Nevertheless, in the *Essai* (c. 80) her heroic exploits were treated very differently from the way they were handled in his lampoon *La Pucelle*, and were accorded at least an embarrassed respect. In the renunciation of the throne by Queen Christina of Sweden he celebrated the victory of urbanism, and gave somewhat smug approval to renunciations of thrones in general. In his judgment (*Essai*, c. 188), it furnished the finest example of the real superiority of the arts, politeness and the mature society over greatness that is merely great position. He pronounced the French *tiers état* to be the *fonds de la nation*, which was without particular interest (*Essai*, c. 175). He gave this opinion in connection with his account of the last States-General to meet in France, in 1614; and in so doing he struck a faint note (though certainly without any revolutionary intention) suggesting the political claims of the middle classes that would eventually appear. His immediate concern was only the peaceful enjoyment and unhindered development of a middle-class civilisation under the protection of a strong monarchical rule. The values that crowned this civilisation, as far as he was concerned, were the useful and the elegant; and this latter, which included all the charms of a refined social life and the accepted standards of art, was in his eyes undoubtedly the highest. But the useful (the epitome of economic and technical activity and the prosperity that accompanied it) was the necessary first step towards the refinement of taste. And so Voltaire had already looked round upon all that was destined in the nineteenth century to become the object of the most diligent methodical research as the practical and material basis for modern culture; yet not with the eyes of the scientific economic and social historian, but simply with the pleasurable gaze of a comfortably placed bourgeois. All around him, men were already busying themselves with these things out of practical interest, but he was the first to have the courage to admit them into written history and to explain that they were the really important part of it.

He was able to do this by virtue of massive reading, though often of a very insufficient and unsystematic kind. But he knew how to ask questions, and how to work out causal connections. In his account of Tamerlane, he is struck by the fact that the cities of the Orient were just as easy to rebuild as they were to destroy. He put forward the suggestion that this was possible because of the sun-baked bricks (*Essai*, c. 88). Again, he had no doubt that the herring trade at Amsterdam was an important fact in world history (*Essai*, c. 164).

He was just as eager to notice the alterations in coinage and the problems of population as the invention of new weapons of war, the changes in the construction of city streets, and in the riding and travelling habits of good society. His historical curiosity descended even to the manner of beard worn by men; in fact, Voltaire wanted to have exact knowledge about everything.[1] Nor must it be overlooked that he came to history from the theatre. This helps to explain his delight in the dramatic and exotic scenes of history, and the colourful externals of historical life. But beneath the gay costume of his historical characters there moved only what the enlightened thinker chose to call reason or unreason, taste or barbarism. This feeling for the picturesque detail of the past stands in contrast to the insufficiency of the *leitmotivs* at work in the Enlightenment, rather as a coloured jacket stands to a colourless book. Voltaire was lacking in the antiquarian's love and reverence for concrete things. Without something of these qualities, these things remain mere costume and could not become the genuine clothing of historical man. Yet the important and fruitful result was, nevertheless, that he aroused a boundless curiosity for all that concerned the past. So here too, Voltaire led right up to the threshold of historism, whose task it became to infuse life into the mass of material that he had collected.

The same is true of the other success achieved by his interest in history, which, perhaps, ranks still higher than his achievements in the cultural field. It may be said that he was one of the first thinkers of the Enlightenment (though preceded by Hume in 1742[2]) to discover the power of opinion in history. There can be no doubt that he considered it part of the sphere called by him, as we have already noted, the sphere of custom, which he regarded as the source of all variety in history. He says in the *Essai* (Remarques II) that the history of opinion needs to be written. By so doing, all the chaos of events, factions, revolutions and crimes would become worthy of attracting the gaze of the wise. We have seen how he included religion as one of the chief causative factors in history; and religion, according to his intellectual outlook, was nothing but opinion. Opinion, he was persuaded, led to the crusades; though he added, with a descent into personal pragmatism, that the Popes had only stirred up the crusading spirit for their own interests. Yet Voltaire had to admit in a flash of recognition that priestly calculation alone would not have been enough to send the nations to the East, unless they had also

---

[1] *C'est un exercice incessant de la raison qui a besoin de voir clair en tout*, says Lanson in his *Voltaire* (p. 120), in the course of his very readable chapter on Voltaire as a historian. He tends, though, to read rather too much of nineteenth-century positivism into him.

[2] In the *Essay on British Government*.

been moved by very powerful and generally-held ideas—though these were, in his opinion, utterly false. He held that the errors of opinion should be described as the doctors described the plague at Marseilles, although it had been cured. In Islam, he saw the greatest change that had ever been brought about upon this earth by the force of opinion. Opinion had also been responsible for making the laws that were often so different in places not at all far off from one another, so that what was held to be true and good on one shore might well be considered false and bad on the opposite one. In view of all this confused welter of powerful opinions, there bore down steadily upon Voltaire a feeling that the proud and self-confident Enlightenment might be powerless in the face of the mighty power of ideas and ideals in history. He added, in his observations upon the irrational multiplicity of laws, that there is contradiction everywhere. We sail in a ship which is constantly beset by contrary winds. Thus he was indeed capable of discovering the power of opinion in history, but not able to comprehend it. For as interpreted by him, it belonged rather to the pathology, than to the ordinary course, of history.

Voltaire was led to this discovery by the desire for more power to be given to the new opinions held by thinkers of the Enlightenment, for they considered their most redoubtable opponent to be the dominance of false and unreasonable opinions. In the scepticism that often came over him with regard to this opposition, however, there was a force at work that was producing in Voltaire what may be looked upon as the heritage of the seventeenth century. This was a certain realistic sobriety of outlook, a lack of illusions with respect to the world and the life of man, not characteristic indeed of all the seventeenth century figures, but more especially of its politicians, and inherited by their successors in the political field. Frederick the Great would not have been able to become a friend of Voltaire's unless the two men had understood one another on this score. The enlightened ideal they held in common was free of utopianism and of any over-valuation of human nature, which they saw in all its nakedness, Frederick with an even more stubborn scepticism than Voltaire. And as this produced in Frederick's life an unreconciled cleavage between political realism and humanitarianism ideals, so also was Voltaire's interpretation of history rent by the same division. For the gulf between the great realm of unreason and the small kingdom of reason opened up by their mechanistic psychology was only increased and kept open by their cold sense of reality, which often rose to the point of contempt for man himself.

For the same reason, there was a cleavage in Voltaire's understanding of the sphere which, along with the power of opinion, presented also in his eyes the strongest causal effects and decisions in universal history—namely the State, power politics and war. He saw its exterior as it really was, in all its naked ugliness; and, as we shall see in a moment, he could to a certain extent enter into a rational understanding of the motives behind political actions. Nevertheless, he could never come to comprehend them from the inside, because his mechanistic and egotistical thinking did not provide the key to the specific existence of all the objective creations of the human mind and spirit.

He certainly wanted the State to be strong and independent, more especially independent of any ecclesiastical influence, but only as an instrument of civilisation, or, as the language of the Enlightenment expressed it, of 'happiness' for the nations. His contempt for the dull and superstitious *populace* whose helot-like status he accepted as an unalterable necessity for the possibility of any higher kind of life, could on occasions be melted by a sudden wave of natural kindliness or social sensibility. But behind the 'happiness' of the nations there lurked only too clearly his own personal happiness and comfort. Thus the general standard by which he judged political affairs was set by asking the one question: what can the State do for me and for my beloved enlightened society?

Such egotistical individualism could, as a rule, only understand the life of the State in personal terms. Voltaire could not understand the great statesmen in their own right. He could only see the personalities of rulers in terms of wisdom or folly, peacefulness or rapacity, bringers of prosperity or calamity in the history of the world—and mostly of calamity. In this personal form, the dependence of cultural life upon the State was something of which he became at any rate superficially aware.[1] The historical writing of the period was in general personal in tone and pragmatic in outlook, with its tendency to ascribe all the important events of political life to the conscious motives and aims of the transacting parties. To this Voltaire added an inquisitiveness into the petty and all-too-human motives, and a proneness to see romantic and picturesque causes for great events, which betrayed his theatrical origins.

But for the most part, what Voltaire called attention to in political affairs was the predominance of force. In the *Essai* (c. 33), he says that force has created everything in this world. It was in this moralistic form that his shrewd realism recognised the importance of political power in the life of history. The supra-personal background,

---

[1] No doubt he also brought out the free constitutions of the Italian and German cities as a reason for their thriving cultures (Sakmann, *Voltaires Geistesart usw.*, p. 336), but more from hatred of cultureless despotisms than from reflection upon the links between culture and state.

the specific structure and tendencies of individual States, were accordingly thrust on one side and ignored. Voltaire depicts his individual rulers and statesmen as arising directly, like the heroes of French drama, from the general run of humanity. Any of these heroes could equally well have lived at another time, at any period that was more or less at an equal stage of rational development. It was only his feeling for the vivid, for the gay variety of manners and customs, that spread something like an individual historical atmosphere round the violent deeds of political man. One further point may be noted. His basically unheroic and pacifist attitude is now and again interrupted by a naive pride in the notable deeds of Frenchmen. But the combination of world citizenship and national feeling which Voltaire already embodied, and which inspired his *Siècle de Louis XIV*, was far more deeply rooted in the cultural, than in the political, nation of France.

And yet there was a means of acquiring historical knowledge that would have led him out of the moralising personal approach into a more objective judgment of political actions. This was the doctrine of *raison d'état*, the reasons and interests of particular States, founded by Machiavelli, much developed in the seventeenth century, and by the eighteenth century well-known to all politicians and to those who were interested in the politics of the time. The formula produced by the Duke of Rohan, 'The princes command their peoples, but interests command the princes', represented the essence of this doctrine. This suggested to the historian that in searching for the motives behind the actions of States he should not in the first place look for those of a personal nature, whether moral or immoral, but for those which arose from the factual necessity for a State to maintain its existence. The later historism, starting with Ranke, was able to incorporate this doctrine as a matter of course into the perspective with which it viewed the large objective pictures that included and conditioned its treatment of detail. But during the previous century this doctrine led an intellectually isolated existence. It certainly influenced political practice, and provoked consideration of its technique; but it never broke completely through the barrier of thought-forms founded upon Natural Law. It all depended now on the attitude that would be taken towards this doctrine by the historians of the Enlightenment. Right in front of their eyes was the practice of the European Powers based upon it; but in their hearts they cherished the happiness of the human race as their ethical goal. In this dilemma they pursued a characteristically eclectic course. They gave a personal colouring to the actions prompted by the *raison d'état* which they could not explain away in the pages of history, by underlining the selfish interests of the holders of power in maintaining their own position and influence. If there arose a case when all personal considerations clearly gave way before the weight of great decisions objectively brought about by reasons of State, this was noted with a certain respect, but not ascribed to anything deeper than the peculiar characteristics of the particular State. According to this view, the *raison d'état* worked within the life of history either in a mechanical way, like some *deus ex machina*, or as a special variety of the usual self-centred interests. This was, of course, intimately connected with the stage then reached in the development of the modern State. The absolutist State still appeared to contemporaries too much in the guise of an isolated power-mechanism, whose ideals were directed towards the general weal, but which was in practice an estate managed by its rulers along strictly rational lines, according to their good or bad personal motives.

We have already sketched in a general way Voltaire's application of the doctrine of reasons of State to the writing of history. He applied it often and without stint, and in so doing once more displayed the continuing influence of the seventeenth-century spirit, with its sober matter-of-factness and harshness. 'The interests of the State are the sovereign reason of kings' (*Essai*, c. 174). 'When interests are at stake, princes can forget both insults and benefits' (*Essai*, c. 125). 'Politics overcome all passions in state councils' (*Essai*, c. 176). 'Everything gives way to interest' (*Essai*, c. 184). All this has a familiar ring to those who know the literature of the *ragione di stato* since the time of Botero. It lay behind the actions of Francis I, Henry IV, Richelieu, the Pope and so on. But Voltaire transferred this doctrine even to the times before the Renaissance, and made use of it in his contest with the Christian Church. Decius, Maximian and Diocletian, he held, had all only persecuted the Christians for reasons of State, because they supported rival Caesars; Diocletian was far from being religiously intolerant (*Essai*, c. 8). Even the Christian persecutions in Japan, he maintained, were motivated by reasons of State (*Essai*, c. 196). It is not surprising that he also uttered the harsh Machiavellian dictum: 'Religion, where princes are concerned, is almost always a matter of their interests' (*Essai*, c. 173, and similarly c. 178).

Voltaire applied the doctrine of political necessity most felicitously and significantly to the man whom, of all the French rulers, he had closest to his heart, namely Henry IV. He agreed that, in ordinary circumstances, a change of religion undertaken so obviously in his own interests would have cast a slur upon his honour. In this case, however, the interests had been so great and so closely bound up with the kingdom's welfare that the best of his Calvinist advisers themselves counselled him to adopt the religion that was so hateful to them. Several politicians then considered that Henry IV, once in power, should have acted like Elizabeth of England and freed France from Rome, as the only means of raising her political and economic states. But, as Voltaire particularly pointed out, Henry IV was not 'in the same circumstances' as Elizabeth; he had no national parliament, as she had, who shared her interests, and he also had insufficient money and arms, while he still had to continue the struggle with Philip II and the League (*Essai*, c. 174).

This example perhaps confirms the saying that a man only understands what he loves. Voltaire loved Henry IV and abominated Philip II. His judgment upon the latter was thus an exact reflection of a personal moralising attitude. Religion, Voltaire maintained, was only a mask, and his campaign against the Netherlands had been nothing but blood-thirsty despotism (*Essai*, c. 163 f.). So it remains true that although the doctrine of reasons of State could throw light on a number of individual cases of political action, it could not, as far as Voltaire was concerned, illuminate the whole complex of dynamic relationship between States. The realism of the politician who had given birth to this doctrine, and the moralism of the Enlightenment, were not suitable for an organic fusion.

Let us now review the course we have followed. On the whole, Voltaire's enlightened thinking was able to put the great mass of historical phenomena that had become rigid with convention into a melting-pot, as it were, and give it a thorough stirring. In so doing, he won a victory for the independence and autonomy of historical thought. He extended the horizon of historical interest to universal proportions, bringing within it everything of human concern. He aroused a desire to compare, to trace analogies, to ponder on the causes of variety in spite of the obvious likeness of the things compared; and here and there he stirred up a feeling for the specific structure of each historical creation, and for the links between the various cultural phenomena. Moreover, he succeeded in evoking a unified sense of world history as a whole, over and above all its individual manifestations, through the idea of a perfection of reason. This, as he showed, made it possible to see the course of Western history more especially as a gradual ascent to a higher level of culture, which had gathered speed in its later stages, but whose ultimate success was not a matter of certainty. This upward trend was viewed as a struggle towards achieving the highest benefits, caused and conditioned more particularly by the power of the State and by the opinions and ideas of men; and this view, along with the universality of his interest, constituted the most promising element latent in Voltaire's historical approach. But his sense of history as a whole was narrow, defective, and limited by the mechanistic concepts of contemporary philosophy and by the selfish demands of

French bourgeois society; with the result that genuine historical man, in all the richness of his varied characteristics, was never able to come fully into his own. The crucible therefore failed to compound the juxtaposed collection of historical phenomena in any age into a living blend controlled by a pattern of master-ideas. Thus a victory was achieved for a sense of universality, and a feeling that the life of history was an intellectual and spiritual whole; but there was no satisfactory solution to the incalculable problem of individuality, present both on the large and on the small scale; and instead of a living development of the individual, Voltaire could only offer the mechanical substitute of perfection.

Voltaire's historical picture tended, by the impetus of its own dialectic, to be transcended, and yet to go on exerting an influence at the very point where it seemed to be superseded. Voltaire had succeeded, as scarcely any of his predecessors, in sharpening men's awareness of the irrational character of historical life. The astonishment at the marvels of history which soon came over him never went beyond a resigned shrug of the shoulders. This is what the world is like, he would say to himself; it consists of contradictions, and can never be anything else (Art. 'Contradictions' in *Dict. philos.*). But the energy with which he searched out these contradictions was bound to result in a more insistent effort to reach a deeper understanding of them.

Furthermore, we saw that there was in Voltaire an unresolved contradiction. On the one hand, there was his lively interest in all things human at all stages of development, and the active power of his *homo sum*; on the other, the mechanically handled standard of values of a settled judgment, which divided the life of history into an enormous rubbish heap and a very small pile of precious metals. Or, as Voltaire himself expressed it at the close of his most tedious work, the *Annales de l'Empire*, (which is nonetheless spiced with all kinds of malicious touches): In a long chain of rocks and precipices, there are some fertile valleys to be seen. This contrast between the tendencies in history which linked things together, and those which seemed to divide them from one another, faced the Enlightenment with an urgent challenge to find some higher level of unity. This could only be produced by a new inner life, involving a radical revolution and reordering of all the psychological powers and resources of reflective human beings.

Chapter three

Montesquieu

A writer who wishes to present a clear account of the stage-by-stage transformation of the rational Enlightenment into the historical outlook has to consider whether he shall portray Montesquieu as coming before or after Voltaire. In point of life-span and activity, Montesquieu (1689–1755) comes immediately before Voltaire (b. 1694). And if we only take into account and compare the literary works of these authors which directly affected the interpretation of history in that period and in the following years, Voltaire must be put first with his *Considérations sur la grandeur et la décadence des Romains* of 1734. For the popular *History of Charles XII*, published by Voltaire as early as 1731, though a very powerful literary production and a picturesque account of a remarkable contemporary hero, contained nothing of the specifically new and original contribution that he made to the treatment of history. This new outlook was probably already building up in the thirties and forties. The *Siècle de Louis XIV* appeared in its first form in 1735–9, and the first fragments of the *Essai* in 1745. But before he could present these great works to the world in their complete form, Montesquieu had already appeared on the scene with his most successful enterprise, and had published his *Esprit des lois* in 1748, after almost two decades of preparation.

Nevertheless, we have decided to take Montesquieu as coming after Voltaire, for if viewed from the intellectual, rather than the strictly chronological point of view, Montesquieu certainly follows Voltaire. The latter drew the new insights he contributed to historical thought and knowledge from the treasures of the Enlightenment. But Montesquieu, both in his political and in his historical thinking, is more of a twin-headed Janus. He is one of those borderland figures, and much more difficult to grasp and understand than Voltaire. One can survey him again and again, pondering whether he should be placed in the eighteenth century, in the company of the Enlightenment where his thought-pattern would seem to place him, or in a world of reaction, in which by his social and political interests and ideals he would seem to belong. Or again, he may be seen as the man who transcended the thought of the Enlightenment, almost the unconscious practitioner of a Gothic or Romantic art, the pioneer of modern thought about political liberty and constitutional theory. At times one is forced to admit that the oftener he is read, the less certain does it become what he is really aiming at.[1] Since there can be no doubt about Montesquieu's pre-eminence as a thinker of great intellectual ability, all this points to unusual tensions and a fruitful wealth of motive behind all his thinking, though he never perhaps succeeded in reducing it to a state of balance—a wealth that is not to be discovered in Voltaire. One thing is certain: in subsequent times, men have continued to find more intellectual food in Montesquieu than in Voltaire. Voltaire's writings and thoughts can by the charm of their form still find readers today, but the charm is that of the inimitable art of a bygone age. On the other hand, Montesquieu's judgements, in spite of their old-fashioned dress, can still provoke to thought by reason of their lively content. Voltaire's questions, however varied and whimsical their effect on the reader, are usually answered by him in a clear and obvious manner, and his answers are no longer of anything but historical interest. The questions raised by Montesquieu, however, have been taken up and discussed again and again, and many of his weighty pronouncements can still have meaning for the searcher after historical connections in the world of today.

A glance at the personalities and careers of the two men is sufficient to explain the difference between their respective influence on history. In spite of a rather more eventful youth and a more even and serene old age, Voltaire's life from beginning to end was all of a piece, a mixture of enjoyment, intellectual activity and struggle, though even work and struggle became an indispensable part of enjoyment in the highly developed civilisation of this epoch. Montesquieu, too, tasted these pleasures, especially in his youth, and his *Lettres persanes* of 1721 and the racy poems of his youthful period reflect in satirical form, with humour and sensitivity, some of his experience in the licentious world of the Rococo period. But already in the *Lettres persanes* a deeper note was sounding—a prelude to his later thought and to his satire; and in a way that was quite different from Voltaire's, enjoyment, work and struggle then occupied separate compartments in his life. Montesquieu set a greater distance than Voltaire between

---

[1] Morf in the foreword to the 5th ed. of Hettner's *Literaturgeschichte des 18. Jahrhunderts*, part 2 (1894). He quotes Villemain and Bonnetière in the same sense.

his inner life and the outward flux of life in the world. He led a private existence of a simpler kind and concentrated with full intellectual power and deep practical assiduity on the task of a thoughtful and reflective mind in search of guiding principles. His office as President of the Parliament of Bordeaux, which came to him as a child of the *noblesse de robe* in 1716, very soon became irksome to him. He gave it up in 1726, but as the squire of the castle of La Brède, he faithfully maintained the corporative outlook of the parliamentary aristocracy. He represented a type of French nobleman that was already becoming rarer, refusing to be enticed by the allurements of the court, and became a scholar in a spirit of noble independence. The long European journeys he undertook from the years 1728 to 1731 bore the character of serious voyages of research, as his recently discovered travel notes and collections of material prove.[1] Then for many years on end he concentrated on his own special life's work (for the *Considérations* were only a preliminary excursus for the *Esprit des lois*) unceasingly collecting and reading, and mentally combining all that he had read and seen and experienced, often tiring himself out on the toughest material, until he had finally scaled the heights, where he could breathe with relief and say: 'Now everything falls into line with my principles' (28, 6 and preface).[2] By this manner of life, Montesquieu gave one of the finest examples of modern scholarship, with a combination of the thinker and the researcher entirely dedicated to his task. Voltaire may have read fully as much as he; but in his case, the transfer of what he read into his own thought took place so speedily and in such cursory fashion that he only extracted a part of its nutriment. Montesquieu has also been reproached for passing too rapidly from observation to explanatory principle. From the point of view of modern methodical research, this may well be true. But he stands head and shoulders above his own time, and more particularly above the activities of the French Enlightenment, by virtue of the perseverance with which he preceded all his deductive thinking by a process of inductive research.

In order to arrive at a fuller understanding not only of this procedure, but also of its final aims and of what was peculiar to him and prophetic for the future (and a considerable advance on Voltaire's interpretation of history), we will take a glance at the intellectual currents of thought in which he was involved, and see how he compares with Voltaire.

The Enlightenment judged the world of history according to a standard based upon an eternally valid reason that was free of all

---

[1] *Voyages*, 2 vols, 1894–6.

[2] All subsequent quotations giving figures only refer to the books and chapters of the *Esprit des lois*.

religious and metaphysical ingredients. It had arisen out of the intellectual movements of the seventeenth century, out of an exaggeration of the old thinking based upon Natural Law as produced by Cartesianism, by the extinction of confessional fanaticism, and by the rise of the natural sciences which looked for and discovered simple general laws. But there was also another strain of thought peculiar to the seventeenth century, which we have already alluded to in connection with Voltaire, namely the sober and stern sense of reality. This was especially the governing principle of the politicians; and when transferred to the sphere of historical studies, was marked by an avid hunger for facts and a tendency to collect enormous masses of material. Between the formative and simplifying spirit of Natural Law and the masses of empirical material, there was a gulf which the somewhat rigid and ponderous manner of the seventeenth century had not as yet succeeded in bridging. Even Leibniz's thought, with all its wider implications, was not altogether able to penetrate the vast stores of knowledge he had accumulated. Further, there was no means of bridging the similar gulf between the very sober and empirical outlook of practical politics and the general theories of the State based upon Natural Law. This practical political outlook, however, had produced a literature for its own use in which affairs of State were presented in a very different light from that of the general political theory of the time. We refer to the literature of the *raison d'état* and the doctrine of political expediency, the importance of which is dealt with in my book *Die Idee der Staatsräson*. The State of the theorist, as based upon Natural Law, was here confronted with the real State and genuine political activity, with all its efforts to maintain power, its calculation of the means required and the moves and manoeuvres of opponents, with all its ruthlessness and lack of scruple, and all its craftiness and trickery. Of course some practical considerations also found their way into the theoretical outlook, just as some elements of Natural Law were incorporated in the practical manuals on statecraft. This was perfectly possible, because on either side, in Natural Law as well as in practical politics, there was a highly utilitarian spirit abroad, prepared to use first one weapon and then another and not above making sudden changes from one thought-pattern to another. But there was no possibility of an inner fusion between the two.

In historical writing too, particularly in contemporary history, the doctrine of political expediency and the concrete interest of the State was apt to come in here and there; and in his great work on contemporary history, which drew material from the papers of the chief actors in it, Pufendorf set it up on the grand scale as the principle for understanding political actions—though not without a certain harshness and onesidedness. The best feature in Boling-broke's rather shallow *Letters on the Study and Use of History* (1735) was the survey of recent political history from the standpoint of political expediency. As we have already seen, Voltaire also knew and used this doctrine, but only for the most part in an external way, along with his other standards of judgment. It must in fact have been pretty generally known at that period, for in the same years that saw the beginning of Voltaire's and Montesquieu's great historical studies, there appeared the last great inclusive work on the doctrine of political interests, Rousset's textbook *Les Intérêts présents et les prétentions des puissances de l'Europe* (1st ed., 1733, 3rd impr., 1741).

It can easily be shown that Montesquieu was familiar with this literature.[1] But there was more than literature available to him, there was the living and contemporary spectacle of the statecraft and power politics of Louis XIV and the Regency. This grew to be one of the very strongest influences in the shaping of his thought, for the general effect of the War of the Spanish Succession, the profound exhaustion it left behind, the last sad years of Louis XIV, and the troubled times of the Regency had caused much heart-searching amongst French people, and had been a powerful incentive to new ideas. The new mature movement of the Enlightenment was in no small measure a protest against the power politics inherited from the seventeenth century. Abbé Saint-Pierre's treatise on permanent peace was published in 1713. 'I am no longer interested in wars, but in men', Montesquieu once remarked (*Pensées et fragments*, 1, 301). His first philosophy of history, which, though immature, was full of

---

[1] In his *Montesquieu e Machiavelli* (1912), Levi-Malvano undertakes an instructive examination of the specially close relationship between Montesquieu and Machiavelli without, however, exhausting this theme. Particularly valuable is his demonstration of the influence exercised by many thoughts in the *Discorsi* upon the *Considérations* and the *Esprit des lois*. One of the most important works in political theory from the early seventeenth century, Boccalini's *Bilancia politica*, is quoted by Montesquieu in his *Pensées et fragments*, 2, p. 357. On his list of books to be read, there was also the Duke of Rohan's *Interest des Princes et Estats de la Chrestienté* 1638 (*Pensées et fragments*, 1, 31). In what is said in *Esprit* 21, 30 about Machiavellism and *coups d'état*, we catch a glimpse of an allusion to Gabriel Naudé's manual on Machiavellian theory, the *Considérations politiques sur les coups d'état* of 1639. A camp-follower of the seventeenth-century 'Tacitists', who dealt with political theory along the lines of Tacitus, was the republican-minded Englishman Thomas Gordon, whose translation of Tacitus, with appended discourses, appeared in 1728. Dédieu, in his *Montesquieu et la tradition politique anglaise en France* (1909), p. 287, demonstrates the probability that Montesquieu made use of this work. In addition, there is the use of the various slogans employed in the literature of political theory, such as *nécessités de l'état, raison d'état, intérêt de l'état, maximes d'état, bienséance*. Finally, there is his verdict on Pufendorf's Great Elector (*Voyages*, 2, 202): '*C'est le Tacite de l'Allemagne. Il démêle fort bien les divers intérêts de la cour de Berlin.*'

promising thought, was deliberately directed against what he saw
before his eyes in the shape of statecraft and power politics. The
Lettres persanes of 1721 already suggest this here and there; but it did
not find its full expression till the essay 'De la Politique',[1] which was
written soon after, but did not become known till 1892.

So discredited was the word 'politics' at this period, that Montesquieu treats it as equivalent to statecraft, devoid of all honesty and
faith. 'It is useless', he begins, 'to attack politics direct by saying how
much it goes against morality, reason and righteousness'. For
politics, he maintained, would continue to exist as long as there
were passions which kept politics independent of the restraints of
law. The matter must be approached differently, and it must be
proved to the politicians that their petty devices and evil practices
were of no significance when measured against the general trend of
events. It was really quite irrelevant as far as the final outcome was
concerned whether this or that particular man was at the helm, or
this or that particular decision was taken. For he held that over all
the separate actions of individuals in the social life of men there ruled
a superior power, a *caractère commun*, an *âme universelle*, in the
shape of an endless chain of causes stretching through the centuries
and constantly producing new ramifications.

> As soon as the dominating key-note is sounded and accepted,
> it alone is sovereign, and everything the ruling powers, the
> authorities and the peoples do or imagine, whether in rebellion
> against the accepted key-note or in conformity with it, is
> always strictly related to it; and it will continue to rule until
> completely destroyed.

And when this will happen, he maintained, can never be foreseen or
calculated because of the multiplicity of interacting causes. Today,
the spirit of obedience was in universal control. The princes had no
need to be specially able, for this spirit ruled on their behalf; and
whatever they might do (good, evil, or indifferent) the result was
much the same in the end.

This was a real young man's philosophy, passionately radical and
one-sided, and blind to the dubious consequences of its own theses.
Montesquieu wanted to disarm the rascality of statesmen, and to
work for morality by methods that were beyond good and evil. But
this extreme collectivist and fatalistic interpretation of history could
only lead to an even greater moral indifference. It was the expression
of an upsurging and ambivalent train of thought in him, coming from
the depths of his being, and destined to influence him throughout
his life. On the one hand, there was an ardent moralism, which

[1] *Mélanges inédits de Montesquieu*, 1892, pp. 157 ff.

attacked the world of thought and the spheres of activity created by Machiavelli and the modern statesmen at its most unsavoury point; but beyond this, there was an unusually urgent demand for causal thinking, combining the sense of an incalculable and impenetrable multiplicity of active causes with a sense of large general groups of causes and effects, and comprehending both the boundless sea and the chief currents prevailing in it. Both of these tendencies, the moralistic, with its hatred of the politics of power and conquest, and the causal determinism, with its call for the application of the newly discovered orderliness of nature to the needs of human life, belonged to the essence of the Enlightenment, more especially the French Enlightenment. In each of its thinkers, however, this dualism took on an individual form. In Montesquieu, it struck deeper root than in Voltaire. His youthful work showed that he had emotional strength, though it was as yet of a rather primitive kind. But it now came about that his very contact with the world of the 'politicians' was to lead to a great enrichment of his thought. What he attacked in them was the odious and often petty ways of day-to-day power politics—what is called Machiavellianism in the specific sense. But Machiavelli had also taught that a statesman should make an empirical study of actual men and the causes generally at work in the life of the State. He often carried out an enquiry into causes of the profoundest kind, not really in order to discover a new picture of the world (though this did come as an incidental fruit of his teaching) but from the practical motives of a statesman, behind which there indeed lay a particular personal ideal of the State. Montesquieu's moralism did not by any means arise, as was the case with so many other thinkers in the Enlightenment, simply from his needs as an individual; it was also deeply concerned with the woes and the weal of the great social communities. Thus it came about that he was also prepared to learn from Machiavelli's state-utilitarianism and empiricism, and therefore honoured Machiavelli as 'a great man'.[1]

It is not necessary for our purpose to trace all the connections that have been established between Montesquieu's and Machiavelli's thought. Our aim is simply to understand the interpretation of history as reflected more particularly in these two great works. But for this purpose, we have now reached the moment when it will be as well to compare Montesquieu's approach with the line marked out by Machiavelli from an angle which, as far as I know, has not so far received attention.

---

[1] We may adduce from the *Correspondance de Montesquieu*, 2, 369, a further testimony to the special importance of Machiavelli for Montesquieu. He offers a compliment to Hénault, '*qui me touche comme les grâces et m'instruit comme Machiavel*'.

If we compare the general questions posed by the *Esprit des lois*, and even the *Considérations* which were derived from it, with Machiavelli's *The Prince* and his *Discourse on Livy*, an inner relationship between them is at once discernible. Machiavelli divides States up according to their form of government, and asks the following questions both of republics and of principalities: What particular means are requisite for maintaining them in being, what laws are useful for this purpose, what mistakes must they avoid, and what are the causes of their decline and fall? There is a faint suggestion of this same scheme in the *Considérations*, as well as throughout the main portion of the *Esprit des lois*. Incidentally, we may glance at the literature on the *ragione di stato* and *arcana imperii* which had flourished during the seventeenth century. Here too, the generally dominant question is what are the means most suited to the particular position and form of a State, through which it may best be preserved. In particular, since the time of Zuccoli and Settala, there had been discussion of the political expediency that was applicable to monarchies, aristocracies and democracies, or to their debased forms, when they had become tyrannies. For each of these types of State a scheme of governing principles and standards of behaviour had been worked out. In the ultimate analysis, this way of looking at things went back to Aristotle and the fifth book of his *Politics*.

In the *Considérations*, which we shall later examine in more detail, Montesquieu was only concerned with the Romans. It had a more far-reaching aim than Machiavelli's *Discorsi*, which is indeed never mentioned in this book, but which certainly influenced him. Whilst Machiavelli was primarily concerned with the doctrine of statesmanship, though he did in fact work a philosophy of history into it, Montesquieu deliberately strove for an interpretation of the whole historical destiny of the Romans along philosophical lines. But he uses as his means the doctrine of statesmanship sketched by Machiavelli, for throughout this work his first consideration is the political maxim governing the Romans' actions, for which Polybius was his principal source. He pays attention to their *principes toujours constants*, and what a *république sage* may and may not do, and what would be harmful to it. There are also some thoughts woven in on the best method of conquest.

And what is the leading train of thought in the *Esprit des lois*? Montesquieu says in his preface that the result of his enquiries has been the recognition that mankind was not simply being led by their moods and caprices through the boundless variety of laws and customs that surround them.[1] This, as we shall subsequently show, was

[1] In his *Lettres persanes* (no. 129) there is this further comment: '*La plupart des législateurs ont été des hommes bornés que le hasard a mis à la tête des autres, et qui*

indeed a result that rose far above the narrow confines of any doctrine of statesmanship and pointed the way to a new land of thought. And yet its basis was still the old technical question of the reasonable means of effecting the desired purpose in political action. He goes on to say that he is not writing in order to censure any institutions that may happen to exist in a particular country. Each nation will find in his book *les raisons de ses maximes*, and the only man who should propose alterations is the one who can scan the entire constitution of a State with a *coup de génie*. Again we have a great thought, pregnant with new ideas; but again it is rooted in the inherited insights of the *ancien régime* statesmanship, in the examination of the particular concrete interests of individual States—in other words, the *raisons de ses maximes*. We have already seen that along with this individualising doctrine of the interests of the State, which considered each one in its specific historical particularity, a schematic doctrine also flourished in the seventeenth century, which suppressed the individual aspects and was only concerned to ask what was politically advisable for the preservation of the particular constitutional forms, whether it was monarchy, or aristocracy, or democracy. And it is sufficiently well known that a large part of this study by Montesquieu consists of working out, for each of the constitutional forms dealt with, what kind of dispositions, customs, institutions and maxims of government will be required to maintain and preserve it.[1] He is never tired of repeating that the same fundamental principles which might well be harmful in a democracy will work well in an aristocracy. For example, fortifications will protect a monarchy, but despotisms should be afraid of having fortifications (9, 5). The distribution of benefits among people is harmful in a democracy, but may be useful in an aristocracy (5, 8).

Moreover, the famous Chapter 6 of Book II on the English Constitution is particularly illuminating in this connection. It does not belong to the part of the book that deals with general and vital principles in a schematic fashion, but rather to the more individualising sections, where the author examines from the point of view of

n'ont presque consulté que leurs préjugés et leurs fantaisies'. This reference enables us to assess the significant development undergone by Montesquieu's thought since his early days. This letter from the *Lettres persanes*, with its inner freedom of sentiment, was indeed expressing fundamental ideas of the later Montesquieu, particularly the thought that if it was ever necessary to alter existing laws, this should only be done 'in fear and trembling'.

[1] In his *Montesquieu et la tradition politique anglaise en France* (1908), p. 132 n., and *Montesquieu* (1913), pp. 50 ff., Dédieu has called attention to Doria, *Vita civile*, 1710, as a possible source for Montesquieu's thoughts on this subject. Doria teaches, for example, that the virtues of its citizens is the principle of a republic, ambition that of a monarchy, etc. But in this doctrine Doria is only expounding the principles of the older political theory.

political expediency the particular concrete tasks of specific States, and the means necessary to their fulfilment. For he starts from the assumption that every State has, apart from its general task of maintaining itself (*de se maintenir*, Machiavelli's *mantenere*), another special and peculiar task—which, in the case of the English nation, is the achievement of political liberty. But then, as is very well known, his inclination to schematise distorted the image of the English Constitution and its history. For the time being we will leave on one side the controversial question whether in this chapter Montesquieu was really depicting his own personal ideal for a State and stating a personal confession of faith. But it must be noticed that we are dealing here with two traditional questions peculiar to the literature of statesmanship and political expediency. In the first place, with the question, what special interests a specific State possesses; and then with the question, what technical arrangements are required to realise a particular political value, namely *la liberté politique*. In that older literature, such questions were dealt with rather as a modern general staff will work out marching orders and operational plans for certain possible eventualities. Already, Machiavelli had liked to present his doctrine of statesmanship in this form. Here, as he generally did, Montesquieu quite obviously linked on to this traditional doctrine of statesmanship. The conclusion to be drawn from this, however, is that Montesquieu's praise of the English Constitution must not be taken in too immediately a personal, literal, or absolute sense. He is only concerned in the first place to say that, assuming political liberty to be the highest aim for a State, the English Constitution must be held up as a model; that the English State, in so far as it depended on the laws, had indeed achieved that aim. It is not to be denied that there may well be a warm and intimate note of the most personal kind running through this chapter. But it is also marked by the political relativism represented by the line of thought established by Machiavelli, the power to come to grips with the most varied situations and tasks.

What Montesquieu has to offer is statesmanship of the highest degree that was possible at that time. It is a guide to statesmanship, a continuation of the line begun by Machiavelli; and it represents the climax (and as far as the main theme is concerned, the end) of this development. For the similar literature that appeared after Montesquieu, such as Bielfeld's *Institutions politiques*,[1] are no longer of any importance in the history of thought.

But the greatness of Montesquieu's achievement consisted in pressing into the service of his project all the scholarly and scientific

[1] On this topic cf. my short essay: 'Bielfeld als Lehrer der Staatskunst' in the *Zeitschrift für öffentliches Recht*, VI, 4.

information available in his day. His intention was to give the statesman the most thorough knowledge of the life of the State and the best and most reliable maxims founded upon this knowledge. The older doctrines of statesmanship had often drawn these maxims from the foreground experience of practical politics. Montesquieu wanted to draw upon a much deeper background, upon the ultimate laws governing the whole life of history. He used history and natural science, geography and ethnology, the teachings of contemporary philosophy and psychology that had become common knowledge, and not least his own experiences, playing upon them all rather as an organ player makes full use of all the stops and registers in his instrument. From the humanist tradition came his massive knowledge of the authors of antiquity, and his classical respect for the exemplary nature of the forms and patterns of the ancient world. From the travel literature of his own time came his attraction for comparing the circumstances and conditions of exotic races and States; and from his own travels he had acquired a knowledge of modern Europe. The study of natural science undertaken in his youth had given him familiarity with the results of research in this field. The growing political interest, since the Regency, in the revitalising of the ancient French institutions suppressed under the absolute monarchy, gave him his intense preoccupation with their most ancient roots, and with the source-literature of the barbarian centuries. And finally, the life and atmosphere of French society, the salons, his reading of Montaigne and other gifted men who knew the world and human nature, and, first and foremost, his own disposition, gave him a mental versatility and a gentle openmindedness and tolerance towards the strange tricks played by the human psyche.

Voltaire, like Montesquieu, possessed a universal, though less thorough, acquaintance with the sources of knowledge for his period, yet used them in a completely different way. For him, they were weapons to be used in the one great single-minded struggle between the eternally valid reason and the multifarious forces of human unreason. In this perspective, the causative factors such as time and place, climate, soil, the form of political constitution, customs and so on were indeed not forgotten, but receded into the background compared with the main dualistic theme. In Voltaire, the interpretation of history based upon Natural Law, based upon reason, the one steady guiding star amid all the variety of life, enjoyed its greatest triumph.[1] But in Montesquieu, the two powerful

[1] 'Voltaire will never write a good history', we read in the *Pensées et fragments*, 2, 59, 'he is like the monks, who do not handle their subject for its own sake, but for the reputation of their Order. Voltaire writes on behalf of his own monastery'.

main currents of the preceding centuries, the current of a rational Natural Law, and the empirical and realistic current, finally came together and united.

Thus Montesquieu's work was not only the climax and final stage of the thought-pattern and literature initiated by Machiavelli, which sought to give guidance to actual States based on empirical analysis, but also a climax of the thought-pattern and literature based upon the general ideals of Natural Law, intent upon discovering the best kind of State. For its leading star remained justice and the harmony of politics and morals; and it therefore viewed the State not only from above, with the eyes of a statesman, but also from below, having in mind the needs of the governed and the individual person. But the statesman's view was predominant, and so there was the remarkable spectacle of political realism, which Montesquieu had learnt from Machiavelli, being given a new twist under the Frenchman's influence. It moved away from the sphere of pure power politics, though it never quite lost sight of it, and took possession of the new field of justice, civic freedom and order, and the borderland between political and individual life. The spirit of middle-class enlightenment flowed in to occupy the territory originally carved out by Machiavelli. The idea of statesmanship created by him broadened out into the art of the lawgiver, embracing all social and human needs as far as they had any connection with the State.

It lies outside our purpose to evaluate this new statesmanship and its problems. Nor can we consider the intellectual struggles of Montesquieu as a person which are here disclosed,[1] except insofar as they serve to throw light upon our main question, what the uniting of these two streams of thought undertaken by Montesquieu achieved towards a new and deeper understanding of history.

But first, the contrast between the thinking of the rationalistic Natural Law and the empirical realism has to be stated more clearly. There already existed within the doctrine of Natural Law going back to the Stoics a contrast between an absolute Natural Law derived from God-given human reason, whose utterances were of eternal validity, and a relative and differential Natural Law, which, without denying the absolute norms in principle, yet paid regard to the actual imperfections of human nature and the manifold particularities of social life.[2] In the further development of this thought, it was therefore possible to lay stress sometimes upon the absolute and

---

[1] This theme has been handled with great interest and often felicity in Klemperer's work on Montesquieu (2 vols, 1914–15), but there is a certain element of expressionistic exuberance about his writing.

[2] Troeltsch, 'Das stoisch-christliche Naturrecht und das moderne profane Naturrecht', *Hist. Zeitschrift*, 106 and *Collected Writings*, 4, pp. 166 ff.

sometimes upon the relative aspect. In Voltaire and the French Enlightenment as represented by him, the absolute aspect triumphed. The imperfections and peculiarities seemed, in comparison with the demands of reason, to be only more or less regrettable hindrances which could never indeed be entirely removed, because they were backed by the superior power of actual human nature, but which could here and there be brought closer by 'perfectionism' to the ideal reason, the ideal of the true and higher nature in man.

The empirical realism, however, originating in Machiavelli, proceeded firmly along the path already travelled by the relative and differential strain of thought based upon Natural Law. It took men and things naturalistically, as they really are, and in a cool and purposeful way supplied practical solutions to the problems of life. While remaining true to itself, it contented itself, as Machiavelli and his adherents had done, with making polite bows to the absolutist theories of nature and reason. For the most part, however, thinkers attempted a compromise between the naturalistic standpoint and the notion of an absolutely valid law of reason. This can be seen in both Hobbes and Spinoza. But as long as the concept of an absolute law of nature remained fixed and unvarying, these compromises were bound to remain intrinsically incomplete. And the very idea of 'Nature' was bound therefore to fluctuate permanently between two concepts—an irrational or supra-rational power over all life and the source of all reality, or a rational power that worked in and through the mind of man. From now on, we shall call these two extremes respectively naturalism and rationalism.

Even Montesquieu did not altogether transcend such compromises and such hesitations. His strong sense of reality had always made him refuse one of the main tenets of thought based upon Natural Law—namely, the assumption that the State had come about through some kind of social contract. But there is sufficient, though not very frequent, testimony to his belief in an absolute law of nature. He says in the *Considérations* (c. 22, conclusion), that the great division between spiritual and temporal power, which forms the basis for peace among the nations, is founded not only on religion, but also on reason and nature. In the *Esprit des lois* (25, 7), he remarks that Plato says on the subject of the gods all that 'the light of nature' has ever been able to produce in an intelligible way upon matters of religion. And in the 26th Book, where he begins to deal with the composition of all the kinds of law by which men are ruled, *le droit naturel* decisively occupies the first place. It follows from Natural Law, for example, that since all men are born equal, slavery is 'against nature' (15, 7).

But Montesquieu immediately goes on to say that in certain

countries with hot climates, slavery can yet be based upon a *raison naturelle*. And this brings us close to the naturalistic conception of nature, which could not but recognise the fluctuating effects of irrational and physical forces upon human life, and was then free to declare it reasonable to comply with them. In this way a relative reason came to be recognised alongside of the absolute reason. The laws founded upon absolute reason were, from our present-day point of view, no more than norms and ideals for human thought and action. But the laws given or recognised by relative reason, even where they bore the character of norms and not merely of causal consequences, were based upon natural causal connections to which human reason must needs accommodate itself.

And this brings us to the obscurity in Montesquieu's thought caused by the juxtaposition of naturalism and rationalism, an obscurity that is particularly characteristic of the great discussion on laws in general which opens his work.

Laws, the author states, are the necessary relationships that flow from the nature of things.[1] All beings have laws, even deity itself—and so does the material world. The animals have their laws, and human beings have theirs.

This would appear to posit the strictest principle of causality, seeing that even God invariably obeys the laws He has laid down. And yet Montesquieu at once vigorously attacks those who hold that all actions in the world can be traced back to a blind fate. For the rationalist in him, believing in a timeless reason remote from the ordinary causal chain of things, was at strife with the deterministic consequences of his premises. The laws, or (as we should call them) the norms, of reason, would need to be as invariable as the laws of motion and the theorems of mathematics in the material world, if they were to satisfy these rationalistic requirements. Montesquieu could only prove his thesis by confusing 'law' in the sense of norms and 'law' in the sense of causal relationships and mathematical statements.[2] Today, for example, we should consider the concepts of right and wrong as norms whose content had been produced by the development from lower to higher stages of human life and were likely to change and develop still further. For Montesquieu, however, they ranked as eternally valid, along with the truths of mathematics. Thus he could write: 'To say that there is no right and wrong except what is prescribed or forbidden by positive law would be like saying, before one has drawn a circle, that not all radii are of the

[1] On the relationship between 'relationships' and 'laws' in Montesquieu, cf. M. Ritter, *Entwicklung der Geschichtswissenschaft*, p. 211.

[2] On this point cf. also Barckhausen, *Montesquieu, ses idées et ses œuvres* (1907), p. 40.

same length'. And so he interpreted the contradictions he found between positive laws and the so-called law of nature as a hard-and-fast distinction between a world of variable, and a world of invariable, norms (26, 3 and 4).[1]

Under the spell of the pattern of thought based upon Natural Law, Montesquieu was therefore unable to realise the lack of clarity produced by this confusion of the different meanings of law. He was not even alerted to his error by the fact (which he himself proceeded to explain in detail) that man infringes the laws of reason at every point, whereas his physical nature is subject to unbreakable laws. The reason for this, he explained, was that man as a free intelligence was subject to ignorance and error, and as a sentient creature to a thousand different passions.

But it must be admitted (and this was one of Montesquieu's greatest achievements) that he was able to give much deeper thought and a quite different explanation from Voltaire's to the interplay between this ignorance, error and passion in the life of history. He had a more genuine and original scientific desire to find causal connections than Voltaire. Where the latter was content, with the complacent arrogance of the Enlightenment, to see sense and nonsense lying as a rule side by side, and to accept the irrational in history with a sigh and a shrug of the shoulders as something fated by nature, Montesquieu made energetic attempts to discover some reason even in the irrational. He did this in the first place by showing that there were traces of reasonableness making themselves felt in spite of everything even in the historical phenomena which conflicted with the laws of reason. We may once again recall his great saying in the preface that caprice was not the only thing that led men through the unbounded variety of law and custom. Everywhere and again and again he had discovered that rational and irrational motives are interlinked. Even the Iroquois, who ate those they took prisoner, says Montesquieu at the beginning of his book (1, 3), have a native legal system. They send

[1] It is one of Montesquieu's small inconsistencies that in the immediately preceding chapter 26, 2, he expressly assigns an unalterable character only to 'divine law'. But then in 26, 14 we have the following unequivocal statement: '*La défense des lois de la nature est invariable parce qu'elle dépend d'une chose invariable*'. Barckhausen gives a pretty example of how Montesquieu, even as he worked, was still wrestling with the problem of how to reconcile reason as interpreted by Natural Law with the wealth of historical variety (*Montesquieu, etc.*, 1907, p. 233, from the papers of La Brède). The 11th paragraph of I, 3 was originally to have run: 'La raison humaine donne des lois politiques et civiles à tous les peuples de la Terre'. It was altered to: 'La loi en général est la Raison humaine *en tant* qu'elle gouverne tous les peuples de la Terre'. The rationalism was thus toned down, though not removed. Cf. also *Pensées et fragments*, 1, 381 on the *lois invariables et fondamentales* which should prevail in political life, though admittedly this is not always so.

and receive ambassadors and recognise certain rights in war and peace; unfortunately (he had to add in the spirit of *raison naturelle*), this legal system was not built upon the true principles. Just as there are many wise things that are done in a very foolish manner, so there are also foolish things that are carried out with great wisdom (28, 25). Some of the best-known features of his thought are the respect he showed for the customs of the different peoples as they have come into their present form, his advice to preserve them where they were not directly harmful, and his warning against any forcible attempt to alter them by law. For a people, he says, know, love and defend their customs more than their laws (10, 11). Although he mostly explained the origin and growth of laws along pragmatic lines (in which he differed profoundly from Savigny's later doctrine of the national spirit), ascribing it to the deliberate will of the law-giver, he admitted that there was also the influence of concrete circumstance; and he was already thinking along collective lines when considering the origins of customs and manners.[1] He pro-nounced them to be the work of the nation in general (19, 14). Else-where, he says that customs take their origin in nature, and the accent of nature is the sweetest of all voices (26, 4). The examples he had in mind here show that the idea of nature still has a connota-tion based upon Natural Law, because the customs he is alluding to corresponded to what would be called natural morality. But this reference to 'the sweetest of all voices' already had overtones and an atmosphere going beyond rationalism and pointing forward to a quite new and much more intimate relationship with history.

This was the first germinal sign of a new feeling for life, and a deeper and warmer conception of nature. Even in his youthful *Lettres persanes* (No. 53) he had appealed against the conformist and enslaving spirit of society to 'nature, who expresses herself with such variety and appears in so many forms'.[2] But the time was not yet ripe for a complete yielding to this new feeling. Although he was already conscious of its deep-down urges, in the bright light of consciousness it was outweighed by the need to justify his respect for the irrationalities of history by utilitarian and rational arguments. The practical power of the irrational was by no means unknown to the thinkers of the Enlightenment in general. Voltaire had certainly

[1] Not indeed without some exceptions. '*Lycurgue . . . forma les manières*', he says in 19, 16. Here, however, as we shall have to emphasise again later on, he was depending in classicist fashion on the ancient tradition. He deals in the same pragmatic way with the Chinese lawgivers in this passage, depending upon the literature of travellers.

[2] Cf. also his thoughts on the upbringing of children, in which he anticipates Rousseau—*Pensées et fragments*, 2, 307. 'Votre art trouble le procédé de la Nature . . . *laissez former le corps et l'esprit par la Nature!*'

noted the remarkable mixture of contrary qualities within the same historical phenomenon, and had observed that good and evil could flow from the same source. Montesquieu went one better than Voltaire in showing that this irrational element could also be useful to the State. For the whole great tradition founded by Machiavelli and fed by the doctrines of statesmanship belonging to the ancient world began here to assume an extremely modern shape. This doctrine had always taught that it was necessary to make allowance for the passions, follies and weaknesses of man. In his youthful work, the *Dissertation* of 1716 on the religious policy of the Romans, which was strongly influenced by Machiavelli,[1] Montesquieu had written: 'Polybius reckons superstition as one of the advantages that the Roman people had over other nations. For what seems ridiculous to the wise is often necessary for the foolish'.[2] In the *Considérations* (c. 4) we read: 'There is nothing so powerful as a republic like Rome or Lacedaemonia, where the laws are observed not out of fear or out of respect for reason, but by the forces of passion'.[3] Or in very similar tones in the *Esprit des lois* (19, 27) he writes of his much-admired England: 'This nation, who are constantly in a heated state about something, could be more easily led through their passions than through their reason, which never has a very great effect on the minds of men'.[4]

It would appear, then, that Montesquieu confessed to a certain notable powerlessness in reason. But should his remarks be interpreted in this downright fashion? Did his rationalism come to an end at this point and capitulate before the power of the irrational mental forces at work in history?[5] Is this the point at which the high narrow ridge is crossed which separates the works of the Enlightenment from those of historism? This can surely not be seriously

[1] Cf. Levi–Malvano, *Montesquieu e Machiavelli*, p. 67.

[2] The way in which political theory and an enlightened outlook dwelt side by side in him is shown very characteristically by another dictum on superstition in the *Pensées et fragments*, 1, 390: 'Nothing is more calculated to produce harmful prejudices than superstition; and if it has sometimes happened that wise lawgivers have used it to their own advantage, the human race has then lost a thousand times more than it has gained in the proceedings.'

[3] Cf. also *Pensées et fragments*, 2, 225.

[4] There is a somewhat similar judgement on England, '*une nation impatiente, sage dans sa fureur même*', in the *Lettres persanes*, no. 136—that is, before his journey to England the influence of which upon the development of his thought must not be exaggerated.

[5] In *Pensées et fragments* 2, 133, there is the following exclamatory passage: 'What a remarkable thing! Hardly ever is it reason that brings about reasonable things; and hardly ever do we come to reason through reason itself.' But the example he then gives of the vanity of two Roman matrons as the cause of a beneficial change in the constitution shows an almost primitive kind of pragmatism.

maintained. The close connection of Montesquieu's thought with the older doctrines of statesmanship would rather lead to a different interpretation of his words on the power of the passions. This power had long ago been known by those who used to be called 'politicians', and even Machiavelli had learnt to take them into account. They saw the passions as none other than the fiery steed whom reason, as rider, had to learn to direct, at times restraining them, at other times allowing them a free rein. But reason thought of as the rider was not quite identical to reason as conceived by the Enlightenment. Rather was it in the first place *raison d'état*, the interests of the State and of the powers that be, a strictly practical use of all available means, even the irrational ones, of achieving and maintaining power. But it could well happen, and the process began with Machiavelli, that this *raison d'état* was thought of in deeper terms and filled with an ethical content, and its goal became the ideal of a healthy and vigorous life for the State and its people, and a more perfect social constitution for its citizens. Then it was possible at this point for the reason of the Enlightenment to join in and to weave humanitarian and eudaemonistic ends into this ideal of a State. This happened, for instance, with Frederick the Great. But in his case, the practical aims of power politics and the eudaemonistic ends became so widely sundered that the latter threatened finally to vanish into the limbo of the unattainable. For with Frederick, foreign policy, power politics, κατ' ἐξοχήν [by clear preference] held the primacy. But for the jurist in Montesquieu, on the contrary, domestic policy was primary. There is a personal sound about his dictum that next to the Christian religion, the best political and civic laws are the greatest good that men can either receive or give to others (24, 1).

Therefore Montesquieu saw the statesman in the first place not as a power politician, but as a wise lawgiver, who works out from the irrational practical material with which he is constantly being presented the best constitution possible in the circumstances. The horse, as we saw, may be irrational, but the rider must be rational. Hence the remark we have already quoted from the *Considérations*, to the effect that in Rome and Sparta passion rather than reason had been the real basis of the strong political bond between the State and its citizens. To this was added the significant remark: 'For then there is joined to the wisdom of a good government the entire power that usually belongs only to a faction'. And the same is true of his picture of the English nation, swayed by its powerful passions. He points out that if it were not for this free play of all the passions (hatred, envy, jealousy, greed for gain and a strong desire for personal success) the State would be like a man exhausted by illness, who is without passions simply because he is without strength. Even

107

this irrational spectacle which he presented with such vigour and ingenuity, and almost in the colours of the later historism, rests in the last resort on a rational, or one might say rationalistic, principle. For Montesquieu's aim is to show (19, 27) 'how laws can contribute to the shaping of the customs, manners and character of a nation'. In the English Constitution as interpreted by him, it was the machinery for the separation of powers, which he presented so ingeniously and yet with such an artificial rationalism, that was calculated to make possible the development of all the nation's powers, edifying and unedifying, and in the end ensure that everything would work out for the best. And even the interplay of these various forces is set out as such a wonderful piece of interlocking machinery that we sense the want of a certain breath of life which belongs to actual history.

Yet in spite of his often attested faith in the formative power of the wise lawgiver, Montesquieu was far removed from the banal opinions of contemporary rationalism, which was always searching behind every historical event to find some purposeful agent at work. The depth of his insight rests upon his realisation that the general and the personal, the environment and the individual, always exist in a state of mutual interaction. He knew the formative power not only of lawgivers, but also of institutions. But how naively mechanical was his attempt to balance these two factors against each other as a matter of principle! In the first chapter of the *Considérations*, we are told that when republics are set up it is the heads of republics who make the institutions; but subsequently, it is the institution that makes the heads of the republic.

All this goes to show that an essential feature of his interpretation of history was the combination of a personalistic pragmatism (the idea of the importance of human beings acting with deliberate purpose) and a pragmatism of institutions and all other extra-personal causes in general. But this pragmatism remained under the spell of a thought-pattern that was both mechanistic and utilitarian. Historical causes were sharply marked off from one another, and each was considered strictly by itself. As a skilled mechanician he was well aware that reality does not always correspond to the calculated effects. 'Just as there are frictions in the mechanical world, which often alter or prevent the working of the theory, so too do politics have their frictions' (17, 8). As an active and purposeful politician, he was not content merely to look at the world of history for the sake of pure observation and knowledge. It is therefore quite understandable that he should have succeeded in painting such an extraordinarily rich and inclusive picture of historical causality, and yet prove unable, at any rate in the main sections of his work, to fuse it from the inside into a living and developing whole. For what did political men of the *ancien régime*, beginning with Machiavelli, care about the ultimate and intimate connections between the various aspects of life, inasmuch as they already knew all the relationships that could be of any importance for the statesman's actions? It was Montesquieu's tremendous achievement to have extended the knowledge of such causes to the limits of what was then possible. The prevailing spirit of his work was one of political utilitarianism on the broadest possible empirical basis. Again and again he stands out like the topmost peak in the movement that began with Machiavelli, and which aimed at founding a rational statesmanship upon an empirical basis. Once more, however, it must be emphasised that this was like a mountain massif which has lost half of its mass through a landslide, and now stands half exposed to view. For it was not possible for this pacifistically-minded young protagonist of the Enlightenment to enter with full interest and understanding into the meaning of foreign policy or the problems of power and war, without which even the domestic life of a State could not be fully understood, least of all by one who hated the great armies and the rivalry in armaments that were typical of his own time (13, 17).

It was of the essence of the political utilitarianism activating his researches that it could be both the source of his historical insight and a limitation to it. It drove him on to dig deeper and deeper for the foundations of given fact on which the lawgiver must build—the psychological, historical and natural factors with which he had to reckon. But it also misled him at the same time to give these factors a certain mechanical and conveniently manageable character, sufficient for practical purposes, but insufficient for a full historical understanding and sympathetic reconstruction of historical events. It is well known that one of his leading ideas, the influence of climate on the differing characters of various peoples and on their various arrangements and institutions, suffered from just such a mechanical treatment. To be sure, it was a great feat to take up again systematically, in the wider geographical setting of his own day, the question of climatic influence, which Bodin and others had asked themselves in connection with the attempted solutions of the ancient world but had only answered in a rather primitive fashion.[1] But now Montesquieu's main interest centred on the direct and peculiar relationships between climate, national character and lawmaking, which were often very crudely construed. Because he did not see that

---

[1] Dédieu, *Montesquieu et la tradition politique anglaise en France* (1909), pp. 212 ff., seems to me to have shown that Montesquieu took the physiological basis of his doctrine from the work by the English doctor Arbuthnot, published in 1733, on the effects of the air on health. But the broad application of this doctrine to political and social life was Montesquieu's own contribution.

these singular relationships were an integral part of a general stream of historical evolution, he ended by subjecting them to doctrinaire generalisations and strange exaggerations. For example, he ascribed the Englishman's mania for suicide to the climate (14, 12f.).[1] He thought he had discovered in the climatic differences between Europe and Asia 'the great reason for the weakness of Asia and the strength of Europe, for Europe's freedom and Asia's slavery' (17, 3). Here, Voltaire, who had been annoyed by the naturalism of Montesquieu's teaching on climate, which offered a deep threat to his own enlightened doctrine of the will, showed that his was historically the more promising outlook. It was not climate, he maintained in opposition to Montesquieu, but the achievements of the Greeks, that had given Europe a superiority over the rest of the globe. 'If Xerxes had been victorious at Salamis, we should perhaps still be barbarians.'

Montesquieu's doctrine of climate led to certain deterministic conclusions that were to set up a notable tension with his ideas of political utilitarianism and enlightenment. 'If it is true', he writes at the beginning of Book 14, the first to be devoted to the doctrine of climate, 'that the character of the mind and the passions of the heart are extremely different in the different climates of the world, then laws must correspond both to these differences of passion and to those of character (*doivent être relatives*).' Note the ambivalence of this language, which can be interpreted either as a purely historical statement of cause and effect, or as a maxim for the lawgiver. This ambiguity does in fact run through all that follows, and at times the deterministic sense predominates.[2] 'There are climates in which the psychic factor is so powerful that morality is practically powerless against it' (16, 8). Yet again, he could call upon the rational lawgiver not only to take into account the peculiarities of the climate, but even to join battle with them wherever they were harmful to natural morality.

> Whenever the physical effects of certain climates are at variance with the natural laws governing the sexes and man as a thinking creature, then it is the lawgiver's business to make civic laws that

[1] On this point he had been preceded by Dubos; Lombard, *L'Abbé Dubos*, pp. 250 and 327.

[2] At the end of 16, 2, there is a remark appearing at first sight to imply that climate is a *cause suprême* which conditions all *raisons humaines*; and this is also how Klemperer interprets 2, 157. But before this Dédieu, *Montesquieu* (1913), p. 309, had made it seem probable that in this passage, only added to the edition of 1753, the *cause suprême* should rather be interpreted to mean the divine governance of the world. The addition is rather unorganically inserted, and equivocal in its wording. Did Montesquieu perhaps do this on purpose, in order to pacify and at the same time mislead the ecclesiastical critics of his theory of climate?

overcome the effects of the climate, and restore the natural laws to power (16, 12).

Seldom can one look as clearly as in these divergent judgements into the gulf between these two trends in Montesquieu's thought, the naturalistic–empirical, and the rationalist falling back upon Natural Law. And this procedure was hardly calculated to arrive at an unambiguous concept of 'nature', or of its relationship to history. He himself was so deeply concerned at this divergence between nature conceived as reason and nature as a determinative power of compulsion, between the light and the dark side of the eighteenth-century world picture, that this problem, this struggle between the *causes morales* and the *causes physiques* may well rank as one of the basic themes of his thought.[1] He proved unable to resolve this conflict within himself and work out his theory of climate in a logical and organic fashion. It looked as if this cleavage was likely to force all subsequent historical thinking along new lines. It can be said of Montesquieu, as of Voltaire, that the inner dialectic connected with the unsolved problems of the Enlightenment was passed on as a stimulus to the attempts of historism to arrive at solutions.

But Montesquieu certainly demonstrated in the grand manner what could be achieved at the stage of the Enlightenment by a combination of naturalistic and rationalist thought as applied to history. Both lines of thought demonstrated the need for recognising causal connections, which was peculiarly characteristic of the Enlightenment. The pattern of thought possessing the greater interior strength within the French Enlightenment at that time was probably still the rationalistic. With Voltaire, it predominated to such an extent that the rich interplay of historical variety became a mere kaleidoscopic procession. It was Montesquieu's great achievement that, apart from the fragmented aspects of both thought-patterns which we have noted in him, he strove to bring the two together with wide open arms and bring about a mutual interpenetration. He sought to combine the empirical sense of the manifold variety in human affairs and their innumerable specific causes, with the sense of a rational unity presiding over this multiplicity and ultimately explaining it. He searched for the supreme laws which could be seen to be the spring from which all this variety flowed. The final result, as he says at the beginning of the *Esprit*, is that every difference becomes a uniformity, and every variation a constant. Lurking in the background, one can feel this boldest of all philosophical urges—the desire to do justice both to being and becoming; but it was still

---

[1] Cf. Klemperer, *Montesquieu* 1, 30; Dédieu, *Montesquieu et la tradition politique anglaise en France* (1909), pp. 197 ff.

under the spell of the mechanistic thought-forms belonging to that period.

Something of this sort was the basis of the great historical sketch contained in the *Considérations*, in which he attempted to grasp the whole mighty drama of the rise and fall of Rome as a unified process governed by universal laws. This theme was suited above all others to stir up historical thought and spur men on to enquire into causes. The history of this enquiry from the time of Biondo and Machiavelli to the year 1664, when Saint-Évremond wrote his *Réflexions sur les divers génies du peuple Romain dans les divers temps de la République*, and to Bossuet's *Discours* in 1681, shows all the changes that took place in the thought concerned with historical causes from the time of the Renaissance onwards.[1] Montesquieu no doubt learnt a great deal from this book. Although only equipped with a rather summary psychology, Saint-Évremond was able to follow the transformation in the 'spirit' of the Roman people, from a rough but powerful devotion to the State, to the rise of particular individual and selfish interests. In so doing, he was able to subsume all the detail under one general question. *Je cherche moins à décrire les combats qu'à faire connaître les génies* (*Œuvres*, 1714, 1, 287). In the matter of seeking causes, Bossuet had gone still further, and had likewise laid it down as a matter of principle that enquiry into *les causes universelles* was more important than the usual personal and pragmatic enquiry into the characters of the actors in history (III, 7, conclusion). Both of these writers had thus methodically prepared the way for looking at the destinies of the Roman people as a whole. What was new in them was their intention not only to seek for what might be politically useful (as had been predominantly the case with Machiavelli) but also to acquire historical knowledge. Further, there was something new in the rather freer and more independent relationship to classical tradition (though it was not yet a genuinely critical attitude) leading them to group their material according to the dictates of their own reflective subjectivity. Saint-Évremond had already begun to have critical doubts about the authority of Livy, but Montesquieu did not follow him in this, for he was far too credulous about his sources. But he outbid both his forerunners[2] in the passionate intensity with which he sought to discover general causes.

[1] Cf. Rehm, *Der Untergang Roms im abendländischen Denken* (1930), who even goes back into antiquity in his examination of the causes.

[2] In his article, 'Montesquieu, Bossuet et Polybe' in *Mélanges Ch. Andler* (1924), Duraffours deals with Montesquieu's detailed polemic against Bossuet's clericalism, and also with the significance of Polybius' interpretation of history for both of them.

The world is not ruled by chance; you can see this with the Romans, who had a long run of good fortune when they followed a particular plan, and an unbroken series of disasters when they changed over to a different plan.

Machiavelli too, in his *Discorsi* (II, 1), had seen the true reasons for Roman greatness to lie not in their *fortuna*, but in their *virtù*, though he subsequently went on (II, 29) to ascribe a demonic power to *fortuna*; and in the *Principe* (c. 25), he divides the ascendancy over human actions between *fortuna* and *virtù*. He could not rise as yet to a general and coherent theory of causes. But the extent to which the demand for causes, and the self-confidence of the human mind in its ability to explain life, had increased, is well demonstrated by what Montesquieu goes on to say, in words that had already caught the attention of the youthful Frederick the Great.

There are general causes, either physical or moral, at work in every monarchy, either to raise, or to maintain, or to cast down. All accidental happenings are subordinate to these laws, and if the hazards of one battle (that is, a particular cause) have ruined a State, there must always be a general cause responsible for the downfall of this State in one single battle. *En un mot, l'allure principale entraîne avec elle tous les accidents particuliers* (c. 18).

This was the maturest statement of his theory of historical causation, which we have already met with in his youthful essay 'De la Politique'.

When applied to Roman history, this principle produced a picture that can be represented as follows: The Roman Republic became a world power by constantly applying a unified and constantly practised system of splendid maxims, all calculated to strengthen the State. This was how the 'spirit of the Romans' showed itself in action. We shall have to return to his doctrine of the human mind and spirit; at this point, it is enough to note that in order to give the strongest and simplest possible expression to his theory of general causes and the *allure principale*, he represents this 'spirit of the Romans' as an amazing composite of properties and characteristics that was, so to speak, there almost from the beginning. This was really a retrograde step when compared with Saint-Évremond's outlook, which had specifically based itself on the various stages passed through at different periods by the Romans. Montesquieu felt an urge, however, to compress this complex of causes, and therefore takes a comprehensive view of the cause that brought about the downfall of this Roman spirit—insofar as it was the spirit of a free State. 'The vast size of the Empire destroyed the republic'; 'it was nothing but the size of the republic that led to disaster' (c. 9).[1] Under the pressing demands of the tasks imposed on Rome when it became a world empire, the old maxims had to be abandoned. Characteristically enough, Montesquieu made this into a regular law of political life, valid not only for Rome but universally. 'Experience has always shown that good laws, which have made a small republic great, become a burden as soon as it increases its size, because these laws were naturally adapted to making a great nation, but not so suitable for governing it under the new conditions' (c. 9). It was thus necessary to change to a new form of government to rule the empire. But the maxims followed under this new form of government were opposed to the original maxims, and led in the end to the downfall of the imperial greatness (c. 18). Thus Rome perished by reason of her own greatness.

Once only did he insert into this iron chain of causation a link of somewhat softer metal. He says at the end of chapter 9 that 'Rome was made to expand . . . she lost her freedom because she brought her work to an end too soon'. Would it then have been possible, if the speed of conquest had been slowed down, to have attained full greatness without losing freedom? But Montesquieu did not follow up this wishful thinking that gently pressed upon his mind, and so the main impression left by him is one of inescapable destiny.

In spite of an inclination to make mechanical simplifications, this powerful picture of the broad course of history possesses permanently valid features. Above all, it was of the greatest value historically that personalistic pragmatism (though Montesquieu sometimes gave way to it in details) should yet be in the main transcended by a balance and interplay of general causes, in comparison with which the random peculiarities or mistakes of individuals appear of small importance. So he writes about the fall of the republic that it is unreasonable to ascribe it to any particular person's ambition, but it must be laid to the account of man in general, who, in proportion as he enjoys more power, becomes greedy for more power still (c. 11). But Montesquieu now proceeded to add to the distinctive force of the human drive for power the destructive effect of the situations that had created this urge, and so ruined Rome through the very success of her achievements. 'The mistakes made by statesmen are not always the result of voluntary choice: they are often the necessary consequences of the situation they are in, where inconveniences of one sort and another produce further inconveniences' (c. 18).

As his search after more and more all-embracing causes took him into higher and higher regions of thought, Montesquieu rose to the point of descrying a great historical destiny which was working itself

[1] We shall omit the accompanying causes that Montesquieu also adduces.

out. This must not indeed be interpreted, as some have done, in a too modern fashion.[1] For Montesquieu was still too much under the spell of mechanical causality, which had ruled over learned thought since the time of Descartes, as well as of the old cyclical theory of history. This was first formulated by Polybius, and renewed by Machiavelli. It thought of the destinies of States and peoples as passing through an unending succession of recurring rise, decline and fall.[2] Montesquieu's thought was also still too much bound up with a political resentment against great empires and policies of conquest in general.[3] But it was a sign of greatness in him that he did not allow himself to be swept away by this attitude into a general and moralistic resentment against this Roman spirit as a whole, which seemed to be marked out for conquest. He was prevented from taking such a line by an inherited and also well-founded admiration for the original virtues of Rome. Moreover, the manner in which these virtues had their necessary place in a shrewd, balanced and effective system of powers, attracted the rationalist bent of his mind; and this side of Roman life had a great attraction for the thinkers of the Enlightenment. Montesquieu could therefore survey the whole course of Roman history both with admiration and with repugnance. In his intimate writings (*Pensées et fragments*, 2, 234; cf. also 1, 133), he expresses the opinion that the establishment of the Roman Empire was the longest conspiracy ever perpetrated against the universe. And deeper feeling was added to this conception by the sinister thought, implied rather than expressed, that the final fate of Rome might well one day be the final fate of France. Perhaps this was even his ultimate hidden motive for the powerful drive behind his search for causes, for he hated the despotism of the contemporary French monarchy.[4] Taken as a whole, Montesquieu's thought probably represents the highest degree of historical awareness that was possible at this stage of the Enlightenment.

Furthermore, his thought reminds us again of Machiavelli and his

---

[1] Klemperer.

[2] The cyclic theory is clearly formulated in *Pensées et fragments*, 1, 114 (cf. also 1, 278). This cyclic movement, somewhat reminiscent of Vico's, Montesquieu thought he could discern in 'almost all the nations of the world'. It included the stages of barbarism, conquest, State policing, the extension of power based upon this, its subsequent refinement and internal weakening—which was followed by conquest and a return to barbarism. In another passage (*Pensées et fragments*, 2, 201), he does indeed hold forth against another cyclic theory, the one that begins with the stage of happy innocence. But to judge by the places in which these passages occur, it would seem that the first is distinctly later in point of time, and probably took shape after the completion of the *Considérations*.

[3] This motive is rightly brought out by Barckhausen, in his *Montesquieu* (1907), pp. 200 ff., though rather too one-sidedly.

[4] Cf. Rehm, *Der Untergang Roms im abendländischen Denken*, pp. 99 f.

doctrine of political expediency. Practical maxims and laws, as he had shown, can guide the human urge towards power into successful channels. If situations change, so must the maxims, if misfortune is to be avoided. Hence to a very large extent the actions of statesmen must be governed by the *necessità* of situations. Machiavelli had not indeed generalised this thought to suggest that Rome's expansive power was in itself the cause of her downfall.[1] Montesquieu was the first to add this weighty consideration[2] by fusing the Enlightenment's aversion to conquest, in a most ingenious and fertile fashion, with the demand for adequate causes, which was equally characteristic of the Enlightenment. In so doing, Montesquieu was also the first to give a higher significance to Machiavelli's thought considered as a philosophy of history.

The above comparison of Machiavelli's and Montesquieu's thought brings us back to the problem of relativism, which we have already considered in another context. We saw that laws suitable for one situation could be harmful in another. This led to the practical conclusion that in politics the statesman should aim not at the absolute and permanent best, but at what is relatively best, taking the time and all the circumstances into account. Montesquieu quotes Plutarch (19, 21) to the effect that Solon was once asked whether the laws he had given the Athenians were the best possible; to which he replied that they were the best the Athenians were prepared to tolerate. A fine answer, says Montesquieu, which should be taken to heart by all lawgivers. And so even for laws, it was not possible to expect more than a *bonté relative*.

This political relativism was one of the pointers to the coming historism. Yet just because it was political, and satisfied with practical solutions, it was not sufficient to break the ascendancy of absolute standards based upon Natural Law in the life of the State and in the outlook upon history. But in all concrete individual cases, it could give answers that were gradually bound to shake belief in those standards. Montesquieu still occupied a position midway between the absolute and the relativistic trends of thought, and sometimes one and sometimes the other would prevail. There are some surprisingly clear-cut relativistic admissions in his thought. As early as the *Lettres persanes* (No. 75), we find him saying that what is true at one time may be erroneous at another.

> Expressions such as good, beautiful, noble, perfect, are attributes of objects, and are always relative to the beings who are

[1] Rightly stressed by Klemperer, 1, 175.
[2] For a related judgement from the Middle Ages (Engelbert von Admont), cf. Rehm, pp. 40 and 103.

contemplating them. It is necessary to get this principle firmly into our heads, for it is the cure for most prejudices (*Pensées et fragments*, 2, 476, and *Oeuvres*, p. p. Laboulaye, 7, 160).[1]

But even in applying this principle to the aesthetic field, he was once again (as we have already seen in his attitude to Natural Law) inconsistent. He worshipped the classicist's ideal of simplicity in art, and saw artistic 'perfection' as an achievement of the Greeks and, at a considerable distance behind, the masters of the Renaissance who learnt from them. Now and again, to be sure, he could also admire a piece of Gothic architecture, for he himself inhabited a Gothic castle, as he once apologetically observed. Perhaps there was already some admixture here of traditionalist pride and of what we shall subsequently call 'Pre-Romanticism'. But the degree of general approval he was prepared to mete out to Gothic art in a relativistic way was confined to the opinion that it represented 'the taste of the ignorant', and was therefore typical of the primitive, as well as the decadent, in art.[2] Here, too, his belief in the cyclic nature of history cropped up once again.

On the other hand, there was a freer development of his relativism in the religious sphere. From the beginning, the loosening up of dogmatic thought and the rise of free thinking had been closely connected as early as Machiavelli's time with political relativism, and he was certainly the first person to give a powerful impetus to this movement. Since the sixteenth century, the notion of political expediency had been undermining belief in the absolute values of any particular confession or creed. For it led to a tendency towards assessing all things according to their practical value for politics, their 'relative benefit' to the State. This could in certain circumstances even lead one back to the Church, if one had started by being a freethinker—not indeed to a personal faith, but rather to an enlightened recognition of its usefulness to the State and to society. And in the more recent history of Europe, it must surely be acknowledged that to a considerable degree the maintenance of positive Christianity has been largely due to the support of political expediency—spiritually very questionable, but by its nature very powerful. Montesquieu was one of those who began as a freethinker and never ceased to be one, yet as a political man learnt to affirm the value of Christianity and of the Church. He went so far as to pronounce Richelieu's policy of

[1] There is a further discussion in Klemperer (1, 91 ff.) on this relativism of Montesquieu's and Malebranche's influence upon him.

[2] Cf. *Voyages*, 1, 43, 97, 156, 158, 169, 229 ff.; 2, 6, 185 (Cologne Cathedral), 303 ff., 351, 367 ff., etc. *Correspondance*, 1, 403 (La Brède Castle). It would appear from this that he even considered Egyptian art to be 'Gothic' and that of Rome in her decadent period.

alliance with the Protestants old-fashioned, for France, in his opinion, would never have more deadly enemies than they were (*Voyages*, 2, 206). This judgement was based upon a political relativism, which saw the change that had come about in the world situation since Richelieu's time through the growth of opposing interests between England and France. But there is evidence that along with this political relativism, there was also a specifically religious relativism at work, already suggestive of Lessing's tolerant attitude. In the original draft of his *Esprit des lois* (25, 9), there was a passage which he struck out before the manuscript went to the press in deference to the censorship. 'We can look upon God as a king who has many nations in his realm, and they all bring their tribute to his feet, and all speak to him in their own language.'[1] But there are many passages in the printed version too that echo the same thought. For example, he gives it as his opinion (24, 24) that Montezuma's dictum that the Spaniards' religion was good for their own country, but so was the Mexicans' religion for theirs, is by no means absurd. For legislators cannot avoid the necessity of taking into account what nature has created before they came on the scene. In another passage (19, 18), he gives it as his opinion that Christianity is not at all likely ever to become established in China, for manners, customs, laws and religion have been fused into such a unity in that country that any new conqueror would be brought under their spell.

Here too, Montesquieu discovered one of those large general causes for which he was searching. In the process, he was bound to assume, adopt and build upon thoughts that had long been in the air, a certain 'spirit' behind the events of history, just as we saw in the case of Voltaire. It was not at all in his line to suspect the presence of mysterious and mystical first causes. His rationalism was always nourished upon reality, and was clear-eyed enough to descry an inner connection between phenomena everywhere, but was also intent upon interpreting this in as clear and evident terms as possible, in strict accord with the natural facts. The definition of what he understood in a general way by his title *L'Esprit des lois* was in this respect quite characteristic.[2] 'This spirit consists of the different relationships (*rapports*) that can exist between the laws and a whole variety of things' (1, 3). In other words, it meant to him the totality of causal relationships between legislation and life. His insistent de-

[1] Barckhausen, *Montesquieu, etc.* (1907), p. 244; *Pensées et fragments*, 1, 186 and 2, 498. Cf. also his letter to Warburton in 1754 on Bolingbroke's anti-religious writings (*Correspondance*, 2, 528): '*Celui qui attaque la religion révélée, n'attaque que la religion révélée; mais celui qui attaque la religion naturelle, attaque toutes les religions du monde*'.

[2] On the supposed influence of Doria (*Vita civile*, 1710), who already used the catchword 'the spirit of the laws', cf. Dédieu, *Montesquieu* (1913), p. 67.

mand for causes did not hark back from the tangible to the intangible, to a something that lay hidden in the background, but went forwards from the tangible to what would seem to be constantly produced by the continually changing interplay of tangible factors, to what he called the *esprit général* of a nation. In the chapter of his book devoted to this theme, and furnished with all the pointed epigram of which he was so fond, he says (19, 4): 'A multitude of things exercise an influence upon men—climate, religion, laws, the maxims of government, the example of the past, customs and manners. From these there arises an *esprit général*, the resultant of them all'.[1] And he goes on to show that the general spirits of particular nations differ from one another by reason of the different blending of these factors in each of them. Savages, for example, are almost totally under the control of nature and climate; in Sparta of old, custom set the tone; in Rome, a blend of custom and political maxims. We may therefore conclude that each national spirit has its dominant characteristics; yet these only constitute a typical factor, which may in single cases be particularly pronounced, but not an entirely individual and unique attribute. The various ingredients in the different national spirits are conceived just as typically as the moral categories of the virtues, such as honour and fear, on which Montesquieu constructed his psychology of the three political forms of republicanism, monarchy and despotism. One certainly feels, as one reads his *Considérations* and is caught up in his exposition of the Roman 'spirit', that he had created a quite individual and vital conception; but the theoretical methods he employed in his interpretation did not as yet enable him to get at the heart of this individuality.

Yet they would have sufficed at least to set his feet upon the road travelled by the later doctrines of national ethos, in the main with fruitful results, though not unmixed with error. That is to say, it would have been possible for him to treat the *esprit général* not only as the product of such and such factors, but also as an effective cause of specific phenomena in the life of a nation. He made some attempts in this direction, notably in the *Considérations*.[2] It should be noted,

---

[1] In the *Pensées et fragments*, 2, 170, there is a definition of the *Volksgeist* that is still narrower: '*J'appelle génie d'une nation les mœurs et le caractère d'esprit de différents peuples dirigés par l'influence d'une même cour et d'une même capitale*'. Montesquieu was a very spirited observer of the influence that a great capital like Paris could have on the *esprit général* of the French nation: '*C'est Paris qui fait les François: sans Paris, la Normandie, la Picardie, l'Artois seroient allemandes comme l'Allemagne; sans Paris, la Bourgogne et la Franche-Comté seroient suisses comme les Suisses etc.*'. *Pensées et fragments*, 1, 154.

[2] Cf. c. 14, closing remarks, where the mourning of the Roman people for Germanicus's death serves to characterise the *génie du peuple Romain*; and c. 15, where the fearful tyranny of the emperor is deduced from the *esprit général* of the Romans. Thus Hildegard Trescher's criticism (in 'Montesquieus Einfluss auf die

moreover, that he did view customs and manners as a whole as derived from the national life; and we may recall his ingenious sketch of the English national character in the *Esprit des lois* (19, 27), with its attention to both great and small, even down to the details of daily life, as well as its full recognition of the higher intellectual and spiritual creations. But it is thoroughly typical of his pragmatic outlook that in this sketch there was no attempt to demonstrate the powerful effect of the national spirit upon the national life, but only to trace the influence of the laws on the formation of the national character.

Fundamentally, moreover, he was looking at the problem of the national spirit not with historical but with political eyes. The basic political utilitarianism of his outlook won the day. He was of the opinion that the legislator must get to know the national spirit, pay heed to it and handle it tenderly. Even in the *Considérations* we find him writing: 'There is in every nation an *esprit général*, on which the power [of the government] itself is based; and if it injures this spirit, it is doing injury to itself' (c. 22). Again, he wrote in the *Esprit des lois* (19, 12): 'Laws are laid down: customs are inspired. The latter are more dependent upon the *esprit général*, the former upon particular institutions. It is therefore just as dangerous, nay, more dangerous, to upset the *esprit général* than to alter a particular institution'. A people would only be made unhappy if you robbed them by force of their cherished customs (19, 14). True, this deep political insight into the tender and sensitive nature of the irrational forces in the national spirit was in sharp contrast to the incipient rationalistic zeal of the enlightened despot. Montesquieu criticised the violent behaviour of Peter the Great in Russia (19, 17), and thus by implication he criticised in advance Joseph II and the legislators of the French Revolution. But these insights stemmed from the traditions of political doctrine that had already seen the importance of respecting the irrational in politics. Not that he by any means renounced the idea that the legislator should remould the national spirit, if he found it to have undesirable political features; he only put on one side as unpractical the attempt to do so by law. He was of the opinion that when necessary, the peoples themselves must be made to change their customs (19, 14). 'The lawgiver', so he concluded, 'must follow the spirit of the nation, if it is not contrary to the principles of government' (19, 5). In case of conflict, then, the primacy would be given to these principles. But what did these principles consist of? Not indeed

philosophischen Grundlagen der Staatslehre Hegels', thesis, Leipzig, 1917, p. 83), that 'Montesquieu *never* derives single phenomena in history from the whole cultural background', is somewhat too sweeping. For the interpretations so far put upon Montesquieu's doctrine of the *Volksgeist*, cf. Rosenzweig, *Hegel und der Staat* (1920), 1, pp. 224 ff.

principles belonging to individual States in the sense of political doctrine in later history, but the schematically formulated principles of the three forms of government, which it was one of the chief aims of his book to place upon a reasoned footing. Yet at this very point we are conscious of the stirring of a certain new spirit, which we have once before had occasion to note, when he follows the above statement of principle by these words: 'For we all do best what we do freely in pursuance of our own *génie naturel*'. Perhaps this was the most significant remark for the future in the whole of his book; and it sprang from direct experience, from the national spirit of the French nation as it now began to be conscious of itself. What profit is it to the State, he asks, if it brings a spirit of pedantry into a nation whose nature is naturally happy? Leave people to carry out the unimportant things reliably and the important things happily.

If Voltaire more often spoke of the spirit of the age than of the spirit of peoples, it was the reverse with Montesquieu. This difference was connected with the difference between their fundamental purposes. Voltaire looked at history in a more temporal perspective, because he was concerned to follow out the fortunes of his ideal of reason, its struggles, defeats and victories, down the ages and up to his own day. Only in this very restricted respect may it be said that Voltaire's thought and outlook was more historical than that of Montesquieu, who saw things more in spatial dimensions, spread out, as it were, over a large surface. This was because his concern was to employ them as a source of politically useful doctrine, and in general extract from history a political system. On the few occasions (cf. for example 31, 13) when he expressly mentions the 'spirit of the age', he shows himself entirely capable of doing justice to the impact of a particular time; and the purely historical parts of his work, the *Considérations* and the concluding chapters in the *Esprit des lois* devoted to the feudal system, show this even more decisively. One of the finest pieces of historical observation in the whole of his work was his demonstration that a particular institution may well disappear in the course of time, but the spirit embodied in it may still continue to work. He showed, for example, that the common laws of the migration period disappeared, because the feudal system made them inapplicable, but the 'spirit' of these laws, namely the right to settle most things by fines, still remained in force. 'The spirit of the law rather than the law itself was obeyed' (28, 9).

If, as he once remarked, each century has its *génie particulier* (*Pensées et fragments*, 2, 141), this gives rise to the great methodological principle that one must banish from the mind the customary conceptions of one's own period before one can rightly understand the past. There has been no more frequent criticism of the historical writing of the Enlightenment than that it proved unable to achieve this detachment. This was no doubt a real failure; yet it is important to note that by its discovery of the manifold variety of the historical world, the widely differing 'spirits' of different ages, peoples and things, the writers of the Enlightenment did at least establish the basic principle that it is not permissible to judge unfamiliar material by the standards of one's own time and environment. We have already noted in Voltaire (see above, p. 73) a certain stirring of this spirit. Montesquieu gave it more definite expression: 'To carry over into distant centuries all the notions of the century in which you happen to live, is the most fruitful of all the sources of error' (30, 14).

Taken all round, Montesquieu was more successful than Voltaire in refining the doctrine of the 'spirit' of nations, ages and institutions, and in spite of the limitations of his schematic psychology he succeeded in directing attention more strongly to the individual element. He was not in the first place concerned, as Voltaire was, to work out the contrast between unenlightened and enlightened periods, between phenomena of unreason and reason, and so to enjoy thoroughly the good fortune of his own time. His approach was dominated by a stricter intention to search for causes behind the strange and manifold appearances of the historical world; and he respected the complexity of causes which had produced, and was bound to produce, such wide variety and difference in history, though he was not as yet able to rise to a full appreciation of the wholly and genuinely individual. He was not prepared, like Voltaire, simply to accept the multifarious and often irrational character of the historical scene with a shrug of the shoulders, as the result of the incompleteness of man's natural equipment. But it is possible to sense in his work an implied feeling of awe for the historical cosmos, for its drama, governed by great and simple fundamental laws, which produce all this variety and are not contradicted even by the strangest and most heterogeneous elements among this diversity. Deep down, as we have already ventured to suggest, this awe was a thing of the spirit, whose source was a nascent feeling of new life astir in the world. But as far as he was concerned, he could only justify this by his conscious feeling of responsibility as a rational politician, who makes allowance from his lofty rational standpoint for all that is irrational, and turns it to good use.

This survey should have sufficiently indicated Montesquieu's attitude towards the two basic ideas of the future historism—the idea of individuality, and the idea of development. The most natural way for understanding the individual in history is that of aesthetic sensibility, which finds in the very manifold variety of human phenomena, even if conflicting with traditional notions of beauty, something beautiful and full of charm. And the natural thirst for knowledge in every antiquarian with a turn for research, and for every traveller with a real zest for travel, has always contained this latent propensity for genuine historical sensitivity. Left to itself, it could always produce simple pictures of human life in their historical setting which were a faithful reflection of the individual. Such pictures had been produced from the days of Herodotus onwards. This development could not, however, come to full flower as long as the individual variety of life so clearly demonstrated by experience was still dominated by thought based upon Natural Law, which insisted upon the superior authority of the norms based upon the unity, and universal, timeless validity, of reason. In this setting, the individual element in history and life could only be recognised as a fact, here and there perhaps unconsciously or half-consciously greeted with affection, but never accorded a whole-hearted approach and placed in the centre of philosophical thought. No one denied that individuality was in fact there, but its essential right to exist was doubtful, or at best a matter of indifference. Even the doctrines of statesmanship which, since Machiavelli had taught respect for the individual factor, never managed to go beyond a utilitarian relation to it, as we have already seen.

Nor did Montesquieu succeed in general in transcending these limitations. The political thinker and lawgiver in him studied the individual aspects of nations, periods, and institutions for the practical purposes of legislation of a rational kind, taking into account the existence of these factual differences. Again, the rationalist in him was inclined to effect some mental simplification of the gay variety of life as he encountered it, and classify it under categories such as religion, honour, trade, agriculture and so on. This has already been noted by Moriz Ritter: 'The real active forces would seem to be portrayed not as vital living persons, but rather as abstractions'.[1] Montesquieu had an overmastering passion for simplification in the interests of causal discoveries. He remarks in the *Considérations* (c. 1) that men have at all times had the same passions. The circumstances producing the great changes are indeed different, but the causes are always the same.

With such an interpretation of historical man (none other than the one which had always held the field) the individual mind of the historical person, who is also striving to bring unity to its actions and thoughts, which are often so greatly at variance, was bound to remain a sealed book to Montesquieu. This can be seen in his relationship to Machiavelli. Montesquieu treated him as he treated the thought-pattern of historical persons in general, under the dominant

[1] *Entwicklung der Geschichtswissenschaft*, p. 227.

influence of Natural Law. He treated them not as structures that had grown to their present form, but pulled them apart, praised one piece, criticised another, and pigeon-holed them to suit the categories of Natural Law and a universal moral outlook. True, Montesquieu could produce brilliant and lively portraits of historical characters. His *Réflexions sur le caractère de quelques princes* are among the most attractive pieces of his unpublished works, which have only come to light in recent times (*Mélanges inédits*, 171 ff.). But these are more or less timeless psychological works of art, sketched from the political viewpoint to assess how far such and such a mixed character was fit to discharge his allotted task, and what successes or failures were bound to occur. The individual persons only appear on the scene as more or less clock-work figures of a particular kind of construction, though this in no way diminishes his acute understanding of the importance to be attributed to the 'mixtures' of good and bad qualities which would always occur. These pictures were more the product of his critical intellect than his powers of sympathetic intuition.

Here, we have one of those cases in the history of thought when the intellectual climate of a period holds back or diverts the development of inborn capacities and urges which in another period might well have come to splendid fruition. Under the cover of Montesquieu's ruling rationalism there was developing the germ of a new feeling for life drawing its nourishment from within. This was often more clearly expressed in his intimate writings than in his published works. Opinions are formed not by the mind, but by the heart: this is one of the sayings found in his works with the richest significance for the future.[1] And so behind the consciously utilitarian and the abstract trend of his thought derived from the tradition and spirit of the age, there was alive in him at a deeper level a primal element of historical sensitivity, a joy in manifold variety and individuality. One can sense this even in his insatiable curiosity for the mastery of constant new varieties in the historical field. But he himself gave clear expression to this inclination. When in Genoa on his journey to Italy in 1729 he heard a foreign lady abuse the bad manners of the Genoese ladies, he remarked: 'I should be very annoyed if all human beings were like myself or like one another. One travels in order to observe a variety of ways and manners, and not in order to criticise them' (*Voyages*, I, 138, cf. also 2, 78). He could also be saddened by the excessive

---

[1] *Mélanges inédits*, 145. Cf. also *Pensées et fragments*, 1, 29: '*Ce n'est pas notre esprit, c'est notre âme qui nous conduit*'. On another occasion, in a more rationalistic and reflective mood, he restricted this somewhat to: '*Comme le cœur conduit l'esprit, l'esprit à son tour, conduit le cœur. Il faut donc perfectionner l'esprit*' (*Pensées et fragments*, 1, 158).

regularity of modern house-construction, and even in the lay-out of gardens, which he often saw as mere copies of Le Nôtre. Our houses, he remarks with a sigh, are like our characters (*Pensées et fragments*, 2, 78). After his stay in England, where he acquired a new taste for English gardens, he had his park at La Brède remodelled along English lines (Viau, *Hist. de Montesquieu*, 131 f.). A writer of strong individuality comes most easily to appreciate individual worth and creative power through a sensitiveness to his own work and style; and this is certainly true of Montesquieu. He was conscious of the harshness of his style, which demanded a good deal of forbearance from readers used to the smooth contemporary taste, and refused to be judged by this style. A man of intellect, he remarked, is a *creator* of expressions, and clothes his thought in his *own* dress. A man who writes well does not write as others have written, but as *he himself* writes, and often a bad manner of speech may make him a good speaker (*Pensées et fragments*, 2, 7).

Yet it was denied to him to feel the really creative side of the individual forms and structures in history. At this point he remained under the spell of mechanistic causality imposed by Descartes and the later seventeenth century. But once again there took place in him a process of historical dialectic whereby a thought that has reached maximum intensity bursts through its casing and scatters forth seed for something entirely new. For Montesquieu, by the unprecedented energy he displayed in his search for causal explanation among the multiplicity of possible physical and mental factors, was able to give the individual creation a higher value than ever before. In so doing, he was often able, through his propensity for rating dominant general causes above the subsidiary particular causes, to give the contemporary picture a certain specific sharpness of contour. None of the criticism levelled from Voltaire onwards at the artificial sharpness of these contours and at Montesquieu's over-hastiness in causal explanation can diminish his impressive achievements in the history of thought. He was responsible for forcing historical research to embark upon new explorations, and to come much more thoroughly to terms with individual phenomena in history than ever before. He compelled historians to approach their subject-matter with the surmise that its background contained a complex of ramifying causes,[1] so that the apparently anomalous and perverse began to make sense as the underlying causes were revealed.

In historical thought, the idea of individuality and the idea of development are very closely associated. To put it more accurately,

[1] '*Il y a peu de faits dans le monde qui ne dépendent de tant de circonstances qu'il faudrait l'éternité du monde pour qu'ils arrivassent une seconde fois*', he says in the *Pensées et fragments*, 2, 309.

out of all the possible ideas of development, the historical notion of individuality demands as its complement a quite distinct concept of development. It must be one that adds to the notion of a purely biological development, including the plant world (in fact, an evolution from innate tendencies), the marks of mental spontaneity in what develops, and its plastic capacity to change its form under the influence of specific factors. In this double requirement, necessity and freedom are everywhere indissolubly fused together. It remains for us to enquire how far Montesquieu succeeded in approaching this concept of development which historism created.

Montesquieu's prime task was to clarify for himself the essence and the changing forms of political institutions, and the social institutions with which they were allied. The way in which he understood their essential features conditioned the way in which he interpreted their changes, or, in modern language, their development. The essence of an institution, however, resides in its individuality. This will certainly always display certain typical, comparable and more generally recurrent features, but also what is entirely individual and incomparable. As we have seen, Montesquieu, in spite of his acute sense of the endless and manifold variety of phenomena, never succeeded in understanding the altogether individual. His gaze was so fixed upon the typical and the comparable that he could not but consider the forms of the State as the highest institutions, subordinating to them everything else he studied, which appeared to him as artificial mechanisms of a self-balancing kind. He once said this in so many words of monarchy, which he compared to 'the finest machine', because it could manage with a minimum of *vertu*, just as a good mechanism could manage with a minimum of wheels and motive-power (3, 5). In the machinery of the different forms of State he saw that there had been at work from the beginning one variable factor. He made a distinction between the nature and the principles of a particular form, understanding by nature 'their specific structure', that is to say, their visible outward form, and by principle, the particular human drives by which they move and work—*vertu* in a republic (a further development of Machiavelli's *virtù*), honour in a monarchy, fear in a despotism (3, 1 ff.). These drives are subject to alteration, either increasing or diminishing, and so changing the structure of the State for the time being; but one cannot possibly call this process, so carefully observed by Montesquieu, 'development'. For he never emerged from his mechanical attitude to it all, though he undoubtedly took an important step towards the idea of development by substituting (as we have already noted in another context) for the personalistic pragmatism characteristic of the Enlightenment a considerable degree of objective pragmatism. That is to say, he interpreted political and social conditions and changes less as the resultant of rational or irrational action on the part of individuals, and more as the outcome of material necessity, the effect of objective factors such as climate, soil, difference of locality and so on. Laws and other institutions could thus have effects that were not foreseen, they could fail to fit into the existing system, and so call urgently for alteration. So there could come in at this point what Montesquieu once called in a great phrase *la force des choses* (28, 43). He repeatedly notes with acute perception that often this only happens gradually, in imperceptible transitions. 'It often takes several centuries to prepare these changes; then at a certain point events mature and the revolution takes place' (28, 39). Already we begin to catch a breath of the true evolutionary outlook.[1] But if we are right in our interpretation of his thought, he was less consciously inclined to watch thoughtfully the gradual development, growth and alteration than to explain these changes as the result of alterations in definite complex causes, chief of which were his favourite general factors, such as forms of government with their specific principles, climate, soil and so on. He was concerned with tangible, circumscribed causality. The course of events thus described by him would be better interpreted as alteration or adjustment to fit changed circumstances, rather than as genuine development. Let us look at one or two examples.

A monarchy, Montesquieu says (8, 17), must be of moderate size. If it were small, it would transform itself into a republic. If it were very extensive, the grandees of the country would no longer be under the eye of the prince, yet would remain protected against the prompt execution of the laws and customs (which, he believes, derive from the monarchy itself), and would cease to obey. He then gives as examples the kingdoms of Charlemagne, Alexander and Attila. To prevent such a kingdom from dissolution, it may be advisable to proceed at once to the establishment of an unlimited despotism. True, this describes a typical historical process, yet not in the fluid form of a development, but rather in the solid form of a transformation that can be assessed in mechanical terms.

Further on (11, 13), he says that a State can alter in two ways, either by improvement in the constitution, or by deterioration through corruption. If it conserves its principles (he means those that are specific to the particular form of constitution), and the constitution changes, then the State improves, but if it loses its principles in

---

[1] Cf. also *Pensées et fragments*, 1, 307, where he pokes fun at the popular pragmatism which considers the kings of primitive ages to have been the inventors of the useful arts, whereas the most widespread arts have only thriven through 'imperceptible advances' by the efforts of nameless discoverers. Here again, it is possible that Montesquieu was influenced by Vico.

the course of constitutional change, then the constitution itself becomes corrupted. Here again, what we have is a straight-line process,
rather than a natural river-like, winding development.

Just as Machiavelli had once done, Montesquieu emphasised the
typical and the constantly recurrent in these processes, because, like
his great predecessor, he was concerned to extract from history
maxims for political action. This politically utilitarian motive was
enough to hold him in bondage to the old interpretation, according
to which, looked at from a higher point of view, every great political
structure is always in a cyclic movement either of ascent or descent.
We saw this in our review of the *Considérations*. Montesquieu did
indeed avoid the danger of dealing too schematically with this cycle,
by reason of the endless wealth of interesting variety he discovered.
And the cyclical theory itself enabled him to escape another pitfall
that might well have lain on the road to a historical thought-pattern
that was fully evolutionary, namely the temptation to construct a
scheme of steady human progress rising step by step to ever higher
reaches. Although, like Voltaire, he was in practice a forerunner in
championing progress, he knew as yet nothing of the idea of progress
belonging to the later Enlightenment.[1] He was immune to this
through mixed motives of a different kind from those of Voltaire.
But both men breathed the atmosphere of the early eighteenth century, in which, despite all the progress men thought they had made,
a more general faith in progress as part of a philosophical view of
history was not yet ready to come into full flower. Society was still
thoroughly aristocratic in composition and outlook. Aristocracies,
however, think in terms of maintaining or reconstituting the status
quo, and not in terms of continuous progress, which might pass
beyond them and leave them behind. They are more inclined to
think of the danger of their own decline, and this could easily
strengthen the notion of a cyclical movement in all human affairs.
And lastly, the sober sense of reality that we found in both Voltaire
and Montesquieu as a common heritage of the seventeenth century
could easily blend with the aristocratic outlook, and prove an ob-
stacle in the way towards a belief in progress.

For all that, we have not yet said the last word about Montesquieu's attitude to the idea of development. Psychological motives of
a special kind might well lead him to abandon his restricted circle of
intellectual enquiry into causes in the face of a specific historical
course of events, and be attentive to genuine historical growth and

[1] Even Delvaille, in his *Histoire de l'idée de progrès* (1910), in spite of all his
efforts to find traces in Montesquieu of the idea of progress, has finally to admit
this point. Cf. also Bach, 'Entwicklung der französischen Geschichtsauffassung
im 18. Jahrhundert' (1932), p. 45.

development. We must therefore search further afield, and look at some things we have already considered in a new connection.

In Montesquieu's works, there are three great historical worlds that stand out in a particularly bright and warm light, and were his special favourites: republican Rome, constitutional England, and the Teutonic-French Middle Ages. And in his treatment of each of these worlds he can be seen, on closer inspection, to have made use of a particular attitude and criterion of judgment; and other sides of his mind also came into play.

He surveyed the Roman world with the enthusiasm of a classicist. The virtue that he regarded as the principle of the republic was not virtue in the usual moral sense, but rather political virtue, or civil virtue—'renunciation of self and love for the laws and for the fatherland' (4, 5). What the ancients achieved in their own good time 'gives us cause for astonishment, petty souls that we are' (4, 4). On another occasion he says that he feels solidly confirmed in his maxims when he has the Romans on his side (6, 15). One can never forget the achievements of the Romans: even today, in their capital city the newer palaces are being passed over, while the ancient ruins are being sought out (11, 13). And when one examines the splendid historical picture he drew in the *Considérations* of the rise and decline of Rome, one feels a breath of the authentic classicist atmosphere on every side, in spite of the newer sources of knowledge on which he drew, and a genuine dependence upon ancient tradition. The new element he introduced was his original method of research into causes, his skill in bringing the detail of laws, institutions and political events into precise connection with one another from a political point of view. He was then able to extract a general principle concerning the steady extension of power, namely that the growing size of Rome was bound to shatter its own foundation, the very principles upon which the republic was founded. But within this network of causes there was also something that the ancient authors, especially Montesquieu's favourite Florus, had already noted about the greatness and decline of Rome, something that was faithfully preserved alongside the other material. Apart from the pragmatical thought of Polybius, who was certainly of great importance to Montesquieu, it was a highly moralistic way of looking at history that these authors had employed, in the sense of an ethic that dealt with the development of power and fame. They connected the heyday of Rome with the heroic quality of civic virtue and the wisdom of the Senate, and the decline of Rome with the corruptive effect of riches and luxury, the ambitions of the demagogues and the unbridled licence of the party spirit. What lay behind all this was only gradually revealed.

Montesquieu has often been rightly criticised for a too credulous attitude to his narrative sources. He could indeed transcend them where his political understanding of the material threw light upon them, and made a beginning in this direction in his *Considérations*, which pointed out the importance of paying attention to the whole context of institutions; yet to a large extent he kept the over-painting to which people had become accustomed through the humanist traditions of the schools. Once, indeed, he did launch out in vigorous criticism against them, and reproached Livy with scattering flowers on the mighty colossus of antiquity (*Consid.*, c. 5); but he did not really effect a clean break with the traditional approach. Niebuhr was the first to do so, and bring about a deeper understanding of growth and development and the quiet transformations that take place in history.

Montesquieu saw England in a more independent way, and not under the influence of humanist tradition. Here he had seen with his own eyes vigorous life actually going on in the present, with contradictions that nevertheless worked together remarkably on the whole to produce a national and constitutional spirit of striking character, whose effects were traceable in everything great and small. He was able to reproduce some idea of all this in a lively and individual manner, though still strongly imbued with his theories of general causation (climate in particular). But his inclination towards mechanistic explanation entirely got the better of him when he drew up a sketch of the English constitution, in reliance upon Locke and other writers. He was swept away by the task of producing an accurate assessment, in terms of statesmanship and fine calculation of the exact balance of powers, checks and counter-checks, needed to bring about *liberté politique*. This time, it was not a classicist tradition that prevented the breakthrough of historical thought, but the tradition of doctrinaire statesmanship with too calculating, utilitarian and deliberate an outlook to permit the beginnings of its understanding of historical individualism to unfold still further.

But there was yet a third tradition alive in Montesquieu, which now helped him to look with fresh eyes at the third favourite subject of his thought, namely the Teutonic-French Middle Ages. This was the tradition of the French nobility, which had been aroused to new life in the time of the Regency. Both as a descendant of a tolerably ancient noble family (cf. *Pensées et fragments*, I, 9), and as a member of the *noblesse de robe*, he was inclined to look to this heritage as the source of his most direct political ideals. Not that we should see his enthusiasm for Roman *vertu* as the direct outcome of this descent. His own inclinations were probably more nearly represented by the idealised picture of English liberty that he constructed. Yet even this ideal, as we have seen, had something artificial and self-conscious about it. Moreover, at the very beginning of his work, he pronounced it to be a great stroke of luck if the laws, which needed to be tailored to the needs of a particular people, were also found to fit another nation (1, 3; cf. also what was said about civic law under 29, 13). This stands in the way of our accepting the old opinion that his favourite idealised picture of the English constitution represented his own personal preference.[1] As Morf has shown,[2] his own predilections lay rather within the framework of the French setting, with all its given historical circumstance. He was directly concerned to preserve the intermediate powers of aristocracy as a bulwark of freedom against modern absolutism (2, 4; 8, 6; cf. also 23, 24). Republican virtue and the preservation of liberty through a neat separation of powers were by comparison fine theories on which he lavished merely a Platonic love. The origins of English freedom were already traced back by him to the forests of Germany; and this inclination was due not only to a long-standing tradition and favourite opinion among political thinkers, especially in England,[3] but also to his own personal needs. He wished to provide a reasoned historical basis for all the freedom that was possible in his time (English freedom no less than the remnants of French freedom) by showing its line of descent. This need is echoed in the often recurring phrase 'our German ancestors', which Voltaire reproached him with. It was not the voice of blood that made him speak like this—he who was a Gascon; nor was it a romantic longing, or a preference for things German. In his travel-diaries of 1729, Germany cuts a rather poor figure. But his thirst for knowledge drove him on to reconstruct what things must once have been like in Europe. Thus he wanted to visit Hungary too in the course of his travels, because he was of the opinion (*P. et fr.*, 1, 22), that all European States had once been as Hungary now was, 'and because I wanted to see the customs of our fathers'. This was a feeling for a world that had grown to its present stature, a genuinely

---

[1] Cf. also the reservations that he himself makes at the end of the chapter describing the English Constitution (11, 6). He says (1) that he does not want to examine whether the English really enjoy the freedom depicted by him, but only to show that it is established by their laws; (2) that one can manage with even a more moderate amount of political liberty, and that '*l'excès même de la raison n'est pas toujours désirable*'. Cf. also Klemperer, *Montesquieu*, 2, 98. But Hildegard Trescher's able work still exaggerates somewhat in saying (p. 39) that Montesquieu 'holds up the English Constitution as a model for all States'. One may perhaps surmise that he would have liked to do this if his relativistic conscience had not forbidden him to do so. He understood the virtues of political resignation: 'The best of all constitutions is usually the one you live under, and a sensible man will have an affection for it', he says in *Pensées et fragments*, 1, 416.

[2] *Archiv für die Studien der neueren Sprachen*, 113, 391.

[3] Hölzle, *Idee einer altgermanischen Freiheit vor Montesquieu*, 1925.

historical feeling for the connection between past, present and the whole context of Western culture. He was not ashamed of his barbarian ancestors; on the other hand, he refused to deify them.

His quite unromantic attitude to the Middle Ages, and his thoroughly modern reflective outlook and taste, are well shown by his complaints at the 'cold, dry, hard, insipid' writings of those days which he had had to labour through; the only thing to do, he says, is to devour them, as Saturn in the fable was said to have devoured stones (30, 11). Here, in this material from the Middle Ages, he was up against the toughest wood, and needed to do some steady boring to work through to the necessary knowledge. And this was really a blessing. For here there was no ready-made picture, as there had been of antiquity, which exercised a compelling power on the cultivated reader, nor, as in England, material belonging to a modern State and easy to present in clear form, but a whole mass of historical events that had to be brought into shape for the first time. Knowledge of the period had been notably increased (particularly of the Frankish period and the French Middle Ages) by the learned work and editions published by the Benedictines and other researchers in the late seventeenth century. There had been an awakening of critical sense with regard to this traditional material, which gave this work an importance of a pioneering kind for European historical scholarship. A start had also been made with the formative process, the attempt to bring the past history of the Middle Ages and the present political life of France into some sort of clear common perspective, when Montesquieu began his research. Men were on the eve of discovering the idea of developmental thought in history. And it must be noted that everywhere, with Montesquieu himself as well as with his predecessors, it was with political standards and requirements that the attempt was made to get beyond the merely antiquarian detailed criticism of the past. The past needed an infusion of living blood from the present, by means of independent thought and endeavour, in order to make some advance to historical thought in terms of genuine development.

Yet it remained an advance only to the threshold, in spite of all the links that had already been forged between the past and the present. We must become acquainted with some of these in order to enter into a proper appreciation of Montesquieu's farther-reaching achievements, and even to see their connections with the history of developmental thought as a whole.

The problem we are concerned with here is a big one, and still a living issue today. It centres round the relationship between the Frankish-German and the Gallo-Roman roots of French society and political life, and examines the degree of causal significance and permanent value that should be ascribed to both. In Montesquieu's time, anyone who approved the centralising absolute monarchy naturally felt attracted by the Roman roots; anyone who felt oppressed by it (for example, the aspiring part of the French nobility) was bound to incline towards the Germanic origins. This historical battle had already been joined in a primitive fashion by François Hotman during the Huguenot wars, in his book *Francogallia* (1573). He was disposed to glorify the Franks as bringers of freedom to the Gauls under Roman oppression, and to derive from this the demand for a monarchy resting upon popular sovereignty. And now, as Montesquieu started his work, there were two very different writers (to select only those who were most directly connected with his thought) who had just taken up this problem, one of whom answered it in a Frankish-Germanic, the other in a Roman sense. The two were respectively Count Boulainvilliers and Abbé Dubos. Boulainvilliers' *Histoire de l'ancien gouvernement de la France* appeared five years after his death, in 1727 (three vols); the Abbé's *Histoire critique de l'établissement de la monarchie française dans les Gaules* in 1734, (though we are here using it in the two-volume edition of 1742).

We are less concerned with their content than with the question of their significance as preliminary stages towards a fully evolutionary conception of history. It is enough to note that Boulainvilliers maintained with stubborn defiance that he was in the direct line of inheritance from the Franks, and saw in them not only the conquerors of Gaul and the founders and only legitimate occupants of a free polity with an elective monarchy, but also the ancestors of the true French nobility. And he then went on to follow out the process by which the rulers of subsequent dynasties (apart from the much idealised Charlemagne) began increasingly to oppress this nobility and infringe their rights, setting up their own despotic power instead and watering down the nobility by the creation of a new artificial paper-nobility recruited from the ranks of former bondmen, the Gallic population who had once upon a time been subjected by the Franks. In this account of events, a tremendous process extending over centuries, unfolding at first slowly, but later with increasing speed, was presented as a single unity! The author maintained (3, 135) that Richelieu and Louis XIV had completed in thirty years what previous kings had not managed to achieve in 1200. To this extent this theme may be seen as a stage towards evolutionary historical thought. But in events as here depicted there are no criteria of genuine historical development. For there was a complete lack of the material forces at work from within that could combine necessity and freedom and act as a bridge between one condition and another. Instead, the picture painted is one of an ideal exemplary original state—exemplary at least on the political side, for there is full admission that the bearers of this heritage were thoroughly ignorant and barbarous (3, 137). And this condition is transformed by the conscious actions of ambitious monarchs with a thirst for power, who were able to succeed because the nobles were heedless and lazy (1, 179, 327, etc.). This is nothing but pure personal pragmatism. And it is combined with the old scheme inherited from antiquity of a golden age destroyed through the sins and errors of humanity. Yet there were still possible ways of effecting a transition from this defiant traditionalism to an understanding of history in relative terms. Everywhere he compared the bad contemporary state with the good old days of the past; and in so doing he could reproach the historians of his own time (in particular the Jesuit Daniel, author of the *Histoire de France* (1703)) with 'bringing in the most remote and least comparable facts from the past and applying them to the present', whereas all ages had their own special excellencies, which did not pass on to subsequent generations (1, 322). He then came closer still to the position taken up by Montesquieu in the words of his preface, where he says that not all kinds of laws are necessarily good for a nation. The laws of Athens or Lacedaemonia, he maintained, though recognised as masterpieces of the human mind, would be monstrous in our State, and our usages would be intolerable in England and Poland. The safest rule, then, must be to follow the example of what has previously taken place and been successfully managed in our own society. He therefore surveyed his own evil time with some pain, but not with any feeling of radical rejection; for it too, as he was ready to admit, possessed its own particular excellences (3, 205). Thus he was seized by something like a sense of heroic destiny, which sees the approaching inevitable decline of all that is splendid. 'The omens for an even greater decadence in French honour (he means the ancient Frankish noble blood) are all too clear' (3, 205). In another passage (2, 270), he remarks that all States have their inevitable destinies, just as much as individuals. Just as a freeborn man might well, through force of circumstance, fall into bondage, so can a State, in spite of the soundness of its original laws. And at this point he anticipates Montesquieu, by reminding the reader of the fate of the Romans, who destroyed their freedom through their own armed power, never again to arise from their despicable servitude.

The works of this race-conscious and stubborn nobleman bore further signs of far-ranging historical thought.[1] For Gobineau ac-

---

[1] Cf. Hölzle, p. 57, on the idea represented by him and adopted from English thought of an inclusive Germanic common liberty, from which he then derived the broad features of both the English and the German constitutional institutions.

tually saw him as the forerunner, though in very incomplete form, of his own theory of race.[1] But the fundamental idea in Boulainvilliers' interpretation of history, the *droit primordial* of the first conqueror and its destruction through the thirst for dominance among the kings, was and remained crude and unsuitable for the tasks of the future historism. In working this out, even he was not able to be altogether logical. For in admitting the rights of the first conqueror, he also had to admit that this could equally be used to justify the rise of the unlimited royal power which he so ardently detested. And so here and there he borrowed a little from the traditional Natural Law and fell back upon 'the natural freedom of man' (1, 255); but this brought him into glaring contradiction with his much-emphasised rights of the conqueror. All the same, considered as a whole, his work exhibits a certain natural freshness in spite of its traditional feeling, and acted as one of the ferments that were destined to produce a new relationship to the world of history. Montesquieu gladly let the ferment work in himself, and was happy to recognise the *simplicité* and *ingénuité de l'ancienne noblesse* which spoke through Boulainvilliers' writings (30, 10). Boulainvilliers' attempt to do justice to a piece of mediaeval history spurred Montesquieu on to make a better attempt at it himself.

Whilst taking Boulainvilliers' book as a conspiracy against the Third Estate, he saw Abbé Dubos' book as a conspiracy against the nobility. Dubos had a much better scholarly equipment than Boulainvilliers. He tried his utmost to do justice to all the demands of critical erudition that had been put forward by the scholarship of the late seventeenth century. But try as he might to give a factual basis to the chain of events leading up to the establishment of the Frankish monarchy, and however sensitive and attractive his approach might be,[2] the preconceived dominating tendencies we have already noted penetrated just as strongly into his work as into Boulainvilliers', and caused even his ripest scholarship to be distorted in their favour, even to the point of drawing on his imagination for source-material when it was not forthcoming. His concern was to contradict Boulainvilliers' thesis of the seignorial rights of the Frankish conquerors. Those seignorial rights, the detested rights of the *seigneurie* and the hereditary rights of jurisdiction, were in his opinion a usurpation by the tyrannous overlords of the ninth and tenth centuries (*Discours prélimin.*, 1, 39 and 2, 608). Up to that time, he maintained, the social

For other components of his historical thinking (the spirit of the peoples, the common thought-forms of a century, his interest in the history of morals), cf. the points on Voltaire noted above.

[1] Schemann, *Gobineaus Rassenwerk*, pp. 475 ff.

[2] For a very happy treatment of this, see Thierry, *Récits des temps Mérovingiens*, I, 68.

framework and political arrangements of the Romans had continued unaltered in their essentials, apart from the special privileges enjoyed by the Franks, who were not very numerous. It now became his further concern to show that there was a precise legal continuity between the *Imperium Romanum* and the Frankish kings, and that they had gained dominion over Gaul proper not as conquering popular monarchs but as *officiers de l'Empire* (2, 76), and had finally received a formal cession of it at the hands of Justinian. So the present kings of France were the legitimate successors of Augustus and Tiberius, whom Jesus Christ himself had recognised as legitimate sovereigns. They were thus the only modern kings who could boast that their rights had come down to them directly from the ancient Roman Empire! (2, 370 f.). The reader can perhaps guess what degree of smoothing over and adjustment had been required to establish this connection and turn the wild Clovis into a civilised figure. On the other hand, there was partial truth in the theme of the continuity in the Roman institutions; and Alfons Dopsch, who has taken it up again in recent times, has mentioned Dubos as one of his predecessors in this field.

This attempt to show a large-scale continuity in the life of history, an attempt that was carried through with so much learned energy, already sounds a modern historical note. Fueter in his history of recent historiography (p. 329) has compared Dubos' achievement with that of Justus Möser. As regards his work on the French monarchy, this verdict can, as we shall presently show, only be maintained with some reserve. But Dubos' general position within the early French Enlightenment is indeed somewhat reminiscent of Möser's appearance on the scene, inasmuch as he was an independent thinker who sought out new ways destined to lead far beyond the bounds of the Enlightenment. At this point we must consider his *Réflexions critiques sur la poésie et la peinture* (first published 1719, but here used in the three-volume edition of 1740), which later even influenced Lessing. Here he had already broken a lance against the regularity of the French Classicism in support of the importance of sentiment, the passions, and inborn genius in the field of art. He did this in deliberate opposition to the Cartesian, mathematical, deductive spirit that was largely dominant at that time in the world of thought, and in deliberate alliance with the empirical inductive methods of natural science and the sensualistic philosophy of the English thinkers. The result of this was to give his doctrine of genius, and all the conclusions stemming from it concerning the causes of the rise and fall of cultures, a downright naturalistic character. For he explained the existence of periods rich in genius or poor in genius simply by physical causes, through the influence of changing factors such as climate, air, or soil. Thus he was a direct forerunner of Montesquieu by virtue of his theory of climate; and in general he was more a forerunner of the later positivism[1] than of the later historism, although he anticipated the latter by his vital feeling for the power of the irrational, which he already possessed by virtue of his aesthetic interests. But one might almost say that he rationalised the irrational and remained within the limitations of thought based upon Natural Law, in that he substituted for a timeless reason an equally timeless *sentiment* as the judge of aesthetic values.[2] And his power and strength of will were not sufficient to penetrate the whole field of history with his new pattern of thought. Thus his historical thinking on the subject of the French monarchy stands in a very different position from his work on the theory of aesthetics.

To start with, he had been employed in the minor service of French diplomacy. He knew what political expediency and the interests of the State meant, and had had close practical relations with it as official publicist. With some political side-glances at conquering trading republics, he had during the War of the Spanish Succession written a book on the League of Cambrai, and so was fully acquainted with the doctrines of statecraft. He was also specially interested in what was then known as the *état* of a country, the structure of its official bodies, its administrative and legal machinery, taxation, politics and so on. All this was very useful for his book, which treated these matters with particular thoroughness and clarity, and was in many respects a pioneer work for this Romano-Germanic transitional period, and is thoroughly suggestive of Möser's later work. Yet what profoundly divides Dubos' work from Möser's is his irresistible inclination to modernise the mentality of the past.[3] These people living during the time of the great migrations were depicted by him in the political and social dress of the seventeenth and eighteenth centuries. A certain degree of barbarism was of course admitted by him, but he represented the Franks as much more potentially cultured than the other Germanic tribes; and they were, therefore, so to speak, 'adopted' by the *nation Romaine* (2, 227). Gaul of the later Roman period appears like a modern France, in a

[1] His attractive and learned biographer Lombard (*L'Abbé Dubos, un initiateur de la pensée moderne*, 1913) brings this out most sympathetically.

[2] 'It is remarkable to observe how feeling takes the same place with our author as reason does with Boileau' (H. von Stein, *Entstehung der neueren Ästhetik*, p. 238).

[3] Lombard notices this point, too, on p. 399, yet ascribes to him, strangely enough, on p. 401 a philosophical *sens de la différence des temps*. In his aesthetic works, however there are far more traces of it. Cf. also on Dubos, Cassirer, *Philosophie der Aufklärung*, p. 397, and Finsler, *Homer in der Neuzeit*, pp. 233 ff.

highly civilised state, but going to rack and ruin through civil wars and bad government, until it finally found a 'protector' in the Frankish kings. His arguments often suggested that there was a time-lessly valid law and polity of the nations, and a political almanac of the migration periods, which could be just as neatly and fully drawn up as any modern calendar of Dubos' own period. This spirit of a modern civil servant sought to explain the wars and power politics of that age with a wealth of often highly ingenious analogies taken from the new system of European States. For example, he compared Clovis' supposed dual position as a Frankish popular king and as a Roman imperial official with that of King William III of England, who had remained at the same time Captain-General of the Nether-lands. To illustrate the confused coexistence of different national common laws in France he hit upon the delightful analogy of the Turkey of his own day, where the Sultans' policies maintained a simi-lar condition. He went on to ask, entirely in the spirit of contem-porary statesmanship: 'Why should not our first kings also have kept their subjects in a state of national division for reasons of policy?' (2, 385).

This discovery of analogies for the understanding of contemporary conditions through political expert knowledge was, therefore, a principal means of cognition in Abbé Dubos' historical thinking. It rested upon the tacit assumption that the political life of all not positively barbarian times possessed certain typical and constantly recurrent features. And his attention was centred, not so much on the individual, as on the typical features. Because of this tendency, Dubos' enterprising attempt to trace a greater element of continuity through the centuries lost some of its genuine historical value. For with him, as with Montesquieu, the background of thought was still the old cyclical doctrine,[1] the belief in a recurrence of the same, or very similar, events. This was a doctrine easily combined with a per-sonalising, as well as a material, pragmatism. Dubos' work partakes of both kinds. He would never have undertaken to fill out the gaps in historical tradition by such daring hypotheses, or have attempted to restore a smooth connection in political and legal structure between the Roman Imperium and the Frankish monarchy, with all good faith in his own methods, unless that idea had been dominated by the conviction that political life in the ancient and in the modern world was essentially one and the same. With him, as with Montesquieu, a material and factual pragmatism predominated over the more primi-tive and purely personal kind. We have to thank Dubos for the valuable extension of historical interest in the composition of institu-tions and the changes they undergo. The critical caution that is

[1] Cf. his *Réflexions critiques* (ed. 1740), 2, 319, and Lombard, p. 255.

lacking in his work could only come in when a thorough sense of the genuinely individual had prevailed in historical thought.

We come back now to Montesquieu. Dubos' work was a kind of hymn in praise of the undivided political power handed down by the Roman emperors to the Frankish kings, and as such was bound to clash violently with Montesquieu's favourite political idea, that a separation of powers in the State was thoroughly healthy.[1] There were certain further contentions of Dubos, which, contrary to his general trend, he treated with ridicule; and of these he would probably have been most provoked by the suggestion that the seignorial rights and hereditary jurisdictions had first been created by the usurpers of the ninth and tenth centuries. For this was where he set about working out the origins of the intermediate aristocratic powers which he valued so highly. If these still possessed some value in his own time, their origin in the feudal system and its preceding stages could not have been quite unreasonable or barbaric. This was the question he put to himself, suggested no doubt by political interest, but not without highly valuable historical results. Then there was the further question of the jurist in him who was so eager to know the origins of French law and French justice in general, and the causes for the division of France into two zones, one of common law and one of Roman law. To these questions the last three books of his *Esprit des lois* were devoted. Their character of pure historical research marks them off as different from the rest of the work, with its systematic arrangement, and makes them somewhat out of place in the whole. But what was a fault from the literary point of view contributed greatly to the fame of the book as a piece of historical thinking. For it burst the bonds of the political manual, which assumed a certain static character for what was in fact the constant flux of history. But here Montesquieu felt the attraction of the dramatic flux of events, because they, and they alone, contained the rational meaning and purpose for which he was searching. The errors and mistakes of detail he committed in the course of this search are not here to the point. The value lay in the establishment of a new historical method.

Montesquieu explained (30, 19) that it was impossible to penetrate into our system of constitutional law unless one had first acquired a complete understanding of the laws and customs of the Germanic peoples. He asked himself what were the origins of the seignorial patrimonial rights of jurisdiction in his own day, traced them back to the elaborate system of primitive and compensatory law among the Germanic tribes, and proceeded to carry out a patient examination of this institution's further development. In the midst of this

[1] Cf. Dédieu, *Montesquieu et la tradition politique anglaise en France* (1909), p. 158.

task, we find him exclaiming with the joy of a discoverer: 'Ah, now I begin to see the actual birth of seignorial jurisdiction' (30, 20). This led him to the conclusion that these jurisdictions did not owe their origin to any usurpation, but were derived from the earliest traceable institutions and not from any subsequent debasement of them (30, 22). There are many possible objections to the correctness of this account of the genesis of manorial jurisdiction. It is possible, moreover, to surmise a certain political bias in his rejection of Dubos' pragmatic and moralising explanation of the facts. But it was a genuine achievement of genius to make this deliberate rejection and to be able to resurrect a still living portion of the past by means of a slow change of its original institutions through forces coming from within them. By using these methods, he added with a touch of justifiable pride, it was possible to observe 'generation', 'the birth of law', among most peoples as a general process. By these methods he went beyond his own previous achievements, and beyond the pragmatic methods he had elsewhere mostly employed. In so doing, he compared peoples to individuals, as had been done by Boulainvilliers and a number of others before. But he made the comparison in such a way that the individual, alongside the typical, now entered into its proper rights. For he pointed out that peoples, like individuals, have their *suite d'idées*, their *manière de penser totale*, their beginning, middle and end (*P. et fr.*, 1, 193).

Then there was the further question of trial by combat in the Middle Ages, the fact that 'our forefathers' would hand over their honour, fortune and life itself more readily to chance than to the operations of reason (28, 17 ff.). Once again, he found the explanation, from the historical point of view, in their *manière de penser*, their way of bringing war under the control of certain rules and seeing its outcome as a work of providence, and in their special sense of honour as a warrior people. 'There was some reason behind the practice of trial by single combat, for it was founded upon experience.' Cowardice in a warlike people would naturally rank as a ground for suspicion that there might be other faults as well. He also found in the spread of trial by single combat a reason for the disappearance of the authority of written law, for trial by combat was henceforth held to be a sufficient means of judicial proof. He also had some very suggestive ideas to put forward about the origins and transformations of the *point d'honneur*. He went on to trace 'the wonderful system of knighthood' back to trial by combat and the belief that magic herbs could be used to influence the results. There was certainly considerable simplification and pragmatism at work here to derive the whole system, including its magic horses, paladins, fairies and so on from such slender material. He also linked this on to the rise of the distinctive *esprit de galanterie* in the Middle Ages, which created a relationship between the sexes unknown to the ancient world. But his general purpose was 'to trace the monstrous institution of trial by combat back to the principles behind it, and so to discover the solid substance in such a strange system of jurisprudence'. For Montesquieu believed that 'men are basically reasonable, and disposed to bring even their prejudices under certain rules' (28, 23). This was still a rationalist reaction, but of a kind that prepared the way for a fuller understanding of the irrational and the individual.

Voltaire had taught that there was a constant struggle going on between reason and unreason, in the course of which the Middle Ages became the mediator of the irrational. Montesquieu was rather concerned to teach the accommodation of reason to unreason in the course of history, so that the Middle Ages were to be regarded as by no means a mere barbarism devoid of all reasonable elements. Voltaire thought it ridiculous that each place should have its own particular law; but Montesquieu explained this by the intoxicating idea of local sovereignty, which at that period had a firm hold upon everybody, and was of the opinion that it would have been unwise to have created a single unified book of laws for a time when men's outlook was so different (28, 37). Once again, this was not yet historism, but a piece of political utilitarianism, of the subtlest kind taught by Machiavelli, which took men as it found them, and not as it would have liked them to be. This kind of accommodation of reason to the irrationalities of history did not indeed reduce the stable reason of Natural Law to a really fluid state, but it did render it considerably more malleable. To treat reason in a more fluid fashion meant to let it become more individualised, to recognise it in the thousand different forms it assumes, and to see in each something unique and irreplaceable in its sheer individuality. This creative process of looking with new eyes and new amazement at all things, as though each one were a fresh revelation of the spirit, was something that Montesquieu could not as yet aspire to. Or should we rather say that he had already made tentative efforts in that direction?

In the course of these enquiries Montesquieu was once gripped by the genuinely historical feeling that in the feudal system of the Middle Ages there was a phenomenon that had never existed in the world before, and was never to exist again (30, 1). Nowadays, to be sure, we should qualify that statement by referring to analogous systems and feudal developments in other cultures and among other peoples. And yet the Western mediaeval feudal system possesses a quite individual character. This feeling for unique individuality in general was a great achievement, for it sharpened Montesquieu's awareness that its effects were not always definitely good or bad, but had often been a mixture of both. Thus there came to him an even loftier sense of reverence for the great creations which were living embodiments of the spirit.

> One can now watch the unfolding drama of the feudal system. It is as though an ancient oak-tree stood there before our eyes. The foliage is visible from afar, and as one approaches, the trunk comes into sight; but the roots remain hidden. You must dig down into the earth to find them.

The peculiar feature in Montesquieu is thus his failure to attain to any general new relationship to history going beyond political utilitarianism and rationalism, except in a particular historical field. Here, there was a new awakening both of individuality and of the concept of development; though the taste for rationalism did not entirely disappear, for the search after meaning even in the irrational, though often very fleeting and purely utilitarian, was still under the spell of pragmatism. Montesquieu's mental world might be compared to one of those remarkable settlements high up in the mountains, where the mountain ridges are in general the natural barriers, but do not constitute an absolutely final barrier. Their origins, their interests, and their trade relationships all point the inhabitants naturally to one particular side of the ridge, for this is the direction in which they look out on life. But they also have pastures on the far side of the mountains, up to which they drive their flocks at a favourable time of the year; and the paths they make serve to open up relationships for future traffic with the world that lies beyond.

Looking out from this new world waiting to be opened up, Herder already had an inkling of this double outlook in Montesquieu, when he pronounced the classic judgment on the *Esprit des lois*, that this noble and gigantic work was like a Gothic building erected in the taste of its own philosophical century (1774, *Works*, 5, 565).

Montesquieu's work proved to be more far-reaching than he either wished or thought possible. His most powerful effect on history was to produce a new respect for its creations, a new sense that on all sides there were new discoveries to be made as to the meaning and framework of events which had hitherto escaped notice. At least there were some signs of these effects in his own country during this period. He was certainly admired; but in the main, people preferred to follow as a guide to the future the broad highway of the Enlightenment, with its assured signposts.[1] Yet as the following chapter will

---

[1] Characteristic of this is the reception accorded to his work in the circle of his closest friends. A good deal of instructive light is thrown upon this in the *Correspondance de Montesquieu*, II (1914). The achievements of his study of the

show, the trends towards historism which he represented were not an entirely isolated phenomenon in the field of French thought.

Middle Ages were greeted with astonishment, but not appreciated at a deeper level (cf. also Laboulaye's note on 30, 1: *Œuvres*, 5, 415). The chief interest was in his political maxims. The dangers inherent in his methods for the pure ideals of the Enlightenment were most acutely felt by Helvetius (*Correspondance*, II, 16 ff. and 565 ff.: '*Sa manière est éblouissante. C'est avec le plus grand de génie qu'il a formé l'alliage des vérités et des préjugés*'). Cf. also on Helvetius's criticism, Wahl, 'Montesquieu als Vorläufer von Aktion und Reaktion', *Hist. Zeitschrift*, 109, 144 ff.

Chapter four

Other Historical Thought in France during and after the Time of Voltaire and Montesquieu

In the person of Montesquieu, the French spirit made an indispensable contribution to the origin of historism. Of subsequent French thinkers and scholars, Rousseau was the only one whose work subsequently played an essential part in the lives of those Germans who were destined to stir up the new sense of history in their own country.

Yet we cannot break off the sequence of French thinkers too abruptly at this juncture. True, the great French philosophy of history belonging to the second half of the century, beginning with Turgot's *Discours sur les progrès successifs de l'esprit humain* in 1750 and culminating in Condorcet's *Esquisse d'un tableau historique des progrès de l'esprit humain* (1794), belongs rather to the early history of positivism than to that of historism. Its general note is not so much the individual as the typical and universally valid; and progress towards a great perfection in humanity, which was one of its tenets, was conceived more as a process resting upon general laws. They observed the connecting links leading from one stage of this progress to the next more accurately and reflectively than Voltaire, and so undoubtedly furthered the advance of evolutionary historical thought in general.[1] But they fitted it too narrowly into a schematic framework of progress, which became even more dominant in the second half of the century. This tendency may be largely viewed as the result of the spectacle offered to philosophers by the active development of enlightened despotism at this period. When governments themselves, after centuries of unreasonable rule, now at last began to listen to the voice of reason, this opened up unsuspected hopes for further advances in the future. And this mood was destined, through

[1] A more detailed treatment in Breysig, *Die Meister der entwickelnden Geschichtsforschung* (1936), pp. 84 ff.

144

the French Revolution, to become a real intoxication, in which reason herself appeared to be assuming the task of forming anew the powers of government. Thus it came about that the path of interpretation in terms of universal history opened up by Condorcet diverged further from the ways of historical thought that we are following up than did the line previously pursued by his master Turgot. For in Turgot, in spite of his inclination towards a 'mechanism of moral causality' (*Works*, 2, 213), there was still a certain realism concerning the doctrine of political expediency, which had continued ever since Machiavelli, to look upon complexes of political interest in a morphological manner, as representing to some extent natural growths. His sketches of a 'political geography' (*Works*, 2, 166 ff.), which were important as a pointer towards modern geopolitics, were full of pregnant questions, such as the relationship between the extent of a particular territory and its internal administration and form of government, or the suggestion that religions could be divided into types according to their current relationships with politics and their propagandist, or non-propagandist, character. In taking this line, Turgot was continuing the methods of Montesquieu, but with the intention of refining them, as he observed the onesidedness of his doctrine of climate; and as Dilthey has shown, he is somewhat reminiscent of Herder in his capacity to take a broad, quick look at a subject. He is even more reminiscent of him in that he still believed in a divine providence at work over the whole course of history; though he interpreted it in a markedly more mechanical and regular fashion than Herder, and pictured it more in terms of a vast army on the march, directed by some mighty genius (*Works*, 2, 225).

In Condorcet, with his anti-ecclesiastical attitude, divine providence disappeared from the scene and was replaced by the purely natural laws of progress, 'almost' (to quote his still slightly cautious language) 'as certain as those of the natural sciences' (pp. 244 and 327), leading up to a most fervent faith in the unlimited perfectibility of the human race. Though the sense of the concrete in the creations of history did not altogether disappear, it tended to be eclipsed. Turgot had certainly displayed it, though in a typifying rather than an individualising manner; and in the later positivism of the nineteenth century it was to reappear, though again confined to the typical. Condorcet was deeply concerned to show that human reason was an equally infallible natural power, not unlike the force of gravity, already at work in primitive times in a rudimentary form, and slowly but surely permeating human nature in spite of all the hindrances. It was always advancing, and never retreating; compelled, indeed, to compromise with its opponents as it went forward, but with its eyes

145

fixed upon a uniform future for the whole of humanity. Powerful as was the spirit in which Condorcet completed his work while he lay there in prison, awaiting the sentence of death, it only touches the fringe of our subject, and serves principally to reveal the gulf that separated positivism from the nascent historism.

Condorcet represents, in fact, the utmost that the Enlightenment, left to its own resources, was able to achieve towards a more satisfactory world view of history. As far as we shall be concerned with the rise of historism in Germany, neither Turgot nor Condorcet are of any direct significance. Turgot's sketches of universal history were not published till 1808, when his collected works first appeared. We will now follow in summary form the products of French intellectual life in the second half of the century, insofar as they contribute, either by analogy or by their influence, to our understanding of the movement in Germany.

Even in the writings of Turgot and Condorcet, for all their preference for mechanical laws and their belief that history can be treated by methods similar to those of the research scientist, their factual interpretation of historical changes often passes over into a more dynamic form. As Cassirer has shown in his *Philosophie der Aufklärung* (1932), the involuntary turning away from the mechanical and the abstract towards a more dynamic and materialistic pattern of thought was characteristic of the French Enlightenment in general in the second half of the century. It was present in Buffon's *Histoire naturelle* (1749 ff.) in a fashion that was destined to show further fruitful development in Herder and in Goethe's evolutionary thought. But alongside it, there could also still exist in France an extreme rationalism, and a certain materialism was also developing. A limited transformation of the intellectual outlook in the Enlightenment was a tribute paid by it to the general transformation of the Western outlook that was perceptible on every side.

A principal witness to this is Diderot, one of the most dynamic among French thinkers, who could hover between materialism and idealism, and yet become a pioneer in a poetry concerned with the passions, in a more lively, though perhaps not very profound, style. He must be set alongside Rousseau, whose effect was even more powerful. But they were not the men to bring about a new movement in historical thought, for they still had not broken through the basic assumption of the unchanging nature of reason. True, reason was now interpreted, along the lines of the English sensualists and under the influence of the rising naturalistic outlook, less as the epitome of truths and more as a power that must come to grips with the sub-rational forces of human nature, which were now seen to be of a much richer content. But there was still a belief that reason made certain demands and led to certain truths that were universally valid for all time.

Rousseau, too, was caught up in this error. We shall see later on his importance for those who were to arouse the new sense of history in Germany, though he acted more as a stimulant than as a genuine leader of thought. Here, we shall be content to put the facts in summary form. His radical cultural criticism contained in the two *Discours* of 1750 and 1754 certainly shook the self-satisfaction of the Enlightenment and led to a deeper level of reflection. Moreover, with his anti-conventional and independent character, Rousseau did an incalculable service for the rights of the individual. He was a pioneer in this experience, and he gave countless people the courage to make use of his example, and, with a stirring of the inner man, to become sensitive to life all round them in a more individual fashion. Again, he was responsible for a new and vigorous outlook that set everything individual in a higher total context, which he called nature, and embraced with ardent affection. This conception of a living connection between the individual and nature, though it never became explicit in him, was yet able to give immeasurable reinforcement to the fervent search for new links between the world and the human heart. But he himself did not succeed in finding the way that led to the world of history. The ideal man, the unspoilt child of nature, and the virtuous human heart which he preached, was only an inverted form of the Enlightenment's 'normal man'. Solely because of his effects, and not because of his teaching (or only to a very minor extent) is it possible to rank Rousseau as one of those who aroused the sense of the individual which was so greatly needed by the future historism. In his *Contrat social* of 1782, which proposed the goal of freedom but ended in the despotism of the *volonté générale*, it was fully evident that his thought was still tied to the normative spirit of Natural Law.

Thus the broad paths of French thought in the second half of the century do not as yet lead to the country we are seeking; but there are stirrings of a tentative kind in that direction, and they are a step towards the achievements of Herder.

As a contemporary of Voltaire, the youthful A. J. Goguet was essaying a general cultural history of early man, from primitive times to the heyday of Greece, entitled: *De l'Origine des loix, des arts et des sciences et de leur progrès chez les anciens peuples* (3 vols, 1758; German translation by Hamberger: *Untersuchungen von dem Ursprung der Gesetze, Künste und Wissenschaften, wie auch ihrem Wachstum bei den alten Völkern*, 3 vols, 1760–2).[1] He produced an

---

[1] The monograph on him by Emil Spiess in *Studien aus dem Gebiete von Kirche und Kultur. Festschrift Gustav Schnürer*, 1930, does him rather too much honour. Cf. also Unger, *Hamann*, pp. 653 ff., and Justi, *Winckelmann* vol. 2, pt. 3, p. 71.

innocuous mixture of certain ideas of the Enlightenment and a faith in the Church, and was therefore much more uncritical of the biblical tradition than Voltaire. But he was much more devoted to the perfectibility of mankind, and much more diligent and penetrating than Voltaire in his concrete research. He contrived to produce questions that still concern research into the early history of mankind—such questions as the techniques of agriculture, the arts of writing and calculation, what people wore on their heads, the wearing of rings, how the obelisks were built, and so on. Indeed, he even went on to ask how Moses could have managed to burn the golden calf. He taught that civilisation had arisen step by step, from the rude conditions of an almost animal life. Man, driven on by necessity, had ascended with strict continuity, until he had reached the climax of the much-belauded heights of the last hundred years. Goguet did not set up any general laws, but sought as a rule to explain progress along pragmatic and practical lines. He looked at the individual, the 'spirit' of things, the opinions and thought-forms of particular peoples, in a somewhat summary way, but was again inclined to derive them from external circumstances. But the boundless curiosity of the middle-class Enlightenment for everything human bore good fruit in him, leading him to institute comparisons with the primitive American Indians, and to compare the ancient Germanic and the ancient Czech civilisations, although in a rather vague fashion. He is thus somewhat reminiscent of Lafitau, though there is already a more modern touch about his work. Herder, who sometimes mentions Goguet, may well have been influenced not only by some of the detail, but more especially by the conception that all thought is interlinked through tradition, and the belief that nothing achieved by tradition is ever really lost.

Boulanger made a different approach to the problems of early human history, combining both the attitude of the Enlightenment and the outlook of Vico. In 1758 he had to give up his profession as a road engineer and bridge-builder on account of poor health, and threw himself with dilettante self-dedication into the study of early times, learnt the necessary ancient languages one after another, and was compared by one of his friends[1] to the silk-worm, which spins around its own body and covers everything with its threads. It is possible that he knew Vico's work,[2] and had his attention called by it to the influence that the vast natural catastrophes of early times must have had on the shaping of early man. It was quite in keeping with Vico's approach, too, when he published his first work anonymously, *Recherches sur l'origine du despotisme oriental* (1761), and

[1] *Gazette littéraire de l'Europe*, 7, 207 ff. (1765).
[2] Cf. Croce, *Philosophie Vicos*, p. 243, and *Bibliografia Vichiana*, p. 50.

expressed the methodical principle that antiquity was not to be judged by the mendacious tales of the later historians, but should be studied from its customs and usages. But his belief in the original goodness and reasonableness of primitive man immediately toned down all he derived from these historians, making him see the hated Eastern despotism as a debased product of theocracy, and the latter as a perversion of the good forms of belief and practice built up by man after the occurrence of those early natural catastrophes.

But the Flood would give his imagination no rest. He proceeded to throw light upon its significance for the history of mankind from a quite new direction, in a second work which came out posthumously, *L'Antiquité dévoilée par ses usages* (3 vols, 1766) (3 vols in German: *Das durch seine Gebräuche aufgedeckte Altertum*, 1766). As a road engineer he had been observant of the variations in the surface of the earth, and had ascribed them to the Flood. Furthermore, he saw the long-term effects of this tremendous disaster in the disruption of capacity for thought in a confused humanity, and in a legacy of fear and horror that had left their mark in minute detail on the religions, customs and political institutions of the peoples. To such an extent that he even saw the ascetic practices of monks as an after-effect produced by fear, although the real reasons for it had long ago been forgotten. He collected an astonishing amount of material bearing upon religious rites that were in some way or other connected with water, in order to prove his thesis. He wanted to free mankind from the century-long anxieties that had oppressed them by disclosing their real causes, which lay in the distant past. All this strikes us to start with as a vast piece of dilettantism. All the same, there is food for thought in the fact that Herder wrote to Hamann in 1766 that 'this work appeals to me a great deal'. For what interested him in this book was the attempt to throw light upon the deeper levels of human history, and especially the history of primitive times, which had normally remained hidden from the ordinary scholastic learning. This was a world of obscure emotions, which must nevertheless have given the impulse towards many religious and social structures whose origins had long been forgotten. True history, as Boulanger observes, is hidden behind the curtains of time. Boulanger's was an attempt to demonstrate in one breath not only the very primitive origins of specific things and their continuance in altered form down the ages; to give not only the history of opinions, but of the inward disposition from which they arose; and to study not the abstract man of Natural Law but the real primitive man of early history.

All this was calculated, no doubt, to whet the curiosity of a Herder[1]

[1] Cf. the fragmentary essay written in youth: 'Zur Geschichte der Wissenschaften aus Boulanger', in his *Works*, 32, 153. The criticisms of Boulanger's

(who did not at the time know of the much greater Vico) and stir him up to take a peep himself behind the curtains of time.

Apart from the main current of the French Enlightenment which flowed through the Parisian salons, there were other tendencies in France of interest to us here, traceable perhaps to three main roots: a pure and simple interest in antiquity as such; a deliberate cultivation of an inherited aristocratic interest in memories of the Middle Ages; and a newly aroused interest over almost the whole of Europe, about the middle of the eighteenth century, in the primitive history of the nations, and not only mankind in a general way, as analysed by Voltaire and Goguet, or as idealised by Rousseau, or as shrouded in darkness and horror by Boulanger, but in the early and middle period of European history, and particularly the northern peoples, who were perhaps of more significance to the contemporary world than the Indians and South Sea Islanders.

Even in the middle of the strictly classical period of Louis XIV, there had been a continuance of Gothic building in the country (E. Lanson, *Le Goût du moyen âge en France au 18. siècle*, 1926, p. 8), and the cultured art collector Abbé Marolles had been able to build up an unprejudiced taste for the beauties of Gothic architecture (see Weisbach's article on him in the *Deutscher Rundschau*, Nov. 1929).

There was likewise at the same period a growth of interest in the one-time poetry of the troubadours; and throughout the century it was kept perceptibly, though not strongly, alive, till the eve of the Revolution, when the French nobles in their growing uneasiness were thrown back more and more upon their past, and the interest became even livelier (Baldensperger, *Le Genre troubadour. Études d'hist. littéraire*, I, 1907). As we have already seen, Boulainvilliers in the early part of the century was a witness to this traditionalist attention to the values of aristocracy, and Montesquieu in his own particular way also fostered this interest. Even before the appearance of his *Esprit des lois*, De la Curne de Sainte Palaye had been concerned with the collecting of troubadour songs. He had begun with a grandiose rehabilitation of the honour of mediaeval knighthood; and in November 1746 he produced in the *Académie des inscriptions et belles lettres* the first of his five *Mémoires sur l'ancienne chevalerie* (they then appeared in vol. 20 of the *Mémoires de littérature* of the gen. Akademie, 1753). This was a remarkable book, full of material, and the work of a very well-read man. He looked at chivalry as it were through the spectacles of a nobleman in the Rococo period with a chivalrous outlook. He took a fervent delight in glorifying all its achievements, institutions and virtues, and ended by expressing

fanciful treatment of his material was more sharply expressed in his later utterances on this subject.

regret that the ancient knights of those ignorant and barbarous times could not have had 'the cultured mind nurtured in reason', by virtue of which they could have become ideal men, superior even to those envisaged by Plato. 'They loved glory, but they did not know the true glory.' Thus he could not altogether cut loose from the timeless standards of reason cherished by the Enlightenment. But we shall see how he was able to influence English thought, and by that means exercise an indirect effect upon Germany too, including Herder.

And so since the middle of the eighteenth century, France too had had a revival of popularity in the chivalry of the Middle Ages as represented in literature and artistic taste, alongside the material from other countries which had hitherto been the most popular. Whether this fashion can already be called Pre-Romantic depends upon the degree to which there might be some real feeling for this new atmosphere—though it must be admitted that this was in fact mostly lacking. But a group of younger poets, who since 1760 had been in revolt against the philosophy of the Enlightenment, and who shared a strict Catholic faith, or traditionalist theocratic outlook, and a lively subjectivity, can be rightly regarded as a genuine prelude to the later Catholic French Romanticism (cf. Kurt Wais, *Das anti-philosophische Weltbild des französischen Sturm und Drang*, 1934).[1]

Living far apart from one another in the country, these young poets were not in a position to exercise any central influence on French intellectual life. On the fringe of this movement there was an achievement which did not so much affect France as the nordic countries, and acted almost like the discovery of a new and unknown world. This was the book written by the young Genevan Mallet, *Introduction à l'histoire de Dannemarc* (1755), which opened up the world of wonder and giants to be found in the Edda and the ancient heroic nordic sagas. He had come to Copenhagen, and there he put together in an orderly form what the antiquarians of the seventeenth and early eighteenth centuries had collected and suggested by way of conjecture.[2] We are not concerned here with what he derived from them and their sources (Snorro Sturleson and others) about the

---

[1] It seems surprising that Wais, who ventures to transfer the term 'Sturm und Drang' to the French movement discovered by him, yet rejects the term 'Pre-Romantics' for the movements of the eighteenth century which preceded the real Romanticism of the early nineteenth century. We cannot dispense with such concepts, however loose they may be, if we want to grasp the connecting links between different individual structures. Pre-Romantic is no more to be equated with Romantic than Pre-Raphaelite with Raphael; nevertheless, from the historical point of view they are closely connected.

[2] For the connections between Mallet's work and the Norse renaissance in Denmark, cf. Leopold Magon, *Ein Jahrhundert geistiger und literarischer Beziehungen zwischen Deutschland und Skandinavien 1750–1850*, I, 1926.

actual facts of ancient nordic history, and the possible origins of King Odin and his Ases, or Asiatics in Asia. But he also looked at this world in a new light, and saw a genuine history behind the fabulous material of the sagas. This new point of view was reached not only through the guidance of Montesquieu, for whom he had the greatest respect, but also through his own attitude, which certainly amounted to what could already be called a gift of empathy for this kind of research. Yet he remained essentially a man of the Enlightenment, who held fast to the basic belief in Natural Law and the universal equality of human nature, and supported the enlightened reason of his own day against the monstrous errors of rude primitive times. Moreover, he adopted Montesquieu's bold policy of looking everywhere for causes, and deriving manifold variety from the simplest initial principles. Even his interest in nordic history was linked up with Montesquieu's celebrated saying that the origins of English freedom went back to the forests of Germania, and to his verdict on the solid virtues produced by a northern climate (*Esprit*, 14, 2). Mallet's particular outlook, which had already been approximately achieved by others too, now led for the first time into a mixed world of principles based on Natural Law, doctrines derived from Montesquieu, and prejudices dear to the heart of the antiquary, namely the opinion that the originally good monotheism of primitive times had nowhere retained its purity, but had left its most substantial mark in the north, where the climate helped to restrain the passions. But his own independent achievement, which can still be valued in the light of present-day knowledge, was the discovery of a specific ancient nordic human culture. True, Mallet, as a son of the Enlightenment, followed its manifestations at a certain distance; but there was nevertheless a growing delight in following all its details and so building up a well-rounded colourful picture of the ancient nordic life and its time, a picture which, as far as we know, had never been sketched in such individual detail by any contemporary writer. Mallet was indeed a pioneer in the art which Jacob Burckhardt was to bring to perfection a century later. His picture of the nordic peoples represented them as full-blooded, with strong nerves, not easily roused, though passionate when thoroughly stirred; but otherwise inclined to be phlegmatic and indolent; revolting against all arbitrary authority, open-hearted and even generous from self-confidence; and disinclined for everything that demanded more patience than action. Only war gave them the excitement they needed, and stamped their religion, their laws, their prejudices and their enthusiasms (pp. 250 ff.). In Mallet's view (an amplification of Tacitus), there was a profound difference between northern and southern peoples in their attitude to women; and it was probable that the northern nations had contributed most to the spirit of moderation and chivalry in relation to women (in short, the knightly temper and its taste for gallantry) as they spread and settled all over Western Europe (pp. 197 ff.). The mingling of conqueror and conquered had, in Mallet's view, produced the customs and the general ethos that still held sway over Europe (p. 6).

This outlook was also based on methodical reflection upon the proper task of the historian, for which both Montesquieu and Voltaire had given the impulse. Moreover, it shows how fruitful could be the fashionable curiosity about the 'spirit and customs' of a nation, which they both helped to popularise, when it was not applied with any feeling of enlightened superiority, but with genuine historical sympathy. This was how he set out his programme in the preface to his book: to portray the actions of peoples, princes, conquerors and lawgivers, without knowing the thoughts, the character and the spirit that inspired them, would be merely to present a skeleton history, and to watch dumb wandering shades moving about in darkness, instead of living and speaking with men. Only by combining the two, political and military history with the history of customs and opinions, would it be possible to arrive at the *corps d'histoire véritablement utile et complet* (p. 35). In practice, as we saw in Voltaire's case and shall see again subsequently, all the great historians of the Enlightenment attempted this combination, though they only succeeded in setting the two elements side by side, rather than combining them into a whole. In Mallet's words there is already a suggestion that some such combination would be necessary in order to bring political and military history to life as well. He himself was not capable of effecting it, and he continued to treat the factual content of traditional history quite uncritically and pragmatically. But he succeeded in achieving a true and accurate insight into the new world opening up before him, an insight whose methods were destined to have far-reaching influence. 'The most credulous author, however much he may distort the history of his century through a bias towards the marvellous, does nevertheless give us a picture of it without meaning to do so.' So it was possible and necessary, he held, to use even the most fanciful poets of ancient times as material for history, for they 'unwittingly' reflected the thought and customs of their age (pp. 35 f.). Thus an insight arrived at by Vico came to life again at this later stage.

There must have been some special enthusiasm at work in the mind of this young Genevan, who had drifted so far North; as this new world suddenly opened up before him, in order to make it possible, in spite of the dominance of the idea of Natural Law in the outlook of the Enlightenment, to effect a breakthrough in historical thought, at least in this one particular place. As far as France was concerned, the appearance of this book in Copenhagen seems to have had practically no effect; but it was otherwise in England and Germany, where it aroused a fashionable mania for things northern, and filled the poets with new enthusiasm for nordic subjects. And so the youthful Herder's wish, which he expressed in 1765 when he called attention to a German translation of Mallet's book (*Works*, 3, 73 ff.), 'that the book might become the armoury for a new German genius', was in fact fulfilled. Later on (1778, 8, 390), when he came to know more about Mallet's original nordic source-material, he was more critical about his over-painting of the picture. But there can be no doubt that Herder was powerfully stirred by the book. Goethe knew it too (*Dicht. u. Wahrh.*, III, 12). External and theatrical as this literary fashion set by Mallet may have been, it yet contributed to loosening up the framework of thought in the Enlightenment, and preparing the way for a historical sense of the individual.

In France, however, the Enlightenment was moving with almost logical necessity towards its greatest and most fatal victory in the French Revolution of 1789. Here was the most hotly-disputed territory; here was a society in a state of intellectual and social excitement, kept away from the political power of the state and filled with the strongest desire to conquer it; here, then, we should expect the drama of history to be at its most lively. But the same abstract principles of an unalterable Natural Law, now turned into an effective instrument of universal struggle, froze history and historical thought into a fixed and static state.

A representative of this double tendency now at work in the *Esprit classique* is to be found in the small guide to the writing of history entitled *De la Manière d'écrire l'histoire*, published in 1783 by that prolific writer the Abbé de Mably.[1] He laid it down in this book that the most important requirement for the writing of history was a knowledge of Natural Law (*droit naturel*), without which there was no standard for judging right and wrong in the events of history. He held that it was the historian's business to depict the struggles of vice with virtue, and the frequent temporary victories of vice, but also the constant counter-attacks by virtue that ensued. The Abbé was disposed to place more value upon this kind of ability to pronounce

[1] A German translation by Salzmann of Strassburg, with a foreword by Schlözer, appeared in 1784. An earlier work by Mably, *De l'Étude de l'histoire à Monseigneur le Prince de Parme* (Nouv. éd., 1778), treated history, in the frivolous fashion common during the Enlightenment, as a collection of examples for princes, and as a warning to carry through measures of *égalité* in their respective States. For further information on the rationalistic or materialistic historians of France before and during the Revolution see Bach, 'Entwicklung der französischen Geschichtsauffassung im 18. Jahrhundert', thesis, Freiburg, 1932.

judgements than he was upon the qualifications of erudition. He pontificated in the most presumptuous way against the whole historical writings of the Enlightenment, from Voltaire to Gibbon. It was all superficial chatter. The Abbé showed not the smallest trace of any contact with those slight Pre-Romantic stirrings of the spirit which we have been exploring. The fact that he does not even mention them in order to criticise them shows how little they had so far penetrated the world of thought. It was reserved for the German mind to take them up and deepen them, and to give the decisive direction to historical thought.

Chapter five

Enlightenment Historiography in England

England was the mother country of the Enlightenment, which aimed essentially at proving its new human ideals not only through pure reason, but also by finding them in history seen through the eyes of reason. As a result the new outlook on history created in this way became the prelude to what historism was later to develop step by step. Both Voltaire and Montesquieu were strongly influenced by England. When considering their historical standpoint we pointed out the stage at which they came to the end of the means of knowledge available to the Enlightenment, and new solutions were being prepared beneath the surface. A contribution to these new solutions had been made at an earlier date by the Platonic doctrines of Shaftesbury, though for a long while it remained practically unused. But now in the middle and the second half of the eighteenth century historical writing in England reached a high point of development through the labours of David Hume, Edward Gibbon and William Robertson.[1] But their inspiration was not Shaftesbury, with his emphasis on the formative principle latent within all living structures, but Locke, the founder of the sensualist and empirical wing of the Enlightenment. Even from this standpoint, as we suggested in our discussion of Shaftesbury, it was possible to discover new territory in the search for historical knowledge. It proved feasible to go beyond the framework of Natural Law in explaining historical material, by critically probing man's inward intellectual and spiritual life as it

[1] We shall likewise leave on one side the great English collective undertaking, the *Universal History from the Earliest Account of the Time to the Present*, 1736 ff., as well as its later German versions in various different revisions. In the inclusion of all the non-Christian peoples, it was indeed carrying out a fundamental idea of the Enlightenment, but it remained almost entirely on the factual level. Cf. F. Borkenau-Pollak, 'A Universal History of the World, etc.', typescript thesis, Leipzig, 1924.

156

really was and showed itself in history. It will now become clear to us whether this critical probing was in every respect adequate, as we see how these Englishmen set about with unusual energy to discover new ways of acquiring knowledge of the past and putting it to good use. We shall take for fuller analysis the work of David Hume (1711–76), because it rests upon the strongest intellectual basis and the greatest variety of motives. But we must also grasp the essential features of Gibbon's and Robertson's conceptions of history in order to understand the strong and the weak points in the English historical writing of the Enlightenment, and see to what extent it was limited by contemporary conditions, and to what extent it was forward-looking as well.

I Hume

With Hume, the construction of a philosophy preceded his writing of history. It represented the work of a young man of genius, for he did not add to it at all in later years.

In 1739–40 there appeared his great achievement, *A Treatise of Human Nature*, but it was scarcely noticed by his contemporaries. Then in 1748 came the definitive work, to which he subsequently gave the title *An Enquiry Concerning Human Understanding*, and which became so famous. His various collections of essays, appearing between 1741 and 1752, broke new ground in the historical world; and when he became librarian in Edinburgh, it was to this that he devoted his chief energies till 1762.

Even as a pure philosopher, Hume had begun to pass beyond the bounds of the Enlightenment. He always remained a son of the Enlightenment, and wherever we hear him passing judgement upon the human material of history, we still catch the voice of the old stable, non-progressive reason, 'grounded in the nature of things, eternal and unyielding' (*Enquiry Concerning the Principle of Morals*). But his great achievement was to produce a notable limitation to its sphere of action by denying its creative character, and only allotting it the task of separating truth from error; and then to proceed to examine and purify the deep-seated creative sources of 'sentiment' and 'taste' that arise in the human being. There is a clear connection here with Shaftesbury; and as he was also a historical thinker, he would have been the very man to take the decisive step and to recognise the creative powers of the mind as also individual powers, if only his 'reason' had not still been bound down by thinking based upon Natural Law. He did not effect the breakthrough to an experience of the whole psyche, to a full consciousness of its total make-up, together with its individual content. His intellectualism only allowed him to discover the positive meaning of the soul's irrational powers, and focus them more accurately, so revealing the limits of what was possible to reason. He showed that the indispensable background for reason, without which it was incapable of passing judgment on life, was observation and experience. As his experience grew, he saw the factual content of reason in men change and undergo purification. But this process, which was definitely one of purification rather than of development, could only approximate to the ideal of a fully cleansed reason, because of the innate and incurable weakness of human nature, which he was never tired of emphasising. And so there came about in this profound and extremely honest thinker a quite peculiar blend of trust in reason and scepticism, each of which imposed certain limitations upon the other. He relied on reason, and could yet be sceptical about any one of its pronouncements, because experience taught him that it could be obscured by ineradicable human weakness. As the ethos of his nature developed he tended to be ruthless in showing up these weaknesses, and yet to go on believing firmly and cheerfully in the goodness in mankind.

With the help of this reason drawn from experience, he applied three incisive criticisms, which not only shattered the prop that had hitherto supported rationalism, but also influenced historical thought, sometimes by way of restriction, and sometimes by way of advance. These were the criticism of the concept of substance; the criticism of the law of causality, and the criticism of natural theology. We shall have cause to go into this last in some detail. Hume's attempt to destroy the concept of substance shows with particular clarity that he had not yet had an experience of the totality of psychological life. For he even split up the substance of personality into a mere bundle of sensations and images (as someone has remarked) and so created a psychology without a soul, whereby the irrational psychological forces, which he himself described as creative, were turned into mere complexes. The fact that they nevertheless remained creative and meaningful seemed to him to be one of those mysteries of wise nature impenetrable to human understanding (cf. *Human Understanding*, V, 2).

This dissolution of the substance of personality was to have an effect on historical thought, as we shall presently see; it acted like an over-powerful dissolving acid. But his criticism of the law of causality was certainly of service to all later historical thought. Kant was to take it up subsequently at a deeper level. Hume denied that it possessed the character of necessity, and derived it from the habit of seeing the same recurrent sequence of events always connected with one another. Henceforward, anyone who made this criticism his own was likely to be freed from the stultifying notion that all human life and action was controlled by blind mechanical necessity, and could be on the look-out for other inner connecting links in the life of history. This was to become evident later on in Herder. Hume himself, starting out from a sober and sceptical empiricism, did not as yet feel this need. In practice, he restored what he had destroyed as a matter of theory by the doctrine that we could nevertheless believe in the undemonstrable law of cause and effect because this belief has been implanted in us as an instinct by the wisdom of nature, and gives us practical certainty. For Hume was always thoroughly English in being at one and the same time empirical and utilitarian in outlook. He was always ready to tone down any consequences of his views and even his ideals that threatened to be dangerous, and to accommodate them to the necessities of life as he understood them. At all points his endeavour was to observe the facts carefully, conscientiously, and without partisanship, and quietly to assess their usefulness or harmfulness for his ethical and political ideals. And so he was able to look out on the world of history with much more freedom and less prejudice than the average rationalist of the Enlightenment. Yet the genuine feeling for life belonging to the Enlightenment remained almost unbroken in him, the feeling that the life of humanity had reached a peak, and that reason was of practical usefulness for everything calculated to sustain life at this high level. Even fictions and irrational things could be useful for this purpose. In this study of both the irrational and the sub-rational spheres in man and in history, Hume came into direct touch with the thought of Montesquieu, whose *Esprit des lois* he valued very highly, and with whom he also corresponded. He and Montesquieu can be placed in the first rank of those who, using the means available during the Enlightenment period, made as much progress as was then possible in acquiring a really understanding grasp of the historical world. But it must be added that they were only able to do so because behind the utilitarianism they used to justify their historical interest there lay a natural inclination to rejoice in the richness of the human scene, the *variety of mankind*, to use Hume's own language. In possessing this, they had the essentially charismatic outlook that belongs to all true historians. In his essay on the study of history, Hume says that there can surely be no more splendid spectacle than that of the human race, seen in its true colours, and without disguise. And he even quotes, as first and foremost among the advantages brought by this study, that it *amuses the fancy*. In discussing the two other advantages of historical study, he also included the intellectual and moral advantages, that it *improves the understanding* and *strengthens virtue.* Along with other more commonplace thoughts such as those plentifully scattered throughout Bolingbroke's *Letters on the Study and Use of History* (1735), Hume added a note of deeper historical understanding. He was perhaps one of the first to become aware that modern learning at its best is historical learning. True, he was only able to express this somewhat pedantically by saying that a large part of our so highly prized erudition is nothing but acquaintance with historical facts. He went on to say that we should remain children in understanding if we did not possess the experience of all past ages and nations. A man well versed in history could, he maintained, feel as though he had been alive since the very beginning of the world. And finally, he expected history to have more powerful moral effects than either poetry or philosophy.

It is clear, then, how important the writing of history was for Hume in the total setting of his life's work; in fact he considered it of almost equal importance with his philosophy. Admittedly, his philosophy had a stronger influence than his historical writing on the further development of thought. It may be said with Kant that Hume aroused men from a dogmatic slumber, and spurred them on to attempt new solutions to ancient philosophical questions. His historical writing, on the other hand, in spite of all the great qualities imparted to it by his specific methods, remained bound down by the limitations of Natural Law. He was still in the grip of the old fundamental prejudice, recently revived by Locke, that human nature had remained the same in all ages. He says in the *Enquiry Concerning Human Understanding* (VIII, 1):

> Would you know the sentiments, inclinations, and course of life of the Greeks and Romans? Study well the temper and actions of the French and English: You cannot be much mistaken in transferring to the former *most* of the observations which you have made with regard to the latter. Mankind are so much the same, in all times and places, that history informs us of nothing new or strange in this particular.

Thus what was to be learnt from history could, in the nature of the case, not be anything individual, but only typical and general. True, history does always contain plenty of the latter, but it does not suffice for an understanding at depth. His own natural and so-to-speak naive feeling for the *variety of mankind* might nevertheless have been able to produce extremely lively pictures of the persons and features of the past, as all the great genuine historians have done. He even once made a minor theoretical attempt to turn aside into the paths of Shaftesbury, and in his essay, *The Sceptic*, spoke of *the particular fabric or structure of the mind*, which indubitably led to dif-

160

ferent appreciations of beauty and value. And in his *Enquiry Concerning the Principles of Morals*, Sect. VIII, he spoke of mysterious and inexplicable psychological qualities possessed by many a man—an *I-know-not-what* in them. But he did not follow up this idea, which would have led on to a problem of individuality. His own conscious bent was far more towards making the highly moving spectacle of human culture in all its manifold variety intelligible in terms of general laws, and not through considering the individual. He once wrote in *A Dialogue* that the Rhine flows northwards, and the Rhône southwards; yet both rise in the same mountains, and the opposite directions they take are governed by the same law of gravity. The differences of inclination in the ground they flow through is also responsible for all the differences in their flow. In the same way, he held, the moral value-judgements and inclinations of the different nations vary; but there is no variability in the first principle, the original ideas of what is worth pursuing. To be sure, Hume was careful to concede that not everything could be traced back to general rules. But in the exceptions, he only saw chance at work; and for him, chance was only another word for causes that were as yet undetermined. And so the task seemed to him to be 'to find a guiding thread through human nature, and so be able to disentangle all its confusions'. He goes on to say, in the section of his most famous work we have already quoted:

> But were there no uniformity in human actions, and were every experiment, which we could form of this kind, irregular and anomalous, it were impossible to collect any general observations concerning mankind; and no experience, however accurately digested by reflection, would ever serve to any purpose.

And so, according to Hume, what was required for a knowledge of history was a psychology of the typical in human nature. As he says in his essay *Of National Characters*, nature in her abundance could mix the same ingredients with the greatest degree of variety. Yet they remained the same, and the organ that scrutinised them remained the self-same reason. For in spite of Hume's searching disclosure of the elements of observation and experience embodied in it, and in spite of the human failings that often obscured it, reason did not lose the stable and timeless character it had always possessed in his eyes. Yet it did not prevent him from making the typical mistakes of the historians during the Enlightenment period, namely over-hasty generalisation and an inclination to see everywhere cause and effect. But his dissolution of man's intellectual make-up into a bundle of ideas led to the transformation of the whole life and history of the universe into a countless number of psychological complexes controlled by general laws. Hume has been rightly called one of the fathers of modern positivism. As Dilthey once remarked (*Schriften*, 2, 358), he introduced that trend of positivism which, in contrast to the French writers Turgot and Condorcet, derived its regularities not from the external world, but from inner experience. But this inner experience did not penetrate to the psychological depths. When worked with Hume's tools, the material of experience could not yield what it proved able to do subsequently in other hands. Such material remained in the category of unchanging reason, bound down under the limitations of mechanical causality, and so could only disclose a part of its content, and no more than the foreground of events. It could reveal only in part, and nothing as a whole—except where wholeness positively forced itself upon his attention.

We ourselves should only be dealing with parts, and not with wholes, if we were to rest content, in our effort to make Hume's interpretation of history generally intelligible, with what has so far been set out on his tendencies and the pattern of his thought. All intellectual theories are the product of personality and experience, the particular experience undergone by a personality of a specific kind at a particular moment of time, which is then impregnated with all the life of past history available in that particular cultural milieu. We have already gathered a general idea of Hume's inheritance and cast of mind. There was a strong tradition of Natural Law based upon reason, considerably loosened up by Hume's sceptical empiricism, yet by no means fundamentally rejected; and there was a somewhat narrow alliance between simple experience and critical reason, which he put at the disposal of mankind by means of a psychology dealing in nothing but general laws. But this abstract picture at once comes to life as soon as we are confronted with Hume's actual experience as a British citizen in the middle of the eighteenth century. His essays and his *History of England* are soaked through and through with an experience full of great concreteness, and penetrated with individual feeling. The substance may be briefly summarised as follows. Life in England today enjoys greater advantages than have been previously enjoyed by any nation in any age. In the whole of the world's history (*Of the Protestant Succession*) there has never been a time when so many millions have had a life suitable to the dignity of human nature. We have a quite unusual and most fortunate form of government, public liberty, and yet a healthy balance between authority and freedom, which prevents the latter from running to excess; freedom of thought and an unfanatical mental outlook; personal security, prosperity and wealth through trade and industry, and refinement in the arts and sciences, which springs from intellectual culture. And all these—'industry, knowledge and humanity, are linked together by an indissoluble chain'; they help one another, and depend on the social support of 'that middling rank of men, who are the best and firmest basis of public liberty' (*Of Refinement in the Arts*, as well as numerous passages in the other essays and in the *History*). Though Hume shared in this proud optimism, he was too profound and serious a thinker to go all the way with it. He saw shadows in the picture, albeit not the same ones we should note today when we remember Walpole's system of corruption, and still more, the social and economic revolution that was just beginning to make itself felt. The Englishman of that time did not concern himself very much with this as yet, and Hume, as a representative of the rising middle classes, was inclined to direct his social attention more to the upper than the lower levels. He was concerned, though, about the apparently harmful effects of the rising National Debt, as well as the continued existence of latent sympathies for the Stuarts. Guided, though not altogether dominated, by the traditional cyclic theory of history, he saw the regular procession of rise, prosperity and decline at work and judged there must also come a time in England when the soil would be exhausted. But this was not his deepest concern. His originality as a thinker and his propensities for greatness as a historian are shown rather by the inclination of his mind towards the past, and to the question imperatively and unerringly pressed upon him by the urge for truth, the question as to how this rare and fortunate state of affairs had come about in England. All his historical writings—not only the *History of England* but also the *Natural History of Religion* and even the great essay dealing with the history of population, *Of the Populousness of Ancient Nations* —may be regarded as tacitly guided by this underlying question.

The result of his researches turned out to be the remarkable fact, which he was never tired of confronting, that the origins of the present English *liberty* were to be found in something highly repugnant to his nature—in the religious enthusiasm of the Puritans. Hume says in his *History* (1762 ed., 4, 125) that the authority of the crown was so absolute in Elizabeth's time that the precious flame of freedom could only be kindled and kept alight by the Puritans. It was to this sect, whose principles seemed so *frivolous* and whose customs appeared so ridiculous, that Englishmen owed the whole of their constitutional freedom. Even in James I's day, things were so difficult that the patriots would have despaired of continuing their struggle against the crown if they had not been impelled by religious motives, inspiring them with a courage that was triumphant over any kind of human opposition (5, 74). He then declines to accept a comparison between Pym and Hampden, the protagonists of freedom, and the heroes who upheld liberty in ancient times. For the latter, he held (5, 259 ff.), were men of high culture, whereas these Englishmen were besmirched with the lowest and most vulgar hypocrisies, and used a mysterious jargon. This was 'the deep draught of intoxicating poison' (5, 295), which, in the revolution of 1641, drove all classes to the wildest excesses, overthrew the most stable political institutions, and yet produced, as its final result, the Englishman's freedom.

Historism later on sought to understand these powerful phenomena, with their destructive and creative aspects, in terms of the development of inner individual powers, though these also correspond to certain broad types. Hume took them as a challenge to discover the basis for a psychology of the human soul, and to use this experience for the formulation of certain general and permanently valid doctrines. His first collection of essays published in 1741 already contains the essay *Of Superstition and Enthusiasm*, which extended the special historical picture of an Englishman who was a representative of the Enlightenment and a friend of freedom to form a picture of general religious psychology. He begins by reminding us of the old truth, *corruptio optimi pessima*, and applies it to the harmful effects of superstition and enthusiasm, which are corruptions of true religion. But this psychology is of a conflicting nature. Superstition grows out of terror and fear of unknown powers, which are then imagined; and this is added to by weakness, melancholy and ignorance. But by the same token there is also a human disposition that leads through unwarranted arrogance, luxurious well-being, and stubbornness of spirit, to the error of enthusiasm. Here, too, the imagination gets to work and dreams of things—particularly direct divine promptings, which are not in accord with any beauties or joys of this world. In this way ignorance is wedded to hope, pride, presumption and imagination. But now there emerges a quite different relationship, that of superstition and enthusiasm to priestcraft. Superstition is the real soil in which it grows; and the stronger the element of superstition in a particular religion, the higher the authority of the priestly body, whilst enthusiasm is just as far, and usually rather further, alien to their authority as are sound reason and philosophy. For the enthusiast has no need of any human mediator between himself and the divinity. By means of comparison with other analogous movements in the history of religion, such as the Anabaptists in Germany, the Camisards in France, the Levellers and Covenanters in England and Scotland, Hume then draws the further conclusion that when they first arise, the enthusiast religions are indeed more virulent and violent than the superstitious ones, though after a short time they tend to become milder and more moderate. Their violence was like that of the thunderstorm, which works itself out and then leaves the air calmer and fresher than it was before; whilst, on the other hand, superstition creeps in unnoticed and little by little, and prepares men for the tyranny of priestcraft. This led Hume on to a third and last conclusion, which was this: superstition is an enemy of civic freedom, but enthusiasm is well disposed towards it. The Independents and the Deists in England were sharply opposed in their religious principles, but nevertheless united in their enthusiasm for the Commonwealth.

Political liberty and enlightenment as the fruit of the most violent upheavals and the most dubious and erroneous human courses of belief and action—this was perhaps the historical experience on which the whole of Hume's psychology was based. But his historical thought and research were nothing more nor less than applied psychology. More precisely, they were an attempt to confirm his picture of human nature through history. The transformation by which Puritan enthusiasm turned into English enlightenment and parliamentary freedom served Hume as an experimental scientific proof of the working out of cause and effect in certain specific religious phenomena. One cannot call this development in the historical sense, for there is no mention of any developing substance which constitutes it, the individual human being in his totality, and the community that has grown up out of such material. Hume's interest was centred rather on particular and separate human qualities and dispositions looked at in isolation; he breaks man up into bundles of ideas and strivings and he does the same with religious history. It becomes a kind of meteorology, in which regularly recurrent sequences may be explained in terms of cause and effect only to the extent that a sceptical and cautious observer ventures to do so. But all enquiry into cause and effect in history, from whatever standpoint it is pursued, is interfused with certain values that are both a help and a hindrance to it. Here, the hindrance is clear enough. Hume assumes the existence of a 'true religion', namely the deistic approach of a purified reason, and uses it as a standard by which to proclaim regretfully that all other religion, which is full of superstition or enthusiasm, is nothing more than corruption. His prejudiced outlook upon value prevented him as yet from asking the deeper historical question whether what he was pleased to call superstition and enthusiasm did not also contain a something essential to every religion. Even the wonderful and striking transformation of the English spirit, which led from enthusiasm to enlightenment, remained in his eyes nothing more than an incident of psychological reassurance. This kind of meteorological psychology was all he apparently needed to reassure him in a general way about the mysteries of human nature and history.

Hume once expressed the fine thought that the human heart is made to reconcile contradictions (*Of the Parties of Great Britain*). It is a thought that lay on the fringe of his own awareness; but it remained as far as he was concerned no more than an amiable empirical statement; he did not go on to use it as a key to the psychological make-up of man as a whole. The essay *Of Superstition and Enthusiasm* became the germ-cell for his famous *Natural History of Religion* (1757). This went far beyond the bare confrontation of two religious types, and asked the much deeper question of the general origin of religion in human nature, since it did not appear to have arisen, like self-regard, the sexual urge, love for one's children, gratitude and so on, from an original instinct or from some directly natural influence. Yet there were peoples (if one could trust what travellers and historians had related) entirely without religious concepts. By approaching the matter in this way, and making religion a particular phenomenon within the human race, though apparently embracing the majority of mankind, Hume set religion apart from morals at the outset (clearly to its disadvantage), for he based morality upon a universal human disposition deeply rooted in feeling (*Enquiry Concerning the Principles of Morals*). So it only remained to him to explain religion in causal terms, as a secondary product of specific psychic factors, and linked up with specific stages of culture. He taught that polytheism or the worship of idols was necessarily the first and most ancient religion. Man was a creature who lived in a state of anxiety, impelled by desires and passions, incapable as yet of tracing cause and effect and so by reflection arriving at belief in some higher being. He was a creature who hovered between fear and hope, who saw the unknown causes of his good and ill fortune as beings of a human kind, but possessed of more than human power and cunning, who were to be worshipped in fear and trembling. Thus far Hume's thought showed connections with Vico's deeper psychology of primitive man; but its further developments were along pragmatic lines. In the long run (so Hume taught), these ideas proved insufficient for humanity; and the exaggerated glorification of these beings finally focused in the picture of a single almighty and eternal deity. But this theism, born of sensual motives, superstitious fear and self-abasement, possessed no guarantee of permanence, and could easily sink back into idolatry, raise itself once more above that level, and then once again go into decline. It is characteristic of his distaste for the theological conceptions of God that in many respects he preferred polytheism as practised by the Greeks and Romans. In Hume's view, the doctrine of monotheism led to intolerance of other religions, whilst all idol-worshippers, he held, possessed a certain spirit of accommodation. In a milder form, presented as a contrast between tolerant heathenism and an intolerant priestcraft, this notion became the common property of a rationalist interpretation of history; and even Herder did not altogether avoid it. Hume, however, combined it with another value-judgment that runs through the centuries. He fell back on Machiavelli's doctrine of the slavish effects of Christianity, and in contrast to this considered the mythologies of the ancient world not altogether devoid of sense. For this world of the gods, connected with man's own sensual and reasonable nature, only of finer stuff and more powerful than man, bore such a natural look that it might well have seemed to men to be more than likely. It was a poetical religion, full of light, brightness and encouragement.

This view has something of a slight historical sympathy about it, though it is by no means a romantic longing for the gods of Greece. It was a prelude to many a subsequent attitude, up to the time of Nietzsche and the present day, all of them somehow linked up with the spirit of the Enlightenment. But the most immediate religious expression of the latter was deism, the rational conception of God. This was nothing but a loose abstract superstructure to suit the severely law-abiding nature of the universe, decked out with the predicates of unfathomable wisdom and reason, but out of the reach of all genuine religious contact. The feeling of the Enlightenment for strict causality, and its pragmatic need for the presumption of ends and purposes behind the order of things, were linked together in deism in a somewhat external and inorganic fashion. Hume represented this deism in holding it natural, if not absolutely necessary, to conclude from the unity prevailing in the universe that there must be one single and undivided world intelligence. But he gave this deism a new direction, which pierced the thinking based upon Natural Law at a new point; though once again, as was thoroughly characteristic of Hume, he did it without himself becoming altogether liberated from the restrictions of this outlook.

Deism so far, as represented by Herbert of Cherbury, had been constructed purely on a basis of Natural Law, that is to say, it believed there was a natural and reasonable basis for belief in one God. This was part of the eternal content of the truths of reason. It might at any time be obscured by decay or distortion, but always came to life again as soon as reason was once more victorious. But now Hume came on the scene with his powerful and devastating demonstration that the monotheism of the nations of whose history we have any knowledge did not arise from the light of reason, but out of the darkness of idolatry, out of the obscure welter of anxiety, struggle, fear and vengefulness characteristic of early man. This view not only struck at belief in the Christian revelation in Jesus Christ, but also at the ancient world's belief in a timeless and stable human

167

reason always at work in the world. Man (according to Hume) had only risen by gradual stages from the lower to the higher.

This seemed to open the door wide to a natural history of the human mind and spirit in terms of development, tracing the advance from barbarism to culture. And in actual fact, this work of Hume's did produce an immeasurable effect. But we must notice the limitations in this progressive thought which prevented it from demonstrating development in the sense belonging to the later outlook of historism. The deepest and strongest limitation lay in his psychology, which spoke only of mental constituents and their mechanical interaction, but never of mental wholes which were capable of developing out of some central point deep down in the individual. Only in Hume's sympathetic judgement of Greek religion did we catch sight of a breath of real historical insight and an individualising approach. For the rest, however, we could only discern in his picture of development the interplay of the same human emotions and impulses that can be explained in terms of law as action and counteraction, periodic increase and decrease. The timeless activity of a stable reason was here replaced by the timeless activity of unvarying impulses and passions. This was a much more dynamic picture, and to that extent nearer to historical reality than the pictures controlled exclusively by Natural Law. Moreover, it gave a true account of many typical developments in the history of religion. But apart from that one small exception, the individual nature in its specific appearances and phenomena remained unnoticed and uncomprehended, even as it had been by Natural Law. To this extent we can speak here of a residuum of this pattern of thought.

Moreover, as we have already implied, Hume was not able to carry through his own developmental thought with any thoroughness. Mankind, as we have seen, was only to progress by gradual stages from the lower to the higher. But we are also told that polytheism and theism (the theism, mark you, of the historical religions) constantly fluctuate in history, yet not with a gradual upward movement, but rather in a series of gradual ups and downs. This was a recurrence of the old cyclic theory, the return of the same material in history; and this again was a residuum of the Natural Law pattern of thought, with its general belief not only in the stable nature of reason, but also in the timeless similarity of human nature.

And now for the third residuum. Hume considered the theism of the positive religions so loose and unstable, because it was only supported by the unreasonable and superstitious beliefs of the masses. He showed with reference to belief in Jehovah that these religions only arrived as it were by chance at a state of correspondence with the basic principles of reason, although the way followed was one of the narrowest possible subservience. This was why it seemed to him so easy for theism to sink back again into polytheism. In Hume's view, then, there was a deep gulf between the irrational and the rational kind of theism, or, as we must now call it for the sake of clarity, deism, as known to Hume's contemporaries. It goes without saying that in making this distinction he counted the philosophers of the ancient world on his side. But the number of these, even in his own time, he reckoned as astonishingly small. The great mass were, in his view, ignorant and unenlightened: the whole of mankind, in fact, with very few exceptions. It was granted to these few to be able to arrive by a process of logical argument at the existence of an invisible but rational power. In the face of his own scepticism (as is further shown by his Dialogues on Natural Religion) this recognition was not a complete certainty, but the only one that it was possible to attain along rational lines of thought. The reason that was his guide at this point was none other, however, than the stable reason of Natural Law, which must always pronounce the same truths, insofar as it could be set free from all the disturbances produced by the senses and the emotions. Hume's discovery of the sphere of action occupied by the irrational and sub-rational forces had the effect of confining the province of this reason in history to an almost epoch-making extent, but it did not affect its essential qualities. He may be said to have transcended rationalism in a quantitative, though not in a qualitative, manner—or only qualitative to the extent that he introduced into the thought of his own day a thorn of doubt as to the theory of the available means of knowing.

His deism, which he held to be the only 'true religion', was not indeed a genuine religion, but a matter of knowledge. At a deeper level, one would not deny that from his youth onwards the restless searching, questioning and doubting, and the dubious affirmations, had something genuinely religious about them; but at a conscious level, Hume held that religion was not even necessary for the conduct of one's life. He was satisfied with morality, which he held to be the primary possession of human nature. Yet in conclusion he could pronounce (though not quite in accordance with his thoughts at the outset) that a people with no religion of any kind, if such were ever discovered, would be little above the animal level.

Thus his inner aversion to the positive religions did not prevent him from admitting that they were the bonds of society, albeit extremely imperfect ones. His utilitarianism and penetrating feeling for the weaknesses and imperfections of man could not but admit as much, which saved him from becoming a hater of the human race. Although he had consigned all the ancient conceptions of Stoicism and Natural Law to the sphere of naturalistic psychology, he still believed in innate moral feelings in humanity (though these remained in the first place mixed and polluted), feelings which were gradually purified by reason in accordance with the principles of social progress. It is typical of the basic trend of his character, and its firm anchorage in the English character, that Hume was most strongly captivated not by the problems of individual ethics and the moral personality, but by those of social ethics. He therefore turned his special attention to the moral feelings and impulses useful to society. Here he was constantly aware of the opposition from the self-centred and crude impulses of the lower man. But society and the State, he held, were not only based upon these. He saw their origins and their continuance as something markedly different from the anxieties, fears, etc. which had produced and still sustained the positive religions. But it is a fundamental feature in his interpretation of history to employ the same methods of empirical observation, historical study and knowledge of primitive peoples, by which he had attempted to throw light upon the emergence of religion, to analyse the origins of society as well. At this point naturalistic motives once more came strongly into play, along with the moral impulses of sympathy and social usefulness. This did not perhaps apply to original human society in general, which he viewed as an original phenomenon of a common life that had very few, and very easily satisfied, requirements (*Treatise on Human Nature*); but it did hold good of the rise of States, *governments* and *authority*. According to Hume, war itself, with its need for military leadership, had been instrumental in producing this, as the outcome of the mutual struggles between the hordes. He says in *Of the Origin of Government* that in time of war one man wins authority over the crowd, accustoms them to subjection, and, if he is clever and just, he establishes his authority by a blend of force and consent. His subjects find out the advantages of their new condition when they see that he brings them a new assurance of justice, and a feeling of obligation is gradually aroused in them. Thus the monarchical State, resting upon military power, is the earliest form. Republics arose through abuse of monarchical and despotic power. *Camps are the true mothers of cities* (*Treatise*). This saying is an exact counterpart to the hard words at the end of the *Natural History of Religion: Ignorance is the mother of devotion*; but they were nearer to historical reality than this saying, which ignores the original religious bent of mankind.

Moreover, the naturalistic teaching of Hume about the origins of the State did not remain altogether free of pragmatic features and elements derived from Natural Law (particularly in the *Treatise*). But just as his teaching on the history of religion had dealt the death-blow to any rationalistic picture of natural theology, so here too any idea of the origin of the State in some sort of contract had to go by the board. (There is a more detailed presentation of the argument in *Of the Original Contract*.) Shaftesbury and others had been his predecessors in this rejection of the contract theory, but it continued to exist after Hume's time, because the scholars' rejection of a false doctrine does not at once bring about its extinction in history. In the final resort, it could only be done away with by new historical experience and a new historical consciousness. But Hume must certainly be ranked as one of the most powerful pioneers in this new consciousness, if only by reason of the two breaches he effected in the world of history as constructed upon a rationalistic basis rooted in Natural Law.

The new historical consciousness of the nineteenth century certainly did not rest alone upon an understanding of the factor of political power in history, but it was this understanding that brought it for the first time, so to speak, to completeness. Hume already possessed it without, however, its most essential ingredient, the sense of individuality and individual development. He says in *Of the Original Contract* that the world is in a constant state of transition from smaller to larger, and then from larger to smaller kingdoms, on account of migrations and new settlements. Is there anything else to be seen in these events, he asks, but *force and violence*? But then time and custom do their work upon the human disposition, and authority, law and obligation grow up out of what was originally usurpation or rebellion. It is custom that determines the particular direction to be taken by a newly recognised condition, and this is by 'general instinct'; but the process is assisted by the interest of mankind in a secure state of law and order (*Treatise*). Hume sees the historical process fulfilling itself in this swing of the pendulum between the soldier's rule by the sword and the original social and moral needs of humanity. True, there is still a flicker here, as in his reconstruction of religious history, of the old cyclic theory, the belief in the constant recurrence in history of the same pattern of events. But sometimes, though not always, there was genuine historical experience at the root of such belief. The swing of the pendulum between the invasion of force and a condition of law and order, which Hume assumes in political history, could be much more truly explained on a basis of history than a swing between theism and polytheism, as set out by him in his survey of religious development. At all events this was a much truer and better-focused picture than Voltaire's, which had chiefly presented only the meaningless nature of these brutal struggles for power, and the impotence of reason when confronted with them. Hume's dualism re-established a connecting link and a polarity between them, and a polarity between the basic forces of naturalism and moralism in history. There was thus no need for mankind to despair at the constant breakthrough of destructive forces, for quiet forces were also constantly at work to remodel the work of the destroyer into new structures. Even military power could, in certain emergencies, be reckoned as a friend to the rescue. In his essay *Of the Original Contract*, Hume says that in chaotic conditions any sensible man would be glad to have a general at the head of an army in order to give the people the leader that they are incapable of choosing for themselves.

It is clear, then, that Hume did not take at all a doctrinaire view of the swing between the various holders of power, forms of State and political constitutions. He probably considered liberty, as eventually achieved in England, the most blessed 'perfection of civil society' (*Of the Origin of Government*). But historical experience taught him that it also required a basis of authority for its very existence, and that there was a perpetual inner struggle in every State between the claims of authority and freedom; and neither of them could win an outright victory, even in an oriental despotism, where there were always some remnants of individual and collective freedom. In cases where authority had been seriously abused, even Hume recognised a natural right of resistance. But his immediate concern was always to bridge the gulf again as soon as possible, and to lay it down as a rule that in struggles between authority and freedom, authority was the prime consideration. This was not only a statement of historical fact, but also a value-judgement. For, seeing that death was bound to be the inevitable end of everything, even political life, he would rather see his free England sink into the euthanasia of an absolute monarchy than perish in the convulsions of a purely popular seizure of power (*Whether the British Government Inclines more to Absolute Monarchy or to a Republic*).

Shaftesbury, under the intoxication of the newly-won English liberty, had thought that the free development of the mind, the arts, and knowledge could only be permanently assured in a free State. This was a thought that had once upon a time stirred men's minds in the days of the early Roman Empire. It was born both of factual observation and of a sense of values, in a situation where the latter could easily influence the interpretation put upon the former. Here, Hume tried to let simple experience speak for itself. He asked whether the arts did not flourish even under the priestly tyranny of modern Rome; and whether the arts and learning had not achieved their chief progress in Florence since the Medici had been in power. Yet he admitted that absolutist France was the only people, apart from the Greeks, to produce at one and the same time philosophers, poets, artists, historians and so on. It is clear that value-judgements influenced by contemporary conditions also entered into Hume's opinions, when he reckoned that modern France had reached a higher level of total development than even the Greeks, who for their part had far surpassed the English (*Of Civil Liberty*). In his essay *Of the Rise and Progress of the Arts and Sciences*, he returned once more to this theme, and sought to use a careful critical sense to arrive at some general rules of experience. Yet in spite of many perceptive individual observations, he only arrived in the end at the questionable conclusion that the arts and sciences did indeed first arise in republics, but could also be transplanted to other civilised monarchies, and that a republic was more favourable to the growth of the sciences, whilst a civilised monarchy was more suitable to the fine arts. But this was a problem amenable only to a more individualising treatment than was possible to his limited means of knowledge.

Hume's most strenuous endeavour was to harmonise the findings of experience with the norms of reason. In truth, his empiricism was apt at times to get the better of his still surviving rationalism in the course of this struggle, while at other times the rationalism would be victorious, though on each occasion he always made characteristically generous concessions to the defeated cause. His artistic taste was both rationalistic and normative. Experience, however, taught him that on closer examination the manifold varieties of taste among different men and peoples in various ages were much greater than appeared at first sight (*Of the Standard of Taste*). What attitude then should be adopted? Should all that did not agree with present taste be rejected? Should we put away the pictures of our ancestors because they wore laced collars, frills and hooped petticoats? For empiricism and knowledge of the world had clearly made the men of the eighteenth century so tolerant that Hume, knowing his public, could reject this suggestion with a smile. We should not be disturbed by innocent peculiarities of custom and habit such as we find in the artistic works of the past. Moreover, we should overlook the speculative errors of religion, and the absurdities of belief about the gods of the heathen could well be ignored in a critical appreciation of their poetry. But where bigotry and superstition showed their face, or where there were ideas of morality and decorum that wounded our finer feelings, our judgement must be that there was a real distortion of the artistic values. And Hume was not disposed even to except Homer and the Greek tragedians altogether from this somewhat unsympathetic and narrow verdict. Once again, it was the standards of truth enjoined by a timeless reason which caused him to reject phenomena that were not in keeping with them.

Everywhere, then, we find the Enlightenment striving to bring the manifold variety of historical phenomena under general truths and principles of regularity. Hume's first success, as we have seen, was in the sphere of political life, where he discovered genuine types of historical phenomenon. True, they could only be very general, and as a rule he took good care not to generalise too much on the basis of single historical facts. He showed that his empiricism was genuine by the fact that he never for one moment forgot the limitations of human experience. He himself says in the essay *Of Civil Liberty* that we have too little experience, and the world is still too much in its youth, for us to be able to establish general truths in political life that would hold good for all time. How can we know what degrees of virtue or vice mankind is capable of, or what could be expected of it if there should come about some great revolution in education, habit, or principles?

Thus equipped, with his undogmatic and deliberately openminded attitude, his treasures of scholarly skill, his empirical psychology, which yet strove to get a general view, inseparably combined with the values and ideals of the Enlightenment, Hume became one of the greatest historiographers of his nation. We will use as our text the form in which his three works appeared in 1762 under the title *The History of England*,[1] in which a good deal of revision and knitting together of loose ends had taken place. And we shall make an attempt to grasp the special qualities of his achievement, and the stage that it represents in the preliminary history of historism.

Voltaire's *Le Siècle de Louis XIV* had been published in 1751; and in 1754 there was published the first volume of Hume's first work written between 1752 and 1754, on the Stuart period. On this account

---

[1] *The History of England under the Stuarts* had come out in two volumes in 1754 and 1756; the *History under the Tudors* in 1759, and the *Earlier History from Julius Caesar to the Accession of Henry VII*, in two volumes in 1761. Metz, *D. Hume*, pp. 41 ff. He and others are wrong in thinking that the first unified edition of the whole work came out in 1763. I have in front of me the six-volume quarto edition of 1762. Hume himself testifies in his autobiographical sketch that when he revised the History of the Stuarts he altered more than a hundred passages in a Tory direction. See on this point Burton, *Life and Correspondence of David Hume* (1846), 2, 73 ff. Even the expression *superstition* was often toned down into *religion*. Our present task does not require us to go more fully into these variant readings. A short reference may be made to the monographs that have so far appeared on Hume's interpretation of history: Goebel, *Das Philosophische in Humes Geschichte von England*, 1897; Daiches, 'Verhältnis der Geschichtsschreibung Humes zu seiner praktischen Philosophie', thesis, Leipzig, 1903; Goldstein, *Die empiristische Geschichtsffauassung Humes*, Darmstädter Habilitationsschrift, 1902; Wegrich, 'Geschichtsauffassung D. Humes im Rahmen seines philosophischen Systems', thesis, Cologne, 1926. The best of these is Goldstein. Wegrich's book is spoilt by unpleasant philosophical jargon, and its phenomenological critique obscures the phenomenon of Hume himself to such an extent that one has great difficulty in discerning it. Black, *The Art of History* (1926), also has a good chapter on Hume.

he has been looked upon by some as an imitator of Voltaire. Hume had already contradicted this supposition in a letter of 5 November 1755 (Metz, *Hume*, p. 395), where he writes: 'The truth is that my history was already planned and to a large extent written down before the publication of that excellent work.' It is true that he was mistaken in the date he ascribes to Voltaire's work; but we can trust the word of this truth-loving man, who was singularly free from vanity, when he says that he first learnt of Voltaire's work when his own was well under way. It may be assumed that he then confirmed and followed up its findings in the direction taken by his own work; but this does not in any way impugn the originality of his achievement.

Great historical writing always grows from history that is actually in the making, that is, from life; and it receives its basic trend from the struggles and aims with which the author is himself surrounded. His view of things alters according to whether he is writing in peaceful or in stormy times, and whether he is recording victorious events or seeking to uncover the reasons for the fearful experiences he has undergone. In history written during the Enlightenment, there is a mixture of features belonging to calm and to stormy times. There was a belief that decisive victories had already been won, and that progress could continue in the same direction, though the final goal had not yet been reached. We already know what Hume's basic attitude was—that of a careful and critically-minded conqueror, who saw himself, for all the inadequate powers with which nature had endowed him as a human being, at a peak of human development. We are using a word that is rather glibly employed to denote any historical development; but we have still to ask whether it was 'development' in our full historical sense of the word that Hume was portraying. In his *Natural History of Religion* the first requirement is lacking—namely the individual substratum from which all development proceeds. Hume, who had dissolved the notion of substance, only depicted the changes in typical psychological complexes, and not the essential alterations in mental and spiritual entities. In his *History of England*, the individual entity was there ready made, for it was no less than the English people.

Hume was a Scot, and possessed many innate antipathies to the English character; but he was also unsparing in criticism of his own people for their one-time barbarism. His theory had a dissolving effect: the nation was nothing but a collection of individuals who were subjected to the same causes (*Of National Character*). But his feelings proved stronger than his theories, and the book is nevertheless shot through with English national spirit, though it is of a very modern and rational type, rather than something deeply rooted in sentiment. This can be seen from the manner in which he passed judgement upon the political union of Scotland with England, which he held to be merely the victory of reasonable statecraft. For the Scots, as he says at one point (6, 187), had up till then possessed very incomplete notions of law and liberty.

This suggests the meaning that Hume descried in English history as a whole. He viewed it as a progress from *government of will* to *government of laws* (2, 149). His purpose, which became clearer as the work proceeded, was to portray this painful and unattractive process which yet had a happy ending, in all its complications and all its phases. To begin with, so to speak, he had taken the bull by the horns and tackled the Stuart period, which was vital to his under-lying purpose; but as he went on he was forced more and more to go back to the earlier periods, in themselves much less attractive to him, in order to complete the search for the chain of causes that had led up to *government of laws*. What started as a basic political question thus became the general theme of his book. We owe to Hume some-thing that had hitherto been neglected—a really understanding selec-tion of material and coherent design in his work. Here, he is charac-teristically different from Voltaire, who purported to give a genuine history of civilisation and yet was reluctant to take in the broad masses of political and military material, which had been so funda-mentally neglected, in anything but the traditional manner. Hume too was influenced by the conventions of historical writing, which had always preferred this kind of material. But he infused a higher mean-ing into it by making a definite big political problem the centre of the history to which this material was related.

The very choice of this problem of internal politics was evidence of the Enlightened outlook, which was never interested in the life of the State for its own sake, but only as a means towards an orderly and secure private life for the citizen. Thus Hume could not but view this problem in the light of his ideals and inner psychological assump-tions. He intended his approach to be not only nationalistic and English, but also universally human. His purpose was to show to what a degree of perfection this weak human nature of ours could attain. It was perfection rather than development in our sense that he meant to demonstrate. The idea of perfection, as we saw in both Leibniz and Voltaire, was apt to set limits to genuine historical thought in all the authors of the Enlightenment. And it is character-istic of all Hume's thought that he held this idea without any great illusions about the degree to which such perfection could be either attained or maintained. He says in the *History* in connection with Harrington's *Oceana* (6, 128), that the idea of a perfect and immortal *Commonwealth* would always prove as chimerical as that of a perfect and immortal human being. Yet the idea of perfection was deep

176

down in his blood, for he himself developed his *Idea of a Perfect Commonwealth* in one of his essays. True, he made a realistic beginning with the remark that authority and not reason controls the mass of mankind, and that nothing commands authority unless it has the recommendation of age. But as quite apart from the habits and inclinations of particular men a specific form of government could well be more satisfactory than another, it was quite legitimate to ask which was the most perfect of them all. Who could say what might become practicable in the future? And so it was reasonable to try and approximate present-day constitutions to this ideal as far as it could be done without causing upheavals.

We shall not deal here with the content of this ideal constitution, interesting though it is from the political point of view. It is clear enough that despite all his peculiar feeling for the *Variety of Mankind*, and for the typical and consequential ways in which the varieties of thought and custom had arisen, this did not amount to the recognition of the extent to which all political and historical creations in general were individually shaped and fashioned. In the ultimate analysis, in spite of all Hume's empiricism, the old standards of a timeless reason based upon Natural Law still held the field.

English history, then, is presented as a process of growing perfection in accordance with the laws of psychological and political experience. We have already studied Hume's doctrine of the rhythmic movement of political life, which leads from the forcible seizure of power to gradual acceptance through habit, an accommodation between the ruler and the ruled, and the gradual building up of authority. This picture was perfectly suited to the trend of English history, which had led from the Roman conquest onwards up to the revolution of 1688–9 (the point at which Hume's study ended) in a series of successive rhythmic movements remarkably like the pattern traced by the author. Hume depicted them without overmuch schematisation, and always with a forward look, up to the last movement with which he was most closely concerned, leading from the fanatical enthusiasm of the Puritan rising to the nicely-balanced blend of authority and freedom. Everything in the earlier periods, the old Germanic freedom, *Magna Carta*, the beginnings of Parliament and so on, were specially emphasised by him, but without any overvaluation. He even destroyed the prevailing legends of clearly-shaped Parliamentary rights, either for the Middle Ages or for Tudor times, or for the Stuart period, as these had sometimes been maintained. It was one of the main theses of his work to point out that these rights were a late acquisition, and he stressed this point still further in the complete edition. In so doing, he annoyed all the political parties of his country, but paved the way for an objective

177

treatment of both the Tudor and the Stuart periods. In the process, he was confirmed in his conviction that the course towards human perfection was always extremely lengthy. Hume's mind was very far removed from that of Boulainvilliers in France, for instance, who was intent upon resurrecting from the past some ancient and original inheritance of right and law.

Thus Hume treats English history as a slow and tardy development with much confusion about it, wrought out in blood and tears. Out of the Gothic and feudal inequality of political powers, out of the mixture of authority and anarchy, there eventually emerged the right blend of authority and freedom. Hume also clearly recognised that this process had only been made possible by the great social transformations that had taken place among the English people through the destruction of the feudal nobility, the rise of the gentry, and the growth of the middle classes, the upholders of the new civilisation, who were particularly dear to Hume's heart. The incidental evil effects, the depopulation of the countryside and the unfair treatment of the lower classes, did not indeed altogether escape his attention, but did not stir him deeply. It must be remembered that he was writing at the beginning of the great Industrial Revolution, when as yet there were no dark shadows to disturb his tranquil social conscience.

It must be said in praise of this work, however, that he wrote it not only as a constructive and moralising philosopher, but also as a narrator of history in the grand style. True, his main approach was that of a psychologist and moralist who analysed his material and assessed it in terms of praise or blame. But his joy in the manifold gaiety of the world, with all its events and figures, however repellent they may often have seemed to him, was nevertheless constantly breaking through. His narrative carries the reader along, for it is exciting, stirring and gripping, and the composition is often brilliant. Hume has been criticised for arranging his material in a too external manner according to the reigns of the various kings. This is a more justifiable criticism for the Middle Ages than for the more modern period after the time of Henry VII, when each new reign bore a new character—at least up to the end of Hume's narrative, the revolution of 1688. But even for the Middle Ages the author gives a good picture of what the change of ruler meant on each occasion for the ups and downs of inner political development. Perhaps his most skilful piece of writing was his picture of Queen Elizabeth's career as it gradually took shape. He shows how she never lost the feeling of insecurity, and yet was obliged to become the bulwark of the Protestants in Europe, and how in the process there was a gradual focusing of events towards a decisive struggle with Philip II, till in the end Elizabeth proved courageous enough to recognise the necessity of action and to take the requisite steps (cf. e.g. vol. 4, pp. 45, 127, 185). In the same way Hume succeeded in combining the personal and the general in his account of Charles I's fate, and in showing how his peculiar personal characteristics only became fatal to him because of the particular historical situation in which he was placed, between the absolutist precedents of Tudor times and the new popular spirit that was asserting itself in the cause of freedom (vol. 5, pp. 485 ff.). On closer examination, it becomes clear that in historical climaxes like this there is an intricate mixture of psychological and factual causes at work that have the makings of great historical drama. The thinkers and writers of the Enlightenment were already alert to the prevalence of such destinies, which forced particular individuals to follow a certain definite course. Shakespeare had already begun to have his effect. Montesquieu's and Gibbon's masterly portrayal of the fate of Rome were inspired by this same feeling; and Schiller's dramas, in spite of their strong permeation with the spirit of the Enlightenment, show it even more closely. But in order to gauge the distance between Hume and the later historism with greater accuracy, we must now go on to ask to what extent the sense of individuality in history was really developed in him as he came to grips with his subject. There is no doubt, as we have already seen, that he was prompted by a certain involuntary but fundamental feeling for the English national spirit. But he failed to give any coherent survey of the concrete factors underlying the peculiar English genius, such as geographical conditions, racial composition and special economic factors. His shortcomings are more obvious still when we ask to what extent he was sensitive to the inner core of things, the factual and psychological forces at work, the real 'centres of activity' and the entities which arise from them, which were only perceptible to the spiritual eye. Since the time of Ranke, these entities are usually referred to as ideas, tendencies of the century, objective necessities of the period, or general world conditions. These are expressions with no very clear edge to them, since the entities they represent tend to run into one another. But, if we may again adopt Ranke's words, there is always some spiritual, *real-geistig* process of an individual kind at work, whether it is concerned with the world of motives behind an individual personality, or with the most general movements in the West as a whole; and this is something that can always be felt and seen and recognised in those entities.

In other words, Hume generally showed a clear recognition for the foreground of movements and described it clearly; but his grasp of the background that moved the foreground was much less adequate. The foreground of the action, whether concerned with whole nations or individuals, was illuminated with an inexorable clarity, like pieces on a chessboard. But there is a lack of feeling for those hidden tendencies and movements that slowly but surely bring about historical change. Hume was as yet unable to grasp (if we may once more draw upon Ranke) how great new combinations in world history could arise out of the alliance between the Normans and the Church, between the spirit of chivalry and the spirit of hierarchy, or how the expansion and invasion of France by England (ascribed, as it is by Hume, merely to the Englishman's expansive and untamed vitality) gave the English people their first awareness of the powerful position they occupied, and how those events, though involving individuals, led on to a further development of collective life.

As we have already noted in Montesquieu and Voltaire, the psychological observation of collective intellectual and spiritual phenomena, and the need for determining the causes behind them in the most universal manner, had given rise since the latter part of the seventeenth century to the notion of a 'spirit' behind all human creations; and this conception had been applied to whole periods. Although this idea gradually led by its own weight to a further search for hidden vital forces, within the Enlightenment, however, it did not for the most part go further than a summary assembly of all the obvious intellectual and spiritual peculiarities of a period or a people, and a summary presentation of their effect upon the course of events. Hume's work, too, is full of expressions such as the *romantic spirit* of the Middle Ages, which he saw at work in William the Conqueror's invasion and then as the chief inspiration of the Crusades. More frequently still, he mentions the *spirit of superstition* in mediaeval men, or the *spirit of bigotry* in their clergy. For the most part, he had not much good to say about this *spirit*; he mostly mentions it with a sense of pathological regret. Yet we know that Hume ascribed these phenomena that did not attract him at the deepest level to the innate weaknesses of human nature, and only relatively to those that could be improved. This cold insight was not indeed sufficient for a really generous understanding of what did not attract him. But it gave his historical value-judgements a notably more resigned colouring than could be achieved by Voltaire's bitter resentment. And what Hume felt even more strongly than he as a causative psychological factor was the massive historical importance of the *minds of men*, the intellectual changes that took place from one age to another, the *history of the human mind* (vol. 5, p. 207). For after all, the great changes in the English spirit over the last turn of the century constituted his own chief piece of historical experience, and his own intellectual existence was rooted in them. As he looked out optimistically on his own age, in which politics and war, economics and science, the mechanical and the higher skills, all seemed to work together for the best, he was able to write in words that were full of promise: *the spirit of the age affects all the arts* (*Of Refinement in the Arts*). Even in more primitive times he could now and again go deeper, and see in the revolt of his compatriot, the Scottish national hero Robert Bruce, 'an awakening of the genius of the nation' (vol. 2, p. 120). And so a deep and lively interest could at times take him beyond the boundaries of his own psychology. But as this psychology always contained the same recurrent rearrangement, occasional clarification and refinement of the same static basic intellectual and spiritual powers, the mental life of the individual at the deepest level was bound to remain beyond his comprehension. What he had to say about the spirituality or even the piety of the Middle Ages is among the sorriest and most repellent parts of the work. He therefore completely failed to understand Luther's reformation, for he saw the chief motive for Luther's advent to be the jealousy of the Augustinians against the Dominicans (vol. 3, p. 119). As we have already seen, Hume considered ignorance as the mother of piety, particularly in the superstitious forms of the Middle Ages. True, he had begun to overcome the ancient and erroneous belief cherished by intellectualism, that virtue could be taught, at least in the sphere of genuine worship; but in the neighbouring sphere of the religious life he was still quite unaware that this intellectualism would not hold water.

It is more difficult to grasp the collective picture of spiritual and intellectual life than that of the individual. The direct understanding of one human being by another, which at once produces a distinct picture of the other man's character, is also the central point for the historian if he would make any further progress; it even comes before all psychology in importance. Hume had an understanding of human beings which preceded his psychological theories. These latter dissected the inner life into separable complexes consisting of the same motivating springs of action, and therefore gave his characterisation of historical personalities a very monotonous and typical colouring, in which the individual emerged as the summing up of the typical. And yet his characters did not remain altogether lacking in fire and force. Hume was just the opposite of Voltaire in this respect. Voltaire, in spite of his efforts to search out cause and effect in primitive times, was really bored by barbarian evidences, and was only attracted by civilised man. But Hume, as his history of religion had already shown, had a certain feeling for the primitive man who was only moved by emotion. In this respect he was closer to Montesquieu. He took a genuinely artistic interest in depicting the wild personalities of the Norman rulers and barons of the Middle Ages. He saw them as untamed natural forces, to be regarded with astonishment and fear, though also at times with a certain admiration.

It is indeed difficult to say how much of individual comprehension lay behind these portraits. Dutifully at the end of each reign he would try to give a vigorous general portrait of the ruler. Henry VIII, for example, appears as a mixture of horrible, repulsive characteristics and noble and attractive ones, whose first effect on the reader is not very different from that produced later on by Ranke. Yet the latter saw him in entirely individual terms, whereas Hume regarded him as one of those enigmatical 'mixed' characters compounded by good and evil, wisdom and folly, whom he sceptically acknowledged at the end of his *Natural History of Religion* to be an inexplicable mystery. He felt the same thing about Cromwell. The life-work of this hypocritical fanatic (for that was how Hume saw him) was so closely related to the origins of the new English liberty and yet was so contrary to it, that one gets an impression of hesitation in Hume's portrait; one can well understand the hesitation between purely political comprehension of the facts, appreciation of the man's great qualities, and a profound antipathy for a character in whom all the means and methods he used were only a cloak for his ambitions (cf. vol. 6, p. 58). In the end it was the moral verdict that prevailed (vol. 6, p. 89); but there was no real understanding of the formative centre of this powerful personality.[1]

There was only one way in which Hume could escape from this hesitation—the necessary consequence of his atomising psychology and his powers of political judgement running in separate channels. It was to make a jump, and to separate human and psychological judgements from factual and political judgements of personalities, and in difficult cases to fall back upon the latter. He did this quite deliberately in the case of Elizabeth. First of all he sketched her human weaknesses, and then he went on as follows: 'But the true way to assess her worth is to leave all these considerations on one side and to think of her simply as a rational being who held authority and was called to rule over men' (vol. 4, p. 313).

Hume possessed in a high degree this ability to understand political facts. It was both a sense of the permanent interests of a State, and of the place of political necessity—in fact, the sense of political expediency or 'reason of State' so often mentioned by him in his works. As a moralist, he could not help realising that the overriding of truth, law and custom by political expediency was one of the greatest sources of human unhappiness; but as an empiricist, he saw it as a longstanding and world-wide evil that simply had to be reckoned with (vol. 2, p. 114, etc.). He saw how it cut both ways, but he understood its prevalence and power. Thus he did not fail to realise how

[1] For Hume's picture of Cromwell, compared with Burke's conception of him, cf. Meusel, *Edmund Burke und die Französische Revolution*, pp. 105 ff.

indispensable was England's sea power, though on one occasion he remarks in a tone of civilised warning that trade does not by any means depend solely upon force (vol. 6, p. 165). In general, there is a feeling of a much more political atmosphere in Hume than in Voltaire, though in his writings we took note of many signs of political realism, which was still much in evidence in the eighteenth century. Political realism had marked all the chief historical writers in the political field from Machiavelli and Guicciardini onwards, including Thuanus and Davila, up to Clarendon, who was one of his chief sources. It reminds us of Pufendorf when Hume not infrequently, in an attempt to throw light upon the extremely complicated details of events, develops the political *rationes* of the conflicting parties in a coherent manner and sets them side by side. This was an extension of the custom in the ancient world of throwing light upon the motives of historical characters by putting imaginary speeches into their mouths. Even more modern was another device he used in the writing of history, namely to give from time to time a conspectus of the complete foreign relations of England and Europe. The reader can see the efforts Hume makes to be the intellectual master of his material, and to organise it more effectively, although the subject-matter often held little essential attraction for him.

There is a great deal of political wisdom scattered through this work. But it is to be noted in Hume, as in Voltaire and Montesquieu, that there was not sufficient traditional and realistic understanding of the peculiar and specific interests of States to bring home the fact that these States were themselves living individual entities. And so Hume failed to establish any inner connection between what he was most concerned with in a State (the goal of a constitutional and wisely limited liberty) and the activities of the State purely in the field of power politics.

The lack of coherence between the different historical fields of life that were there to be dealt with is characteristic of the Enlightenment. With nothing but its rational and empirical tools and methods, and its utilitarian goals, it was incapable of establishing any genuine intellectual and spiritual unities. The State as a legal institution, the State as power, the psychology of the constantly recurrent human weaknesses, reflected particularly in religion—all this was dealt with in parallel, as it were, but without the fusing agent that would have combined it into a whole. Like Voltaire, Hume saw that the fundamental causative factors in history were the State and religion. But with the limitations of his mechanical psychology, he failed to bring these two into any kind of organic connection. This lack was all the more perceptible when it came to dealing in addition with the new material opened up by the new interests of the Enlightenment—the progress of civilisation, customs and institutions, technical and economic advance. Hume, too, shared these interests, but they were not predominant with him. Spurred on by Montesquieu, he had devoted special attention to the Anglo-Saxon constitution and to feudalism, and had not neglected finance and the question of prices. In the later volumes he devoted a section in each reign to these topics, as well as to trade, industry, literature, art and customs. This cultural extension of the field traditionally covered in historical writing was thus something which Hume carried out at much the same time as Voltaire. He says in one passage (vol. 4, p. 37) that even trivial events, if they testify to the customs of the period, are often more instructive and entertaining than the great events of war and intercourse between nations, which are nearly always much alike at all times and in all places. But Hume did not proceed in accordance with this tenet. These special sections did not amount to more than an unsatisfactory collection of notes, and did not come up to the level of Voltaire's cultural history. Some sense of the wholeness of life, which was a bond between the State and culture, events and conditions, was no doubt there; and the historical writings of Hume and Voltaire certainly added new members to the body. But there was a lack of the joints that would have given them a living connection with the whole.

At a time when German intellectual life was already turning in the direction of the State and the study of history, German readers at the highest level greeted Hume's works with the greatest respect, whilst also subjecting it to certain characteristic criticisms. On 16 December 1814, Niebuhr wrote to Dore Hensler:

> I gladly recognise Hume's great qualities, and in some respects he is to be preferred to Gibbon. But in the earlier periods I miss even more of the things you feel the lack of; and in the later periods he lacks the sense of what the human hearts of all those men felt whom he regards only as fools and rebels. But in this respect, I must admit, Gibbon is no better.

And Baron vom Stein applauded the work as a pattern of reflection, fair-mindedness and acute perception in its development of the inner political connections between events, as well as praising the highly cultured style. He admitted Hume's lack of warmth and imagination in his descriptions, his inability to bring to life what is not actually present, or remote. Both these critics put their finger most accurately on Hume's greatest deficiency (and this was something shared by the whole Enlightenment) namely, his failure to provide history with any kind of inner soul.[1]

[1] Gerhard und Norvin, *Die Briefe B. G. Niebuhrs*, 2, 514 f., or Botzenhart, *Frh. vom Stein, Staatsgedanken*, p. 107. We may also refer here to a characteristic

In England, in spite of the criticisms constantly directed against his work by the parties, Hume's book continued to be highly regarded. A High Church opponent, stirred up by the continual bad effects of Hume's unreligious handling of history, took it upon himself in the middle of the nineteenth century to make a vigorous attack upon his work.[1] It then became clear, as in Voltaire's case, that the scholarly background of Hume's work was inclined to be weak. It was possible to make severe criticisms of his insufficient acquaintance with conditions in the Middle Ages. And in the collection of his material, he had often suited his own fancies, and had preferred to select from his predecessors (Carte, Tyrrell, Brady and so on) for his narrative of English history. But this is as far as we are concerned a minor criticism, and does not touch the independence of Hume's historical thought. Moreover, as this critic was clearly a partisan, his remarks are somewhat dubious unless they can be supported by further proofs.[2] At all events, Fueter's reproach, that Hume never criticised his sources, is quite unjust.[3] The High-Church critic mentioned above even spoke of falsifications; but there is absolutely no proof of this,

judgement of the youthful Ranke on Hume's work. He was asked by Perthes in 1825 to write a history of England, and remarked in reply: 'I should direct my attention to the whole, and to the process of development running right through it, which is hardly the case with Hume'. Oncken, *Aus Rankes Frühzeit*, p. 30. Incidentally, Ranke agreed with one of Hume's main theses, namely, that in English constitutional law at the time of Charles I 'there was still a good deal that was undefined'. *Epochen der neueren Geschichte*, p. 174.

[1] 'Hume and his influence upon History', in *Quarterly Review*, vol. 73 (1844), pp. 536 ff.

[2] Even the sharp criticism of Hume's methods of work in Black, *The Art of History*, p. 90 f., and Peardon, *The Transition in English Historical Writing 1760–1810*, pp. 21 ff., are apparently based in the main on this essay in the *Quarterly Review*. Hume's use of Th. Carte's *History of England*, which had come out shortly before, in, and after 1747, had been already noted in the *Edinburgh Review*, 53 (1831), p. 15, without the critic however being in any doubt as to the independence of Hume's historical writing.

[3] As examples one might mention the details in 1, 19 on the lack of monastic traditions; 1, 153, on the precarious value of public statutes for showing the real moral conditions; 2, 111, where the figures given are highly fanciful; 2, 397, the faulty use of traditional material on the Wars of the Roses; 4, 95 ff., on the casket letters of Mary Stuart (admittedly given too much credence); 5, 38, Henry IV's grand scheme as represented by Sully; 6, 231, on the typical weaknesses of the accounts of naval battles. Cf. also Wegrich, *op. cit.*, pp. 54 ff. Even more important, in my opinion, are the methods of source-criticism used and developed in his great *Essay of the Populousness of Ancient Nations*. 'The first page of Thucydides', he says, 'is in my opinion the commencement of real history'. Here, too, Hume puts forward incisive criticisms of the numbers given by ancient authors, and enunciates a principle that shows a delicate insight, namely that more attention should be paid to the details given casually and incidentally by ancient authors about the conditions of ordinary life than to what they set out to narrate directly and of set purpose.

at least not in the subjective sense. Hume wanted to uncover the whole truth, though he was unable to understand many aspects of historical life because of his prejudices as a thinker of the Enlightenment, and so he projected himself and his way of thinking into historical persons and events.

In spite of all this, it was Hume's achievement to show both in philosophy and in history the limitations of the Enlightenment in the realm of thought—as far as this thought could learn and direct itself by experience. He knew that there was still some 'inexplicable mystery' at the back of the human being, and that the word 'chance' was only an expression for causes as yet unknown. Voltaire, who reached the same stage of scepticism, preferred to fall back in a mood of enjoyment upon the known world. But Hume, who was the deeper and more vigorous thinker, and possessed greater intellectual probity, laid down his arms when confronted with this unknown sphere. Here Hegel's saying applies to Hume's historical work: empiricism could only fragment its material, but was powerless to put it together. Yet this fragmentation, like the work of Montesquieu, did have the effect of loosening the soil in such a way that it could become more receptive to new seed.

II Gibbon

The intellectual force and the energy of the urge for knowledge of the past is not only the most impressive feature of the great historical work performed by the writers of the Enlightenment, but is also the most important driving force to be considered if we would understand its function in the history of the origin of historism. It was destined to arouse in a new generation whose attitude was radically different the zeal to become the masters of history with an equally great energy, but more penetrating tools. While Hume was able to advance the intellectual movement by the philosophical elements in his historical thinking, Edward Gibbon (1737–94) was even more widely read and more influential as a writer of history. The first volume of *The Decline and Fall of the Roman Empire* appeared in 1776, and the work was completed in 1787.[1] Its lasting influence was partly due to its being based not only on Gibbon's own immensely wide reading of sources, but also on the critical foundations laid by Tillemont, which previous ages had not been able to draw upon. Even today, Gibbon's work can arouse great enthusiasm and at the same time considerable revulsion. But every student in earnest about the study of universal history must come to inward terms with

[1] First ed. in six quarto volumes. The last three appeared in 1788.

Gibbon. And there are two basic ideas which may be reckoned the peculiar legacy of the Enlightenment to historism, and lead straight on to its highest development in Ranke. The first of these is the world historical grasp of his subject shown by Gibbon, and the capacity to penetrate right into it and link together its various parts. He is never content with the external fact of foreign peoples descending upon Rome and laying her waste; he must go on to give some account of each of them, with their own special characteristics and their own peculiar destiny.[1] Thus the work becomes a grandiose review of the various peoples, as seen from the heights of the Capitol, where in 1764 Gibbon had been so impressed by the remains of this mightiest of all empires that he had there and then conceived the idea of his great undertaking. He is already reminiscent of Ranke in the application of his universal interest to the internal lives of the various peoples and in the choice and penetrating treatment of those departments of life which are generally held to be of decisive importance for universal history. As in Voltaire and Hume, the State and religion are placed in the first rank of importance, only more consciously, and with a stronger sense of their primacy. True, Gibbon is less interested in their own particular way of life than in the question that is so typical of the Enlightenment, the question of what they had contributed for good or for evil to the fortunes of the human race. Hence his utilitarian treatment of the life of the State, and his admission of 'useful prejudices' as a legitimate means of ruling and disciplining the masses. Hence also his detailed treatment of Christianity. It would be quite possible to construct from the various relevant chapters of his work a specific, though not complete, history of the Church, together with its dogmas and attendant heresies. But this again is connected with a failing that is specifically characteristic of the Enlightenment. There is no adequate inner coherence or interconnection between the various lines of development, and this is a fault we have already noted in Hume. What a strange effect it produces, for example, when Constantine's rise to power is related almost as though there had been no such thing as Christianity in existence at the time; and then the sluices are, as it were, suddenly raised and the accumulated masses of thought are allowed to pour forth.

The universal thought-pattern of the Enlightenment, as represented by Gibbon, and of historism, as represented by Ranke, went

[1] In *The Autobiographies of E. Gibbon* (1896), p. 332, Gibbon testifies to following in this respect the advice of the Abbé de Mably, (*Manière d'écrire l'histoire* (1783), p. 110), who had advised him not to deal too minutely with the fall of the Eastern Empire, but to deal more thoroughly with the barbarian conquerors. In this case, Mably's extremely trivial book would have had at least this much merit.

back to the same common consciousness that the culture it stood for was not the work and the task of any single people, but belonged to a community of peoples closely bound together by their intellectual outlook and their destinies, the peoples of the Christian West. This was the second basic idea, springing from roots that went far back into the *corpus Christianum*, that linked the Enlightenment with historism. As can be seen for example in Ferguson's *Essay on the History of Civil Society* (1767), it had, in one or another of its nuances, become the common property of the Enlightenment.[1] Gibbon, like Ranke, welcomed the manifold variety as well as the oneness characteristic of this community of peoples. Later on, Ranke was able to expand this idea in a much more intimate and creative fashion than was possible to Gibbon, with the fragmentary sources and tools of knowledge available to the Enlightenment. But he had this idea clearly before his eyes (especially in the *General Observations on the Fall of the Roman Empire in the West*, following upon c. 38), though only in a way that was thoroughly characteristic of the Enlightenment; and he used it as a hinge for his conception of world history as a whole. For at this point there emerged one of the favourite doctrines of the Enlightenment, already taken up by Shaftesbury, and by Hume (though only in a limited form), that *liberty and letters*, political freedom and culture, normally belonged together, and that despotism was inimical to culture. Working on this idea, Gibbon came to the following conclusions.

In this present age, we have returned (though in a much larger and more assured way) to the happy condition of a closely-connected group of nations, living independently, yet on the same cultural level and in mutual emulation; to the condition, in fact, from which this great culture originally sprang. The small family of the Greek States with their *happy mixture of union and independence*, became a prototype for Gibbon of the modern West (c. 53, conclusion; cf. also c. 2, conclusion and c. 3, conclusion). With the advent of the Roman Empire, however, the world not only became a prison for all who were the enemies of the absolute monarch (c. 3, conclusion), but also gradually lost its vigour through a process of internal poisoning, in the political, the moral and the intellectual spheres of life. This poison was introduced by the long period of peace and the single pattern of rule, which reduced men to a uniform intellectual level, stifled the fires of genius, and even led to the evaporation of the martial spirit (c. 2, conclusion). We can already sense in this lively judgement something that transcends the mechanical and moralistic thought of the Enlightenment. Yet on another occasion Gibbon

---

[1] '*L'Europe n'est plus qu'une nation composée de plusieurs*', said Montesquieu (*Monarchie universelle* (2 vols, 1891), p. 36).

could fall back into the mechanical pattern followed by his predecessor Montesquieu (in his *General Observations*) where he simplifies the causes of decline into an inexorable law of nature, and specifies the excessive size of the Roman world Empire purely and simply as the active cause of this decline.[1] Against this background, it is all the more surprising to find Gibbon uttering his famous dictum that without question the happiest period of human history lay in the time of the good emperors, between Domitian's death and the accession of Commodus (c. 3). It is often forgotten, however, that there was a tragic background to this saying. We can hardly help asking whether Gibbon had really felt this matter at any depth and sensed its purely tragic side, when he uttered the judgement that the highest level of human happiness was to be found in a cultural period already doomed to decline. For his judgements disclose a certain ambiguous split in the standards by which the writers of the Enlightenment during the later *ancien régime* before 1789 assessed the political destinies of the nations. There was an enthusiasm for freedom and small political entities, and yet there was common agreement about the blessings of enlightened despotism as found in a large empire. And because there was a general readiness to interpret the detail of historical events in a personalistic and moralistic manner, absolute and enlightened rulers of the past always received special commendation. But here, too, the lack of coherence in the historical thought of the Enlightenment is clearly evident. In preference, its thinkers judged according to absolute standards; but they also paid attention to the lessons of practical experience. The absolute norm approved of liberty, but practical experience commended a benevolent absolutism, where the virtue of the ruler could also win the approval of the absolute norm.[2] Not till the rise of historism with its individualising outlook did it become possible to appreciate the full tragedy of the ancient world, which in its very death set free new life

[1] This simplification cannot have occurred to him at the beginning of the work, as shown by the words towards the end of c. 2: '*Whatever evils either reason or declamation have imputed to extensive empire, the power of Rome was attended with some beneficial consequences to mankind*' (consequences which are then described). Perhaps the verdict of the *General Observations* was influenced by Robertson as well as by Montesquieu, for Robertson had written at the beginning of his great introduction to the *History of Charles V*: '*The dominion of the Romans, like that of all great empires, degraded and debased the human species*'.

[2] For a characteristic controversial debate held in Paris in 1777 between Gibbon and the Abbé de Mably, in which the Abbé warmly defended republics, whilst Gibbon defended monarchy, cf. *The Autobiographies of E. Gibbon*, p. 314. Also on p. 342, some sharp words written in 1791 on the French Revolution and an approval of Burke's *Reflections*, though he was only able to appreciate their practical acuity, but not the deeper spirit that underlay them.

for the future. Only then could these events be seen as a unity and understood with a real sensitiveness to the destinies involved.

True, the Enlightenment already possessed some sense of historical destiny, which could be felt in Montesquieu's book on Rome and in his disciple Gibbon's great work. There can be no doubt that they were both deeply gripped by the tragedy which they attempted to explain in moralistic terms, and by the mechanical laws of cause and effect. But as soon as Gibbon comes to the detailed narrative of events, the sense of destiny seems to fade away before the moralistic and censorial judgements pronounced upon the various actors in the scene. In the years of his youth that were spent in Lausanne, Gibbon had imbibed the French tastes and had even seen Voltaire take a part on the stage. Again and again his historical works remind us of the theatrical scenes of a classical tragedy; and the rhetorical brilliance of the diction, tightly controlled as it is, is yet apt at times to become wearisome. And the atmosphere becomes cold, if not positively icy, whenever his pen is directed by an inner revulsion, whenever he describes the conflict between paganism and Christianity and the penetration by Christianity of the already rotten body of the Roman Empire. It is not true to say that Gibbon lays the chief blame for the fall of the empire upon Christianity,[1] for the 'slow and secret poison' was seen to have been long at work in its vitals. But it is certainly his opinion that Constantine's conversion to Christianity hastened the decline (*General Observations*). Gibbon's industry was indefatigable, and he wrestled with his material much more seriously than Voltaire. But there was a pitiless severity about the way he probed the results of Christianity in history from the earliest times onwards as far as the revival of reason and scholarship in the fifteenth century. He does not see this as the development of individual vital forces, but only as the interaction of certain specific human impulses, passions, reflections and artifices, conceived almost as though they were cogs in a vast machine.

In reading Gibbon's work, however, we are struck by the thoroughness with which he treats these particular dogmatic controversies. The theologian Robertson, when writing the history of Charles

---

[1] This is in disagreement with Bury, in the introduction to his edition of Gibbon, p. xxxviii; Rehm, *Untergang Roms im abendländischen Denken*, p. 125, and McCloy, *Gibbon's Antagonism to Christianity* (1933), p. 13 and p. 50. On the other hand, Black rightly interprets Gibbon's thought (*The Art of History* (1926), pp. 170 ff.), and so does Trude Benz, *Die Anthropologie in der Geschichtsschreibung des 18. Jahrhunderts* (1932), pp. 71 ff. Moreover, the testimony of one of his autobiographies ('*as I believed and as I still believe, that the propagation of the gospel and triumph of the church are inseparably connected with the decline of Roman Monarchy*'; *Autobiographies of E. Gibbon*, p. 285), does not contradict the interpretation here put forward.

V, gave it as his opinion that the dogmatic detail of the Reformation period might well be left to ecclesiastical historians. Voltaire in his *Siècle de Louis XIV* did indeed give a superficial and reluctant treatment of the theological struggles in this period, which he considered a disgrace to human reason. But in general the historians of the Enlightenment disliked to go into the details of these matters, which were repugnant to their essential outlook. What was the reason that prompted Gibbon, with his irreligious attitude, to undertake such an expansion, which was almost on the scale of a universal history of thought? The important Jewish philologist of the nineteenth century, Jacob Bernays, in his remarks on Gibbon (*Gesammelte Abhandlungen*, 1885, p. 215), which are very acute and shrewd, hazards a guess at the answer. During his unformed youthful period, Gibbon allowed himself in 1753 to be persuaded to go over to the Roman Catholic Church; but a year later, when his father had sent him abroad to Lausanne, he reverted to Protestantism. On each occasion, this seems to have been more of an intellectual than a religious decision. But the experience was a powerful one, and its effects lingered on in the interest the author now began to take in the Church's dogma. Such a deep concern, as Bernays appositely remarks, 'can only be ascribed to an interest that had cooled down after a period of heat; it could not possibly be the mark of a radical indifference'.

There was a sphere of historical development in which Montesquieu had already passed beyond the limitations of pragmatic explanation when he depicted the history of patrimonial justice as the gradual transformation of what was originally legal institutions. The world of jurisprudence was something that to a certain extent even the intellectual outlook of the Enlightenment was able to treat along genetic lines, because the historical actions of individuals were here somewhat in the background. Chapter 44 of Gibbon's work, treating the history of Roman jurisprudence from Romulus to Justinian, has earned the admiration even of the great nineteenth-century jurists. But it was not by any means free from a certain moralistic pragmatism. And masterly as is the composition, it has rightly been noted that there is a lack of inner connection with the rest of the work.[1]

---

[1] Ritter, *Entwicklung der Geschichtswissenschaft*, p. 302. Cf. also the valuable remarks on Gibbon in K. J. Neumann, *Entwicklung und Aufgaben der alten Geschichte* (1910), pp. 90 ff. Ringeling's dissertation delivered at Rostock in 1915, 'Pragmatismus in Edw. Gibbons Geschichte vom Verfall und Untergang des römischen Reiches', ascribes far too modern an outlook to him. There is a penetrating analysis of Gibbon's interpretation of the Middle Ages by Falco, *La polemica sul medio evo*, I, 1933. He, too, as we have done, stresses the incoherent

And in general, throughout this mighty mass of material ranging over one and a half millennia, and handled with consummate art, the selection and division of the subject-matter is lacking in the inner unity that would have made it a work of great historical individuality in its total compass. It was indeed only right and proper to follow the destinies of the Eastern Empire up to the fall of Constantinople; and it was a necessary part of universal history to trace the further fortunes of the various peoples interwoven in the story. But the further destinies of Rome and Italy were no longer part of the decline and fall of the Roman Empire and their story breaks off quite unorganically at the end of the Middle Ages. It was through a sentimental feeling, which the first conception of the work had aroused, that the author was induced to bring the story to an artificial close with the last chapters devoted to the city of Rome, Rienzo's adventure, the Papacy, and the final ruin of Ancient Rome. In reality, the original conception of the work in the year 1764, going up to the fall of the city of Rome, and not concerned with the Holy Roman Empire, really comes to the fore again in these chapters (cf. *The Autobiographies of E. Gibbon*, pp. 270, 302 and 405).

The work as a whole was the creation of strong feeling and great mental vigour rather than psychological depth. The strong feeling was merely a sentiment of grief at the extinction of values dear to the Enlightenment, softened by a sense of good fortune in the present. Something of the typical high-class English gentleman of taste came out again in Gibbon, a type that Shaftesbury had formerly tried to deepen and spiritualise. In Gibbon, it produced an appreciative intellectualism of the highest power that was completely self-confident. Anyone who would acquaint himself with Gibbon's intense intellectual energy, together with his complacency and self-assurance, should turn to his autobiographical memoirs. Looking back on his life's work, in the midst of his pride of intellect, he does indeed wonder at one point whether after all he did not root up some flowers of imagination, some graceful errors, along with the weeds of prejudice (p. 344). This showed a slight awareness of tendencies that were already beginning to affect his contemporaries; it was an unobtrusive sign that the Enlightenment was beginning to have some suspicions of its own limitations.

nature of the construction; but he then overstresses (on pp. 254 ff.) Gibbon's tendency towards anti-pragmatic interpretations. Yet his final judgment on p. 264 is that '*l'opera è irrimediabilmente statica*'. A youthful work of Dilthey's on Gibbon (*Westermanns Monatshefte*, 21 (1867), 135 ff., under the pseudonym W. Hoffner), is interesting even today for the sake of the man who wrote it. But it gives more of a sketch of Gibbon's life than a critical evaluation of his work, and is somewhat panegyrical in tone.

III Robertson

As we turn to the third great historian of the Enlightenment, William Robertson (1721–93), we shall do well to look back a moment at the special way in which the Enlightenment's chief title to fame, its universal historical writing, was embodied in the work of Hume and Gibbon. Hume's interest embraced the whole of humanity in its rise from barbarism to civilisation, and approached religious history from this angle. Yet in his *History of England* he was not able, in spite of the universal interest that underlay it, to give more than a rather incomplete idea of its universal involvement with the general history of the West; moreover, this was an aspect on which he did not carry out enough research. Gibbon wove the history of the other nations into the story of Rome with a universal grasp; but the means at his disposal did not allow him to give an inner unity to his work as a whole. In Robertson's work, however, although it hardly manages to rise above the limitations in knowledge and standards of value that are characteristic of the Enlightenment, and is inferior to both Hume and Gibbon in its total intellectual power, there is a certain perceptible progress in the handling of universal history. This is why we have left the consideration of his writings until now, although in point of time he preceded Gibbon. His history of Scotland came out in two volumes in 1759, shortly after the first part of Hume's work, and received an extremely warm welcome in his country.[1] In Europe, his fame rested upon his greatest work, *The History of the Emperor Charles V* (1769, 3 vols). Apart from a work produced in old age about the ancient world's knowledge of India (1791), his last major historical work was the *History of America*, which was published in its first 2-volume form in 1777.[2]

All these three works have a definite vein of universal history running through them, and are the achievement of a born historian. Robertson's talent does indeed fall short of genius; but it shows a high degree of respect for the phenomena of a world that is ever in movement, and even (as far as it can grasp it) for its specific and individual qualities, on which all true historical objectivity must be based. This respect for fact, and a conscientiousness that had already led him to probe the archives, earned for Robertson the complimentary verdict (in Black's *The Art of History*, p. 122),[3] that he was

[1] Cf. B. Pier, 'W. Robertson als Historiker und Geschichtsphilosoph', thesis, Münster, 1929.

[2] Some excerpts on Virginia and New England were added later on from his literary remains. We are using the three-volume edition of 1790.

[3] Pier has shown (*loc. cit.*) that along with many direct successes in the use of source material, there were also a good many failures.

the most impeccable historian of the eighteenth century. The three works, however, show an organic development of his sense of the universal in history. First he shows how Scotland, his mother country, did not grow in isolation, but in a European setting; then he deals with European history as such, and finally the New World as it originally was, as well as its transformation by the powers of the Old World. A further organic feature of his work is that in the main all three books concentrate on the sixteenth century, and so attempt to give a penetrating study in universal history of the first order, and from many angles, of a whole period. At this point Voltaire's hints in his 'Idée générale du seizième siècle', chapter 118 of his *Essai*, bore their fruit.

But the reason for Robertson's intense interest in the sixteenth century was not exclusively connected with the Enlightenment. He says in his *History of Scotland* that this was the period when the world was awaking from its lethargy, when the human mind was becoming aware of its own powers, and was breaking the bonds of authority. He interpreted this process purely as one of improvement, *improvement of the human mind*. In Luther's Reformation, he saw one of the greatest events in human history; but he assessed it (though with greater warmth and sympathy than Hume) in purely rationalistic terms as a breakthrough to freer and more rational thinking about the deity. Religious problems as such did not hold any deeper attractions for him. He was content for his own historical purposes with an equable belief in a guiding world-providence, which included both the Enlightened and the Christian outlook in a rather loose embrace, but did not link them in any organic fashion. This providence, he held, could be observed at work in the great turning-points, and made for general progress; and taking a more restricted line than Gibbon, he was prepared to leave dogmatic questions to the ecclesiastical historian.

We may ask whether he really recognised any 'problems' in the genuine and deeper sense of the word. Well, he examined each question that he posed with serious thoroughness; but he usually contrived to answer it so satisfactorily and plausibly, putting one cause so elegantly together with another, that there was no mystery left in the matter, and that everything fitted in harmoniously stage by stage into the general pattern of progress. Even the introduction to the history of Scotland in the sixteenth century is couched in these same terms, and so more especially is the masterly introduction to the history of Charles V, with its retrospect over the dark scene of the Middle Ages, and the gradually dawning light. The author gives us a wonderful story of the steady progress that was taking place in Europe, in the course of which he is able to do much greater justice to the positive effects of the crusades and chivalry than his sceptical successor Gibbon. A whole series of lengthy developments in the State, constitutional, legal, economic, social and cultural, are related with great skill and in the pleasantest of styles. The causal importance of institutions in the life of the whole was powerfully worked out, sometimes even with a touch of exaggeration. Incidentally, Robertson's pragmatic tendencies were sometimes in evidence here, turning unconscious developments into deliberately intended change. It was thoroughly characteristic of the Enlightenment, too, to see knowledge and trade as the two most powerful levers of progress. Robertson's capacity for sketching in the broad lines and lighting them up with significant detail is all the more to be respected in that it is based upon great knowledge and mastery of his material. There is no mistaking his advance upon Voltaire, who with his smaller knowledge was yet much rasher in his assertions. And Robertson was much more successful in adducing factual support for his broad delineation of political and military struggles for power. He would compare the regulated cabinet warfare and the strife between political interests of his own day, which were yet subject to reasonable limits, with the lawless and limitless wars of earlier times; and in so doing he would reveal how the construction of a European balance of power represented a degree of progress beyond anything that had been previously achieved. This political balance, which kept even power politics within reasonable bounds, seemed to him to be the *great secret of modern politics* (*History of Scotland*). We noticed in Gibbon a similar feeling for the cultural importance of the more recent European political systems, and saw it as a bridge connecting him with Ranke. Robertson likewise saw in the formation of a political balance of power that was favourable to culture the universal historical significance of the struggle for power between Charles V and Francis I. When he comes to the detailed narrative, however, which is essentially based upon the Renaissance historians, he does not show the same broad skill as in the introduction. It proceeds in a somewhat narrow perspective from one action to another, and though making clear enough distinctions between practical interests and human passions as motives, it is deficient in any large ideas which would draw the whole together. As a true son of the Enlightenment, he could shape the general *improvement* of humanity into an artistic drama, but the hour when political history would come fully alive had not yet struck.

Only in his *History of Scotland* did the narrative of struggles for power strike a somewhat more lively and individual note. As a faithful Scot, he naturally had the destinies of his own country very much at heart. He was moved by the dramatic story that had led from the isolated battleground of a wild mediaeval feudalism and the personal rule of the nobility to an interlinking with English history in the sixteenth century. Scotland had then been transformed by the development of the new European political system until it was finally ripe for union with England. Not without a touch of sorrow he discussed the possibility at the conclusion of his work that the Scottish language might have flourished in a separate country as did the manifold dialects in ancient Greece. But he expressed a decided preference for becoming one with the English nation, rather than continuing in the half-and-half existence of the seventeenth century. He judged that the results would benefit both the freedom and the essential genius of Scotland.

But he at once repressed this slightly romantic tendency, of which he was already aware. He is clearly at pains to give an accurate account of the particular and specific along with the simpler and more general laws that govern the progress of mankind. And this clear intention warns him not to apply the ideas of the present to the past. Voltaire and Montesquieu had also pronounced this warning, and Robertson was only taking Montesquieu's causal methods a step further, but with a claim to increased accuracy in detailed research, and a growing sense of the manifold variety of the causes that were constantly at work. 'But the passion of that great man for system sometimes rendered him inattentive to research', as the author rightly says in the *History of America* (vol. 3, p. 379). Thus Robertson avoided the onesidedness of Montesquieu's theory of climate, whilst showing an awareness of geographical conditioning. Above all, he was concerned like Voltaire to search for moral and political causes, and see how they fitted together into a pattern. Yet the past continued to be worth research, in his estimation, not for its inherent value, but only as a means of getting to know more about the rise of modern civilisation and acquiring a completer picture of the species *homo sapiens*. Fundamentally, then, his attitude to the past was causal, and not evaluative. At any rate the values of the past which he recognised were only the approximate values of a reason that was still in process of gradual purification. In his *History of Scotland*, it was only possible for this feeling to come through as it were by the way. He viewed the earlier history of his own nation with quite un-romantic eyes. He expresses the opinion at the outset that the earliest times should either be ignored as quite fabulous, or handed over to the credulity of the antiquarian. Nations, like human beings, only reached maturity by stages, and what took place in their childhood or early youth should not be recalled to memory.

Yet later on he broke this basic principle in his *History of America*, where he analysed the primitive stages of the Indians' history, and the somewhat higher level of the half-cultured Mexicans and Peruvians with great care, and from all the sources that were then available. Here, he was not frightened off by the fabulous nature of the traditional material. Rather was he enticed by the task of finding reliable material to demonstrate the lowest stages of the great process of human improvement. Rousseau's thesis of the ideal state of man in his natural condition had roused the opposition of the Enlightened thinkers. Voltaire had taken the lead, followed by the Swiss author Iselin, who in 1764 had collected a good deal of material bearing on primitive conditions that told against Rousseau, but without taking the problem down to a deeper level. Then in 1767, Ferguson had undertaken a more delicate examination of the stages in primitive cultures. Robertson now stepped into the ranks, and likewise came down fairly and squarely against Rousseau. Here, too, he gave most careful consideration to any special features that he discovered; but his leading theme was that all the specific features in the primitive American peoples were only secondary as compared with the general human types exemplified by them, which were valid for all nations. He contested the conclusions drawn from the similarity of customs in certain old Germanic and Indian tribes, that they must therefore be related and have sprung from the same origins. These likenesses, he held, were more probably to be explained as the result of the same way of life and the same stage of culture. 'A tribe of savages on the banks of the Danube must be very much like a tribe on the plains of the Mississippi' (*History of America*, I, 26; cf. also *History of Charles V*, Note 6 on Sect. I). Ferguson's analysis of the primitive peoples had started out from the same point. Both these theses must be reckoned an advance on the wild uncritical speculation such as even Lafitau had indulged in, with his genealogical hypothesis. Like Hume's related theory of the history of religion, these ideas paved the way for a comparative science of cultural stages. Once again, as with Hume, we stand at the beginning of a positivist attitude to history, based only upon the development of types. But the outlook based upon Natural Law still showed its influence in Robertson's assumption that the similarity in human nature everywhere showed itself in the similarity of the progressive cultural stages. 'The human mind holding the same course in the New World as in the Old, might have advanced by the same successive steps' (*Hist. of Am.*, 3, 171). 'A human being as originally shaped by the hand of nature is everywhere the same', whether he grows up among the wildest of savages or in the most civilised of nations. The capacity for *improvement* seemed to be the same; and the talents and virtues to which it was applied seemed to depend largely upon the contemporary circumstances of society (*Hist. of Am.*, 2, 188). Thus

Robertson saw in the feudal constitution of ancient Mexico an exact counterpart to the feudalism of Europe in the Middle Ages. Comparisons of this kind could only be fruitful if the new feeling for types growing out of an empirical approach could be combined with a new and more vital sense of the individual. Robertson was lacking in this, and no conscientious description of peculiarities alone could take its place. But such a sense was not altogether lacking in the intellectual life of England as a whole in the eighteenth century, as we shall now see in examining the remarkable spectacle of the English Pre-Romantics.

Chapter six

The English Pre-Romantics, Ferguson and Burke

I The English Pre-Romantics

It belongs to the essence of historical development that it only becomes possible through a process of polarity, through an unceasing tension between opposing tendencies. Great intellectual movements, when they first arise, become established and dominant, and indeed often seem to take on an absolute character and prevail at any rate for the time being against all opposing forces. In truth, closer examination often shows that from the start there has been at work alongside and in the background some force of another kind operating in a different direction. This force looks beyond to a more distant future, and is often closely and widely connected with the dominant movement, but is destined at some point to take its place, in order then to recommence the same process of rise and eventual dissolution: 'Formation, transformation—an everlasting entertainment of the eternal mind.' It depends on the character of the observer whether this overpowering drama spells out a meaningful or a meaningless history, a world of consolation or a world of despair, whether it leads to a resigned relativism or to a faithful devotion to an idea, in spite of its threatened extinction. This belief may rely on the faith, apart from anything else, that even what appears to perish in this dialectic of development is never quite extinguished, but goes on working 'at a higher level'.

The eighteenth century provides one of the greatest examples of the process whereby a new intellectual and spiritual force appears to effect an absolute conquest for a certain period, yet is accompanied from the very start by an opposite tendency which later causes its dissolution. The century of the Enlightenment and of rationalism was never merely this and no more. From the very start, it bore within itself the germs that would spring to life as Romanticism, irrationalism and historism in the nineteenth century. This is observable on all sides in Europe, as we have already seen in France; and in general literature this has been shown by a Frenchman, Paul van Tieghem, in his book *Le Préromantisme, Études d'histoire littéraire européenne* (2 vols, Paris 1924), where the material is handled with great felicity, though not with entire satisfaction as far as the Enlightenment is concerned.

A certain polarity, however, marks not only the development of Western intellectual life as a whole, but also the separate individual lives of the nations. Each people has hidden within it certain polarities of character and opposing tendencies, often dwelling side by side in the same breast, scales of the same balance, as it were, that may move up or down. The particular call of the period, or a common situation arising from the great contradictions in the common life of the West, can make the balance go up or down. It was a genuinely English trait that the spirit of the Enlightenment, which led the counteraction to the age of religious wars, should have taken the form of empiricism and sensualism under the influence of Locke, Hume and others. It was typically English, too, that the opposite of the characteristic English *common sense* (which we can perhaps represent summarily as a need for the romantic and the aesthetic) should not simply have perished under the victorious impact of the enlightened outlook, but should have survived and gradually re-asserted its influence. At the beginning of the eighteenth century, that is even before the climax of the English Enlightenment, we noted in Shaftesbury the first strong stirrings in this direction, though closely intertwined at the same time with its opposite pole, the enlightened outlook. But the contrary tendency was also at work, for in Pope, the classical poet of English enlightened taste, the opposite romantic–aesthetic trend was not altogether dead. Even his mind had a place in it, as has been well said, for doubt, mystery and infinity.[1] Shakespeare was indeed strongly attacked by the authors of the Enlightenment on account of his offences against good taste; but at the same time he was always continuously admired. He remained the English poet *par excellence*, who gave the most vigorous expression to everything that fell outside the bounds of English *common sense*. He was enough by himself to keep the countervailing tendencies alive over against the influence of the Enlightenment.

But not more than half alive, it must be admitted. It was decisive for the character of the movement we have to depict that it never transcended the limitations imposed by the outlook of its authors.

[1] Crane Brinton, *The Political Ideas of the English Romanticists* (1926), p. 11. Phelps, *The Beginning of the English Romantic Movement* (1899) quotes on p. 18 from Pope's letter of 1716 the following sentence: '*The more I examine my own mind, the more romantic I find myself*'.

In other words, it remained a movement of cultured and refined men of taste; and that in spite of many respects in which it was deepened, and in particular one outstanding phenomenon which we shall have to describe in conclusion. It would indeed have been possible to follow up the line pursued by Shaftesbury. He had succeeded not only in being a man of taste of the first order, but also in not merely enjoying, but also understanding what he enjoyed at a deep metaphysical level, and with a broad world outlook that was truly religious in its compass. But in typically English fashion, it seemed more proper to satisfy these new stirrings of life in a quite untheoretical manner, and gently to discard, with an instinctive sureness of touch, all that stood in the way, yet without engaging in basic conflict with it. The capacities for drive and radical intellectual revolution inherent in the English character had spent its force for a long time in the seventeenth century. But what had eventually emerged, the cool deism and intellectualism of the Enlightenment, with its leanings towards clear and simple statements of universal law, did not satisfy the sensitive spirit as it now emerged in a more untrammelled guise; nor did it satisfy the needs of cultured taste for the attractions of manifold variety.

Step by step, taste and feeling now proceeded to shape their own forms of expression, though without necessarily being untrue to the spirit of the Enlightenment. They were blissfully satisfied with the new little world that then came into being, and without the slightest suspicion that this new little world would open out into a new intellectual world for the whole of the West. At this point Shaftesbury, with his original enthusiasm for the beauty of nature's spontaneous creations, was able to exercise a direct effect upon his fellow-countrymen. Addison, Pope and he together expressed the thoughts that were then embodied and developed in the English garden from 1720 onwards.[1] The strictly formal garden design of French-Italian taste gave way to a delight in the charms of a more free and uncontrolled nature, whether in its milder or in its wilder mood. It is incidentally worth remembering that there had been some earlier traces of this feeling even in the seventeenth century in the shepherd poetry and art of Ruysdaels, Salvator Rosas and others. Contemporary with the first English gardens were the first stirrings in literature that have been called Romanticist.[2] In architecture,[3] the first

[1] Marie Luise Gothein, *Geschichte der Gartenkunst* (1926 ed.), 2, 367 ff.

[2] Phelps, *loc. cit.*, and Henry A. Beers, *A History of English Romanticism in the 18th century*, 1899.

[3] The older work by Eastlake, *A History of the Gothic Revival* (1872) has been superseded by Kenneth Clark's *The Gothic Revival* (1928), and by Alfred Neumeyer's book (which also has references to England) *Die Erweckung der Gotik in der deutschen Kunst des späten 18. Jahrhunderts* (*Repert. f. Kunstwissenschaft*,

half of the eighteenth century was the period when the Renaissance forms had so established their ascendancy that there came about a pause (almost a temporary vacuum) in the further development of the local Gothic style. Throughout the seventeenth century, the norms of the Palladian style had been largely triumphant as far as public buildings were concerned. But alongside it, in private building and in the University city of Oxford, with its High Church traditionist outlook, the hallowed Gothic style was still being used for the new colleges. In the seventeenth century, too, there had been a small school of antiquarians who had kept alive an interest in the Gothic, not so much out of love for it as a style as out of reverence for its antiquity. But in their ranks there was also something of a gap about the middle of the eighteenth century. The taste of the Enlightenment, for which everything smacking of the Gothic was sheer mediaeval barbarism, seemed to have been victorious all along the line. Yet as early as 1740 a young Englishman called Thomas Gray could on his travels express admiration for Rheims Cathedral, and surrender to a mood of romantic colouring in Italy. Gray was one of those men who may be of importance in a time of transition, not as productive writers, but as the living central figures in groups of friends who help to spread a movement when it has once caught on. His travelling-companion on this journey, Horace Walpole, the witty and much-travelled son of Robert Walpole, suddenly roused the attention of the public by the gradual transformation and extension of his country house at Strawberry Hill, near Windsor, into a Gothic building, or rather a picturesque complex of buildings, in a style which became known as Rococo–Gothic. It was thoroughly eclectic and artificial in feeling: in the dining-hall, for example, you sat at altar tables. And Horace Walpole's famous novel *The Castle of Otranto*, published in 1765, makes an equally artificially mediaeval and wild impression, for it is full of the trappings of mediaeval horrific romance; but it was first in a line which eventually led on to the happy and skilful evocation of the past that culminated in the novels of Walter Scott.

For Horace Walpole himself, as has rightly been noted, all this was sport rather than profound and vital need, for he remained the polished man of the eighteenth-century Enlightenment. But the fact that he had successors shows that he had been led on by a happy instinct towards a change in mental outlook that was already underway. Perhaps we should incidentally distinguish between the subsidiary element of whimsical fancy and the collector's zeal for the rare or exotic, which even Shaftesbury had noticed among his fellow-

vol. 49, 1928). Both these works treat their material from the point of view of the history of thought.

countrymen, and genuine English traditionalism. This latter could be surrounded by all the towering testimonies to the past, and could preserve most piously all its outmoded forms in politics and in jurisprudence, even while its head was full of the very latest notions of Enlightenment. The splendid continuity of English development, which was symbolised even by externals, thus became a seedbed for a feeling for historical traditions. It was always unconsciously in the background, but awoke significantly to full consciousness just after the short period when the taste of the Enlightenment had apparently been victorious over the whole field. It would seem that in real life things have to run their full course to arouse the opposition into action at the right moment. Here, as everywhere, the Enlightenment showed itself to be the indispensable means of producing a strong reaction that would stir up countervailing forces.

It was the Englishman's eyes, and the Englishman's interest in concrete things, that sought for new pastures and found them in the English garden and Gothic buildings. As Neumeyer has pointed out, everywhere that English gardens appeared, you can also be certain to find Gothic architecture soon putting in an appearance. The broad trends of feeling that followed in their wake could, however, extend their influence in a great variety of directions. In his *History of English Thought in the 18th century* (1876 and many subsequent editions), Leslie Stephen called attention to the connection between Romanticism, sentimentalism and Naturalism particularly prominent in the second half of the century, but also observable before this time. What he called Naturalism was the longing for the nature that had been proclaimed by Rousseau since the middle of the century. It was neither more nor less than a kind of inverted civilisation, a sentimental dream-picture of natural simplicity that arose by way of reaction, a picture thought to represent what had once existed either among primitive peoples, or in the early days of the great civilisations. As was natural enough against the classical background, men's attention was first of all directed to Homer and his world.[1] As early as 1735 Blackwell could write: 'The pleasure which we receive from a representation of *natural* and *simple* manners is irresistible and enchanting' (*Life and Writings of Homer*, p. 24), when he published anonymously his study of the life and writings of Homer. This was translated into German in 1766 by Johann Heinrich Voss, and in this form made a fresh impact upon German readers. He was bold enough to call attention once again to an 'old opinion' that poetry

[1] The fundamental work for Homeric interpretation in the eighteenth century is G. Finsler's *Homer in der Neuzeit von Dante bis Goethe*, 1912; only it is somewhat overloaded with subsidiary detail, and so does not always clearly bring out movements of thought from the historical point of view.

existed before prose (pp. 38–49 in translation). Earlier on, Vico had arrived at this same important result, but from a deeper study of antiquity, and had drawn conclusions that radically upset historical thought based upon Natural Law. But Blackwell did not command any such revolutionary insight, though he probably gave some encouragement to Hamann's later and famous dictum, which proved so fruitful for Herder, that poetry was the mother tongue of the human race.[1] Blackwell goes on to say with a new insight that all original writers were only at their best when using their mother tongue and speaking of things that were thoroughly familiar to them. Renaissance authors who had written in Latin were a proof, to his mind, that it was not possible to reach a peak of excellence if one attempted to express oneself in some other medium, even if the language and the imagery were better than one's own. He saw a people's destinies, customs and language as linked together in a chain, and acting and reacting upon one another. Thus it was necessary, in order to understand Homer, to place oneself among his audience, in the company of a warrior people who would fain hear something of the heroic deeds of their ancestors. It was therefore quite wrong to take offence, as the more refined taste of our own day was inclined to do, at the blunt and natural language used by Homer. When he calls the princely Menelaus βοὴν ἀγαθός (a good 'loud-hailer') this is not to be criticised as unseemly, as has sometimes happened, but should be much commended, because the army commanders of those days needed a powerful voice. Along with this remarkably early breakthrough to a freshly individualising historical standpoint, which was yet still slightly pragmatic in approach, Blackwell's book admittedly contained many uncritical and sweeping generalisations about the Egyptian and Phoenician sources of Homeric wisdom and fantasy. Yet even this was a step forward towards a history of Eastern culture that would link together the peoples of the Ancient East.

Taken all round then, the picture is one of warm currents of air invading the cold climate of the English Enlightenment, and on every side penetrating existing conventions. At this point it would be well to ask how far the stormy religious revivalism of the brothers Wesley and Whitefield in the Methodist movement influenced these developments. In Germany, pietism was to show itself one of the strongest forces inspiring the new intellectual trends. One of the Wesleys learnt about the German brotherhood in 1740; but their movement,

---

[1] For Hamann's knowledge of Blackwell, cf. Unger, *Hamann*, pp. 215, 641, 658. Herder became acquainted with Blackwell as early as 1765 (*Works*, 18, 424 and 593). Winckelmann called Blackwell's work 'one of the finest books in the world' (to Hagedorn, 16 November 1758, *Works*, 11, 508).

although it had a powerful effect on the masses, did not sink as deeply as the more individualist German pietism into the channels of the inner life. But it certainly helped to bring about a change in the mental atmosphere by creating a strong reaction against the spirit of the Enlightenment.

At all events there was soon to be a combination of pure piety with new, original and creative taste in the shape of a book by the Oxford Professor and Archdeacon Robert Lowth, *De sacra poesi Hebraeorum*. It appeared in 1753 at the same time as Horace Walpole was beginning his experiments in the neo-Gothic; and it was a religious, scholarly and aesthetically serious counterblast to his dilettante frivolities. It need hardly be said that in his work, too, the novel elements appeared side by side with much that was still stubbornly conventional and traditional. He took the old watchword of Horace's poetics, which placed severe limitations on the character of poetry, *aut prodesse volunt aut delectare poetae*, and gave it a more pointed utilitarian direction by the phrase *prodesse delectando*. He had himself tried this recipe for poetry, and showed in his didactic poem *Choice of Hercules* (1747) that he had no real poetic power (Phelps, p. 72). As an orthodox theologian, he felt bound to adhere to an allegorical and mystical interpretation of the Song of Songs. But he went far beyond all conventional methods of treating the Bible hitherto in use when he proceeded to show that the poetic form and content of the Old Testament tradition as a whole were one great unity, of a wonderful and unique kind, and went on to interpret its details in a really attractive fashion. He was more particularly concerned with two genuinely historical questions, the origins of Hebrew poetry, and its specific character in comparison with other national poetries. As a theologian who believed in revelation, his first concern was to show the divine source of Hebrew poetry. It had not been contrived by human ingenuity, he held, but had come down from heaven, and had from the start attained complete maturity. But along with this contention he introduced something of a comparative and evolutionary psychology such as Hume was already applying. In order to throw light upon the origin of this poetry as a whole, which was as dark as the waters of the Nile, he directed his attention to other nations, and found that everywhere sacred poetry with its hymns and songs had been the earliest stage, and that all later poetry strove to go back to it *veluti ad germanam patriam*. He derived it from the original position of mankind as a whole, and from powerful mental excitements and disturbances (*Poeseos origo . . . ad religionem omnino videtur referenda . . . [Poesis] . . . non aetatis alicujus aut gentis propria sed universi humani generis, vehementioribus humanae mentis affectibus necessario tribuenda est*). Adam, he held, could scarcely be imagined without some use of poetry. As with Blackwell, only more definitely and boldly, we can see that this is a stage towards Hamann's and Herder's conviction that poetry was the mother tongue of the human race.[1]

And Herder was also destined to be deeply impressed with Lowth's attempt to capture the peculiar character of Hebrew poetry, its *propria indoles*. Following up Blackwell's vision, he maintained that we must sink ourselves entirely in the life and thought of this people, for whom religion governed everything—the state, the laws, justice and everyday life. It was not enough to be content with translations, we must go back to the sources, *qui proprium etiam ac suum quendam saporem habent*. Then we should see clearly the splendour of much that was at present dark and obscure. In the pictures drawn by the bards and prophets of Israel, he saw in his mind's eye the stony land of Palestine, with its mountain streams that rose in annual flood from the snows of Lebanon; a land inhabited by a peasant and shepherd people with a nobility of tribe and race, strongly marked off from their neighbours by their laws and their religion. Lowth was extraordinarily successful in bringing out the earthy quality and the scent of the soil in this poetry. Anyone who took offence at the smell of dung and common people that sometimes pervades it (*oleant plebeculam et stercus*), simply had no feeling for the power of these pictures.

Lowth's book was perhaps the most intellectually important product of the whole Pre-Romantic movement in England. It was free of all dilettantism and superficiality of taste, and had the indirect result of contributing to the liberation of historical research from the bonds of theology by displaying the purely human and historical content and value of the Bible. It set forth a genuine science of the humanities, and gave it new organs. The same can be said, though in a slightly smaller degree, of the attractive essay *On the Original Genius and Writings of Homer*, which Robert Wood first printed in 1769 as a manuscript for friends, and which appeared in an enlarged form after his death, in 1775. Lowth, it would seem, had only divined the spirit of the East from his study; but now this much-travelled and classically cultured Englishman was to show the world

[1] In the English studies following this line of thought upon the primitive poetry of the nations, which were of importance to Herder, we must include Brown, *A Dissertation on the Rise, Union and Power, the Progressions, Separations and Corruptions of Poetry and Music* (1763), translated by Eschenburg in 1769 under the title *Betrachtungen über die Poesie und Musik*. It starts from the connection between poetry, music and the dance among the North American aborigines, then applies the observations made in constructive and pragmatic fashion to other peoples. Herder, in his *Geist der hebräischen Poesie* (*Works*, 12, 177), rightly recognised both the fruitful fundamental ideas and the weaknesses in Brown's treatment of this theme.

the worth of his fellow-countrymen's extensive travels for the discovery of new historical values. In 1743 and 1751 he had travelled through Greece and the Near East, including Egypt, with Homer in his hand and heart, and could announce with much greater eloquence and conviction than Blackwell that up till now Homer had not been properly understood. It was necessary to pay more attention to the *Ionian point of view*, and the special characteristics of the Ionian earth and the Ionian sky. One must have seen the Bedouins in all their savage cruelty and cunning, and yet with their open-hearted hospitality, and their poets reciting their verses under the open skies of the Arabian desert, to have any idea of the world in which Homer was rooted, and which he reproduced with incomparable fidelity and veracity, as a *faithful mirror of life*. His main thesis, then, was that the heroic and patriarchal customs were quite comparable with those of the Bedouins today, because Eastern life was so unchanging that the cultural stages of primaeval life had still been preserved. Thus when we are disgusted by many things in the customs and manners of Homer's heroes, as in life today in the East, this must not be ascribed to any capricious peculiarities in the period or the country, but simply to certain common factors, such as soil, climate and the spirit of the laws of society at an undeveloped stage.

At this point Montesquieu's disturbing influence also played a part, although Wood did not consider his particular attempt to explain Eastern customs near enough to actual life. Comparing him with Montesquieu, one can see that there has been visible progress in English historical insight. Wood, like Montesquieu, also wanted to explain historical phenomena by peculiarities of time, place, climate and so on; but at this point Montesquieu's rather cold analysis gave way to a warmer emotional interest and a certain degree of ability to identify himself with a completely different world of the past. This difference, this great gulf between periods and cultures, must first of all be strongly felt if one was to be able to enter with all one's heart into the remote past. Up till now, with the exception of Vico, Blackwell and a few others, Homer had been considered along the lines of Natural Law as a timeless classical phenomenon of great didactic value. Wood was quite right to make fun of those who discovered in Homer a whole political and moral system, without regard for the character of the age in which he lived. Even Vico had recognised that Homer should never be treated as a handbook of wisdom. And it is indeed quite possible that some knowledge of Vico's discoveries had reached the English Homeric scholars. For a few years before the appearance of Wood's book, the *Gazette littéraire de l'Europe* had carried an article enlarging on Vico's interpretation of Homer, and his view of its barbaric character and the absence from it of anything that might be called 'a secret wisdom'.[1]

This Englishman was prevented by the sense of superiority that still clung to the outlook of the Enlightenment from feeling completely at home in the world of Homer. Again and again he emphasises that this world of Homer's and the society of the East at the present time represented something imperfect; and there are the usual expressions of regret that under an oppressive despotism it is not possible 'to maintain the natural rights of man'. Wood saw the gulf separating the world of Homer and the East from the civilised West, not as a different stage of development in individual cultural habits and attitudes, but as a lack of perfection. He therefore apologised for Homer's faults as belonging to a primitive period which must nevertheless be studied in order to appreciate the beauties of Homer.

We will refrain from quoting any further testimonies to the normative, rationalistic and classicistic sides of this thought. But his lively admixture of unfettered delight and relish for the products of foreign culture is reminiscent of a specifically English outlook that is still in evidence today. However liberal, tolerant and interested the Englishman may be in the ways of foreign nations, it is mostly with the reservation that he is himself superior, and so are the standards by which he judges life. Goethe was wont to jest that the Englishman would take his kettle for making tea even to the summit of Mount Etna! But Goethe, too, in the years of 'Sturm und Drang' experienced Wood's interpretation of Homer as a liberation. He expressed his enthusiastic approval when he reviewed the German translation (which might have been undertaken even at his own suggestion[2]) that was published in his native city of Frankfurt in 1773 in the *Frankfurter Gelehrten Anzeigen*; and in his old age, when writing *Dichtung und Wahrheit*, he could still say:

> We could now see in these poems [of Homer] no mere thrilling but somewhat inflated account of a heroic world, but the reflection of truth from a primitive age that was yet eternally present; and we did our best to appropriate its treasures.

Herder also spoke with gratitude of Wood's achievement in preserv-

---

[1] B. Croce, *Philosophie Vicos*, p. 244. Yet Bentley and Blackwell had already begun to contest the Stoics' interpretation of Homer as the epitome of all knowledge. See Finsler, *Homer in der Neuzeit*, p. 355.

[2] He mentions in *Dichtung und Wahrheit*, 3, 12, that his circle of friends first heard of Wood when a copy of his work, which was then hard to obtain, was reviewed in a Göttingen periodical. It was, in fact, a review by Heyne in the *Göttinger Anzeigen* (1770), no. 32, which was reprinted at the beginning of the German edition of 1773. The initiative for such a translation might have possibly come from Goethe. The translation was prepared by the son of the Frankfurt Counsellor Michaelis (Unger, *Hamann*, 301).

ing the natural wildness and beauty of Homer 'which was unnoticed by the blinking eyes of the scholastics and classicists' (1777;
Works, 9,534; cf. also Unger, *Hamann*, p. 302).

The two basic books in Western culture, the Bible and Homer,
were thus set in a new light by Blackwell, Lowth and Wood, a light
that had hitherto been obscured by thought based upon the principles of Natural Law. The battle for precedence between Homer
and Vergil, which the judges of art waged as a symbol of a still
greater battle, began to incline in favour of Homer. The norms of
classical taste did indeed continue to hold sway, but were at least
temporarily forgotten wherever the charms of the past began to
exercise their sway. Without being totally disloyal to their own times
and their spirit of rationalism, people now began to take delight in
the contrasts provided by the irrational, not as yet weakened by
civilisation, in the primitive and early periods of human history; and
especially in their own particular nation and all its early racial components. Mediaevalism, primitivism, Celtomania, Germanomania
and septentriomania are recently coined terms for these various
passions that came to the fore in England from the middle of the
eighteenth century onwards. There were two French books whose
acquaintance we have already made—P. H. Mallet's *Introduction à
l'histoire de Dannemarc*, 1755 (translated by Percy in 1770) and
De la Curne de Sainte-Palaye's *Mémoires sur l'ancienne chevalerie*.
Both these books had a stirring and exciting effect on Englishmen,
for they served as an introduction to the almost unknown and
gigantic world of the Edda, and the heroic tales of the ancient
North. We shall only select from these efforts what is most representative and at the same time important for the German movement;
but we would also refer the reader to Phelps's and Beer's account and
Peardon, *The Transition in English Historical Writing* (1933).

The anonymously published *Letters on Chivalry and Romance* of
Bishop Richard Hurd, which appeared in 1762, would certainly
seem to have exercised a powerful effect, both on Hamann (cf.
Unger, 910, 933) and Herder (*Geschichtsphilosophie* of 1774). Hurd
was a friend of Thomas Gray, who had once been Horace Walpole's
travelling-companion about 1740 and had admired the Gothic
cathedral of Rheims. Sainte-Palaye's book had been of considerable
service to him.[1] But it did not cut loose from the timeless standards of
reason so dear to the Enlightenment; nor in many respects did Hurd,
who made such good use of it. For in his enthusiasm for all things
Gothic and romantic in poetry he soon overshot the mark and
simply inverted the normative classical ideals of art, which it was his

---

[1] This work had also contributed towards Robertson's favourable judgement on
chivalry (see pp. 194–5 above).

concern to oppose, in maintaining that Gothic customs and folklore were more suited to the purposes of poetry than the classical. But even this thesis is suggestive of the creative idea that is reminiscent of Blackwell, Lowth and Wood, namely the existence of a close connection between the specific structure and the specific poetry of an age, and that even the political and social structures of a particular period contain necessary links between cause and effect. Voltaire and Hume had both already seen the truth of this for the Middle Ages, but only in a somewhat external fashion; they had not been inclined to apply it intrinsically. Even Hurd showed that he still had links with the historical outlook of the Enlightenment in the somewhat flat and almost mathematically simple way in which he constructed his chain of cause and effect. According to his interpretation, the splitting up of Europe had produced the feudal system, with its warlike spirit; and this again had produced the age of chivalry, with its jousting and notions of knightly honour, which should not, however, be looked upon as absurd and fanciful, but should be considered useful in fulfilling a purpose for that particular period. He held that 'the principles of feudalism were bound to end in this development'. The 'spirit of chivalry' was thus a fire that was soon extinguished, but the spirit of romance which it kindled continued to burn on into the more polished ages of civilisation. At this point he ventures the happy suggestion that Ariosto, Tasso, Spenser and Milton—yes, and even Shakespeare—should be grouped together as poets in the Gothic tradition; and he pronounced Shakespeare to be greater when using Gothic material and contrivances than when drawing upon a classical background. This judgement may still find a sympathetic echo at the present time, when the simple and the primitive formulas have again come into favour, and there has been a weakening of the feeling for a creative synthesis between the Gothic and the classical spirit—though Shakespeare does indeed engulf them both in his immensity.

Hurd as a child of the eighteenth century was more modest in his apology for chivalry and Gothic taste, and more resigned to their disappearance. Though he judged them to have contributed more to poetry than the world of the classics, he was equally convinced that they were gone for good and all, and that in this age of reason no poet would be well advised to deal in Gothic fictions, which could only be effective where they were rooted in popular beliefs. He expressed the view that the revolution in taste had produced a fair proportion of *good sense*; and that through it we had lost *a world of fine fabling*. This conclusion is noteworthy, for it is so particularly in accordance with a period of transition, where there was such a constant coming and going and clash of opinions. At this very point

Hurd was involved in a new revolution of taste, which yet had its roots in the past, and showed that there was life in the old world still. His warning concerning the mere trappings of Gothic taste, which perhaps had Horace Walpole in view, was profoundly justified in the light of history; but when it is closely examined, it is clearly seen to be another piece of his Enlightenment thinking that made him utter this warning against leaving the territory of that which had been once and for all given and certified by the spirit of the age.

But the following passage will show that there was in Hurd's work a really new achievement in genuine historical thought. 'When an architect examines a Gothic structure by Grecian rules, he finds nothing but deformity. But the Gothic architecture has its own rules, by which, when it comes to be examined, it is seen to have its merits, as well as the Grecian' (Letter VIII). The relevant question was not which of the two was the truest and most genuine taste, but rather whether there was not some meaning and some plan in both of them when they were examined according to the principles on which they were based. The substance of this remark was the same as the truth that came home so clearly to the youthful Goethe in the cathedral at Strassburg ten years later. Thus Goethe was not the first, as has sometimes been supposed, to discover the specific laws and values of the Gothic; only in Goethe's case, the discovery burst forth from the volcanic depths of a new attitude to the whole world, whereas the Englishman's was rather something that grew from the well-tended garden soil of a refined culture.

Stimulated by the work of Sainte-Palaye, Hurd took a further step that was full of promise. Sainte-Palaye himself had been (rather remarkably, perhaps) stirred by a word thrown out by Frederick the Great,[1] directing attention to the analogy between the heroic days of Homer and those of the knights-errant. It was Hurd's opinion that the common cause was to be found in the fragmentation of the state in ancient Greece, as in feudal Europe. He stated the case in rather summary fashion; and the thinkers of the Enlightenment had already been concerned with comparing different cultures. Hume based his history of religion upon it, and had even compared Germanic penal laws with those of ancient Greece (*The History of England* (1762), I, 157). Hurd, however, anticipated the modern attempts at a typology and this comparison seemed to give him a greater understanding of the individual in the midst of the typical. At this point he broke

---

[1] Sainte-Palaye's *Mémoires* close with a quotation from the *Mém. pour servir à l'hist. de la maison de Brandebourg: 'On faisoit dans ces siècles grossiers le même cas de l'adresse du corps, que l'on en fit du temps de Homère'*, etc. For the wording (which has been insignificantly altered), compare *Œuvres de Fréd. le Grand* (ed. Preuss), 1, 12.

through the pragmatic habit of mind that had clung to him up till now, by which he had been inclined to derive great effects from causes of a rather superficial kind. He now explained that there was some active force preceding all habits and forms of government and independent of them all. This he called *the different humour and genius of the East and West*, to be seen in a comparison between Greek and Western chivalry, where the woman held a position among the Greeks very different from her position in the Christian Middle Ages. This was a point to which Mallet had already called attention. But it is worth noting how simply and naturally the Englishman's sound sense and good taste took the doctrine of the spirit of the age, long in use among the thinkers of the Enlightenment, and raised it to the level of a broad inclusive conception, namely the idea that behind all the great historical cultures, and behind the obvious workings of cause and effect, there lay some final formative ferment that had set the whole development in train.

In comparison with Lowth's more serious research, Hurd's work was only a happily conceived and spirited essay. Neither he nor the English historians who had entered the lists against Hume's under-valuation of the Middle Ages (such men as O'Conor, Lyttelton, Gilbert Stuart, Pinkerton and so on—for whom cf. Peardon), had the necessary power to apply the new tendencies and principles to history in the grand manner. Thomas Warton, along with his brother Joseph, had been the most deliberate in striking the new note of sentimental romanticism, and had championed the cause of chivalry before Hurd in his *Observations on the Faery Queen* (1754). But in his great *History of English Poetry* (1774–81), though a major pioneer attempt in this kind of writing, even he was not able to get beyond Hurd's fundamental outlook in his evaluation of mediaeval culture. His approach was in fact less bold than Hurd's and more strongly loaded with residues from the Enlightenment. But his suggestions about the origins of the Gothic spirit were hazardous and some-times rather fanciful. He was inclined to derive it from the Arabs, and agreed with Mallet in tracing it back to Goths who had once upon a time migrated under Odin from Asia. Yet slowly and quietly, side by side with the continuance of historiography written in the spirit of the Enlightenment and its development into positivism, there was a steady progress in England from now onwards towards historism, although many cross currents still flowed between the two.

Thus the ideas that were tending towards a new historical attitude were connected all round with the need for a new poetry and a new art that should draw more deeply upon the feelings and the imagina-tion. This was a need generally felt in the intellectual life of the West, more or less strongly perceptible since the middle of the century in all the countries of Europe. But England, so fortunate in her rich possession of Shakespeare, led the field in the demand that the poet should not be a mere imitator, but an original creator.

Quite early on, in the time of Pope and Addison, this idea was stirring, and was even somewhat hesitantly felt by these two Classical poets. The aged poet Young crowned his life's work by sending forth into the world his final message, *Conjectures on Original Composition*. (Cf. Brandl's essay on the subject in the *Jahrbuch der deutschen Shakespearegesellschaft*, vol. 39, 1903). This appeal reached Germany in a translation as early as 1760, and rang forth there almost like a cry. His essential idea, that imitation destroys the whole individuality of the soul, and that the original poet shares something of the plant's nature, not only gave the 'Sturm und Drang' generation a most welcome encouragement, but became in addition one of the germinal notions of the future historism. Young confined himself to the poet's task in maintaining that it was both right and possible for him to have something of genius to unfold to the contemporary world; but he also from time to time glanced with friendly understanding at the mediaeval scholastic, in whose constricted outlook there was nevertheless a great deal of deep and original wisdom. But it is characteristic of the transitional character of his thought that he handled the problem of genius in history in such a timeless manner. He saw genius present at all times, but looked at it as the 'sunshine' of a particular period that favoured it as a matter of chance, and as an accessory to ordinary life. He thought it only needed courage to burst the bonds of imitation and set genius free. But the youthful Goethe at Strassburg saw genius as aware of its own timeless nature, and this was his fundamental attitude, and the point from which his further development started.

The position now reached, both in England and in Germany, was that only the apparently genuine, or half-genuine, insofar as it was charged with the strongest feeling, could strike home and have the effect of a revelation. This was true of Macpherson's publications on Ossian, which raised a storm in the years between 1760 and 1763, and to a certain extent of Percy's famous collection of ballads, the *Reliques of Ancient English Poetry*, which appeared in 1765. He continued a tradition of ballad collecting which goes back to the beginning of the eighteenth century. Like most of his predecessors, he considered himself at liberty to 'comb the hair' of the old ballads by means of modernisations and insertions. For as yet no one dared to present himself or the public with the unkempt looks of antiquity. *Simplicity* and *sentiment* were the qualities looked for in these old ballads (Shenstone in an exchange of letters with Percy, edited by Hecht, p. 6); and Percy wanted to satisfy men's curiosity as to the stages through which barbarism had developed into civilisation. This again shows in what a confused half-light the Enlightenment, sentimentalism and mediaevalism were groping. Percy was not only interested in the English national heritage, but was something of a dilettante forerunner of Herder in his zeal for collecting the ancient poetry of the most diverse nations throughout the world. In so doing he incidentally satisfied the fashionable craze for all things Chinese in the eighteenth century. The powerful effect produced by his collection of ballads (which was quite unexpected, even by himself) showed that the Pre-Romantic movement in England was now at its height.

It lacked the revolutionary passion, the world-shaking depth and universality of the German 'Sturm und Drang'. But it should never be forgotten that England led the way in this new historical evaluation of the past.

II Ferguson

It was something of a weakness in the English Pre-Romantics, that they never became quite free from the shackles of thought that belonged to the Enlightenment. But the relationship between the English Enlightenment and English Pre-Romanticism was not confined to a mere unorganised medley of thoughts drawn from these two sources, lying side by side as it were in the same breast. We have seen this tendency in the Pre-Romantics hitherto; and on the other hand even in Gibbon and Robertson we saw one or two gleams of Pre-Romantic origin flit across the scene. We must now return once more to Hume, and consider the possibility that his bold empiricism and scepticism opened up for historical thought. It may well be that he prepared the way for seeing that there were stronger and more sensitive spiritual forces at work than he had allowed for. He had disturbed the widespread illusions of rationalism and disclosed the general power of instinct and the irrational drives in the soul; yet he had not fully understood them, because he mentally stood apart from them in an attitude of critical rationalism. The man who could bridge this gulf would be able to penetrate deeper into the heart of history along the way that Hume had prepared. In this process, the Pre-Romantic discovery of historical values that had hitherto been neglected might well lose its peculiar character as an aesthetic movement, and broaden out into a more general and lively picture of history as a whole. In other words, there might well be a possible synthesis between the advances made by Hume and those made by the Pre-Romantics. And to a certain extent a synthesis was in fact effected by two thinkers, individually very different and not at all closely related, Adam Ferguson and Edmund Burke. They exercised a very different historical influence, and whereas the former was only successful in the world of scholarship, Burke's reputation was universal.

Ferguson (1723–1816) was Professor of Moral Philosophy in the University of Edinburgh. He is the third Scot (along with Hume and Robertson) of leading intellectual rank to make a serious contribution to English intellectual life and pass on something of importance to a wider European circle and relevant to our problems in particular. He was also the friend of another great Scot who exercised a powerful influence in history, Adam Smith, whose sphere of thought touches at certain points upon our problems, but who is yet a little too far apart to come within our selection. Ferguson published his *Essay on the History of Civil Society* in 1766. As early as 1768 a bad German translation was produced with the title: *Versuch über die Geschichte der bürgerlichen Gesellschaft* (Leipzig, 1768). It was not a literary masterpiece like those produced by the three great English historians of the Enlightenment. It suffered from prolixity, many trivial side-issues, and a clumsy and laborious style. But despite the heaviness of the portrayal, some vigorous and fertile thoughts of a fundamental kind did manage to come through. Ferguson is usually remembered as one of the pioneers in an attempt to deal with the development of forms of human society along sociological and positive lines. He tried to trace this development from the primitive level to higher culture both empirically and constructively, and to understand it as the operation of general laws. In so doing, he not only followed the hints thrown out by Montesquieu, but also the lines laid down by Hume. He stressed the power of instinct in the growth of society, and was ahead of Robertson in his evaluation of the primitive American peoples. Then, under the strong influence of Lafitau's methods, he brought all this into close connection with Tacitus' information about the ancient Germans, and with early accounts of Rome and Sparta. He showed a special interest in the changes undergone by society through increasing social differentiation.

But along with these lines of research, which tended rather in the direction of positivism, Ferguson also put forward important ideas bearing upon our particular problems. With a new insight drawn from Hume's doctrine of instinct, he energetically opposed the widespread pragmatism which sought to explain the origins and transformations of political structures as the outcome of conscious human purpose. He was of the opinion that the institutions of society were very obscure and remote in origin, and arose from natural impulses, not from human speculations. Men, groping as it were in the dark were often brought up against institutions that were not purposely intended, but were rather the indirect result of their activity. He recalled Cromwell's saying, that man never climbs so high as when he does not know where he is going; and one realises the extremely English quality of this great saying. Thus Ferguson too rejected out of hand the theory that the State had come into being through a contract. The constitutions of Rome and Sparta, which had been the favourite objects of pragmatic political discussion, he considered to be based not upon the designs of individuals, but on the situation and the genius of the whole people. Vico had formerly come forward as the solitary representative of such views. But now the mental climate of the century had altered to such an extent that here and there, and apparently quite spontaneously, a trend of thought in this direction was observable.

And so Ferguson, approaching his material with freshness and without prejudice, took up the suggestions put forward by the Pre-Romantics and drew certain conclusions from the language of the primitive races. These testified to the fact that man was by nature a poet; and no artificial alterations could improve on the beauty of the splendid unstudied songs of the primitive peoples. He touched on the same problem that had occupied Hurd shortly before, and examined the question whether modern poetry based upon imitation of the classics had resulted in gain, or whether it had on the whole lost more through sacrificing the natural lines of thought. Ferguson's answer was more accurate and cautious than Hurd's, and would even satisfy the historical sensitivities of today. He explained that this was really a matter of individual judgement, but that without the example and models of ancient learning customs and politics would have been quite different from what they are at present. And although both Roman literature and modern literature smack of the Greek originals, men would not either then or now have drawn upon those sources unless they had at the same time been constantly opening up new resources within themselves and their own contemporary world.

He thus roundly affirmed the importance of the ancient element for the history of modern culture and its development. But with the same sureness of touch he also stressed the equally great importance of the life and customs of the Middle Ages. For the basis of that which is nowadays respected as the rules of warfare and the common law of nations lay in the feelings that find expression in the popular tales of knights-errant and in the love-stories, as well as in the contemporary customs of Europe. Whatever may be the origin of these ideas, which can be either so lofty or so ridiculous, they had a lasting effect upon our manners and customs. He saw a combination of the hero and the saint in the men of the Middle Ages; and although he still acknowledged the importance of the ancient world's contribution, there was already some suggestion of the threefold elements of Germanism, Christianity and Antiquity which modern thought sees as factors in Western culture.

With the same surprising lack of prejudice and an absence of either Enlightened or Romantic presuppositions, Ferguson worked out a comparison between the starting and the end-points of this process, between barbarism and civilisation. We often cannot understand how men could exist under the wretched conditions of barbarian life; and yet each age has its consolations as well as its sufferings. To the stern judges of contemporary habits who condemned the luxury of modern times he pointed out that the standards of judgement they delighted in were no more than contemporary. The man who nowadays condemns the use of the coach would very likely in earlier times have condemned the wearing of shoes. If a palace was held to be unnatural, well then, so was a hut. Rousseau had been radical enough to maintain such a thesis.[1] But Ferguson now tackled the problem of modern civilisation at a deeper level than had been possible for Rousseau. He was just beginning to experience the early stages of the English industrial and technical revolution, the replacement of manual work by machinery, and the increasing division of labour which was destined to rob the individual of a good deal of the mental and spiritual satisfaction he had formerly found in his work. Ferguson was aware of these dangers, however clearly he saw the processes of technical improvement at work before his very eyes; and he was of the opinion that the outward effects of the division of labour would be to disrupt the bonds of society, for it would in the end simply consist of separate elements in which there was no longer any of the spiritual inspiration that should be the leading force among the nations.

And perhaps this was Ferguson's most vital contribution to historical thought. He saw, even more clearly than his contemporary Boulanger, that the spiritual attitude of men was ultimately the decisive factor in the rise and fall of peoples and States—that force which Machiavelli had once sought to comprehend as *virtù* and which Ranke would later call the moral energies of a nation. Here again Ferguson transcended both the Enlightenment and Pre-Romanticism. He rejected the eudaemonism of private life, which had been largely accepted by the former, and was not content, as the latter had been, with purely aesthetic or sentimental delight in the new values discovered in the past. He may not have been very happy in his expression of what he took to be the basic law of history and indi-

[1] '*Le premier qui si fit des habits ou logement se donna en cela des choses peu nécessaires*' etc. *Discours sur l'origine de l'inégalité parmi les hommes*, I.

vidual life; but he saw the essential truth that States and peoples flourish when their members possess not only mental and spiritual vitality, but also a strong sense of political community. Even in the England of his day this seemed to him to be lacking. He observed a tendency to think of the individual with pity and sympathy, but seldom with vigour of the whole body politic. But a political philosophy that only paid attention to good order and security for persons and property, without regard to the political character of its citizens, was only cultivating their taste for enjoyment and their acquisitive propensities, and was rendering them unfit for the common weal. We build walls (he once said) and then weaken the spirits of those who should be their defenders. Looked at from this moral and political standpoint, even war lost the character of an inherited vice, which it had held in the eyes of the Enlightenment, and revealed its positive and creative aspects. He showed the disapproval of the large all-conquering States that had been typical of the Enlightenment since the days of Shaftesbury and Montesquieu; but he pleaded for a system of smaller States in which there could be an element of mutual tension that would make for all-round vitality. He explained that nations were fortunate in having to maintain the courage of their inhabitants in order to remain powerful and secure. Their constitutions must be shaped both so as to take into account the possibility of external war, and so as to maintain a state of peace at home. And without the jealousies between nations and the practice of war, even civic society would hardly have come into being.

Notes like these were a sign of a new age of historical thought, giving due importance to the State and to the inner forces that sustain it. Ferguson did not indeed possess the penetrative power or the imagination to give full and individual vitality to his important advances in historical thought and the idea of development, or to his unprejudiced evaluation of historical phenomena. He was only to show his capacities to the full in 1783, when he published his extensive 3-volume *History of the Progress and Termination of the Roman Republic*.[1] In this work, he pursued his basic theme and traced the fall of the republic to the decline in the public spirit; and he did so not merely in a moralising strain, but also with an eye to dynamic causes, such as the increase in the size of the State (cf. Montesquieu) and social changes within the community. But when it came to the figure of Caesar, his standards proved inadequate. The fall of Caesar is instructive, in that it shows how incapable the thinkers of the Enlightenment were of combining political and moral criticism in a higher unity, and of weaving the actions of individuals and the des-

---

[1] A German translation in 4 vols, 1785 (*Geschichte des Fortgangs und Untergangs der römischen Republik*).

tiny of the whole into a single organic texture. It was abundantly clear to Ferguson that the time 'was seasonable' to the conversion of the republic into a monarchy. But as he could see no other motive at work in Caesar but personal vanity, he considered it unjustifiable to excuse the overthrow of the republic on the grounds that it had become impossible any longer to preserve it (vol. 3, pp. 36, 324).

Thus Ferguson's work supports the view that the new ferments in historical thinking produced by the Pre-Romantic movement were not strong enough to effect a total transformation of the historical outlook belonging to the Enlightenment. His *Essay on the History of Civil Society* showed that it was easier to get beyond the conventions of the Enlightenment[1] than to achieve a new attitude to such a concrete problem of universal history as the career of Caesar. But it was again a thoroughly English trait that the demand for a new pattern of historical thought should arise, not in the sphere of scientific reflection, but with regard to the public life of an individual figure of exceptional power.

A greater contemporary of Ferguson's[2] was Edmund Burke. From the midst of actual political life, he was to confirm Ferguson's main thesis of the importance of the public spirit in history. He was able to bring such a degree of passion and creative power to bear on these problems that he could treat them at a much deeper level, and became a figure of European importance who had a lasting influence on historical thought in the future.

III Burke

In the context of the history of thought, Edmund Burke's activities can be seen more directly than Ferguson's as a branch of the Pre-Romantic movement; and they concerned a sphere that had so far been neglected by that movement—the life of the State. Burke's early life has recently had new light thrown upon it in a study by Samuels (*The Early Life, Correspondence and Writings of the Rt. Hon. Edmund*

---

[1] It is understandable that his friend Hume was dissatisfied with the book and called for its suppression. Cf. Leslie Stephen, *History of English Thought in the 18th Century* (1876), 2, 214. Stephen passes over what seems to us to be the important ideas in this book, as does the analysis of Delvaille, *Essai sur l'histoire de l'idée de progrès* (1910), pp. 473 ff. On the other hand, Trude Benz, in her *Anthropologie in der Geschichtsschreibung des 18. Jahrhunderts* (1932), rightly recognises on p. 83 that Ferguson was already clearing the way for the individual aspect of historical events.

[2] For other parallel figures in eighteenth-century England of lesser importance (Butler, 1726, Tucker, 1781), cf. Mario Einaudi, *Edmund Burke e l'indirizzo storico nelle scienze politiche* (1930), pp. 17 and 25 ff.

Burke, 1923). Along with the usual classical background, there are some clearly Romantic features, such as the reading of mediaeval romances dealing with chivalry, and a lively delight in Gothic architecture and ivy-covered ruins. His youthful piece of work on the origin of our ideas of the beautiful and sublime appeared in 1756, but belonged to a much earlier date, and may even have been written when he was only nineteen (Samuels, pp. 137, 141, 213). It was to attract Lessing's and Herder's attention,[1] and was destined to win an important place in the history of aesthetic theories. Its basic ideas showed that it was part of the general revolution of taste then taking place in the aesthetic sphere both in England and in Germany, parallel with and related to the changes we have been tracing in the field of historical thought. Everywhere there were signs of a revolt against the rigid norms of traditional artistic taste and a reaching out to a livelier art able to express a new indwelling spirit. For Burke's view was that the starting-point should be, not the works of art themselves, but the spiritual stirrings within the human being, if one was to arrive at any satisfactory aesthetic laws. This was very much after the heart of all who were finding new life in Homer, the Bible and the romantic poetry of chivalry, by learning to understand them in terms of the particular mental and spiritual outlook of the ages to which they belonged. But so far none of these precursors in the attempt to understand art and history in a more individualising fashion had applied these new principles to the central sphere of historical life, namely the State. This was a task which did not appear to the cultured men of the eighteenth century in general either very enticing or very urgent. True, Montesquieu had already paved the way, but the means at his disposal were inadequate. It was then the task of Möser to infuse new life into the nature of the State in Germany. In England, this was the achievement of Burke, who used Ferguson's tentative approaches to the subject and built much more solidly upon them. All the thinkers we have named were in fact pioneers rather than completers of their task. But England was the nation that offered the most favourable conditions for a more solid study, for it was of all the nations in Europe the best integrated; that is to say, the nation who had best succeeded in combining the interests of society with the interests and institutions of the State.

In the years of the French Revolution, Burke completed his work and service as an active politician; but he began his work as a historian. His *Essay Towards an Abridgement of the English History* was produced in those same middle 1750s when Hume was still working on his great history. But it remained a fragment which broke off at the year 1216, and was never given to the world until 1812, when it

[1] Cf. on this point Frieda Braune, *E. Burke in Deutschland* (1917), pp. 6 ff.

was published posthumously in his collected works. A hundred years ago, when the new school of historical criticism was flourishing in Germany under Ranke, Lappenberg rightly regretted that this promising attempt of Burke's to write the history of his nation was never completed (*Geschichte von England*, I, 1834, lxxiv). For although it often failed to get beyond a pragmatic standpoint, it yet revealed the stirrings of a new historical sense that went beyond anything Hume had written under the influence of the Enlightenment. At this point Burke unconsciously reveals his innermost nature, for his work does not contain any of the Enlightenment's condemnation of the Middle Ages for their barbaric ignorance. Moreover, he takes a clearly religious attitude in tracing the workings of providence in the destiny of nations, in his respect for the achievements of religion even in primitive times, from the time of the Druids up to the cultural contribution of the monasteries and the pilgrimages to the Holy Land, and in his general inclination to assess the people and the affairs of the Middle Ages in milder and more generous terms. But most clearly of all, and even more strongly than Hume, Burke shows a feeling for all that is institutional in the past, seeing in it the roots of our modern institutions, and for the way that it has gradually risen to a higher stage from very rough and obscure beginnings. Here, both Hume and Burke owed much to Montesquieu's powerful influence; and Burke praised him as the greatest genius of our age. In two particular problems that he set himself one can especially see Montesquieu's methods at work in the study of 'the generation' of law. The case of Thomas à Becket was the occasion for an excursion on the history of the power and jurisdiction of the Church from the end of the ancient world onwards. Moreover, he was delighted to search out the earliest and very scanty sources of the jurisprudence from which all the nations of today derive benefit. He showed how they had originally been muddied by much superstition and brute force, and how in course of time and with the help of favourable circumstances they had gradually become cleansed. No doubt there was something here too of the Enlightenment's joy in the *improvement of the law*. But it was a genuine piece of historical insight to see where the two chief deficiencies had hitherto been in the treatment of English law: first, in the failure to realise that it had remained essentially the same from time immemorial; and secondly, that it had remained essentially free of foreign influence.

In combating these mistakes, Burke would have had Hume on his side. But even in this youthful piece of work one can see the germ of a profound difference from Hume's pattern of thought, which was later to be consciously developed. In spite of his naturalistic interpretation of the origins and development of the State, Hume had always remained attached to the idea of Natural Law—which was really rational law. He continued to believe 'that ideas of primitive equality are engraven in the hearts of all men'. He made this affirmation on the occasion of John Ball's insurrection in the reign of Richard II— John Ball, who might be counted one of the first Levellers. He revolted in horror at the idea of a populace free to do its own sweet will (*The History of England*, vol. 2, pp. 245 and 248), yet felt unable as a rationalist to deny a natural claim to equality. Later on, in 1791, when he was standing out against the human rights claimed by the French Revolution, Burke reproached Hume with this (*Thoughts on French Affairs*). And if we enquire what attitude is taken to the ideas of Natural Law in his youthful work, we shall not indeed find any explicit attack on them, but rather a tacit abandonment and their substitution by historical explanations; for it is clear that as early as this Burke's innate attitude was moving away from those concepts. His third youthful work, *The Vindication of Natural Society*, which appeared anonymously in 1756, showed an even more marked tendency in this direction. It was a satire, and as satire, not a particularly successful attack against the effects of Bolingbroke's enlightened philosophy. Bolingbroke had undertaken to root out the positive religions with the weapons of pure reason; so Burke, masking himself under this particular style, intended to reduce the matter *ad absurdum* by showing how the same insipid sophistic methods could also be used to throw doubt upon the value of any ordered political life for man, and to recommend the primitive condition of statelessness as the ultimate human ideal. At that time he was probably not yet aware of Rousseau's earnest efforts only a short while before (in 1750)[1] to preach precisely this reversal of all the usual values. Yet Rousseau was destined to be the very man whose intellectual and spiritual after-effects Burke was to make it his chief life's work to combat. We get a glimpse of a remarkable and yet quite understandable interlacing of the intellectual worlds that are here at strife. In reality, both Rousseau and Burke were fighting the same enemy, for Rousseau had also administered a sharp blow to the spirit of the Enlightenment by his criticisms of modern civilisation. But Rousseau was both a man of feeling and a rationalist, and fought with rationalist weapons and methods of thought. He never became aware that this world of natural humanity he so earnestly longed for could never be won by these weapons. Thus it came about that Rousseau only saw and attacked as it were the exterior of the enemy position, but failed to perceive the enemy that dwelt in his own breast. On the scale of world history, however, he was able to have some effect in spite of these

[1] Cf. Lennox, *Edmund Burke und sein politisches Arbeitsfeld 1760 bis 1790* (1923), p. 20.

contradictions, though the inconsistencies were always there in full force. Burke's intellectual structure was much less complicated and perhaps less interesting for the psychological analyst. But he, too, did his best to take a world-wide standpoint, because his one great obsession was to seek out the enemy in his central position and disarm him. This innermost enemy who must be slain in order to understand human life and history on a deeper level was the spirit of Natural Law, further exaggerated by the Enlightenment. It was the measurement of all things according to a supposedly eternal reason, which was yet confined within the limits of the contemporary horizon, and exalted the intellect whilst neglecting the deeper places of the human soul.

When Burke published his *Vindication* in 1765 he lifted the mask and gave his foe a name. He says in the preface that by using Bolingbroke's methods one could equally well criticise creation itself 'by *our* ideas of reason and fitness', when it would appear no better than foolishness. Such reasoning had a certain air of plausibility, but this only arose from its

> beaten circle of ordinary experience, that is admirably suited to the narrow capacities of some, and to the laziness of others. But this advantage is in great measure lost, when a painful, comprehensive survey of a very complicated matter, and which requires a great variety of considerations, is to be made; when we must seek in a profound subject, not only for arguments, but for new materials of argument, their measures and their method of arrangement; when we must go out of the sphere of our ordinary ideas, and when we can never walk sure but by being sensible of our blindness.

To quit the circle of our ordinary ideas meant searching expectantly for new tools of thought and knocking at the doors of a new intellectual and spiritual age. It might perhaps be objected that the time-honoured theological Christian standpoint gave an assured basis for a protest against pure rationalism, and an appeal to insights that were superior to all reason.

Now it is not to be denied that there is a certain continuity between Burke's outlook and the traditional Christian approach. But there is an equally clear continuity with English empiricism and scepticism as so effectively handled by Hume, and now given a further creative development by Burke. Hume had not indeed altogether transcended rationalism, but he had confined its operation within certain limits. He had uttered a warning against the misleading deductions of our own reason; and although he did not give the irrational powers of the soul any predominant function in his own thought, he did accord them an important role in human life and history. And in his practical tendencies, as well as in his conservative realism and feeling for authority, Hume very often gives us a fore-taste of Burke. Many of his sayings might indeed have been uttered by Burke. For example, the saying that if there existed truths that were harmful to the State, then they had better be allowed to give way to harmless errors and be relegated to eternal silence (*Enquiry Concerning the Principles of Morals*); or that other saying that a wise administrator should show respect for things that bear the mark of age (*Idea of a Perfect Commonwealth*). Hume and Burke were at one in their admiration for the constitutional position brought about by the revolution of 1688; and both of them might be called conservative Whigs in their essential outlook.

It is not certain whether Burke read Hume's other works, as well as his *History* (cf. Lennox, p. 106). But the point is of no great importance, for Hume's thought could well have been in the air and have been spread by conversation and travel. But there can be no doubt that as far as they bear upon the State and upon history, Hume's works were an immediate stepping-stone to Burke in the history of thought. It was Hume who loosened up the rigid dogmas that had sprung from the concept of Natural Law through his psychological and historical analysis of social and political procedures and transformations, by his discovery of the 'Instincts' operating through them. And in following this line he had also shown a sense of the practical and the useful in political life (all that had been tested by experience), something that was as a matter of course part of the Englishman's inheritance. But although his empiricism could be theoretically very radical, yet it had remained of the old utilitarian kind that belongs to statesmen, treating men superficially, and their impulses and passions as material that could be dealt with along mechanical lines. Hence his mechanical formula for the balance between *authority* and *liberty*.

To step from Hume's picture of political life to Burke's is like seeing a piece of country first in the cold bare light of dawn, and then under the early rays of the warm morning sun. Burke's political thought developed as straight as a die from its roots in his youthful writings to his many Parliamentary battles which first made him famous, and then on to its full stature in his struggle against the French Revolution, especially as mirrored in his *Reflections on the Revolution in France* of 1790. The decisive advance was that Burke did not view the State in a general and abstract manner, like the thinkers bound down by Natural Law, nor empirically, mechanically, and from the utilitarian angle, like Hume. He could share Hume's sense of the concrete structure of the English State as set up in 1688, but could also look at this concrete and living State not only through the eyes of a practical politician, but also as one who loved his country, one who was aware of its religious needs, whose heart went out to it imaginatively with a goodness rooted deep in the love of its past. The State as a useful institution, which Burke had always upheld, now took on an aspect of beauty and goodness as well, something that could benefit the inner life of men, because it had grown like a noble tree through the centuries, a work of nature cared for by providence, not a mere work of human caprice and conceited human reason. Over against the most arrogant expression of the spirit of Natural Law as embodied in the declaration of human and civic rights in 1789 and the revolutionary reconstruction of France, there rose up in protest one of the ancient States shaped by history, but with new spiritual weapons which set it in a new light. The dangers embodied in these revolutionary ideas, which were already forcing their way into England, were brought into the full light of day by its worthiest representative, the champion of all that was finest in the nation. These values, now adorned with imagination and reverence of the past, also concealed the specific interests of particular social classes, who were intent upon preserving the rights that had come down to them. This was the State of 'the saints and the knights of chivalry', of the English aristocracy and the English High Church, crowned by the monarchy, which Burke was now defending with burning hatred against this egalitarian democracy of France. But the depth of his hatred was only the measure of his affection for the beloved treasures that were being threatened. The saints and the knights whom he defended with conscious idealisation and a certain deliberate blindness to their serious deficiencies were symbols of an attitude to the life of the State that was at once deeply devout and intensely chivalrous.

If one were to attempt to derive all Burke's judgements upon the values of human life, politics and history from one single concept, one might perhaps call it piety towards the world—world-piety. He was prepared to accept the world as he found it, with all its deep abysses and disadvantages, with a faith in the ultimate meaning and harmony of the universe and a devoted sense of his own duty to fulfil the tasks that life had laid upon him. World-piety also meant a love for it in all its natural growth, this world into which he had been born, with all his relations of dependence to it. Looked at through the eyes of understanding love, these were no longer seen as fetters upon personal development, but rather as a protection and covering for its natural nakedness. This was 'that mutual dependence which Providence has ordained that all men should have on one another' (*Thoughts on French Affairs*, 1791). He incidentally reproached Louis

XVI for having grossly failed to recognise this natural and mutual dependence when he cut himself loose from the nobility, his natural support, and threw himself into the arms of the Third Estate. The historian of today would perhaps be less disposed to criticise this action in itself, for the choice was probably unavoidable; he would rather criticise the way in which it was carried out. This shows that Burke's conservative world-piety was not by itself always competent to pronounce judgment upon historical actions of decisive importance. But it represented the fundamental attitude the future historism needed in order to extract from this irrationally developing world of history a rationality that could not be found solely by pure reason, but only through all the human powers and abilities working together in concert.

Shaftesbury, in whom we saw one of the roots of historism, already had this world-piety. It reached its deepest and richest expression in Goethe, and in Ranke its most universal application to the world of history. In Shaftesbury and in Goethe, it went back to a Neo-Platonic view of the world, and in Burke to a positively Christian outlook. Herder's generous historical appreciation of the world was rooted both in Neo-Platonism and in Christianity; and in Ranke, too, these sources were firmly united. In each of these great pioneers of the new feeling for history there was the specific individual attitude, set in a particular historical world from which it drew assistance and direction, but which also imposed certain limitations upon it. This environment was not something rigid and externally given, but something also shaped from within by the man himself, rather like a suit of clothes whose material came from outside, but which is cut and shaped upon the man's body. Here, too, there was what Burke called *mutual dependence*. All this only shows how differently Hume and Burke saw and experienced this world of England, with its parliamentary and aristocratic government—though when looked at externally, it was one and the same for both of them.

These observations were preparatory to our main task, which is to consider more precisely how far Burke's kind of world-piety and his individual reaction to his environment enabled him to understand historical life in the way historism did later on.

His world-piety removed the deeper roots of the outlook based upon Natural Law by giving the higher powers in history primacy over the conscious rational will of man. This had indeed been done by the old interpretation of history along the lines of Christian theology, though it had never quite freed itself from the shackles of Natural Law. It could therefore only view the providence that directed history as a God who interfered from outside. True, it is possible to interpret a good many of Burke's sayings in this sense;

yet there is already something different about his interpretation, often difficult to define because of a certain haziness in his ideas, yet easy enough to feel. To put it briefly, there is already a sense of immanence, or, more accurately, a combination of immanence and transcendence, gradually making itself felt.[1] This is a sense of the divine forces at work from within the world process itself, and of the indissoluble links between this world and the next. One feels it in the way that Burke handles the doctrine of the social contract in his *Reflections*. As a Whig who had been influenced by Locke, he held to the letter of it, but gave it another interpretation which removed its basis in Natural Law. For Burke, the contract on which the individual State rested was only, as he expressed it, a clause in the great primal contract of eternal community which bound together the higher and the lower natures, the visible and the invisible world. This was a mystico-religious conception, according to which all life had been linked together from the beginning by bonds that were both immanent and transcendent; it was not, like Locke's conception of the contract, something that could be modified as a social arrangement by each new generation. And it was this concept that was decisive for Burke in all questions concerning the life of the State. As a conservative with a firm religious life and faith, Burke could not but recognise that the true basis was positive law, as shaped by the manifold forces of real life, and (to use a favourite expression of his) confirmed by *prescription*. Never must we lose sight of the practical statesman in Burke, who saw that the consecration of law through *prescription* afforded the surest pledge for the security of both private and public life. By practical instinct, and not by a relapse into any theories of Natural Law, he recognised the right of rebellion in extreme cases (as in 1688) against tyranny and the forcible suppression of the law. For how otherwise could the law be restored? But his advice was not to theorise on the subject, and not to spend too long looking down into this dark abyss. For in such cases it was not so much a question of law as of political sagacity. This doctrine not only linked up with Hume's teaching, but also sounded a note of the mediaeval right of resistance to tyranny; yet its roots went deeper down into history as a whole.

Let us attempt once more to characterise the essence of Burke's political thought in a few words. It was a revitalised traditionalism, and not yet historism;[2] it represents the highest stage reached by the traditional approach in general. For here it is no longer merely naive

---

[1] Noted in the perceptive book by Cobban, *Edmund Burke and the Revolt against the 18th Century* (1929), p. 86.

[2] This point is missed in the otherwise helpful and perceptive work by Einaudi, *Edm. Burke e l'indirizzo storico . . . .*

and unreflecting, but conscious of itself; and this it could only become as a counterblast to the Enlightenment, which considered itself so free of tradition. His dictum: 'Reverence for antiquity is congenial to the human spirit' expressed a primal fact of human psychology, which may be suppressed, but is bound to reassert itself. But the chief evidence that it does represent the highest stage of this traditional outlook lies in its concern with the inner psychological life of man, and not merely with the faithful preservation of the institutions, customs, rights and so on that had been handed down the centuries. This psychological life circulates through a people like a blood-stream, builds up something interconnected and organic in the body of the State and society as a whole. And this psychological life no longer seemed to Burke, as it had to all others up till then, including Hume, a juxtaposition of rational and irrational mechanisms, but a unity in which feeling and thought, the conscious and the unconscious, the inherited factor and the individual will, blend with one another. He saw the danger that 'the hair-splitting subtleties of reason' would fail to recognise the wisdom hidden in the natural voice of sentiment. 'Wisdom without reflection and above it' (*Reflections*), was the quintessence of his teaching on the creative forces in history and in the life of the State. According to another characteristic saying of his, politics should be conducted not according to human reason, but according to human nature, of which reason only forms a part, and by no means the largest part. This view of the past and the present blended them more intimately than the usual traditionalism could possibly do, and made them more forward-looking. And at the same time there was a strong pervasive suggestion that a truly living political and national community went far beyond merely political ends, and involved a real community of culture. It was thus that Burke arrived at the famous definition of 'society' which was to the specifically English mind identical with the State:

> It is a partnership in all science; a partnership in all art; a partnership in every virtue, and in all perfection. As the ends of such a partnership cannot be obtained in many generations, it becomes a partnership not only between those who are living, but between those who are living, those who are dead, and those who are to be born (*Reflections*).

This is the original wording; but the Gentz translation of 1793, using the gilded language of the Goethe period, had a profound effect on the Romantic movement in Germany (cf. my *Weltbürgertum und Nationalstaat*, 7, p. 40).

There is no doubt then about the vitality, the historical vitality, of the State in Burke's writings, and that to a very high degree. But was there also as with historism a full realisation of the concept of individuality and development? Certainly the English *commonwealth* itself appears as a living whole with full individuality, shaped over the centuries by inner formative forces. And in the history of political thought this must always rank as an epoch-making breakthrough to a quite new way of looking at the State, and one that was far nearer to reality (Cobban rightly emphasises this point). But in a history of historical thought such as we are here attempting, we must also call attention to the limitations of this breakthrough. Burke's nature was simple, naive, and creative: he viewed the specific form that his own State had acquired in the course of its historical existence from the standpoint of practical experience and with loving sympathy; and this attitude was unconscious, rather than a deliberate attempt to look with the comparative eye of one who is seeking for individuality at every point. Thus he was inclined to give the picture so presented an absolute value, and set it up as a canon for modern European States in general. In the *Reflections* he advises the French to imitate the English constitution. In so doing, he forgot his own doctrine, that the form of government for a particular country ought to be in accordance with its customs and circumstances. He did not stop to ask whether France was capable of resuscitating the antiquated institutions which had cracked at so many points, or whether the French nobility had the spirit to rise to the level of their English counterparts. True, in what he subsequently wrote, Burke did not repeat his advice to imitate the English Constitution of 1688; but this did not denote any radical change in his outlook, only a practical recognition that such a policy was now impossible to carry out in view of the flood-level reached by the French Revolution, which left England no alternative but a life-and-death struggle with France.

Burke's individualising mind failed him in this basic question because he was obsessed by the task of resistance. His opponents seemed to him to be the representatives of utter darkness, and his own cause the one and only light. Burke, who stood and wrote in a time of transition half-way between the Enlightenment and the Romantic Movement, succumbed to the danger of a dualistic division of the world's history into periods of light and periods of darkness— a temptation to which both the Enlightenment and the Romantics also succumbed. Yet it must not be forgotten that in other affairs where he could take a freer view, Burke's clear, vigorous and intuitive mind showed a brilliant capacity for grasping the individuality of things, as in his statesmanlike support of the North American colonies in their struggle for freedom. Here, he had the wisdom to draw a clear distinction between the specific desires of the New England colonists for freedom, derived from their radical Protestant sectarianism, and the pride in their freedom taken by the Southern planters, based upon their consciousness as a slave-owning aristocracy.

> Burke's analysis of the essential determinative characteristics in the American people is an astonishing achievement. His words contain almost everything that later knowledge has enabled historians to say on this subject (Lennox, p. 182).

The mood of truggle against the French Revolution was also calculated to inhibit the sense of change and development which we saw at work in his youthful study of English history of the early Middle Ages. In his *Reflections* he spread a certain attractive haze over the whole of England's past history, a haze through which the constitution, the pride of his country and his own heart appeared in all essentials as a structure that had been completed centuries ago, though constantly being added to by the contributions of countless men, both living and dead. Thus Burke looked at the constitution both statically and dynamically, just as his favourite ideas of *prescription* and *presumption*, which he exalted as the most reliable of all the law's credentials in every department of life, combined both static and dynamic elements.

We may ask whether he considered there was likely to be any material change in things in the future. He certainly saw life as growth through adjustment to new circumstances, both in the past and the future, an adjustment that was happiest when it proceeded almost unnoticed. He was also prepared to put his hand to an individual improvement here and there, but would also be anxious to keep a protective hand over the whole. Electoral reform in England was something that he opposed. Hume, although further away from historism in his inner disposition, was nevertheless led by his naturalistic and mechanical ideas of development to have a stronger feeling for change. He could look sceptically at the future, and could even speak of the coming 'euthanasia' of the English Constitution in the arms of an absolute monarchy. 'There will be no such euthanasia', Burke cried out in indignation. Perhaps this was his final word, for it stands at the end of the fourth letter *On a Regicide Peace*, which he died without completing (cf. Meusel, *E. Burke und die franz. Revol.* (1913), p. 49). This was a proud and noble protest. It sprang from one who was utterly convinced of the inner vitality of the English Constitution, who believed in it with his last breath, though with a belief that insisted on giving it an absolute value.

Starting from such premises, Burke could not do justice to those new forces of historical development that were active on his opponent's side. There are some words in the *Reflections* that bring this out even more clearly than the judgments we have already quoted on what was desirable and possible for France. Burke is seeking to justify his hatred of the spirit of 1789 on general historical grounds:

> History consists, for the greater part, of the miseries brought upon the world by pride, ambition, avarice, revenge, lust, sedition, hypocrisy, ungoverned zeal and all the train of disorderly appetites. . . . These vices are the *causes* of those storms. Religion, morals, laws, prerogatives, liberties, privileges, rights of men are the pretexts.[1]

Burke thus showed himself unable to pierce behind the foreground of the dramatic events in France, and fell a victim to the weakness typical of all thought with a naive and unhistorical attitude; he could not see anything but the evil motives at work among the enemy. But the dynamic power of historical storms is always something more than the mere interplay of disruptive human passions.

There were other features in Burke's historical thought, which look, from the point of view of historism, like dross deposited by relics of Natural Law within a mighty process of melting. But from this time onwards, it would be the golden elements in Burke's thinking that would command men's attention. It was his great political passion that raised him head and shoulders above those who were proclaiming the new Pre-Romantic tastes in England. Their direct influence upon him up to the last is shown by his famous apotheosis of the Middle Ages' chivalrous spirit in his *Reflections* (pp. 113 ff.; in Gentz, 1, 105 ff.), which he held up in the face of all 'sophisters, economists and calculators' of his century. But whereas the Pre-Romantics enjoyed the Middle Ages as an aesthetic spectacle quite unconnected with the enlightened present, there was something much more powerful coming to fruition in Burke—something we seemed to catch a glimpse of in bud in the writings of Ferguson. This was a deep inner feeling of the continuity in life, and the oneness of past and present. He expressed the opinion that if ever this mixed system compounded of opinion and feeling, originating in the chivalry of old, were to disappear, the loss would be incalculable. For it was this system that had given modern Europe its character, which had raised it above all the States of Asia, and quite possibly above even the most brilliant achievements of the ancient world. A proper pride in subordination, dignified obedience, true service from the heart, which could even infuse a spark of freedom into bondage, 'chastity of honour'—these were constructive spiritual forces that Burke descried in mediaeval chivalry, and felt to be at work in himself and in

---

[1] The same interpretation occurs at the end of the *Appeal from the New to the Old Whigs. Eadem semper causa, libido et avaritia et mutandarum rerum amor*, etc.

his idealised English State. Although these were not, as they seemed to him, the only values that had given the Western States their character, they were certainly indispensable values for making the most of this character and maintaining it down the ages. They were still alive in the ethos of the modern officer's profession; and the inner renewal of the State's vitality (which was Burke's greatest contribution to the development of the new historical outlook) certainly had its roots in his strong sense of the virtues born of chivalry.

The German Movement

Chapter seven

A Preliminary Look at the German Movement: Lessing and Winckelmann

We now turn to the great German movement, within which the new sense of history, which we have called historism, was destined to reach its first large-scale expression. The tentative efforts we have so far been considering in various parts of Europe were taken up into this movement, but it far surpassed them all. In order to focus sufficiently on the decisive developments, it will now be necessary to exercise some selection in our material. Basically, this was a general European movement of growth, which set in somewhat later in Germany, but speedily developed and matured there in surprising fashion. In order to show its generally European character, we have also examined and quoted from the works of French and English authors of lesser importance, especially those who were contributory to the German movement. We shall now concentrate on the real pioneers of historism in Germany, whose achievements by themselves balance all the other work by men of lesser stature in the same direction, but without the same degree of creative power. New elements of thought were certainly springing to life everywhere. There was J. F. Christ in Leipzig, with his new archeological interests, and his new interpretation of Machiavelli (Justi, *Winckelmann*, 1, pt 2, pp. 345 ff., and Meinecke, *Idee der Staatsräson*, p. 365, now vol. 1, p. 344 in his *Works*); Chladenius in Erlangen, with his theme of the historian's 'viewpoint' (R. Unger, *Ges. Studien*, I, pp. 98 ff.). Such men were already by the middle of the century, or even earlier, beginning to create a stir. Baumgarten's aesthetics witness to a movement that was at least closely related to the new sense of history. The rise of the new German poetry from Klopstock onwards, and its significance as an expression of a new feeling for the life of the individual, is a matter of common knowledge; so is the influence of pietism upon it, and the growth of a new, though somewhat narrow, appreciation of the work of ancient German poetry and the life of the past. The analogy between all this and the slightly earlier English Pre-Romantics is clear enough. Any account of the rise of historism in Germany which aimed at an exclusive treatment of the material (such as falls outside our present purpose) would also have to take account of the important critical achievements in theology and philology by men such as Semler, Michaelis and Heyne; it would also have to deal with the further developments of historical thought among German professional historians especially in the so-called Göttingen school—men like Gatterer, Schlözer, Spittler and Heeren.[1] The tradition of German scholarship had always been one of thoroughness. Now, inspired by the work of Montesquieu and the historians of the Western European Enlightenment, and linking up with the great world-histories of the English writers, German thought turned towards the universal and embraced the whole of humanity. But in so doing, it was, like its English forerunners, more successful in dealing with the material content than with the inner life of history. These German thinkers showed praiseworthy seriousness in their approach and great critical sobriety; but most of all are they to be commended for encouraging a study of the political sciences and so arousing a new sense of the historical importance of the State. Baron vom Stein and Rehberg had both sat at their feet. But even with them, that new sense was still bound down by a utilitarian and moralistic attitude. The historical writings of the four men referred to above all reflect the particular intellectual changes of the second half of the century.

---

[1] The older work by Wesendonck, *Die Begründung der neueren deutschen Geschichtsschreibung durch Gatterer und Schlözer* (1876), seriously over-values their achievement and blissfully ignores some of the main questions at issue. Recently, much good work has been done (though still with some over-valuation of the Göttingen school and the achievements of other contemporary historians and literary historians) by von Lempicki, *Geschichte der deutschen Literaturwissenschaft bis zum Ende des 18. Jahrhunderts* (1920), and by Trude Benz, *Die Anthropologie in der Geschichtsschreibung des 18. Jahrhunderts* (1932). We must be grateful for W. Nigg's useful piece of work, *Die Kirchengeschichtsschreibung, Grundzüge ihrer historischen Entwicklung* (1934); cf. my review in the *Hist. Zeitschrift*, 150, 315 ff. Then I must call attention, in response to a suggestion by W. Gurlitt, to recent research work on the history of music, following the successful lead of historism. First among German books must be mentioned Forkel, *Allgemeine Geschichte der Musik* (1788 and 1801), influenced by Herder and the Göttingen school. On his work, see Gurlitt, *Zeitschrift f. Musikwiss.*, 1, 574 ff.; Trude Benz, pp. 146 ff., and Edelhoff, 'J. N. Forkel', thesis, Freiburg, 1932. Further literature: E. Hegar, *Die Anfänge der neueren Musikgeschichtsschreibung um 1770* (by Gerbert, Burney and Hawkins) (*Sammlung musikwiss. Abhandl*, vol. 7, 1932); H. Osthoff, 'Die Anfänge der Musikgeschichtsschreibung in Deutschland' (*Acta musicologica* 5, 1933); W. Gurlitt, *F. J. Fétis und seine Rolle in der Geschichte der Musikwissensch.* (*Lütticher Kongressbericht der Internat. Ges. f. Musikwiss.*, 1930).

Heeren's work more especially reached a commendable level, and showed signs of awareness that there were new needs in the field of history; but none of these four produced work of sufficient originality and power as to demand detailed examination for our present purposes.

Finally, we can also omit the historical writings of Johannes v. Müller. His work was not original: if we may be allowed the metaphor, he was more like a sponge which absorbed many of the contemporary trends and then squeezed them out again. He held a position midway between pragmatism and historism, and there are features in his work reminiscent of Herder's and even Ranke's historical outlook, with its basis in religion. The intensive study by Requadt (*Joh. v. Müller und der Frühhistorismus*, 1929) gives an attractive and fair-minded account of his work, but does not sufficiently stress its weaknesses.

We will now turn our attention, then, to the great figures of the German movement. It soon becomes clear that from our point of view they fall into two groups, of which one, at any rate when considered as a whole, was only indirectly preparatory to historism by a general raising of the level of German intellectual life. The others were the direct protagonists of an early form of historism, though it still retained residues from the older patterns of thought. The first group consists of Lessing, Winckelmann, Schiller and Kant; the second, of Möser, Herder and Goethe. The former can be summarily treated, but the latter will need our fullest attention and understanding. The brief treatment of the first group must not be taken to imply that we wish to play down their intellectual achievements as a whole. Historism is not a kind of saving faith which puts anything not strictly belonging to it into a lower class. Quite apart from historism, Schiller's relationship to the historical world was so profound and original that the present author might well be tempted to view him as one of the most attractive problems for a future full-length study. In relation to the second group, Schiller will come into the picture as Goethe's close friend, but not primarily as a historical thinker. Likewise Kant's rationalistic and progressistic conception of history will not here concern us, in spite of its revolutionary effects on philosophical thought and so indirectly on the further developments of historical thinking. But something must be said about Lessing and especially about Winckelmann, if only to correct some of the views that have hitherto prevailed about their specific services to new forms of historical thought.

The inner dividing-line between these two groups will at once become apparent when we turn to Lessing. There is a contrast between those whose thought is principally directed towards certain ideals, and those who, without losing sight of related ideals and often touching upon them, nevertheless apply their main creative efforts to the mysteries of individuality in life and in history, and so open the way to historism. We shall therefore divide the great German movement into a more idealistic, and a more individualising, group of thinkers.

In Lessing's *Nathan der Weise*, the portrait that finally emerges as the fruit of mature wisdom is that of an ideal, rather than an individual, man—'the good man', whether he be Christian, Jew or Muslim. For Lessing, the art of portraiture was of minor importance, for it could presumably display the ideal of a particular man, but not that of man in general (Justi, *Winckelmann*, 2, pt 3, p. 212). It would certainly be wrong to suggest that he had no power to feel or depict the individual in any way whatsoever. Tellheim and Minna are beings of flesh and blood, with an inner individual personality. In spite of the rationalistic features in his judgment upon Shakespeare, as Gundolf has shown he was nevertheless profoundly moved by his uniqueness and universality. 'The smallest of his beauties is stamped with a something that immediately proclaims to the whole world: "I am from the hand of Shakespeare". And woe to the extraneous beauty that presumes to stand beside it!' (*Dramaturgie*, Sec. 73). In *Nathan*, Lessing makes Saladin say:

> Ich habe nie verlangt
> Dass allen Bäumen *eine* Rinde wachse.[1]

But even these words, when compared with the general meaning of the work, show that there were certain limitations in the author's understanding of individuality. For it only looks in a friendly and tolerant manner at the differences in men produced by environment and education, the outward bark, as it were, which is of no real consequence, and not at the inner heart, the essence of 'the good man'. All Lessing's thought about the highest values in life and in history was controlled by the search for the basic ethical motives at work in this contentious human nature, which was yet so full of deep tenderness and a yearning for love. Here, the methods of Montesquieu were of great service to Lessing, his emphasis on the differences between States, their customs, their moral precepts and their religions, and their derivation from the varieties of climate. Lessing was intent upon so coming to terms with all these differences that it might be possible to arrive at an ideal of pure humanity that rose above them all, at least for those 'who had risen above popular prejudices'.

---

[1] I have never desired that all trees should grow one single bark.

In Lessing, it was not by any means a matter of applying a species of general enlightened morality after the manner of the Stoic tradition. The illuminative power of his ideal sprang from an inner source of light, from esoteric thoughts about the relationship between God, the world and man that were mystical in character, and only now and again lifted the veil from the divine mystery. The recent study by Leisegang (*Lessings Weltanschauung*, 1931) has given a convincing account of his well-rounded system of thought. He shows that in Lessing's thought the personal God and the sum-total of the universe are one and the same, and God develops in and with the world—a prelude, in fact, to the philosophy of identity. And in his opinion, it is this idea of development that also marks off Lessing from Spinoza, with whom Lessing, in his famous conversation with Jacobi, once acknowledged his kinship in rather general terms. Already Dilthey (*Erlebnis und Dichtung*, p. 129) had said that Lessing, in the idea of development contained in his *Erziehung des Menschengeschlechts* (*Education of the Human Race*) of 1780, had prepared the way in the world of scholarship for the great German movement that led on to Hegel. The path followed by Lessing might well lead on to Hegel, but hardly to Goethe or Ranke. For the esoteric central idea of his *Education of the Human Race* was not the individualising concept of development upheld by historism, it was only the concept of perfectionism through a normative ideal already represented in Leibniz, and also in cruder form in the Enlightenment. Leisegang has shown the influence of Ferguson's *Essay on the History of Civil Society* of 1766 upon the conception of the *Erziehung des Menschengeschlechts*. Ferguson released Lessing from the despair he had hitherto felt as to the meaning of history. Yet it was not the elements preparatory to historism which we noted in Ferguson that had this effect; it was rather the idea of progress in history. Lessing was now able to see his ever-developing deity not in static terms, but like Leibniz before him as an endless growing progress. Yet the stages of this upward journey were not conceived by him in individual terms, but only in the character of normative truths. The visible goal in Lessing's eyes was the ideal man as depicted in *Nathan der Weise*, the man who does good for the sake of goodness. We cannot agree with Dilthey's verdict that 'in this world-process the full rights of the individual are also preserved'. A certain degree of mild forbearance was the most Lessing was prepared to grant to all the gay exterior wrappings and outer bark in his sole concern for the inner kernel. He had not yet discovered that the outer bark and the inner core in the individual unity of the human being and his creations are not so easily to be separated from one another.

It is important to see the distinction between the perfectionism of the Enlightenment, even where it was conceived in terms of an autonomous development, and the individualising conception of development that constitutes the outlook of historism. Yet we only need to glance at Lessing's pioneer work towards a new intellectual life in Germany to become aware that underneath the apparent division between these two lines of thought a latent community of ideas must have been at work. The dynamic power of his mind, which broke through all the remnants of intellectualism and rationalism that still clung to him, forged an inner bond with what was to follow. This dynamic also found expression in his *Erziehung des Menschengeschlechts*, in which he showed, under the outward form of the divine plan for human education, how the power of reason is at work (like the plant that grows through and splits the wall) gradually making its influence felt, and using all sorts of roundabout but necessary ways. This work had a stimulating effect as a sketch of the history of religion down the ages, not unlike that produced by Hume's naturalistic approach.[1]

Then in 1764 came Winckelmann's *Geschichte der Kunst des Altertums*,[2] producing a deeper effect upon historical thought, although Winckelmann was still, like Lessing, essentially on this side of the dividing-line between normative thinking and a full historism. For however unambiguous the main principles of thought may appear to the critical eye, the very fact that they bear the impress of a definite individual writing from the depths of his soul means that they may always take an unexpected turn leading into a new intellectual and spiritual country.

In order to understand this new turn, we must first of all take up a widely held opinion and see it in proper perspective. It has been commonly maintained that Winckelmann's new historical sense was already in evidence in his discovery of a succession of styles in art, and the connections between the life of art and the whole life of a nation, particularly with its political destinies. In making this discovery, it is maintained, he superseded both the hitherto prevailing antiquarian approach to works of art, as well as the more reflective and argumentative. Now this was certainly an incontestably great achievement. But it must be noted that, taken by itself, it does not lift Winckelmann's work above the framework of enlightened historiography. It should be strongly emphasised that the Enlightenment already possessed, alongside the perfectionist approach, a

---

[1] Fittbogen has given us a helpful work on the religion of Lessing (1923), in which (p. 203) he calls him 'the father of the history of religion'; but he forgets that Hume had pioneered the way before him. Nor must we forget the attempt made by Lafitau.

[2] *A History of Art in the Ancient World.*

theory that has been called the 'life cycle theory', which could already have been used to understand the course of human events on a large scale.[1] It could already speak in terms of the growth, maturity and decline of human creations, as we have seen in Montesquieu's and Gibbon's treatment of the destinies of Rome. And in Winckelmann's youthful essay of 1751, entirely in the manner of the Enlightenment (*Works*, vol. 12, 1829), this conception was also applied to empires and states. His distinguished biographer, Justi (2nd ed., vol. 3, pp. 78 ff.), has shown that in the sphere of art Winckelmann had a forerunner in the person of the French connoisseur Count Caylus, who had begun to study the national taste as a basis for art, and the shift in this national taste according to the general principles of growth from youth to maturity. His criteria were less well-defined, and his tools less effective than Winckelmann's; but the principles laid down in his *Recueil d'Antiquités Égyptiennes, Étrusques, Grecques et Romaines* (I, 1761) showed a certain kinship with those of Winckelmann. Moreover, the causes connecting the artistic life of a particular people with their life as a whole, and making it dependent upon the latter, were the same in Winckelmann as in Montesquieu and Voltaire, namely climate, political constitution, national character and the spirit of the age. In Winckelmann, too, there was a touch of Montesquieu's inclination to picture causes in clockwork terms, for example in the direct connection that he boldly makes between the national character and climate and soil;[2] or in his discussion of the reasons why Etruscan art reached a somewhat higher level than that of the Oriental peoples, but did not come up to the level of Greek art. For each separate cause was treated here as a distinctive and definite force producing specific effects.

One of Winckelmann's chief ideas was that political liberty played an important part in the world of art. As well as the grace of God, which called forth in men a sense of bodily beauty and so led to truer notions of beauty, there was the element of political liberty, from which art 'as it were' received its life, and the loss of which 'necessarily' meant the decline of art. We are already familiar with this idea of the lively effects of liberty and the stultifying results of despotism, which runs through the eighteenth century; it was part of the common stock of the Enlightenment, and was only now and again called into question (by Hume, for instance). Shaftesbury had formerly proclaimed it from his truly English standpoint in his

---

[1] Trude Benz is quite right on this point in *Die Anthropologie in der Geschichtsschreibung des 18. Jahrhunderts* (1932), p. 101.

[2] 'The nature of every country has given its native-born inhabitants, as well as its immigrants, a specific form and a similar pattern of thought'—explaining the idea of imitation of Greek works of art etc. (*Works*, 1, 125).

watchword *liberty and letters*; but on the continent, where absolutism was the order of the day, the doctrine was often only given a very ineffective and theoretical assent. There is no reason to doubt the genuineness of Winckelmann's feeling for liberty. It is perfectly understandable as the result of his hard upbringing and youth in his native Brandenburg. Yet this passion for liberty, not unconnected with his own sorrowful experience, would not have prevented him from leaving his beloved Rome and joyfully accepting a call to Berlin from Frederick the Great in 1765, if only it had been couched in acceptable terms. In his history of art he could impress on his contemporaries that the decline of Greek art from its greatest heights took place in the period when liberty perished under the rule of the Diadochi; but this was only because he did not know much about the great achievements of Hellenistic art, and would not in any case have been able to appreciate them in the light of his own standards. And yet he had to record the fact that in the midst of the general artistic decline, there was a further period of flourishing activity in Sicily under Agathocles and Hiero II. But he simply accepted this fact without seeing that it threw considerable doubt upon the invariable validity of his thesis. In reality, his praise of political liberty as the source of all exalted thinking, true distinction and great art reflected the attitude of a very unpolitical man. In practice, his naive and happy nature[1] was satisfied with the liberty provided in Rome (in spite of the Inquisition) in his friendly intercourse with the cardinals, to whom he could speak his mind quite freely. He had only to take care not to call the Pope Antichrist in public (to Count Bünau, 12 May 1757, *Works*, 10, 196). All the same, we should recognise that his thesis of liberty as a necessary basis for art did hold good within certain limits. It had developed not only out of his enthusiasm for ancient Greece, but also from his critical attitude to the luxuriance of Baroque and Rococo art. It was a true and delicate piece of historical perception to sense the change in art from Raphael and Michelangelo to Bernini as linked with the change in the political atmosphere from the comparative freedom of the Renaissance to the subservience of a courtisan society. His successful analysis of the styles in ancient art was closely connected with his distaste for Baroque and Rococo art in comparison; and he used the analogy of this change in contemporary artistic taste in his examination of ancient works of art, and in classifying them under their historical periods. Thus Winckelmann's disapproval of his own times, which he refused to consider either politically or artistically great, helped to guide him through the changes and chances of artistic history.

---

[1] 'I am not often unhappy', he wrote to Heyne in the year of his death (13 January 1768) (*Works*, 11, p. 455).

His survey of the Renaissance (for Winckelmann and his time pre-eminently 'the age of restoration in the arts and sciences') led him on to a further refinement of the Enlightenment's attitude to history. We have already encountered the doctrine of the 'spirit of the age', up till now treated in a rather external manner by the historians of the Enlightenment. It had easily passed over into nothing more than a general account of the degree to which either reason or unreason appeared to be the ruling spirit of any particular period. In 1755, when Winckelmann exchanged his caterpillar existence in Germany for his butterfly life in Rome, and felt himself to be 'a late developer', this question gradually became a matter of indifference. He was only concerned to know what degree of artistic value each age could produce. He began to notice that the rise of Etruscan art from the first primitive stage to the second improved stage was probably contemporary with the advances in Greek art; and this brought his mind back to the Renaissance. He then went on to argue that as in that period, so in earlier times, the stirrings of new life did not take place in one country alone, and spread abroad from there, but in the human race at large, and over the whole range of human nature. 'It would seem that in those days a universal spirit was poured out over peoples with different manners and customs, which worked more particularly in art and filled it with new life and enthusiasm.' Here, all of a sudden, you feel the presence of creative spiritual power at work in the life of the nations, reaching beyond any one people. Such power can be appreciated in terms of an inner living process rather than explained in terms of particular causes.

But these signs of a new historical sensitivity do not by themselves suffice to rank Winckelmann among the immediate pioneers of historism. Justi (vol. 3, pt 2, p. 105) makes a very apposite comment when he remarks that 'the prevailing mood in this great work is distinctly anti-historical'. His history of art was very much restricted by dogma, which measured all events by the absolute values of Christianity. There was only *one* beauty, Winckelmann held, of timeless validity, because it is embodied and developed in nature itself. The grace of heaven, political liberty and the character of the nation were all happily combined in the Greeks at the time of Praxiteles and Pheidias. All other periods of artistic history were only a foil to show up all the more brightly the truth of this doctrine. As we have already seen, it was current practice everywhere in the Enlightenment to compare the different cultures, seek out resemblances, and explain differences in terms of simple and unambiguous causes. Just as the Enlightenment was everywhere at pains to discover why in this case reason, and in another case unreason, should have prevailed, Winckelmann strove to establish why only Greece, and no other country, with the possible exception of Raphael's Italy, should have attained the peak of artistic beauty—for after all, Raphael's art was only an imitation of the Greek. Even this search for causes, and in general almost everything that may be regarded as 'historical' in his attitude, was only a means to an end. The sole purpose was to display the absolute worth of Greek art at its highest. The first words of his preface make this abundantly clear. 'I do not intend,' [he writes] 'to give a mere narrative of artistic periods and the changes they contain. I take the word "history" in its wider sense, the sense it bears in the Greek language; and my purpose is to attempt to build up a system of artistic doctrine.' Thus history in the wider sense meant to him merely all information, knowledge and science of any kind whatsoever. He distinguished from this 'history in the narrower sense', which he dealt with in the second part of his work, though it only covered the history of the Greeks. The sub-title ran as follows: 'considered from the point of view of the external events affecting the Greeks'; and the chief theme was the influence of their changing political fortunes on art, viewed from the standpoint of his thesis of liberty. The first volume covered the essential characteristics and the inner changes of Greek art in four stages, which he called the older style, the high style, the beautiful style, and the imitative style. These he considered to be part of his 'system', the essential broad view, not history 'in the narrower sense'. Here one can clearly see the dividing line that marks him off from true historism; for the latter would never tolerate this separation of inner changes from external influences. It would be at pains to integrate them into one current of development. It would thus recognise only one single conception of history, namely the history of development. Here in Winckelmann we have a classical example of that incoherence between the various factors in development which we have so often noted in the historical writings of the Enlightenment. The only difference is that there the incoherence is chiefly due to incapacity, whereas in Winckelmann it is more due to the author's distaste for certain aspects of his subject. Greek art was in his eyes a sanctuary that must be freed from all profane associations and be contemplated and venerated in pure isolation.

'There is only *one* beauty, just as there is only *one* goodness', wrote Winckelmann (Justi, vol. 3, pt 2, p. 167). This normative beauty is exactly analogous to the normative reason of the Enlightenment. We have seen this as the climax of the pattern of thought based upon Natural Law inherited from antiquity, stretched to such an extreme that it has often looked like collapsing. In art and poetry too, ever since men began to reflect about them, there had always been some norms of taste, and the *Querelle des anciens et des modernes*, which had been carried on in France at the turn of the century, had been solely concerned with the question whether the standards of the ancients or the moderns should prevail. Winckelmann's powerful support achieved a victory for the Greek norm of beauty—perhaps the last and finest victory of the spirit of normative absolutism. And it was destined to be won by this purest and most ardent admirer of the ancient Greeks. This triumph was also a triumph for the antique pattern of thought in general.

Let us make the dividing line between Winckelmann and historism still clearer. There can be no question of his having any conception either of developmental or individualising ideas. True, his discovery of a succession of styles, and his profound examination of the changes undergone by art, had given a powerful impetus to a fully developmental treatment of its history. Yet however epoch-making his methods might be, his conception of development, like Lessing's outline of religious history, was limited by the notion of perfection. It only differed from the versions current in the Enlightenment in that it placed this perfection in a romanticised past—a past that must be regarded with yearning. Yet in spite of all his exhortations to living artists to imitate this past perfection, it was to all intents and purposes a vanished and irrecoverable world. Winckelmann viewed this past, in the striking words of the conclusion to his book: 'as a lover standing on the sea shore watches her beloved sailing away from her; she has no hope of ever seeing him again, yet her weeping eyes follow him into the distance, and think they can see his likeness mirrored in the sails as the ship draws further and further away.' The contrast between Winckelmann's views and historism comes out even more strongly in his attitude to the individual in art. The greatness of Greek art, and its exemplary nature for all time, seemed to him to lie precisely in the fact that it sought the ideal, and not the individual. This could be regarded as a 'composite epitome' of all the beauty that existed in scattered form among individuals; and it reminds us of the somewhat similar view put forward by Shaftesbury. Not till the period of decline did the artist, in Winckelmann's opinion, begin to 'occupy himself with the sculpture of individual heads and busts, or what would now be called portraits'. These he regarded as no more than 'diligent pieces of work'. This indifference to portraiture, which he shared with Lessing, is in itself enough to show where these two great masters stood from the point of view of historical thought.

Yet in spite of all this, Winckelmann's work is a landmark in the prehistory of historism. This last and finest product of the spirit of Natural Law and normative thinking contained the seeds of a new outlook that burst through the casing of the old. The dialectic of historical development, the growth of hitherto prevailing tendencies until they reach bursting-point and release something new, was to come into operation at this juncture. Winckelmann's most personal and important achievement, more significant and fruitful than all his consideration of underlying causes and even his discovery of successive styles in art, was his whole-hearted devotion to the historical world of artistic creations, his intense desire to grasp its meaning, the steady activity of all his intellectual and spiritual powers alongside of the critical and more specifically optical and artistic faculties. Once the critical and optical work had been accomplished, his whole soul (what he called 'the inner sense') would brood over the work of art, until he reached the point where the sensual passed over into a super-sensual or divine awareness, where the Platonic Eros came into action, and the material work of art became a symbol and a revelation of the divine. This is what he called 'the contemplation of that beauty which comes forth from God and leads to God', in which 'the figures that represent humanity in its higher forms seem to become the veil and vesture of pure contemplative spirits and heavenly powers'.

One further point may be added in order to round off our understanding of Winckelmann. The complete blending of the spiritual and the sensual, which astonished the world, was just as deeply rooted in the senses as it was sublimely exalted to the supersensual. His artistic sense and his zest for life, which constantly led him to strive for 'heroic friendships' after the pattern of the ancients, were nourished by a certain erotic disposition, a sensual delight in the youthful body. But this sensual–supersensual wooer of the arts would in the end agree with Plato that 'the highest cannot be represented in visible form'.

The decisive point as far as we are concerned is that in Winckelmann the combination of intellectualism and rationalism in the approach to an object, such as characterised the artistic critics of his time and the historians of the Enlightenment, was now almost completely eclipsed by the rise of metaphysical appreciation. 'Beauty is one of nature's great secrets, whose effects we all see and feel; but if it is a question of forming a clear and universal conception of it, then it must be ranked among the unexplained truths.' Hume and Voltaire had also spoken of the inexplicable mysteries of history, but had despaired of developing any means of deepening their knowledge in this direction. Winckelmann, on the other hand, spoke of the mystery of beauty in the certainty that the soul, if not the understanding, could have access to it. The idea of beauty comes to us, he maintained, more through impressions than reasons. Still less could it be acquired from books. He himself was one of the best read men of his time, and the intense preoccupation with books in his hard upbringing as depicted by Justi makes extremely painful reading. But with a touch of genius he was able at the crucial moment to shake off the dust of books and soar into the world of Platonic ideals in which beauty had its being. He had a foretaste of the experience of the modern top-ranking scholar, who must perforce bear the burden of a long cultural tradition based upon much bookreading. Winckelmann knew that in this respect the Greeks had fared better than the moderns. 'They had one vanity the less in their world; they could not pride themselves on their great book-learning.'

Winckelmann thus anticipated something of the psychological sensibility for a historical creation that the future historism was to require as its own peculiar avenue to knowledge. His indifference to the individual, just because it was the product of deep insight, did not therefore in the long run prevent his work from arousing precisely this feeling for the individual. For every individuality is a whole, and only intelligible as such. Winckelmann did not indeed sense the individual, but he had a strong feeling for wholeness in art. As he taught in his treatise on the capacity for the Perception of Beauty in Art (1763), the 'inner sense' comes from a sense of the whole, and not from a perception of separate parts then added together to make a whole, as a 'grammatical brain' would like to do. He could not yet realise the historical character of a piece of art that he embraced with such love because it still remained in his eyes a revelation that was supra-historical. Yet the very fact that he could see these creations as a whole, as great coherent unities, paved the way for a fully historical approach that took account also of their individuality. The simple statement at the beginning of the second part, that the author's purpose was to give a history of art, rather than of artists, had a revolutionary effect in its refusal to adopt a line of personal pragmatism. We have already had occasion to mention a similar thought in Leibniz (cf. above pp. 28–9). Winckelmann's tremendous influence upon his contemporaries shows that they sensed in him the movement of a new spirit.

The sympathetic insight into Greek art achieved by Winckelmann was the outcome of the new German spirit in concert with the reaction already under way against the prevailing Romano-French normative outlook. Already Ranke observes that 'the return to a proper appreciation of the art of antiquity may be traced back to the national antagonism against the academic approach of the artist which had been derived from the Romance nations' (*Works*, 51–52, p. 543, obituary notice on Böhmer, 1868). There was also perhaps something of a Germanic strain about the first stirrings of sympathetic insight into Homer and the Bible which we noticed in the English Pre-Romantics. We may also perhaps regard as generally Germanic a certain tendency towards freedom and subjectivity, and a disposition to champion them openly, and if necessary pugnaciously, against all precepts to the contrary. This kind of friction is precisely what mostly brings out the best in the German character, because controversy leads to a mutual interaction and a healthy cross-fertilisation with the more formal spirit of the Romance nations. Winckelmann indeed did not draw upon that spirit which he encountered in his contemporary world, but rather direct from the spirit of the ancient world which had been the original source of Romanticism. Goethe, who was a congenial spirit, has given us an incomparable appreciation of the antique and pagan element in Winckelmann. And his canonisation of the Greek standards of beauty denoted, as we have already observed, a victory for the ancient ways of thought. Yet even where Winckelmann seemed to be most pagan and most attached to the ancient world, he was still a German, although an unusual one, by reason of the free and almost naively childlike single-mindedness of his inmost genius. And even when he had to become a Roman Catholic in order to go to Rome, he preserved something of the German Protestant heritage. Even in Rome, he sang for his own edification, as it were, a morning hymn from a Protestant hymn-book. And may it not be said that his great achievement in the history of thought (the sympathetic understanding of Greek art) also had a touch of German Protestant sentiment about it?

In order to arrive at a complete understanding of the connection between the canonisation of this art and its further effects, we must assess the position rather more broadly. It may perhaps be said that it was easiest to exercise this new power of sympathetic insight in the first place in the sphere of art, because there was no disturbing factor here, at any rate for a receptive spirit. Any other kind of sympathetic insight of a historical kind is liable, however, to be a patchwork, and cannot succeed in completely bridging and transcending what appears to be strange to the onlooker. This was to become particularly evident in the difficulty felt by the growing historism in understanding the life of the State. But with complete sympathetic insight into the perfect work of art, such as Winckelmann managed to achieve, there was an inner urge to give absolute value to what he so dearly loved. And it is to be noted that this very canonisation by Winckelmann of the highest achievements in Greek art and culture led on to the new German humanism and classicism, which shone forth right into the nineteenth century as one of the strongest formative influences in culture, and still leaves traces of its effects even today. Goethe, Schiller, Hölderlin and Wilhelm von Humboldt all looked through the eyes of Winckelmann at 'the noble simplicity and tranquil greatness' of Greek art, with reverence and with love; and they considered that in the Greek ideal mankind had reached the highest standards of humanity. It would be difficult to put into words the energy, spiritual delight and serenity imparted to them by this belief. This belief represented the deepest and most fervent of all the new inspirations that had come to modern man from the men of antiquity since the Renaissance. It became the integrating element in the highest achievements of the Goethe period. But it stood in a certain contradiction to the tendencies of the nascent historism, which was now to expand during this selfsame Goethe period. For this new outlook stood for individual examination, even of the highest creations of culture; whereas Winckelmann's normative classicism had taught that man must rise above the troublous realm of the individual into the pure air of the ideal, following the ideas of Plato, who had likewise left the individual far behind. But the Platonic element in Winckelmann reminds us of the Platonist Shaftesbury,[1] who was also a favourite author of Winckelmann's, in whom we have traced one of the roots of historism; and the Platonic and Neo-Platonic thread in the texture of the growing historism will stand out more clearly as we proceed. And so the most wonderful part of the great German movement is to see how the idealising and personalising effects of the Platonic and Neo-Platonic attitude to life go on working side by side until in Goethe they even blend and become one. Is this a radical contradiction, or a vital union of opposites? We are on the threshold of one of the mysteries in the history of thought—a mystery we shall keep in mind as we now turn to the immediate pioneers of historism.

[1] Cf. Justi, vol. 2, pt 1, 211, and Vallentin, *Winckelmann* (1931), p. 165. We will not enter into controversy here over the often exaggerated interpretations of Vallentin, who belongs to the school of Stefan George.

Chapter eight

Möser

Whatever differences there were between Voltaire, Montesquieu and Hume in their general contribution to historical thought, they had all agreed in maintaining that the power of the irrational in history was, as a matter of fact, tremendous. Voltaire had reluctantly admitted as much; Montesquieu and Hume had calmly recognised it, with a fuller understanding of what was everywhere obvious—the mixture of rational and irrational forces. But it had not occurred to any of them that this mixture was not understandable in mechanical terms, but only by following the course of individual lives. All three were richly endowed with interest in the external individual variety of the historical scene, Voltaire with the curiosity typical of the Enlightenment, Montesquieu and Hume with an incipient delight in sheer variety for its own sake. But they were not able as yet to appreciate the unique value of the individual.

In order to disclose this individual worth, it was necessary to reveal the interior aspects of the individual. This could only come about through a change in psychological attitude, a new inner experience. There had to be a certain softening up and blending of the psychological faculties to form a free and more dependable whole. It was all a matter of overcoming the sharp mechanical dualism between reason and understanding on one side, and drives, inclinations and passions on the other, and aiming at an understanding of the psychological unity and wholeness of man; and as a first step, giving the irrational forces in psychological life a higher place in the scheme of things than had so far been allotted to them. Sentiment had to win its proper status alongside thought and man be accepted as a creature who feels, in the midst of a rationalism that prided itself on reason. This came about as a natural reaction. For every emancipation produces effects that have wider consequences, and liberates

250

in any particular sphere the forces hitherto held in bondage by the yoke that is now thrown off. Reason, now become autonomous, strove to conquer the whole of life and free it from all its former shackles; but in so doing it mobilised the whole of life, and aroused in it forces that now came and took their places alongside reason. This was all connected with the changes in social life that had first made themselves felt in Europe about the turn of the century, in particular the rise of the middle classes and the birth of a new middle-class spirit. It was as though new landscapes were being opened up alongside the still valid provinces of Natural Law, landscapes in which disposition, feeling and imagination flourished, and new individual values were disclosed. This is a process we have already seen at work in Shaftesbury and the English Pre-Romantics. Even France did not remain altogether lifeless; and there were thinkers and poets with a freshness of outlook, such as Saint-Évremond and Marivaux, before the time of Rousseau. It should never be forgotten what a powerful impulse was given to the German spirit by this first loosening up of the hard soil of Natural Law in Western Europe. But Germany now went further and dug down deeper. There had already come down from Leibniz a specific German philosophy, which, in spite of its mathematical tendencies, taught how to combine the unity and harmony of the universe with an ever-changing individual multiplicity. Leibniz, Shaftesbury, Saint-Évremond, Marivaux and Montesquieu, and finally Rousseau, with his criticisms of modern rationalising civilisation and his ardent longing for a humanity of greater naturalness—all these influences co-operated in Germany to form the mind and spirit of the man we are now to consider, Justus Möser. He began to look at the historical world with new eyes at much the same time as Herder, in the period following the Seven Years War, and was the older of the two. Indeed, if we count his first approaches to this field, he was in fact slightly the earlier.

We cannot therefore follow Dilthey in his somewhat misleading statement that Möser was a 'powerful autochthonous figure'. On his own showing, these West European influences were so clearly at work in his mental make-up that they cannot be merely ignored. But there was a powerful autochthonous root, a quite original vein which steadily made its way little by little through all contemporary influences, fed by a very special and remarkable background. The individual, the local and the European all fused together in him to produce the brilliant phenomenon that already delighted the youthful Goethe.

Möser was born in the bishopric of Osnabrück in 1720, and lived there till 1794, the year in which he died. It was the very epitome of all that was old-fashioned in the old German Empire—a characteristic that had been better preserved by the smaller territories than by the larger. You could read in it layer by layer a history that extended over a thousand years. The way of life was reminiscent of ancient Germanic customs; so were the lay-out of the city *ut fons ut nemus placuit*, and the structure of the peasants' houses. Möser has given us an unforgettable portrait of the Osnabrück farmer's wife sitting as she had been accustomed through long tradition in the middle of the house and keeping a close watch on all that went on around her. Above her were the later social institutions, such as seignorial rights and serfdom, a cathedral chapter, the knights, the city and the middle-class citizens with their autonomous institutions; and above them again a divided system of sovereignty, which had only taken on its curious form since the end of the religious wars. There had been a Catholic and a Protestant bishop alternately since 1648, the latter always from the house of the Guelphs. The most recent social class, from which Möser himself originated, was what Bruno Krusch has named 'the learned patriciate'[1] of the city. This was a new and very powerful creation, though it had in fact no legal status. In 1773 there were thirty-three lawyers with university degrees out of a population of barely 6,000. They provided the secretaries, lawyers and so on for the various departments that dealt with the affairs of the city. The official seats on the city council were reserved for the nobility, but the main burden of work even in Möser's time fell on the families of the learned patriciate—an arrangement for which he himself was partly responsible. They held together and helped one another, and Möser had already received his first appointment as secretary while still an undergraduate in 1741. They were rising in the social world and in comfortable circumstances; and they also cultivated intellectual interests. We are somewhat reminded here of Montesquieu's 'parliamentary aristocracy' although there was no question in Germany of a *noblesse de robe*. But this whole class of scholarly officials among the citizens were the supporters of the new German culture, and then became the first middle-class representatives of the new German education and later on the protagonists for a share in the life of the State. Such political pretensions were as yet scarcely on the horizon in Möser's time and circle. People could still be satisfied with the outward respect they enjoyed and take advantage of the opposition that arose between the various ancient aristocratic

[1] 'J. Möser und die Osnabrücker Gesellschaft', *Mitteilungen des Vereins für Gesch. . . . Osnabrücks*, 34 (1909). For a view of this historical environment as a whole, see the attractive work of Ulrike Brünauer, *J. Möser* (1933). My own chapter, which was written before the appearance of this work, is largely in agreement with its interpretation. The chapter on Möser in G. A. Walz, *Die Staatsidee des Rationalismus und der Romantik, etc.* (1928) seems to me less satisfactory.

powers superimposed above one another. There were no less than three of these rivalries—between the sovereign power and the Estates; within the Estates themselves, between the Cathedral Chapter and the Knights; and within the sovereign power, between the Catholic and the Protestant principles. And all three were intensified by the tendency of the Guelphs to secularise the bishopric entirely and annex it to their own domains.

Möser contrived to be the servant of nearly all these powers simultaneously. He became *advocatus patriae*, corporation lawyer to the knights and government Junior Counsel, under which modest title he led the administration; but as an ordinary lawyer he was also able to help both the Estates and the government. This unusual position disposed him in a conservative and relativist direction, and made him something of an opportunist; yet his mind was never completely absorbed by these twists and shifts, or immersed in the general atmosphere of the 'gelehrtes Patriziat'. He remained in it, and it is noticeable in his work, but he grew beyond its restrictions by virtue of a genuine inner idealism, which was always prepared to tackle with good will the daily task, yet irradiated it and filled it with an inner warmth. This tall, handsome man could take this life merrily and deeply. He could serve this world faithfully and diligently, not as a moralist who was merely scrupulous about detail, but as a man of profoundly moral nature all through. He enjoyed the confidence of his masters and the love of his fellow-citizens, and desired no higher rewards than those which came his way. But he was in fact possessed of an original power to make the historical world in which he lived conscious of itself, and to give it a voice. Let us see how his sense of history developed.

His relationship to history was, as may be surmised, closely connected with his manner of life, and they influenced one another reciprocally, though his life had more effect upon his historical sense than vice versa. The basis of this sense was his love for the past history of his native place and all that still remained of the past. He had the antiquarian's delight in the charm and the fragrance of things from a bygone age—a human impulse which may be just as insistent in the man who is so inclined as the bent for drawing, or music, or observing the stars. There were of course lawyers, judges, and teachers with some knowledge of antiquity, researchers into old legal matters, collectors of old books and manuscripts, in his native place and elsewhere, both before and after his time. He came from a family who, as it were, laid these interests upon him as a heritage. His father was head of the Osnabrück Chancery, and wanted his son to begin with a learned dissertation, something like *de successione foeminarum in feudis praesertim Osnabrugensibus*. His *History of*

Osnabrück (begun in 1762 and published in 1768 and the following years), and the many historical essays produced in his *Patriotic Phantasies* for the benefit of his fellow-countrymen were published in the *Osnabrückische Intelligenzblätter*, founded by him in 1766 and continued until the year 1782. They consist for the most part of a continuous account of the history of this locality and its firm roots in the soil of the past. He taught what was traditional, for he himself was the embodiment of tradition. He loved what was old, as a man loves the garden of his parents' home, where he used to play as a child. But traditionalism is not necessarily historism. Traditionalism may do no more than confine itself to a stubborn cultivation and maintenance of the old soil that supports the life of the community, whilst naively allowing the thought-pattern based upon Natural Law and reason to prevail at all points outside this restricted territory. Historism, on the other hand, comprises more and more the whole of thought and the whole outlook upon the world. In order to find its way to historism, Möser's love for the things of old needed to become a deliberate, critical, comparative, reflecting love. And this transformation came about through contact with the thinkers of the Enlightenment, contacts that were both friendly and hostile.

In his youth, the effect of the Enlightenment upon him was both friendly and enlivening.[1] The remarkable mixture of enlightenment and sentimentality began about the middle of the century to penetrate into the middle-class circles of Germany. As an undergraduate at Göttingen and afterwards, Möser wrote some rather stiff and sentimental verse. He also devoured the Frenchmen Saint-Évremond and Marivaux, and the Englishman Shaftesbury. From Gottsched he picked up some knowledge by the way, and came under the influence of Haller, Hagedorn, Günther and more especially Klopstock; until he finally discovered the deeper powers of poetry in Shakespeare and Homer, in whom he sensed that nature, rising above all theories, had shown what art really is, namely the art that is immanent in nature herself.

This is how he came to see the matter in later years. In his youth, as was still the usual practice everywhere, he was content to take the world of sentiment and the irrational on trust from his teachers, accepting their somewhat specious and eudaemonistic arguments, praising 'a happy ignorance' as the sustainer of all things working together for the best, and preferring the 'comforting error' of a belief in immortality to any truth that would upset it (1745). But this very attitude also provided him with weapons to justify and idealise the despised barbarism of the past. In the preface to his tragedy *Arminius*

[1] Valuable dates for his development up to 1762 are given by W. Pleister in *Mitteilungen des Vereins für Gesch. . . . Osnabrücks*, vol. 50.

(1749), he makes us prick up our ears by the following judgement. 'I am not of the opinion that our forefathers were such dolts as they are commonly held to have been at a superficial reading of Tacitus' (*Works*, vol. 9, p. 204). His sense of individual nuances was already active when he speaks of the fine 'Wölkungen' ('clouding') in his hero's actions. Our attention is at once arrested by this coining of a new word.

It has been noticed in a very felicitous piece of writing[1] how the various elements in Möser's education all had a part in the formation of his language. First they were only in an external relationship, lying as it were side by side; then, as a result of mutual opposition and alliance they managed to blend, and so eventually produce a creative synthesis from what appeared to be incompatible antitheses. For a long time, however, in spite of the early evidence of his antiquarian interests, Möser continued to write a polished High German after the manner of Gottsched, betraying perhaps the influence of a French education, but without any kind of local colouring. Not till his history of Osnabrück did the influence of his native dialect and the attempt to achieve a sense of antiquity and 'a taste of the soil'[2] really make itself felt. Then the conscious struggle began against the French spirit. But this had been an indispensable element in shaping his own mental powers and making him aware of his native roots; and its effects were perceptible right up to the end in the rhetorical and dramatic forcibleness of his style. The old was now transcended, but also 'taken up' into the new. The transition took place much more slowly and tardily than was to be the case with Goethe's transition from the Leipzig to the Strassburg style. But quite apart from the difference in the talents of the two men, Möser had to make his way through harder ground.

In 1756, when he finished the essay begun years earlier on *The Value of Well-balanced Inclinations and Passions* (9, 3 ff), he was still writing in the flashy and overloaded manner adopted from Marivaux. In its content, too, this essay had been influenced by English and French psychology. But taking this as his guide, Möser pushed forward into a new psychological territory of which he was to become increasingly the master.

This came about (and it could scarcely have been otherwise) on the basis of rationalistic and sentimentalist principles. It had now decidedly become the contemporary fashion to let oneself go in tender feelings, while at the same time closely observing the play of these feelings. The various mental powers—understanding, disposition,

---

[1] Laging, 'J. Mösers Prosa', *ibid.*, 39 (1916).

[2] This was Möser's own expression (1, 87), recorded by his pupil Rehberg (*Schriften*, 4, 245).

passion, virtue—were all put like larger or smaller weights into the scales which inclined first one way and then the other, with the eventual purpose of carrying out Shaftesbury's teaching by lessening the weight of sheer intellect and 'weakening a prejudice that makes virtue the sole fruit of reason'. For even lofty impulses and inclinations already carry us along the road to virtue. Möser went still further in joining the ranks of those who distinguished between virtue in the specifically moral sense, and virtue in the more general sense, as 'the good properties of any particular thing'. This latter definition would then include cruelty as a 'good property' of the tyrant. He was in fact reviving the ancient world's conception of ἀρετή and Machiavelli's Renaissance idea of *virtù*, though not entirely, for he still strongly maintained the moral criterion—whether this 'virtue' was to be used for good or for evil. But all his efforts were bent upon showing the power of the whole man in action. He was prepared for the objection that his views confused the difference between natural and moral feeling. 'But there is the same relationship between these two as we find between the soul and the body, which are continually interacting, without our being able to mark out any clear boundary-line between the one and the other.' This affirmation took him down into deeper regions, where the mystery of the unity and interpenetration of mind and body began to loom up, though the ordinary rationalism was content to ignore it altogether. But it was not at all his way to attempt to strip the veil from this mystery in any speculative or analytical spirit. He had a joyful confidence that everything in the world fitted into the perfection of the whole, so that 'even the spheres that seem to be furthest apart have a relationship to this whole'. We are at once reminded of Leibniz and Shaftesbury, to both of whom Möser makes reference in this passage. He then takes up a thought which constantly recurs in his writings, a thought that may be called a key to the gate of historism. 'Our mixed passions', he remarks, 'are often like a stirring piece of music, in which we feel the beauty of the whole without counting the separate sounds'.

This was the first form taken by his doctrine of the 'total impression' which should be our guide. He explained in 1767 (vol. 1, p. 196) that under a magnifying-glass many things appeared crude, fearsome and repulsive which to the unassisted eye seemed fair and lovely in form. 'Does not an admixture of cruelty belong to true bravery, just as lamp-black is a necessary ingredient in grey colouring? Must there not be a streak of avarice in the householder's character to make him economical? Is not some degree of falsity necessary for mistrust, and some degree of mistrust requisite for prudence?'

Hence the whole may be good and fair, whilst the separate threads that compose it are very ugly. So Möser's conclusion was that he should abide by the whole, and rejoice in it. Thus the cheerful optimism engendered by the Enlightenment was to be increased by the rising tide of sensitivity and later on deepened and completed by the majestic touch of Goethe. Its essence was this joyful affirmation of the wholeness of things and the world that contained them, in spite of knowing or suspecting that there were beneath the surface many obscurities and problems, and many partial aspects of reality.

Up till now, however, no one had applied this principle of 'total impression' where historical and political matters were concerned. In a simple and unconscious way, of course, it had often been applied, but not with logical consistency, for the judgment was constantly being upset by the fixed ideas inherited from the thought-pattern based upon Natural Law, which disturbed the freshness of the impressions. Möser was quite clear in the first place that the things of practical everyday life could not be reached simply by the use of inherited notions. The learned scholar, he remarks (4, 25), uses a series of separate and definite ideas and evolves from them rules which, when put to the test, will never stand up against the 'total impression'. But the commander, who has viewed the enemy positions a thousand times, adds one general impression to another, adds incalculable mass to incalculable mass, and produces a result that cannot be assessed in finite terms.

In Möser's view, this was true for the actions of practical life. But as a researcher into history, this theory of 'total impressions' brought home to him the inadequacy of the ideas hitherto applied to the past. In their modern form he saw that they could not be simply applied without more ado to the relationships of the past, which were often so different in kind and expressed in a different language. We may recall that even Leibniz had touched on this problem (cf. above pp. 27 f.). He had written to Nicolai in 1767 (vol. 10, p. 149): 'the clothing in words, and the modern ideas connected with them, give the historical writer endless trouble'. What changes, for instance, had taken place in the idea of 'liberty': in one period, it had represented the beggar's law—*liberi et pauperes*, mentioned together as one group; in the following period it had become something of a privilege, and, finally, a title of honour. He felt the poverty of language as deeply as only a man with creative linguistic talent could feel it. But he drew comfort from the overflow of new life produced by the awakening of German poetry, realising that words are not the only medium through which man can communicate with man. The competent reader can 'reach out sympathetically to the author, and draw out from his soul all that remained hidden in it'. And when the reader thinks he has hit upon a truth, he must go deeper and deeper, and assume that there are many hidden folds and aspects to be discovered; he must so press its soul that it will yield up all its content. The soul must become full of ardour and affection as it confronts its grand subject (vol. 4, pp. 5 ff.).

Thus 'total impressions' are one of the means of acquiring true knowledge. They are based upon a wealth of experience, but they can be evoked in a mere moment, rather as the wine-dealer can immediately taste the origin and vintage of a particular wine (vol. 4, p. 12), or the wool merchant can distinguish the yarns spun by different families (vol. 2, p. 127). The other method of cognition is to proceed step by step and with all the powers of the soul to enter sympathetically into the subject as intensively as possible. Or, as he also expressed it (vol. 4, p. 13), one must 'construct tangents' to things. One can make contact with the human face in a flash by means of ten thousand 'tangents' which are nevertheless ineffable; it all depends on the number available, and on whether they are the right ones. Möser states this proposition in the first place with regard to tastes. But he also constructed such tangents to the past, only with the important difference that in this case he did not expect to record any total impression 'in a flash', but only through long and patient insight and sympathy with the things he was studying. Only an inner love for these things and a delight in the past could produce the patience required for such a task. There had been no lack of antiquarian interest before Möser's time, as we have already noted. But it fell to Möser to combine this love for the past with the new love for human affairs arising from the increased psychological communion among men and the new prominence given to all the irrational powers of the inner man; and it was Möser who opened men's eyes to the broad totality that embraces both men and things.

None of the other great historians of the Enlightenment had pointed out this close connection, not even Montesquieu, whom Möser greatly respected. Montesquieu had certainly not lacked an antiquarian's love for the past and devotion to its study; but his inner powers of sympathy and insight had been inhibited by his rationalism. However, we have seen that the way had been prepared in Western Europe from the 1750s onwards by the English Pre-Romantics and the youthful Mallet. There was another young German historian, a friend of Möser's, who was much valued by Herder, but died quite young—Thomas Abbt by name. He had something of the new sensitivity and inner warmth, but he lacked the antiquarian's steady interest in the remains of the past, a knowledge of the necessary sources, and a capacity for close observation; and his historical writing therefore succumbed to the generalising spirit of the Enlightenment. Möser's criticisms of these deficiencies is of universal significance because it shows with peculiar clarity the gulf between the historians of the Enlightenment and history in the new manner (vol. 10, p. 147, letter to Nicolai, 5 April 1767).

A man such as he was could not merely copy; he must needs see the originals for himself, and his eye would always see more than any of his predecessors had descried. It was an altogether rash undertaking to attempt to dress up history written by others by skill of style and power of thought. Such a work will always have a certain long-windedness about it. *Both of these qualities can be as it were engendered only by a long and attentive contemplation of the original.*

'Engendered, as it were'—these words usher in the whole new method of writing history by means of a purposeful attention to the original, combined with the help of the unconscious, creative, psychological powers.

Because this new method of working aimed at a deepening of insight, it demanded in the first place a certain limitation of the task. The historian should only consider himself at liberty to rise to the universal after he had massed all his powers to deal with the smallest detail. And even the smallest detail, if seen in truly historical depth, can serve as a stepping-stone to the universal. On the other hand, the universal conspectus of history practised by Voltaire and imitated by Abbt and Iselin in Germany only won its renown for breadth of treatment by its rapid review of peoples and periods, which summarised the individual aspects of history under a number of general ideas that were typical of the Enlightenment. Möser produced a delightful parody of this procedure. 'I asked Abbt', he tells us, 'whether it might not be a good idea for him to place his armchair[1] under the apple-tree in paradise and from this point of vantage watch the gradually evolving nations gather round him, and then let his pen take up what he beheld in these scenes from early history.'

Another piece of advice Möser gave his friend Abbt may serve to take us a step further into an appreciation of his early historism. He told his friend that 'he would like to study Rome attentively in the first place as a village and work on the hypothesis that citizens had been evolved from peasants; because this assumption that peasant rights had developed into civic rights would be uncommonly useful to him. And in truth nothing makes Roman history seem more probable than the gradual changes brought about by the degeneration of its notions on the tenure of land.' One can see the projection

---

[1] Abbt, in the foreword to the *Geschichte des menschlichen Geschlechts*, I (1766), had spoken of the armchair in which the thoughtful reader might be sitting.

of Niebuhr's shadow;[1] one can sense the possibilities of Möser's methods—the massing of great powers to deal with a single small detail, the absorption with the original historical phenomenon that will lead on intuitively to an insight into universal phenomena by the use of analogy. To start with, it might only be intuitions that came in a flash; but these were fruitful enough to warrant that 'slow and patient examination' referred to above.

But there were also wider implications: The transformation of peasant rights into civic rights, the conversion of one institution, or one legal system, into something different and new, was a kind of Moses' staff stretched forth over things, bringing life and movement to what had hitherto been static and petrified. Up till now, the sole authority had resided in Natural Law, one and the same everywhere, eternal and unchanging, and in positive law, which had developed very differently in different places. Its early history had mostly seemed to be important only insofar as it established its validity, and only as it affected its existence rather than its genesis. Even when an anti-quarian interest came in and drew attention to the changes in legal institutions, German scholarship did not do more than note these changes, and could not get beyond a merely pragmatic guess at their causes. Here, Montesquieu was the first to make a genuine advance by directing attention to the real process of development, the genesis of laws, the evolution of positive law from rights that had originated quite differently. To be sure, he had done this in the first place to satisfy the practical demands of politics in order to justify things which he himself loved, but which were called in question by the spirit of the times. But as he worked at this task he had acquired a new feeling for the charm and specific values of this processs of development. And this point brings out more clearly than any other the positive encouragement which Montesquieu's work gave to Möser. For Möser, like Montesquieu, was indeed to follow this new line through practical and social considerations. He had noted the same evolution of a law from a right that was originally quite different, when he was led in the course of practical administration to examine the question of serfdom, which the spirit of the age had begun to revolt against. He realised that what had once been public legal institutions had changed into private rights, and private legal rela-tionships had been affected and altered by public legal factors. How could this have come about? Möser began to ask himself new questions about the *dynamic* causes of this transformation, and this

[1] For Niebuhr's relationship to Möser, cf. the brief remarks by Hempel, in 'J. Mösers Wirkung auf seine Zeitgenossen', *Mitteilungen des Vereins für Gesch. . . . Osnabrücks*, 54 (1933), pp. 33 and 53, where there is also other most useful material for the early nineteenth century.

led him to put together his splendid *History of Osnabrück*, which aimed at giving an account, not as it were of a number of doctors assembled round a body, but of the body itself, its various vicissitudes, its original constitution, the assaults it had suffered, the changes and chances that had befallen it in the course of its natural life. In the course of this enquiry he discovered the real object of a genuine history dealing with the life of a State or a nation—the portrayal of a people's entire political development. He was dealing with Osnabrück, but he had the whole German people in mind, and proudly claimed in his introduction that his treatment of the particular example he had chosen would give 'an entirely new turn' to German history as a whole.

The picture that emerged was somewhat as follows: The body of free landowners in early times, whose wars were carried on by a general levy, lost its close-knit character and power of resistance through the changes taking place in the nature of warfare and armies since the reign of Louis the Pious due to the rise of the feudal military service. They acquired the power to subject free men to servitude, to loosen the local and corporate bonds, and gradually to set up a territorial State. 'People will think', says Möser, in a letter to Nicolai in 1778 (vol. 10, p. 174), 'that we are talking too much about militias and regular armies; yet this is the only thing that provides one with a clue—and for the history of a small country it is sometimes only too obvious a clue. But I cannot help it: the moral thread in history is a childish affair and is apt to snap; but this line holds secure.'

The moral thread—that was the leading idea in the old thought-pattern based upon reason and pragmatism, according to which the Enlightenment wrote its history. 'My distaste for all moral observations', wrote Möser two years later in the preface to the second part of his *History of Osnabrück* (vol. 7, p. vi), 'has increased as the work has advanced. Moral considerations belong to the history of humanity, and not to the history of a State. In the latter, it is purely a matter of politics'. There was a touch of irony in his allowing a history of humanity to indulge in moralising. For, as he says further on, this kind of universal human history has no power because it treats the participants not as fellow-members of a State or as shareholders (a word to which we shall have to return), but merely as human beings. 'I should like the peasant also to be able to use this history, and see whether and at what points the political arrangements were for him or against him'. For the moment, we will leave on one side the utilitarian motive for his historical research which comes in here. The essential point is that Möser was deliberately parting company with the basic assumptions not only of the Enlightenment's historical writing, but of the enlightened outlook as a whole. The person who interests him is not an abstract and generalised man, who is the same at all times, whose actions can be judged according to the universal standards of reason, but the concrete, historically conditioned man with his particular joys and sorrows, who must be understood as a specific person. This is the first historical vision to possess real power. The peasant whose life is rooted in the soil is pitted against the pallid philosopher of the city.

This is something we need to appreciate rather more deeply. Starting out from Möser's friendly contacts with the spirit of the age, and its influence upon him, we saw his increasing inner capacity to take in 'total impressions' consisting of a network of innumerable rational and irrational threads. This led on to a deepening of the intellectual and spiritual elements in his antiquarian interests, and to the recognition of the great dynamic causes at work in history. But even hostile contacts with the spirit of the age can be fruitful, for it is sometimes only through conflict that new ideas are able to emerge.

We have already noted the importance of Möser's intercourse with practical life in the development of his historical sense. His was the permanent task of *advocatus patriae*, along with all his other obligations involving work with things derived from the past and needing to be accommodated to the present; and he constantly had to deal with matters such as tithe serfdom, rights and charters of pasturage and markets, guild privileges and so on. Here, it was of decisive importance for his practical as well as his theoretical training that at this particular period all kinds of modern, unhistorical ideas and tendencies claiming absolute validity were invading this ancient institutional world, and that Möser often had to ask himself whether they were likely to be helpful or harmful in their results. The ideas of enlightened despotism and the French philosophy of enlightenment were both demanding entry into the quiet territorial backwater of this little North German State. In the purely intellectual world, and more especially in art and literature, a new and more liberal day was already dawning; but in the State and in society the old principles of reason and Natural Law were now for the first time coming forward with a claim to exclusive dominion and demanding reforms, either in the direction of State subjects domesticated and ruled by reason, or in the direction of a universal humanity conceived in timeless and abstract terms. At the back of the trends of enlightened despotism the real driving force was political expediency in its modern form; and behind the tendencies of enlightened philosophy the rising claims of the middle classes. The ideal motivation for both these tendencies was a not very deep, but mostly honest enough, eudaemonism. The love of mankind and human happiness were the first watchwords of this outlook. Following upon this, however, there came the second demand, which already had a touch of the revolutionary about it. Contemporary philosophy began to dissociate itself from the more limited efforts of enlightened despotism, and to advance the claims of innate human rights over against the State, and to insist on their restoration. These ideas have been called unhistorical, because they went beyond the actual development of history and ignored the real historical man. Nevertheless, they had sufficient historical force behind them to advance the status of man to a considerable degree and bring about notable changes in the world. Who would have suspected as much, when they were first put forward in Germany after the appearance of Rousseau's *Contrat Social* in 1762? Möser was later to experience the bursting forth of these ideas in the French Revolution, and devoted his last written work to opposing them. But in the fruitful years after the Seven Years War, his novel conceptions were brought to maturity by the very conflict that he engaged in with the outlook that immediately preceded them, namely the trends set by the administrators of the Enlightenment and the philanthropic attitudes of the period.

At heart, Möser was not as far removed from these fashionable ideas as his heat in controverting them might suggest. For he too was full of love for humanity, and he too, like the average enlightened thinker, was all in favour of what was universally useful. But there was a decidedly new slant about his philanthropy and utilitarianism, in that he did not choose as the object of his concern the ideal man, but man as he met him in his occupation. It might be the peasant or the farm hand, who still followed a thousand-year-old custom and manured his fields with grass sods, although forbidden to do so by a well-meaning government; the farm hand from Osnabrück, whose efforts to earn a quick fortune by seasonal work in Holland made him work so hard that he aged prematurely; the housewife, who sat inside the house and did her spinning while keeping an eye on the servants; the shopkeeper who induced the peasants to buy all sorts of unnecessary trash—and so forth. He looked these people (to adopt an expression of Luther's) 'in the mouth'; he knew what they felt, what made them merry, or industrious, or lazy, and what gave them assurance and peace in the hour of death. Before and after Möser's time, there were thousands of other officials, country parsons and doctors who knew the intimate ways of the people as well as he did; but their knowledge was inarticulate. There was also the literature of the moralising weeklies, there were the stories by Gellert and other authors about the common people, but seeing them as it were from city windows, and looking down on them in a somewhat dogmatic and patronising fashion. But the novel and original element in Möser's approach was that he built up these pictures of popular life with a full understanding of the soil from which they sprang, and was continually reflecting upon their meaning and context, their origins, purpose and aims, and always in a mood of living delight in things, which raised him above the level of Montesquieu's assessment of the institutions that were rooted in the soil. Thus he created a warm picture of the world, teeming with colour and variety, yet forming a well-rounded whole in which both the individual and the typical fitted in as part of nature, that is to say, a work of art produced by man in harmony with nature. The bishopric of Osnabrück, with barely 120,000 inhabitants, became for Möser a microcosm of the historical world of men in general.

For Möser concluded that wherever the State and society were based upon primitive agriculture, similar developments to those in the ancient Saxon territory must have taken place. The original free landowning community must have been transformed by the necessities of war, and new forms must gradually and necessarily have stepped into their place. Mention has already been made of Möser's judgment upon Rome, with its suggestions of Niebuhr. He prophesied (wrongly, as it turned out) that the American colonists fighting against England would be drawn into militarism by the very circumstances of the war, as Germany had been in the days of the feudal system (vol. 10, p. 174).

Everywhere he was on the look-out for historical analogies in the life that he himself was leading, without closing his eyes to the existence of other forms of State on a different basis from that of free landowners. The historians of the Enlightenment had already begun to compare, seek for analogies, and note differences; but in spite of an accompanying interest in the manifold variety of the human scene in general (*The Variety of Mankind*), they had not succeeded in doing more than analyse in terms of cause and effect. With Möser, however, along with the feeling for the typical and the recurrent already expressed by the historians of the Enlightenment, there emerges a new sense of the individual. Everywhere within these analogies he discerned the richest individual differences in arrangements, customs and patterns of thought, including those of the particular man, which were often so various 'that many people will immediately establish countless connections with a specific idea, whereas others will hardly be aware of a single one' (vol. 5, p. 310). 'A man cannot even appropriate the words of another so that they have in his life the same truth as when uttered by the other' (vol. 9, p. 150). In these ways he was already penetrating to the problem of the specific individual personality, though his interest was primarily political, and so more strongly directed to the individuality of the political structures created by man.[1] He saw their manifold variety, however, as a source of greater vitality. Would it not, he asks, make for a greater variety in human virtues and a stronger development of the spiritual resources, if every large or small society of citizens laid down its own laws and was less inclined to model itself according to some 'general plan'? (vol. 3, p. 68; 1777). He recalled the example of the small Greek republics, and denied that Voltaire had any right to make fun of the two neighbouring villages which had different legal systems (vol. 2, p. 23).

And so as the years went on Möser waged an ever-increasing battle against the 'general plan', against the gentlemen of the 'General Department', against the zeal for regulation displayed by the princes' councillors, against the 'lofty line taken by the would-be philosophers'; and finally, when he was an old man, against the legislators of the French National Assembly. Thus, even before the Revolution, Möser was forging the mental weapons which have served since the Revolution to defend the historic rights of the individual in State and society against the general rights of man. There was often a great deal of entrenched selfishness behind this defence of an ancient world rich in cultural values against a historical destiny that demanded its re-shaping, as we have already seen in the battle waged by Burke. We are reminded of K. L. von Haller's reproachful speech when we find Möser as early as 1772 complaining about 'the insolent attacks on human reason, the destruction of private property, and the infringement of freedom' (vol. 2, p. 23). But we begin to see here more clearly than formerly the link between the history of thought and that of the practical world, between ideas and personal interests, when we recognise that these struggles were the means of gaining a knowledge of what we have called 'historical individuality'.

It would be difficult to fix the exact point at which Möser had reached this revolutionary conviction, for the change had been steadily taking place in him since the end of the 1750s, just as the bud gradually unfolds into the flower. When he began his history of Osnabrück in 1762, this development was already at work in him, but had not as yet reached the stage of a deep and solid conviction, such as a conflict with opponents is likely to produce. In the stirring period after the Seven Years War two movements were at work in Germany. On the one hand, there was enlightened despotism and enlightened philosophy asserting their general claim upon public life;

[1] What Baron says in his commendable article, 'J. Mösers Individualitäts-prinzip', *Hist. Zeitschrift*, 130, 50, is therefore not quite accurate: 'The individual variety he looked for in history was first and foremost only the particularity of *external* relationships; *man*, however, he saw as the same astute political being in all periods.'

on the other, there was the following counterblast of the youngest generation, who launched the 'Sturm und Drang' movement upon the world. Möser was no supporter of 'Sturm und Drang', and its supporters (particularly those of the first subjective period) directed their earliest attacks elsewhere than against the State, which was the contemporary arena of the enlightened legislator, and only here and there did they make any impression upon it. But Möser, whose main intent was to wrest the State from the grasp of these legislators, saw which way the wind was blowing, and realised that it was in his favour. He realised that he could make use of this new and ingenious doctrine of the 'Sturm und Drang', and with a touch of genius applied it there and then to the State. In 1772 (vol. 2, p. 21), we find him writing:

> Every day we hear it said how restrictive to genius are all these general rules and regulations, and how severely they fall short of the ideal and so prevent the new generation from rising above the common ruck of mankind; and yet these critics would desire to bring the constitution of the State, the noblest of all creations, once again under the sway of a few general laws. They wish it to take on the uniform beauty of a French drama; they want it to be something you can draw up on a sheet of paper, in elevation, ground-plan and cross-section, so that the gentlemen in the State department can at once have a convenient little yardstick for quickly taking the measurements of everyone and everything.

The meaning is clear enough. What is right for the talented individual must also be fair enough for the State. It too should live by its specific individual law, rather than by general rules. Thus Möser paved the way for what was probably the most important and effective of all the new applications of this new feeling for the individual—namely the conception of States as individualities.[1]

The spicy expression he adopted for what we call 'historical individuality' still had something of an old-world flavour about it He called it 'local reason' (vol. 6, p. 86).

> When I light upon an ancient custom or habit which will not fit in with newer ways, I go about for a while thinking to

---

[1] This and the above remarks on Baron disproves the opinion of Stefansky who wrote ('J. Mösers Geschichtsauffassung', *Euphorion*, 28, 28); 'Neither the State itself, nor the single individual in the State, forms an individual magnitude'. Stefansky is only right in making the point that Möser did not as yet see the full implications of the principle of individuality as applied to the State and the individual. Stefansky also distorts Möser's relationship to the irrational. Yet his work contains much good material.

myself: 'The men of old were after all no fools', until I find some reasonable explanation for it; then I mostly (but not always) turn the tables of ridicule on the modern folk who seek to decry the ancients and all who still cling to their prejudices, often without really knowing the full facts (vol. 5, p. 144).

It is worth remembering that already Bodin (*De re publica*, 1. V., c. 6) made reference to a *locorum ac regionum ratio* that it was advisable for the statesman to respect. And Montesquieu, in the preface to his *Esprit des lois*, laid down the great heuristic principle that the endless variety of law and custom was certainly not only due to human 'caprice'. This was a pattern of thought that could take note of irrational and individual phenomena, but was not yet in a position to sense their specific worth. This has been named the 'negative historical thought' (Gunnar Rexius, *Hist. Zeitschrift*, vol. 107, p. 500). Möser seems indeed to have shared it to the extent of even reckoning that superstition had a positive value—for instance, the old belief that an angel on the wing might cut himself on your knife if you left it with the sharp edge upwards. Yet even here there is a feeling of something new creeping in. There are flashes of exaggerated poetical humour, as when Möser suggests in a charming picture of this kind of superstition that the people of olden times as it were tied wooden blocks on the keys in order not to lose them. Sensitivity, a new feeling for beauty, and utilitarianism were the contemporary ideas that Möser adopted and made his own. He saw the old Saxon world of the peasant proprietor beneath his oaks and lime-trees as the positive value of the past protruding into the present. It exercised a powerful effect on him, but he could at first only express it in the language and thought-forms of his own age. So he arrived at this idea of 'local reason', which was yet more than a mere idea, because he filled it with his poetical love. We are reminded here of Burke. Möser, exactly like Burke, assumed that there was a meeting-point in history between the beautiful, the useful and the reasonable.

Later on, it was Hegel who worked out in the grand manner this coincidence between the historical and the reasonable. Möser's 'local reason' is by no means the same thing as Hegel's 'historical reason'. When stripped of its poetical associations, it does not signify in the first place anything more than man's adaptation to the manifold and varying necessities of life, which are yet fundamentally simple and repetitive in pattern. To be sure, there was at the back of this Möser's deep and universal confidence that in obeying the necessities of nature, man was also obeying the command of God, for nature was the embodiment of a divine reason. In his notable discussion with

Frederick the Great on the German language and German literature (vol. 9, p. 146),[1] a scene in which not only two kinds of taste, but also two world views and two epochs were at strife, Möser maintained that the Almighty Creator is the source of all the world's manifold variety. And we are reminded at this point that before the Enlightenment which Frederick represented, Leibniz and Shaftesbury had both taught that the Deity should be adored as the source of all the beauty and delightful variety of life. And Möser followed their footsteps in reshaping the ancient natural and rational law into a Natural Law that was concretely historical, poetical in temper, and based upon firm metaphysical foundations, though it still had something of the utilitarian about its foreground colouring. But in thus acquiring the capacity to sense the individual in history as derived from God, Möser was also preparing the way that led on to Hegel's cosmic reason.

Möser's line of thought now impinged upon the historical pragmatism that had so far been dominant at its weakest place. The attitude of the historians, as Möser had put it, was that of a number of doctors gathered round a patient's body, discussing the external injuries, blows and wounds inflicted upon it, but quite oblivious of the living body itself, with its blood-circulation and metabolism. In his historical narrative, Möser had played down the personal motives of particular actors in the scene, and had concentrated attention upon the collective behaviour of groups and communities. To a large extent he replaced causal explanations in terms of motives, character, or external chance by the idea of factual necessity. For instance, he took the case of Adelard, the 'unwise minister' of Louis the Pious (vol. 6, p. 319), which could certainly be partly explained by personal weaknesses, but then developed a snowball effect which eventually turned the old situation into something entirely new. Nature and necessity, as we have already seen, are the most powerful forces in history. No doubt there was still something of the old pragmatic pattern of thought in such phrases as 'the great plan of the ancients' (vol. 6, p. 98), 'the wise purposes of the nations' (vol. 6, p. 140), the 'mistakes' the ancient Saxons would have noticed (vol. 6, p. 151), and so on. But Möser undoubtedly rendered an outstanding service to historical research in this decisive advance upon Montesquieu's line of approach in the sphere of legal, social and economic institutions. He opened the way to a genetic treatment of those institutions which constitute the main framework of history.

Linked with this was an advance in what we have called actual pragmatism. It had been the custom, wherever the motives of

[1] A critical new impression by Schüddekopf in 1902 (*Deutsche Literaturdenkmäler*, 122), p. 14.

individual actors were not sufficient for explaining things, to look for objective and material causes of a very mechanical kind. They were usually located in some very primitively conceived single and obvious events, such as wars, disturbances, changes of place and so on. These were also used to explain the changes in institutions, so that there was no possibility of advancing beyond a purely descriptive and external treatment. Möser burst through this barrier, and opened men's eyes to the immanent causes for change, steadily and silently at work, and so prepared the way for a genuinely genetic understanding.

Yet he firmly adhered to the word 'pragmatic' for this new kind of historical writing, for at that period the word stood for the ideal of a truly scientific history, though this was an expression understood in various ways by different people. Thus he says about a history of artisan institutions and guilds that badly needed to be written: 'Such a history could be treated thoroughly pragmatically. For the origin of any particular institution is a witness to the necessities of the age, the way people acted, fought and thought, dressed and fed themselves' (vol. 1, p. 148; 1767). But an even more precise and personal term was the expression 'natural history', which he liked to use for his manner of writing. 'In a word, it is the natural history of this connection that one thinks of as pragmatic historical writing' (vol. 7, p. vi, foreword to part 2 of the *History of Osnabrück*; cf. also vol. 10, pp. 174 ff.). Words like these brought him once more into contact with the spirits of the modern age, who were so fervently seeking a return to 'nature'. Many of them only found in nature an image of their own indeterminate subjectivity. But Möser did not have to discover afresh the objective power residing in the idea of nature, nor did he allow this to oppress his spirit. For to him, nature was, like the peasant, very down to earth as well as poetical.

Möser was incidentally able to make some other discoveries of general significance. His new manner of looking at the phenomena of life and history individually and dynamically might have led to a thoughtful and ingenious contemplation of separate objects, and a defence of separateness falling back upon the comforting thought that everything was a part of the general creative scheme of life. A student of Shaftesbury and Leibniz, he knew they had conceived this universal primaeval cause; and he might well, as Herder did soon afterwards, have taken a further step and presented the view of individual detail on top of pages of combinations taken from universal history. But that would have been a hazardous proceeding for one of Möser's nature. As we have already seen, he was frightened by the sombre pattern of history as written by the authors of the

Enlightenment. He also showed his masterly abilities in his power to limit his subject, though he achieved the utmost that was possible within the bounds that he had set himself. While concentrating on the concrete history of the State and its people he managed also to give some general perspective and to range the historical phenomena under higher principles of unity.

In the first place he solved what had always been a problem in the older methods of writing history—the time-honoured or conventional division into periods. Möser showed such skill in his division into periods that he continued to bind them together by inner connecting threads and specific individual links, so that the period became a unified historical whole with its own individuality. There had indeed been some attempts to divide time into epochs marked by some substantial *motif* ever since the beginning of the Enlightenment, notably in the historical work of Dubos, even in Boulainvilliers, in Voltaire and in Robertson, to whose example Möser himself referred.[1] Gatterer at Göttingen used the 'method of epochs in favour with recent writers', but in a rather rough and ready, external manner ('Vom historischen Plan' in vol. I of his *Allg. histor. Bibliothek*, 1767, p. 42). Then some unknown reviewer of Abbt's *History of the Human Race* in Gatterer's *Allg. histor. Bibliothek* (vol. 4, 1767) may also have helped Möser's thought on this subject. To the question whether it was possible to give a general history the unity of a work of art, he answered with a definite affirmative, and expressed his wish to have at least a whole period of general history treated according to the rules of an epic poem. Möser took up this idea and gave it vitality and depth. He called it giving history the form, the power and the movement of an epic (vol. 4, pp. 149 ff., vol. 5, pp. 76 ff.). His *History of Osnabrück* was intended to have this effect because it raised the destinies of the body of common landowners to the level of a grand unity (vol. 6, p. x). Moreover, the individual periods were also treated in the epic manner, with a movement that clearly took its inspiration from the new style in poetry. Thus a period would no longer be the life-span of a particular royal family, but would cover a fundamental change in imperial history. Möser maintained that the history of the German Empire ought to begin with the perpetual peace of 1495 because it ushered in a quite new empire; and by way of introduction, the beginnings, progress and final dismemberment of the older empire ought to be presented as 'a single process', and a necessary prelude to the new. Without such a unity, the history of the Empire would be like a snake cut up into a hundred pieces and merely held together by a bit of skin. There was perhaps a

[1] For the attempts made in Mosheim's Ecclesiastical History, cf. E. Seeberg, *G. Arnold*, p. 596.

note of rather forced and no longer quite confident imperial patriotism in this melancholy attempt to restore the unity of the poor Imperial serpent.

Möser rejected the division of his material according to dynasties and reigns, but this was the division that had been used by Hume not long before in his great historical work. Möser, who obtained the book during his stay in England in 1764, felt that he was superior to Hume in other respects as well. He wrote to Abbt in 1764: 'I have often rejoiced in England at being able to untie the knot where Hume confessed himself completely ignorant.'[1] He was referring specifically to his new dynamic method of understanding the structural changes in the great social bodies. And yet Hume may well have exercised a certain influence upon Möser's principles for the division of periods. It will be recalled that Hume had transcended his own external scheme of division by coming to realise that political history exhibits a rhythmic alternation of forcible exercises of power followed by legal consolidation.

Möser shared this opinion. At the beginning of a period, he held, freedom and oppression were usually in opposition. But then they combined to produce some substantial creation (a monarchy, or democracy, or republic) which subsequently increased in power, lost its vigour, declined and finally fell. Summing the matter up boldly and confidently, Möser wrote: 'In France, it was the monarchs who were victorious; in England, the nobles and the freemen; in Germany the servants of the crown.' This was how the matter was bound to appear to the government Junior Counsel and lawyer of the local corporations at the close of the *ancien régime* in Osnabrück. The history formed a whole, yet within that whole there were periods, Möser held, which were big enough to be suitable for epic treatment, for example 'the period before Charlemagne—the heyday of the free nobility', with its significant pattern of balanced powers, but also its mistakes, which led to its gradual decline.

This example may perhaps demonstrate the danger of this new method of dealing with historical periods. There was a risk that the author's own ideals might become a strait-jacket for the history of the past. But this transfer to the world of history of the new aesthetic methods applied to works of art proved uncommonly fruitful. Lessing's new theory taught that attention must be paid not only to the inner unity of the action, but also to the exact context and the homogeneity of all the individual features. And Winckelmann had taught a little before this that the unity and integrity of a work of art could only be felt by sympathetic identification with it. Moreover, he had shown how to recognise the common 'style' belonging to the products

[1] Göttsching, *J. Mösers Entwicklung zum Publizisten*, p. 48; cf. also p. 40.

of a particular period. And Möser had been very eager to learn all
that he could from Winckelmann.[1] With his readiness to look at the
'original' in history as attentively and lovingly as one would at a work
of art, he soon became aware that it was one and the self-same spirit
that expressed itself through all the phenomena of a period, whether
lofty or humble. When reflecting upon the struggle between the territorial principalities and the cities from the fourteenth to the sixteenth
centuries, he came to realise what a close connection there was
between the struggles of the cities to assert their power as economic
units (although they ended in failure) and their heyday in the field of
art. 'It may be boldly asserted that the Germans reached a simultaneous climax in trade and in the Gothic style at that period' (vol. 1,
p. 340; 1767). Thus Möser, with his sense of the connecting links
between the vital activities of a period, anticipated Goethe's work on
German art and German ways, and recognised the beauty of the
Gothic style, 'its strength, its boldness, and its magnificence'. And his
famous foreword of 1768 to the first part of his *History of Osnabrück*
(vol. 6, p. xxi), shows that it was nothing less than artistic intuition
that enabled Möser to divine this consensus of testimony in a
period:

> The clothing of the period, the style of each constitution, each
> law, and I would venture to say each word from the past, can
> give the greatest satisfaction to the art-lover. The history of
> religion, jurisprudence, philosophy, the arts and belles lettres is
> assuredly inseparable from the history of the State. . . . There
> is a close connection between the styles of all the arts: even the
> dispatches and the love-letters of Cardinal Richelieu. Every war
> has its own particular tone, and State affairs have their specific
> colouring, dress and manner in their connections with religion
> and the sciences. Russia provides us with daily examples of this;
> and the readiness of the French genius is as evident in affairs
> of State as it is in the novel. It can even be pursued in
> subterranean fashion along the line that follows up a rich
> metallic vein and exploits it to good purpose.

'Every age has its style', as we read once again later on in the
History of Osnabrück (vol. 7, p. 16). We know that even the historians
of the Enlightenment, headed by Voltaire, had discovered a 'spirit of
the age', though they had not developed that finer feeling for the
structural and the all-pervasive spirit of a period which Möser now
exhibited. The habit of noticing and comparing the different characteristics of the various peoples was older still. Later on, this led to the
Romantic doctrine of the creative *Volksgeist*—narrower and more

[1] See the evidence in Göttsching, p. 51.

272

nationalistic than Möser's outlook, which took both the spirit of the age and the nation into account. The Romantic doctrine of the historical school of jurisprudence led later on to a wrong under-valuation of the supranational connections and influences in history, and remained basically attached to an interpretation of history along the lines of Natural Law, paradoxical as it may appear. For they replaced the belief in a stable and universal human nature by belief in the unchanging nature of a whole people or nation. They then felt this to be something individual in a much more intimate and mystical way than the very unmystical, but extremely wide-awake, Möser. Yet it would seem that Möser, with his presentiment of the close permanent interaction between the *Zeitstil* and the *Volksstil*, the style of the period and the style of a people, was more in tune with the authentic music of history than these Romantics who were so in love with the *Volksgeist*, the spirit of the people.

If Möser had further pursued the aesthetic capacities aroused in him by contact with the new poetry, he would very likely have used the new and more powerful means of knowledge to surpass Voltaire's achievements in basing political history upon a broad foundation of cultural history. But he was primarily interested in the common life of men in political communities. He was therefore satisfied if the historian 'took with him only as much of the artistic and cultural history as he needs in order to do justice to the changes in political forms and fashions' (vol. 6, p. xxii). In writing his *History of Osna-brück*, he even used less of this material than his insights into its connection with history expressed in other contexts would have led us to expect. It should be noted that his selection and grouping of historical material, with political history in the centre, and cultural history on the fringe, yet treated in close structural connection, constituted a prototype for the main line of German historians from Ranke onwards and up to the present day. The justification for this approach can only be found in the central importance of the State for all other aspects of life. Möser did not indeed make this a matter of principle, but he wrote history in this way because his life reflected the experience of a statesman.

In retrospect, it will be seen that the new historical pattern of thought already had a considerable number of achievements to its credit. There was the new empirical intuitive approach, or (to use Möser's phrase) 'total impression', with innumerable tangents making contact with things of all kind; and blended with this was the doctrine of 'local reason'. Then there was his insight into the dynamic changes wrought by material necessity; his perception of the typical and the individual in history, lying side by side, and interwoven; his application of the doctrine of specific genius to political structures, and his discovery of the true subject-matter of political and national history; the application of the epic principle in the division of historical periods, resulting in the formation of new and large supra-individual historical entities, which at once led to the deeper recognition of a contemporary style that shaped all the events of the age; the interaction between the style of a period and the style of a particular people; and finally a new principle of selection and grouping for the material of history.

As well as these general innovations in method, there were also fruitful suggestions for applying the new ideas to particular provinces of life. 'I wish there were someone who studied languages in the same way that Winckelmann studies the ancient world' (vol. 10, p. 150; 1767). Or Möser would have the idea, perhaps inspired by Goguet, that someone should write a history of the plough (vol. 10, p. 179; 1779).

In all these achievements, Möser's experiences of local patriotism and statesmanship combined with the new impulses of the German spirit fertilised by the thought of Western Europe. The leading motive was his local patriotism and sense of statesmanship; but behind it there was a mental and spiritual urge that provided the deeper springs of action.

Looking at Möser as a whole, you get the impression of a beautiful bud unfolding steadily into full bloom, to produce a result of the highest historical value—yet failing in the end to do so because of the climatic environment. There were various obstacles to growth: in spite of all the new lines of thought making up the full historism, which Möser had either conceived or expressed or at least suggested, with a touch of real genius, they had not yielded their full potential. Something more was needed than a new and all-inclusive historical insight into the material, namely a greater capacity for critical research. Ranke's subsequent and truly remarkable achievements were only made possible by the methods evolved in philology since the humanist movement. By using these methods, it became possible to distinguish in documents of the past between the genuine and the spurious, the original and the derivative; and they could then be used in conjunction with the new ways of studying the individual and irrational in history, its genetic character and the interplay of action and destiny. It was precisely this philological criticism that provided such incomparable help for the study of the individual. But Möser was modest enough to realise that criticism was his weakest point. 'No one has better cause than myself to be humble and teachable, for I am more and more aware that I have come to historical studies too late in life, and have been too neglectful of historical criticism.' He realised that this was why he had often mistaken a mere idea for the truth (vol. 10, p. 256). There is no need to cite specific proofs of this. Yet the 'certain feeling for truth' which had to make up for this deficiency did nevertheless enable Möser to produce great and valuable results.

But quite apart from the pruning of his ideas which critical capacity would have provided, even his most original and fertile thoughts were prevented from having the fullest application in matters of great importance. We have only to compare Möser for a moment with his contemporaries, Goethe and Herder, who did most to change the intellectual outlook. It at once becomes evident that he had a priceless advantage over them in access to the historical world through his professional links with the State. He very soon acquired an understanding of the powerful passions at work in politics; but there was one ardent passion in which he himself was lacking—the passionate and conscious impact of a great creative individuality, without which the deepest recesses of the historical world cannot in the last resort be explored. Ranke's subsequent achievements presuppose not only Möser's work, but that of Herder and Goethe and the Romantics. Möser's inability to go with the subjectivist 'Sturm und Drang' movement had both a favourable and an unfavourable effect on his achievements as a historian. He was certainly able on occasions to recognise the importance of the creative individual. We have only to recall his saying about the general who acts creatively as a result of 'total impressions'. But it was apt to retreat into the background in the face of the pressure of material necessity, which he certainly understood profoundly in its dynamic aspects, but was still inclined to interpret in too utilitarian terms. It was no doubt his peculiar gift to be able to view political and social life with eyes that had been opened by the artistic sensibilities of the new European and German intellectual movement. But in his case, the artistic sense was overshadowed by the utilitarianism with which the Enlightenment had viewed the State and society. Furthermore, it must be questioned whether the State and society as they confronted Möser were such as to exhibit their fullest potentialities and vitality. It surely required the powerful revelation of some great political and social drama, such as faced Burke. But Möser lived within the confines of a small German State; it was from this standpoint that he reviewed what had hitherto been the strongest power in German history, political absolutism; and from this angle he was more likely to see its defects than its achievements. At all events he made intensive use of a fairly long stay in England during 1763 and 1764 to absorb the picture of a system in which political power was quite differently organised and applied. But it now becomes clear that we cannot reach a final understanding of Möser's interpretation of history, including both its merits, its limitations and its lack of balance, until we have had a closer look at what has so far only been indicated in general terms. We must examine in greater detail his attitude to the State, and his political ideals and maxims. And to do justice to Möser's particular habit of mind, we shall have to consider in the same context his attitude to religion.

Möser's world of political thought was made up of two elements. When considered in naked isolation, they may seem to be different in kind, and here and there to have produced minor inconsistencies; but he fused them together in such a way that there can be no question of any deep rift in his political character. One of these elements was a deeply felt political ideal, already tinged with a touch of Romanticism because it sprang from a yearning for an idealised past stirred up by the remnants of past ages that still surrounded him. The other element was a statesmanlike sense of what the State required at any particular moment, the concept of political expediency or political interest, the content of which varies according to differences of time and place. Yet it reigns supreme as a formal law in the life of the State, and will inevitably break through sooner or later, in spite of any temporary eclipses. Machiavelli had been the first to discover this law, and yet had been able to combine it with a personal political ideal drawn from a glorified past. And Möser continued to do likewise.

We have already seen the youthful zeal with which Möser entered the lists in 1749 on behalf of his Germanic forefathers. This was a bold and novel step, but was in keeping with the new Pre-Romantic interest in the earlier ages arising in many parts of Europe. For Möser, this was no more than an enthusiastic interest in the golden age of Saxony, which he held to have prevailed before the conquests of Charlemagne, when the 'common landowners' constituted the State. It may well be that Montesquieu's saying about the origins of English liberty in the forests of Germania, which had such immeasurable effects on political thought and endeavour, also kindled a spark in Möser, and fused his half-conscious feelings and impressions into definite ideas.[1] In contrast to Montesquieu, he applied the words, in a narrower sense dictated by his local patriotism, directly to the Saxons (vol. 5, p. 121), and expressed his opinion that there had been a deep constitutional difference between the Suevi and the Saxons. Preferring 'the genuine happiness of a free nation' to all the achievements of the plastic arts, he saw in the ancient Saxon State the sup-

---

[1] The first testimony to Möser's ideal of liberty, expressed in quite general terms, in his essay of 1756 on the value of well-balanced inclinations etc. (9, 35), does not however show any signs of influence by Montesquieu's dictum.

reme creation of the human intelligence, 'a structure all parts of which were built according to the highest ideals'. In comparison, the small Greek republics were assuredly no more than dolls' houses. 'We have to thank the Saxons for the spirit of freedom, and the skill to preserve fully our property against all the attacks of superior power and the desire for domination.' Once indeed (vol. 5, p. 85), he mentions the period of Charlemagne (the man who destroyed Saxon liberty) as a golden age, but only because the king concerned himself with the welfare of the common landowners. And in his *History of Osnabrück* (vol. 6, pp. 192 ff.; cf. also vol. 6, p. xi), he traces the sinister decline to the institutions set up by Charlemagne. At any rate, Möser places upon the shoulders of Charlemagne's successors the beginning of the descent from the one-time splendour of the constitution under the free landowners to the ruins of his own day, splendid and worth preserving as they were. There can be no doubt that he regarded this sequence of events in German history with deep and passionate sorrow as a *ruere in servitium*.

In his *History of Osnabrück*, he says in a note tinged with a penetrating though somewhat veiled bitterness (vol. 6, p. 185): 'True freedom will never endure being judged or taxed in any cases that occur except through its own freely chosen companions. It has often happened that a nation has lost this right; but to lose it without realising the loss and even uttering one sigh over it, this is the truly astonishing thing.' 'What we have today', he says in another passage (vol. 6, p. 193), 'is at best a freedom that bears the marks of condescension.' When he once more surveyed his favourite class, the peasants, his ideal of ancient Saxon freedom is suffused with a Rousseau-like distaste for the over-refinement of an unnatural civilisation. 'It is to be observed nowadays that none of the hundreds of obedient servants has any of the dignity and assurance of the peasant' (vol. 6, p. 99; cf. vol. 1, p. 233). But he himself inhabited 'the gilded cells of the townsman', and belonged to the 'servants of the crown', who had been victorious in Germany and were now supreme. He thought it a 'terrible consequence' that after the complete collapse of the militia and national honour the peasant was forced to pay taxes for his lord's campaigns, even when they were the lord's sole concern, and of no benefit at all to the country (vol. 6, pp. 339 ff.). Yet Möser fulfilled the duties of his own corporational posts and served the sovereign authorities with exemplary wisdom and fairness, without rebelling against the sorry system of bureaucratic officials and clerks whose servant he was. He even served it with unmistakable pleasure. How is such a contradiction to be explained?

His daughter once said of him: 'My father hates the pen-pushers and the gamblers, although he is fond of writing and gaming himself' (vol. 4, p. 3). As Krusch has shown, he even played for very high stakes. His was a full nature, a mixture of vitality and rationality, something of a rogue and yet a judge of morals all in one, reminding us in many ways of Goethe's combination of a happy nature with a serious attitude to life. Möser was capable of forming ideals in sharp contradiction to the world around him, but also capable of serving this world, with its mixture of good and evil, with a gay resignation and a serious sense of duty. And so in the eternal conflict between ideal and destiny with which man is confronted, he contrived not to deny the ideal, but also to put up with life as it came to him, often in very different shape, and recognise what was relatively good in it. And so at the end of his history (vol. 7, 2, p. 187), he could view what, in the light of his ideals, could only be called a pitiful facet of German history—the absolutist and particularist State, in which both common freedom and imperial power and greatness had perished—with a certain degree of commendation, though the undertone of resignation, the acceptance of a *pis-aller*, is clearly there. 'It is a great, but often unrecognised, piece of good fortune that the sovereign ruler wields equal power over the whole territory', so that he can 'bring peace, security and justice to his common subjects', hold the higher privileged Estates in check, and make it to their own advantage to support the supreme authorities.[1] It was Möser's particular political art to hold a steady balance between the interests of the sovereign authority and the Estates. As we have already noted, his various offices could influence him both in a conservative and in a relativist direction.

Such a temperament was surely well suited to handling historical narrative. Even the modern historian has to hold his various standards of judgement in careful balance. By the use of induction, and by absorption in his material, he gains some conception of the full potentialities of the individual development he is examining, of its immanent goals and ideals, which are occasionally attained, but not often completely, and sometimes not at all. But he must never only measure the past with the teleological standard of an ideal, or he will certainly distort it. He must therefore apply a second standard as well, the dynamic standard, which takes account of the forces that have actually come into play and the causes that have been at work. This will give the historian a patient appreciation of what might by nature have grown straight and fair, but which force of events has twisted. With his ideal wish for an upright growth of German free-

---

[1] There is a similar though somewhat harsher and ironical reference to this 'good fortune' in the foreword to part I, 6, XVIII. I cannot find any evidence for a substantial turning away from absolutism, as Sadowski assumes in his 'J. Möser als Politiker', thesis, Königsberg, 1921, p. 62.

dom and greatness clearly in mind, Möser could yet deal carefully and sympathetically with the children of the German nation, even when their growth had been sadly distorted.

Perhaps, therefore, one of the greatest traits in Möser was that in spite of his romantic ideals and his resentment against his own age, and of many individual features tinged with reaction, he never became a dogmatic reactionary. He never divided the world into a sharply sundered heaven and hell, but recognised the flux of things and bowed before the dynamic power of 'nature and necessity'. Perfect historism also implies the capacity to be resigned, and requires respect for destiny. It signifies something that Möser said about Charlemagne, the destroyer of Saxon freedom: 'It is lost labour to discuss whether his enterprises were just or unjust, once he had won the victory. Good fortune and greatness raise him above the level of the common standards of judgement' (vol. 6, p. 165). It was significant, too, that he also ranked the peasant higher in worth and power than the obedient servant, yet was willing to admit that the German peasant could not compare with his English or Dutch counterpart, and would probably never 'reassert his national worth' (vol. 6, p. 98). Although Möser was by nature no friend of cities, and was wont to praise the ancient Saxons for having resisted the introduction of money and a municipal constitution (vol. 6, p. 127), he could (as we have already noted in another context) do justice to the greatness of the German city civilisation in the later Middle Ages; and he could bewail the fate that had destroyed this splendid creation of the German spirit, and with it the possibility of forming a powerful German Lower Chamber (vol. 1, p. 338). And although he was wearing himself out in a struggle against the spirit of the age, he could yet applaud the historical force of 'the self-chosen and self-made opinions of men'. He raised the question whether it would not be a good idea 'to have a general revolution in the minds of men every hundred years in order to produce a ferment among the law-abiding mass of mankind, and use it to bring about better results than we have at present' (vol. 1, p. 428; 1770). This was his most daring flight, his freest imaginative venture with the future, his most confident insight into the capacity of the spirit for creative renewal. Once again, we feel a breath of the influence that was reaching him from the 'Sturm und Drang'.

And finally, Möser adopted this attitude to the greatest historical phenomenon of his day—the Frederician monarchy. Here again, considerable self-mastery was required. If he applied the standards of his ancient Saxon freedom, or compared it with the easy tolerance of his idyllic little Osnabrück world, it was bound to seem more or less intolerable to him. He felt wounded, not only in his political, but also in his aesthetic sensibilities, with their strong convictions of individuality, at the sight of something that had come into existence through war and martial valour. 'Our whole military set-up leaves no room for personal bravery; the fate of nations is now decided by soulless masses hurled into battle. . . . Such an organisation must necessarily suppress all individual variety and perfection, the qualities which alone make a nation great' (vol. 1, p. 397; 1770). Moreover, when he took up his pen in 1781 against King Frederick in defence of the German language and literature, he did not hesitate to point to the impoverishment of the whole field of intellectual life brought about by this royal absolutism, which was directly responsible for 'this machine-like State'. But the greatest historical forces always have a dual and divisive effect, producing at the same time both weal and woe. Möser was alert to this in Frederick's case, no less than with Charlemagne. He felt and acknowledged its influence on his own historical writing when he confessed in the following weighty words:

> Our own historical style has been improved by this affair, as we have watched Prussia come to the fore and learnt to appreciate our own history all the more fully in consequence. When we acquire a stronger sense of national interest, we shall be more sensitive still to these matters and express them to greater effect.[1]

Thus Möser was well aware that great historical writing receives its strongest impulse from a rational life that is caught up in some strong turmoil, whether it be prosperous or disastrous. It was no mere chance that the decisive deepening of his own personal touch took place in the very years when King Frederick's heroic self-assertion provided the Germans after a long time with their first great historical experience.[2] These events led to a notable and fruitful tension in Möser's historical thought. In the historical phenomenon of Frederick's monarchy, he was confronted by something that evoked in him both a positive and a negative attitude. This was the incentive that drove him to take the narrow field of the bishopric of Osnabrück and bore down to its deepest levels, thus laying bare all the layers of German development, right down to the oldest—and in his view the most valuable. Möser then acquired not only some idea of the power of a great national interest, but also came to recognise the force of circumstance that had up till then impeded this interest, but need not continue for all time to bar its path. The question

[1] Vol. 9, p. 156; Schüddekopf, p. 23.
[2] This is also rightly stressed by Brandi, in his Introduction to Möser's Selected Writings: J. Möser, *Gesellschaft und Staat*, p. xxx.

whether the ancient Saxon common liberties from which Möser had set out were really to be valued as highly as in his estimation is not relevant to our present purpose. What is beyond doubt is that he had produced a splendid synthesis between a sensitiveness to values and an examination of causes.

The historical writing of the Enlightenment had also produced such syntheses. But their universal values were an abstract and bloodless affair compared with Möser's lively and concrete sensitivity, and their causal sequences were mostly of an external and pragmatic kind, whereas Möser's 'nature and necessity' often rose to a deep awareness of historical destiny such as the Enlightenment only occasionally, and in fact rarely, reached. We would refer the reader once again to what has been said about Montesquieu, Hume and Gibbon.

This powerful sense of the dynamic embodied in 'nature and necessity' was blended with the second of the elements on which Möser's political thought was based—the old idea, active since the time of Machiavelli, of political interest and expediency. We even caught the sound of the words 'national interests', which occur just as frequently in Möser as 'the interests of State', 'causes of State', or 'statecraft'. In his youth, Möser's political and historical reading had extended to Machiavelli and to Pufendorf's introductory history of the chief empires and States, which gave a detailed account of interests of State. His moral attitude and his ardent zeal for the common welfare were proof against any Machiavellism in the narrower sense. But its early influence certainly gave him an understanding of the special character of political actions. Even in his first tentative literary efforts produced in the middle forties he once spoke of 'the eternal principles' of the statesman, 'which form the basis of all his enterprises' (Pleister, p. 42; also Göttsching, *J. Mösers Entwicklung zum Publizisten*, 1935, pp. 15 ff.).

We have followed the later history of this doctrine in the Enlightenment, and seen how it was in most cases treated in a mechanical and utilitarian fashion, far removed from the inner vitality subsequently infused into it by Ranke. In Möser, there are indeed some unusual applications of this doctrine. For example, at the beginning of his history of Osnabrück he advances daring arguments to prove that the political interests of the ancient Saxons between the Weser and the Rhine and the ancient Germans (whom he equates with the Suevi) were not identical. But the useful results obtained from this doctrine preponderate over any minor eccentricities; so that he was able to work out the significance of the *statutum in favorem principum* of 1231–2, and show how it constituted the great turning-point in the internal development of the empire. There may perhaps have been a touch of exaggeration, but Möser certainly had a very keen eye for the essentials. The statute, he rightly tells us, 'went against the emperor's true interests' (vol. 1, p. 393), and brought about a 'change in the political interest of all the princes' (vol. 7, 2, pp. 57 ff.). Previously, 'they had completely destroyed the former chain of jurisdiction and dependence stretching from the supreme head of the empire down to the humblest of its members'; but now, 'they suddenly changed their policy' and sought to subject once again to the supreme territorial authority formed from the ruins of the old military organisation the free communities they had themselves set up.

This example makes it clear that Möser's new dynamic sense was considerably developed by the old doctrine of State interest. It was this doctrine that first made him realise at this point how changes in military organisation caused the disintegration of common liberties and imperial unity and led to the rise of the territorial states and their rulers. And as we should expect from Möser, the doctrine itself was given a more dynamic character. For he expounded it as the natural outcome of the changes in military service which he previously described, and then as the driving-force for a progressive transformation of Germany into territorial states. Here, then, we also have one of the most important turning-points in historical thought, as we watch this development in the idea of political expediency and see its effect upon the growing historism.

Möser's political and historical thinking was generally imbued with the idea that the higher necessities of State condition the lives of individuals and groups, and may rightly do so. For the sake of the health and strength of the whole body, he held that we must be prepared to take individual suffering in our stride. At this point Möser, who in private life was the kindest and most good-humoured of men, could become hard and even cruel in his attitude. The fact that the unhealthy lives led by the seasonal workers in Holland and the Osnabrück miners brought them to ill-health and early death did not in the least disconcert him. 'Our state finances', he remarks indifferently, 'are not in the least damaged by this' (vol. 1, p. 180); such a man 'dies an honourable death' (vol. 1, p. 195). He demanded that illegitimate children should lose in social status, that there should be church penance for promiscuous girls, and that suicides should not be buried in consecrated ground. Moreover, he rejected vaccination for small-pox on the grounds that Providence had not sent the disease into this world without a reason, namely to prevent over-population (vol. 4, p. 64). To be sure, not all his remarks are to be taken literally, for the humorous rogue in him often had a hand in them, and he allowed himself in his patriotic phantasies a certain amount of hoodwinking of his readers, which were all part of his *façon de parler* (vol. 3, pp. 3 ff.). But all these demands do indeed reflect his basic attitude.

More characteristic still is his interpretation of law. He was well aware that positive, formal law is often in glaring contradiction to our practical sense of justice, and that *summum jus* can be *summa injuria*. But he was inexorably opposed to any attempt to set practical justice against formal law, and to hold that the latter, as demanded by legal necessity, was imperative for the preservation of human peace and quiet. Möser even maintained that actual justice, like actual truth, could well be dispensed with in this world (vol. 4, pp. 112 ff.; 1780). 'But formal law and formal truth (which is what society has declared to be true) can never be dispensed with.' These were pronouncements that he threw out in his old age in paradoxical ill-humour against the growing tendencies of the time, which threatened with their universal human brotherhood and unwritten rights of man to hand over almost all the established order to the demands of mere subjectivism. Yet he too was a lover of men, and the idea of political necessity which he championed so adamantly was ultimately rooted in his realisation of the frailty of human nature. It was out of sympathy for this frailty that he was prepared to set up the unbending human decree as a shield for the body of society. He would have had Burke on his side; and even Hume's strong sense of authority would not have absolutely rejected this line of thought.

It was typically conservative thinking. As we have already indicated, Möser was not quite free of an opportunist consideration for the ruling classes. Over the question of serfdom, his writings and pronouncements were such that at home he could well be taken as its opponent, whilst to the outside world he appeared to be its defender (vol. 3, p. 4). Yet he admitted to his friend Nicolai in 1778 that he would certainly have waged open war against the system 'if the Ministry of the day and the whole countryside had not consisted entirely of landowners whose love and confidence I cannot forfeit without doing damage to all present institutions' (vol. 10, p. 170). Such were 'the very important local reasons' that decided his attitude—and local reason was always more important in his eyes than universal reason. But it would be quite unjust to accuse him on this account of servility. As a lawyer, he was accustomed to look at questions from two sides, and to decide what seemed practicable according to the particular time and circumstances. Yet it remains questionable how he could reconcile serfdom (which he had himself publicly defended) with his ideals of ancient Saxon common liberty. At this point there would seem to be an intolerable tension between the two poles of his historical and political thought, between political idealism and political expediency. But the contradiction can be resolved.

For his ideal of ancient Saxon common liberty did not in principle include the freedom of all who were then alive, but only the liberties, or (as he preferred to call it) the 'honour' of the landowner or freeholder. The younger sons he assumed to have gone off as a rule on adventures, unless they were poor-spirited enough to become farm hands (vol. 1, p. 332). But however much this arrangement seemed to him to be modelled upon nature, his evolutionary thought-pattern forced him also to admit that it was 'in the course of nature' for this situation to change when the great migrations came to an end (vol. 4, pp. 209 ff.). The necessary changes in the military system led to an extension of the military service, the joining up of freeholds, and the beginning of agricultural holdings of free or bond tenants.

But there was one line of thought that Möser built in to this evolutionary interpretation of the 'course of nature', betraying its connections with the old scheme of Natural Law, although it outgrew its limitations. This was the tacit assumption of a social contract as the basis of the original State built up round the landowners. But the very fact that he restricted its operation to the owners of land deprived it of the abstract colourlessness of the usual contract theories, and made it nothing more nor less than an agreement of those who first acquired land to defend their possessions in common. Möser also expressly conceded that this may have been nothing more than a tacit agreement (vol. 3, p. 296); and in so doing he came a step closer to the purely historical conception of the origin of the State, which traces it back to innumerable conscious and unconscious acts of corporate consent by mankind, and ultimately to a common impulse towards society. But it would seem to us to be a superfluous relic of pragmatism to describe this in any way as an 'agreement' or 'contract', as it is clearly in the nature of a gradual development whose earliest beginnings are impossible to trace. But Möser used this rather out-of-date conception as a firm basis for his ideal State made up of free peasant farmers. For the same reason he assumed a second social contract, agreed upon by the first acquirers of land with their descendants and later migrants, by which they were only entitled to a lower status, and became vassals, tenant farmers, farm servants and so on. In Möser's eyes, all this was part of the natural course of events.

In the state of nature the relationships between parents and children, masters and servants are the first to exist; and this dependent relationship may well have been the basis of a tacit contract. Everything else would seem to have followed from the

parent and master's power; and all that the children and
servants earned belonged to their natural lords (vol. 5, p. 145).

The same line of argument also served to justify serfdom. It becomes more and more evident at this point that Möser is not only
looking for historical origins, but also searching for arguments in
defence of his own political world against the corrosive spirit of the
age. We have already suggested that it is reminiscent of Ludwig von
Haller's impassioned struggle on behalf of all traditional law in the
face of the claims of reason and universal human rights. It might
almost have been Haller who wrote this naturalistic sentence penned
in 1790 against the ideas of the French Revolution, in which Möser
shows his unwillingness to extend the rights of man so widely as to
understand by that term all that is just, reasonable, human and fitting.
'In my opinion, the rights of man consist in the authorisation to take
possession of all that is unoccupied and to defend all that has been so
acquired' (vol. 5, pp. 201 ff.). Yet this must not blind us to the profounder difference between Möser and Haller. To Haller, the finest
political constitution was that of a State under the patrimonial
sovereignty of a single powerful prince; to Möser, it was that of a
commonwealth of free peasant proprietors. And Möser was from the
genuinely historical point of view far ahead of the younger Haller in
his capacity to think in evolutionary terms, and find room in his
picture of the State for the dynamic and transforming forces of
actual necessity at work in the events of history. But both men still
sang the song of *beati possidentes*; and Möser's purely naturalistic
interpretation of history and the origins of the State thus became
somewhat tinged with a certain materialism, which was also predominant in Haller's later doctrines.

Looking back over our survey of Möser's thought, we can indeed
discern this rift between the evolutionary and the conservative elements, between his ideals and the necessities (political or otherwise)
which re-shaped these ideals in actual life. Was it really possible, on
the basis of Möser's political ideals and his doctrine of the twofold
social contract, to have a full understanding of the historical position
of his own period?

To a certain extent, he undoubtedly managed to do so through the
introduction of a dynamic 'nature and necessity'. He contrived to
accommodate himself, although reluctantly, to the territorial princely
States. In spite of his enthusiasm for the more primitive natural
economy, he could appreciate the virtues of a city civilisation, a
money economy and a powerful middle class, at any rate with full
historical understanding, if not with complete sympathy. Peasant and
citizen, prince and nobleman—they none of them had cause to com-

plain of too harsh a treatment in his interpretation of history and of the State. But the princely servants of bureaucracy, who were now at the helm, were much more hardly dealt with. Yet he was unwilling to apply to them the self-criticism directed against his own class, or suggest that they should be abolished outright. But the man who owned nothing was assigned to a thankless and static role in history; he was destined for ever to be a servant, and to have an inferior legal status. He declared in 1791 (vol. 5, p. 178) that this class would be guilty of sharp practice if they wished by sheer force of numbers to abolish the present constitution and gain for themselves a position of equality, as men and before the law, with the original conquerors. Yet, as Möser could not altogether conceal from himself, force of circumstance was working on behalf of these propertiless masses, and demanding some share for them in the State. This was where Möser's political ideals were irreconcilably at variance with what was taking historical shape under his very eyes.

This is shown in striking fashion by Möser's much-discussed 'limited liability' theory, which also reveals the utilitarian vein in his thought. He constantly compares the State to a joint stock company. The first freeholders, according to this theory, contributed their land as 'land-shares'. The later development of the cities then added the citizens' 'money-shares'. The person who had no shares to contribute (so the stern doctrine ran) could make no claim for political rights, or for any voice in politics, for there are no universal human rights, or only in the restricted sense of the right to defend one's property, which we have already noted. Yet Möser admitted in 1774, long before the French Revolution, that development of the territorial State in Germany would give a place to the classes who owned no property and bring them closer to the State. When the taxes on profit and wealth were no longer sufficient to equip and maintain the armed forces, personal taxes had been introduced, and so at last every person had become a member of the great State-company, or (as we now say) a subject of a particular land. And so there arose that general mixture of civic and human rights in which we seem now, with our philosophical legislation, to drift about with no guiding hand at the helm (vol. 3, p. 295; cf. also vol. 6, p. 69). Thus there was now added to the land-and money-shares entitling a man to a part in the State-company, a 'personal-share', or 'Leibaktie', as Möser called it.

But he himself lost his bearings with regard to this development, though he could not deny that it had in fact taken place. He could not be reconciled to it, but in the face of the French Revolution hardened his original theory that only the shareholders possessed of solid land or money had any right to make changes in the State-company. He admitted that there might well be States based purely upon humanity, such as the Jesuit State in Paraguay. 'But such a constitution gives too little play to the nobler passions, and is only useful for the sheep-like section of mankind' (vol. 5, p. 200). It seemed to Möser, with his ideal of the full-blooded and many-sided individual who was yet linked up in a body with others, that all he most valued was being threatened by this democratic process of levelling.

It is perhaps part of the essence of modern historism that its development was bound up with a certain critical uneasiness about its own age and its prevailing ideals, and an interest in ideas for improving human life, and the life of the State. Rousseau was the first to criticise the culture of his own time, but he did not succeed in deriving the ideal he held up instead from any genuine historical source. Möser and Herder derived it from the past, and in a way which gave considerable weight to the manifold individual varieties of liberty, though hardly covering their full range. But the ideal which was a stimulating source of energy to the new historism proved to start with a hindrance to its development. For it brought back a static element into history just when it was beginning to be handled in a more dynamic fashion. It threatened to adopt some real or imaginary condition in the past as the yardstick for history and for the present; and to a large extent it succeeded in doing so. Again and again in the early days of historism the idea of a golden age acted both as an incentive, and as a hindrance, to pure historical thought. This static element was in fact the continuous bridge that connected historism with the interpretation of history in terms of Natural Law; it was to some extent a piece of Natural Law converted to a new use. But it was impossible along this line to come to a full understanding of one's own time, or to a just evaluation of the individual forces or evolutionary tendencies at work in it. For the ideas so forcibly expressed in the French Revolution, which Möser opposed, were a very individual, powerful and lively expression of history, in spite of their abstract and generalising form. We have already contrasted them with the traditionalism of Burke, which, though not pointing back to a specific ideal period in the past, was nevertheless a good deal in bondage to the past.

The limitations of Möser's historical understanding are no less clearly shown in his attitude to religion as a phenomenon in history. Both in relation to religion in general and Christianity in particular, there was the same dual polarity between the ideal and the exigencies of politics. The champions of a naked political expediency since the time of Machiavelli have usually seen religion as an *instrumentum regni*; and this was also true of Montesquieu. But it had been common ground among the writers of the Enlightenment (apart from

Hume) that there existed a natural and very simple religion with a belief in one God, and that this was a universal possession of mankind. Möser adopted both beliefs and combined them in an early Latin composition entitled *De veterum Germanorum et Gallorum Theologia mystica et populari* 1749 (vol. 9, pp. 179 ff.). Here, he explains that according to Tacitus the Germans had only worshipped *one god*; but after the coming of Caesar they had embraced the worship of many gods. Hence he concluded that alongside the purer *religio mystica* there must have been a *religio popularis*, introduced *pro ratione status politici*. This was a production thoroughly characteristic of the Enlightenment,[1] but its theme was still active in his thoughts in 1762, when he sent a letter 'To the Vicar in Savoy, to be given to J. J. Rousseau' (vol. 5, pp. 231 ff.). In this, Möser maintained in opposition to Rousseau that all the lawgivers and founders of great States had held the natural religion to be insufficient for the basis of a civic society, and had therefore been forced to take refuge in gods and other contrivances, or in a positive religion of some kind. 'We are all part of the vulgar mob; and God has wisely bridled us in the soul rather than by the nose. . . . Our religion is meant for the common herd, and not for angels.' This is how he represented the divine policy towards the kingdom of men.

Thus Möser's attitude was different in a slight but quite important degree from that of the enlightened writers, who saw the positive religions as the work of calculating priests and legislators. He applied the pragmatic method of searching out causes to God Himself, representing Him as carrying out in this world a policy which clearly had wise ends in view. This teleological explanation of the irrational events in history was a relic of the Christian doctrine of the divine plan of salvation, and was still destined (as we shall see in Herder) to play a great part in the growth of historism. For the rest, Möser did not make any special use of this doctrine, because he was able to find other and better means of expressing the irrational element in history in a palatable form. But as far as religion was concerned, he held fast to the teleological conception that, in the ultimate analysis, its manifold historical varieties were due to the workings of Providence. He was thus able to trace it back, like Montesquieu, to the variety of human needs and circumstances (vol. 6, p. 74), but could not summon up any genuine historical feeling for it. It was from this standpoint that he later on dealt with the problem of tolerance, which need not concern us here.

Yet Möser, too, possessed a religious ideal, drawn as he thought from history, though it was indeed an ideal thoroughly permeated

[1] Related to Semler's distinction between public and private religion. Cf. on this point E. Seeberg, *G. Arnold*, pp. 602 ff.

with political motives and desires. This was the religion of the ancient Saxons, as he imagined it to have been. One of the most important passages in his history of Osnabrück is the speech that he puts into the mouth of the defeated Saxons, addressed by them to Charlemagne—using in modern form an ancient historical device (vol. 6, p. 188):

> The truth of the Christian religion does not bind any man to accept it; it is therefore not equally suitable for all peoples and all constitutions. Each has its own aim and therefore its own truth. The Saxons' is liberty; and the Christian religion is certainly not in accord with this aim, for a Saxon is bound by honour, but a Christian by love; yet the latter is not as sure a human guide as the former.

This was the direct reproach Möser made against the Christian religion, that it seemed to have unduly weakened the idea of honour (vol. 6, p. 50). The commandments given by Moses to a nomadic people were not suitable for settled landowners (vol. 6, p. 163; vol. 5, p. 195). And he even went an important step further, and attacked Christianity not only from the standpoint of the past, for having forced itself upon people whom it did not suit, but also for its present effects. We have already seen how Möser championed the maintenance of fixed Estates and the rights of individuals against the levelling philosophy of the age and against any general creed of human rights and universal love. He now realised perfectly clearly that these originated in the Christian religion, and had been taken up by contemporary philosophy. In earlier times, he had explained (vol. 5, pp. 119 ff.; cf. vol. 5, p. 195 and vol. 6, xix), no free landowner or citizen had to be afraid of torture.

> It was only the gradual preponderance of a mixed population, as well as the Christian religion and philosophy, which removed all political differences between men and lumped together the nobleman, citizen and serf under the one name of human beings, that brought about the introduction of torture for everyone.[1]

There is a gentle reminder here of Machiavelli, who reproached the Christian religion (in the face of his political ideal of *virtù*) with having made men unmanly. One can also see the recurring gap

---

[1] Elsewhere in the *History of Osnabrück* (6, 69), however, he can makes the point that the old rights were not transformed by human love and Christianity, but by the changes in military service, 'automatically and quite unnoticed'. It would seem, then, that he thought differently at different times on this particular subject.

between Christian thought and thought based upon reasons of State. Möser saw it as politically expedient and necessary that the inequalities between the different classes should be maintained, and was suspicious of Christianity for being the source of the newfangled notions of equality.

Did this mean that Möser was radically opposed to the Christian religion? Far from it. On account of certain of his utterances he has even been extolled (although very onesidedly) as an apologist for the Christian faith (Blanckmeister, 1885). After all, this was the religion in which his countrymen had been nurtured for a thousand years, and it had therefore become rooted in the soil, a part of the 'local reason'. He bowed before the accomplished fact, even though it was not in keeping with his own ideal. We noted this in his attitude to the princely States. As far as his own intimate personal needs were concerned, they were probably more in line with the Vicar of Savoy's natural religion. But his relativist sense, his observation of life as it actually was, combined with his sense of political expediency, made him aware that Christianity, which gave simple people support and comfort in the hour of death, was an irreplaceable source of political and social vitality. In one passage (vol. 5, p. 87), he says that the real cause of decline in our days is that religion is ceasing to be a discipline. The most conclusive statement of his religious attitude occurs in another passage (vol. 5, p. 284):

> Moreover, I would beg the reader. . . . not to accuse me of irreligion if I only look at religious opinions in the light of their advantage or disadvantage to the State. This is an aspect that has always seemed very important to me, seeing that God also seeks to advance the well-being of States through religion, and has given us a revelation not for his own benefit, but for ours. I adopt this attitude with an honest intention and with respect for the fundamentals of theology, which are outside my province.

He was certainly convinced that Christianity must be believed if it is to come to life in man, and he did his best, as far as he himself was concerned, to believe in the fact of the Christian revelation.[1] But from his premises of political utilitarianism, how could he rise to a personal faith in that revelation, such as is required by positive Christianity? He could only regard it as relatively, but not absolutely or eternally, valid.

At no point does the dividing-line between Möser and the fully

[1] In his missive to the Chief Rabbi at Utrecht in 1773 (5, 261), he wrote: 'You are a philosopher who would like to believe in the immortality of the soul, and I am also [*sic*] a Christian, who believes it by revelation'.

developed historism stand out so clearly as in this attitude of his to Christianity. He had certainly begun to feel that religion does not exist in one single form, but may well take on many, and that there must be different religions just as there are different languages. In short, he saw religion as belonging to the sphere of political individualities, or (as he would have said) 'local reason'. Möser shared Lessing's opinion that each religion had its own specific truth. But in adopting this view he was still bound down by what has been called 'a negative historical thought-pattern'. That is to say, there is full recognition of the value of the irrational vital forces for the State, for society, and for individual life; but there is a failure to recognise, and especially to feel, the specific worth of religion, or to appreciate its autonomous status, which raises it above all mundane purposes. Even Möser's aesthetic powers were not enough to overcome the limitations of this utilitarian outlook; and his own religious sensibilities were limited by a rationalistic theism.

In order to see once more where Möser developed from a purely negative thought-pattern into positive historical thinking and feeling, it is necessary to go back to what he had most at heart, to the State and society in the concrete form in which he met them in actual life.

Does it not look as though what we last saw of his theory of the State as a joint stock company was diametrically opposed to the specific ideas of the State as seen by the mature historism? Surely Burke had already waxed indignant against the materialistic and egotistical conception of the State as an insurance or mercantile company. Here too, no doubt, Möser continued to pay tribute to the utilitarian spirit of the current rationalism. Again, one must bear in mind that the pioneer seldom succeeds in entirely transforming any particular ancient body of thought at one fell swoop. It must also be remembered that, as Möser himself discovered, language often lags behind actual feeling and experience. The new structure of historical concepts begun by Möser had not yet found its full means of expression. In actual fact, Möser regarded the State with a much livelier interest and warmer feelings than a shareholder usually displays towards his company. This was only a picture used by him to bring out the close connection between the citizens as members of the nation and the State, and the inseparable relationship between rights and duties.[1] Möser, like Adam Müller after him, wanted the State to be 'a great, energetic, constantly active and living whole'. He complained that the old emperors had allowed the empire to become a prey to the princes; he regretted that the free cities had not sub-

[1] Cf. Hölzle, 'J. Möser über Staat und Freiheit', in the memorial essay on G. von Below, *Aus Politik und Geschichte*, p. 172.

sequently created a strong German Lower Chamber and over-
seas commercial empire, like England. He criticised the absolutist
mechanically-run State, and he longed for great affairs, and a strong
sense of national interests to bring new vigour into the intellectual
life of his time. This was how he saw England, as he looked out upon
it from Germany:

> The humblest person here (in England) makes the general
> welfare his private concern. All the satires, comedies, moral
> exhortations, and often even the sermons, are closely bound up
> with affairs of State. And it is this lively interest which imparts
> energy to the people in England and enables them to aim higher
> than others who write in cold blood, and merely for some
> commendable reason (vol. 3, p. 96).

In England you could hear all manner of wild animals roaring in
the forests, and rejoice in the voice of nature. 'But in the little
summer-house where we children of the neighbourhood gather, even
the chirping of a house-cricket is disturbing.'

Möser's inner thoughts sought to escape in such wishful imagery
from the narrow restrictions of the time and the place in which he
lived; yet he was neither able nor willing to escape from them. He
wanted to remain rooted in his own soil and steeped in 'local reason'.
But it became apparent that the small bishopric of Osnabrück, which
had revealed to him so many historical secrets, could not give him all
the inspiration and driving-force available in a large political entity.
The greatest political asset that he acquired from his studies was a
revival of the German principle of partnership in the life of the
State, which had become so sadly neglected; and in this respect he
was the forerunner of Baron vom Stein. But in the small-scale relationships that belonged to his native air, politics and society were so
much one and the same thing that he hit upon the subsidiary idea of
comparing the State to a joint stock company. His political expediency was thus much more an interior matter concerned with
maintaining the fine naturally developed individuality of a small
social organism, than an affair of external policy, where there was
nothing much for it to bite upon. For (as he wrote with a shrug of the
shoulders in his reply to Frederick the Great) there would be no
Curtius[1] among his compatriots willing to leap to his death (vol. 9,
p. 139). One of the most fruitful of all his insights was his understanding of the connection between the development of internal
affairs in Germany and the changes in warfare and the composition
of the fighting forces. If he had gone one step further, he would have
reached Ranke's doctrine of the primary importance of foreign policy

---

[1] Famous legendary Roman figure who jumped into a chasm of the Forum.

in shaping the internal constitution of a State. But Möser did not progress to this point because he had little general experience of foreign politics. And what he did know, he interpreted just as superficially as the average thinker of the Enlightenment, who treated everything in a moralising strain.[1]

Möser had yearnings for something on a larger and fuller scale, but they were not of the all-consuming kind. He could remain quite satisfied in the society of his Osnabrück farmers. This no doubt was a sign of his historical feeling and identification with what time and place had specifically to offer him. But along with this, there was the risk of a traditionalist acceptance of all historical institutions. Although Möser will always be reckoned a conservative reformer, he never completely avoided this danger, any more than Burke, and this weakness was an anticipation of failings in the historism which followed.

Another weakness was relativism. Möser was already saying: 'Everything in the world is, after all, only relatively fine and grand, and the acorn has precedence over the olive' (vol. 9, p. 141). In so saying, he was defending Goethe's Götz against Frederick the Great's damning judgement, that it was 'a fine and distinguished product of our native soil'. But in this affirmation, Möser was also expressing the sum of the historical wisdom acquired in the course of a life-time. And here it is obvious that such a relativism does not necessarily lead to a virtuosity that is ready to affirm anything whatsoever in history, or (which comes to the same thing) nothing at all, with positive certainty. Here, Möser was much more inclined to affirm with the greatest force and zest the solid soil of the historical land that had nourished his life, and made him one of its 'fine and noble products'. A small place, but my own, he might well have said. He was the first example of a devotion to the small which can deepen into a worldwide outlook on a grand scale. The small things he studied yielded up to him their utmost meaning, as he extracted from them all that they contained in concrete and individual historical material; and he used all his discoveries as a symbol and example of individuality and dynamic force in general, teaching men to view the particular *sub specie aeterni*. In this we must rank him along with Herder as an early pioneer of historism.

'Phantasies', was Goethe's verdict, 'although it is all closely bound up with the actual and the possible'. This combination of imagina-

[1] 1, 399 (1770): 'Most of the causes of war nowadays are insults, which generally concern a single person, or demands which a single person alone is justified in making, but in which millions of men are forced to participate. But however fortunately the war may turn out, they have absolutely nothing to gain from it'. Cf. also 1, 99 (1769) on the 'folly' of the war and power politics of the Hanseatic League.

tion and actuality, nourished by all the mental and spiritual powers, led to a pure contemplation that in the end even raises it above all utilitarianism. Here again, Goethe was able to express something of Möser's secret in the words he wrote in *Dichtung und Wahrheit*, at the end of book 13: 'He is always above his subject, and can deal gaily and lightly even with the most serious material'.

Chapter nine

Herder

Introduction

Möser, Herder[1] and Goethe were the three greatest and most effective among the first pioneers of the new sense of history in the eighteenth century. Looked at from a distance, the achievements of these three great men have much in common in the fundamentals of their thought. But they stand apart from each with wonderful distinctness when considered from the point of view of the basic human and psychic qualities that went into their making. It was also characteristic of the new historical thought that it created quite specific uniform principles for understanding history, and yet was fed by a whole variety of most individual motives and talents. And so it must continue to be today, unless it is to degenerate into a mere routine scholarly technique.

What Möser contributed was the talent of a mature human being whose powers had grown steadily over a long period to form a strong and harmonious habit of mind. With a sure touch he succeeded in combining the concrete experience of a practical profession with the new forces now working at a deeper level in the Enlightenment, to produce a blend of the homely attachment to native soil and the wider European spirit. Herder, on the other hand, considered both as a man and in the development of his powers, strikes us as an inharmonious and puzzling personality. He never struck firm roots in any profession or in any particular place. As he himself says in a mood of

[1] This chapter is based, of course, on a study of the whole of Herder's writings bearing upon his historical thinking. But the vast richness of his thought, with all its intricacies, nuances and contradictions, compels us (within the limits of this present work) to confine ourselves to a selection of what seems most essential. We are only concerned here with the main structural lines of this thought. The quotations are from Suphan's edition of Herder's works.

self-reflection (vol. 8, p. 328), he was 'driven by a vague unrest that sought another world, but never found it'. Even in old age he was quite clearly portraying himself in the character of Petrarch, when he called him one of those tender souls who seek rest on every side but never find it (vol. 17, p. 266 and vol. 18, pp. 362 ff.). The revealing admissions he made about himself are to be found in the travel journal of that most intensive period round about 1769, when he travelled by ship from Riga to France. There, we can see his tendency to acute depression, his violent rebounds to the opposite extreme, his ardent ambition and his essentially tumultuous and restless inner nature. He was no fully developed personality, like Möser and later on Goethe, but a one-sided character, the type of the mere scholar who becomes a problem to himself, who possesses Faust-like longings for a full-blooded humanity, but does not possess the strength and determination to escape from the limited world of the study. At this period, when he was only twenty-five, Herder had already embarked on revolutionary thought of the most fruitful kind. During the journey, grandiose plans and outlines for works that still move the intellectual world were wildly revolving in his mind. The most exalted and inclusive of these projects, a kind of general denominator for all his achievements in historical thought, bore the title: 'A general history of the human soul in all periods and ages. What a book!' (vol. 4, p. 368). And it should be particularly noted (for it serves as a key to a fuller understanding of Herder's total achievement) that the purpose of this plan for future research went far beyond any mere contemplation of ideas to satisfy his personal thirst for knowledge. They were intended to mould, educate and benefit the whole human race. In all Herder's purely historical work, the same fundamental motives were at work, the same ethical and pedagogical purposes as those of the Enlightenment, to which Rousseau and Möser had so much contributed. But he became conscious here of a weakness in his mental disposition, which was indeed a necessary foil to its strength, and distinguished him both from Möser and from Goethe. Herder was somewhat lacking in the sensuous power to see the forms of life and history in their concrete specific particularity and their stark actuality. He had not enough of the realist and the empiricist about him. 'I have not the sort of mind that can observe: I can only contemplate and speculate' (vol. 4, p. 366).

> Why have I deserved as a result of my past circumstances to be only capable of seeing *shadows*, instead of being able to sense real things? . . . Everywhere I suffer from an anticipatory imagination, which strays from the truth and kills all enjoyment by making it seem dull and flat (vol. 4, p. 446).

No doubt this excess of imagination was connected with a further weakness, obvious to and much criticised by his readers, namely a deficiency in clarity of ideas and logical coherence. It was only a consistent desire for these that was apparently absent from Herder's make-up; he was certainly not lacking in power and acuteness of intellect, of which he could give abundant proof in particular instances. Herder himself could see this excessive imagination as a fault; but it was no empty and capricious faculty producing only phantoms. It did not simply bypass reality, but went beyond the real and actual (which it incidentally treated somewhat inaccurately) and then deliberately down into the psychic depths of human life where the creations of the real world have their birth. Here, in the recesses of his own soul, he heard the echoes and faint overtones of sounds that no human being had so far heard. He did not, like the great masters of the human soul in the past, confine himself to self-observation, or the observation of timeless human interior processes. The historical, the mutable, the strange and the often misunderstood psychological processes, with the mystery of their genesis that no man had yet plumbed—these were what attracted him. He was intent upon writing 'a history of the human soul in general', as Hume had been before him, but in a more profound sense; and for all these reasons he was able to discover with a real stroke of genius new provinces in the life of history as a whole, and become the creator of a new method of 'sympathetic identification' ('Einfühlung'—a word that he himself invented); and by the use of this method, all the fields of history he did not himself cover were gradually able to be explored.

For he himself was not able to throw light upon more than a part of the historical world. In order to get our general bearings, we will confine ourselves first of all to the essential features. Fundamentally, Herder's strongest bent lay in the direction of aesthetics; but his capacity for entering into the psychological phenomena of history was by aesthetic receptiveness rather than by active artistic production. He was lacking in the power to give adequate form to his ideas; his poetry was equally defective in this respect, and so were his interpretation and description of things historical. The new wonders of the inner life of history which he discovered were never focused in a clear historical light because he never took the trouble to put them into sharper conceptual form. The light he kindled was a flickering one, wavering and changing a good deal during the course of his life. From the beginning, the ethical and pedagogic motivation, at times combined with a strongly religious strain, was predominant; but in the later stages of his development, it became increasingly a hindrance to his great and almost unique capacity (in spite of all his deficiencies) to 'feel himself into' historical life. And specific contemporary experiences were working powerfully in the same direction. The ethical standards of a spiritualised Enlightenment, which Herder kept working out in more and more definite form, no longer did complete justice either to the whole historical process, or to his individual perceptions; and he gradually dispensed with a good deal that seemed to him to be important as a young seeker after truth.

It is thus possible to mark at least three stages in his conception of history, which we shall then have to consider more particularly. The first stage embraces the twelve years from 1764 to 1776—the years in Riga (1764–9), the years of travel (1769–71), which brought him together with Goethe at Strassburg, and the period of the consistorial council in Bückeburg (1771–6). This was a period of rapid and vigorous rise; and it can be further divided into the early period and the Bückeburg period. In this period Herder produced his greatest work as a historical thinker and pioneer of historism, the sketch possessing an almost visionary power entitled: *Auch eine Philosophie der Geschichte zur Bildung der Menschheit*, written in 1773, and published in 1774 (vol. 5, pp. 475 ff.). In spite of the new religious ferment at work in the Bückeburg period, it can be regarded as the natural climax of his early years, and can therefore be closely linked up with this from the genetic point of view. The second stage, including the first fifteen years at Weimar (1776–91), when the influence of Goethe was at its most fruitful, saw the production of his major work, the *Ideen zur Philosophie der Geschichte der Menschheit* (1784–91, vols 13 and 14). This is a powerful book, which had a tremendous effect on his contemporaries, but is no longer so impressive today. As we shall see, it contains in its first parts a further addition of new and important conceptions; but later on it shows increasing signs of a rift between the aesthetic-contemplative and the ethical standpoints, as we have already noted; until finally in the third stage, this leads on to the *Briefe zur Beförderung der Humanität* (1793–7, vols 17 and 18), and the *Adrastea* (1801–3, vols 23 and 24), where the ethical standard finally predominates. It is clear that for our present purposes the first stage must occupy the chief place.

I The Early Years

Sensitive and unstable natures such as Herder's might easily have languished in other periods. In order to bring out all its potential genius, there had to be a conjunction of intellectual and spiritual influences that happened particularly to suit his specific character. It will be sufficient at this point merely to allude to three of them (the

Enlightenment, pietism and Platonism) as the three chief spiritual forces of a general nature to which Herder was indebted. About the middle of the eighteenth century they were often to be found working in parallel in Germany, but in Herder they coincided. He had the peculiar and rare good fortune to be confronted with great representatives both of the Enlightenment and of pietism, who had already burst the narrow limitations of both of them and had begun to open up new paths. In the Enlightenment, there were Montesquieu, Hume and especially Rousseau; in pietism, there was the personal example of his friend and teacher Hamann. Herder was zealous in making extracts from Montesquieu (vol. 4, p. 508), and in the early days at Riga venerated him as a great master; but he then soon outgrew his teaching. Yet he was greatly impressed by Montesquieu's method of collecting, arranging, and thinking through the details (tracing reason back to yet more fundamental reasons) in order to get at the heart of the matter. And the youthful Herder was spurred on by the energy derived from his attempt to work with the limited tools of the Enlightenment to arrive at a more universal and deeper understanding of the mind, or the 'Metaphysics of laws', as he was already calling it. In so doing, he would finally burst the shackles of mechanistic causal thought, which Montesquieu had already begun to loosen (*Gedanken bei Lesung Montesquieu's*, 1769; vol. 4, pp. 464 ff.; cf. also vol. 5, pp. 565 ff.).

As we saw in Hume and his criticism of the laws of causality, the Enlightenment was already in a fair way to bursting these shackles. The new and disturbing questions being raised exercised a strong effect upon Herder. As he wrote later on (vol. 8, 466): 'Hume has shown, by raising certain metaphysical doubts, that the link between cause and effect is mental: it is something that cannot be seen but only supposed or concluded. That is to say, it cannot really be recognised historically, but only philosophically.' It should be noted that the distinction between 'historical' and 'philosophical' does not bear the same sense in this passage as it would today. Herder meant by it that Hume had enabled him to look for causal connections not simply through pragmatic observation, but in the realm of inner mental processes. This is perhaps the most important testimony we have to the fruitfulness of Hume's thought. In his youth, Herder had also been gripped by Hume's historical works, and had pronounced him to be the greatest historian he knew (vol. 32, p. 27); but this judgement was not an enduring one. Yet Hume's detached comparative psychology as applied to historical phenomena, although not in harmony with Herder's own psychological make-up, did lead him on to problems that captured his attention. Hume's *Natural History of Religion* (1757) had thrown new light upon the primitive history of mankind, which he had depicted as crude and savage. But the very fact that Hume had set out from the thought-pattern and opinions of primitive peoples, and had raised the problem of their ascent from lower to higher levels, spurred Herder both to follow up this line and to contest Hume's findings.

But in the person of Rousseau there had already been a powerful opponent to Herder's suggestion that the human race had substantially progressed. 'Rousseau's voice was heard as though from the desert', wrote Herder in 1774 (vol. 5, p. 643). Already in his *Discours* of 1750 and 1754, Rousseau had suddenly shattered the pride of the Enlightenment at its very climax of raising the great problem of whether the advance of human civilisation was for the good of human life as a whole, or the opposite; and had given an answer in no uncertain terms. In Riga, the youthful Herder had already been profoundly gripped by this teaching (vol. 32, p. 41). This problem, and more still Rousseau's positive thesis that the natural man was humanity at its best, and that cultured and civilised man had lost his paradise and his true youth, was one that preoccupied Herder from this time onwards. Turning back to Hume's sober views (H. to Kant, 1767, *H's Lebensbild*, vol. 1, pt 2, p. 297), he was rightly in some doubt whether the natural man constructed by Rousseau's rationalistic methods was anything more than a romantic picture (*Reisejournal*, 1769; vol. 4, p. 364). But Rousseau's error was one of those productive mistakes in the history of thought; and in Herder's life and work, though there continued to be a mixture of truth and error, it was nevertheless transformed into the most valuable fruit. Moreover, Rousseau himself had derived from his mistake about the character of natural man, held with such fanatical tenacity, a great truth which Herder then appropriated and deepened—namely the recognition that there were very marked diversities within human nature. This led to doubts about the doctrines of Natural Law, which had always held human nature to be uniform, and to the further conclusion that the natural man had only been transformed into the civilised man as the result of a long and complicated mental development.

Montesquieu and Hume had likewise observed the historical changes in human nature, but only those that were externally visible, and only the differences in general types. But at any rate as historians they proved unable to go down into the interior world of individuality, the psychological depths of man or the ultimate profundities of history. Yet Rousseau, as we have seen, in spite of his failure to achieve a fully historical attitude, was able by laying bare his own incomparable individuality to help in arousing the new feeling for all that was individual. And exactly the same is true of German pietism. Oblivious of any world of historical development, it limited the inner spiritual life of the soul exclusively to its relationship with God, though this included all the lively interplay of higher and lower powers, sensual and sinful impulses, and longings for grace. In the narrow days of his youth in East Prussia, Herder experienced such contradictions in this pietism, and to begin with suffered so severely from its most rigid forms that a permanent tension was set up in his religious life. But then in 1764 he met a man in Königsberg called Hamann, whose pietism was a deep and powerful personal experience, and yet he had been able to take a decisive step into a new spiritual country. In Hamann, Herder was confronted with the disturbing figure of an original and independent thinker of great psychological and spiritual force. Here was a man who discerned in the sensual impulses and passions, hitherto considered sinful or dangerous by the pious, a mysterious wellspring of power; who had a new and powerful sense of the God-given unity of body and soul, and so raised the value of the irrational to a new level; and who began to survey the world of history with this new fund of vitality, though his thought was still shaped by dogmas and principles firmly based upon the Bible. His saying (influenced no doubt by the English Pre-Romantics) that poetry is the mother-tongue of the human race (*Works*, vol. 2, p. 258), also became a leading motif for Herder. His other saying: 'Why should we become copyists when we can all be originals?' (*Works*, vol. 2, pp. 196 ff.), put him on the right road for understanding the thinkers of old, namely by making it quite clear how different they were from the men of his day. The fact that this difference rested upon the diversity of historical circumstances was strongly brought out by Montesquieu and others, and emphasised by Hamann himself. He advised Herder to 'study philosophy according to the shades of the different periods, minds, generations and peoples' (*Works*, vol. 2, p. 15). The close contacts between Hamann's and Herder's thought cannot indeed be explained simply by the teacher–pupil relationship. Herder certainly needed for his further development an exchange of ideas with Hamann, and criticism from him. But here, as also later on and even more fruitfully between Herder and Goethe, it was a question of one original mind working upon another. If we might use a mechanical analogy to illustrate a psychological effect, it was as though a billiard-ball in motion collided with another at rest, and communicated to it its own motion. Herder was of a more sensitive disposition and more universal interests than Hamann, and so was in closer affinity with the Enlightenment than Hamann, who was radically opposed to it.

But the common features in these two men's outlook go back to a common source, namely Platonism—using that word in the widest sense. We have already mentioned this as the third great influence in

Herder's life; and by this term we mean more especially the effects produced all down the centuries by Neo-Platonism right up to Leibniz and Shaftesbury, while not forgetting that it was on Protestant soil that this Neo-Platonism underwent its further development. Hence it came about that the deepest thoughts of Protestantism, and the pietism to which these had given birth in conjunction with mysticism, stressing the direct relationship between men and God, could blend with the Neo-Platonic tradition. And Herder in his youth had been influenced by the developments of Neo-Platonism in a mystical direction.[1] But this was not his natural line of country. 'Their light burns with a smoky flame', he wrote to Lavater in 1775 (from Herder's posthumous papers, vol. 2, p. 126); and this divergence increased with the years. On the other hand the clear and deep insights of Leibniz and Shaftesbury ('the new Plato', as Herder once called the latter) cast their spell upon him from his youth onwards. In 1787, when he wrote his dialogue *God*, where he conceives of the All as a system of living forces operating by the eternal principles of wisdom, goodness and beauty, Herder thinks particularly of the sweet hours of his youth spent in poring over Leibniz, Shaftesbury and Plato 'in what was more than mere reverie' (vol. 16, p. 571). We shall meet further testimony to this connection later on.[2]

Among the predecessors and contemporaries who put Herder in the way of a sensitive Platonic outlook upon the world in general, we must also include Winckelmann. Pursuing the line of 'inner sensitivity' developed by Shaftesbury, he had taught men how to see the beauties of Greek art with a new vision. And going a step further than Shaftesbury, he had been the first to show the stage-by-stage development of Greek art as a great historical phenomenon; though he proceeded then to single out the stage of its maturity, lift it out of the time sequence, and canonise it as the only possible pattern for all time. But Herder had been warned against this by Hamann's advice not to imitate antiquity. He saw with unerring insight that Winckelmann's history was 'more of a didactic system than a history can

[1] The earliest version of his youthful poem 'Die Natur' (29, 114), to which Spranger called my attention, reads:
'Blessed indeed am I, in the midst of this world so full of life divine,
At the centre of so many creatures full of the life of God.'

[2] Hatch's interpretation of 'the influence of Shaftesbury upon Herder' is somewhat superficial in *Studien zur vergleichenden Literaturgesch.*, ed. W. Koch, I, 1 (1901). It contains numerous suggested parallels between their respective thoughts, but they are not always capable of substantiation. The most interesting is the reference from Herder's *Theolog. Briefe* (10, 305), where he compares Leibniz and Shaftesbury, and recognises his own greater affinity with Shaftesbury (cf. also p. 5, n. 1 above). Other outbursts on the part of Herder against Leibniz do not amount to much, as is shown by R. Sommer, *Geschichte der deutschen Psychologie und Ästhetik*, pp. 307 ff.

afford to be' (vol. 2, p. 123), 'a historical metaphysics of the beautiful' rather than 'a genuine history' (vol. 3, p. 10). But Winckelmann's sympathetic approach to art impressed Herder deeply, and spurred him on to become a 'Winckelmann for literature'. It has been shown that Winckelmann influenced Herder even in his vocabulary.[1] Whether in eager imitation or in opposition, Herder remained in life-long debt to this great man.

To the three chief mental influences (the Enlightenment, Pietism and Platonism) there must be added a fourth, centred round the great personality of Shakespeare, 'about whom I can go on and on whenever I have occasion to mention him' (to Merk, 1770, *Lebensbild*, vol. 3, pt 1, p. 232). It was his effect upon the soul of the youthful Herder that set it vibrating in harmony with its own inner genius. Already in Riga, Herder acquired an appreciation of Shakespeare which was destined to become more and more influential in all his subsequent historical thinking. He came to realise that such a phenomenon could not possibly be judged by the hitherto accepted standards of the Enlightenment. It could never be assessed according to its details, but only in its full-grown totality. Shakespeare was 'a genius in whom the detailed ornament is nothing, and the great rugged structure of the plot is everything' (vol. 4, p. 284). His essay on Shakespeare, which appeared in a German art periodical in 1773, was a pioneer study in the field of modern aesthetics. In it one can see even more clearly the importance attached by Herder to Shakespeare's poetry as a symbol of the historical world and as a medium for interpreting his own historical thought. And at this point Platonism and Shakespeare came together. It might be said that he looked at Shakespeare through eyes accustomed to Platonism. For he saw each of Shakespeare's works as 'permeated by a universal soul', and each of them became in his eyes a universe in itself. The whole of Shakespeare might be called 'Spinoza's colossus—Pan—the universe' (vol. 5, pp. 208 ff.). In earlier drafts of the essay, Shakespeare was fairly and squarely interpreted as a history of the world, of nature and of humanity—a truer history than that of the textbooks. But the reasons for Shakespeare's work being 'so full, so complete, so vital—a meeting-point for all the world' were based upon such new and profound thinking that they can only be examined in the context of the new historical outlook arrived at by Herder.

And finally, along with these four principal sources from which the youthful Herder drew spiritual nourishment, there were the subsidiary influences that we have already seen at work among the

---

[1] Arnold E. Berger, *Der junge Herder und Winckelmann* (*Studien zur deutschen Philologie*, 1903), pp. 85 ff. Cf. also on Herder and Winckelmann, Fester, *Rousseau und die deutsche Geschichtsphilosophie*, p. 52.

English Pre-Romantics since the middle of the century. They were subsidiary in the sense that they did not produce any intellectual master of the very first rank; but they were closely related to Herder's intellectual development, for they threw a new and warmer light upon just those problems that were destined to spur him on to a still deeper wrestling. Primitive poetry, popular poetry, Homer, the Old Testament, the individuality of the races, especially the Nordic races, the Middle Ages—all these themes of the English Pre-Romantics were to occupy Herder from this time forward. He became acquainted with their productions partly as a young man and partly in later years. Hamann had studied them eagerly in his early days, and so was able to act here too as a mediator; and all that we have examined in considering the French Pre-Romantics and the research into primitive history also became available to Herder.

Herder's reading as a young man was gigantic. But he devoured books in a very different spirit from the Enlightenment, with its insatiable thirst for sheer knowledge. He could also be carping and petty in criticism, like any contentious scholar of the period. But there swept through his being a torment of inner desire for direct sympathetic insight into the life of the past. He read for his soul's sake, as the Christian seeking salvation might read his Bible. He used the commentators of the past only as signposts to the original springs of life, and attacked them furiously if they did not fall in with his own instinctive interpretations. He read in the compulsive spirit of a man who intends to extract from history the last ounce of meaning it can offer to a seeker after God. No one before him had read history in this spirit.

But there were also various factors in his immediate environment which contributed to this new relationship to the world of history. It has been rightly pointed out that in the years spent at Riga (1764–9) there were two strong contemporary influences directly connected with a still living past (Stavenhagen, *Herder in Riga*, Abhandl. d. Herderinstituts zu Riga I, 1 ff.). In the first place, it was here that Herder acquired the direct experience that led to the new interpretation of primitive and popular poetry, issuing in his new line of thought about nationality. And partly connected with this there was his relationship to the State, for it was here that he took up a new attitude destined to remain with him for the rest of his life, and constituting the problematical side of his approach to history.

It is a reasonable and highly probable assumption on the part of Stavenhagen that Herder was present at the Latvian sun-festival on St John's Eve 1765, held in the estate of a Riga friend of his near Jägelsee. Women and girls collected the magic herbs; songs were led by a leader and taken up by the chorus, and there were round dances under blazing tar-barrels. At any rate several years later Herder attributed the 'real genesis' of his enthusiasm for Ossian and the songs of the savages to an experience of this kind, in which he had seen 'the living remains of this ancient savage singing, rhythmic movement and dancing among still living peoples', not yet altogether mutilated by modern customs (vol. 5, p. 170). Ideas from Rousseau and Hamann may well have disposed him in this direction; but the singing and dancing of primitive man must probably have been seen by Herder himself, visible to his senses and stirring up an endless chain of feeling, in order to become from that moment onwards the typical primitive image which Herder exalts again and again in the course of his historical thought. For Möser, the pattern had been set by the Saxon peasant of old in the oak-shaded courtyard; for Herder, it was this flash of experience (perhaps only on one single occasion) that spoke to him of the past and continued to flicker all his life long (cf. vol. 24, p. 42). With Möser, the growth of his conception of history was slow and peaceful, nourished by delightful everyday objective impressions from contemporary life; with Herder, during those same years, it was thoroughly turbulent, and arose from a subjective habit of mind that seized its necessary sustenance wherever it could be found in the world. In the Latvians and the Baltic Germans, Herder could witness in a bodily form a clash between the two spheres that Rousseau had very theoretically and artificially set over against each other—nature, or at any rate a life near to nature, and civilisation. Here, the pressure upon a small subjugated people by a large ruling nation was so striking that Herder soon began to ask himself how long this popular culture, with its original language, songs and customs, could possibly last in face of the corrosive or destructive influence of modern ways (vol. 5, p. 170). There is no evidence from Herder's early years that, in addition to the regrets at the disappearance of an ancient and aesthetically valuable culture, there were also complaints of small nationalities being suppressed by the power policies of large and warlike peoples. In the later period, such complaints occur with striking frequency, and Herder was always ready to associate Latvians, Kurlanders, Prussians, Lithuanians and Slavs together in the list. So much so that it suggests Herder could trace some element of ancient Prussian blood in himself, with its love of songs and singing, its terrible seriousness and its melancholy complaints (*Adrastea*, vol. 23, p. 467). All this points to a tenacious preservation of his earliest experiences, and a capacity to develop them. Later on, in the early decades of the nineteenth century, the sons of the East heard a call from the lips of Herder and the professors inspired by him, a call to awake to their own nationality. In short, Herder's doctrine of nationality was born in that same Eastern world where it was destined subsequently to have its most powerful effect.

As we shall see, it was to be the special contemporary influences of the eighties and nineties that would sharpen Herder's thought in a political direction; but there was already some point of contact in the experiences of his early period. In the same way that Herder's early experience of pietism and religion had two sides to it (the artificial external side and the genuine creative sources within him) there was also an ambiguity about his experiences of the State. Livonia represented in his eyes the land of freedom, for in Prussia he had hanging over him the threat of military service. He seems never to have quite got over the resentment connected with it. From this point onwards, he looked upon his Prussian home, 'the subjected fatherland' (vol. 29, pp. 321 ff., 1769), almost with the attitude of an emigrant. Not that he had at this time fundamentally rejected the enlightened despotism represented in Prussia by a most powerful personality that impressed even Herder. He could regard Frederick as a means towards achieving freedom, and in 1769 he even had some ambitious thoughts about possible activities in Russia which would only be feasible within the framework of this system (vol. 4, p. 403). But his criticism of the Prussian State was more than mere resentment, for it was based upon an argument that did not indeed do justice to the vitality and developmental possibilities of this State, but did certainly fasten upon its weakest point. Herder was perhaps the first person to light upon it because it flowed from the depths of his own new-found sense of nationality. In 1769 (vol. 4, p. 473), he gave it as his opinion that Frederick's monarchy allowed no national feeling and did not build up a nation, but rested solely upon the personal views of the reigning monarch. As he remarks in his travel journal (vol. 4, p. 405): 'The States of the King of Prussia will know no happiness until they are partitioned into a fraternal union. . . . And then where will his empire be? But where is the empire of Pyrrhus? Is there not great resemblance between the two?' It is interesting to see the wishful thinking that pictures a peaceful federalism cropping up at this point. It clearly had connections with the first political stirrings in Germany after the Seven Years War and with the history of the Prussian-German problem;[1] but it is more important still as a pointer to the general direction of Herder's historical thought.

Livonia and Riga, however, also offered positive pictures to set against the Frederician State. There was self-government in the Estates, the corporations and the municipalities, with roots going back far into the past. And as Herder wrote later on, all this was

[1] Cf. *Weltbürgertum und Nationalstaat*, 7, 336, note 2.

vitalised by a common spirit that he would have liked to arouse in every city, village, institute and school (Stavenhagen, p. 18). 'The spirit of the Hanseatic cities has departed from Northern Europe; who will bring it back again?' he complains in his travel journal of 1749 (vol. 4, p. 406). Yet he had experienced some few remains of this spirit even in Riga, and wished to write a factual history of the Hanseatic cities; for which he would have had Möser's warmest approval. But such matters affected Herder and Möser so very differently, in spite of their common feeling for them. Möser, stimulated by political life, became the first political historian of Germany to see the life of the State with new eyes, because he was interested in it at heart. But for Herder, the life of the State remained a marginal, though never an indifferent, sphere of interest. Yet in both cases, the thought bore historical fruit. Möser's influence was passed on via Baron vom Stein; Herder's was instrumental not only in arousing the Eastern nationalities, but in the nationalisation of political life in general. Thus from the very start the new historism worked creatively in actual life. The most intensive *vita contemplativa* can often have the deepest effect upon the *vita activa*.

We have seen something of the constellation of intellectual and spiritual influences in Herder's early period, and something of the setting and the atmosphere in which he grew up. We have seen that the impressions he received were never merely received, but at once shaped into new forms. It will now be as well to follow the pattern of these threads a stage further, so as to have a clearer picture of the root-structure, that is to say the inner motives at work up till about 1774.[1] How were these connected with the two new basic thoughts of historism—the idea of individuality and the idea of development?

The starting-point must be where Herder took his plunge into the world of the past. To judge by his youthful compositions (vol. 32, pp. 1 ff.), there can be no doubt that under the influence of Rousseau, Hamann and the English Pre-Romantics, though with the most personal impulse and energy, he launched straight into the earliest periods of mankind and the most primitive elements in man, both in the present and the past. The child, primitive man in his natural state, and the common people were the sources from which all else was derived, because he drew from them by throwing himself into them. Into what other vessels but these could a man like Herder at this period, under the impulse of warm but vague feelings, and repelled by the cold intellectual rationalism of the day, have poured his in-

---

[1] We are only using occasional testimonies from somewhat later years insofar as they either continue or express more forcibly what Herder had already been thinking.

most self? In one of his earliest essays (vol. 32, pp. 14 ff.), he writes: 'The voice of feeling is like the speech of children and happy animals in the wild state—monotonous, true, and in tune with nature'. The maxim of his educational work in Riga was to treat the child as a child, and not as an immature grown-up (Stavenhagen, pp. 17 ff.). It may be surmised that such doctrine was an aftermath of Rousseau's *Émile* (1762), and more particularly his own powerful childish experiences, and his youthful revolts against unsympathetic pressure. For through the whole of his subsequent career there was the thought that the impressions of youth ('the dawn of life') mostly set the direction for our whole life's course. 'They weave the basic tissue, to which later events and maturer reason add the pattern' (vol. 9, p. 478). This frequently recurring image of dawn, carrying imponderable overtones of thought and feeling, might almost stand as a symbol for the whole of Herder's historical thinking and his entire life's work. This deep interest in the dawn of his own childhood bore a fundamental relationship to his new feeling for 'the dawn of history' (vol. 6, p. 70). He developed this in his Archaeology of the East, begun in 1769, and the subsequent *Älteste Urkunde des Menschengeschlechts* (1774–6), where he wrote significantly: 'The child and the common people—the noblest part of humanity' (vol. 6, p. 309). On the sea voyage of 1769, he interpreted the seafolks' love of miraculous tales in terms of the child's psyche as a phenomenon of primitive man; whereas the great Hume in his *Natural History of Religion*, with a pragmatism characteristic of the Enlightenment, had explained the superstitions of seamen as due to the many strange events of a seafaring life. But Herder at once linked up this piece of intuitive perception with an ingenious idea that embraced all times and peoples, and called it 'the capacity for poetic invention' (vol. 4, p. 360). Out of this there developed quite spontaneously a kind of phylogenetic principle for the history of thought. In the fragments that he wrote on recent German literature (2nd. ed. 1768; vol. 2, p. 69), he says that the human race and a human being in childhood resemble one another; and some years later, in more definite terms: 'The childhood of each individual is at the same time the childhood of the whole race' (*Ält. Urk.*, vol. 7, p. 29; likewise vol. 6, p. 269).

We may suppose that when Herder in Riga began to make this comparison between life and history, he only had in mind an equation between the child and natural man conceived still in somewhat Rousseau-like terms (cf. vol. 32, pp. 15, 17, 41). But then it would seem that the fascinating picture of national life and culture among the Letts led him on to the wider idea of the nation in general, which henceforward dominated his historical thinking, so getting away from the atomistic remnants of Natural Law that clung to Rousseau's doctrine. Within the compass of our theme we can merely hint at the way this gave rise to Herder's great achievement in bringing about a new aesthetic understanding of the most ancient poetry, and poetry as a whole. Resuming our main line of enquiry, we are trying to show how the principles of the nascent historism (individuality and development) as shaped by Herder were closely connected with this new aesthetic sense, as well as with the underlying ideas of childhood, primitive man, and nation.

This can be seen in Herder's youthful essays on the ode and the history of lyric poetry. 'The firstborn child of feeling, the origin of poetry, and its maturest flower, is the ode.' This origin he held to be wrapped in the sacred obscurity of the East. 'The most sensitive feelings', he continues on the subject of poetry, 'are perhaps completely *individual*, or at any rate extremely unlike in their national expressions' (vol. 32, p. 62). And then comes something of decisive importance. Herder admits that others before him had considered the beauty of an ode to lie in its individual circumstances (vol. 32, p. 65); and Horace had been particularly praised in this respect. But critics had only gone halfway in their appreciation of individuality; and others had committed what Herder ridiculed as a complete contradiction—they had tried to imitate Horace. The new and revolutionary element in Herder's thought was the declaration that the individual was inimitable; and this he stated in much more definite and fundamental terms than the English Pre-Romantics before him. Just as a child (we may interpret his thoughts) cannot be imitated by a grown-up, or primitive man by civilised man, or one people by another, so the Horatian Ode cannot be imitated by a modern poet. The German should not strive to produce the cedars of Lebanon, the vines of Greece or the laurels of Greece, but content himself with the crab-apples of his own sacred forests (vol. 32, p. 67). The ode had assumed Protean forms among the various nations; and perhaps only the aesthetic magic mirror was capable of recognising the same living spirit under so many different forms (vol. 32, p. 63).

The same life in different forms, and each of them inimitable: this insight exemplified by the study of the ode had led Herder to a universally valid principle applicable to the whole of history, and of revolutionary significance. Hitherto the prevailing yardstick for assessing works of art, though claiming to have absolute validity, had in fact merely crystallised the taste of its own period. This standard had been already shaken, notably by the English Pre-Romantics; but it was now completely shattered. And the repercussions extended to all cultural values, to everything that was held by any nation at any period to be 'good, beautiful, useful, pleasant or true'. Herder very soon became aware of the tremendously shattering effect on all

historical thought produced by this principle, and at first it was not
without some misgivings that he followed the new path.

> Are not truth, beauty, and moral goodness always one and the
> same? Yes; and yet one can see that principles for which at
> one period any man would have shed his last drop of blood,
> have at another period been condemned to the rubbish-heap in
> that same nation. . . . Such scepticism would almost seem to
> lead us into mistrusting our own tastes and feelings (vol. 32,
> p. 29).

At this point he breaks off, for in 1766 he could get no further; this
awareness had brought him to the brink of a bottomless pit of mere
relativism. But only for a moment, for the new vital quality that the
primitive stages of humanity had already acquired for Herder was
already too powerful to cause any hesitation about the validity of the
changing forms. He felt a warm love and enthusiasm for these
original forms (the child, primitive man, and the nation), a love that
appreciated their inimitable worth and therefore refused to have
them dressed up for imitation by a false romanticism. This was the
starting-point of Herder's evolutionary thinking, and the 'genetic'
principle which from this time onwards he never ceased to expound.
And we, too, are genetically connected with these origins, as the grey-
haired old man is with the child, and the tree with its roots. The novel
element in this idea was not the intellectually comprehensible content,
for the analogy with the stages of human life, the '*Lebensaltertheorie*',
had often been taken up by the Enlightenment. What was new was
the deep and satisfying sense of being rooted in a universal process of
germination, growth and activity common to all things human. Thus
the first form assumed by Herder's developmental thought was vegetative and biological, though we use the latter word with some hesitation, for the modern meaning of the word was very far from Herder's
mind. For him, life was and always remained a physical and metaphysical process. But for this very reason the earliest stages of developing life were endowed with a special significance and dignity,
because they were nearer to the mystery of the primal source.

> Just as the tree grows from its roots, so must it be possible to
> derive the growth and flowering of an art from its earliest
> origins, which contain the whole essence of its later products,
> just as in the corn-seed the whole plant with all its parts lies
> wrapped together; and I do not see how it would be possible
> to derive from some *later* condition any explanation with the
> same *genetic* force as my own (vol. 32, pp. 86ff.).

It must be admitted in criticism of this first stage of Herder's

developmental thinking that it is still confined to a purely evolutionary conception, exaggerating the importance of the earliest stage and
not doing justice to the possibilities of transformations or additions
brought in subsequently through the emergence and operation of
new factors in the course of history. One might almost suppose
that Herder had been influenced by Leibniz's doctrine of monads.
which had viewed each single monad reverentially as a living entity
directly descended from God, and yet had seen it in isolation, pursuing its own lonely destiny.

But Herder's early thought was also in opposition to the pattern
based upon Natural Law, which delighted in deriving the essence of
things from their finished and fully rounded forms. Yet his excessive
emphasis on the origins was in fact a relic of this static thinking. As
so often happens, new ideas first make their appearance as a radical
reversal of old ones, and therefore suffer from a certain onesidedness. But even this onesidedness was fruitful in the realm of method,
because it compelled thinkers to study historical structures more
from within than from without and to approach them with intuitive
sympathy. Herder directed brilliant criticism against the traditional
method of accounting for the origins of poetry by deriving it from the
scanty, later accounts provided by the written tradition. In that
case, he observed (using the words of Hamann), this part of history
would remain a field of dead men's bones. Certainly these accounts
must be used as a guide in seeing

> how these things *may* have come about in view of their similar-
> ity with others, and in accordance with the pattern of those
> times; but then one must go on to ask whether the pattern set
> by specific circumstances does not bring one to a kind of
> *necessity*—the way in which things *must* have come about (vol.
> 32, p. 92).

Even Winckelmann had said that for the origins of art among all
peoples 'the first seed must necessarily have been present' (Arnold
Berger, *loc. cit.*, 101). Herder deepened this idea and set up a new
ideal for historical research, namely to study historical structures
such as poetry and see them as the products of an innermost necessity. Yet for the youthful Herder, this necessity could never be of a
mechanical, but of a living kind, which could only be understood by
a process of sympathetic identification. Thus he also rejected what
seemed to him the mechanical hypothesis of a migration of the arts
and sciences, and the ultimate derivation from a single source. He
demanded that the seed producing the arts and sciences should be
sought for among every people (vol. 32, p. 95). This brings us to the
very source of Herder's doctrine, and that of the later Romantic

Movement—the idea of the creative 'Volksgeist', the national spirit. Subsequent knowledge has diminished the value of this doctrine, and brought back an emphasis upon receptivity and the assimilation of foreign cultural material by specific peoples. Herder himself, whose doctrine of national spirit remained a somewhat fluctuating concept, but at any rate did not become dogmatically rigid, soon also turned his attention to the migrations and assimilations of cultural material. As early as 1769 (vol. 4, p. 477), we find him saying that in all periods false imitations and blendings with other nations have destroyed whole peoples; yet a nation remains incomplete if it does not practise any imitation of others. To anticipate for a moment, we may mention that he even committed the same mistake in dealing with the earliest records of the human race as he had himself criticised earlier on, in that he attributed the whole religious development of the Near East and the Greeks to one single original revelation. But for the early stages in a new line of historical thinking, it was absolutely necessary on heuristic grounds to narrow the field of vision, while at the same time looking deeper and studying the individualities of the various peoples and their own way of life with a really devoted interest.

We must now get a clearer picture of the psychological origins of this new feeling for individuality and development. As we have already indicated, Herder went back first of all with such vehemence to the childish years and the obscure beginnings because this was where his own soul found its most accurate counterpart. For during these years he was engaged in a passionate process of self-scrutiny, going back into the dark and mysterious regions of his own childhood, into the 'wondrous cavern' where 'tinder and flame lie close together' (vol. 32, p. 102), 'where there is suddenly so much in our soul that with regard to most ideas we seem to be asleep beside a spring of water' (vol. 5, p. 61), where in fathomless depths there are unknown forces sleeping like unborn kings (vol. 2, p. 258). It should be noted that a long process in the history of thought is here reaching fulfilment. Around the turn of the seventeenth and eighteenth centuries, first among Englishmen and then in Leibniz, attention was directed to the irrational powers of the soul, the drives, emotions and passions. At first it was for the most part simple observation, dissection and assessment of their relative uses. Shaftesbury was already showing a deeper understanding, but not yet experiencing it in any violently subjective manner. Vico had gone deeper, but had not tried to understand by a process of subjective and sympathetic identification. Then Hume's sober reason had uncovered the creative character of sentiment and taste. Hamann and Herder now became aware with all the force of their souls of what creative depths lay in them, and they

312

thus formed part of a European development, and might be compared to the daring storm-troops who storm a breach already prepared by the careful work of the engineers. And so through all the changes and chances of a life-time, Herder's leading purpose was always 'to grasp the world from the standpoint of the human soul' (H. Unger, *Novalis und Kleist*, p. 4). Soul was understood in the sense Hamann used the term, as inseparably bound up with the sensual nature of man. Herder wrote to Moses Mendelssohn in 1769 (*Lebensbild*, vol. 2, p. 108) that it is mere idle fancy to assume an incorporeal human soul or a non-sensual human nature. This all-round awareness of human nature as a psychosomatic whole is one of the most important elements in the new historical thought.

This triumphant new attitude to life had now to set about organising victory and drawing out the logical results of its triumph over a rationalism based upon Natural Law. The first step was a negative one—namely to show its deficiencies. Thus in 1768 Herder wrote on the subject of Christian Wolf, the leading figure in rationalism, who was indeed linked with the thought of Leibniz, but had neglected the most promising parts of Leibniz's psychology:

> The darkest regions of the soul, from which most human inventions arise, have had no light at all thrown upon them by
> Wolf. He talks of the lower powers of the soul as though it
> were a spirit divorced from a body; but has any superior power
> of the soul ever received the spirit of invention by mere
> inspiration? (vol. 32, p. 157).

Ten years later, he added these words: 'Such an abyss of obscure feelings, forces and impulses is something which fills our bright, serene philosophy with the deepest horror' (vol. 8, p. 179). But now it was also incumbent upon him to show positively the essence of the reason that had been dethroned from its sole sovereignty, and to define its relationship to the soul as a whole. Reason, Herder went on to explain, is no separate and isolated power working on its own, but a *direction of all the powers* proper to the species of man. At this point he was attracted, as usual, to the world of the child; and he concluded that even in the early stages, man, just because he is human, must be possessed of reason, and not merely a capacity for acquiring reason, as Rousseau had maintained. 'To think reasonably does not necessarily imply to think with full-grown reason' (*Ursprung der Sprache*, pub. 1772, vol. 5, p. 31). This at once led on to the thought of a development taking place in man himself. And the way in which the youthful Herder looked at the development of the individual personality corresponded exactly to the course of development envisaged by him in the historical field. First of all, there had been a tendency towards restricting the subject-matter and going down deeper. This had led to an exaggeration of the importance to be attached to the original seed. But subsequently Herder came to a more balanced view of the influence of environment upon the transformations taking place in the seed. He wrote to Mendelssohn in 1769 (*Lebensbild*, vol. 2, p. 110):

> Just as we are unable to provide ourselves with a new sense, so we are unable to supply ourselves with powers, acquirements or perfections of a materially new kind. . . . . There can only be modifications of what was already there in full potentiality, but without any new attributes; there can be alterations in the composition, but not in the essence of the soul.

There is an important shade of difference in the words written nine years later:

> The deeper anyone goes down into himself, into the structure and origins of his noblest thoughts, the more he will be inclined to say: 'What I am, I have become. I have grown like a tree: the seed was there, but the air, the soil and all the elements that were not produced by me must have contributed to forming the seed, the fruit and the tree' (1778, vol. 8, p. 198).

It is through development that something wonderful takes place, whereby the selfsame man does not remain the same. Herder with his impetuous nature felt this more deeply than others, as he stood at the climax of his first experiences in life, and could therefore say: 'A man at different periods of his life is not the same man. He thinks differently after he has come to feel differently' (1775, vol. 8, p. 307). This was the ultimate conclusion to which a combination of the principles of individuality and development could lead; and what Herder here expresses is the ultimate refinement of feeling for the subtle shades of the individual. One can only fully understand Herder's application of this refined feeling to the historical world by realising how Herder appeared to himself as constantly in a state of flux, constantly changing, and so highly individual from moment to moment. In his treatise on the origins of language (vol. 5, p. 124), he remarks that no two men speak in exactly the same way. No two painters or poets treat the same subject in exactly the same way, even though confronted with one and the same object (1778, vol. 8, p. 188). This had already been proclaimed by Hume in his *Natural History of Religion*, where he had said that no two people have exactly the same religious conceptions. Hume had spoken as a detached and clear-sighted empiricist; Herder's voice was that of a man feeling the mystery of life from within his own breast.

In this massive differentiation and individualisation of life, sweeping even the individual life into the general flux of things, was there any room left for an understanding of the other person? For the youthful Herder, all understanding of another could only proceed from the understanding of oneself. We can now appreciate the enormous importance for historical insight of this subjective concern with the depths of one's own soul, in which both pietism and the influence of Hamann played their part. 'The degree of depth in our feelings for ourselves conditions the degree of our sympathy with others; for it is only ourselves that we can as it were project into others' (1778, vol. 8, p. 200). 'Only soul can discover soul; only a genius can understand, stimulate or censure another genius' (1775, vol. 8, p. 527).

But a further advance in thought was needed to make possible this sympathetic understanding of another person and to avoid the chaotic fragmentation to which an exaggerated stress on individuality might easily lead. It would only be possible to understand the other man by breaking down the rigid division between subject and object, by realising that everything is interconnected and works together, not only in a causal and mechanical sense, as the Enlightenment had also perceived, but by virtue of an inner community of being and oneness of the whole. This idea could only be conceptually expressed in a very approximate, intuitive and emotive manner, but it could easily be grasped in terms of experience. This was the old Platonic and Neo-Platonic philosophy of life, held by mystics and pantheists, by Shaftesbury and by Leibniz; Herder was bold enough to proclaim: 'The first thought in the first human soul is intimately linked up with the last thought in the last human being' (vol. 5, p. 135). And in even more general and universal terms:

> Everywhere in nature there are no hard and fast divisions. Everything passes by imperceptible transitions and with mutual interpenetration from one state to another; and not a doubt but the creative life in all its shapes and forms and channels is but one spirit and one vital flame (1778, vol. 8, p. 178).

'Σύμπνοια πάντα' he notes with delight in his *Wahrheiten aus Leibniz*, written in 1770: 'Everything fits in together, and God discerns in the smallest of substances the entire course of things in the whole world' (cf. p. 21 above). This was the voice not only of ancient philosophy, but of a new and original experience, a flowing out or self-projection into the world of the soul stirred to its depths. By a process of self-scrutiny, Herder had found out how to pull down all the artificial divisions between the higher and lower powers of the soul still maintained by the Enlightenment. Henceforward he could only see history, nature and the whole universe in the light of his own soul.

From a higher standpoint, it then became necessary to discount some of the divisions between the individuality of specific peoples, which the youthful Herder had at first been inclined to erect. One particular people always remained in his eyes, a people who had grown in their own particular manner; but we have already seen that he recognised not only false and distorting acquisitions, but good and beneficial ones as well. He was inclined, though, to cling to some of the old mechanistic language, and call these imitations of foreign cultures. Quite early on Herder was thus confronted by a twofold aim. On the one hand, he wanted to 'reconstitute' synthetically the spirit of each age and each people, with its own specific qualities; on the other hand, he wanted to look beyond this to the 'chain of modifications' begun in the earliest times, and still continuing in our own (vol. 32, p. 27). This is what he called 'the continuous thread of human culture extended through all peoples and periods' (vol. 3, p. 397). And this is what he then set out to grasp and to interpret over the whole of its immense extension with a positively indefatigable energy. As we have seen, this was no new undertaking, nor was the idea of the chain original. Voltaire had already used it, and Herder, in what is most likely his earliest reference to it (vol. 32, p. 27; probably written in 1766), alludes to Voltaire and the credit that should go to him for recognising this 'spirit of events'. He mentioned others also (amongst them Goguet and Montesquieu) who had 'called attention to the continuous development of the conditions and fruits of the human race' (vol. 6, p. 327). The great service rendered by the Enlightenment had been to propose the task of understanding its dogma of the unity of human culture. But the means at their disposal, limited as they were by mechanical concepts and thought based upon Natural Law, were insufficient for accomplishing it. Now, however, Herder came on the scene with his new means of approach, which belonged to the current of thought parallel to the Enlightenment, namely the Neo-Platonic tradition. Its fundamental idea was to view the world and nature as a living cosmos of forces originating from God, and to feel it as such; and to appreciate the necessity for comprehending both its unity in God and its manifold variety in experience. One of the boldest ideas occurring to Herder as a young man during the sea voyage of 1769 was that even the natural science of his day was confronted with the new task of grasping the inner necessity involved in the outward order of things. What if a man should succeed in laying his hand upon the 'chain of being that runs through nature', and so become an interpreter of God! (vol. 4, p. 381). This was also a thought (as we shall see in examining his work on ideas during the eighties) which continued to obsess his mind. Meanwhile, however, it was a mighty achievement to grasp even the history of humanity in the spirit of Neo-Platonism as a union of inner vitality and necessity. The crucial moment had come in the history of thought, because there were new ferments lying ready to hand for the further developments in this Neo-Platonic pattern. For up till now, it had not been able to grasp concrete history to the full, because it still lay under the pressure of the prevailing notions based upon Natural Law. It had therefore been unable to apply the principles of individuality and development to history. Just as Möser had transcended these limitations in his remarkably different hypotheses relating to the history of his own people and country, which were both more concrete and more limited, so it was the peculiar gift of Herder to overcome them in world history by virtue of his capacity for universal sympathy and awareness.

And now, leaving on one side the tentative explorations of Herder's youthful period in the realm of universal history, we must move on to the climax of his early work, the outline written down at Bückeburg in 1774 of *Auch eine Philosophie der Geschichte zur Bildung der Menschheit*. But to reach this it is necessary to pass through an important intermediate stage in his thoughts on the subject of universal history, represented by the *Fragmente zu einer Archäologie des Morgenlandes* (vol. 6, pp. 1 ff., partly composed while still in Riga, from 1769 onwards), and later condensed into the *Älteste Urkunde des Menschengeschlechts* (vol. I, 1774; vol. 6, pp. 193 ff.).

Like every other thinker of the eighteenth century concerned with universal history, Herder had to face the question of the origins of monotheism. This question took precedence over all others, because it would provide a standard for assessing all other events in history. The Enlightenment had secularised historical thought, set aside the standards of Christian dogma, and taught that history (including the history of religion) should be interpreted entirely in terms of man's inner world of mental processes. Herder took the same line, but used the new psychological means and methods of research he had discovered, including what he had derived from Hamann's pietism. And he was enough of a theologian to be able to weigh afresh the possibilities of a supernatural revelation, which Lafitau had taken as his starting-point, for comparative religious enquiry. Thus it was a devious route that Herder pursued in this matter. At one time in his youth he intended to 'look at all religions in the first place as natural phenomena' (vol. 32, p. 146). He was even so much in the grip of the naturalistic explanation of all religion produced by Hume that he

317

was inclined to see the main impulses towards religion in the fear and awe engendered by the harsh and crude events of the world (vol. 32, p. 105). In between whiles, however, he would admit that the People of Israel had been vouchsafed a 'supernatural revelation' of religious knowledge; yet he was at pains to explain this word of God as imparted entirely through sensuous channels, and as suited to the capacities of primitive man, with his strong sensuous equipment (vol. 32, pp. 128 ff.). He moved quietly forward in his individualising historical thought, as can be seen in his fragmentary *Archäologie des Morgenlandes*. Here, using the fruits of German and English research, Herder attempted to work out the topographical and the national elements in the biblical account of creation, with due regard to their Eastern setting, but 'free from any physical or dogmatic systems' (vol. 6, p. 37), full of youthful enthusiasm for this youthful period of the human race. It must be admitted that in his excess of aesthetic feeling he tended to see in the noble oriental of the early biblical period mostly himself writ large.

In this general picture, however, he did not conceive of the original divine revelation to the East, as it appeared to him in connection with the institution of the days of the week and the sabbath, as anything particularly supernatural or in any way pre-eminent over other divine revelations in history. He viewed it as an interior human process, a response to divinely given powers.

> When God gave the human race the noble gift of insight into the nature of things and the scheme of creation, he never meant it to be for the purpose of a revelation: it was simply a bounteous addition to the powers he had given the human spirit (vol. 6, p. 88).

But when he came to Bückeburg, and there in 1773 remodelled his previous efforts on Eastern archaeology into a new work entitled *Älteste Urkunde des Menschengeschlechts*, he once more shifted his standpoint. This was the period when the theological side of Herder, who had still delivered sermons of an enlightened kind in Riga, was now directly caught up deep down in himself in a wave of pietistic devotion, which had up till now only influenced him indirectly. True, he was never a dogmatic believer, even in a reduced or pietistic sense. But his new-found religiosity now saw clearer traces of divine providence both in humanity and in history; he was even prepared to see it directly and very specially at work in the primitive revelation of the creation story. It became something raised above the general revelation of God in nature and the works of man. To be sure, this has been doubted, since Haym called attention to the fact (Horst Stephan, *Herder in Bückeburg*, pp. 123 ff.). It has been suggested that the revelation of God in nature and his 'educative voice' to the first man had in fact been rolled into one. It is indeed not possible to be quite certain about the meaning of Herder's individual sentences,[1] for they are wandering and confused in style, and sometimes contradictory, if taken in their literal sense. One must rather concentrate attention on the ardently presented basic concept of the whole work. which makes it clear that Herder saw in the revelation given in the earliest documents a special and unique act of God in man and on behalf of man. For it was in this, and not in any general God-given capacity for hearing the voice of God, that he saw the root of all such Eastern religions as were known to him, and even of the Greek religious outlook. In his youthful period at Riga, Herder had pondered rather more realistically over the origin of the non-Israelite religions, and had attempted, like Hume, to explain it along the lines of a universal comparative psychology of primitive man. But now it seemed to him that a specific act of God, though discernible in its purest state among the people of Israel, was also recognisably present elsewhere, in less pure or very impure forms, but still nevertheless recognisable; and that this was the seed which had led to the mighty branching development of the whole world of diverse peoples.

But at this point we are surely reminded of the Enlightenment's conception of a pure natural religion of humanity, distorted by later developments. If this was only an attempt to secularise the idea of a primitive revelation, Herder may perhaps have been prompted to put it once more into theological terms in order to move closer to Lafitau's standpoint.

Thus he saw in the further course of history and round about the original place of revelation (in Persia, Chaldea, Egypt, Arabia and so on) sometimes decadent tribes, and sometimes new and flourishing offshoots, but all from the self-same root (vol. 6, p. 472). It was singular enough that the thought which had started in the most fanciful fashion along biological and vegetative lines should at the same time appear as an extension of theology. Once again, however, it is instructive in the involved dialectic of the history of thought to note that it was precisely this theological approach which compelled Herder in one particular respect to burst through the too narrow limits that he had originally set for his ideas of development. Hitherto,

[1] In 6, 265 he protests against the cry that 'God should and must reveal himself through nature only', and says 'the voice of some master teacher must have contributed to the creation of this picture' (i.e. of revelation through nature). But in 6, 286 he says: 'No word, no command, no counsel—only a silent example, a deed' (i.e. by God). It may accordingly be conceded that this 'master's voice' may only have been used in a figurative sense. But this second sentence is quite consonant with the idea of a once-for-all revelation in action, rather than in word.

he had tended to bury and lose himself in the separate growths of individual peoples; now, he was confronted with the more promising task (more fruitful in method, though often wrongheaded in content) of following up the migrations of the highest forms of culture from one people to another. He would have to observe the national assimilations and transformations and show the universal connections, along with the peculiar characteristics of each nation. The method as Herder worked it out in detail was indeed distinctly lacking in discipline. No doubt he despised the mechanical links of the hitherto prevailing pragmatism, with its utilitarian motivation and intelligible physical causes. He replaced it by a fabric of metaphysical and vitalistic forces. But there was a remnant of pragmatism and Natural Law still at work in him, a naive inclination to pass over all the difficulties concerned with tradition by the use of his own methods of enquiry. He simplified the issues in a glib and over-hasty fashion and produced solutions to historical problems, apparently without any suspicion of the complicated character of historical structures. One has only to read his wild interpretations of Egyptian antiquity, in which he attributed everything he encountered to the 'archetype' of the most ancient deposit. His manner of procedure might well be called a topsy-turvy revitalised pragmatism. The new feeling for the irrational, individual and vegetative elements in human life was still contained within the old shell. And it could only reach its fullest possible depth, as we saw in the case of Möser, when it came to respect tradition and use the methods that were to be taught by critical scholarship.

This theological approach to the most ancient traditions again narrowed down Herder's developmental thinking in another respect. For what he depicted was nearly always the history of degeneration or disorderly growth in the midst of an endlessly rich development of the pure original revelation. The old scheme of paradise and the fall, or the golden age and the subsequent decline, once more made its appearance. We might indeed sum the matter up by saying that his theological belief in the original divine revelation dating from the Bückeburg period would scarcely have come to life, if the picture of the original primitive man in his child-like purity (man in the first flush of dawn) had not long since disclosed what seemed to be a kind of primitive revelation to the human race. But from both of these revelations, it must have appeared to Herder that the subsequent path of history was a descent.

Yet Herder's optimistic inner nature could not rest content with the pessimistic gloom of a theory that assumed a universal decline. As has already been noted, his ardent love for the early years of humanity and of childhood seemed to put them beyond price just because they were unrepeatable and inimitable. This rejection of a romantic longing for the rejuvenation of the past is already a sign that Herder had within him lively forces working against any dogmatic cultivation of the past. It testifies to the strength of his new feeling for the individual, which strove to be active not only in the dawn and early years of the human race, but throughout the whole history of humanity. This sense of individuality was chiefly rooted in aesthetic feeling. Nature had richly endowed Herder with a capacity to feel and taste and savour everything in the field of the poetic. Now when he began to be aware of a specific religious need at Bückeburg, his deepened sense of the holy became fused with his sense of the beautiful. Once again, the *Älteste Urkunde* shows how his sense of the religious and aesthetic values of primitive times had become one with his special feeling for nature. Herder perhaps represents the climax of that peculiar kind of feeling for nature characteristic of his own day, which no longer rings true to us in our generation. At that period, the human heart overflowed with fervour and enthusiasm over the phenomena of nature that are still just as splendid and beautiful; but (to pick out only one of the characteristic nuances of this feeling) it rejoiced in the harmony between a good and wise God and the natural beauty that revealed Him, and in man's awareness of his higher calling, his universal outlook and his sense of religious need. Thus Herder could quite naturally combine the idea of the original revelation with the impression made upon primitive man by the dawning of a new day, because he was in fact projecting his own feelings into the earliest period of humanity (vol. 6, pp. 262 f.). His heart overflowed within him when he reflected that it was still possible to receive the revelation of a new dawn with the same unspoilt simplicity as early man enjoyed (vol. 6, p. 260).

This feeling for nature, half sensuous and half teleological, which brought nature, God and man together into a relationship partaking both of holiness and of beauty, was in the background of Herder's relationship to the historical world when he began to compose his sketch of the philosophy of history in 1773. Later on, when he was working out his great project of historical ideas in the eighties, he treated this as an immature youthful effort (to Heyne 9 January 1786, *Letters*, vol. 2, p. 199). In truth, something he said elsewhere is more relevant:

> The first unprejudiced work of an author is . . . usually his best; the blossom is just opening, his soul still has the first flush of dawn. Much is still full and measureless feeling, which later on will become brooding or mature thought that has lost its youthful freshness (vol. 8, p. 209).

II The Philosophy of History, 1774

By way of resuming what we have so far surveyed, we may say that there were three main ideas or tendencies which Herder brought to his work.

First, the organic idea of development, now no longer confined to a single people, but extending over a whole group of nations, and so leading on towards an idea of universal human development.

Then there is the idea of the most ancient development as a development for the worse—a fall from original purity. In the first place, it was apparently proved by the later outcome of the original revelation; then it was closely linked up with the criticism initiated by Rousseau and deepened by Hamann and Herder relating to their own age, and the revolt of the irrational full-blooded human powers against the cold rationality of the Enlightenment and the mechanising trends of civilisation.

The third line of thought was the product of this revival of the deeper and more creative powers of the soul. It was to some extent a counterpart and correction to the second idea, in that it set the bleak perspective of the fall in a somewhat more cheerful light. In its religious aspect, it proclaimed that God not only revealed Himself in primitive times, but reveals Himself today and always, and that there is no such thing as an age without God. In its aesthetic aspect, it stood for an undiminished openness to all the individual variety, beauty and vitality of human affairs, though this feeling was not everywhere of the same strength. The increasing trust in God during these years then enabled Herder to carry over this aesthetic feeling to historical phenomena which before then and subsequently were out of his reach. It thus became possible to weave connecting threads of a teleological kind between all these elements and so develop an all-round sense of universal history.

A comparison between these three leading ideas and the methods hitherto in use for universal history shows that the position was broadly as follows. Herder's thought linked up with the ancient traditional doctrine of a golden age followed by a decline; it also linked up with the Christian doctrine (recently expounded with such power by Bossuet) of a divine plan of salvation for man in history. Both these doctrines assumed that the whole of human destiny was embraced in one great circular movement, ending with the eschatological hope or belief in the return of an ideal and final state, whether in this world or in the world to come. And thirdly, there had been since the time of Polybius another purely empirical doctrine of circular history, which envisaged the constant recurrence of typical human

322

cycles. Herder also recognised this doctrine as valid of the lives of individual nations and perhaps even for every human enterprise (vol. 5, p. 588, preparatory work for the *Sketch* of 1774). But it seemed to him so obvious that he appears rather to have assumed it than explicitly stated it in his exposition. He was bound, however, to oppose the fourth and newest doctrine of the Enlightenment, championed by Voltaire. This doctrine represented history, in the light of its own standard of reason, as a constant struggle between reason and unreason, and evaluated it in terms of the 'perfection' attained by its own age. Herder was even more strongly bound to oppose the more optimistic beliefs of other enlightened thinkers in the ascent and steady progress of the human race.

In all these doctrines there still survived the old conception of Natural Law, and the equality of human nature at all periods. Thus the powers and capacities resident in this nature remained identical: it was only the relative strength or preponderance of one or the other of the component elements in different men and different periods that was liable to vary; and this variability might then lead to a rise or a fall or cyclic recurrence, with a repetition of previous patterns, which made imitation possible.

Herder certainly adopted the general framework of the first and second of these doctrines; but he filled them with an entirely new content. He added the two interconnected ideas of the inimitable individuality of all historical creations, and their constant recurrence in the process of human development—a process which embraced them, sustained them, and fused them into a higher unity.

Let us now take a closer look at Herder's *Sketch*, and see how he effected a smooth combination of organic development from below and divine guidance from above, leading on from one stage to another; and let us note the way in which the use he makes of these new ideas produces further fruitful thoughts which serve to knit the development together and provide standards of judgement for points of detail.

'What a well-chosen garden it was which God set aside for the training of these first and tenderest of human plants!' (vol. 5, p. 480). This was the characteristic picture he drew of the patriarchal age, 'the golden age of the human race', when growth was carefully tended by the divine hand. Yet it was no mere poetical fantasy; for it at once led Herder on to dispute the very unidyllic picture of oriental despotism as actually portrayed by the French Enlightenment, by Voltaire and Rousseau and Boulanger and others, in their customary glaring colours. Montesquieu had taught that fear was the basis of all despotic government. But at this point one sees the rigid generalised ideas which the Enlightenment was inclined to clamp upon history beginning to thaw under the gentle warmth of a sensitive soul who loved and therefore understood all that was human. No doubt, as Herder admitted, the patriarchal age was pre-eminently one where reverence, example and authority were supreme. But is there not a stage in every human life when everything has to be learnt under authority? It might well be that oriental despotism had often produced the most appalling results; but it was surely possible that the earliest sons of the East had been the happiest and most teachable of pupils under the gentle hand of a paternal rule.

This was clearly an uncritical and idealised picture, though it led to methodological results of a useful kind. We can make the same comment upon it as Herder made in ridiculing the Enlightenment's ideas about priestcraft and stupidity among ancient peoples: 'Dost thou not see in each of thy so-called mistakes a vehicle—perhaps the only possible vehicle—for good?' This was a justifiable warning against judging the religious feelings of the Ancient East by those of one's own time. They must be understood in the light of their own historical circumstances, which would soon banish the spectres of priestcraft and stupidity. Furthermore, this constituted a principle of far-reaching significance and a means of knitting all his understanding of historical development into a whole. Without it, Herder would not have been able to forge his chain of universal history. This principle had to do with a mysterious phenomenon going far back into the past—the strange fact that whatever seems to us by any standards to be good or bad, an excellence or a defect, undergoes a transposition of values in the course of growth. The good then appears to be the necessary condition for the bad, and the bad the necessary condition for the good. This insight must have been shared by the profounder thinkers in all periods; yet it could be very differently interpreted. The clear-sighted realist Machiavelli gave it as his opinion that in any institution, however necessary and useful it may originally have been, there always lurks a hidden evil (*Disc.*, III, 11). Conversely, it is well-known that he himself expected good results from means admitted to be in themselves thoroughly evil. In Neo-Platonism, the lower was thought to proceed from the higher or even the highest sources, and was constantly striving to return thither. Hence the idea that reason could turn even that which was evil to good purpose was an indispensable middle term between the lower and the higher worlds. And Plotinus did in fact express this very thought (F. Koch, *Goethe und Plotin*, p. 200; *Enn.* III, pp. 2, 5). Likewise for the faithful Christian, it had always been an absolutely necessary link between his conception of God and his knowledge of the world that God allows evil to happen and uses it for His own good purposes. As Hamann expressed it (Unger, *Hamann*, p. 208),

God uses the base and worthless as instruments of His hidden will. And Leibniz in his *Theodicy* expressly taught that it has been ordained from on high that sin and misfortune should not be completely excluded from the nature of things, but that they are of practically no significance in comparison with the good, and can even be used to serve a higher good. Shaftesbury was of the same opinion. Vico, we may recall, worked on the fundamental principle that the limited emotions and passions of men were used by God to produce a higher level of culture. The thinkers of the Enlightenment, in their more prosaic and utilitarian way, also consoled themselves at times by observing that good results sometimes flowed from evil things. The idea was then continued in its sharpest tension through the doctrine of Hegel, though still with an underlying note of comfort and consolation—the doctrine of the 'cunning of reason', which could use even the unreasonable in its service. And at the end of the nineteenth century, the idea was generalised, without any particular association with value-judgements, in Wilhelm Wundt's doctrine of heterogeneous purpose, according to which the results of an action carried out with a particular purpose always contain side-effects, which lead to new results that were not originally intended.

Thus there was a gradual toning down of the poignant experience that lent a tragic, if not demonic, character to all history (the conviction that good and evil could be bound up together in a causal nexus), into a more dispassionate and scientific assessment of cause and effect. But the question of their metaphysical significance was mostly answered decisively in terms of feeling by the doctrines of Christianity. Such a pathos, which saw a downright incomprehensible deity bringing good as it were out of a destructive blind tempest, could not arise in Herder even in his Bückeburg period. His conception of God was too gentle and too tinged with deism and sentimentality to make a radical attack on the problem of how sin could be allowed by God and even be used by Him as an instrument. But he was vigorous enough and sufficiently above the purely rational approach to grasp the conception that God as the educator of man could sometimes lead him to the goal by dark and devious ways. God as educator, unsearchable in His will, though here and there we could get a glimpse of it—this was the middle position adopted by Herder, half-way between deism and positive Christianity. He used it to project his own pedagogic ethos, and that of the age, into his conception of the deity; and he thought that it provided him with the key to an approximate understanding of the framework of universal history. He saw the history of the world as a 'theatre in which you can see a guiding purpose on earth being enacted. Although we cannot see the ultimate purpose, it is a stage for the divine action, even though we only glimpse it through the chinks and in fragmentary snatches of a scene' (vol. 5, p. 513).

Thus the concept of heterogeneous purposes, expressed in modern terms, but still controlled by providence, became the linking idea in the development of world history. 'Peak and valley lie side by side. Round about the noble Spartans dwell the inhumanly treated helots . . . defects and virtues ever dwell together' (vol. 5, p. 508). Always the aim is to awaken man's powers, even through stages of barbarism: 'if it attains some purpose, it is better than to be dead alive and moulder in decay' (vol. 5, p. 516). Luther's work was bound to take place in an atmosphere of stormy passion, for a quiet progress of the human spirit towards the improvement of the world is 'hardly anything but a phantom of our minds, and never God's way in nature' (vol. 5, p. 532). Thus the distinctive excellencies of a people such as the Egyptians or the Greeks could not be cultivated without certain specific deficiencies. Herder rather characteristically shrank from admitting the stern logical conclusion that this was a direct divine ordinance. 'Providence, you see, has not positively required this; it has only arranged to attain its ultimate purpose through this alternation, through the arousal of new forces and powers and the dying out of others' (vol. 5, p. 507). But he could avoid that stern conclusion because his position was different from that of the positive Christian. Apart from his fluctuating treatment of the original revelation (vol. 5, p. 566) and the growth of Christianity (vol. 5, p. 517 f.), Herder was unwilling to recognise any supernatural interference of God in history. In his theological writings of the Bückeburg period he could perhaps adopt a tone of more positive belief about the genesis and significance of Christianity (cf. e.g. vol. 7, p. 388). But now, in his philosophy of history, he sought as far as possible to exclude the theological approach. 'If we take the whole analogy of nature, where do we see God acting in any other way but through nature?' (vol. 5, p. 521).

Although Herder was no doubt at one with the thinkers of the Enlightenment in this respect, he felt that his deeper recognition of the connection between defects and virtues was in point of principle opposed to their outlook. Herder saw them 'with the childish scales of the century in their hands', weighing virtues and vices against each other, and dealing out praise and blame in their mighty pronouncements upon the nations. But he was the first to recognise (even before Hegel) that what struck the Enlightenment as sad and repulsive in history could more properly be regarded as tragic. Here again, one can see how profoundly he had been influenced by the spirit of Shakespeare.

But it was the deeper conception of development in his *Sketch* of

1774 that sharpened his sense of the inseparable intermixture of good and evil qualities, actions and results in every nation. This deeper note was provided by getting rid of the divisions separating the various peoples, as the very task of writing a universal history compelled him to establish much closer interior bonds between the nations figuring in the history of the world. 'If only I can succeed [he says] in showing how the most disparate scenes are interrelated, how they grow out of one another and blend with one another; how in detail everything seems fleeting, and only becomes a means towards an end when viewed in sequence' (vol. 5, p. 513). 'The Egyptians could not have come into being without the oriental background; the Greeks built upon their foundations, and the Romans raised themselves upon the shoulders of the entire world.' So one people was seen as a necessary stage in growth towards another, and not merely, as the Enlightenment had thought, the teacher of another; and Herder, swept along by the dim surmise of a divine plan of education for the world, now felt these deeper links with peculiar power. But he was unable to take more than a bird's eye view of them, and could thus only get an incomplete understanding of the concrete historical connecting links, and the spiritual or political causes at work in the relations between one nation and another. A very general link was provided by his 'stage of life' theory. This was an ancient theory, used by Florus and Augustine, and latterly by Iselin, comparing the different stages in the life of a nation to the different stages in a single human life.[1] But there were also some echoes of his own experience and his thoughts in youth when he traced the different stages of humanity as far as the Romans according to the analogy of human life. The Near East then represented the childhood, the Greeks the youth, and the Romans the period of maturity. But where did old age come in? The only justifiable element in this analogy was the underlying thought that the whole Ancient World from the Near East to the Roman Empire formed a historical unity within the total compass of human history.

There was another fruitful idea which Herder used to illustrate this theory of stages. The Egyptian hated the Oriental, and the Greek the Egyptian; yet the one would not have been what he was without the other. 'Their very hatred was a mark of development and advance, a step up the ladder!' (vol. 5, p. 489). In so saying, Herder was touching on Hegel's basic principle of historical dialectic, the fact that historical development needs to break up into apparently hostile

---

[1] In the meanwhile, Ferguson had rightly observed in his *Essay on the History of Civil Society* that it was not permissible simply to compare the life-span of States with that of a single human being, because society was renewed with the advent of each fresh generation.

opposites in order to make possible a further genuine and continuous advance.

Historical dialectic demands a supra-personal view of things, especially where they are in hostile contact. The historical writers of the Enlightenment, with their personalistic pragmatism, only had eyes as a rule for the human actors whose behaviour seemed purposeful or purposeless, successful and unsuccessful. It is instructive to compare Herder's short passage on the Emperor Julian with what is said about him by Voltaire in his essay on this subject (vol. 5, p. 518). According to Voltaire, Julian saw the defects of Christianity, but for reasons of State he had to consider the superstitions of the majority; and if he had lived longer, he might have revived the strength of the Empire. Herder, on the other hand, sees the spectacle of a great supra-individual battle between the various religions, and the needs of a decadent age for religion in some shape or form. However, he too has a slight lapse into pragmatism, as was still liable to occur at times, when he overstresses the subtle statecraft of Julian. But this was of no avail; the hour had struck for the victory of a universal religion over the narrow national religions that had so far held the field. Nowadays, to be sure, one can grant rather more universal tendencies to the competing non-Christian religions than Herder was willing to allow. But the superiority of his view over Voltaire's is abundantly evident.

For Herder, Christianity was the most powerful ferment in universal history that providence ever gave to the human race. Humanity, however, provided the substratum for the development he wished to demonstrate. The Enlightenment had begun by taking humanity as such in the widest sense as the object of historical enquiry. But in its pride of reason, it had handled the theme most capriciously as the centre and climax of world history in general, in spite of all the revolutionary modern knowledge about the universe. Herder's cosmic thought, however, which we have already examined in its early stages, looked beyond humanity and saw the whole universe being shaped by the forces of divine guidance, and treated man's belief that he was the centre of the universe as an illusion (albeit a delightful one) because it was a well-spring of life (vol. 5, p. 559). The efforts of the Enlightenment to 'collect material about the human race from the ends of the earth' were not altogether rejected by Herder, in spite of some ironical comment (vol. 5, p. 567). He even saw in their work a preliminary step towards a future 'history of humanity in the highest sense', which he no doubt envisaged as embracing the whole globe. But his *Sketch* of 1774 nevertheless excluded the peoples of the Near and Middle East, and more decidedly still, the primitive races, from its purview, although the critical curiosity of the Enlightenment, and even Herder's own warm interest, had already given them some attention. This cannot altogether be explained by the traditions of universal history, or the lingering effects of the old doctrine of the four world empires. Rather was Herder guided by the true underlying awareness of the continuity and singularity of the cultural development originating in the Ancient Near East and extending to the West of the present day. This was the same basic awareness that was subsequently destined to shape Ranke's conception of world history. In making this selection from the universal development of the human race, Herder was therefore simply concentrating attention upon the history of *our* world, our own specific destiny.

Herder wrote this small book with the trepidation of one who was intent upon divining from the past millennia the origins and the meaning of his own times and his own destiny. The nearer the narrative came to the affairs of the West, the more frequently do we hear the word 'destiny' ring out like a mighty hammer-blow. Significantly, he already gives the heading 'The harvest of destiny for the Ancient World' to the Romans and their achievements in breaking down the divisions separating one nation from another (vol. 5, p. 500). The concept of destiny was one of the weapons he forged in order to break in pieces the presumptuous pride in reason developed by the Enlightenment. He deals ironically with their loud-voiced praise for the age of the Renaissance as the peak of human culture. In the face of this exaggerated extolling of human reason, Herder maintained that 'it was much less a matter of reason, and rather—if I may so put it—a blind fate that shaped and guided the course of things and brought about this general world-wide change' (vol. 5, p. 530). 'It is all one great work of destiny, irrespective of the schemes and hopes and actions of men. Do you not see, you little ant, that you are only crawling on the great wheel of fate?' (vol. 5, p. 531). An educational catchword of the time was: 'Education for humanity'. This was also one of the basic motives urging Herder on to the task, and forcibly expressed in the title of his book. But he was so swept away with his own concept of fate that he now even subordinated to it his own pedagogical enthusiasm. 'Unless all I have written from beginning to end is in vain, it is clear that the creation and progress of a people is never anything but a work of fate, the result of thousands of interlinking causes, just like all the elements in which they live' (vol. 5, p. 539). The closer he approached the presentation of his own time, the more passionately humble, resigned and overwhelmed he grew as he beheld that fate and his own place in it. 'In our place we are both the purpose and the tool of fate' (vol. 5, p. 557). And finally, passing over some other thoughts, these concluding words: 'I am nothing, but the whole is everything. As blind instruments, we

329

belong to it'; 'we all have the illusion of freedom in action, yet we know not what or why'. Thus I myself, he reflected, am no more than a mere letter in God's great book (vol. 5, pp. 585 ff.).

In these references it would seem that we have brought together all the elements of Herder's concept of destiny. On one occasion, he gathered all three together into one great triple chord, as he reflected upon the origins of the Reformation: 'There on a grand scale, here on a small; chance, destiny and divinity!' (vol. 5, p. 531).

One must beware of subjecting Herder's misty and fluctuating thought to any too precise a conceptual analysis. In Herder's 'destiny' it is perhaps possible to see an expression in a more all-embracing, unified, deeper and yet more mysterious form, of what he had elsewhere viewed as a natural and organic development controlled by providence. Fate is indeed 'blind', but only as seen from man's side, not from God's, for it is from Him that it proceeds. The notion combines strict deterministic causality with a sense of teleology. And to this must be added, over and above his favourite biological causality observable in growth, the inscrutable causality embodied in a thousand and one chances which contribute to the making of any great change. Yet it is no mere chance that Herder speaks more of 'the threads of development' in the more remote periods, but prefers the notion of destiny for more modern times. For the inscrutable causality due to chance only impressed itself upon him through the clearer and fuller knowledge of his own days. He wished to look at things on a large and not on a small scale, and so boldly lumped chance together with all the other elements in his developmental thought so as to include everything from chance to divinity, and from the common stuff of earth to the transcendental. We are thus all the more able to understand his feelings of insignificance, dependence and subjection in the face of destiny, and yet the yearning for consolation which went with them.

Starting out from this feeling, Herder had to answer the question whether this development was purposive, and if so, in what direction; whether there was such a thing as progress towards higher levels, which could then perhaps only be thought of as 'an advance towards more virtues and blessedness for particular men' (vol. 5, p. 511). This had been Iselin's view in his attempted history of humanity in 1764. Herder, schooled by Rousseau and Hamann in the criticism of his own age, had no difficulty in refuting this illusion in a few trenchant sentences. He had no doubt that such an argument involved exalting and inventing the facts, distorting the proportions or suppressing the inconvenient. It meant taking Enlightenment for blessedness and more refined ideas for virtue. A deeper look into history and the human heart could not warrant belief in a progressive improvement of this world. The Enlightenment's notion of reason was not firmly anchored in the absolute. It was therefore by its inmost nature inclined at times to swing over into a hopeless scepticism. And it would then see in the richer picture of human life unfolded by the increased knowledge of the time a confused and patternless interplay of light and shadow, a mere Penelope's web. And this was what the basic Voltairean interpretation of history amounted to if taken in a pessimistic sense. Even Herder would hardly have escaped this scepticism unless he had taken up two positive positions against it. First, there was his feeling for the potentiality of growth in all life. 'Seest thou that growing tree, that man who struggles upwards? He must pass through different ages and stages; all is clearly onward movement, one effort after another in continuous growth!' (vol. 5, p. 512). Thus in Herder's view history could only be interpreted, not as the Enlightened did by the fate of individuals, but by looking at the whole; not by personal, but by trans-personal judgements. The other position taken up by Herder was that his conception of growth and continuity was firmly rooted in the sphere of the absolute and transcendent, which was more or less non-existent with the Enlightenment. Without a belief in divine providence in history, Herder's idea of growth would also have succumbed to a helpless relativism. Later on, as we shall see, Goethe managed to find a freer but equally firm anchorage in the absolute. But for Herder, the narrower conception of a fatherly providence was indispensable.

Thus Herder's answer to the question of progress in history was an affirmation of 'advance and development in a higher direction' (vol. 5, p. 512). But where was he to place the developments of his own time in this growth, this branching tree of world history? We know how critical he was of his age, with its superficial and arrogant intellectualism and its weakened vitality. In this study, these criticisms became passionate and embittered, and this may perhaps be connected with the new religious position reached as a result of his experiences at Bückeburg. His outpourings against the Enlightenment altogether disrupted the conception of the *Sketch* as a whole. Yet now and again he made a great effort to understand. He pointed out that we do not necessarily have all the vices and virtues of the past simply because we do not possess its poise, its strength and resilience, its spaciousness and elemental power (vol. 5, p. 555). In other words, the weaknesses of his own time were to be ascribed to inevitable biological causes. Taking up his picture of the tree, he represented the present generation as the thinner and lighter twigs at the top, which tremble and whisper in every breeze. His consoling afterthought was that the sun's rays (meaning the Enlightenment) played so beautifully through our leaves that we were able to see, and let our gentle rustling be heard, far and wide; but this sounded frankly ironical. His portrayal of what he was willing to consider great, beautiful and unique in his own gracious and civilised period became in the end a mordant satire.

What was it, then, that could finally lift him above a mood of decadence—or, more accurately, an unsatisfying final stage of growth beyond which no advance was possible? Deep down, it was his own new and powerful feeling of vitality streaming through him in this 'Sturm und Drang' period, his own consciousness of unexhausted, and largely untapped, productive powers. He could therefore prophesy for the doctor of his day, as well as for other professions, rich possibilities in their work by virtue of that 'vital sap that flows from the heart' (vol. 5, p. 571). But in order to justify his reviving optimism in theoretical terms, Herder needed that peculiar combination of biological and teleological-transcendental standpoints which raised the whole historical process above the level of a mere object of knowledge on to the plane of religious faith. This was the belief that 'with the emergence of the human race a larger over-all divine plan became possible than any single creature could conceivably comprehend' (vol. 5, p. 558). It was only a short step from this to a full Christian philosophy of history. As Herder confided to Lavater in June 1774 (*Aus Herders Nachlass*, vol. 2, p. 110, cf. *Herders Briefe an Hamann*, p. 80, May 1774), there was a second part of his history of philosophy to follow, which would be a key to unlock the first; and this key would be 'Religion, Christ, the end of the world with a blessed and glorious consummation'. But however significant this thought may be of the exalted religious mood of that period, it is equally significant that Herder did not carry it out. 'I don't know if I shall ever write it', he added in his letter to Lavater. In the midst of all this longing for the supernatural, there was a steady trend of thought to the natural course of events in history which would have made it difficult for him to profess as a historian what he would have been ready to confess as a theologian.

'My brothers, let us work with happy and courageous hearts even in the midst of clouds, for we are working for a great future' (vol. 5, p. 580). These words faintly suggest the eschatological appeal of the Christian plan of salvation; but they also suggest that Herder's new historical thoughts were not mere thought, but also resolve. His new historism was from the start closely bound up with the urge for creative cultural activity.

Up till now, our consideration of the *Sketch* of 1774 has revolved round the problems of Herder's ideas of development. Because of the swift-flowing and even tempestuous course of his work, directed as it was to the future, it was natural that this vital dynamic element, rather than the associated idea of individuality, should predominate. But Herder would have been completely untrue to himself if he had not meanwhile also been constantly aware of the latter idea, and often expressed it in characteristic fashion. So the first point to be considered is the connection between the single individual and the whole stream of development. The Enlightenment, with its personalistic and pragmatic outlook, had not been able to face this question in any depth. It had placed side by side, in a completely unorganic juxtaposition, the actions of the individual and the results produced by the *esprit général*, which it had already discovered. Herder's picture of the universe, drawing its sustenance from ancient philosophy, and dissolving all things into one great whole, also blended the action of the individual with the whole stream of development to such a degree that, as we have seen, he could exclaim: 'I am nothing: the whole is everything'. But it would be fundamentally wrong to read this as a kind of collectivism in which the individual counted for nothing, and the consummation of the whole was everything. For this movement of the whole was only brought about through the combined actions of innumerable separate forces. In Herder's universal picture, the 'whole' was always a sum-total whose living content was an innumerable series of parts, even down to the smallest, including the incalculable sum of all the separate forces, and above all the divine guidance which controlled them in hidden fashion and wove them into a unity. Thus in Herder the dependence of the individual on the historical process as a whole was expressed in a sense of religious dependence upon God; and this gave it a degree of individual consolation which a purely empirical feeling of dependence would not have given him. And so he completes his recognition of the relationship between the individual and the whole in the following words: 'Whatever I may be! A call reaches from heaven to earth that I in my place, like everything, have some significance. With powers to spare for the whole, and happy only as I respond to these powers' (vol. 5, p. 561).

But even this picture needs further completion to fill out Herder's account of the relationship between the individual and the life of the whole. It will be as well to recall what was said above about the psychological origins of the new feeling for individuality and development. Herder's new and deeper sense of the ego, blending the rational and irrational powers into a unity, was also required to guarantee the individual his value and his achievements in the midst of the dominant total process. Psychologically considered, this 'call from heaven to earth' presupposed, and was perhaps preceded by, a call from the depths of Herder's own soul, protesting against being a mere cog in a mechanical process. This was precisely what he had against the Enlightenment, that its philosophy encouraged men 'to feel themselves increasingly day by day to be machines'. In the face of this, his watchword was : 'Heart! Warmth! Blood! Humanity! Life!' (vol. 5, p. 538). These words are an accurate expression, as it were in a number of big leaps, of the ascent from the deepest spiritual life of the individual to the history of the human race.

But it was no more than a series of big leaps. For neither in this *Sketch*, nor previously nor subsequently, did Herder contrive to make full use of the idea of individuality in history. True, he could criticise the Enlightenment in this same connection. Its philosophy, he maintained, was so concerned with the domain of law, that it confined its attention to 'the splendour and excellence of the general' and passed over 'the individual, in which alone the *species facti* consists' (vol. 5, p. 536). And in even more universal terms (vol. 5, p. 505): 'In a certain respect, every human perfection, when considered in national, secular and accurate terms, is individual'. In these words Herder gives some indication of the narrower and wider circles which the concept of individuality will have to cover in history in order to take account of the supra-individual forces surrounding the individual, such as the nation, and more especially the influences of the century. Moreover, he was sharply aware of the problem for the theory of knowledge presented by the individual *a priori*, the problem confronting the single observer when he tries to find words for that which can scarcely be apprehended, when he attempts to grasp the character of a nation in its full depth, or even more when he explores the great ocean of whole tracts of time (vol. 5, p. 502). Most of these attempts he characterised as 'flat and imperfect word-silhouettes'.

Individuum est ineffabile. This was Herder's deepest conclusion, arising from the depths of his own dark currents of thought and feeling, when he attempted to grasp the individuality of history by means of his own method of sympathetic identification. He felt far more on the subject than he was able to express effectively in words. His spiritual sensibility was too delicate, too restless and too hasty to look this individuality steadily in the face, as the less talented Möser had contrived to do. Herder's glance passed cursorily over 'the men who make history', over the great representatives and pioneers of general development. Only at the close does he seem to realise rather late in the day that these men, too, are a phenomenon of history requiring his verdict upon them. In order to balance his dislike of Frederick the Great, he adds:

No great personality through whom destiny brings about
changes can indeed be judged in all his actions and thoughts by

the common standards applied to ordinary people. There are exceptions belonging to a higher species, and nearly everything of note in this world comes about through these exceptions (vol. 5, pp. 583 ff.).

These words show that Herder was ingeniously improvising a new principle for judging the creative figures in history, in contradistinction to the practice of the Enlightenment. But he never seemed to feel the attraction of dwelling at length on any single personality. Not even when discussing the rise of Christianity, although he cautiously remarks that it will 'remain a wonder for all time'.

Even Luther is only one among many Luthers who had risen before his time and perished (vol. 5, p. 532). This *Sketch*, with its fleeting succession of great figures and tendencies, accordingly produces a more collectivist impression than Herder really intended at heart. But there was undoubtedly this defect in his otherwise incomparable feeling for the individual which was constantly bursting into new life. He could reproduce the individual features of a work of art or a special achievement, including that of nations (especially primitive peoples), and those of great systems and periods with lightning speed and sympathetic insight, though in fleeting fashion rather than lingering detail; but when it came to the ramifications and depths of a self-contained personality, Herder was hardly ever able to give it at all adequate expression. He could indeed clearly see the task methodically laid out before him, the need to let it grow genetically from its inner germ and shaped by its environment, as early as the Riga period, when he was writing about Thomas Abbt and spoke in the introduction of 'portraying another man's soul' (vol. 2, p. 257). But in his later years, when he conceived a stronger desire to grasp the single figure in history, he seldom had the requisite power. It was part and parcel of Herder's own tragic life. The man who was endowed with such wonderful gifts and such a delicate sense of form was never able to form himself, and therefore found it so difficult to understand the fully formed individual personality. The man who was once instrumental in arousing the personality of Goethe appears in the end, alongside that towering growth, as no more than a withered stump.

As far then as the execution of the project of 1774 is concerned, and in its relationship to the concept of individuality, its real achievement lay in working out the individuality of collective forces, the effects of national spirit and the temper of an age enshrined in the total processes of history, which Herder was also able to personalise. 'The whole nature of the soul, which governs all and shapes all the tendencies and inner powers, and even colours the most indifferent actions' ... 'feel your way into everything' (vol. 5, p. 503).

And so Herder approached his task with even greater psychological depth and emotion than Möser had shown in his introduction to the *History of Osnabrück*. He proceeded to take up the task which the Enlightenment had prepared the way for, but never undertaken, the task of understanding the spirit of nations and the spirit of an age as real psychological entities, as structures controlled by central formative forces, and working out a satisfactory solution to the problems connected with them. The attempt had very variable results, depending on the extent of Herder's knowledge and freedom from prejudice. His heart was always more warmly engaged with the earlier rather than the later cultures. But the age of the patriarchs and the Eastern peoples could only be depicted to a great extent in fanciful colours. He only glanced hurriedly at the Greeks and Romans, but here the treatment, though containing many gaps, was rather more certain in its outlines. Yet there was a real touch of genius, and real methodological inspiration, in his refusal to represent their essential character in static terms, or to over-simplify. Just because he took a fleeting glimpse, he also saw the fleeting elements in them. He observes (vol. 5, p. 504) that no two moments in the world's history are identical, and that the Egyptians, Romans and Greeks must not be thought of as always having been the same.

We will pause a moment at his picture of the Greek world, as an example of Herder's reconstruction of a national spirit.[1] First he glances shortly and rapidly at the favourable climate and the racial background, the advantageous situation on the Mediterranean between the Phoenicians and the Egyptians, 'where everything came together from the two extremities, and gave them material for their easy and splendid remoulding'. This spontaneity, arising from the depths of the Greek character, seems to Herder to be the real force that uses the impulses and opportunities provided by external circumstances and expresses itself, in spite of the manifold divisions, in the successful creation of a 'general Greek spirit', 'unity and manifold variety, constituting a splendid whole' (vol. 5, p. 497). This Greek picture was a reflection of the great universal picture taken over by Herder from the Neo-Platonic tradition by way of Leibniz and Shaftesbury; for this had also been based upon unity and variety, a reshaping of the available forces, and a splendid wholeness.

The recognition of the individual and unique character of the

[1] In accordance with our principles of selection, we shall omit Herder's interpretation of the Greek heritage in general, as set forth in his Fragments on the more recent German literature of 1766–8 and in other works of his. It will be enough to say that in this field, too, he was able to develop his new sense of the natural growth of the individual psychological powers of the various peoples, and so laid the stress (according to his principles with which we are already acquainted) on the early period of Greek culture.

Greek culture and its development shattered the classical ideal that Winckelmann had claimed as its permanent legacy. True, Herder could also call it 'the first pattern and exemplar of all beauty, grace and simplicity' (vol. 5, p. 498), but declared it to be unrepeatable, and so individual that a modern man could not even identify himself adequately with the Greeks in feeling (ibid., p. 543). And Herder inveighed most emphatically against Winckelmann's method of judging the Egyptian works of art by Greek standards, as well as against the idolatry which was practised concerning the Greeks and Romans (ibid., pp. 491, 566).

Herder's greatest contribution to a sympathetic reassessment of the individual spirit of an epoch, boldly challenging all accepted opinions, was in respect of the Middle Ages. To a certain extent, he even took up the cudgels against himself, against the antipathies he had previously expressed. For up till now, his views had fluctuated between an attempt to understand the Middle Ages, strictly on principle, as the necessary expression of the needs belonging to that particular time (vol. 3, pp. 401, 424), and a feeling of revulsion against the 'monstrosities of Gothic and monastic taste' (ibid., pp. 432, 465; vol. 4, p. 216). But now, as we have already seen, there had arisen in England a new feeling for the romantic charm of the Middle Ages and the Gothic style. In his *Letters on Chivalry and Romance* (1762), Hurd had compared the spirit of Northern chivalry with the heroic age of the Greeks. This had provided a springboard for the much later doctrine which saw in the Middle Ages not one, but several, stages of cultural development. Herder admitted that there were some legitimate points of comparison between the two epochs, but would not commit himself to any further identification of types. He was even more decisive than Hurd in his opinion that the Middle Ages had their own peculiar and specific character. The spirit of Northern chivalry, he maintained, was something peculiar to itself (vol. 5, p. 523), without parallel down the centuries. And without altogether losing sight of the dark and oppressive side of the Gothic spirit, he could yet call it great, rich, thoughtful and mighty, a marvel of the human spirit, and assuredly an instrument of providence (vol. 5, p. 522). Herder saw a spiritual bond linking everything together, whereas Voltaire and Hume had only seen the Middle Ages as a combination of various kinds of unreason.

What was it that brought about this change of judgement, which might well appear epoch-making in the history of the interpretations put upon the Middle Ages? Herder has rightly been viewed as a precursor and pioneer of Romanticism: can he also be seen as a forerunner of the Romantic idealisation of the Middle Ages?

Well, only in a very restricted sense. The sympathetic feeling for certain features of the Middle Ages, which had by this time been aroused in Germany as well, was derived from other sources than the later Romantic sympathy. The first stage of this movement was marked by the work of Bodmer, about the middle of the century, and was inwardly related to the contemporary Pre-Romantic stirrings in England. The second stage was ushered in by the 'Sturm und Drang' movement, during Herder and Goethe's time at Strasburg, memorable especially for Goethe's *Götz von Berlichingen* and the imitations that followed it. 'Sturm und Drang' and the Romantic outlook had this in common, that they were repelled by the rationalistic spirit and the civilised polish of the eighteenth century. But the champions of 'Sturm und Drang', carrying on the mood derived from Rousseau, admired in their mediaeval heroes the simple, full-blooded natural man and the law of the free and strong personality who had grown according to nature; though they transposed him into a new, closer, and more familiarly German historical setting. The Romantics, on the other hand, reacting against the political ideals of the French Revolution based upon the law of reason, longed for a return of the whole mediaeval atmosphere, with a way of life intimately bound up with religion and the hierarchy of Estates.

Möser, although no champion of 'Sturm und Drang', had begun by belauding the Middle Ages for the strong natures they produced and for the system of feuds and private wars, but from motives nearer to those of 'Sturm und Drang' than to Romanticism. Perhaps Herder had him in mind, without mentioning him by name, when he praised the Middle Ages for their 'knightly pride, as well as for pride of craftsmanship, their confidence in themselves, stability and essential virility' (vol. 5, p. 525). But this delight in the solid though rough vitality of the Middle Ages was not his only motive. We have already expressly emphasised that he did not turn a blind eye to the barbarity of the Middle Ages, or to their dark and oppressive aspects. But he saw these barbaric times as a necessary 'fermentation of human powers, a great cure for the whole species through powerful movement', and regarded them as the soil from which the present orderly Europe had sprung. Looking at them from the point of universal historical development, he saw the Middle Ages as a definite and natural stage in the growth of the great tree of world-history. This was going a step further than Möser. 'The trunk stretched from the East to Rome. Now it put forth branches and twigs; none of them as solid as the trunk, but spreading more broadly, lighter and higher' (vol. 5, p. 528). These words contain an intuitive appraisal of the early beginnings in the Middle Ages of the modern and even less solid culture. Thus Herder evaluated the Middle Ages in dynamic terms, and not as a static still-life picture, as they appeared later on to the Romantics. In order to understand this achievement, we must take all the elements in his developmental thought into account, including both the organic and the teleological. But since his concept of development and his concept of individuality were now firmly wedded, the latter could also be given full weight. The Middle Ages were not to be represented, as many Enlightened writers seemed to think, like an untrimmed block of stone, which had then to be rounded and smoothed off by the art of the moderns. 'Nothing in the whole of God's kingdom . . . is a mere means: all is both a means and an end, and so it is most assuredly with these centuries' (vol. 5, p. 527). Herder may well have been more successful in his attempted universal history at bringing out the value of the Middle Ages as a stage of development than in its own intrinsic qualities; but he was fully sensible of the latter, and even this was an epoch-making advance.

This thought brings us to the climax of Herder's historical outlook, and of the early historism it represents. And from this point we look across to the heights that lie beyond, culminating in the achievements of Ranke. If the developmental aspect was taken to be the norm and extended to an idea of progress, any historical phenomenon was apt to appear nothing but a means to an end. If its individuality was exclusively stressed, then everything tended to become an end in itself. There was also a danger (into which the Romantic evaluation of the Middle Ages subsequently fell) of becoming an absolute norm restricting any further growth in the present. Although Herder too fell into a false idealisation of primitive times, he was a great enough historian to realise from the start that those days could never return. He could therefore stress their relative value, and could apply the same relativism to all historical structures. This can be seen for instance in his treatment of the theme of happiness. 'Happiness' was the question-begging watchword of the period for the realisation of human wishes and ideals; and it smacked of a certain smug satisfaction for single individuals. But as the thought-pattern based upon Natural Law pictured all individuals as homogeneous, this happiness could only be pictured in universal terms. Herder, however, (vol. 5, p. 509) explained that human nature was not a receptacle for an absolute, independent and unchanging content of happiness, as defined by the philosopher.

> Everywhere human nature draws to itself as much happiness as it can; it is a malleable clay, and can form itself in different fashions under varying circumstances, needs and pressures. Even the picture of happiness changes with every change of condition and under every different sky.

So Herder arrives at this great dictum: 'Every nation has in itself its own centre of happiness, just as every sphere has its centre of gravity'.

This once more raises the problem of historical relativism. In order not to leave men utterly without standards or guidance in respect of the apparent justification of any and every point of view, this relativism needs certain counter-weights. Justus Möser, with his robust and healthy good sense, freely admitted, in a spirit of true Germanic equity, that other nations had just the same right to develop their own culture as had the Germans, and therefore managed to avoid having to offer a profounder justification of his relativism. The sensitive Herder, on the other hand, lacking the protection of this sturdy and naive vitality, needed some aesthetic and metaphysical or religious guiding principles. His feeling for the organic world, expressed in all his aesthetic discoveries, told him that the specific worth and beauty of any purposeful creation, however various in hue these purposes might seem, was after all only like the leaves, blossom and fruit on one great human tree, and were intended by nature to be so. But to Herder, nature was not some mechanical and extraneous power standing over against us, but a power that fully included everything human, infused with the life of God and guided by God. The Christian plan of salvation and the Christian philosophy of history were still absolutely indispensable in the eyes of Herder, the former pupil of Hamann. Only it needed to be somewhat loosened, infused with the idea of individuality and development, and blended with a confident renunciation of all visible progress or expectation of human perfectibility. All this was expressed in the following words:

> Is not goodness scattered far and wide throughout the earth?
> Because no single human form or zone could contain it all, it
> was divided into a thousand forms, and—like an eternal Pro-
> teus—it changes its shape throughout all regions and centuries;
> but through all the changes, it strives for the greater virtue
> and happiness of the individual, though humanity still remains
> human, and yet a plan, a forward-striving plan, is visible; this is
> my great theme!

Herder's *Sketch* of 1774 has been rightly called 'the splendid charter of historism' (Stadelmann, *Der historische Sinn bei Herder*, p. 28). It was the most successful synthesis of historical thought he ever achieved. Never again was there to be such a close and organic fusion of the aesthetic sympathy which probed the mysteries of development and individuality, and the ethical and pedagogical purpose. And this was indeed only made possible by the blending agency of the Christian scheme of salvation that had such an influence upon Herder during these years of increased religiosity. To be sure, the addition of the idea of growth did to a large extent secularise the pattern of thought—but not entirely. Thus from the standpoint of a later historism, there still remained too much transcendence in his outlook. Herder was not fully successful in attaining his own goal, which was to represent God as acting solely through nature. He had intended to portray history in entirely immanent terms, although these would be based upon fundamentally metaphysical powers; he failed because his ardent longing kept looking for the providential 'plan', if only to divine it as an act of faith.

And there is still a close link between his ethical will and his historical sympathy. It can be seen initially in his relationship to the State. He can still see the Eastern despotism of early times as a living phenomenon, with its bright and its shady sides. But then he comes out later on with the bitter verdict that despotism is 'the all-devouring jaws that engulf everything, establishing what it is pleased to call peace and obedience, but what is actually death and a uniform grinding to powder' (vol. 5, p. 516). With passionate resentment he saw the contemporary State simply as a mechanism propelled by fear and money (ibid. p. 547), nothing more than a machine, and its army still more so as a 'hired machine, without any thought or power or will of its own' (ibid., p. 534). He looked with a particularly unfriendly eye at Frederick the Great's enlightened despotism and militarism (ibid., p. 535). This was not the frame of mind in which to understand the State as an individual and self-developing structure. Thus Herder was unable to do justice to its tremendous power in the interplay of historical forces. True, he had sufficient insight into the heterogeneous nature of purpose to be able to admit that even the tree of modern statecraft might bear some good fruit (ibid., p. 578). But that was only a strong consolation for the future: it did not give him an understanding of the past.

Moreover, his fresh and youthful sense of nationality in the interpretation of contemporary history had also come up against a cliff that threatened to cleave it asunder, because his ethical ideals prevented him from carrying it through to full historical completion. We know that Herder's enthusiasm had been aroused by the nation in the early dawn of history, where in modern parlance we should call it folk-custom rather than a fully developed nationality. He was in danger of making this type into an absolute, and interpreting its transformation into a modern nation as a loosening and levelling process. 'National characteristics, where are you?' he asks. Taking up the words of the Enlightened, and holding them up to ridicule, he says that of course nowadays we have no fatherland, but are the friends of the whole human race and citizens of the entire world (ibid., p. 551). The supranational movement of the Enlightenment, with its obliteration of all national character, was what he rebelled against; but he was thereby blinded to the specific life that belongs to a modern nation, and failed to realise that the Enlightenment could remodel this, yet could not extinguish it.

But were not the ethical ideals of this movement also at work in Herder himself, though at a deeper personal level, due to his new vitality of approach? There is no gainsaying the fact that the humanitarian ideals of the later Herder, whose derivation from the Enlightenment cannot be doubted, are already in evidence at the end of his youthful essay of 1774.[1] For there he expresses the wish for a contemporary Socrates, a Socrates for the human race, 'to teach with light and clarity, as Socrates could not do in *his* age; to exhort as to a love of humanity which, if it could come to pass, would truly be *more than a love of one's country or one's fellow-citizens*' (ibid., p. 569). The ideal he here recognises might well appear unattainable from the human point of view. But it was undoubtedly something he cherished and looked up to. And this shows that his sense of full-grown individual national spirit, 'a limited nationalism' as he had already labelled it (ibid., p. 510), was not to be the last word in his philosophy of history. Was it possible for Herder and his age to find an organic method for overcoming this tension between humanity and nationality? We shall attempt to give an answer to this question in our survey of his subsequent historical thought.

III Herder's Ideas for the Philosophy of History in the 1780s

The question that must be constantly asked of Herder's world of thought is the same question he himself asked of the historical phenomenon that he came to understand most profoundly, namely the early poetry of the primitive peoples. He rescued it even more vigorously than the English Pre-Romantics from the isolated compartment of art to which it had hitherto been confined, and brought it down to the level of an actual experience of a living individual people with all its manifold impulses and mysterious undercurrents of feeling. It never happened to Herder, as to so many other philosophers, that thought pursued its way in an atmosphere of detached and rarified logic. With Herder, thought was always sublimated experience, the experience of a man who was infinitely receptive, yet infinitely sensitive to injury and resenting an offence for a long time.

[1] There are earlier traces still according to Rud. Lehmann, 'Herders Humani-tätsbegriff', *Kantstudien*, 24 (1920), 244 ff.

All the pains and joys of his most intimate personal life left their permanent impress on the different stages of his historical thought. We have already seen how the narrow East Prussian days of his youth, the period at Riga, the religious ardour of the time at Bückeburg, all gave Herder particular perspectives into the world of history. And now, from 1776 onwards, there was to be the Weimar period.

Here, too, he was dogged by what seemed to be his destiny. It seemed to be his nature to long for intimate links with his environment, yet never or seldom to be able to achieve them. We shall pass over his ordinary professional life in those first years, and only call attention to the basic experiences mirrored in the most comprehensive and ambitious of his historical writings, the *Ideen zur Philosophie der Geschichte der Menschheit*, which appeared in four parts between 1784 and 1791. For without a knowledge of these experiences, the peculiar rift which runs through this work is unintelligible. We are already aware of its nature: it was the cleavage between the contemplative and the ethical-pedagogic motifs.[1] But it was increased by a strange simultaneous intensification of both of them, so that one can hardly help asking what experience lay at the back of it all.

One influence was Herder's happiness at the renewal of his friendship with Goethe since 1783, this time on a mutual give-and-take basis. Both men had now left the explosive youthful years of 'Sturm und Drang' behind them. But its permanent legacy was a deep yearning for nature, and for the divine in nature, a deep desire for a sense of oneness with what had issued from the divine and what was permeated by the divine breath. What was new, however, in both men, was a firm intention not simply to be content with feeling, but to launch out into vigorous inductive research. They were determined to discover all that human quest could discover about the mysteries of nature, its unity and order in things both small and great. The great advance in the natural sciences since the seventeenth century had once given an immeasurably strong impulse to the Enlightenment in Western Europe. Now it kindled the enthusiasm of the great intellectual counter-movement in Germany, which had begun with the 'Sturm und Drang'. Only things were bound to work out differently on these two occasions. In the former, the natural sciences had taught a mechanical thought-pattern; in the latter, they were balanced by dynamic and vitalistic needs justifying themselves on metaphysical grounds. 'Nature' had now become the common denominator for soul, *phusis* (in the sense of the organic body) and

---

[1] Here, too, we must confie our observations to a selection of the points that could be covered. For the most part, the hesitations and variations in Herder's thinking in the different parts of his works have been well brought out in some detail by Haym's acute analysis of the material.

universe; and so the laws operative in nature could no longer be purely mechanical.

The ambition to become 'the interpreter of the deity' in nature as well had already seized the youthful Herder, as we have seen, on the sea voyage of 1769, and once again during the Bückeburg period (*Unterrichtsplan für Zeschau*, vol. 5, p. 396). Now he discovered in Goethe a fellow-pilgrim along the same way. 'Our daily conversation', Goethe related in subsequent years, 'was concerned with the earliest stages of the dry land emerging from the seas and the most primitive forms of organic life that developed upon it' (*Vorwort zur Morphologie*, 1807). The two men agreed in principle that humanity and nature belonged together as a single unified cosmos of active forces derived from one divine original source, and developing through many stages.[1] Goethe saw this in more pantheistic, and Herder in more theistic terms; yet it is clear that in both of them it was the old Neo-Platonic picture of the world come to life again, and showing its undying creative power in the new and fruitful empirical research it inspired in both Goethe and Herder.

Goethe's chief interest lay in nature in the physical sense, though without ever forgetting the human heart and its ultimate unison with the whole of nature. It was not till later, as we shall see, that he developed a greater interest in things historical. On the other hand, genuine history had always been Herder's chief field of interest for research. But now the main theme of his philosophy of history was to set the whole history of humanity within the entire process of nature as far as it could be grasped by man, and to apprehend the whole in genetic terms. The work had been conceived before the renewal of his friendship with Goethe, but had been enormously strengthened and encouraged by it.

Was it, however, possible for Herder to achieve such an anchoring of history in nature? As a first step, it would have been necessary for Herder's conception of nature to become something clearer and more circumscribed than it was. His conception, like Goethe's, combined soul, organic life and the universe, as we have already noted. But it was not given to Herder, as it was to Goethe, to respect the laws of organic life, and yet to maintain its metaphysical foundations. He was much more inclined than Goethe to obliterate the boundary between immanence and transcendence, which the genius of Goethe was mostly able to preserve, and declared much to belong to nature which went beyond the essence of immanental law. True, when he

---

[1] A preliminary stage towards this idea was represented by the thinking of Reimarus, discussed by R. Sommer in *Grundzüge einer Geschichte der deutschen Psychologie und Ästhetik von Wolff und Baumgarten bis Kant und Schiller*, 1892. Cf. especially pp. 92 ff. and p. 110.

spoke of nature, what he meant in the first place was something non-mechanical, to be understood in terms of growth and organism; and here he was at one with Goethe. But in order to follow this up into the historical field, Herder would have needed a capacity for pure contemplation such as Goethe possessed, a certain ability to stand back from the immediate pains and vicissitudes, wishes and aims, of his own time. But of this Herder was not capable. Anyone who reads his philosophy of history especially in its later parts, with an eye to its content of experience, and allows it to make its due impression, cannot but admit that this is the voice of a man who is suffering heavily in the Germany of his days under the general social and political conditions of his own time. And we get the impression of a suffering that was more than the distaste of the shirker for the military yoke of Prussia, and more than indignation against the absolutism of the military State.

The eighties brought an intensification of these antipathies. There was the struggle between the spirit of the age and the remnants of the Middle Ages in social life, in particular the relics of serfdom; the awakening of national political feeling in connection with the North German League of Princes; the dawning realisation that the whole of Germany was ignominiously pining away as a result of the decay and antediluvian conditions that had prevailed for many centuries; there were all the pre-revolutionary stirrings of political unrest rather than an active will to reform, subsequently increased by the outbreak of the French Revolution. All these are perceptible in his philosophy of history, more particularly in the portions suppressed as a result of Goethe's advice. All this belongs to the documents of the political awakening of Germany, though to begin with it could only express itself as resentment. We are only concerned at this point with its effect on historical thought. Was it possible, among the feudal relics of a Germany that had had a military superstructure imposed from above, for a rising and increasingly enlightened middle class to achieve any peaceful and positive historical relationship to the political past of Germany and the West? Möser had done his utmost to achieve sympathetic insight into the specific political destiny of his own people; yet his efforts ended in a mood of calm but mournful resignation. Herder was possessed of great sympathetic insight, and was also a moral educator of mankind; but his very sensitive and stormy temperament prevented him from coming into really close sympathetic contact with the political phenomena of Germany and the West in days gone by. Thus there was now a yawning gulf in his interpretation of history. Whilst the Neo-Platonic element, exalted to a level of thought concerned with individuality and development, set itself the sublime goal of fusing the whole of humanity's historical experience with the divinely ordered cosmos of nature, the Enlightened element allowed an important part of this experience to coagulate and become rigid before it ever reached the melting-pot.

The *Sketch* of 1774 had already shown how incapable Herder was of subjecting the political phenomena of his own time to his new method of sympathetic insight into the individual, and understanding from the inside. But at that date the hiatus between political and general history had been to some extent bridged over by his great conception briefly summarised in the words 'chance, fate, deity'. By means of his form of the Christian scheme of salvation, and the insight into the great variety of ends that was bound up with it, Herder had been able to accept what was for him the darker aspect of history as well, with its wars and power politics. He had been confident that God's hand could be traced even in the storms and passions of history; in short, he had been able to understand the tragic character of history on an extensive scale. In addition, his splendid sense of natural growth in history enabled him to arrive at a grandiose historical relativism which saw every epoch both as a means and as an end in itself, as an individual entity, and yet as a stage in a further development. In spite of the weak places in the structure, the new sense of history was suddenly raised above all the hindrances and prejudices of the contemporary world.

Many of the thoughts and expressions in his philosophy of history written during the 1780s, as well as the minor earlier compositions of the Weimar period, are reminiscent of this inspired conception. But the pillars on which the whole structure should rest were very differently, and very inadequately, distributed. True, the sense of growth, the sense of 'natural history' in history as a whole, had now (as we have noted) taken on cosmic proportions. With the help of Goethe, this supporting pillar had become uncommonly strong. So strong, in fact, that this work was able to act as a powerful incentive to the natural sciences towards the discovery of larger areas of Natural Law in their own fields. But the balancing pillar, which would have to bear the weight of political resentments that had meanwhile grown so much stronger, had itself become notably weaker. The reassurances in the face of all the evil in history, though not absolutely lacking, had now receded into the background; and with them the means for a better understanding of the unwelcome and extraneous elements in history, which we saw to be growing under the heightened Christian experience of the Bückeburg period, and to be reflected in the study of 1774. Now, however, Herder made less frequent use of the idea of a multiplicity and variety of purposes. Towards the end of the work, there is even a judgement based upon a rationalistic ethic that seems to run in an opposite direction. After a sharp criticism of the crusades and strongly qualified praise of their effects on European culture, Herder adds: 'In general, an event can only result in genuine and permanent good insofar as it is in correspondence with reason' (vol. 14, p. 476).

Here, there are obviously clear indications of a changed attitude to Christianity. Herder's theology had always been something of a pendulum-swing between the two poles of divine mystery and a purely human religion. But now the religious impetus given by the time at Bückeburg began to weaken, perhaps because of all the vexations and complications, and the collisions between his ideals and the affairs of everyday life encountered in his professional work as superintendent-general. The judgements on Christianity contained in his philosophy of history suggest a colder, more critical attitude nearer to that of the Enlightenment. It was characteristic of Herder to defend Gibbon's 'masterpiece' against the reproach of a hostile attitude to Christianity (vol. 14, p. 330). Herder's approach to Jesus was noticeably more realistic than in the *Sketch* of 1774, which had hinted at mysterious origins. Now, he was represented as coming from a definite historical environment, as a teacher of 'the most genuine humanity'. But Herder went on to trace a degenerate development of this pure religion, with its devotion to humanity, until it became a worship of His person, ultimately leading on to papacy. Here, he went far beyond anything suggested by Gottfried Arnold, and even discerned the beginnings of corruption among the early disciples (vol. 14, pp. 290 ff., and the unprinted paragraphs, ibid., pp. 500 ff. and 556). Here, Herder was speaking as a rationalist; but from the point of view of national individuality, which had been one of his discoveries, he also began to cast doubts upon the effects of Christianity. He argued that the introduction of Christianity had been inimical to the essential character of the Nordic nations at the stage they had then reached; nay, it had been positively harmful, for it had robbed them of their own spirit (ibid., p. 384 and the unprinted paragraphs, ibid., p. 517). The forcible conversion of the Saxons, Slavs, Prussians, Kurlanders and Esthonians now appeared to Herder as a permanent blot upon a debased Christianity (unprinted paragraphs, ibid., p. 537; cf. also the *Humanitätsbriefe*, vol. 18, p. 222). The bold and sweeping nature of this judgement exceeded even the mania for the Northern peoples which was rife among the English Pre-Romantics.

This cooling off in his Christian religious fervour did not, however, secularise his historical thought to the point of completely abandoning the Christian scheme of salvation. The influence of the general teleological outlook of the period was far too strong. Moreover, Lessing's *Erziehung des Menschengeschlechts*, which appeared in

1780, showed him that it was possible to enlarge the Christian scheme so as to embrace a general theistic outlook. Thus there are (more particularly in the first parts of the work) strong theistic tendencies (vol. III, p. 13, pp. 7 ff.). Herder looked upon the animals as brothers of the human race, though he did not acknowledge the descent of man from an animal line (ibid., pp. 109, 114, 256). But he connected the ascent of man from an animal level with a direct 'creative word of power:—Creatures, arise from the earth!' (ibid., p. 136). He allowed direct divine assistance to have become rarer in subsequent periods to the same extent as humanity began to discover its own powers; but he held that even in later times the greatest effects on earth arose through unexplained circumstances, or were accompanied by them (ibid., p. 198). As the work proceeded, however, Herder's tendency was to explain the whole of human history as a pure natural history of human powers, impulses and actions (vol. 14, p. 145). He emphatically rejected any idea of seeking for 'a limited and secret plan of providence', and any 'philosophy of final ends', and insisted upon treating every historical phenomenon as nothing more than a natural event (ibid., pp. 200, 202).

There has thus been a disposition in some quarters to speak of a universal determinism in Herder (Delvaille, *Hist. de l'idée de progrès*, p. 594). We scarcely need to repeat that there can be no question of Herder's entertaining a purely mechanical causal view of reality. Although he may sometimes have called attention to causality of a mechanical kind, this always had as its general background a picture of interwoven vital forces of immensely rich texture working from within. Only in this sense would it be right to speak of Herder's naturalism.

The progressive secularisation of his thought and the increasing interpretation of history in terms of nature were now, however, balanced by the simultaneous irruption of a rationalism loaded with resentment and bitterness. Yet Herder's thought is so full of contradictions and so imbued with vitality that the rationalism of his system of ideas is of a refined and spiritualised character. The classical spirit of Weimar spoke at this point in a new language and forged for itself in this work one of its first great forms of expression. The 'Sturm und Drang' movement had released the forces of the inner intellectual and spiritual life. These now began to search for new educational ideals, some moderating discipline, some restraint upon all that was over-exuberant, though without losing any of the new springs of life that had been released; and the ideal of humanity was the answer. We have already seen the tentative approach towards this ideal in the *Sketch* of 1774. In the great work, it appears as a new supporting pillar in Herder's historical fabric. The meaning and purpose of historical development is the realisation of humanity, as we shall see more fully when we examine the content of this ideal. It should be noted that the more Christian and transcendent teleology of 1774 has now been replaced by a more worldly teleological principle. Furthermore, we should note that the ideal of humanity, insofar as it was the personal possession of Herder, represents so to speak the positive aspect over against what we have already seen as a negative, namely his inability to reach any inner understanding of the political world and its struggles for power. In the face of this world, for which Herder had no love, and often expressed a positive hatred, he now set up the banner of humanity. In other words, the motives at work were those of the Enlightenment, with its very unpolitical outlook and its emphasis on the happiness of the individual. These were by no means new to Herder, but they now won for themselves a broader sphere of action.[1] The desire to look at things in a trans-personal manner, which was so much to the fore in the *Sketch* of 1774, now recedes into the background.

It is generally recognised that Herder's fluctuating thought-pattern makes it difficult to arrive at any exact definition of his ideal of humanity. He seems to see it rather vaguely in terms of happiness, religion, reason and similar ideas. Shaftesbury's influence is discernible in a notion that constantly recurs—namely, that humanity is born of a harmony between beauty and morality. 'Clear truth, pure beauty, free and active love' was how Herder once described humanity in an earlier work (vol. 13, p. 201), thus revealing the fervour with which he would have liked to embrace all that was highest in mankind under this concept. But this highest level has to be achieved: it was not simply given by God to the human race at the start, though God has no doubt given him an inclination towards it. Man is 'although not yet formed for humanity, nonetheless, malleable in that direction' (ibid., p. 147). 'From the beginning of life our soul seems to have only one task, namely to cultivate the inner form and fashion of humanity' (ibid., p. 187). Here again, we get glimpses of Shaftesbury's thought. His great purpose was to understand every historical phenomenon as a natural product and in the ultimate analysis as proceeding from the divine initiative. This compelled him to show how humanity was the expression of the divine, the impress by which God could be known on earth, and so necessarily embodied in man's

[1] There is a misleading sentence in K. Bittner's *Herders Geschichtsphilosophie und die Slaven*, p. 55: 'Herder's ideal for humanity was social, while Goethe's, Schiller's and Humboldt's was individualistic', for Herder's ideal implicitly included the individual element, too. The right view is taken by Schubert, *Goethe und Hegel*, p. 101. Cf. also Haym, 2, 222 for the antinomy between the individualistic sense of the ideal for humanity ('the purpose of history is the single person') and its application to the human race as a whole.

natural disposition. Herder thought he could discern seven characteristics of this original and natural disposition of man, two of them belonging to *phusis* in the narrower sense; man's physical build, which was apparently much more suited to defence than to attack; and his sexual urge, with its deviation from the animal level, and its inclination towards endearment and loving embrace. The remainder belong to the mental and moral sphere: man as the most understanding of all living creatures; his sympathy, which makes him a social being; his inborn sense of justice and truth; his graceful build (a hint at the ideal of beauty); and finally, urged on by fear and the quest for causation, his propensity for religion, which, whether in true or in false forms, was from the beginning the highest expression of humanity (ibid., pp. 154 ff.).

We shall not attempt to assess this effort to single out the roots of humanity and indicate its essential features by the standards of modern knowledge.[1] We are chiefly concerned with the historical origin of these thoughts, and with the question of how they were applied by Herder to the interpretation of the historical phenomenon of the world. The spirit at work here is an echo of the Stoic belief in Natural Law revived by the Enlightenment: the belief that human nature has a universally valid moral and rational content, which is part and parcel of the human being, and corresponds to the universal reason. Yet Herder's new feeling for the genetic approach can be seen in the fact that he only credited mankind with a disposition towards such reason and morality, but laid the responsibility for its actualisation at the door of the individual historical person in his different gradations and stages. The rationalistic theologian in Herder could not indeed express this in such realistic terms, but had to assign a role to providence. God had not tied men's hands, but had rather allowed them to make mistakes 'so that they might themselves learn how to do better' (vol. 14, p. 210).[2] And what was the result of thus leaving man free to forge his own destiny? Here one can see Herder in the course of his work tossed to and fro between sorrow and optimism. 'It is strange and yet undeniable that among all the inhabitants of this earth the human race is furthest from attaining its destined goal,' so he remarks at the outset (vol. 13, p. 190). But later on we find: 'The course of this history shows that with the growth of true humanity the destructive demons of the human race have diminished in number, and this by virtue of an inner Natural Law of enlightening

[1] Further elements and effects of Herder's ideal for humanity which we can pass over for our present purposes, are to be found in Rud. Lehmann, 'Herders Humanitätsbegriff'.

[2] Incidentally, one of the cases in which he was still using the idea of heterogeneous purposes.

reason and statesmanship' (vol. 14, p. 217). In this connection there was his famous prophesy that even the Slavs, whom he had held up as a pattern of the peace-loving peoples, would once again be freed from the fetters of enslavement (ibid., p. 280). And yet we find in an earlier sketch: 'He who hopes for a political golden century at the end of the world . . . is hoping against human nature and contrary to all historical experience' (vol. 13, p. 468).

Once, under the impetus of the Bückeburg period, Herder had regarded the belief in a tranquil progress of the human spirit towards a better world as a mere phantom. At that time this was a pointer to a tragic concept of history; now, it was an expression of the bitterest disappointment and pain. Formerly, he had trusted in the working of God's providence in history; now, his despair led him to strike out beyond history into the fields of metaphysics and religion. The purpose of our existence with its immediate goal of humanity transcends our life here below. This earth is only a practice-ground or preparatory school for the cultivation of humanity. It is only the bud for a flower that shall be; and the present state of man is probably the connecting link between two worlds. It should be remembered at this point that the habitability of other worlds was a favourite theme for discussion at the time, and that even Kant had considered the possibility that our immortal souls might have other lives to live on other stars. It is thus quite understandable that Herder, with his hazy ideas about nature and his fondness for the transcendental, should maintain this outlook as the only possible philosophy of human history, because it was based upon all the laws of nature (vol. 13, pp. 189–201). The intensive belief in palingenesis current in the German Enlightenment was thus destined to provide the coping-stone for his philosophy of history.

In all this, as we have seen, there was the germ of a personal experience. His ideal of life lay in the direction of gentle and peaceful human relationships, undisturbed progress in intellectual culture, and the development of individuality among the peoples of the world. He was therefore strongly opposed to the 'royal way' of power (vol. 13, p. 378), which he had seen, in both past and present, to be the popular road for those who shaped the destinies of men. In fact, he felt it with all the force of a personal oppression. His opposition was based upon a much more profound and delicate interpretation of life than that of the Enlightenment. But it so happened that he had a peculiar inner aversion to the historical phenomenon of the State as it had actually developed, so much so that it shattered his intention of ascribing every historical event to purely natural origins.

We shall attempt to pick out the solid kernel of Herder's thinking on the subject of the State, though it is often emotionally coloured and expressed in extremely vague language. The only pure product of nature appeared to him to be the family, and political forms based upon it. One might call this Herder's form of the nation–State. 'Nature produces families; so the most natural State is also a single people with a single national character' (vol. 13, p. 384). 'The government of a people is a family, a well-ordered household; it rests upon itself, for it was founded by nature and stands or falls only with the ages' (vol. 14, p. 52). He called this the first stage of natural government, but maintained that it was nevertheless the highest and would be the most permanent (vol. 13, p. 375). In other words, his ideal picture of the political state of a primitive and uncomplicated people remained his ideal of the State in general. It must therefore be remembered, when Herder is called one of the pioneers of the idea embodied in the modern national State, that its origins were in a kind of vitalised Natural Law, and its character in Herder's mind was entirely pacifistic. Any State that had come into existence through conquest was an abomination in his eyes, for it disrupted the material character of the cultures that had arisen from the originating peoples (another echo of his 'folk-thought'). There was no attempt to renew the qualified recognition of Eastern despotism attempted in 1774. Yet he did allow one further second stage of natural government, namely that which was created in answer to specific needs, where the leadership rested upon the free choice of the early tribes and peoples. But in the third stage, that of hereditary governments, Herder was already beginning to be doubtful whether there was any basis for them in Natural Law. In the depths of his heart, however, he answered this question with a decided no. On another occasion he calls these States categorically 'the artificial creations of society' (vol. 13, p. 340). In the parts of the work that were suppressed we read: 'It is fortunate indeed that humanity and the State are not one and the same thing'. 'Serve the State if you have to, and serve humanity if you are able to' (ibid., pp. 455 ff.).

Equally unsatisfactory was Herder's attempt to come to grips with the problem of war in the history of the world. If anything ever was, war certainly was a real and most mighty phenomenon in history going back into the earliest times. Yet Herder was able to declare peace to be the natural state of the human race in its free condition, and war something produced by conditions of need and stress (ibid., p. 322). But we may well ask if there has ever been a time when the human race has not been under some kind of stress.

At this point, we must glance back again at an earlier stage of Herder's thought. Only a few years before, in 1782–3, Herder had struck a very different note about war and politics in his work on the *Spirit of Hebrew Poetry*. This was perhaps his happiest achievement in interpreting the tender spirit of national poetry, with its peculiar and unrepeatable kind of genius. He followed the road in which Lowth had led the way; but though he gave full value to the specific musical qualities of this divinely chosen shepherd-nation's poetry, with all its naturalness of expression, he finally came to the striking conclusion that 'the greater part of their poetry, which has often been called spiritual, is in fact political' (vol. 12, p. 119). And by this, Herder did not simply mean political in the sense of governed by God, for he might well have distinguished this from the usual execrable power politics; but a phenomenon full of heroism, youthful courage, and the subtle craftiness of a newly established hill-people, full of the active, vital poetry of passion, adventure and freedom (vol. 12, p. 168). Thus he was willing to pardon a youthful nation struggling for its freedom a certain recourse to power politics. But wherever, as now in his philosophy of history, he saw despots founding States, or the completely absolutist political machinery of the modern State at work, and using such methods, he rose up in defence of the rights of humanity that were being infringed. That was one of those failures in logicality that are not at all uncommon with romantic natures. It was certainly a great feature in Herder that he could feel the spirit of the fresh young nation as romantic, and yet realise that it could never return. But the genetical principle, which he showed how to apply in such epoch-making fashion to this national spirit, collapsed when it came to dealing with the question of the political origins of the Western peoples. Thus his views upon war were, as we have seen, a relapse into the old conceptions based upon Natural Law and universal reason, and the outlook adopted by Rousseau.

Herder must himself have been aware of the gulf between his genetic and naturalistic, and his humanitarian and eudaemonistic lines of thought. Again and again he sought for methods of bridging this gulf, and for higher regularities in nature which would make it possible to discern a meaning in what appeared to him to be contrary to nature. But when seen in a clearer light, what appeared to him to be against nature was only that which went counter to his ethical ideals and seemed to lie on the darker side of history. Earlier on, his insight into the variety of purposes at work in history had shown him that its shady side must be accepted as inevitable. Now, there rose up in him a new idea, a seed-thought from the philosophy of Shaftesbury, which gained in strength and during the last stage of his life was destined to become the leading motif of his historical thinking. This was the doctrine of a balance of forces in history, which though it might be disturbed, would constantly tend to re-establish itself. It was a law of nature, he now taught, reducible to mathematical certainty, that all actions contrary to true humanity arose from a disturbance of this balance, and were bound in the end to bring about their own ruin (vol. 14, pp. 177, 217 ff. and 500). It was likewise a law of nature that the forces at work in a society operate against one another in wild confusion until 'the opposing principles damp one another down and produce a kind of balance and harmony' (ibid., p. 227). This 'law', when transformed into a working hypothesis, has proved itself to be still serviceable in modern psychology and biology. Moreover, as we shall see in our study of Goethe, it could, when expanded into an original cosmic principle, prove a profound source of nourishment and enlightenment for historical thought. But as soon as it was applied in a direct and hasty manner to concrete historical phenomena, it was in danger of becoming narrowed down into a moral judgement upon the course of this world. The true rhythm of historical movement is too complicated and ambiguous to be universally reducible to Herder's principle of balance. It was rather the product of a desire for the quick satisfaction of his pressing ethical needs than of an effort to arrive at knowledge in its purest form.

This was, therefore, a vigorous attempt by Herder to fuse his ethical ideals for humanity with his conception of nature. His conception of nature had grown out of a combination of extremely original discoveries with a Neo-Platonic pattern of thought. It was certainly original (though Herder no doubt owed something to contemporary influences) to recognise the contribution made by the pristine *Volkstum* through its special spiritual and intellectual productivity, and to weave this so easily into the Neo-Platonic world-scheme of eternally active vital forces, the 'invisible heavenly spirit of light and fire', which penetrate all things living and constitute the original unity of the soul with all the forces of matter (vol. 13, p. 175 f.). The ideal of humanity could then be represented as the finest flower that this interplay of forces upon earth could produce, and so be taken up quite naturally into this general world view. But as soon as it was put forward as an absolute, instead of an ideal conditioned by the age, and was applied as a categorical ethical standard to the history of the past, there were clear signs of the rift between Herder's conception of nature and his ideals of humanity which we have already noted. True, his historism also showed him at the same time that humanity as seen in the events of history is just as much of a Proteus as poetry. Nevertheless, the ideal of humanity which Herder cherished in his own breast remained the yardstick for his treatment of the political side of world history. Thus from the point of view of the development of historism, this moralistic assessment makes his great philosophy of history a retrograde step as compared with the *Sketch* of 1774. And along with this moralism, there was a considerable recurrence of pragmatism—a tendency to explain historical processes by very limited individual motives and causes.

Herder's *Ideas for the Philosophy of the History of Mankind* then, is like some great ocean, not so much perpetually in upheaval as constantly traversed by currents and counter-currents. For Herder's splendid sense of the individual development and the individual finished product was especially prominent where he was concerned with great collective individualities. His greatest strength was his ability to think in terms of whole peoples and the spirit that inspired them. Let us look briefly and selectively at some of the achievements of his philosophy of history in this direction.

About 1774 Herder altered his fundamental philosophy of history and began to ask new basic questions. He was led on now to put the succession of the peoples who followed one another down the ages on a far wider footing. At that period, the question of the origins and destiny of our own Western world had considerably restricted the choice of material, and the peoples of the Middle and Far East had been largely left on one side. But now came the new outlook which saw human history as growing out of the universal cosmic life. The earth was seen to be a star among other stars, the special bearer of a life that had risen step by step to its human climax. And this new outlook was concerned to include everything that bore a human face. True, Herder did not completely succeed in embracing the full width of the material; but at least he took into account all the known peoples who had produced a specific and well-developed culture. Alongside the Greeks, whom he again delineated in very delicate colours, at any rate with the intention of avoiding any false idealisation, he now gave special prominence to the picture of Arab culture, that 'fragrant shrub springing up from the dry ground' (vol. 14, p. 425). He saw it as a centre of light in the darkness, and as a reflection of his own most cherished ideals. It would seem that here, too, Herder was influenced by English writers. In his historical writings, Hume had already extolled the Arabs of the Middle Ages (vol. 1, pp. 209, 345). Then Thomas Warton, in his *History of English Poetry* (1774 ff.), which was much valued by Herder (vol. 8, p. 397), had stressed the connection between Arabic culture and the romantic poetry of the Middle Ages. (The author was not the first to point out this connection, but intended to be the first to furnish convincing evidence.) Herder had perforce to accept in Mahomet and Islam a good deal that was repugnant to him; but his heart warmed towards them because they seemed to him both to display a genuinely poetical national spirit, and to be the chief, if not the only, standard-bearers of enlightenment during the Middle Ages (vol. 14, p. 447). He therefore most deliberately underlined their vitalising and enlightening effect on the Western world of the Middle Ages, which Herder now saw in much darker colours than in 1774.[1] This is only one example of his sense of linkage between all the peoples, and the broad traditional connection between the various cultures, 'the golden chain of culture' (vol. 13, p. 353), which was so strong and fruitful at that period, and which was also widely present in his philosophy of history.

Standing apart from these traditional connections, there were the Eastern Asiatic peoples, whom Herder now brought for the first time into his overall picture. But the very fact of treating them separately made it more difficult for him to understand them. He was not particularly successful in portraying the Eastern Asiatic cultures. From the start, he was not favourably disposed towards the Mongols, and proceeded at this point to adopt the rigid external categories of the Enlightenment, such as barbarism, despotism, useful arts, refined letters, crude splendour and so on. Here, he entirely forsook his own method of sympathetic identification. There was rather more of this, however, in his picture of the Indo-Brahman culture. And yet he had an ardent desire to understand this completely foreign world of the East more deeply, individually and dynamically from within; and this bursts forth in the words in which he refers to it: 'What a wonderful and strange thing it is, that which we call the genetic spirit and character of a people. It is inexplicable and inextinguishable: as old as the nation and the land that it inhabited' (vol. 14, p. 38).

These words also contain the essence of his doctrine of the *Volksgeist*,[2] the national spirit. It was centred in the first place (like its precursors in the Enlightenment) on a permanent character and essence among the peoples, a something that remained in spite of all the changes. It was supported by a more universal feeling for the manifold variety of individuality to be found among the peoples than was shown by the later teaching of the school of historical law, which took its origins in a fervent preoccupation with the peculiar qualities and creative genius of their own specific German spirit. But it anticipated, though with less mysticism, the Romantic feeling for the irrational and mysterious element in the spirit of a nation. Like the Romantics, it regarded the national spirit as an invisible mark that

[1] Midway between the dynamic interpretation of the Middle Ages in the *Sketch* of 1774 and the more moralistic one in the *Study of Ideas*, stand the observations on the Middle Ages in his prize essay of 1778 on the effects of poetry on the habits and manners of peoples (8, 397 ff.), and in the essay of 1780 on the influence of the government on learning (9, 337 ff. and 391 ff.).

[2] Herder dealt with this theme again in more detail in his *Humanitätsbriefe*, 18 and 58; cf. also 18 and 146. Cf. also Lempicki, *Gesch. der deutschen Literaturwissenschaft*, pp. 387 ff.

was imprinted upon the concrete features and products of a people, only in a rather freer and looser and less doctrinaire manner—one might call it a kind of inspiration. Herder also treated with less rigidity than the later Romantics the question whether the national spirit was something ineradicable and unquenchable. He certainly affirmed this in the passage we have quoted, but was also somewhat doubtful whether the specific character of a people could not be subject to change (vol. 14, p. 643, from an early sketch). And his love for a pure popular heritage which had not been subject to any disturbances did not prevent him at this point, any more than it had previously, from recognising the healthiness of 'fresh inoculations of a people at the right moment' (as in the case of the Norman Conquest of England) (ibid., p. 381). Moreover, the idea of the national spirit received a further special meaning at the hands of Herder through the addition of his favourite term 'genetic'. This word has a good many overtones, things that he could only feel or dimly surmise without being able to give them distinct expression, and could only as it were fondly embrace in this word. It stands for the idea of vital growth instead of static existence; and not only takes in the specific and unrepeatable developments of history, but also the original creative source from which all life springs. Furthermore, it contains the whole range of greater and lesser causality which governs the development and essence of a structure such as a nationality. As we have already seen, Herder did not understand this in any mechanical sense, but derived it once again from the mighty creative ground and origin of all life.

> Great Mother Nature, to what trifles hast thou knit the destinies of our human race! One change in the shape of the human head and brain, *one* small alteration in the organisational structure and the nerves brought about by climate, racial characteristics and custom—and you have a change in the entire destinies of the world, the sum-total of what humanity does and suffers everywhere upon this earth! (vol. 14, p. 39).

The persistent elements in the genetic processes and the facts of inheritance were already attracting Herder's attention (vol. 13, pp. 282, 308; vol. 14, p. 8; cf. also vol. 4, pp. 206, 210, 213; and later on, vol. 18, p. 368). But he adopted a much more critical attitude to the now emerging concept of race, which had recently (1775) been broached in the first instance by Kant. His ideal of humanity revolted against this idea, for he regarded it as likely to drag humanity down again to a purely animal level, though in so doing it must be admitted that he failed to reckon with the tremendous causal significance of race. It seemed to Herder to be ignoble even to speak of races among mankind (vol. 13, p. 151). He held that all the racial colours ran together, and in the end we were left with nothing but different shades in one great picture (ibid., pp. 257 ff.). The true carrier of the great collective genetical process was and remained for him the nation and, beyond that, humanity as a whole.

'The genetic force' (he writes in one of his leading sentences), 'is the mother of all creations upon earth, and the climate is only an additional friendly or hostile influence' (ibid., p. 273). Climate 'does not compel, but only inclines'. By climate, however, he understood an epitome of forces and influences of a terrestrial kind, to which flora and fauna also contributed, and which was bound up with all living creatures in a network of mutual exchange. Man, however, could also bring about alterations in it by artificial means (ibid., p. 272). Here we touch upon one of the chief merits of his philosophy of history, which has often (and rightly) been commended. Whilst drawing on the whole scientific and geographical work of the century,[1] Herder refined upon the doctrine of the influence of climate and geophysical conditions in general, which had been treated too rigidly and mechanically even by Montesquieu. He made this for the first time something more elastic, by relating it not only to the permanent factors in a specific geographical environment, and their effect on specific peoples, but by opening up the connections between the land surfaces and their movements and migrations. This led to a new and fruitful insight into the symbiosis existing between all forms of life, and stimulated research which is still today discovering new and unsuspected connections. And all this, to Herder's prophetic eye, took place by a series of mutual interactions. Climate affects man, but man also has a transforming effect upon climate, and even the operation of the climate soon becomes inseparably fused with a specific interior counteraction on the part of the living entities affected. Once again we should note the decisive change of thought since Montesquieu. Even he had spoken of man's counter-effects on climate, but only of such as were under the conscious rational control of the lawgiver's will. For Herder, they arose rather out of the living sum-total of all creatures, and had a creative effect even upon climate.[2] 'Whatever be the action of the climate, every man, animal and plant has its own climate; for each of them takes up all the external effects in its own fashion and transforms them in its own organic manner' (vol. 13, p. 277). He proposed to call this individual

[1] Cf. on this point Grundmann, *Die geographischen und völkerkundlichen Quellen und Anschauungen in Herders Ideen etc.* (1900).

[2] So he had already recognised what Rothacker has characterised as a creative 'response' of man to geographical conditions in his *Geschichtsphilosophie* (1934), p. 52.

character of a creature its genius (ibid., p. 279 from the *Sketch*). We see his old conception of individuality rekindled and extended to the whole living world. It is not clear how far he intended to give prominence to the really individual character of a separate creature above and beyond the typical characteristics of the species. It is rather the view of an enthusiast, carried away by the unison, and yet the separate tones and tunes, of all existence. It is a kind of vitalism based upon a metaphysical Neo-Platonism, dividing by virtue of its individual outlook, yet bringing all things together again at this deeper level. As he says in the *Sketch*, one might well remark of the whole range of existing things right up to man, in a spirit free from all prejudice: 'The radiant image of God is present in everything that exists, closely wedded to its material form' (ibid., p. 274).

As we have already noted, this conception did not succeed in permeating the whole world of history. There was still the gulf between nature and culture pointed out by Rousseau; and the diverse character of the old Platonic–Neo-Platonic and equally ancient rationalistic, tradition of Natural Law, which had pervaded the whole development of Western thought since antiquity, was still evident in the different standards employed by Herder himself.

When we examine his whole interpretation of recent history, as portrayed in the concluding sections of the unfinished work, it is evident that Herder was continually having to jump over ditches in order to pass from one to another of his principles. His concept of nationality, developed on the basis of the study of early beginnings, the 'flush of dawn' idea, is certainly not adequate (as he had to admit to himself) to serve as a guideline for the understanding of this period. Since the end of the Ancient World he had felt the lack of 'that beneficent basis of simplicity and goodness' (vol. 14, p. 485) which he had so often, though not universally, felt among the peoples of ancient days. The original peoples were violently intermingled and largely split into fragments; and from these fragments there arose 'the European republic of today, the greatest commonwealth our earth has ever known' (vol. 14, p. 555—from the suppressed portion). We are already acquainted with this idea as the common ground of historical feeling shared by the Enlightenment and the early historism. But a man like Herder was also aware of its darker side. 'All the signs in Europe point to a gradual extinction of national character' (ibid., p. 288). He had expressed this opinion as early as 1774. And yet, in glaring contrast to this, he could, as we have seen, again express the hope that the Slav peoples would once more succeed in achieving the free development of their nationality. In order to substantiate this hope, he had to make a jump from his own peculiar national ideal to an ideal of humanity, and build his hopes at one and the same time upon a future peaceful European association of nations and the development of a universal European humanitarianism. But this hope was undermined by his scepticism whether such a condition would ever be attained, and by his sorrow at the disappearance of so many genuine popular cultures. It was clear once again, as in 1774, that there was no road from Herder's picture of the early cultures to his view of the problems constituted by those of a later period.

In spite of this dualism, and therefore the pain with which it was written, this account of the whole development of Western history since the end of the Ancient World remains a splendid achievement. Following in the footsteps of Voltaire and Robertson, he showed how modern Europe had developed out of the most unfavourable and difficult circumstances and conditions. But Herder's work succeeded in combining in a much more intimate and lively manner all the natural elements, especially the geographical, intellectual, political and economic (though trade was somewhat overstressed). To Herder's penetrating eye, chance events and general tendencies all seemed to work in with one another, though this was often somewhat obscured by the pragmatic and moralising observations passed upon individual items. But never before had the great subject of humanity and its historical character been treated at one and the same time with such vital depths and penetration and such cosmic breadth. And in this respect it served as a powerful pattern and incentive to all future research. There is a movement in the whole story, and great richness of colour throughout; there is the most lively perception of all the forces at work, sustained by a desire for culture that has an absolute belief in its own human worth. Both of these, the new perception and the sense of worth and desire for civilised humanity, must have had a powerful effect on his contemporaries. Later, in 1828, Goethe bore witness to the unbelievable effect that this work of Herder's had on the national culture, to such an extent that after a few decades the Germans had as good as forgotten the source from which their new inspiration had come. If the *Sketch* of 1774 was Herder's greatest contribution to the growth of historism, his *Ideas on the Philosophy of Universal History*, on the other hand, was the work that produced the greatest general effect. Admittedly, there was bound to be a certain ambivalence in the effects produced by all Herder's writings, for they suited not only the historianising, but also the moralising interpretation of history. The Schlossers[1] and Rottecks of the early nineteenth century could

---

[1] It is true that Schlosser (*Gesch. des 18. Jahrhunderts*, vol. 4, pt 4, 194 ff.) roundly denies that Herder had the qualities of a historian; yet he declares his *Ideen* to be like 'a light shining in the darkness' as compared with the efforts of the Romantics.

have quoted Herder in support, when they sat in judgement on the political part of world history and championed the rights of humanity.

IV The Late Period

The development of Herder's historical writings might be compared to a rose, which reaches its freshest beauty as it first unfolds from the bud. As it develops more fully, there is already a suggestion of drooping; and in its third stage it threatens to lose its petals, yet can still evoke in every single leaf the remembrance of its first loveliness.

After 1789 it was a question of really nothing but depressing or painful experiences working upon the soul of a sensitive man. First and foremost, there was the tremendous impression made upon Herder by the French Revolution and the world-shaking events that followed it. At first it was a subject for great enthusiasm, though he did not dare express this outwardly in too obvious a fashion; but as with so many others, though in Herder's case rather later on, this gave way to disappointment and a growing horror at the unleashed demons of naked force, despotism and warfare. He wrote in Schiller's *Horen*, in 1795, with obvious reference to the Jacobins, that 'there are men who bring misfortune', 'brazen, proud and insolent men who think they are called upon to re-order all things and stamp their image upon all mankind . . . It is as well that these demons . . . do not often appear; a very few of them could spread misfortune over genera-tions' (vol. 18, pp. 417 ff.). Or, as he wrote in the *Humanitätsbriefe* in 1794, 'we are standing on the brink of an abyss of barbarism' (vol. 17, p. 249). A year before his death he wrote in the *Adrastea* (1802): 'And in *our* day—who does not think of the closing years of the eighteenth century with a feeling of dumb horror?' (vol. 23, p. 486). He had long ago become disgusted with the conservative monarchy of the *ancien régime*, but this counterblast was utterly shattering. It is one of the greatest of trials for the historically-minded thinker when he is unable to descry in any of the contending camps of the con-temporary forces any single point of hope for the future. One would have needed, like the Romantics, to be younger than Herder to see nevertheless a new world of political ideals in the making. But Herder, with his ideals of humanity forged in the stress of 'Sturm und Drang' in days gone by, could only feel himself homeless in the political world of the moment. In natural reaction against this state of affairs, his feelings for his German fatherland might well surge forth with startling strength. But, as we have already noted, he himself had not succeeded in discovering any historically based and effective syn-thesis between nationality and humanity. None the less, he belongs to the spiritual forerunners of such a synthesis, which was in the end worked out in the course of the Prussian rise to power. But Herder died before the dawning of the day that would see this development.

Moreover, he became spiritually and intellectually a lonely man. His friendship with Goethe cooled off after 1793, and there was a positive breach in 1795. But the opposition to the Kantian philosophy, in which Herder did his best to requite the wound that Kant had inflicted on him by his harsh criticism of his philosophy of history, estranged him at the same time from the further development of the whole German intellectual movement which now centred on Kant. Herder, with his deep sense of the inner unity of all the psychic and intellectual powers of mankind, would not and could not understand the necessity which nevertheless existed, and which was pointed out by Kant when he disclosed the inherent limits to this unity.

It is moving to see how Herder, in spite of being worn out with grief and bodily suffering, could not cease to wrestle with the great fundamental problems of history, revolving them again and again in his mind, and repeatedly attempting to give an adequate expression to individual historical phenomena. There was a passion and a sense of personal and intellectual need in his preoccupation with the world of history, such as was often particularly evident in the historical writings of the Enlightenment and historism in its early stages, though with Herder it was exaggerated to an almost nervous extreme. This was a quality in which the later and more mature historism of the nineteenth and early twentieth centuries, with its often dull approach and routine procedures, was sometimes singularly lacking.

The *Briefe zur Beförderung der Humanität* (*Letters on the Promotion of Humanity*) (1793–7) can be considered from the purely historical point of view as a natural conclusion to his philosophy of history of the eighties (in spite of their variegated contents) and as a substitute for the final part that was never written. These letters arose from the need for treating individual themes raised in that work more thoroughly, and mostly with an ethical and pedagogical purpose. The work of his old age, the *Adrastea* (1801–2) continued this same line of thought, but the essays were thin and insipid and excitable in tone—the expression of a wounded heart. They were reminiscent of the repeated attempts of a sick bird to flap its wings. There were some tender, refined and profound thoughts, but they floundered amid a mass of formless outpourings, though there were still traces of genius. And although they do not add anything material to our knowledge of Herder's thought, we cannot altogether pass over this last effort to put it into shape. There were still some glowing embers from the earlier fire.

Right up to the last, it is clear that the substructure of Herder's new historical sense was the Platonic–Neo-Platonic world view. Leibniz had formerly been one of those from whom he had received it, and Herder gratefully remembers him in the *Adrastea*. But the objections now raised against him show that Herder did not feel him to be Neo-Platonic enough. He sensed in Leibniz a certain temporal element, a tendency towards a more mathematic world of thought, and the 'fine thread of propriety'. The concept of harmony worked out by Leibniz was too dualistic for Herder, and his monads were too remote from our spiritual experience. And so the Platonists, mystics, magicians, Spinozans and so forth 'could not get away from the feeling that the world is a *single* whole, even in respect of what we call matter, and is informed by *one* single spirit'. Even Leibniz's final causes 'appeared to them to be no more than a limited human point of view, for in the eternal world everything must needs serve both as a means and an end for everything else' (vol. 23, p. 484). From this standpoint, a light is thrown back on the great idea in the *Sketch* of 1774 which was so important for historism—the idea that as in the Kingdom of God in general, so also in history, everything is simultaneously both means and end (cf. also vol. 18, pp. 19 ff. on mysticism and Neo-Platonism).

Now, however, Herder did not find it as easy as formerly to understand in the light of such a universal outlook and *sub specie aeterni* the individual phenomena of history in their specific settings and interconnections, and yet draw comfort and reassurance from the progress of the whole. His inner nature, with its restless 'tension between mournful consciousness of finality and ardent longing for the eternal' (H. Unger, *Novalis und Kleist*, p. 78), was not of a sort that could maintain in perpetuity the balance once achieved between these two. We have already noted this in his philosophy of history and seen how the temporal events of history exercised a divisive effect upon his philosophy. Even more disturbing to his peace of mind were the events of world history during the nineties. 'History is like the thread of an endless screw, an evil confusion, unless it is enlightened by reason and ordered by morality' (vol. 23, p. 50). But reason and morality, to which he now clung as the saving principles of order, were ideas from the treasury of the Enlightenment and the ideals of humanity, and stood so to speak on a lower and more human level than the exalted assurance concerning the history of the world nourished by Neo-Platonism, which he had expressed in 1774 in that watchword 'chance, destiny, divinity'.

Herder did not exactly lose faith in his old age in this idea of destiny which blended with the notions of chance and divinity. But he turned it in a different direction, and more towards the sphere of ethics. In one of the essays in his *Adrastea* on fables he characterises a group of fables as 'demonic or destiny-fables' because they 'portray the higher processes of destiny among living beings'. In other words, the course of nature does not always suffice for clearly demonstrating why such-and-such a thing is bound to follow as a necessary consequence of something else. At this point, there comes into play the great and loftier sequence of events which are sometimes called chance and sometimes destiny, and show why this or that particular thing has come, if not precisely *out of*, at any rate *after*, something else, by reason of a higher ordering of events.

> In the finest fables of this sort our souls become as great
> and wide as creation; Adrastea (= Nemesis) is, we feel, the
> power that works in hidden fashion to deal out justice in all
> things, guide all things, and govern all things. She watches over
> the oppressed and casts down the wrongdoer; she avenges and
> she rewards (vol. 23, pp. 265 ff.).

Thus Herder's conception of destiny, once so intangibly and vaguely used to hint at a higher providence in history, was now narrowed down to something more intelligible, to a doctrine we have already seen advanced in his philosophy of history. This was the doctrine of balance, the disturbance and the restoration of equilibrium, or as he again and again calls it in his old age, the doctrine of Nemesis, and the judgement which holds sway over all history and sooner or later brings all wrongdoing and iniquity to account. This idea of Nemesis now became his chief historical compass on the stormy seas of the contemporary world. He now enunciates the theme that history is either nothing but an irrational repetition of external chance events, or it is a world presided over by none other than the goddess Adrastea (Nemesis), that keen-sighted observer, that strict requiter, who administers the loftiest justice and is worthy of the highest veneration (vol. 24, p. 327).

Herder now saw in Herodotus the model of the faithful and unbiased historian who recorded without prejudice the workings of fate (vol. 18, p. 283 and vol. 24, pp. 326 ff.). Recent political history, which he dealt with in several individual essays on historical personalities, was thus reduced to the level of some middle-class tragic drama or moralising character-sketch. Added to which there was a recurrence of the old pragmatism, though in a psychologically rather more refined form (cf. e.g. on Charles XII and Peter the Great, vol. 23, pp. 415 ff.).

Yet he was all the while clearly aware that there was another possible way of understanding political history. This was 'cold history', as handled in the coldest and perhaps cleverest fashion by Machiavelli, a history that forgets all questions of right and wrong, measures the result of certain given forces with the accuracy of a geometrician, and is continually calculating on some plan. Thus Herder critically discussed in his declining years the historical writing of the *ancien régime* which had been guided by the leading idea of reasons of State. He was clear-sighted enough to perceive that this had constituted a great and challenging undertaking. Human powers in relation to their effects and consequences—was not this the most intricate and important problem confronting our human race? It is extremely instructive to hear what Herder has to say by way of answer and criticism to this historical writing, because from the point of view of the history of thought it reveals both the weakness of these authors and the weakness of his own position.

Herder came to the conclusion that this was a problem which could not, generally speaking, be neatly and tidily solved because of the complication of the interacting forces in politics and the inter-mixture with chance at innumerable points. Thus this school of writers often became a school for writers of fiction, making false retrospective calculations on the basis of a glittering success, or a school of despair. In general, however, this was a whetstone for the wits which easily made the mind too sharp and jagged (*Humanitäts-briefe*, vol. 18, pp. 90 ff., cf. also vol. 16, p. 587).

This was a true criticism. Political history based upon political expediency was lacking in inspiration because it was deficient in the sense of forces and currents going beyond conscious and deliberate action, in the feeling for individuality and development in the whole historical process. Herder had begun to arouse this sense, but he did not set himself to breathe this spirit into the writing of political history, or even show any desire to do so. For the State itself did not now appear to him to have any living individuality, but seemed simply to be a human apparatus managed by ambitious and power-seeking men. True, he admitted that even this 'cold history' could often become very warm, and that the good of the fatherland and the honour of the nation could easily be raised to the level of a clarion call. Indeed, he heard this message proclaimed, but he did not believe in it. Every glance that he took into the world of political action only showed him a labyrinth of the most complicated and distasteful affairs. He was thoroughly afraid of the spirit that held everything to be permissible for the welfare of the State, that is (as he understood it), for the benefit of kings and ministers. Humanity, he saw, was only too apt to be forgotten (vol. 18, p. 282).

But this brings us back once more to the break in Herder's histor-ical thinking. We know that there seems at this point to be some profound and general fatality at work. This political writing of history based upon reasons of State, this 'cold history', certainly contained (as we have often emphasised) the germ and starting-point for a vital and inspired understanding of the large-scale political history of the world in terms of the individual. But neither the political nor the intellectual climate was favourable to its growth. The absolutist State, which was chiefly reflected in such historical writing, was itself too cold and calculating, still too narrowly based upon a small social class, still too little permeated by any national life, to be viewed as anything else but cold by those who served it as historians. And the intellectual atmosphere, with its ideas of Natural Law, its pragmatism, and its psychology which failed to take account of the full life of the soul, was directly calculated to represent the world of political authority and action as a self-contained interplay of political craft or ineptitude. The three great Englishmen of the Enlightenment, Hume, Gibbon and Robertson, who had gone furthest in presenting political history in scrupulously factual terms, leave us nevertheless with a feeling of coldness and emptiness. In the great battle begun in the eighteenth century for a breakthrough towards a more inspired and warm-blooded kind of thinking, and so a deeper interpretation of history, Herder had probably made the most notable advance up till now. But even he had come to a despairing halt before the walls of the contemporary political world, now more than ever under attack from the onslaughts of a revolutionary age. Herder himself had not fought this battle for a complete breakthrough to a finish, nor had he completely overcome the shackles of Natural Law. It was still thought based upon Natural Law in a refined form when he set up his ideal of humanity, and then the allied idea of Nemesis, as an absolute standard over against the whole of political history.

The gap could not be filled until a great change came over the climate of opinion with the end of the wars of revolution and national revolt. It was a gap that Herder, as a son of the eighteenth century, was not able to fill. Ranke, bringing to the task some of Herder's sympathetic insight, succeeded in bringing new life and warmth to 'cold history'. The beginnings of a new national spirit in the life of the State opened his eyes to the hidden inner vitality that had existed in spite of all appearances behind the political expediency of the *ancien régime*.

But this process of nationalism had already begun in principle with the French Revolution, and Herder's relationship to it was not entirely confined to first greeting it with enthusiasm and then later on holding out his shield of Nemesis against it. When he saw how a whole people, whose ideas of humanity he himself shared, exaggerated them to the point of delusion and did the most monstrous things under their spell, his historical thinking took yet another turn which brought it very near to the irrationalism of the 'Sturm und Drang' period. Testimony to this is to be found in the notable treatise on illusion and madness among human beings to be found in the *Humanitätsbriefe* of 1794 (vol. 17, pp. 226 ff.). His own experiences showed him what a fine line there is between illusion and truth, so that 'even the most careful self-scrutiny hardly enables one to say where the dividing-line comes'. But Herder was disposed to consider illusion and madness as less far apart than is commonly supposed. He saw how the great changes in the world had been wrought by men who were half deluded, and how 'in many a glorious deed and many a successful transaction in life there is some kind of permanent madness'. And now there was this French national madness. 'National madness is a fearsome name. But what has once taken root in a nation, been recognised and exalted by it—how can that be other than the truth? Who could have any doubts about it?' Herder could dimly sense how his own most personal achievement in asserting the specific rights of particular peoples and the national spirit inspiring them would be swept away in the whirlpool of doubt and horror raised by this new spirit of militant nationalism. He hinted to his readers that he was confronting them with the horrible prospect of a world that was becoming a madhouse. He stood aghast before the whole world of the irrational forces in history, both those that were creative and those that were frankly sinister.

As a sympathiser with the 'Sturm und Drang' movement, Herder had only felt the more creative side of these forces, and it was from this that his new historical sense had arisen. But now, in the evening of life, the dark and demonic side made itself more strongly apparent; and this represented a first step towards the deepening of his own interpretation of history. Meanwhile, to be sure, he had not altogether escaped the dangers of moralism in his exhortation to his readers to look history calmly and squarely in the face and discern the workings of illusion and madness within it. He exhorted them not to harp in thoughtless fashion on what had happened a thousand times in history, nor to fear that this was the end of the world. Least of all were they to take sides in hatred and anger with one of the parties involved in this blind frenzy. Time alone could cure the illusions, and a free examination of the truth was the only adequate weapon against it.

The stream of human knowledge is always being purified by a clash of opposites and by strong contrasts. At one point it will diminish, at another it will be intensified; but at length mankind will receive as truth an illusion that has been through a long period of much purification.

There was something of historical dialectic in this exalted treatment of the irrational elements in history.

Here, then, there are once more signs of the great and creative Herder. Once again, he was obsessed by the problem he had already attempted to solve in his philosophy of history—how to treat human history as 'natural history' (taking the term 'nature' in the special sense adopted by Herder). He contemplated writing a work that would portray the individualities of all peoples and stocks (he still avoided using the word 'race') from a genetical standpoint, with due regard to their peculiar and specific ways of life. He would represent the world as a 'great garden, in which peoples grew like plants, in which everything—air, earth, water, sunshine and light—yes, and even the caterpillar creeping upon them and the worm devouring them—was part of the whole' (vol. 18. pp. 246 ff.). But this was to thrust the principle of individuality so much to the fore that it became a peculiar kind of relativism, a recognition of the completely equal status of all peoples and (in modern parlance) races. 'He who explores nature acts upon no order of rank among the creatures he observes, for they are all equally dear and precious to him. So must it also be with the natural explorer of humanity.' Least of all must our European culture serve as a standard of general human goodness and human values. Yet this must not be construed to mean that Herder had given up the ideal of humanity which had arisen from this very European culture. He used it again and again in these gloomy years of his old age as the standard by which alone things could be measured and understood. So there is at this point a reappearance of the old dilemma, the inner contradiction inherent in Herder's world of thought. He wanted to treat historically the life of all the peoples, in a decisive and logical manner which should present the Negro and the European as only two different and equally valuable letters in the great word spelt out by our human race. And yet at the same time, though quite unconsciously, he was giving an absolute value to the finest product of the culture to which he himself belonged. We have noted repeatedly how he had recourse to ethics, and ethics of the noblest kind, in order to subdue the phenomena of history that offended him. But now, and for precisely the same reasons, he took refuge in a radical relativism (and here one can see the two poles of his thought lit up with luminous clarity), a relativism with respect to the manifold varieties of human culture. Like Rousseau before him, he escaped from a disgust with his own times and the excesses of contemporary culture into the world of primitive humanity. He overvalued it, as he had always been inclined to do, out of love for the fresh springs of originality, but also out of a hatred for harshness and presumption (which can be discerned early on, but becomes more burning in his ideas for the philosophy of history), the harshness and presumption with which the colonial European treated the primitive races. And finally, is it not reasonable to suppose that this radical relativism, the recognition of the equal value of all races and peoples, was involuntarily nourished by the principles of equality upheld by the French Revolution, which represented the latest logical consequences of the old Natural Law? The threads of the history of thought are always strangely intertwined, and the disruptive and hostile elements have an unexpected way of producing favourable results. This is something that belongs very much to the dialectic of history. But even this does not suffice to explain the whole, because in isolation it can only offer a bloodless dynamic of ideas. It needed the living and inimitable human being Herder, with all the strong and weak points of his psychic and sensuous constitution, and with all his life's experiences, to weave the web of ideas we have been examining in a way that was so full of genius and yet so incomplete.

We must refrain from giving any further examples of such complexes (but cf. *Adrastea*, vol. 23, p. 89). It may be said in conclusion that even in Herder's old age he was still capable of producing strikingly beautiful late blooms of the most splendid and purest kind in respect to the history of ideas. From poetry, he says in the *Humanitätsbriefe* (vol. 18, p. 137), we certainly acquire a deeper knowledge of periods and nations than from the deceptive and desperate ways of politics and warfare. Herder's first great discovery had been that true poetry is protean in form. It is never final and canonical, but always continues to reveal the fullness of the most varied ties, peoples and individualities. He still had something important to say in his treatise on the difference between the older and newer peoples to be found in their poetry (vol. 18, pp. 1 ff.). There is something light and buoyant, something gentle and sensitive, about these sketches. Aesthetic and historical evaluation, with only a few pieces interspersed of a classical or ethical and humanitarian flavour, were blended together in the closest harmony. Everywhere he tried to discover internal links of development; everywhere he sought out the individual meaning of each poetical production. From 1500 onwards the picture becomes more colourless, because now (apart from Shakespeare) there were no longer any great works to inspire him, and the artificial poetry of these times had long ago ceased to satisfy him (cf. vol. 8, pp. 413 ff.). The works that he had studied during his lifetime appeared to him ever more ineffable and incomprehensible in all the fullness of their content. 'I am constantly assailed by a fear' (he says in this essay, vol. 18, p. 56), 'when I hear a whole nation or period characterised in a few short words; for what a vast multitude of differences is embraced by the word "nation", or "the middle centuries", or "ancient and modern times"! I am equally embarrassed when I hear people using expressions about a whole nation or epoch in general. How little does the person often think or know who is most ready to express his opinion in words!'

We are apt to forget with respect to such confessions (and Herder himself forgot) the extent of his achievement in overcoming the limited outlook of the Enlightenment. For out of resentment against individual phenomena of his time he often became the champion of the earlier Enlightenment and dealt with its representatives in a markedly sympathetic manner. He could even have some commendatory things to say about the historians of the Enlightenment, Robertson, Gibbon and even Voltaire, as fellow-labourers in the field of humanity; and the tone was indeed very different from the ridicule dealt out to them in the *Sketch* of 1774 (vol. 5, p. 524). His words did not betray the extent to which he himself had advanced beyond the heights they had attained (vol. 24, pp. 331 ff.; cf. also vol. 23, p. 217).

In the end, the position with Herder was perhaps rather like that of Columbus: he did not realise that he had discovered a new world.[1] Yet this can hardly be maintained in unqualified terms. In the suppressed portions of the *Humanitätsbriefe*, there is a remark which shows that Herder was fully conscious of the 'immense strides' made in the interpretation and understanding of the Bible and Greek and Roman literature in the course of his lifetime (vol. 18, p. 321).

> The reasons for our advantage are being perceived as with the help of time we have penetrated more deeply into the nature of the material, the content, and purpose of language and expression and history, and concern ourselves with *living in the world of ideas* inhabited by the Greeks and Romans.

He was certainly quick to point out at the same time what he had long ago recognised, namely that this world was no longer our world. And yet he was still stirred by faint hopes that by the effects on the rising generation of the old ideals of liberty a flame could be kindled which would 'as it were arise from the ancient embers and imprint itself to our own times'. This could be regarded as a kind of prognosis of the German revolutionary movement of 1813, for Herder seems to have had a premonitory sense of things to come, and to have possessed the gift that often goes with historical genius.[2] But the most

[1] There were even some utterances by him from earlier years on the science of history raising this question; cf. *Denkmal Winckelmanns* (1778), 8, 466 ff. and 9, 334.

[2] Cf. especially the great prognosis in 18, 289 ff., that the Daemons of Europe might bring things to such a pass that in Abyssinia, China and Japan 'intellectual and animal powers could become combined in a way that we can scarcely imagine'.

important thing for understanding the outlook of his old age is to realise that his newly acquired art of historical understanding was now to serve as a method of 'living in the Greek and Roman world of ideas'. And here we seem to catch the scent of Schiller's Weimar classicism and new humanism, of Goethe as he then was, and the youthful Wilhelm von Humboldt. As seen by one of the stoutest pioneers of historism, the intellectual revolution brought about by it looked like a new-style renaissance of Antiquity, and the means of recreating a world of ideas that should draw its sustenance from the Ancient World. Once more, then, we see the blending of historical and absolute thought, though more intimately and sublimely than before.

Towards the end of the chapter on Winckelmann, we already had occasion to note that the contradiction between the idealising and the individualising trends of thought that runs through the German movement could in actual fact lead to an interlacing of the two. And in order to understand this we may remind ourselves that even in the early stages of Herder's historism he was confronted with the problem of how to set limits to the relativism that immediately arose from the historical outlook, and how to maintain the permanent in the midst of flux, in order to avoid simply going under in the sheer welter and multiplicity of historical phenomena which was only just beginning to be understood in fluid and genetical terms. These naive early explorers of the new territory emerged from the dogmatic trammels of Natural Law which had restricted the thought of previous centuries into the new world of individuality and development; and in so doing, they found a naive fulfilment of their needs, to a large extent in quite unlogical and unreflecting ways, simply by the possession of more solid and permanent ideals. It was the same with Herder in his ideal of humanity, and finally in his idealistic renaissance of the antique spirit. But his most vital inner impulse was and remained that of Platonism and Neo-Platonism, combined with a Christian and Protestant universal faith which had implications (though not realised by him) far beyond the temporal limitations of his human and classical ideals. Was it possible to go further along the road of historism that Herder had pioneered than he himself had managed to, starting out from this universal faith? Goethe was to provide the answer. Of the four great direct effects produced by the mind and spirit of Herder—the effect on Romanticism, on the Slav nationalities, on the humane and natural sciences in general, and on Goethe himself, Goethe must now occupy the foremost place in our study. He had been stirred up by Herder at Strassburg and made aware of his own kindred but much more powerful daemon. And now, developing from the depths of his own resources and over a long span of life the ideas of Herder that were pregnant with the future, he gave them a new impress, thus making them for the first time effective in the secular world, in spite of the limitations which even he was perhaps destined to impose upon them.

'There is something everlasting in all that is beautiful', says Herder in the *Adrastea* (vol. 24, p. 349), after mentioning the names of Plato and Shaftesbury. These words portray the cosmic and aesthetic thought of both Herder and Goethe. In both of them, the sense of the eternal to be found in all beauty also shed its light upon all the structures of history. But just as the finite and temporal limitations of the observer proved a limitation in Herder's thinking, so the same problem was destined to recur and repeat itself in Goethe.

Chapter ten

Goethe

Introduction

Without Goethe, we should not be what we are. There would be no difficulty in demonstrating the truth of this statement, and anyone attempting the task would run the risk of becoming pedantic. Effects like those produced by Goethe, which have changed the whole mental climate, can only be the outcome of an intuitive combination of extensive knowledge and individual inner experience. True, Kant and Hegel led contemporary thinking along new paths which may appear to have made a more recognisably permanent mark than Goethe. Again, Schiller's poetry, although the thought-content is often predominant, has had a deeper effect on the sensitivities of the German heart, at least in the nineteenth century, because its appeal is more immediate and his colours simpler than Goethe's. But no one has had as profound an effect as Goethe on thought and feeling together, on the whole area of the inner life. Not even the Romantics, not even their forerunner Herder, in spite of the great effects they undoubtedly produced over the entire field of experience. And it is on a steady interaction between thought and feeling that the whole historical sense depends. In order to clarify its genesis and development, one must look for its sources of nourishment in the inner lives of men. If one is convinced that the German psyche, and many minds outside Germany, have been profoundly changed by the infusion of Goethe's thought and feeling (though this has sometimes been intermittent, it has always renewed its silent influence), the question immediately arises whether this change has not also benefited the new sense of history and the origin of historism.

It is not a valid objection that Goethe was only marginally a historian, and that his concern with history only represents a small sector of his whole mighty circle of activity. Nor can it be usefully objected that, as we shall show, he again and again throughout the course of his life questioned the value of universal history and our knowledge of it. Goethe was, and could not help being, first and foremost a creative and constructive poet and artist, and then a researcher into nature, who thought that the knowledge of nature which he acquired would also provide a key for understanding the essential life of the whole world. In the *Annalen* of 1817, Goethe designated as the three great subjects of study Nature, Art and Life; there is no mention here of History. But the manner in which he balanced these three great subjects one against the other was bound to lead him sooner or later into history. For he rejected the dangerous and deadly principle of 'art for art's sake', and explained that he valued life above art, which was only an adornment of life. Ultimately, however, life and nature were one in Goethe's eyes, for they constituted the realm of 'living nature', where alone he could breathe freely, a sphere which included the whole world of history. Here, like Herder, he did indeed meet with resistances which his principles of enquiry were not altogether able to overcome. And he therefore certainly did not study history with the same passion as nature and the human heart. Yet he never entirely deserted it, or there would otherwise have been an obvious gap in his universal picture of the world's life. Thus he arrived at a certain discrepancy between his two attitudes to history, which hovered between deep satisfaction and an equally deep dissatisfaction. The first led him on to a splendid development of the historical sense aroused by Herder and Möser; the second, as we shall show, arose not only from Goethe's own problems, but from those of the whole eighteenth century.

But there is a special peculiarity of Goethe's thought which gives a distinctive colouring to this discrepancy in his historical judgement. There is something wonderfully natural, to be sure, about all his thinking. The world of objects needed only to breathe very lightly upon his spirit to evoke an echo and stir him to utterance. Goethe never seems to overstrain himself, he never appears affected, as is so often the case with speculative philosophers or pointed epigram-writers. As Schiller said of Goethe, he only needed to shake the tree quite gently for fully ripe fruit to fall to the ground in abundance. Or, to apply to him a picture used by himself in a letter to Zelter, 1823, where he writes that things have the same effect on him as music does on ordinary folk: the clenched fist is undone and the hand relaxes.

Genuine originality is shown by the fact that only a slight impulse is needed to set it in motion, after which it knows of itself how to follow in its own particular independent fashion the path of truth, excellence and permanence (to Purkinje, 1826).

Thus Goethe could think with such apparent ease because his inner man was capable of the most tremendous activity. He once spoke of the Etna within his breast. All our thinking is based upon an undifferentiated and formless lava of the soul. But Goethe gave to everything conceived by him an unforced form, the famous 'inner form' that suited it as the peel suits the apple and the apple the peel. And yet one often gets a hint of the magma within him precisely in his historical judgements and the discrepancies between them. When compared with one another, they cannot easily be reduced to a common denominator: there is often something divergent and iridescent in the colours. He speaks on one occasion of the quicksilver of his mind, in which the globules easily roll apart, but come together again with equal ease. Thus these historical judgements were apt to be both fluid and solid, both centrifugal and centripetal, at one and the same time. In conversation he could at times give the impression of flitting from one train of thought to another. 'I am already in Erfurt when you think I am still at Weimar. Have I reached eighty years of age for no other purpose but having always to think the same?'

All this helps to explain the marked contradictions to be found in Goethe's historical judgements. Without a doubt, there is a good deal of utterance on the spur of the moment; thought that, so to speak, suddenly overflows. But amid the unexampled pliability of his mind the most unprecedented fact of all is that there is not a single judgement to be found which is not somehow related to the deep calm centre of his soul. For such was the man who had his being deeper down beneath the magma of the surface.

And so Goethe affects us in contradictory, as well as in unified fashion; simply and yet boundlessly; mysteriously yet obviously, at one and the same time—just like nature. The picture of nature sketched by him was also a reflection of his own mind and spirit. As Fichte once observed of *The Daughter*: 'with a vitality that gathers itself together into one, and yet flows forth at the same time into eternity'. In his picture of the gods, man is painting his own portrait. Certainly we can discern in Goethe's thought the broad structural lines which make the details intelligible. But they are of a different quality from those of Kant or Schiller, which are conceptually easier to grasp, or the more wavering lines of Herder or Novalis, which are more to be sensed than seen. It has been said that Goethe looks out into the world, but Herder lends an ear to it (*Suphan*). We may expand what we have said above about Goethe's special gifts of perception and observation, which were as strong in him as the capacity for sensitive feeling was in Herder. Goethe possessed a passionate need for observation, which was never content with a single view of an object, but was always constrained to examine it afresh. This was apt to bring about a rapid shift of standpoint that was not always easy for his audience to follow. The result was that observation, feeling and reflection always worked together in what we commonly call the Goethe thought-process; and this means that in its broad lines it is a peculiar combination of clarity and immeasurable depth, of straightforwardness and an enticing, though not confusing, mysteriousness.

Only by this triad of observation, feeling and reflection could the historical sense reach completeness. Our task is now to explore the extent to which this triad, which is so marked in Goethe, developed into the fullness of the historical outlook.

It would seem that this search will lead us along two lines. On the one hand, it will be imperative to show the step-by-step development of Goethe's relationship to history. But we shall also have to attempt to show the inner connections of his historical thought, and to some extent establish his historical methods. Our procedure will thus resemble the ascent of a mountain, in which to start with the view is confined to the immediate surroundings, though now and again wider glimpses open up; but the whole scene can only be surveyed in tranquillity from the heights.

The Genetic Part

I *The Early Period up to 1775*

For the genetic part of our enquiry, Goethe once put forward a method when in his old age he was speaking of the way in which an 'original artist' should be appreciated (*Art and Antiquity*). First and foremost, we should look at his power and its expression. (In the case of Goethe, this task can only be fulfilled by our treatment of the subject as a whole.) Then we should look at the man's immediate environment, insofar as it hands down to him certain subjects, skills and attitudes; and lastly, we should look further afield and examine not so much the extent of the man's extraneous knowledge, as the use he makes of it. For there are often good influences at work upon the world for centuries before their effects can actually be traced. Goethe maintained to Eckermann in 1828 that it was ridiculous to look for the sources of a famous man's inspiration, for that would be an endless and unnecessary search. But the modern spirit of research would hardly admit this to be true; it would maintain that in this utterance the artist in Goethe was overshadowing the scholar. That may be so. And yet, confronted by such a phenomenon as Goethe, we may well discover that his principle retains its validity. It belongs to the highest degree of genius to combine an endless receptivity with an endless power of remoulding what has been received from within and transforming it into something new and peculiarly its own. Every moment there is something received and something born anew. His own genius develops as it finds permanent sustenance in the genius of historical mankind. This can also be said of Herder and the other great figures we have already examined. But it was a mark of Goethe's superior mental power that he transformed all the nourishment he received from outside more easily, quickly and imperceptibly into his own flesh and blood. We can therefore leave the somewhat divisive question concerning the separate sources of his historical thought in the background and content ourselves with a few indications on the subject. In a general way, there is no difficulty about recognising the mental influences that worked upon Goethe's historical thinking. As far as they were centred round the intellectual and spiritual treasury of the past, they consisted of the Bible, Homer and Shakespeare; as far as they embodied personalities of his own century, they were Leibniz, Shaftesbury, Voltaire, Rousseau, Hamann, Herder and Möser. But if we were to extend the field to the wider spheres of culture, there would be first and foremost Greek antiquity, which all his life served him as a guiding star in nature, art and life, but was only of indirect influence in his historical thought; then there would be the whole movement of the Enlightenment, and Neo-Platonism. Although Goethe in his early years rejected the spirit of the Enlightenment, it nevertheless left permanent marks on his historical thought. As we shall see, he managed to fuse it with his Neo-Platonism—or with what might perhaps be more fitly called his Spinozan thought tinged with Neo-Platonism. In the case of this, the most important of all the elements involved, however, the mere search for the sources of Goethe's inspiration (what he read in his youth, such as Shaftesbury etc.) is likely to prove unsatisfactory. The truth is that he immediately and spontaneously seized upon all that was in accordance with his nature, selecting it from all the other possible constructive material, and shaped it anew for his own purposes. To adopt Goethe's own expression, we may say that there was a wind blowing through the centuries, which was destined to strike him just at this particular point.

The same forces were at work to which Herder was so powerfully wedded. In his case, we mentioned pietism as the third force that affected him, first through the agency of Hamann, and then directly during the Bückeburg period. Goethe, too, came decisively under its influence during the years of his youth. But as compared with the Enlightenment and Neo-Platonism, this was only a secondary influence. Thus he was spared Herder's fate of having to wrestle with theological problems as well in the course of his historical thinking. Goethe only imbibed as it were a whiff of the soul-stirring pietistic movement. But this and his permanent relationship with the Bible ensured that the German Protestant element built up by Luther would form an integral part of Goethe's mentality.

We shall follow Goethe's advice and trace out the influences arising from his immediate environment and the general attitude he inherited from it.

But these influences can never be precisely and completely separated from the man who undergoes them. The man and his milieu together constitute a unified life that has grown up in partnership. When the man's own powers develop, it may divide in its upper parts; but its lower parts reach down to a mysterious combination of germ, root and fertile soil. We must take the place and the time together, for they too are intimately linked in growth. As Goethe was to write later on in his *Theory of Colours*, the generation from which a man comes is often more manifest in him than in the abstract, and the year of his birth is his true horoscope—that is to say, the position of earthly affairs when he is born. This would appear to be the meaning of the ancient Orphic teaching, where there is no hard and fast line between the man and his temporal and local milieu, between the position of the planets and the indivisible form of his individuality, but rather a mysterious fusion of the two.

Goethe was born at Frankfurt about the middle of the eighteenth century. This means that he sprang from a rather decaying, yet thoroughly honourable and colourful past.[1] And among the many-sided aspects of his genius, as he himself strongly affirms, was the basic attraction towards the antiquarian which was so marked in Möser, and which led Goethe as a boy to examine the relics of a former historical life that surrounded him on every hand. We have only to recall the famous pictures in *Dichtung und Wahrheit* (*Fiction and Truth*). And so from the very start Goethe's attitude to the world of history was strongly conditioned. In addition to this, there was the pedantic regimentation of the local life which passed for public life at the time, or rather was a substitute for it. Corresponding to this in Goethe's character was his submissiveness to the existing authorities,

[1] The threads of his relationship to history in his younger days have been analysed more deeply than was possible within the compass of this present book in the careful work by W. Lehmann, *Goethes Geschichtsauffassung in ihren Grundlagen* (1930).

which we also noted in Möser, the 'reverence', as he calls it, to which he was by nature inclined. In later life, this was to be raised to the level of the three great reverences—for what is above us, what is on our level, and what is beneath us. But there was no question of any blind respect, though tradition might seem to have inclined him that way. For his native critical sense was not slow to discover the dead and the harmful elements in the surviving remnants of the past that lay round about him. Later on, as he looked back, he could see why the German poet was bound to be a different man from the English poet in his native land, where the great historical struggles over the centuries had produced a free, lively and proud national life, concerned with the present and highly progressive. Goethe had already felt the force of this in Shakespeare; and in his old age, when reading Walter Scott's novels, he often held forth on the subject. This shows how definitely (though without any trace of envy) he noted this difference, which he characterised as 'a lack of national feeling' in himself (*Dichtung und Wahrheit*). It should be stated at the outset that not only his poetry, but also his historical thinking, was lacking in the direct stimulus that comes from great national and political incentives. The environment in which he grew up served as a field for observation, but did not invite the vital co-operation of his strength and will-power. Even the experience of King Frederick II and the Seven Years War remained no more than an exalting spectacle to be watched, without feeling the temptation to take any personal part in it. 'What did Prussia matter to us? It was the *personality* of the great king that impressed us all.' Here we are already confronted in germinal form with a fundamental attitude of Goethe to the events of political history—the delight in a great personality, combined with indifference to the material concerns of politics.

But the experiences of the Seven Years War in Germany set in train a wave reaction which became one of the great driving forces behind the 'Sturm und Drang' movement. In connection with the well-known judgement expressed by Goethe, and the similar judgement of Möser (see above, pp. 280 ff.), the effect of the Seven Years War may perhaps be expressed as follows: As far as the classes were concerned who were seeking to create a better position for themselves, the life that a man himself led became once again of major importance in Germany. Up till now, the powers in the shape of custom and religion, society and the State, had so channelled the individual's life in traditionally accepted forms that scarcely anyone ventured to raise himself above the general conventional level. But now, in the person of Frederick the Great, who was both a freethinker and a hero, and knew how to order his own destiny, there came the first powerful breach in the world of custom and practice hallowed by tradition. This new experience was so well assimilated that not only the objective power of the State, which he himself served, but also the subjective manner of life, were felt to be important. It is surely possible that this drama of a historical hero witnessed by its contemporaries helped to prepare their minds for Shakespeare's heroic drama. As far as Goethe himself is concerned, this possibility cannot be ignored when one reflects on the quiet, powerful, lifelong effect of Frederick the Great's heroic career on his mind and spirit, an effect that extends even to the closing scenes of *Faust*. But if we consider Shakespeare's effect on Goethe, and its connection with his relationship to history, we are plunged straight into the middle of the great breakthrough of the Strassburg period, into the combined effort of all his mental powers to express themselves originally and reveal for the first time his full individual talent. This talent was indeed original, but it was roused to life by Herder, who had himself already experienced a breakthrough into a new kind of historical thought. But Herder had not been able to impart to Goethe anything beyond what was potentially his already. Yet it is through the long line of great kindred spirits which maintains the intellectual and spiritual life of mankind that Herder was able to arouse these potential gifts. Thus Herder's 'Sturmwind' helped to work out Goethe's destiny.

> Wind mischt vom Grund aus schäumende Wogen . . .
> Schicksal des Menschen, wie gleichst du dem Wind![1]

Herder's guidance of the youthful Goethe at Strassburg took the particular form of introducing him to Shakespeare, and so in a special sense to the world of history. In June 1771 he had expressed the opinion that Shakespeare's dramas must really be understood as history, 'so full, so complete, so alive that they can only belong to the category of actual world events' (vol. 5, p. 236; cf. p. 303 above). It was under this influence that Goethe wrote his effusion for the Shakespeare commemoration day, 14 October 1771:

Shakespeare's theatre is a beautiful casket of treasures in which the history of the world surges past before our eyes, bound by the invisible threads of time. Judged by the accepted canons of style, his plots are no true plots; but his plays all revolve round the mysterious point (which no philosopher has so far been able to locate or define) where the uniqueness of our ego, and the assertive freedom of our will, collide with the necessary course of events as a whole.

[1] The wind uplifts and blends the foaming wave . . .
Oh wind of destiny, thou dost the same in human lives.

The essence of history is thus the struggle between the deeper individuality and its need for freedom and the forces of the objective world. History as a whole is a countless number of individual foci, each charged with energy, and each carrying a particular destiny. But 'a countless number' is putting it too mildly, for these centres of energy are not merely separate and side by side, like men as pictured by the Enlightenment, but are joined together into a great whole which leads its own pre-eminent life.

To what extent is this assertive freedom represented here as a genuine freedom, or is anything and everything in fact subject to necessity? Goethe did not answer this riddle because it was beyond his power. But he proclaimed in the same breath: 'Nature, Nature! There is nothing so natural as Shakespeare's men and women.' This is the first clear indication that history to Goethe meant nothing else than a department of nature in the largest sense. It is well known that as he stood on the threshold of the 'Sturm und Drang' movement, nature meant for Goethe 'inner, ardent, sacred life' (*Werther*)—the irrational and infinitely powerful creative source of everything, high and low, good and evil, to which both of them necessarily belonged, both together, and 'as a whole'. This nature, however, was nothing but the reflection of his own subjective genius in all its stirrings; but it was definitely a subjective approach, a feeling of being indissolubly interwoven with the whole texture of the world.

This rhapsodic conception of nature, and history as a part of nature, was therefore capable not only of subjective enthusiasm, but also of digesting the actual forces and specific phenomena of history. So when Goethe came to Strassburg, the battleground for German and French culture, a new element was added to all the other ferments in the intellectual life of the time which were then bursting the bonds of thinking based upon Natural Law and liberating the irrational powers of the soul in abundance. This was the feeling of 'an emerging Germanity' (*Dichtung und Wahrheit*). The hours that Goethe spent within the cathedral at Strassburg, or contemplating it from outside, during the years 1771–2, belong to the great moments in the history of German thought, for it was a time when something radically new was being proclaimed. Here, if anywhere, was the place where under Herder's stirring influence the new sense of German identity was most likely to 'emerge', as it confronted a work created 'by the strong, rough German soul against the dark priest-ridden background of the Middle Ages'. This was also the first recognition of creative power in the despised Middle Ages, and a first ray of light piercing its darkness; but as far as we can see there was no intention of lightening this darkness as a whole, or giving a new look to the whole of the Middle Ages. Nor does this enthusiastic

confession made in the heat of youth suggest any step towards unravelling Erwin's[1] work according to the method he was to learn later
on, the method of 'deciphering by means of development', and of
examining it in the light of assumptions that make it intelligible. As
Goethe wrote to a friend (Röderer, 21 September 1771), his work,
that of a *great* mind, 'without regard to what others have produced,
must appear with a touch of timelessness about it'. At the time, he
still needed to see great achievements based upon the primal powers
of humanity as sudden and miraculous eruptions. We have already
noticed this timeless trait in Young's doctrine of original genius,
which had such a powerful effect on the 'Sturm und Drang' movement (cf. p. 213 above). At that time, Herder had already got
further by the application of his genetic principle. On the other hand,
Goethe's time-scheme in history seemed still to be, like that of the
Enlightenment, lacking in inner coherence, and as timeless as nature.
In this respect he went far beyond the views of the Enlightenment by
representing nature as an eternal womb for earthly, divine and
demonic forces. Their conception, however, was thought of rather as
an emanation, and in this respect was already in line with the youthful Goethe's picture of the world based upon Neo-Platonic concepts.
This interpretation is substantiated by an entry in a contemporary
diary of his, the *Ephemerides*, expressing his philosophical sympathy
with a *systema emanativum*.

Again, his work on German architecture (1772) does not exactly
indicate any progress in historical thought from the developmental
point of view. It may be said that development was too circum-
stantial a process to suit the hot blood of youth. Yet the idea of
individuality certainly emerges with considerable emphasis, to such
an extent that not only the mediaeval, but also the essentially German character of the architecture retreats somewhat into the background. On the other hand, it is inseparably fused with the concept
that a truly individual phenomenon also bears a certain form and
constitutes a whole.

> How freshly I see it gleaming in the morning sunlight, how
> gladly I could stretch out my arms to it! How harmoniously the
> great masses appear, filled with life in their countless small parts,
> as in all the works of nature, down to the minutest fibril!
> Everything has its *form, everything contributes to the purpose of
> the whole.*

The taste for Gothic architecture was not indeed new. As we have
already seen, it had been awakened in England some decades earlier,
and had already been exemplified in more than one German building,

[1] One of the twelfth-century builders of Strassburg Cathedral.

and even on one occasion used by Frederick the Great, in the Nauener Tor at Potsdam (1755). But it had only been toyed with: there had been not the slightest abandonment of the classical norms, and the Gothic style had only been adopted for the external details, in order to produce a pleasant change and arouse 'agreeable feelings'.

The Englishman Hurd had already gone deeper, and pointed to a specific meaning and underlying plan in Gothic architecture. Whether Goethe knew of him or not (perhaps through Herder), his own powerful sense of the whole went far beyond Hurd's merely friendly and understanding interest. And so, suddenly, what had hitherto been a despised historical structure was discovered to be a meaningful whole, possessing a beauty that had nothing to do with the ruling canons of taste; beautiful because it was the expression of a characteristic way of life; or, more accurately, because it was the product of a primitive 'creative urge' in man and nature, and therefore true and necessary. The ideas of truth, beauty and necessity sounded together here in complete unison, because this was felt to be an achievement of nature on the highest level. The naturalistic pantheism underlying this view was by no means disposed to glorify indiscriminately everything that had been created, but recognised 'countless gradations in nations and individual men'. Let us once again note the rungs on this ladder of nature's activity. First, the irrational creative original source of all things; and then, proceeding from it, gifted men who, 'inspired by an inner, unified, individual, independent sensibility, exercise an effect all round them'; and finally, the works of art created by them, which bear a rational character (though this is not explicitly stated) insofar as they constitute an individually shaped whole to which all the multiplicity of their parts is subordinate. These ideas of wholeness and specific form, and the combination of vitally individual unity and multiplicity, were to constitute the continuous power of Goethe's historical thought once the volcanic fervour of his 'Sturm und Drang' mood had died down.

Thus, during these early years Goethe's relationship to the world of history was rather like a violent general occupation of everything in the historical field that seemed to be homogeneous with his own tumultuous individuality. He hurled himself into history like a swimmer leaping into a boundless sea, in order to let its waves carry him along. So naively did he entrust himself to it that he was hardly aware of any sentimental or romantic attractions.

Do I need any testimony to the fact that I exist and feel? This is the only way I can assess and love and adore the testimonies that confront me, just as thousands have felt before my time the

same things that give me force and strength. . . . From the
bottom of my soul I would fall upon my brother's neck. Moses!
Prophet! Evangelist! Apostle, Spinoza or Machiavelli (to
Pfenninger, 26 April 1774).

This was a very subjective and direct relationship of genius to all the
elements of genius in history, going far beyond convention and
traditional authority. But it was combined with the belief that an
admittedly incomprehensible 'whole' bound all these emanations
together ('the whole world would not fit into your head any better
than into mine'). And it was furthermore linked to the belief that
history could assist in the struggle to possess one's own soul in the
present. For Goethe wrote in his essay on the cathedral that what was
needed was 'scarcely less than a new creation'. This idea of history as
productive of new forms of life was again something basic in his
relationship to the world of history.

In the ardour of 'Sturm und Drang' another more subjective and
tremendous thought was stirring, which must be taken into account
in order to reach a full understanding of the youthful Goethe's feeling
for life and history. This was the belief in autonomous creativity, and
the rejection of the gods which he poured forth in the fragment on
Prometheus written in 1773 and the ode on the same subject. Here,
he even scorns and denies the joy of 'feeling oneself all one deep
down' with the gods and with men, with the world and with heaven;
and he ridicules as an illusion the belief that a divine providence is at
work in history. Thus, there only remains as the dark rulers who have
power over gods and men the almighty forces of time and eternal
fate, whose sole purpose as far as human beings are concerned seems
to be to mould them into men. It may well be, as has been suggested,
that the continuation of the drama projected by Goethe would have
brought peace with the gods and a return 'to an intimate whole'. But
the original ideas of Prometheus were also genuinely representative
of Goethe's thoughts and feelings, and are also echoed in the original
version of *Faust*. All great beliefs grow out of protests and tensions.
So did Goethe's belief in an all-embracing whole grow out of the
protests and assertions of individual sovereignty. He now explained
that this whole was as yet incomprehensible, but he alternated
between an ardent devotion to its pursuit and a defiant rejection of it.
Even later on he was never so presumptuous as to claim complete
comprehension, but his mood of titanic defiance gave way to the insight and prophetic faith of the later Prometheus. 'I see what is lit up,
but not the light itself' (*Pandora*). Moreover there remained with him
from this early promethean period (although expressed in milder
form) a tremendous sense of destiny, of the dark stormclouds that

hang over the human race, indwelt by 'all-powerful time and the eternal fate'.

Gradually, however, Goethe's sense of fate in all that was incomprehensible and overpowering was softened down by an equally strong and soothing sense of the laws of development in nature and history, which could at any rate be approximately understood. But, as we have already seen, the consolation of this developmental thought was lacking in the earliest stages of 'Sturm und Drang', which was (it may be surmised) why his nature reacted in such promethean form against the traditional consolations.

Now, however, at the end of 'Sturm und Drang', the thought of development began to dawn upon him. For he began to be aware that the great Individual was not, as his thoughts on the cathedral in 1771–2 would suggest, a sudden revelation breaking forth from the abyss of nature, but rather something that developed in the mutual interactions of community life and its environment. In the *Beitrag zu Lavaters Physiognom. Fragmenten* (1774–5) he writes:

> The environment has not merely an effect upon man, but man
> also has an effect upon the environment, and by being itself
> modified, it proceeds to cause further modifications all round.
> . . . Nature forms man and he in turn, transforms himself; yet
> this transformation is still something natural.[1]

Yet this sense of the connection between the environment and the individual achieved through his own experience of life was not enough to enable Goethe to appreciate the great personalities to the full in the genuine historical atmosphere of their own times. The *Physiognomische Fragmente* gave brief character-sketches of Scipio, Titus, Tiberius, Brutus and Caesar. They have often been admired, and are indeed worthy of admiration. Yet they are not men of ancient Rome, but rather universal and almost timeless human portraits, and all that was Roman about them was derived from traditional ideas.

But *Götz von Berlichingen* and *Egmont*, it will be objected—do not these contain men and periods and countries interwoven with the most skilful individual and historical colouring? Is there not astonishing historical faithfulness to the atmosphere of the tragic hero— in *Götz*, the rough, cheerful chaos of the decaying Empire, in *Egmont* (which was conceived and begun in the 'Sturm und Drang' period), the strong sensuous life of the Netherlands and their popular

---

[1] See in addition the letter to Auguste, Countess of Stolberg, 13 February 1775, 'because he (Goethe) will not allow his thoughts to shape themselves according to any ideal, but lets his feelings *develop* into capacities through a process of playful struggle'.

aristocracy rooted in the soil? Certainly, but we must explain how it was precisely that he succeeded in creating those pictures, and point out some reservations.

All his life long, Goethe had a specially close relationship to the sixteenth century, and even *Faust* bears witness to it. At that time the similarity with his own period (at any rate as he felt it to be) attracted him to that century. The battle between a naturally strong and genuine humanity and one that was less meritorious, but destined to triumph because it had objective powers of forcible oppression on its side, is represented in *Götz* by the rising princely territorial and bureaucratic State, in *Egmont* by the cold fanaticism of the Spanish despotic monarchy. The self-assertive freedom of the individual ego was here in collision with the necessary course of the whole historical situation (as Shakespeare so often perceived and felt with such profundity), a whole to which the individual remained so closely bound, however much he was in revolt against it. Thus Goethe was projecting his own full-blooded and freedom-seeking personality of the 'Sturm und Drang' into a past where such full-bloodedness had actually existed in even more naive forms. At this point we should not forget the development that took place in Möser, which Goethe so often (and in many other connections too) remembered with gratitude. Möser was the first to venture, in 1770, to praise the days when might was right, 'when our nation was most aware of the noble feelings of honour, showed the greatest bodily virtues, and possessed a specific sense of national greatness', whereas now individual variety and perfection were suppressed (*Works*, vol. 7, pp. 35 ff.).

Thus the spirit expressed in *Götz* is that of the late eighteenth century awakening from the slumber of the ages based upon Natural Law. But people were also jibbing against the goad of the cold power-State, which had domesticated and subjected the individual to authority. Herder had already revolted, and so did Goethe. In *Götz*, he was working out an idea of the State that even stemmed from the soil of the genuine Enlightenment. In the third act (which is even more powerful in feeling in the original form of the play), Götz sketches the picture of an ideal peaceful prince who should bring blessing to his subjects. In the fourth act, Weislingen tells of a conversation with the Emperor. 'We spoke of the welfare of the State. "Oh!" he said, "if only I had had good advisers from the start to direct my restless mind more to the welfare of my individual subjects!" ' To which Adelheid replies: 'He is losing the mind of a ruler.' In this short criticism Goethe managed with a touch of early genius to anticipate the essence of political expediency, which rides roughshod over the happiness of the individual; and furthermore to suggest that the supra-personal powers of fate were, broadly speaking, on the side of the humble opponents of his hero. For his 'mind of the ruler', which the Emperor himself no longer possessed, is the very opponent of Götz. But Goethe's own heart was at this point in sympathy both with Götz and with the Emperor, and he put into their mouths the sentiments of a mid-eighteenth century individualising eudaemonism. The higher power of law and order in the State, which overthrew the robber baron, would only have seemed the better regime if it had also embraced the happiness of the individual.

Primarily, however, this political motive was as unimportant in the creation of *Götz* as it was for *Egmont*, though it is also interwoven with the latter.[1] Nor was the poet primarily concerned with the historical motive of wishing to resurrect a particular piece of the past and its specific values. What he was looking for was some purely human, universal and supra-temporal theme, and he discovered it in the past, as the men of the Enlightenment had done when they ransacked its records. But Goethe effected a vast change in the ideas and content of this supra-human material. For he replaced the generalising thought of the Enlightenment by the individualising approach of the 'Sturm und Drang'. In the Enlightened outlook, the individual who was the object of its eudaemonistic efforts was only an individual in the sense that every atom and every leaf of a tree is individual, that is, composed of the same permanent elements of human nature, though in countless different blends. The vitality of 'Sturm und Drang', shared by the youthful Goethe, could discover beneath these constantly recurring elements, which it could not well deny, a metaphysical bond of union, the hidden spring and source of true individuality, the 'inner kernel of the specific self'. It was in order to defend this that Goethe composed *Götz* and *Egmont*. And the human 'happiness' that is central to the theme is even somewhat reminiscent of the 'highest happiness of men upon this earth' of which Goethe spoke in his old age. Here again, however, the continuity with the Enlightenment is evident. Goethe's doctrine of personality contained the eudaemonistic spirit, but in a deepened form.

The uncommon individual vitality of each character and scene created by Goethe gives these portraits of a past age an inner power and truth, though they do not possess strictly historical verisimilitude. But without doubt they contained a greater degree of historical truth than his character-sketches of the ancient Romans. This was

---

[1] But with an important variant. At the end of the 4th Act, Egmont says: 'He (the king) wants to destroy the inner kernel of their specific self, no doubt with the purpose of making them happier. He wants to destroy them in order that they may become something else, something different'. This sets out in dramatic terms the conflict between the idea of individuality and the rising absolutism that would level everything from motives of eudaemonism.

because Goethe knew how to use the historical sources bearing upon the relevant periods which he consulted for these dramas with simple insight and sensitivity, although it must be admitted that he also idealised them and infused into them something of his own spirit. It is well known that he owed a great deal to Gottfried von Berlichingen's own rough autobiography. A further consideration, however, and perhaps a stronger one, is that the past of the sixteenth century still projected as it were into the contemporary eighteenth century, and could be easily made use of by Goethe, just as Möser could relive the past of his homeland through the ploughland, the meadows and the forests all around him. There were all sorts of decaying remnants of the past in Frankfurt which Goethe as a boy absorbed with all a boy's ardent curiosity. The autumn fair of Frankfurt with its pomp and legal tradition presented him with a picture that came straight out of the sixteenth century. Moreover, the stay-at-home citizens of the old imperial cities such as Frankfurt and Strassburg were not very different in character from their ancestors in the sixteenth century. As late as 1900, a discerning observer of Alsatian local life, Werner Wittich, could see in the humble inhabitant of Strassburg, beneath his modern costume, the old comfortable citizen in an imperial city of 1600. And as he wrote *Götz* and *Egmont*, Goethe had these people closely in mind. It has been rightly noticed that the language used in *Götz* as a whole is neither that of the sixteenth century, nor Goethe's own natural style, as for instance in the personal outpourings of *Werther*, but that it has a more or less old-fashioned flavour. It seems probable that Goethe was influenced here by the language of Luther. But this language, although it was not then spoken, was still much closer to the popular mind and feeling than it is today. In fact what Goethe was accustomed to see and hear in the streets was both past and contemporary.

This brings us to what Goethe says in *Dichtung und Wahrheit* (book 14) about his relationship to the past at this period, which is particularly significant for our present purpose:

> I had a feeling, which became positively overpowering and could not find wonderful enough utterance, that the past and the present were one. I saw them in a way that brought something ghostly into the quality of the present. This feeling is expressed in many of my larger and smaller works, and always has a beneficial effect in my poems, although at the actual moment of direct expression in life it was bound to appear strange, inexplicable and perhaps even unpleasant to the reader.

These are indeed strange words, and for a moment they clutch at our hearts. They depict a little world all on its own, the centre of which we can perhaps understand fairly adequately, but whose fringes are incomprehensibly obscure and shade off into vague forebodings which we must try little by little to clarify. For all further examination of Goethe's historical thinking is really only a commentary on these words. Let us take the two experiences from the year 1774 which Goethe adduces by way of example—the experience at the Cathedral in Cologne, and the experience in the Jabachs' house at Cologne. They could almost be compared to the crucial moments of spiritual awakening in the lives of the pietists. The Jabach experience was often the subject of subsequent discussion between Goethe and Jacobi, who was present at the time. We are therefore in a position to see what a powerful impression it must have made and what good supporting testimony there is to the account in *Dichtung und Wahrheit* (Goethe to Jacobi 21 August 1774, and Jacobi to Goethe 28 December 1812; Conversations 1, 45; *Kunst und Altertum*, jubilee edition 29, 236; also Georg Jacobi's diary in Morris's new edition of *Der junge Goethe*, vol. 4, p. 116).

In the Cologne Cathedral of that period, Goethe was confronted with a ruin which probably first had the effect of reviving the feelings roused by the cathedral at Strassburg, but then forced them to take a different and tragic direction. Midway in its construction this gigantic building had been brought to a halt and as it were petrified, and the architect's original intentions were now lost in labyrinthine obscurity. The frustration that had come upon this mighty act of human willpower in the past oppressed Goethe's spirit. He may well have shuddered as he contemplated this relic of the past that was really there, yet created a feeling of unreality. He was dominated by the 'ghostly' element in the unity between the past and the present.

The experience in the Jabachs' house during those same July days of 1774 was somewhat different. He discovered the home of a patrician family that was now extinct in exactly the same state, and still with the same furnishings, as in the past. A traveller today can find such petrified old families' homes in museums here and there, in Danzig, Milan, Florence and so on, and wanders round them with perhaps slightly damped curiosity, yet with a feeling of friendly invitation. But Goethe's 'over-sensitive feelings' (as he once called them) were stirred into full life by the sight of a Lebrun portrait of the Jabach family confronting him above the mantelpiece, in which the one-time owners looked down at him with all the freshness of the living, although they had long since passed away. Now, however, this did not plunge him into anxious doubts, like the ruined cathedral in Cologne, but rather served to free his spirit from the oppression; and afterwards, as Jacobi tells us, Goethe seems to have been particularly open and resilient in mood. The 'beneficent' element in the unity of past and present was predominant.

This 'oneness', however, leads us rather more generally into the deepest problems of historism. These examples had already shown that this feeling of unity can take on various forms. In *Dichtung und Wahrheit* (book 15), Goethe says again in praise of Möser that he 'connects up' the past with the present, and derives the one from the other. And in the same connection he says about a certain Strassburg teacher, the antiquary and business man Schöpflin: 'He belonged to those fortunate beings who are able to combine the past and the present, and understand how to attach to their contemporary interests their historical knowledge' (book 11).

This is, so to speak, the average intelligible way in which the historian can bring together the past and the present. But this is not the kind of mental connection envisaged in these two experiences of Goethe. To bring together is not the same as to have a sense of complete unity—the mysterious and almost visionary experience to which Goethe bears witness. And because it has this touch of the visionary, and has the power to evoke the past far beyond all familiar and traditional methods, it has nothing to do with the sense of unity between past and present evoked by traditionalism. This sees the present simply as the continuation of a well-proven past. People remain or desire to remain what they were. Thus, it has been said of the French today that they look unhistorically at the past with the eyes of the present, and see it as all of a piece (E. R. Curtius). Of Goethe's mysterious sense of unity between the two one can only say that he had no impulse or desire to extend the past or bring it back to life. We would rather venture to suggest that it was a transcendental experience embracing both past and present, and lifting the poet into a higher sphere in which he was carried up above time, and remained in a state of complete rapture. It is thus understandable that this mood could be helpful in his poetry, but in actual life, which forced him to come down again to the present, it could prove rather uncongenial. His words leave us, however, in no doubt that this was no fleeting experience belonging only to that particular time, but something that was the basis of all his poetry. It is upon this that its human yet divine magic rests; for this feeling of oneness is at bottom identical with the quality that made him a great poet, the power to strip every temporal experience that moved him of its temporal veil and so lift the fleeting moment on to the eternal plane.

Perhaps, then, we have reached the pivotal point where Goethe's poetical feeling is connected to his specific sense of history.

For the question now arises, whether from this point onwards the same mood did not form the basis of his historical thinking, in a more or less clearly conscious manner, after it had been latent for a long time and had then burst forth into full awareness in Cologne. There are two important landmarks to be kept in mind in all further discussion of this matter. First, this mood was clearly something that raised Goethe into the supra-temporal and eternal world. We have already suggested as much in our account of the cathedral experiences, and of *Götz* and *Egmont*. And we called attention to the fact that they seem to have something in common with the historical thought of the Enlightenment, which also had its supra-temporal aspects. Secondly, this experience seems to have had a psychically divisive effect upon Goethe, sometimes producing a kind of ghostly fear, at other times a heightened sense of vitality. May not this throw some light upon the discrepancy between his deep satisfaction and his deep dissatisfaction with history, which was hinted at in our introductory remarks?

This supra-temporal element in the feeling of unity points to still further heights in Goethe's outlook upon the world—the source of the springs that were to feed his conception of history. It is of these that we shall be speaking in the systematic part of this chapter. But for the moment we will continue our excursion through the various stages of Goethe's development.

II *The First Weimar Period and the Journey to Italy*

It is usual to designate the second period in Goethe's life, beginning with his life at Weimar in 1775, as the classicist period. This again is usually subdivided into the early and the mature classical period, ending approximately with Schiller's death in 1805. But for our purposes we must adopt a rather different division. For us, too, his 'Sturm und Drang' attitude to history can be considered as changing just about when he set foot in Weimar. But it would seem that there is a new orientation towards history already discernible at the end of the nineties, prepared for by the experiences of 1789. It appears that from this turning-point onwards, all Goethe's subsequent historical thought and research could be compared to a sea spreading out uniformly from a narrow gulf, with various arms and currents that yet obviously belong to a unified whole.

The interval between 1775 and about 1789 acted like a narrow but very deep river bed which channelled the waters flowing from the original springs of 'Sturm und Drang' into this wider sea. The interval was not as rich in direct contacts with the world of history as the earlier and later periods. *Tasso* and *Iphigenie* cannot, like *Götz* and *Egmont*, be looked at in the light of their historical content. True, the historical field in which they are set was no random choice; but each of them was transformed into an ideal world, as the artistic and human requirements of the poet now demanded. The administration and politics of a small State, with which he now became acquainted through his professional duties (though he also threw his whole personality into them) led him naturally into experiences which were incidentally fruitful for his historical thought. Yet when his duties likewise led him to plan a monument for this little State in the shape of a historical biography of Duke Bernard of Weimar, he was taking on something that lifted him out of this little world into the destinies of Germany and Europe. At this point the thread of interest was broken, and Goethe had neither the desire nor the faith to put into some kind of ordered shape the confused military and political events of the Thirty Years War (1779–82).

To find the appropriate form—this was Goethe's great concern at this period for the aspects of life he was then preoccupied with, namely art and nature. This was not to mean an impoverishment of the content, although the exuberantly sensuous attitude of 'Sturm und Drang' needed to be moderated and completed by a richer contribution from experience. Nor were the newly discovered forms to make his material rigid and static, like the unchanging values of the Enlightenment. But the vitality that had hitherto swept along in a swirling flood now settled down into a steady stream. The demands for freedom of the individual now led to a conscious recognition that any such rights could only be based upon the maintenance of an interior principle of law-abiding discipline. At this point Goethe's orientation to the external world was thoroughly helpful; it was good for him to be confronted by the objective powers and forces that he encountered in his life at Weimar. While becoming more closely acquainted with the specific and conditioned nature of actual life, he was unconsciously seeking in it the inner vitality that he was aware of in himself. Subjectivity and objectivity began to interact in a fruitful manner. And so the inner laws that Goethe sought out everywhere in art and nature did not become laws of static existence, as in the Enlightenment, but laws of development. With the youthful Goethe, it had been a matter of a tremendous explosive dynamic which he saw at work in the creativity of nature, and in the human mind interpreted in natural terms—a dynamic that had been the driving-force of his own poetry. Now, however, this was replaced by the calmer all-embracing power of a genetic understanding of the captivating aspects of art and nature.

We will now try to give a more detailed explanation of this first summary glance at Goethe's early years, taking it stage by stage. The key to the activities of Goethe, both in thought and in self-development, during these years would seem to be his effort to master the superabundant wealth of life that he felt and saw in himself and in the world around him. He had to find orderly principles to regulate it without diminishing or doing violence to any of its rich content. And so he went back methodically, in a certain sense, to the work of the Enlightenment and its predecessor, the movement of the late seventeenth century. They had both attempted to understand the world and its life as the result of simple natural laws, and to bring together the multiplicity of things in order to regulate them. As Goethe wrote to Wieland in 1780, 'you know that as a result of long thought the soul descends from multiplicity into simplicity'. But this simplicity could no longer be as simple as it was thought to be by the laws of mechanics and by Natural Law since the principle of individuality had been discovered. Goethe had discovered it at an early stage, and expressed it more profoundly and passionately in his poetry than ever Herder and Möser had managed to do. And now he held fast to this idea of individuality with fervour, conscious that it was a key to the whole world. He wrote to Lavater in 1780: 'Have I already written to you the words *Individuum est ineffabile*, from which I derive a whole world of meaning?'[1] Even his study of Spinoza, which was now pursued with great zeal, did not tempt him to allow the individual to slip out of sight as a mere modification of the universal absolute substance. He read into Spinoza what was already firmly implanted within himself, and wrote to Jacobi in 1785: 'I recognise a divine character only in and from *rebus singularibus*'. But the driving-power of the concept of individuality itself could not stop at this point. The Cologne essay, as we saw, was inclined to isolate great individual actions with sole reference to the universal womb of nature that produced them. But now, at the end of the 'Sturm und Drang' period, this gave way to the view that individuality is always interacting with all the individualities round about it. Even this insight was not sufficient to fill the gaps that had arisen between the rule of nature's more obscure forces in general and the individualities that burst forth from her as direct creations. It was necessary to work out a more fully connected, clearer and more convincing relationship

---

[1] We have not been able to ascertain the direct origin of this dictum. Joël, in *Wandlungen der Weltanschauung*, 2, 923 ff., ascribes it to Pliny, from whom it was later taken over by the Scholastics. But Eduard Norden, whom I questioned on this point, doubts whether it is of ancient origin, and on enquiring at the *Thesaurusarchiv*, received a negative answer on this point. But the thought expressed in this dictum can, as Ernst Hoffmann has informed me, be traced from Plato (*Theaetetus*, 205e, στοιχεῖον ἄλογον (inexpressible element)) and Aristotle onwards through the Scholastics. During the later Middle Ages, Aristotelian and Neo-Platonic, purely logical and mystical, motifs seem to have become fused together. Cusanus is particularly important in this respect.

between unity and multiplicity. A first stage would seem, if we are right in our interpretation, to have been already reached in the original version of *Faust*—namely an enthusiastic conviction that there is a timeless and eternal interaction and co-operation of all existing forces to form a whole:

> How all things weave one whole together,
> And live and work in one another!
> How heavenly beings sink and rise
> Exchanging golden chalices![1]

Or, as he wrote in the *Satyros* of 1773:

> And rolling up and down there went
> The all and one eternal thing
> Ever changing, ever the same.

The same spectacle is presented, this time to the ear rather than to the eye, by a letter to Knebel in 1784, showing that Goethe's scientific thirst for knowledge was already at work. It is in connection with his osteological researches, which had shown him that human and animal bones were related and, as we shall see, had confirmed the importance of his theory of form; it runs as follows: 'And so we see once again that every creature is a note, a single sound in a great harmony which must be studied as a whole, or each separate element in it is a mere dead letter'.

To this stage also belongs the famous fragment on nature written in 1781–2. Goethe, perhaps in one of his lordly moods, seems to have deliberately played the same game of mystification about its authorship that he represents nature as playing in its mysterious revelations. Whatever the truth may be about the co-operation in this essay of the young Swiss author Tobler, it is certain that we must reckon on the possibility of all its ideas stemming from Goethe. Dilthey has shown (*Ges. Schr.*, II) that Goethe was here specially influenced by Shaftesbury, though he deepened and intensified the thought. Here, as Goethe (in agreement with Herder) always felt to be the case, nature includes human life, and so by implication the whole of history. But here too we see the logical impress of a well-known basic need of Goethe's. History becomes entirely de-temporalised and transformed into an eternal drama played out by 'many motives, though they are never effete, but always active and always manifold in their variety. Everything is simultaneously present in history. It knows no past or future. The present is eternal in its eyes.' Here again we have a transcendental sense of temporal unity, though with a different colouring from the experiences of Cologne Cathedral and the

[1] Trans. by J. Shawcross, *Goethe's Faust* (Allan Wingate, 1959).

Jabachs' house. It was not, like these, evoked by the protrusion of the past into the present, but arose from a deep and arresting general view over the whole of nature and humanity. Thus what Goethe said about nature is also true of this feeling of unity: 'Everything is new, and yet it is still the old'. He could play the same protean game with his experiences and basic ideas as his 'nature' played with all its manifestations.

It need scarcely be said that this essay also contains an acknowledgement of individuality. But it also acknowledges the transience of all individuality, with the consoling thought that it is eternally arising afresh. 'Nature seems to have laid the greatest possible stress upon individuality, yet she cares nothing for the individual.' These words could be interpreted either as sublime indifference to the ever-changing phenomena of nature, or a deep conviction of the creative power that can produce such constant renewal. In fact, both moods are present, but fused into a single whole. Yet the standpoint is too lofty and rarified in atmosphere to allow the world of history, which is here represented as altogether merged in the general life of nature, to dawn on the mind in all its universal realities. In his old age, writing to von Müller in 1828, when he was once again looking at the *Fragment*, Goethe described this insight as only 'comparative', an intermediate stage in the development of his highest thought. He criticised in rather exaggerated terms the fact that at this earlier period he was lacking in his later insight into the two great motive-forces in nature, polarity and gradation. We shall be concerned with these later on. But it may be said at this point that even this more mature view fails to do complete justice to all that is signified by development, both in nature and in history.

Thus after he had turned away from 'Sturm und Drang', and had begun the task of conscious and orderly construction, the pendulum of Goethe's thought first swung over in a speculative and abstract direction. This is borne out by the *Philosophische Studie* of 1784–5.[1] It linked on to the ideas of Spinoza, but only (as Dilthey has shown) in order to transform them at once in the direction of his own new sense of the vitality and inscrutability of the actual world. This work sets forth two methodical principles which could at some future date also be applied to the world of history. First, that the standard for measuring anything alive must never be taken from outside. If it was a question of measuring it, 'the thing itself must provide the standard', which then became something highly intellectual, and could not be discovered by the senses. Secondly, something Goethe had already intuitively recognised in the cathedral essay of 1772, but now expressed more completely and in a clearer conceptual form—

[1] This would seem to us to be the correct date.

the essential characteristics of an organism. 'In every living entity what we call the parts are inseparable from the whole, to such an extent that they can only be understood along with and as a part of the whole.' In this statement we have something that exceeds all the usual powers of comprehension. Goethe realised this, and with an echo of Leibniz (cf. p. 20 above), drew the great conclusion that we must declare even the most limited living being, 'as well as the vast whole in which all existences are included, to be absolutely infinite'. Anyone who henceforward joined in this way of thinking could never again fall back into the methods of the Enlightenment, based upon Natural Law, of measuring the human individual according to the imaginary external standards of static truths founded upon reason. And sooner or later, this atmosphere of supra-rational eternity was bound to seep over into the historical field.

The Italian journey of 1786–7[1] brought a further advance in Goethe's thinking. It is well known that this journey was decided upon as essential for a new breath of life. The atmosphere at Weimar had become too thin and lacking in content for him, not to speak of the other psychological factors which drove him away from that place. His ideas were already in danger of becoming too speculative. They needed to be filled out by what was to Goethe the very stuff of life—the observation of concrete life and all its great phenomena, against which he could test and deepen his theoretically acquired basic principles.

This took place with deliberate onesidedness, and all the other sides of life that Goethe saw in Italy were eclipsed by the over-mastering concentration on nature and art. And it was not even on the whole of the art he had managed to see, but on what came from Greece or was derived from it, or seemed to be linked up with it. We have already noted in our study of Winckelmann that this classicist taste and standard, which was to be continued in the new German humanism, had retained something of the absolutist spirit based upon a universal outlook steeped in Natural Law. This was more understandable in an older man like Winckelmann than in Goethe, whose world had already been invaded by the idea of individuality. This development was only possible because Goethe himself measured

[1] As is well known, the reproduction of Goethe's thoughts from Italy has to contend with some difficulties in respect of source-criticism, since the original diary and letters which formed the foundation for the *Italienische Reise* are only partly extant. I have, of course, consulted the original documents, as far as they are available; but I thought it better to use the revised text of the *Italienische Reise* as well, where the original documents were wanting, since the possible source of errors from this direction would be much less harmful than ignoring completely valuable but possibly touched-up evidence. These references are noted in the text by (*Ital. Reise*).

396

art by the standards of nature, that is to say, his own conception of nature. He came to the conclusion that Greek art was really the only one in keeping with this idea of nature, and was thus the only art that could produce works of inner perfection, harmony of form and essence, and fullness of body and soul. 'These sublime works of art are the highest products of man according to true natural laws. Everything arbitrary or merely fanciful collapses to nothing: here is necessity, here is God' (6 September 1787, *Ital. Reise*).

We must seek to enter fully into the rapturous revelation which burst upon Goethe in Greek art under Italian skies, in order to realise the narrowing effect that it had upon Goethe's mind. In his earlier experience at the Strassburg Cathedral, Goethe had been aware of necessity, truth and beauty, and had seen in them the marks of an organic whole. But now his sense of nature as well as art became detached from Europe north of the Alps by a highly exaggerated view of what form in art and nature, in landscape and the world of men, could offer to the eye of the senses—form conceived according to the classical pattern. For the time being, the external form, which was more persuasive to the senses and more marked in its impression, became more important to Goethe than the 'inner form', in which the Nordic creations were certainly not lacking. In his eyes, it now seemed quite right that Charles Augustus should give up his intention of completing his collection of Rembrandts in Weimar. As Goethe wrote to him in 1787: 'Here in Rome I feel with particular strength how much more interesting this purity and definiteness of form is than our full-blooded crudeness and vague spirituality'.

Goethe's journey to Italy must have aroused in him a passionate need for the perfect, and especially for seeing perfection face to face. This was something which he never felt so strongly at any other time before or after, and something that only one other northerner before Goethe (Winckelmann) had felt with equal strength. So passionate was this yearning for perfection that it even threw Goethe's artistic needs into the shade, and finally resulted in his finding satisfaction only (as he did in his youth, but now in a much clearer and rational fashion) in the bosom of nature herself. He admitted to the Duchess Louise (23 December 1786) that it was easier and more comfortable to observe nature than art, and easier to appraise it. 'The smallest product of nature has its self-contained perfection, and I only need eyes to see it; so I am convinced that I can discover the proportions; I am sure that a true and whole existence is found within a very small compass.' In works of art, on the other hand, the 'best' existed only in the mind of the artist, and was seldom or never attained in actual practice; especially was there a great deal of the traditional in them, which was not as easy to understand and decipher as the laws of living nature. 'The works of nature are always like a word of God uttered for the first time.'

But art is a part of the historical world, and we are bound to enquire what effect it had upon Goethe. His interest in the historical world seems now to have been largely concentrated on art, and art interpreted absolutely in a very particular, and as we should now feel, unhistorical manner. Yet even this did not altogether stand the test of comparison with the works of nature. And the highly historical force of 'tradition' Goethe did not realise for what it really was (a vital power in art) but considered it almost with displeasure as a hindrance to true understanding. In fact Goethe's development would seem to have reached the exact opposite to what we should call historical interest and historical thought. This opposite pole of 'nature' on which he now took his stand was no longer what it had been in the 'Sturm und Drang' period—the obscure and irrational first cause of all life, whose power had at that period been venerated in a summary and tumultuous manner in all the events of history. Now, nature had once again taken on a more rational character, and was interrogated by Goethe along the lines of its clear and intelligible operations. Yet this was a new *ratio*, profoundly different from the reason of the Enlightenment, understood as it had been in mechanical and static terms—an idea which embraced the creative conception of the 'Sturm und Drang' in a refined and 'elevated' form. And so this new conception of nature could well prove in the long run to be the source of new influences that would sooner or later make their impact upon the world of history.

We now come to the great discovery made by Goethe in the Botanical Gardens of Italy, the discovery of the original form of plants and the various changes they had undergone. The question of primitive forms in natural life in general, and of their transformations, was not entirely new. Buffon had already posed it in his pioneer research work with a view to setting out the facts in a more elastic and lively fashion, and this research was now going ahead in West European science; and Herder, perhaps under the influence of Goethe, had already broached the subject tentatively in the first part of his work on the philosophy of history (vol. 13, pp. 49, 67; vol. 14, p. 590). We are not here concerned with what was already known in the observations made by Goethe, or with what must be considered (from the modern scientific standpoint) erroneous about the new elements in his discoveries. The decisive point for our purposes is that he thought he had discovered a law which transcended the mechanical character of the laws of nature as hitherto understood. This new law explained the metamorphoses in plant life not only in terms of physical and chemical antecedents, but principally in terms of their own interior and intimate life-principle. The interrelatedness of all plant life led him on to the idea of a common original type perceptible in all living specimens, the 'supersensuous original plant form'. He therefore posited a relationship between all the external parts of the same plant on the assumption of their original identity. In order, then, to explain the differences that were clearly present, there only remained the straightforward conclusion that they had evolved by gradual development out of the original basic form. This meant that a large field of nature was thrown into a state of flux and changeability; yet it retained a permanent element, namely the original type, which reproduced itself in a thousand varying forms. Thus a new pattern of unity and variety was established. The problem of the apparent contradiction was overcome by an insight into the inner similarities deriving from the necessary vital processes. The idea that each single organ of a plant had the capacity under certain conditions of turning into a plant itself (or in other words developing into a whole) threw light upon a tendency of life to form wholes as a general principle. Goethe visualised the inner powers and the outward conditions as co-operating in this process of growth. As he later expressed himself in his *Geschichte meines botanischen Studiums* (*History of my Botanical Studies*): 'the plants possess a certain mobility and pliability in order that they may be able to adapt themselves to the manifold conditions they may encounter upon this earth, and be able to transform themselves accordingly'.

Once this conception had been formulated, it was bound to extend in some way or other to further departments of nature. As Goethe was already writing to Frau von Stein in 1787, 'the same law could be applied to all things living'. The sequel will show that Goethe already had this law at his fingertips, though he had not yet consciously formulated it, at the time of his entry into Italy. Later on, in his *Geschichte der Farben* (*A History of Colours*), he was to describe the procedure as 'unravelling the secrets of nature through the idea of development'. How far would it go in also unravelling the history of the human race? Goethe was not yet in a position to propound this question as a whole while he was in Italy, because he had enough to do with his researches on nature and art. But he was brought closer to it by reading Vico (though somewhat cursorily) in Naples; at any rate he was left with the strong impression that his works contained 'sibylline forecasts of the good and right that will or ought to come to pass in the future, founded upon the most earnest consideration of traditional material and life as a whole' (*Ital. Reise*). Vico reminded him of Hamann. We must not, however, rate his indebtedness to either of them too high. The sense of inner dynamic movement in the whole of nature, including humanity, possessed by these two men was also native to Goethe. But at this particular moment (the period of Classicism) their special insights into the primitive elements in nature and history meant comparatively little to him.

The method of explaining the great artistic creation in terms of development had been pioneered by Winckelmann. Goethe followed him as though he were entering a newly discovered country on the fringes of civilisation. He writes to Herder in January 1787: 'I constantly keep an eye on the different styles of the various peoples, and the periods during which these styles prevailed'. And as he says in the *Italienische Reise*: 'Winckelmann impresses upon us that we must separate the various periods and recognise the different styles made use of by the different peoples, and see how they were developed in the course of time and finally ended in degeneration'. And in this field 'no judgement is possible unless it is developed historically'. He also applied this new perspective to the Renaissance, to the line of ascent from Mantegna to Titian, to the steps of the pyramid that led up from Raphael's predecessors to Raphael himself, 'who towers head and shoulders above all the rest'. But it now became clear that there were certain unconscious barriers in Goethe to his application of the principle of development. He passed by the art of Giotto. His classical principles became a hindrance. He was fascinated by his expectation of seeing a development of *what was most beautiful* in art. As with Winckelmann, so with Goethe: his conception of development was fettered by the idea of perfectionism. He had something inside him which refused to follow the process of development in art as a whole, or to seek out some peculiar and distinctive value at every stage, even in the lowest. We now begin to get a clearer picture of his selective procedure *vis-à-vis* the historical world, which had been adopted by him at an early stage. But the subjective criteria for selection in the 'Sturm und Drang' period were now replaced by objective ones. The inner regularities that he had found in nature and now transferred to art provided him with an anchorage in the face of the forces within himself, which still had volcanic power. He remembered Rousseau, and how he had been misled by his subjectivism. Often, as he admitted in 1787 (*Ital. Reise*), he considered himself a fool for not having remained loyal to the inner ordinances of nature.

But the world of history in the broader sense could not as yet offer Goethe this anchorage, not even in Italy, where it made such a powerful appeal to him. No doubt, history appealed strongly to his emotions. He records in his diary that 'the spirits of history rise from their grave in a hundred different forms and show me its true shape'. His words about Rome are famous—Rome, where history does not look the same as anywhere else in the world.[1] 'One seems to to be seeing everything, and it all fits into the picture.' And in another passage: 'The whole history of the world is linked up with this place'. 'Roman history speaks to me as though I had actually been present.' Such words may perhaps be interpreted not so much as the inner historical feeling of the deep connections between himself and the whole existence of the West and Rome, as an aesthetic satisfaction at being able to scan, from this centre of so many mighty events, the countless lines of influence that had radiated forth in all directions over the whole world. These had been mostly of the military and political kind, and where Goethe was to come into closer contact with these, he could suddenly display a feeling of revolt against them, and show his hostile attitude towards this sphere of the historical world. He curtly declined an invitation to Sicily to visit the site of one of Hannibal's battles—though he had misheard it; it was in fact Hasdrubal, not Hannibal. He did not want to see any 'departed ghosts' where he now enjoyed a beautiful present. To Goethe, this was an unbearable 'mixing of the past and the present' (*Ital. Reise*). The disturbing dark side of his sense of unity between past and present once again made itself felt.

Yet Goethe could on another occasion look back on Hannibal's career with interest, when he studied the position at Lake Nemi taken up by the German troops whom the campaign of 1744 had brought there. 'A splendid position, which was occupied of old by Hannibal' (to Charles Augustus, 1787). The vivid reconstruction of this memory set Goethe thinking, and at once brought the shades of the past to life.

Generally speaking, wherever historical structure that still protruded into the present could be viewed according to the method adopted for the metamorphoses of plant-life, Goethe could breathe a contented sigh of relief. 'You know my old way of dealing with nature', he wrote to Frau von Stein, 'well, I am dealing with Rome on the same lines'. 'One cannot understand the present without some reference to the past', he said on the subject of the city of Rome and its situation. He clearly saw that this place must originally have been occupied not by a great nation or a mighty prince, but by shepherds and riff-raff (to his friends in Weimar, 25 January 1787).

Goethe was already casting the eyes of genius on Venice on his journey out. As he wrote in his original diary: 'I have observed

---

[1] To Herder, Dec. 1786. The text of the *Ital. Reise*: 'Elsewhere people read from the outside inwards, here people think they can read from the *inside outwards*' is thus a revised version—an importation from Goethe's later feelings. But even the examples given by Goethe in the *Ital. Reise* of this 'reading from the inside outwards' only bear upon the exterior aspects of the Roman power.

things with a quiet and cultivated eye, and have rejoiced in all this abundant life'. Goethe looked at things very differently from the travellers of the Enlightenment, whose outlook was apt to be super-ficial—even Montesquieu, though he had paid close attention to the characteristics and customs of Italy. Goethe, however, could enter deeply into the gay external life of the decadent republic as though it were a plant whose silent growth and orderly development could be defined from its present condition of faded and withered glory. Nothing arbitrary had been at work here, but necessity (Möser's 'nature and necessity') from the very beginning. There had been no single commanding spirit, but the collective power of humanity: 'a whole people' had created and formed it.

> A noble pile! and a necessary and involuntary way of life. This race did not take refuge in these islands just for amusement, nor was it by choice that others were driven to unite with them; it was luck—sheer luck—that made their position so advan-tageous, and that they showed such wisdom at a time when the whole of the Northern World still lay steeped in folly.

It is not difficult to understand how the contemporary Venetian State, with its jealously guarded secrets (viewed by the rest of the world with some astonishment and anxiety) now became clearly intel-ligible to Goethe. He thought that he now understood all these secrets without their having been betrayed to him. Above all, how-ever, he could now interpret in far more genetic and necessary terms the emergence of a marvellous creation from the Middle Ages, which were generally speaking still considered as a dark age—far more so than when he had meditated fifteen years ago before the cathedral at Strassburg. He could now see the rise, ascendancy and decline of the republic as one single phenomenon, to be viewed with a new feeling of oneness between past and present, a phenomenon that was no less venerable in its decline than in its superb site and situation. 'It has succumbed to time—like everything else that has an outward form of existence.'

But such words did not imply that Goethe bowed before the omnipotence of time. Through his observation of nature he had won for himself something that he had always been intent upon—a time-less view of reality, which had now become a firm and intuitive pos-session. It constituted a permanent law behind all the changes and chances of the phenomenal world. And through his contemplation of art, he had discovered timeless and eternal values, whose develop-ment in time and history only interested him insofar as they had given rise to something eternal. It is quite easy to understand how he now thrust away or left on one side everything that was at variance with this comprehensive contemplation of eternal existence, development and decline. Papal and ecclesiastical Rome, for all its gay variety, and for all its intrinsic and universal historical interest, was for him, like so much 'water off a duck's back' (to Frau von Stein, 1787). It did not, however, prevent this and the popular life around him from recording a clear image in his all-seeing eye. All the more so did he detach himself inwardly from the contemporary events in the great world of politics, which already heralded the ending of an old epoch and the coming of a new. Again, however, this did not prevent his keen and penetrating eye from perceiving the connections between things. Frederick the Great's death, indeed, was only recorded with the brief concluding harmonies of an Eroica Symphony: 'How gladly one possesses one's soul in silence when one sees such a man laid to rest'. But in the correspondence with Charles Augustus, Goethe was already calling attention to the danger that through the expansionist policies of Catherine and Joseph France 'might be brought very low'. This decline in France's position as a European power, which the French spirit could not tolerate, was certainly one of the causes of the French Revolution.

But on the whole, Goethe remained true to what he wrote to Herder in December 1786: 'I want to see Rome, that is, the permanent features, and not what changes every ten years'. In his moments of clearest insight into the historical world, he was now chiefly concerned with the enduring and imperishable elements in the past. The Roman ruins affected him differently and more cheerfully than the ruins of Cologne Cathedral had done in former days; and the brighter side of his feeling of unity between past and present now came to the top. The 'presence of the classical soil' (an expression Goethe wished to be understood in the loftiest sense) took possession of him, the 'sensuous and spiritual conviction that here there was, and is, and always will be, something truly great' (*Ital. Reise*). In these loftiest feelings he could also find a natural place for the achievements of the post-Classical ages, papal Rome, St Peter's above all, which fitted into his supra-temporal picture of an enduring creative movement.

This feeling of Goethe's was far greater and more all-embracing than what Gibbon had felt two decades earlier (1764), when he had looked upon the ruins of Rome and had conceived the idea of his great history. Gibbon had gazed in sentimental mood upon the remains of the Capitol, and had listened as a member of the Enlightenment to the singing of the barefoot monks in the one-time temple of Jupiter. Here we see the clear contrast between the dissolving character of historical writing in the Enlightenment, and the synthetic character of Goethe's new approach, with its inclination to find a parable in all things transitory, and its universal rather than purely historical outlook. Goethe did not feel sorrow, but rather exaltation, as he gazed upon this scene. 'We should not be cast down when it is impressed upon us that greatness is transitory; rather should we be enheartened, when we find that the past was once great, to produce something of significance ourselves' (*Ital. Reise*). All the oppressiveness, all the 'ghostly' elements in the past, have now vanished. Goethe's contemplative approach *sub specie aeterni* showed that it could also be fruitful in actual life.

We have seen that Goethe had a stronger universal than historical sense; and it was perhaps because of this that he had a gracious gift not always possessed by the historism that followed him, but nevertheless indispensable to it, if it does not wish to restore merely the dead documentary relics of the past, but its actual revivifying life. The mere written tradition, however full of rich intellectual content, only provides the historian or even the philosopher of history with silhouettes of a bloodless kind, however vivaciously they may be presented, or however acute the critical approach may be. But every real remnant of the past, including the fragments from primitive times, casts an inexpressible spell on the receptive spirit, because here is a piece of bygone life that is yet fully present and can even in some way be interpreted and filled out in terms of contemporary life. And it is precisely to such surviving remnants that the simple antiquarian impulse leading to historical study is in the first instance directed. This was the great advantage Möser had over Herder. He was able to see entirely concrete remnants of the past in the actual life of the present. Goethe, when he was in Rome at this time, read Herder's *Ideas for the Philosophy of the History of Mankind* which had then just come out, and was much impressed by them. He had already given Herder his interest and advice in the course of their preliminary composition at Weimar. But now he became aware of the profound difference between his own and Herder's outlook. As Goethe wrote to him in 1787: 'What you are able through the power of the spirit to gather rapidly together from the traditional heritage, I have to drag laboriously together in my own peculiar way from all the corners of the earth—from mountains, hills and rivers'. Herder was lacking in Goethe's capacity for sensuous actualisation, which enabled him to feel at home everywhere, and to actualise and unify the greatness of the past. But Herder did not lack a longing for this capacity and the complementary need for actuality, and therefore the universal surveys that he carried out with such intellectual power over the whole range of human cultural development were profoundly satisfying even to Goethe. In the first parts of the work Goethe also came across some of his own ideas which he had discussed with Herder (conversation with Falk, 1809). This applied to Herder's almost botanical conception of the blossoming forth of humanity from the successive cosmic stages of development, to his sense of 'the original forms and first germs of things' (*Ideen*, book 2), and of the creative impulse in all living creatures. Where Herder had hovered in his prognosis between hope and scepticism about the future of humanity, Goethe inclined towards scepticism. Herder had once formulated the fearful question 'whether the crowding together of mankind and its increased sense of community had not turned many countries and cities into an almshouse, an artificial infirmary and hospital' (vol. 13, p. 373; cf. also vol. 14, p. 297). Goethe took this up and intensified it to the point of an opinion that as humanitarianism would in the end undoubtedly triumph, the world would become one vast hospital, in which each man would be the compassionate sick-nurse of his neighbour (to Frau von Stein, 8 June 1787). Thus he strengthened Herder's already incipient doubts on the absolute value of his humanitarian ideals. It is possible that in both men something of Rousseau's critique of civilisation was at work.

Let us now return to the starting-point of Goethe's discussions with Herder on the problems of tradition. Here Goethe's sense of actuality was markedly in evidence in his growing scepticism towards all oral and written tradition. In this, the pyrrhonic criticism of the Enlightenment had undoubtedly prepared the way. But Goethe replaced the negative motivation of its scepticism (the contempt for human weaknesses) by a positive one; and this was why his own scepticism soon set itself limits. The imponderable content of his own vitality, the magma of his own nature, soon made him feel the difficulty, if not the impossibility, of one person arriving at a complete understanding of another. 'You may say what you like in favour of oral and written tradition, but only in a very few cases does it suffice; for the peculiar character of any being cannot be imparted, not even in things intellectual or spiritual' (*Ital. Reise*). But it was possible, Goethe concluded, first to take a steady look and form an impression from life, to supplement this by reading and listening, before considering and arriving at a judgment. This was a valid recipe for Goethe, as he again took up his Livy and his Plutarch in Rome. But he was even readier to trust his senses, which were constantly kept on the alert by his reason, with a faith that was later to assume an almost religious character. The critical attitude of historism, although just as deeply sensitive as Goethe to the defective sources and gaps in tradition will, however, see the values of the material handed down from the past and the remains of past ages as more like two scales of a balance, which go gently up and down round an ideal point of equilibrium. But Goethe was perhaps the first to put forward the postulate that the one should be constantly supplemented by the other, in order to come as close as human fallibility will ever manage to the goal of a thoughtful and lively appreciation of the past.[1]

It was one of those fruitful conjunctions, one of the polarities that were of such value to Goethe, that he happened to read Herder's *Ideas for the Philosophy of History* under Roman skies. As a counterpoise to Herder's purely intellectual efforts, and to his philosophy of history as constructed out of traditional material, Goethe could at once draw upon the actual presence of all that still survived from the past in Rome. No wonder, then, that he missed a certain substantial quality in Herder's portrayal of the past (*Ital. Reise*). Among the survivals of the Roman past there was, however, another powerful historical element which up till now had only had a marginal influence upon Goethe, namely the State. And for a brief moment in his life, it would seem, Goethe felt the weighty significance of what the State has meant in history. For his criticism of Herder's picture of Rome is followed by these notable words:

> At the moment, my mind is quietly full of what the State meant in its own right; it is, I think, like one's fatherland, something exclusive. And in comparison with the vast sum-total of the world you would have to weigh the significance of this single phenomenon, which would mean that a great deal would shrink in importance, and dissolve into smoke.

This is followed by a meditation upon the Colosseum (*Ital. Reise*). The 'exclusive' quality of the State and patriotism was something Goethe could not tolerate. The Roman State, symbolised in the steeply rising walls of the Colosseum, certainly impressed Goethe, but he immediately conjured up the picture of the 'vast sum-total of the world', in order to re-establish the true standard by which to judge the relative value of this self-contained entity, and be able once more to breathe the air of freedom.

This brings us to the end of his Italian experiences as far as they concern the theme of this book. Their decisive importance lies not in the detailed material of history they brought to him, which (as we have seen) he allowed to work upon him in a highly selective manner. They were, rather, of importance because this immeasurably enrich-

---

[1] We must not, however, fail to recognise that the words I have quoted from the *Ital. Reise* may arouse suspicions that they have been slightly coloured by a later Goethe.

ing confrontation with nature and the works of man clarified his own method of observation and perception and made him conscious of it. As Goethe wrote in November 1786: 'I have had no entirely new thoughts, nor found anything totally unfamiliar; but the old ideas have become so definite, lively and coherent that they may be considered as new'. Beneath the favourable skies of Italy he learnt to take a clearer view of the individual, which he had formerly succeeded in making his own through the stormy approaches of feeling, and to get a fuller grasp of its form. The full inner vitality and unaccountability of the individual was thus somewhat pushed into the background during his Classical period. But the idea of unity and variety in each visible shape, which he had first conceived in his early days, finally reached its full development. More particularly, there was the influence of his botanical studies, which gave him a new sense of the typical, and its constant blending with the individual. But this fusion, which he could see taking place again and again in nature, could only be recognised by a steady comparison of things with one another, and could only be made intelligible by the concept of development. This thought was precisely expressed by Goethe in a letter to Herder written in December 1786: 'The capacity for discovering similarities in relationship, even when they are remote from one another, and for tracking down the beginnings of things, is a tremendous help to me here'. 'One needs only to look, if one has eyes to see, and everything develops', he says in his diary. These are simple words, but they are uncommonly important for the history of thought, as we shall see at a later stage. In short, the idea of development, aroused by the use of the senses and by comparison, now definitely emerged during this Italian period and linked itself on to the idea of individuality. The two main pillars of the future historism were thus built up side by side in Goethe, not only to bear the weight of history, but of the world's life as a whole. The mighty flux and the wealth of forms in the universe, which Goethe as a young man had felt with such fervour, were thus channelled into orderly lines and subsumed under regular laws. He had reached the goal he had glimpsed when he set foot in Italy—'to seek out truth in its simplest elements' (*Geschichte der Farbenlehre, Theory of Colours*). The immediate historical interest was now concentrated in a narrower field of specific values than in his early period, but it was at the same time much deepened. Whether it would be once more enlarged, and if so how, depended on the interplay between mind and external events in the further destinies of Goethe. A year after his return from Italy the French Revolution broke out. This revolution and its world-shaking results were to constitute the new external events in the life of Goethe.

III *From the French Revolution to the End*

Between the French Revolution and the transformations succeeding it, and the restoration of the old regimes in 1815, Goethe fell out with his own age and with the new historical forces arising in it one after another. He found himself unable to be inwardly at one either with the ideas of universal humanity taking shape in 1789, or with the ideas of 1813 and their combination of nationalist and humanitarian aspirations, in spite of some occasional slight concessions. He only readily accepted into his world picture the intervening phenomenon of Napoleon—all the more so because he had already accepted Frederick the Great, though he scorned the type of State that he had set up. But now the image of Frederick was overlaid by that of Napoleon. And this gave even more grounds for the reproach that from the German standpoint (which was after all where nature had placed him) Goethe had made a false historical and political choice. But anyone who attempts to judge these matters from the standpoint of universal history will readily come to the conclusion that Goethe lost his quarrel with the ideas of his age, and that they have shown him to be in the wrong.

Judged, however, by his own standards for measuring the phenomena of history, Goethe will be seen to have won his case. He had stood out himself and defended his entelechy against forces that were poles apart from it. He did not absorb a single drop of foreign blood, nor did he allow any external influence to bear upon the essential purpose of his life. It was part of the fundamental principles of his outlook upon the world that life rested upon its own foundations, and that all living things carried their law and purpose within themselves. The great and universally active forces of a particular time, which Goethe has been suspected of rejecting, will be seen by a deeper historical judgement to be always pre-eminently dynamic, rather than normative and universally binding. No doubt they may become binding and normative for the individual who thinks that he hears in them the summons of conscience and destiny, especially when it is a matter of defending the most natural form of communal life—that of the nation. A sacrifice of the nation leads to the unnatural and the immoral—for this is a point where nature and ethics are fused together. Goethe was not guilty of making any such sacrifice, in spite of his standing apart from the nationalist movement in politics. He saw the State in general as no more than the overseer and nurturer of civic order and culture; and this outlook prevented him from attaching much importance to efforts aiming at the liberation of the national soil from any particular political dominance. The same peaceful interpretation of authority had made him earlier on equally critical of any attempts to reform the State by forcible means. But in his inmost heart he remained true to German culture, which meant to him all that was highest and most sacred in his nation.

Yet the maintenance of his own law of life against the attacks of extraneous forces did not mean (even in Goethe's view) remaining completely unaffected by them. For his whole attitude to life was based not upon static rigidity, but upon development. And this developmental view was not confined to the unfolding of a germ that already contained within itself all potential growth, but embraced the possibility of a mutual give-and-take with the environment, and even with a hostile environment. This is the interplay of individual mind and environment. His environment, as we have already suggested, was the great events of world history subsequent to 1789. Now, having noted the inner bent of his mind, we must go on to ask how far the external events influenced his attitude to history and contributed to its further development.

A preliminary glance at Goethe's activities from 1789 onwards shows that the effects could only have been indirect rather than direct. The symbol of his attitude was the peasant whom Goethe saw going on with his work in the fields within range of the guns at the siege of Mainz in 1793. 'The individual man in his limited surroundings does not give up his usual immediate concerns, whatever the bulk of mankind may do' (*Annalen*). Amid the fearful collapse of all his familiar world, and as a participant in the campaign of 1792, with which he was forcibly brought into close contact, he clung to his studies (to use his own expression) as to a plank of timber in a shipwreck. What Goethe is alleged to have said about the importance of the cannonade of Valmy in 1792, that it ushered in a new epoch in world history, may really have been uttered, in spite of the critical doubts that have been levelled against it. If so, it was one of those lightning shafts of genius with which Goethe was apt now and again to illuminate spheres which he did not normally enter, by giving them, albeit unwillingly, his momentary attention. His revolutionary poetry does not contain one single hint of this attention to the field of universal history.

Yet these poems, together with other utterances, show that Goethe understood part of the historical causes of the French Revolution—more than the aged Möser—like him in politics the typical type of conservative and gradual reformer, intent on practical reform from above. It is very revealing to note which of the causes of the Revolution Goethe recognised—those that could be directly felt and observed in the common social life of men. As early as 1781 the case of Cagliostro had given him an uncanny feeling that 'our moral and political world is undermined by subterranean passages, cellars and sewers' (to Lavater). He also had an eye for the sufferings of the lower classes, who had to slave in order to keep the upper classes in their comfortable circumstances. If only these upper classes had remained sound and fit for their position and not been deficient in worth and self-respect, the aristocratically-minded poet would probably have contented himself with the reflection that without a certain element of menial service by the lower classes the higher culture of the upper classes would be impossible. But he was assailed by doubt on this positive contribution of the upper classes after the affair of the necklace,[1] which affected him with unusual force. The intrinsic worthlessness of the behaviour horrified him. It is remarkably significant of the high value Goethe always placed upon the visible things in life that when he looked back on events he laid some of the blame upon a decadent external worthlessness in the behaviour of the highest personages in the *ancien régime*. He stressed the simple and unostentatious appearance of Frederick II and Joseph II, and the maxim that the prince is only the highest servant of the State. Marie Antoinette's abandonment of court etiquette seemed to him to be a 'behaviour on the part of the great' that had led directly to sansculottism (1810, cf. my *Idee der Staatsräson*, p. 421 ff., now *Works*, vol. 1, p. 396). Again, with his usual touch of genius, Goethe also broached the profound problem whether the State as rationalised by enlightened despotism would remain permanently capable of upholding a monarchical form of government, that is, whether it would be able to maintain the necessary distance between prince and people, and the necessary *mystique* of the monarchical idea. And yet he never felt the need to follow up these new lines of enquiry, which he was the first to propose, or to penetrate more deeply into the world of political history. He often discovered more in passing than he was willing to elaborate.

For only that which had shape, or was capable of being shaped, attracted him (even against his will) since he had arrived at the new clarity of his intention achieved in Italy. The forms and shapes of life which he sought could only come from the life within, but this life must, to satisfy Goethe, constitute a whole into which all the parts fitted; otherwise it remained a chaos. And the apparent chaos produced by the French Revolution repelled him. Perhaps the noblest of the compositions in which Goethe sought to free himself from the oppression of the revolution was *Die Natürliche Tochter* (*The Natural Daughter*). Although it was quite unable to do justice to the historical

---

[1] A public scandal in France, involving a notorious charlatan, the Bishop of Strassburg and Marie Antoinette (see E. Lavisse, *Histoire de France*, ed. 1910, vol. 14, pp. 137–40, 310).

phenomenon as a whole, it contained the most precise acknowledgement of what the Revolution meant, or failed to mean, for Goethe.
In the fifth act, the monk says first of all:

> As structured stones break loose and fall apart,
> So crumbles into formless rubble
> The outward show of pomp and circumstance.

To which Eugenie replies:

> A sudden overthrow impends
> Upon this kingdom. For the elements designed
> To fit together, forming one great life,
> No more with mutual strength of love embrace,
> Their oneness constantly to renew.

A monstrous event, which Goethe felt to be quite senseless and
destructive, had taken place before his very eyes. He looked upon it
as a necessity of nature, but only in the way that brooks and streams
sometimes join their currents and so produce a flood (letter to
Schiller, 9 March 1802). And Goethe never got rid of this impression.
It caused a deep and permanent rift in his relationship to history,
which he was never afterwards quite able to overcome. And as we
have already emphasised, his attitude had been quite early on ambiguous, as he hovered between a feeling of oppression and a sense of
exaltation. Even in the mild *Xenien*[1] (*Gifts*) which gave vent to so
many of the poet's pains and sorrows hitherto hidden from the world,
there is still a residual shudder from those revolutionary years:

> Nought is more tender than the past;
> Approach it like iron all aglow,
> For straightway it will clearly show
> Our present furnace-blast.

> Three hundred years confront us here,
> Yet, even could we sense their every toil and tear,
> All those long years' experience
> Is packed into these thirty last years torn and tense.

But even that which repels the spirit and seems evil and senseless
can in the long run have a vital effect upon it. At the end of his life,
Goethe himself testified to the historic influence of the Revolution
upon his whole generation, including himself.

The demand for something more significant, for greater world-
characters and universal events to be represented on the stage,
was bound to make itself felt in these latter days. Anyone who

[1] Satirical epigrams by Schiller and Goethe on contemporary writers (1796).

has lived through the Revolution feels impelled towards history. He sees the past in the present, and contemplates it with fresh eyes which bring even the most distant objects into the picture (*Französisches Haupttheater*, 1828; cf. Eckermann 25 February 1824).

As early as 1793, when Goethe was still under the strongest influence of contemporary events, it is remarkable that the figure of Frederick the Great rose up before him as the pattern of what was now to be expected by way of contrast in the contemporary world. For he praised him as the man who controlled *opinion* because he did so through *action* (incomplete Third Letter). And Frederick was destined to appear as the 'king of brazen strength', with that combination of heroism and paganism which must already have impressed the youthful Goethe, in the scene in the second part of *Faust* where the spirits are conjured up, a scene that was most probably composed in that year (Hertz, *Natur und Geist in Goethes Faust*, pp. 15 ff.). And now, about 1795, when the Peace of Basle was signed and Europe and France returned to something like a state of peace, Goethe seems (if our reading of the situation is correct) to have entered upon a period of greater interest in historical subjects, which now came for the first time to occupy an extended position alongside his studies of nature and art—an interest which is then sustained right up to the end. In it, we can see Goethe's involuntary reaction to what he himself had experienced as a matter of history, yet had not been able to reduce to orderly shape. We may conjecture, then, that he began to sample other historical material, approaching it as a mass of which parts at any rate might be capable of organised treatment. For his relationship to the historical world as a whole was still characterised by the words he puts into the mouth of the old priest in his *Unterhaltungen deutscher Ausgewanderten* (*Conversations of German Emigrants*) of 1795: 'I feel neither strong enough nor bold enough to survey history as a whole; and the individual events of this world confuse me.' Yet he undoubtedly had much to relate that was full both of human charm and significance.

Goethe also felt a greater attraction now for material that was important in content, insofar as it was the work of man and comprised the conditions in which human culture developed. For the third Italian journey, which had been planned since 1795, Goethe drew up a programme of specific questions. The answers to these were to form a comprehensive work on Italy, with the history of art as its centre, but with extensive sections projected on the nature of the country and the history of agriculture, as well as political and constitutional affairs. On the second journey in 1790 Goethe had already made a study of the history and constitution of Venice. When he broke off his journey in 1797, without getting beyond Switzerland, he devoted to the preliminary stages of the promised land an extremely extensive interest, embracing a wide knowledge of the country and of its cultural history. This was a sign of the widening of the horizons that had been unduly narrowed down by his classical approach. The inner pains and tensions accompanying this process were apt to produce repercussions. Goethe went through such sudden revulsions against the past that he even burnt his own private correspondence of the year 1797. But he could now stroll through his own home city of Frankfurt, where he had once upon a time experienced so naively the venerable antiquity and the clash between past and present, with the eyes of a researcher directed to the historical stages of progress and to the beginnings of more clearly visible and symbolically significant things, and with the appreciation of a realist, who carried his idealism 'firmly enclosed in a little casket'.

If his eye should chance to fall on something new in the contemporary scene, such as the French soldiers in the streets, his antipathy for the Revolution and for warfare did not prevent him from forming a picture of the fearful power of their nation based upon the detailed observation of their behaviour. 'Everything is firmly directed to one single purpose': this was something he could appreciate as in accordance with his own way of thinking.

To these same years (1795–8) belong Goethe's preoccupation with Benvenuto Cellini's autobiography, which he not only translated but also provided with a historical commentary. He had already been led by a thirst for knowledge or for poetical reasons to read a whole variety of historical source-material and descriptions. But now for the first time he was reading as a research historian, who intended to reproduce and shape the view that emerged from his studies; and his new line of study was a source of much satisfaction to him. 'The time I have been spending in this reshaping of the material has been among the happiest in my life', he wrote to Zelter in 1803.

Thus Goethe emerged into a new period of interest in history. His spirit, which had at first been constrained and oppressed by the impact of the revolutionary earthquake, now began to regain its elasticity. World events indeed continued to roll by on their mighty course but they did not tug at his heartstrings, as they had in the early days. And above all, his fruitful friendship with Schiller released his inner powers into freer activity. Two great historical achievements, the *Geschichte der Farbenlehre* (contemplated in 1798, begun in 1805 and published in 1810), and the *Essai über Winckelmann* (1805), still bear the marks of this particular period. The plan for a prize competition discussed with Schiller in 1801 led him to a study of history on a universal scale, intended to give him a broad view of all the European nations. He began with Spain and Portugal, with the idea of observing things 'well and truly from within'. The natural inner bent of his mind in these years of Classicism was more towards the typical than the individual, and inclined him to an '*a priori* history' (to Schiller in 1798), to 'the permanent elements in mankind', 'to a certain overall unity' in which (as he wrote to Schiller in 1801) the differences between individual cases tended to disappear. But he did not himself pursue these rationalising and psychologising experiments any further.

Then once more world events intervened, with a profound but divisive effect upon Goethe. There was the battle of Jena and the collapse of German liberty; but at the same time there was the construction of a new order by the mightiest man of action of the century, who greeted Goethe at Erfurt in 1808 with the words 'voilà un homme'. The pain and consternation at what had befallen Germany, although not forgotten, was thrust into the background by the admiring confidence that Napoleon would complete his world mission, and that German culture would not be allowed to perish under his rule, if only the Germans themselves made a stand on its behalf. In order to maintain the Germans' consciousness of themselves, Goethe planned as late as 1807, with encouragement from outside, a *Homer of the Germans*, which was to be a kind of historico-religious popular book. How far he now felt called to make himself the leader and guardian of the German spirit in a national mission, is shown by his plan of 1808 to convene a German cultural congress at Weimar (conversation with Woltmann, September 1808). The period after 1806 is particularly rich in profound historical judgements backed by deep feeling, and shows a wide range of historical interests, not only in the human field, but also in all departments of the past. It is as though an unseen hand were gently leading him more deeply into history, so that history as actually experienced by himself would in the end compel him by sheer inner necessity to acknowledge it as an object that could arouse the strongest desires for reducing it to ordered form, and provide him with powers to match them. He would see himself as the carrier of a development which needed a whole epoch as its milieu in order to be thoroughly understood. This was the meaning of *Dichtung und Wahrheit*, on which he had been working since 1810. He was also helped by his desire to bring comfort and pleasure to his own people in their hour of dejection. Thus the work involuntarily became Goethe's contribution to the rising of 1813, although to begin with he did not admit that it was historically justifiable. This represented the climax of Goethe's historical thought and writing.

The Romantic trend of the times was unmistakably at work in this turning of Goethe towards the world of history. The pioneers of Romanticism in the nineties were deeply indebted to Goethe and the spirit of his poems. From the standpoint of the history of thought, the Romantic movement could never have been what it was without the influence of Goethe. It followed him along a path more clearly marked out by him than by anyone else—the path of individuality and development, the attempt to seek out the inner dynamic centre of life in every human phenomenon, and from this centre to reach an understanding of the colourful and manifold variety and richness of form contained in humanity. It is not our present purpose to show how Goethe and the Romantics subsequently followed largely divergent ways. But it is a matter of common knowledge that in the period after 1806 Goethe gladly let himself be led on by the Romantics and their friends to the newly-discovered values of German-Nordic art and poetry.

They helped him to find the way back again out of his narrow Classicism, not so much only into the German-Nordic world, which never again became of primary importance to him, but rather into a universal openness towards the historical world as a whole. This new universalism was something different from the stormy subjective and naturalistic universalism of his early days. It had a certain spiral movement in that direction, but altogether at a higher level; for it took into itself the gains of the Classical period—the doctrine of primitive forms and metamorphoses, and of the accurately observable inner laws by which the changes in form were governed. But these inner laws were now felt more spiritually and ideally than in the Classical period of sensuous delight. Yet this new universalism, and the inclination towards the historical shown by Goethe since 1795, were influenced by the political constellation, the events of the contemporary world. Only there was this difference, that formerly Goethe had been driven into himself by them, whereas now they encouraged him to a freer expansiveness and a more relaxed expression. The liberation of Germany in 1813–14, which Goethe did not desire to bring about, was nevertheless greeted by him, once it was under way, with profound gratitude and deep satisfaction. This is testified to by his festival drama *Des Epimenides Erwachen* (*The Waking of Epimenides*) which hinted at the tragic side of his own situation during this crisis, but contained the reassurance that the gods had kept him in quiet security in order that he might be able to 'feel with integrity'. But as the festival drama shows, Goethe could only have unalloyed feelings over his nation's struggle for freedom insofar as it was a matter of universal humanity, but not in its nationalist and political aspects. And he was from now onwards powerfully attracted towards the universal. This was the deepest psychological effect which the Wars of Liberation had on him. Just as *Dichtung und Wahrheit* was Goethe's reassuring answer for an oppressed Germany in 1806, so the *Westöstliche Divan* (*West-East Divan*) was his answer for 1813–14. For however definitely the specific poetical and human content of this poem stands out, it nevertheless rests upon a deliberately chosen universal basis, and its lines are eloquent of universal historical experiences. As Goethe wrote to Boisserée (14 February 1814): 'It would seem fitting at this time that we should measure our little private circumstances by the immense standard of world history.' Poetry and truth had never before been so organically and deliberately combined by Goethe as in the *Divan*. Once before, in *Götz* and *Egmont*, he had projected his own ego into a period of the past that seemed to have affinities with it. Now, he chose this remote Oriental period in order to get a general grasp of the primitive forms and metamorphoses of historical life in general. He was urged on by a complementary historical need; and he called the Divan 'West–East' because the West was here seeking its home in the East. Thus the notes for the *Westöstliche Divan* were Goethe's last great historical enterprise.

We have called *Dichtung und Wahrheit* the climax of Goethe's historical thought and writing. But it would now appear to be outtopped by the universal philosophy of history contained in the notes for the *Divan*. Yet this trend led the way out of the purely historical into a timeless and supra-temporal sphere towards which Goethe had from the very beginning been impelled. Once again, as we shall see, it was a question of past and present in a single unity; this was what he was looking for, and found, in the 'unchanging East'.

All the subsequent directly historical efforts of Goethe, which continued right up to the end, are an echo of these same tendencies. An example of this is the collected cultural and historical results of his journeys on the Rhine, Main and Neckar in 1814–15, published in his journal *Über Kunst und Altertum* (*Of Art and Antiquity*) in 1816–17. The very title of this journal is significant. It would have been unthinkable in his Classical days to give antiquity an equal place alongside art. There are, moreover, scattered historical observations in the reviews and minor essays of his late period. And, finally, there was the historical cameo inserted into the continuation of his *Italienische Reise* on the subject of Philip Neri, the remarkable saint of the Counter-Reformation (composed in 1829, but sketched out earlier, round about 1810).

Even more important for us, however, than those direct testimonies to Goethe's historical work during his latter years is the wealth of thought scattered through the productions of his old age in the form of aphorisms, letters and conversations—the final arch in the great structure of his universal thinking. Indeed, their ethereal transparency often seems to lift them right above the level of ordinary history, to hover in an atmosphere that arouses ineffable forebodings. However, in comparison with all the facts that he had produced earlier on and was still producing, they only represent the highest degree of sublimation.

This brings us to the end of our survey of Goethe's relationship to history, considered period by period over the whole course of his life. We must now attempt to grasp his historical work systematically in its actual context. In Herder's case, we took a different course, and tried within the successive temporal stages of his work to give a picture of the basic thoughts that were dominant at any particular moment. The very difference in treatment is an indication of the difference in the genesis and structure of these two men's historical thinking. With Herder, the finest flowering was at the dawn of his career; with Goethe, it was in the evening of life. The experiences of the contemporary world had a powerful influence upon both of them, but the effect was in each case different. With Herder, who reacted against them strongly, and in a directly ethical manner, the effect was to fragment his thinking; Goethe assimilated them more slowly and less visibly, but in the long run more intensively, and with a greater degree of fusion. The inner purposefulness and coherence of his total development was incomparably greater.

In the following attempt to systematise Goethe's thought, we shall therefore base ourselves upon his maturest stage of development. The earlier stages, as well as any changes taking place at the time of maturity, can safely be left in the background in our unified picture of the permanent in the midst of change.

Systematic Section

I *The Basic Assumptions*

We are to follow the advice given by Goethe for his own guidance in Italy: 'To seek out truth in its simplest elements.' To be sure, Goethe offers plenty of material for the subtlest possible treatment of his intellectual fabric, and it has been abundantly dissected by all the refinements of modern criticism. But unless it succeeds in clearly bringing out the simple main lines of thought, any such analysis makes Goethe more remote, instead of bringing him nearer to us. We must find our way back out of the immense overload of inherited cultural values, which has been increased by historism, to some method for intellectual control of the material. Historism must itself attempt to heal the wounds it has inflicted.

At every point where he can get a glimpse of the personal, Goethe seeks to structure his higher creations upon the relationship between personality and environment. It is the same when he is trying to discover the story of his own life. Questions must be asked about the time and the place as far as they affect the man, and his elementary reactions to them are to be observed first and foremost, before any of the more subtle connections.

Möser seemed to us to be simply and essentially a scholarly patrician in his homeland of Osnabrück. Winckelmann, as we saw, exchanged his ugly chrysalis existence in North Germany for a butterfly life in Rome. Herder, in spite of (or perhaps because of) his feeling for the universal, the original and the full-grown, did not absorb the local colour of the places he passed through in life nearly as deeply as Goethe, whose life in Frankfurt, Strassburg, Weimar and Italy left permanent traces of the peculiar elements he absorbed from each of them. And they are discernible up to the end in his character and his thought. But he managed to take them up into his own individual colouring, so that one could call him in the same breath a native, yet not a native, of his environment. His Faust, for example, clearly shows traces of the conditions of his life at the time of composition, but is finally subsumed into a higher unity which is assuredly present from the beginning. Even in the case of Goethe's historical thought, it may be said that he contrives to have a specific savour of all manner of times and places, and yet to raise these into a loftier atmosphere without losing their distinctive qualities. In order to understand the whole, we shall do well to reflect on his opinion that in order to experience, we must already by anticipation carry the world within ourselves (to Eckermann, 1824). 'Who can say that he experiences something unless he is an experienced person' (*Jub. ausg.*, vol. 23, p. 307). 'One only sees what one already knows and understands' (conversation with von Müller, 1819). Goethe carried within himself from the start the necessary means for fusing together all that came to him from time and place. He was mystically convinced that there existed a secret primal relationship between the given unity of his spirit and the changing content of his experience.

In order to be able to deal with all the separate elements of his experience, to preserve them, control them and rise superior to them, he had to 'foot it lightly'. 'Don't do anything professionally!' he said to Riemer in 1807; 'that is entirely against the grain as far as I am concerned. I like to do everything I undertake in a playful fashion. . . . I will not make a mere instrument of myself, and every profession is an instrument'. This lighthearted attitude could be most vigorously applied in his own special sphere of artistic criticism, but was also maintained in the easy touch of genius that he applied to his historical thought, as we saw in our opening survey. All his occupations showed the minimum of systematic and logical application. And yet this preliminary trying out of his intellectual strength produced in Goethe a systematic framework of knowledge which can only be indicated with a rather light touch and not too much 'professionalism'.

Our starting-point was Goethe's early antiquarian impulse, already evident in his boyhood. We saw how active he was in Italy and on his other travels, and the diaries and accounts of journeys in his old age show that he was always ready to get out of his carriage and pensively examine an old church or castle, or an old rampart. 'The sight of old implements, weapons, harness, seals and sculpture', Goethe once wrote in his old age (*Der deutsche Gil Blas*) (*The German Gil Blas*), 'always helps us to feel what life must have looked like in the days when they were made and used'. True, when he was only confronted by worn and shapeless remains of the past, his innate need for meaning and coherence in phenomena might make him turn away in revolt. This happened in 1801, when he came upon some reminiscences of Roman and Germanic history in the district of Pyrmont. Yet the power of the primitive urge was shown by his standing still and relapsing once again into that strange mood of union between past and present.

> Turn and twist as one may, or show any amount of distaste for such efforts to make the uncertain even more uncertain, one finds oneself as it were caught up in a magic circle, one identifies the past with the present . . . and ends by feeling in a thoroughly comfortable frame of mind because one thinks for a moment that one has had a direct glimpse of the incomprehensible (*Annalen*).

He then thoughtfully wove this motif, with very little alteration, into his *Wahlverwandtschaften* (II, 2).

An attempt must be made to come to closer grips from many different angles with this feeling of unity that so often came over Goethe. In spite of its highly individual shades and varieties, there was nevertheless, as we have hinted, something of the heritage of the Enlightenment about it. For the Enlightenment had already, in its own way, established a sense of unity between the past and the present. Admittedly, this had only come about through mechanistic lines of thought. The life of history had appeared in principle to be similar in all periods, ruled by the same constant forces of human reason and unreason. The only variation between past and present was the variation in the proportions between these two.

Connected with this sense, however, there was a feeling for the unity of everything human, a universal curiosity and openness for the remotest parts of the human and historical cosmos. We saw this in Voltaire, and we come across it again in Goethe. Even in his old age, and in spite of all that separated him from Voltaire, Goethe called him a universal source of light, and testified emphatically to Eckermann in 1830 what it had cost him to guard against his influence. Voltaire, with his energies directed to culture, meant more to him than Montesquieu, with his political utilitarianism centred upon institutions—though Montesquieu was equally familiar to Goethe.

In general, however, there is no mistaking the points of connection with the Enlightenment which in many respects influenced Goethe's historical thought. Both were more concerned with seeking humanity in history than history in humanity. Only Goethe as he went on his way through life found that the historical elements in humanity came extensively within his purview. A specific common starting-point, which then led him much further afield, was Goethe's feeling for the unity of all things human. He believed that there is a common world of values in the good and the beautiful, applicable to all peoples, 'in which they all necessarily resemble one another' (Notes to the *W.-ö. Divan*). In his old age (*Dicht. und Wahrh.*, I, 4; von Müller, 1881, Eckermann, 1832), Goethe even spoke of the truths of natural religion and a kind of primitive religion of pure nature and reason. Here, he did express himself in a much more spiritual and creative fashion with regard to its primitive phenomena than the men of the Enlightenment had done when they reduced the bare content of a natural religion to a kind of catechism. For Goethe, the common religious ideas of the various peoples, with their everlasting recurrence, were only a thousand individual varieties of a basic form, the mysterious contribution made to life by a higher power, from which an attentive researcher could piece together a kind of alphabet of the world spirit (von Müller, 1818). All the same, as in Herder's original revelation of the 'earliest primitive knowledge', there was something of the Enlightenment, with a mystical and romantic reinterpretation, about this confession made by Goethe in his old age. At that time an open conflict began between the old rationalism and the new Christian faith which held itself to be superior; and Goethe did not hesitate to admit that rationalism corresponded to the assumptions of the most enlightened philosophy (von Müller, 1823). There are other detached historical judgements of Goethe confirming this line of thought. In the commentary on Benvenuto he calls Savonarola a ridiculous monstrosity; and in his *Theory of Colours* he characterises the religious excesses of the English revolutionary period as sheer whimsicality, and 'a monstrosity of the time'. One can almost see

Voltaire looking over his shoulder and smiling in approval. The ultimate motives for this disapproval, however, were not the same as with Voltaire. He had revolted against this superficially, as contrary to reason; Goethe against what he felt in his deepest self to be contrary to nature. Yet there is clearly a connecting line between Voltaire and Goethe. It is hardly necessary to remind ourselves that even Goethe's cosmopolitan view, which (as he once expressed it to Eckermann in 1832) surveyed the landscape like the soaring eagle, grew up in the bosom of the Enlightenment. His conception of the State, which we have repeatedly touched upon, his treatment of the Middle Ages, and many other features show the same colouring in respect of their origins. But nowhere do we get mere residues of the judgements passed by the Enlightenment. Even where this is our first impression, they are charged with a new sensitivity and inner strength which make them stand out above the average of the Enlightenment, just like the comparable features in Herder. But the principle of continuity, which gives the history of thought its inner unity and philosophical value, proves its worth at this point too. It must never be forgotten that the Enlightenment was able to provide Goethe, if not with building-stones, at any rate with a level and prepared site for the construction of his own edifice of world thought.

In the chapter on Möser we showed how the Enlightenment freed human reason from dogma and tradition; and how simultaneously and unwittingly it acted as a summons to all the irrational powers of the psyche.

Sensibility and over-subtle reasoning, pride in the present and a Pre-Romantic dilettantism, went hand in hand together like a strangely unequal couple that copy each other. Then came the deeper breakthrough in 'Sturm und Drang', the growing consciousness of the unity and integral quality of all the psychological powers. Yet along with this, there was the realisation of their individuality, and the origin of all originality and its various gradations in the endless creative depths of nature, in the universe as a whole. The new element, which had never been represented like this before in the history of Western thought, the centre piece in this sequence of ideas, was the strong and definite experience of individuality. It was at once fused by Herder with the idea of development, and the youthful Goethe soon followed suit. This happened against a Protestant background, and was not unconnected with the arousal of personal religious life brought about by pietism. But there was here a more vital view of the universe, transcending the mechanisms of the Enlightenment in its restless dynamic and its production of manifold gradations of natural and spiritual powers from nature's invisible bosom. There was a far stronger sense of their permanent and immanent connection with the

421

universal whole, and a sense that they would some day return to their original source. And there were the ideas in which the stamp of Neo-Platonic thinking once more impressed itself upon the general fabric of Western thought.

Thus the philosophy of life at the basis of Goethe's historical thought (apart from the experience of individuality and its development) is a synthesis of elements from the Enlightenment and from Neo-Platonism. Herder had blended the two previously, though not with such fullness, and the process had been completed by other minds in the eighteenth century. But the peculiar power of Goethe's own experience of individuality was able to add immensely to its depth. In recent times, it has been more and more clearly recognised (notably by Burdach and Franz Koch) how Neo-Platonic Goethe's thinking was all through his life, and to what an extent he even interpreted his beloved Spinoza along these lines. This has incidentally shown that the Neo-Platonic thought was mostly not presented to Goethe as a young man in its original form, but was largely transformed into a Christian, and particularly a pietistic, mysticism. Yet his method of forging these elements afresh for his own purposes, and his incorporation of what suited his inner selectivity, was something highly original. Perhaps the most apt testimony to his Neo-Platonism (if one is needed) is a little-known verse of a theatrical prologue in 1807, belonging to the years of special study devoted by Goethe to Plotinus after 1805, and expressing the sorrows and subsequent recovery of the fatal year 1806–7:

> So in the small as in the great
> Nature is active and the mind of man.
> Both are reflections of the primal light above
> Which all unseen illuminates this world.

What attracted Goethe to the Neo-Platonic philosophy was not only its ability to derive the whole of experience, including the mind of man and its natural environment, from a primal source that was far beyond human ken. It was not only the noble place thus given to nature, or the comforting prospect of development by gradations up to an ever loftier purity and unity of the whole. This might well have been enough for purely speculative needs; but Goethe's inner nature asked more of God. As soon as he had fully understood himself in Italy, he realised that he was intent upon unwearying creation, evolution and self-development, upon constant remodelling of the self, while yet remaining true to himself; upon individuality, which was both malleable and yet permanent; upon the primal forms of nature and humanity created by God, and the thousand changes that they undergo. The Neo-Platonic philosophy was based upon the idea of emanations (or more accurately radiations), rather than development; but it touched upon the principle of individuality, though not in an exhaustive manner, and made demands of an ascetical kind that were foreign to Goethe's nature. Yet it contained so much restless dynamism, and so much room for movement and development for the individual who would otherwise have been so forlorn in the world, that it was capable of forming a starting-point for Goethe's own universal philosophy. And where it blended with Spinoza's outlook was in preserving so much that was stable in the midst of change, so much ultimate permanence rising above all temporary restlessness, that it could even satisfy Goethe, who looked upon all the pressures and turmoils of this world as eternal peace when seen in God, the sovereign Lord of the universe.

Goethe and Plotinus, like Heraclitus before them, were fond of thinking in pictures; and pictorial thinking is a constantly and universally recurrent type in human intellectual life. It leads in itself to a lively and dynamic view of life, whereas abstract conceptual thinking tends to be more static. Furthermore, it can conduce to a feeling for the whole, a sense that scattered things are somehow or other linked to one another, that each individual course of life corresponds to some related course in another part of the universe, and that in spite of all the manifold variety, movement, connection and unity somehow belong to the essence of the world.

Thus Goethe's highest achievement in universal philosophy was the combination of Heraclitic and Eleatic thinking, eternal development, and eternal being—'constancy in the midst of change'. But the only part of the eternal being that could be descried, according to Goethe, was the eternal law of everlasting change. Since his journey to Italy he had concentrated upon this, though without for a moment losing his delight and sympathy in all things temporal and transitory. He could even rejoice in the symbolism of a garden, and marvel 'how the transitory and the permanent are here interwoven' (*Wahlverwandtschaften*, II, 9). But this need for eternal laws was again something that linked him with the Enlightenment, and constituted without a doubt his deepest point of contact with it. Like the Enlightenment, Goethe strove to find a lofty supra-temporal standpoint from which to view the events of time. Only the point was quite differently selected from that of the Enlightenment and much more upon Neo-Platonic lines. It often happens, however, that a man will most strenuously deny a continuity with other thinkers that is nevertheless obviously present. And he will do this particularly when he is seeking to satisfy a need which he holds in common with others, but is trying to satisfy in a different way. Thus it was precisely at this point that Goethe drew the sharpest dividing line between himself and the Enlightenment. He reproached the 'intellectual culture' of the eighteenth century and its 'self-opinionated cleverness' for seeking the eternal laws of being purely by means of the intellect, instead of with the reason, which represented to Goethe the sum-total of all the higher powers of the soul. The laws of being corresponding to a purely intellectual approach could only be lifeless and static: they could not produce a living and dynamic world. As he said to Eckermann in 1829:

> The deity, however, is active in the living and not in the dead;
> in that which is developing and changing, not in that which
> has reached a static state. Thus reason in its tendency towards
> the divine is only concerned with the developing and the
> living; the intellect is concerned rather with that which has
> developed and reached a static state.

Goethe's conception of law was therefore quite different from that of the Enlightenment, and completely devoid of all mathematical elements. As Gundolf very happily expressed it, 'Goethe's laws are themselves individual—delicately elastic formative forces mysteriously residing within the ever-dynamic life'.

Thus Goethe reached within himself an ideal balance between becoming and being, change and permanence, the historical and the supra-historical-eternal. But there remains the great and difficult question, whether this meant that he could do full justice to the phenomena and essential character of the historical world. We must ask whether in the cases where his unifying maxims concerning becoming and being were not quite able to penetrate the world of history, the reason should be sought in the maxims themselves, or in other factors of Goethe's life. This question, which can only be answered as we proceed step by step, is brought closer by a series of adverse judgements uttered by Goethe on the subject of history in general.

II *Goethe's Negative Relationship to History*

The testimonies to Goethe's discontent with history are like a block in the road we should like to travel in our further exploration of his world of historical thought. Even in the glance we took at Goethe's genetical approach, there was a repeated note of vague disenchantment with certain impressions of the past. But up till now, this has been kept in the background by the picture of a developing and constantly more fruitful interest in history on the part of Goethe. There is, however, a chain of pronouncements upon history, stretching from the ridicule in the original version of *Faust* at the rubbish-bin and lumber-room of the past to the verdict of 1828, that universal history is the absurdest thing that ever existed (von Müller). This is such a continuous chain that it would seem to give a repeated 'no' from the depths of Goethe's feelings to anything we might be inclined to affirm about his sense of history. This brings us to one of the most difficult problems in our attempt to understand Goethe.

First, it is necessary to state the motives and arguments and distinguish them from one another, as far as they are discernible behind these verdicts or may be in any other way surmised. It has been suggested that Goethe, like others, was put off from history by the unsatisfactory state of historical writing at that time. But this is in itself a very external and unsatisfying explanation. It may well be that the professional histories written by the German professors of his day bored him. But there were also the splendid historical writings of the Enlightenment, ranging from Voltaire to Gibbon, which Schiller was zealous in imitating. It may be that the enlightened and misleading gloss of these works, so very different from his own out-look upon the world, was seen through by Goethe. But he was also aware from the start of the new efforts towards a deeper and more vital handling of history. Möser's magnificent project for a history of Osnabrück was printed in the same number of *Blätter von deutscher Art und Kunst* (*German Custom and Art*) of 1772–3 that contained Goethe's essay on the Strassburg Cathedral; and Möser, with his new wealth of historical sensitivity, remained for the whole of Goethe's lifetime a man after his own heart. And Herder's *Ideen*, that great new attempt at a sketch of universal history, was read by Goethe in Italy, with some reservations, yet with predominating admiration, as we have already seen. Niebuhr's history of Rome, however, which was first in the field of modern historical writing, was a revelation to Goethe, or at any rate a fulfilment of his own former thirst for knowledge. Nor must it be forgotten that Goethe, as his diaries demonstrate, read not only the modern historians but also those of antiquity—and went back to them again and again. As well as historians, he read source material, such as memoirs and auto-biographies, which provided him with fresh springs of direct historical life. In short, there were enough green pastures and fertile land around him to entice him into history; and he did in fact respond to the enticement.

There is perhaps a second motive of a general kind to be con-sidered, which may have kept Goethe at arm's length from the world of history. We might almost be tempted to say that he approached history with the sovereignty of an artist, and was therefore inclined to despise and condemn the part of history that cannot be artistically viewed and reconstructed. But this would be too summary an explanation. It would at once give rise to the counter-question, why so large a part of history seemed to him to be incapable of this artistic reconstruction. Face to face with nature, Goethe had by no means shown himself only as the formative artist, but also as the thinker and researcher. Though gifted with an artistic eye, he was also capable of strict inductive research into the objective forms and norms of nature. As Cassirer has most happily suggested in his book *Freiheit und Form* (*Freedom and Form*) (p. 382), the primary element in Goethe's character was not the specific artistry, but rather a higher common source for both the artistic and the researching talent, in what may perhaps be called his constructive power.

But some closer enquiry is needed about the grounds for his dissatisfaction with history. First of all, there was certainly something of an objection to the writing of history as carried out up till then, with its pragmatism in the handling of great political events, the so-called 'Haupt- und Staatsaktionen' ('public events and actions of state'). As early as the original *Faust*, Goethe was already making fun of the apposite pragmatic maxims, suitable to be mouthed by puppets. And in the review of Sonnenfels' *Liebe des Vaterlandes* (*Love of the Fatherland*) in 1771 (probably attributable on internal evidence to the hand of Goethe), still more scorn is poured upon the defective manner of explaining the results of great lives like those of Lycurgus, Solon, Numa and so on in terms of clear and specific political principles and purposes. 'Fancy touching upon mysteries (for what great historical data are not mysterious to us?), only dimly accessible to the profoundest sympathetic mind, and producing blissfully clever arguments!' Passing over further detailed testimonies, we may simply say that even in his later years Goethe treated the would-be pragmatic-historical descriptions with irony ('so that is what he thinks?'), and called the whole of written history a euphemism (Rochlitz, 1829).

There was more in this than the revolt of a profounder vitality against the superficial way pragmatism accounted for motives. What Goethe mistrusted was the subjective element, which seemed to him so inseparably bound up with the historical tradition and the historical standpoint. This is specially evident in the famous conversation with the Jena historian Luden on the value of history in 1806. When Luden put forward the possibility of using methods of critical examination to overcome the deficiencies and contradictions in traditional material and so arrive at the truth, Goethe replied that this would only be subjective, and not incontestably objective, truth. He could not help smiling when he saw how scholars used the same acuteness (or lack of it) to reach different historical opinions. Writing to Zelter in 1824, Goethe remarks: 'Therefore everything historical has a strange and uncertain character, and it really becomes comical, when one considers how people convince themselves with complete certainty about the distant past'. Only where he believed he had discovered an objective truth did Goethe, after he had found his true self, feel altogether confident about the foundations of his own attitude. 'My whole contemporary world was at variance with me', he said to Eckermann in 1824, 'for it was entirely preoccupied with a subjective approach, whilst I with my objective endeavours laboured under a disadvantage, and found myself all on my own'. Purely objective truth seemed to Goethe to be provided by the results of his studies of science; also by his work of art that was shaped according to the inner laws of nature. The whole coherence of his philosophy of life (what has been called his objective idealism) comes into the picture at this point. He was 'the God-guided man' who was glad to shun the dim spheres in which subjectivity could not be transcended, in order to work his way up into the unclouded regions of the divine nature.

It is possible to elaborate this point in more detail. Goethe regarded the results of his studies of science as objective because he had seen them with his eyes, grasped them with his senses, and subjected them to full intellectual examination:

> To trust the senses be then bold,
> For nothing false shalt thou behold
> If understanding still her vigil keeps.

He was above all things a man of the sensuous present, though never this alone, for he was wonderfully well equipped both physically and mentally for grasping the phenomena he encountered according to their form and shape, their sensuous appeal and their inner law. As one of his younger friends, Rosette Städel, remarked in 1814, 'the whole of nature, every blade of grass, every word and every glance speaks to him and records itself as feeling and as image in his soul'. This was the 'objective thinking' of which Goethe spoke himself, 'which forms itself and expresses itself always in confrontation with the actual object' (to Boisserée, 1822). Compared with what the actual presence of phenomena could give him, the past might sometimes well seem to him no more than a sealed book. The seals were loosened as soon as his mind could light upon some aspect of humanity that had form, and the power to speak to him in a vital manner; and this was pre-eminently true of a work of art. The historical past as a whole perhaps remained for Goethe something like the dark night-sky against which countless brilliant stars stood out. But the deep darkness behind them was apt to strike him as a repellent chaos:

> E'en though the stars with double brilliance gleam
> Eternally the universe will darkness seem.

These were the deeper reasons for the constant sounding in Goethe of the Pyrrhonic tone of scepticism against historic traditions cultivated by the Enlightenment. It seems paradoxical enough that Goethe, with his sharp eye for anything legendary, who had tried his hand at the criticism of legend in the story of Moses, should at times have championed and defended the legends against modern criticism, despite his dissatisfaction with fallacious and unreliable history. As he said to Eckermann in 1825, modern criticism was now coming along and proclaiming that Lucretia and Mucius Scaevola never existed. What should we make of such pitiful findings, he asked? If the Romans were great enough to invent them, we should at least be great enough to believe in them. It was the same with the Bible. To question what was genuine and non-genuine in its contents was indeed strange. Surely all that was excellent in it, in harmony with the purest in nature and in reason, and still of service to our highest development today, must indeed be genuine. All that was absurd, hollow and stupid, and not productive of any good fruit, must be pronounced non-genuine (Eckermann, 1832).

We begin to have an inkling of how the paradox was resolving itself for Goethe. In his eyes, there was no contradiction between a general distrust of the written tradition, and a confident acceptance of such traditions as proved to him their legitimacy by the vitality of their inner content. To him, they were as 'genuine', as true and objectively valid as the work of art formed in accordance with the inner laws of nature. 'Only that which is fruitful is true.' As Goethe wrote to Zelter in 1829, 'I have noticed that I hold a thought to be true if it is fruitful for me, fits in with my other thinking, and at the same time carries me forward'. In *Dichtung und Wahrheit* (III, 12) he explains:

> When I have appropriated to myself the inner content, the
> sense, the original element, the divine and active and
> imperishable part of a work from the past, I do not allow myself
> to be robbed of this acquisition by any destructive criticisms
> that can only touch the externals of the work.

Here is another characteristic testimony:

> With paintings, but even more with drawings, everything
> depends upon the originality. I mean by originality, not that the
> work is necessarily by the hand of the master to whom it is

428

ascribed, but that its original genius is such that it at any rate deserves the honour of a famous name (to Rochlitz, 1815).

Mere facts did not represent genuine truth to Goethe. 'Everything becomes uncertain', he remarks, 'if one only pays attention to the chance relationships between earthly things' (*Theory of Colours*). He thus drew out the ultimate logical consequences of the Pyrrhonic criticism characteristic of the Enlightenment, and in his own way transcended it. For he constructed for himself a higher law of truth in which there was only room for that which was in accordance with the divine nature, that which was creative, and that which bore the higher kind of fruit. As Cassirer rightly points out in *Goethe und die geschichtliche Welt* (p. 23), he completely changed the doctrine of historical certainty. It might be objected that his attempts to be objective threatened at this point to swing round into a grandiose subjectivity, a kind of belief in inspiration. But the feeling that his own nature was intimately linked with the divine constituted the great source of power in Goethe's thought. Moreover, it was free from the overweening delusion of being able personally to achieve the highest absolute form of truth. 'Truth as identical with the divine can never be directly attained by us' (*Versuch einer Witterungslehre*, 1825); 'We can only catch its reflections by way of example and symbol.' Finally, it is only the language of his own conceptual world that veils from us a kernel of truth that is still valid in his judgements on legendary material. It was profoundly historical insight which showed him that even traditions in legendary form could still possess a value independent of their factual truth. In certain respects, this was an anticipation of the higher historical criticism, which can infuse new life into what criticism merely concerned with genuineness would be disposed to reject.

Goethe's transformation of the doctrine of historical certainty had, however, some further consequences which are still at work and have taken on new life particularly in recent times. It was not the 'facts', but the mental and spiritual content, of the past, discernible only by intuition, that seemed to him truly certain. And the facts appeared to be transitory in comparison with the mental and spiritual content, which was constantly being filled with new life. 'Thoughts return, convictions are renewed; it is only the circumstances that pass away beyond recall' (*Max. und Refl.*). In these judgements, Goethe was justifying in advance the efforts of the modern history of thought. Only the latter remains more sceptical than Goethe: it is conscious of its subjective *a priori* basis, and (apart from the most modern aberrations) its attitude is different from Goethe's on the relationship between criticism and intuition. The modern view holds them to be closely interconnected, and will not apply them separately. Goethe, however, as we have just seen, held them to function along-side one another, but not intermingled; he under-estimated the importance of what he called the criticism of externals—the mere body of tradition. On this particular point, Goethe and critical historism certainly part company. Yet this separation should not be interpreted too deeply or radically. Wherever (as in Niebuhr's *History of Rome*) Goethe encountered criticism and intuition in creative partnership, he was at once won over and felt their close intellectual relationship. 'The separation between fiction and history', Goethe wrote to Niebuhr in 1811, 'is invaluable: it destroys neither of them, but rather enables the value and merit of each to be all the more clearly confirmed'.

Thus Goethe's dissatisfaction with history could also produce positive ferments for his historical thought. But we have not yet completely understood the motives for this dissatisfaction. In his history of the theory of colour he reproached universal history with being incalculable and incommensurable. In so doing, he was also impugning the value of its factual content. Law and chance, he held, were intermingled; but the observer was often put in a position where he confused the two, and this led Goethe once more into voicing his criticism of the subjective character of historical writing. In his *Italian Journey*, he says that nature is the only book in which *every* page contains important material. It is better to turn direct to nature than to search about in the slag-heaps of past centuries (*Annalen*, 1812). And in the conversations of his old age with Chancellor Müller, when he called universal history the absurdest thing in existence, he went on to say: 'I am not concerned whether such-and-such a person dies, or this or that nation perishes; I should be a fool to bother myself about it'.

Goethe's views were not always as unfeeling as that. But the deep dissatisfaction with the material composition of history demon-strated by these and many other sayings was only the expression of his incapacity to master the material of history with as great an intellectual completeness as he reckoned to achieve in the explorable part of nature, where he could confidently go step by step on the heuristic principles of original form and metamorphosis. No doubt, nature and history were ultimately one in Goethe's mind, and history no more than a section of the totality of the divine nature. But after he had learnt to seek this universal life by way of the observation of nature, he applied to the historical field tests that were applicable enough to nature, but not so simply and directly to history. In nature Goethe thought he could descry 'a pure and sound development' of 'the idea that leads on to life'; but in history there was the danger of being 'led astray in a morbid manner from the true path'. He continues (writing to E. H. F. Meyer in 1829):

> And equally, the history of the Churches and nations becomes so confused that the main line of thought, which should accompany the course of the world's history in an extremely pure and clear form, is obscured, disturbed and distorted through considerations of the particular moment, or century, or locality, or various other factors.

Most repulsive of all the elements in history to Goethe was chance, which his innate daemon compelled him to hate from the depths of his soul. Even in the sphere of non-human nature he combated it wherever he came across it. He confessed his aversion to forced explanations of theories of catastrophic change which employed earthquakes, floods and other titanic events, whereas a calmer look at the facts suggested a slow and natural continuous activity (*Annalen*, 1820). In this sphere he could obstinately defend himself against the 'mad eddies' of chance. But in the realm of history he could not use the same weapons. He had no means of recognising and eliminating the turbulent volcanic element, or at least of confining it within strict limits. The birth and death of powerful rulers, the accession of weaklings to thrones that had been occupied by greater predecessors, degeneracies and collapses, petty motives for particular actions— were not all of these the work of chance, which yet produced mighty effects? This recalls Voltaire's historical writings in the Enlightenment, and his reluctance to face up to this coarse and ugly world of chance; whereas Montesquieu's powerful thought had attempted to defy it. Voltaire had eased the way for himself by lingering in the few green valleys of the rocky wilderness of history. And Goethe, in his own particular fashion, was to follow in his footsteps. Both of them, however, being thoroughly realist, were ready to face fairly and squarely the causal importance of chance in history, and the modern historism must do the same. For example, it must firmly and decisively recognise that the death of the Empress of Russia, Elisabeth, in 1762, was a chance event, but for which the destiny of Russia and Germany might well have been quite different.

There might have been an opportunity for Goethe to accord a greater dignity to the element of chance in history. He might have assigned it to the sphere we thought of as a dark storm-layer hanging over humanity, the place where 'almighty time and eternal destiny have their dwelling'. Goethe always possessed this sense of fate, a fate which becomes linked through the element of chance to the inscrutable texture of the world's events and he certainly felt it at work in his own life. Testimony to this is provided by the closing passages of

Dichtung und Wahrheit, where he exalts to the mysterious level of fate the chance that played a part in his journey to Weimar, and the decisive consequences that it had for the course of his subsequent life. Moreover, he conceived humanity as a whole to be in the grip of fate; yet he objected to chance, which appeared to govern a part of historical events. There were certain inhibitions in him at this point which we must try gradually to understand.

Now since Goethe's time there have been repeated attempts to exclude chance altogether from history as something quite unimportant compared with its great regularities. But this has only been achieved either by labouring the concept of law at that particular time and distorting the awkward facts on a bed of Procrustes, or by pronouncing the inconvenient facts to be totally insignificant over against the iron processes of universal law. Goethe did not attempt either of these alternatives. He respected facts, even those which he found awkward. It is again quite evident that even in the negative part of Goethe's relationship to history, there could be something positively true and fruitful.

Goethe was also preserved from any exaggeration of the idea of law, such as Positivism later on betrayed, by the more refined and vital nature of the laws that he himself believed in. They were not, like those of Positivism, discovered by a deductive generalisation of certain experiences, together with the importation of its own temporal ideals into the material of those experiences. On the contrary, Goethe's laws were discovered by sinking himself inductively into the specific life of the phenomena under observation—nature in the first place, and then from nature to the life of man. No doubt his own living ideals of development, and his own individuality, with its typical and universal limitations, played some part in this process. Yet everywhere he sought to discover the inner essence and inner dynamic of things from their own centre of vitality. He saw this kind of individual life, derived from the universal life and permanently interwoven with it, in the smallest and the largest star alike: he saw it everywhere. 'Even in this piece of sugar in front of us', he once said in his old age, 'there is life'.

But was there not after all much more life in what Goethe disliked in history as 'chance' than he was willing to admit? Was there not much more trace of inner regularity in the course of events which seemed first of all, to one nurtured on the Enlightenment, to be no more than the wild confused motion of blind forces that had been let loose on the world? Was it not possible also in the sphere of national and political destiny, with its wars and struggles for power, to replace the explanation in terms of catastrophic change, which Goethe so much disliked, by something more along evolutionary lines? Even during Goethe's lifetime, attempts were beginning to be made within the Romantic Movement, and notably by Adam Müller, to interpret at least the struggles for power among States in aphoristic terms as vital and organic processes. Under the stimulus of Romanticism and the work of Goethe, Ranke had begun to take the lead with writings which uncovered the vital centres and vital laws of politics in typical as well as in individual fashion. This Goethe either could not, or did not want to do. Together with the methodological difference noted above in the relative assessment of criticism and intuition, and with certain effects of normative thought which we shall touch upon later, this really constitutes the only serious dividing-line that separates Goethe from the fully developed historism. And it constituted the chief reason for his dissatisfaction with universal history in general. Viewed in the broad light of the history of thought, Goethe would seem to have possessed the key that would have unlocked this world as well, and to have filled it out with the concepts of primal form and metamorphosis. He had it in his pocket, and yet did not use it. Why was this?

It was because Daemon and Tyche, his mentality and his circumstances, his spirit and his fate, were at mutual odds in this point of his thinking. 'I am a child of peace', he declared; and in these words he expressed one of his deepest needs. His profound understanding of Hamlet's character, 'without the sensuous strength that makes the hero' (*Lehrjahre*, vol. 4, p. 13), suggests something of a self-analysis, although it will scarcely be denied that Goethe himself did possess quite a different kind of heroism.

Goethe grew up in the somewhat decadent comfort of an imperial city in the old Empire, in the unpolitical, peace-loving atmosphere of the eighteenth-century middle class, which had worked its way up out of the Thirty Years War. It built up its culture mainly without help from the State, and also without any State interference; the result was an easy-going juxtaposition of State and culture. The State was looked upon both as the administrative welfare State, which was thoroughly acceptable, and as the warfare State, which did not affect a man personally. It must either be criticised or simply dismissed with a regretful shrug of the shoulders as a foreign world that must be allowed to go its own way. 'Our modern wars', said Goethe in Italy, 'make many people unhappy while they last, and no one happy when they are over.' This was his feeling as he stood on the threshold of a quarter-century of warfare, to which he bowed like a field of wheat before the storm, without ever proving untrue to the natural bent of his disposition. Roethe is quite right in his opinion that Goethe's attitude to war never showed much sign of development. To a certain extent, his poetic talent enabled him to sympathise with the heroism of the warrior (Achilles; Prometheus in *Pandora*); and his insight could enter into the beneficial results of great struggles for the life of the nation, such as those in English history. On one occasion, he even ventured the overstatement that culture was nothing but a higher conception of political and military relationships (von Müller, 1827); and in so saying he at any rate did justice to the causal relationship between culture, the State and war. Moreover, he could declare that 'the events taking place among peoples and their shepherds when they rise up in solidarity' are of the very greatest human importance (*Dicht. und Wahrh.*, book 7). He knew and appreciated this primal phenomenon, yet he was not interested in its deeper manifestations. In spite of his basic nature, he remained true to the Enlightenment on this one point, and entirely shared its judgement that the confused warlike events of particular periods resemble one another, in whatever century they may occur (*Annalen*, 1795). 'Even this world-wide disease that has come down to us from the past I had to suffer and overcome' (to Rochlitz, 1822); this was Goethe's comment on his interest in the campaign of 1792. On the whole, like Herder, Goethe took up the detached attitude of the eighteenth century to all power politics; but he felt less passion and pain about them than Herder.

Thus, Goethe was at one with Herder and the Enlightenment in his convinced assumption that culture is of higher value than the State. The later champions of the Enlightenment went on to work out an ideal State, completely suitable to the cultural and peaceful needs of the individual. Goethe, however, remained faithful to the political realism of an older period, as represented by Möser and others (and even in fits and starts by Voltaire); and this again was due to his fundamental nature. He did not expect the fostering of culture to come from some imaginary ideal State, but from the actual solidly-based State as it existed, which was responsible under all conditions for law and order. And for this purpose he was willing, in accordance with the political traditions of the seventeenth and eighteenth centuries, to grant it the right to exercise political expediency, and in case of need to use methods outside the law. The root of his political thought was well expressed in the words he uttered at the siege of Mainz: 'It's a part of my nature: I would rather commit a wrong than put up with disorder.'

The support of political expediency, as we have already seen on more than one occasion, led on to an examination of historical struggles for power, their meaning and general place in the scheme of things. Even in his early days, Goethe recognised this line of action. In *Götz*, *Egmont* and *Die Natürliche Tochter*, he made his heroes feel the cold touch of political expediency, or what purported to be such, and the daemonic element in it. He brought it out even more strongly in what Faust allows to happen to Philemon and Baucis. In the last years of his life, Goethe came into closer sympathy with practical politics and its traditions. He was willing to accord the rights of political expediency to princes not only for the forcible maintenance of internal order, but also for achieving the requirements of external policy. In his conversation with Chancellor Müller, he justified Prussia in taking her share at the partition of Poland, rejected the judgement of 'the usual platitudinous political moralists', and declared that 'no king keeps his word, nor can he do so, for he must always give way to imperious circumstance. . . . For us poor Philistines the opposite course of action is a duty, but not for the mighty ones of this earth'.

Yet Goethe did not succeed in advancing a single step in his understanding of the confused ways of the world. In his later life he did indeed often follow contemporary political events with remarkable accuracy, but more from a certain sense of duty, which would not allow him to neglect this side of life, than from intrinsic interest. Politics are a matter of destiny as he remarked in agreement with Napoleon in the last weeks of his life (Eckermann); and yet he had deliberately excluded this largest area in which destiny was at work from the compass of his own interests. Even if one took a Machiavellian view, as he said to Zelter in 1827, one could scarcely occupy oneself with world history.[1] This world, in which Machiavelli was the acknowledged master, was to Goethe a world for which his psyche was no match, and which it must not fit, if it was to continue to take up into itself all the rest of the world with profundity and clarity. To be sure, he took into his pantheon all the great political heroes of world history—Caesar, Frederick the Great, Napoleon, and almost even a figure like Tamerlane. But the characteristic thing about Goethe was that he dissociated himself from the details of their practical politics, and only considered them as dynamic forces, who certainly also exercised something of a moral effect upon their age. In this respect he did not in principle differ much from the ordinary naive hero-worshipper.

Yet it is perhaps possible to discover a deeper reason for his disinclination to penetrate at a profounder level into the confused events of history. He was certainly full of relief after 1814, and felt that these were halcyon days of restoration, in which a man could

---

[1] 4 December 1827. He speaks of Walter Scott's Napoleon, and how he 'strictly abstains from all Machiavellian views, *without* which one could indeed hardly wish to have anything at all to do with world history'. The foregoing praise of Walter Scott leaves us in no doubt that the sentence would be more grammatical if we substituted the word 'with' for the word 'without'.

rejoice, as did the young Ranke too. But whereas Ranke, starting out from this point, began to contemplate the world of power politics with a view to understanding it, a particularly deep trait in Goethe held him back from any such course. He was always disposed to be active and creative, and he could not adopt a merely contemplative attitude to any human affairs. As a minister of Charles Augustus, he had helped him at the time of the North German League of Princes[1] in 1785 to direct his master's cautious little-State policy. He would only have been able to enter fully into the tremendous events that followed it with full understanding, if he had had the chance of taking some creative part in them. But this would have meant being untrue to his own genius. On this point, the words he used in 1824 to Chancellor Müller are significant:

> The present condition of the world, with its demand for transparency in all relationships, is very favourable for the development of the individual, if he desires to keep himself to himself. But if he wishes to interfere with the running of the world's machinery, and thinks he can run some part of it according to his own independent ideas or check its working, then he will only come to grief all the more speedily.

Thus it may be said by way of summary that in the last resort it was not Goethe's incapacity for historical judgement, but an incapacity of his inmost self, that was the limiting factor. It was this that prevented him from grasping in the same morphological manner the part of universal history concerned with wars and rumours of war, the turmoils of peoples and the violent overthrow of kings, and from working out its course of development as he had done for nature and the rest of human life. 'Disturb not my circles': this was the message given by the overriding sovereignty of his own personality. Only it is not altogether possible to separate Goethe's own spirit from the spirit of the times, which here speaks with the same voice. For it shows that on this point he was still lingering in the thought-world of his early environment, the atmosphere of the Enlightenment, which in other respects he had so completely transcended. On one occasion (to Knebel in 1817), he even spoke about the events of the Reformation period as 'a lot of confused nonsense'.

This was a judgement that embraced both the political and the ecclesiastical events of the Reformation. And it raises the question whether Goethe's own attitude to Christianity contributed to his reluctance to admit that the history of the world as a whole carried any deeper meaning. If he had been a convinced Christian, he might have been able to find a constructive unity in world history; and as a

[1] Against Joseph II of Austria.

convinced opponent of Christianity, as a pure champion of the Enlightenment in its struggle to promote reason, he might have seen this as the main spiritual and intellectual bond. Even a synthesis of Christianity and Enlightenment, though still incomplete, could have achieved a meaningful interpretation of world history—as was shown by the example of Herder. But Goethe was unable to accept Christianity outright, or reject it outright.

His varying attitude to Christianity may be compared to an ellipse. In youth and in old age he came closest to it; but in the intervening space, the classicist period, he stood at some distance from it, though not so far off but what we can trace a subtle Christian influence even in his *Iphigenie*. Only once (in his youthful period) did this permanent influence affect him decisively in the form of pietist religion, and start to give a specific religiosity to his poems. But this attitude was soon absorbed by a religious outlook permanently tinged with Neo-Platonism. In youth and in old age, Goethe had the deepest veneration for the sublimity of Christ's teachings. But can this be called a purely and specifically religious attitude? Surely there was still some admixture of the Enlightenment's separation between the valuable kernel of Christian morality and the useless husk of Christian dogma. Moreover, in his heart of hearts there was at times a wish that 'this Jewish stuff', the Bible, had been replaced by Homer. 'What a different form humanity would have assumed if this had been the case!' (to Böttiger, about 1790). As he wrote to Herder in 1788:

> It remains true that because of the fairy-tale of Christ the world may last for another 10 million years and no one will reach full understanding, seeing that it takes as much force of knowledge, understanding, and conceptual power to defend it as to attack it. Now the generations blend with one another; the individual is a poor thing, whatever party he belongs to. The *whole* is never a *whole*; and so the human race hovers to and fro in a mean and miserable state. This would not matter if it did not have such a great influence in points that are so essential for humanity.

This is how Goethe felt in his classicist period, when the man of the Ancient World was uppermost. He saw Christianity as a thorn in the flesh of mankind, as the disrupter of the unity of its psychic life. And his own religious needs were concerned with unity and wholeness, the ἕν καὶ πᾶν. In life he could satisfy them, but in world history at this period he could not. Goethe would not seem ever to have completely overcome this sense of religious frustration, even though in old age his thinking once again took on a religious colouring, and he again began to feel more intensely the value of Christian symbols and the 'divine depths of suffering' in the example of Jesus (*Wanderjahre*). But the symbol of the Cross, at any rate insofar as it was the symbol of a sacrifice for sin, remained permanently something that repelled him. From the standpoint of 'pure reason', high above that of the Enlightenment and the rationalists, Goethe could value the Bible as a 'mirror of the world' (to Zelter, 1816). In the last years of his life he praised the teachings of Christ, and more especially the love shown by Christ, in striking terms. But when he compared these with the historical development of Christianity and the Church, genuine Christianity seemed to him as one of the unfulfilled possibilities of world history. He gave his opinion (*Max. und Refl.*) that Christianity had never shown forth its full beauty and purity at any time in political and ecclesiastical history. He called the history of the Church a hodge-podge of error and violence (*Zahme Xenien* and von Müller, 1823), though he went on to admit that he had studied it with the greatest diligence (*Dicht. und Wahrh.*, 3, 11). This bears witness to the fact that Goethe had hoped to find God somehow and somewhere in the history of the Church, but had not done so. Taken as a whole, he was as little satisfied with the historical developments of Christianity as he was with the power politics of States and nations. Here again, then, there is this strange breach of continuity. The primal form of a phenomenon was seen by Goethe as great and splendid, but its subsequent metamorphoses did not satisfy him.

For these and the other previously mentioned reasons, Goethe's world philosophy could not reach a full appreciation of history. This meant that the source of this world philosophy, his very personal and splendid universal religion, reached a critical point. It seemed that the divine nature could not fully penetrate this world, at any rate as far as human understanding could see. The actualisation of our ideas of God, as he said to Riemer in 1811, constitutes true reality. But God (he continued) must indeed have taken human waywardness into account, and allows mankind as it were to continue in it. This was some comfort to him in the face of what he could not understand. Yet this brings us to the limitations of his own human nature. He saw the everlasting gulf 'between idea and experience, which we exert all our strength to span, but in vain. Nevertheless, our ceaseless effort is to bridge this hiatus by means of reason, understanding, imagination, belief, feeling and fancy; and if nothing else succeeds, we try a little folly.' Goethe also observed (in *Max. und Refl.*) that the world will always have a bright and dark side to it. Here we see the dark dualistic background to the picture of the world which he normally saw in such bright colours. The brilliant light of his poetry and his universal philosophy can easily make us forget that he was acquainted with the darker side of life and all its terrors; but for the most part he preferred to bear it and ponder over it in the quiet of his own heart, and then to struggle up from it again with all his inner strength (and principally through will-power and action) into the light of the divine nature in which all things are unified. And this led to what was perhaps the most significant polarity in his life's work. His contempt for universal history, which roundly denied its meaning and value during the times of his estrangement from history, became the profoundest interpreter and guide for the particular treasures of the historical world that his mind was able to make its own. And the paths of understanding opened up by Goethe could be carried further into the provinces of history which he still regarded with scorn.

Goethe once remarked at a moment when he was trying to strike a balance (*Max. und Refl.*):

> In nature, as in all profound studies, whether they concern the past, the present or the future, the deeper one penetrates, the more difficult the problems that emerge. The man who is not afraid, but goes boldly on his way, feels, as his studies prosper, that he is being raised to a higher level, and experiences a sense of inner well-being.

By this kind of bold approach Goethe was enabled in the end, at any rate in principle, to come to terms with those elements in history that he found particularly distasteful, notably the ingredient of chance, which he so much disliked. 'There are always great original forces ceaselessly at work, either through all eternity, or developing in the course of time; and whether they prove helpful or harmful is purely a matter of chance' (*Max. und Refl.*). This has a passive and fatalistic ring about it, but the next moment his active side was once again to the fore: 'This vast reasonable world is to be looked upon as a great immortal individual, which unceasingly works that which is necessary, and so contrives even to get the better of chance' (*ibid.*).[1] And much in the same vein, some words from *Wilhelm Meisters Lehrjahre* (*The Apprenticeship of Wilhelm Meister*) (I, 17) concerning the features of this world woven both of necessity and of chance; yet chance must be guided and made use of by reason. And, finally, a judgement upon chance in which his realism and his optimism are fairly balanced: 'Nothing unreasonable takes place which either understanding or chance cannot set to rights; and nothing reasonable but what a lack of understanding and chance combined can bring it to disaster.'

[1] In the letter to Beulwitz, 18 July 1828, quoted as the 'sublime words of a wise man'.

And so the clouded sky which represented Goethe's picture of history in the earlier stages begins to clear. Yet there is one final cloud to be noticed, not arising from the after-effects of older ways of thought, nor from any obstacles put up by critical or philosophical attitudes, or due to Goethe's own character—like the motives we have so far been examining. This final cloud arose from the deepest and almost sub-human levels of his emotional life, where the groaning and travailing of all creation seemed to meet. This was the sphere of what Goethe designated at various times as 'apprehension', 'the woes of anxious earthly feeling'. It is astonishing (though our astonishment is mingled with respect) that what was the source of his highest happiness, the sight of an emerging idea, the discovery of primal phenomena, and the revelation of the divine in his own nature, should also have been subject to 'apprehension' and feelings of anxiety (*Max. und Refl.*).[1] This kind of apprehension could come upon him with regard to the historical past in general. It already made its appearance, as we noted earlier on (p. 389), at the experience centring round Cologne Cathedral in 1774. The realisation of any idea could arouse it, and still more so its frustration. This effect could be produced by the sight of any meaningless and yet existent phenomena, especially those that at first sight had no clear connection with the rest of life. 'Every strange creature taken out of its own environment', he says in the *Wahlverwandtschaften* (*Elective Affinity*), 'impresses us with a certain feeling of anxiety.'

There was also a kind of no-man's land for Goethe between meaningful and meaningless phenomena. This was the mysterious realm of the daemonic, to which he had devoted lively attention, particularly in his latter years. 'It resembled chance, for it showed no signs of logical sequence; it was like providence, in that it pointed to the general connection of events' (*Dicht. und Wahrh.*, IV, 20). On another occasion he designated it as that which cannot be disposed of by understanding and reason, yet expresses itself in thoroughly positive activity. Natures like Napoleon's and Charles Augustus's seemed to Goethe to be daemonic, whereas he denied any daemonic powers in himself, though admitting that he, too, was subject to their influence (Eckermann, 1831). For he saw the daemonic as active not only in persons, but in a great variety of ways in the whole of nature, visible and invisible. He believed that good and evil proceeded forth from it, often with irresistible power; yet a man must do his best to

---

[1] Simmel's attempt (*Goethe*, p. 122) to explain this 'apprehension' as arising from the logical difficulties that threaten every kind of monism, seems to me to have failed. What comes to light here in Goethe is a primitive human feeling, and a primitive phenomenon in religion generally—the *mysterium tremendum*. This is also how Leisegang interprets it in his *Goethes Denken*, p. 119.

uphold the right against the daemonic (Eckermann, 1831). These and other similar thoughts are a reminder of the obscure dualistic under-current of his universal philosophy. Yet when Eckermann sounded him with regard to this dualistic trait in his idea of the daemonic, he refused to answer, but referred to the incomprehensibility of the Supreme Being. His thoughts bordered here upon the world of the inscrutable. And since Goethe saw the daemonic as active in the whole of nature, and was quite content to research into that which it was possible to discover, there is no reason to suppose that the dae-monic element would particularly have prevented him from tackling the world of history, where it was most palpably at work. Only it is odd that he did not more consciously scent the daemonic at work in political life, where political expediency so often betrays its pre-dominant activity, or even where his own dramas displayed it with such power and fidelity. By so doing, he might have gained access to a more intuitive understanding of large-scale political destinies in the world as a whole. But, as we have already noted, he was careful to steer clear of these broad tendencies; they only interested him insofar as they affected the individual.

There was one further primitive human feeling, which Goethe experienced in an exaggerated form, and which set up a barrier between him and the past. The sight of death and decay, and the protrusion of decomposition into the world of the living, often made Goethe shudder at the world of history and avert his eyes. 'History, even at its best, always has something corpse-like, some smell of the tomb, about it' (projected preface to the third part of *Dichtung und Wahrheit*). 'A man who concerns himself merely with the past is in danger of giving his heart to something that sleeps the sleep of death and has become for us mummified and desiccated' (*Klassiker und Romantiker in Italien*, 1820). We see in *Faust* how Goethe saw the continuing effects of a dead legal system, and the consequent conversion of reason into nonsense, as a positive curse upon life. In his revolt against all burdens imposed by the past, he could even say during his classicist period that the present was the only goddess he worshipped (Fried. Brun 1795). It is strange that in extreme old age he should on one occasion confess to almost the opposite, and say that the present had something absurd and trivial about it, because the ideal was foolishly enough eliminated, as it were, by the real (to Zelter, 1829). But behind this pointed paradox there lay in the end his permanent lofty outlook upon the world, which saw an ever-flowing ideal life at work behind the passing realities of the present, yet immanent in them. And as he saw the real and the ideal interwoven with each other, so he also viewed life and death. For death was no true, that is to say, no final, death, but the means chosen by the Deity to bring new life into being. Goethe himself was, indeed, too full of vitality to take a purely mystical attitude; he was moved to the depths by an alternation of feelings and counterfeelings on the subject of life and death, the past and the present. Thus he was unable to shake himself free of the past, nor did he wish to do so. In the end, he gathered together all his ambivalent feelings about life and death evoked by the past in one great tragic utterance: 'We all live upon the past and perish by reason of the past' (*Max. und Refl.*).

Poetry was Goethe's method of freeing himself inwardly from the weight of experience. He saw this also as the highest task of historical writing, and held that its function was analogous. Like the spear of Telephos, its duty was to heal the wounds it inflicted, and to remove the oppression of the past, which it had itself imposed. 'The writing of history is one way of ridding oneself of the burden of the past' (*Max. und Refl.*).

Goethe can only be understood through the polarities of his thought. In a good few of the motives conditioning his negative attitude to history we have seen ferments at work that were also active in his positive attitude. Thus the negative pole might at any time swing round again into the positive pole, and universal history (that is history as experienced) could even be set up by him as the standard for the present moment, insofar as this present moment was itself full of aspiring life:

> He who lives in universal history,
> Should he conform himself to the present moment?
> Only he who looks into past times and strives to live
> Is worthy to speak and be a poet.

To this we must add the familiar words in denigration of the man who cannot give any account of the events of the last 3000 years; and Goethe's testimony that all the virtue of the past survives and is immortalised in noble actions.

The way is now clear for developing the positive content of Goethe's understanding of history.

III *The Positive Relationship to History*

First and foremost, it must be stated that Goethe was not only able to practise on a magnificent scale the new kind of historical vision brought in by Möser and more strongly still by Herder, but also raised it to the level of a deliberate methodological principle. This was the art of using all the powers of mind and soul, with no single one excluded, and using them in harmony with one another. It is hardly necessary to add that Goethe did not confine this art to history, but aimed at applying it to the whole range of phenomena issuing from the divine nature. In the all-round vision of things, there would thus be a concert of all the powers—'the depths of presentiment, a steady contemplation of the present, mathematical depth, physical accuracy, the heights of reason, acute understanding, a yearning and dynamic fancy, and loving delight in all things sensuous' (*Geschichte der Farbenlehre*).

But how far could all these take him in treating the phenomena of history? Already in his first version of *Faust*, Goethe knew that the presentation of the past reflects the spirit of the gentlemen writing in the present. This subjective *a priori* element in the historian could, as we have seen, be felt by Goethe as a barrier, and could rob him of his pleasure in history. On the other hand, when it acted from the opposite pole it could become a vitalising incentive to look at history with fresh eyes and become a 'creative mirror' for it. Especially was this so in his old age, under the powerful influence of historical events. This brought about a deepening of his feeling for the present, and a search for stronger contact with the past, where he now saw in retrospect the mental changes that had taken place in his own lifetime. And by no means last, there was the mighty working of his own spirit, which was perhaps the most decisive factor of all.

What Goethe says in his *Geschichte der Farbenlehre* is therefore one of the most significant testimonies to his growing consciousness of a new historical sense: 'There can hardly remain any doubt in our day that the history of the world needs from time to time to be re-written.'[1] He demanded a radical departure from the kind of historical judgement passed by the 'self-confident' eighteenth century. Where in their writings, he asked, could one find 'respect for lofty and unattainable gods? Where could one find a feeling for the seriousness of research called to explore the fathomless depths of knowledge? How seldom is there any forbearance towards bold efforts that were unsuccessful, or patience for slow developments!' How seldom in general was there any understanding shown for problematic natures. But the nineteenth century was already on the way to making good the mistakes of the eighteenth 'if only it does not encounter the fate of becoming lost in the opposite tendencies'. That was a premonition of danger that bore the stamp of genius; a danger that the mature historism would become shallow, and accept even the most absurd

---

[1] Cf. on this point his letter to Sartorius of 4 February 1811: 'Someone has said that the history of the world needs from time to time to be re-written; and when was there ever a time when this was as necessary as now!' Who, one wonders, was the first to pronounce these words about the re-writing of history?

phenomenon by a process of glib and relativist accommodation applied to anything and everything.

But Goethe could draw upon the courage to overcome the scepticism towards 'the gentlemen's own (projected) spirit' that constantly assailed him from one of his loftiest and most personally reassuring thoughts about the world and humanity to which he often gave utterance. 'A single person', he wrote to Schiller in 1798, 'cannot grasp nature, although the whole human race together might well be able to do so'. Only all men together, as Jarno says in *Wilhelm Meisters Lehrjahre* (8, 5), constitute humanity; only a concerted effort by all our power can grasp the world. 'Only humanity taken together', he says in *Dichtung und Wahrheit* (book 9), 'is the true man'. We shall not fail to note the peculiar transformation of the Enlightenment's belief in Natural Law and the unchanging truths possessed by humanity. Goethe remodels it and extends it into the dynamic conception that the whole wealth of individually human opinions, with all their liability to error, is yet the place where a supra-empirical and invisible treasury of truth is enshrined.

'And therefore (he continues) the single person can only rejoice in his good fortune, if he has the courage to feel his own identity within the whole.' His highest sense of reality consisted of 'an interior resonance or harmony with the whole' (*Dicht. und Wahrh.*, book 12). This brings us to the central point of importance for showing Goethe's creative achievement in the field of historism. And not in this only, for nature is also included in this whole. But humanity in itself, as far as Goethe was concerned, formed a whole of unending dynamism and variety, a mighty current of life in which the individual does not perish or become a matter of indifference. On the contrary, the individual only rises by developing its own vitality and regularity from the primal source into the total stream of life. Goethe's basic conception of nature and history is that of a vital current of all being saturated with individuality and potentiality. And the individuality of separate phenomena first comes to light with real power in the sphere of history, for in nature it is masked by the types and the species, which are the only things perceptible to the human eye.

In one of his profoundest sayings, however, he remarks that 'in life, the important thing is life itself, and not merely its results'. In the writing of history also (as he remarks in the projected foreword to the third part of *Dichtung und Wahrheit*), the single act and the single person are apt to get lost in the assessment of results. The process of life itself was what counted with Goethe, and 'the absurdity of final causes' was something for which he expressed his hatred (to Zelter, 1830). There must be no 'dragging forward from a final goal', but a 'growing up from the roots' (Simmel, *Goethe*, p. 4). Thus, historical phenomena were to be interpreted primarily in terms of the forces at work, rather than the results brought about by them. Then even the results take on a different look, and are seen to have a deeper and intrinsic necessity.

By this approach, Goethe effected a radical transformation in the pragmatical and utilitarian outlook of history as written during the Enlightenment. It had judged historical actions according to the greater or lesser degree of usefulness produced by their results, and these in their turn according to the range of purposes that had been established by the unvarying reason of humanity. This had created a divide between these purposes and the men who performed the actions. The tendency was to assess the latter, not by their own standards (by the laws of life at work in them) but by what was considered the absolute standard of general and ultimate human purposes and aims. This led to cutting off and isolating the various motives at work in particular historical actions, and to treating them as trigger-mechanisms, regardless of whether they were good or bad, or whether they were based upon passion or upon reason. Moreover, there was an inclination to take no notice of any but the motives lying clearly in the foreground, and to ignore (in the reproachful words of Goethe) 'the unfathomable depths of action'.

It was always easy for this pragmatism to become associated with a moralistic outlook. Moral standards were the easiest for judging the single action. Goethe did not altogether reject moral judgement, wherever it fitted the case; but he was much impressed by Johannes von Müller's *Universal History*, and completely in accord with what Möser had once remarked in criticism of Abbt—that moral judgement was unable to master the history of the world as a whole. As Goethe wrote to Reinhard in 1810: 'It has been brought home to me again and again in my solitary watch-tower that one cannot write a universal history from the moral standpoint.'

Pragmatism itself was nothing but the further development of a naively human attitude to practical life. As a rule, people think this cannot be managed except by concentrating on what is directly apprehensible and understandable and isolating it from all its deeper connections with life. Life is treated as though its parts could be dealt with mechanically, and in so doing, all that cannot be mechanically treated is ignored.

Goethe was well aware of this, and his habit of thought was deliberately set against it, so preparing the way for historism. He wrote as follows to Zelter in 1804:

It must be admitted that men as a whole can only conceive of a together, or side-by-side, relationship; they have no feeling of things being intermingled or inter-penetrating one another. For you only grasp what you can yourself make, and you only comprehend what you can yourself produce. Because in experience everything seems to get fragmented, people come to think that the highest things can also be pieced together from fragments.

Another saying of Goethe's is directed against the same fragmentary manner of thinking: 'The thinker goes wrong particularly by enquiring into cause and effect; both of them together constitute an indivisible phenomenon' (*Max. und Refl.*).

It may perhaps be objected that even modern historical thought cannot dispense with a modicum of fragmenting pragmatism and utilitarianism when it comes to examine, for example, the actions of statesmen. It has first and foremost to note and work out the motives that lie in the foreground; it is bound to apply the standard of achievement and results to the single action, because it is upon these results that the further development of the objective powers of State and society depend. In criticising the tendency to judge by results in the writing of history, Goethe did not wish to 'blame' the historian; in fact, he himself said one or two things from time to time that have a distinctly pragmatic ring about them. But as soon as the judgement of the single event and the further development of the objective powers forgets even for a single moment the deeper laws at work, the soul of history vanishes, and you are left simply with the *caput mortuum* of roughly connected facts. Such deeper laws are not always clearly recognisable but they must always be assumed to be immanent in the stream of life. The man who had taken up into himself the vital currents flowing through Goethe's *Faust* was not likely, however, to be exposed to this danger. We must therefore assess Goethe's contribution to historism higher even than Herder's, because it had more power to remodel human thought and feeling from their very roots, because it grasped the psyche in larger terms and gave it more intensive and delicate scope than Herder, whose own restless spirit was in this respect a hindrance.

Nor did Goethe rest content with the mere contemplation of an eternal growth and change. He touched the emotions, arousing a new and tolerant love for all that is human—for Goethe knew that nothing less than such a love will take us into the heart of things. As he wrote to Reinhard in 1807: 'It is really a synthesis of all our affections that brings everything to life.' Or again (to Jacobi in 1812): 'One does not get to know anything one does not love.' We need to bear in mind the creative quality of this love if we are fully to understand Goethe's profound picture of the 'creative mirror' in the disputation scene of *Faust* (which was not in the end completed). In the frigid atmosphere of thought based upon Natural Law, this love had not been able to thrive. For this kind of thought had always been ready to apply its fixed standards and pass a loveless judgement, where an understanding based upon a deeper insight into the whole process of development, even of what seemed perverted or absurd, would lead to a feeling of human sympathy, and an ability to descry the workings of fate and necessity. This was the new gift of historical 'understanding' we have already seen at work in Möser and Herder; and with Herder and Goethe its source was the new feeling for the universal and the personal, the συμπάθεια τῶν ὅλων (intuitive, sympathetic understanding of the universe). There was indeed a danger that this universal sympathy would become merely soft and formless. In affirming everything human, one might end by affirming nothing with any certainty. When Goethe composed his *Werther* and *Stella*, he was perhaps on the verge of this danger. As we have seen, however, the classicist period of Weimar and the Italian journey gave a new solidity to his thinking, leading him on to see the permanent in the midst of change, and so renewing on a higher level the abiding essence of Natural Law.

The three epoch-making features in Goethe's world scheme of thought and his understanding of history (the fresh view of the current of life, the fresh understanding love for its products, and the fresh shape he gave to the flux of things) are as it were brought together into a single brilliant constellation in the final lines spoken by the Lord in the Prologue to *Faust*:

> The powers of growth, that through all being move,
> Enfold you in the holy bonds of love!
> And to the fitful, shifting shows of sense
> Let living thoughts give shape and permanence.

All life, as Goethe saw it, was a question of primal forms and successive metamorphoses. History too, as he saw it, was bound to follow this same law. But that was where the shade of difference in his relationship to nature and to history became apparent. He thought he could come closer to the primal phenomena in nature than was possible in history. He believed at first that he could actually discover the original form of a plant, until Schiller felt bound to call his attention to the fact that this was not an actual experience, but only an idea. Even so, Goethe believed that he could still see natural phenomena 'face to face, in their fathomless splendour' with his mind's eye. But he never ventured to speak of the primal phenomena of history. At this point he was hindered by all the factors with which we are familiar as the causes of his dissatisfaction with history. Yet he continued to apply his methodological principle of searching for simple but productive basic forms of life, and this proved fruitful even in the field of history. He could hardly do other than involuntarily apply this kind of test to historical material. Only these basic forms—apart from certain fundamental forces—cannot be treated as 'ideas' like that of the primal form in plants, but remain empirically conceived creations of simple structure, yet capable of a high degree of development and adaptability. Provided this distinction is not forgotten, it is legitimate to speak of the simple phenomena discovered by Goethe in history as primal forms.

We have looked at the constituent of history that Goethe was not prepared to derive from such prototypes. But there remained an important field open to them, rising from the lowest natural level to the highest mental and spiritual life of man. Since we are not concerned to catalogue Goethe's works, but simply to characterise his achievements in the realm of history, we shall be content, here as elsewhere, with some representative examples. There is a fundamental feature in Goethe's historical thought which makes it superior to all his successors' without exception—a clarification and refinement of Hamann's basic idea. Goethe maintained that he could glimpse behind all the higher actions of historical man a supremely natural and beneficent power at work, and so could view even the round of everyday life as something hallowed by its primal form. Victor Hehn once pointed this out in an unforgettable way.

> All enjoyment of life is based upon a regular recurrence of
> external things. The alternation of day and night, the seasons of
> the year, blossoming and fruiting, and everything else that comes
> to us periodically to be enjoyed—*these are the real springs of
> earthly life* (*Dicht. und Wahrh.*, book 13).

This natural rhythm was the first of all the primal forms pulsing through all living matter that Goethe's attentive ear was able to catch. This was the 'primal polarity of all existence that pervades and vitalises the endless variety of phenomena' (*Kampagne in Frankreich*), 'the mysterious systole and diastole from which all phenomena develop' (*Geschichte der Farbenlehre*). He was indebted to Kant's knowledge of natural science for this clear perception, but it was already in evidence at an earlier stage in Goethe's own thought. It had already been a concept in the Neo-Platonic system that the movement of the world was an alternation between outgoing and incoming power, between expansion and contraction. Herder too had spoken, in the spirit of Hebrew poetry, of the systole and diastole of the heart and breathing as the most natural of all dimensions (vol. 12, p. 20; cf. also vol. 4, p. 469). Yet Goethe was probably led to this view more particularly by self-observation, by the recognition of the contradictions within himself that he constantly felt resolving themselves into a unity. The pulse of his own being became the pulse of nature. With his hand upon his pulse he could look confidently at life and at history. Thus all divisions were once more brought into a unity, because it was of the nature of all things that had been unified to develop by further division. All would thus be well in the end, for everything, nature and the works of man included, obeyed this law, and any *hubris* in one direction would be corrected and balanced by a swing of the pendulum in the other. We have already seen this swing of the pendulum in history suggested in the later writings of Herder. But his outlook had been coloured by a moralistic judgement of the world, and this narrowing down diminished its immediate validity. With Goethe, however, though the moral aspect was of course included, it remained a cosmic principle, on which all things living and all the wealth of forms mysteriously depended. It served him as an assurance that unity and multiplicity, nature and culture, belonged together, and that there was a divine nature in control of all things. The thought of polarity therefore made it possible for him to come to inward terms with the hidden dualistic components of his universal philosophy, and so to tolerate the daemonic in history without a qualm. It is now evident that Goethe's apparently divided attitude to history did not appear to him to be contradictory, because he could see it as polarity and as a swing of the pendulum, making it possible for any dissatisfaction with history to swing over into the deepest satisfaction. We shall see later on how his thoughts on the meaning and coherence of history were controlled by this doctrine.

In general, however, this attitude brought a certain rhythm and inner serenity into Goethe's contemplation of history.

> Anyone who has rightly understood history will see from a hundred and one examples that the process of spiritualising the physical and giving physical shape to the spiritual has never ceased for one moment, but has pulsated to and fro under the influence of prophets, men of religion, poets, orators, artists and artistic circles. Sometimes this influence has been premature or late in making itself felt; often it has been strictly contemporary (to Eichstädt, 1815).

In his *Geschichte der Farbenlehre*, too, Goethe reflects as to which of the three periods a man of importance goes through in the course of his life does him most credit—his early upbringing, his peculiar personal efforts, or his years of fulfilment. He decided for the first period, principally for the profound reason that the generation from which the man stems is often more characteristically manifested in him than in the generation itself. Modern doctrines of generations are inclined to stress the contrast, rather than the likeness, between successive generations. But Goethe, with his feeling for continuity that had matured in his old age, was of a different opinion. In thus differing, he was also expressing his gratitude to the Enlightenment, in whose bosom his own genius had been nurtured, and was giving confirmation to one of the fundamental ideas underlying this present study. The two subsequent periods, however (the period of contest with his contemporaries and rivals in the field, and the period of completion and fulfilment during which a man's influence upon the world becomes manifest) produce the characteristically new element which in its turn again completes the circle, to become the teacher and helper of another new generation.

This rhythmic view of history was apt to reduce the symptoms of confusion and disintegration in great historical movements, with sublime equanimity, to a uniform prototype. In the *Annalen* for 1794, Goethe depicted in a few brief strokes the great literary revolution of his own time in Germany, and pointed out how it had been accompanied by a strange fragmentation and isolation of individuals. But, he added, 'this is the old story, which has so often happened when there is renewal and new life stirring in what has hitherto been rigid and static. It may therefore serve as an example in literature of what we so often see in political and ecclesiastical life.'

In the suppressed foreword of 1813, it is clear that Goethe also desired to shape his own life story 'according to the laws shown us by the metamorphosis of plants'—namely, their development from the tender root to the blossom, but also their dependence upon the favourable or unfavourable effects of soil and weather. Never before in the field of the world's literature had a great man's individual life been so deeply and consciously realised and depicted in its indissoluble mixture of dependence and independence. It offered future historism the first decisive prototype of biographical presentation and its possibilities. True, it has been felt as a deficiency in Goethe (R. M. Meyer in the Jubilee Edition, 22, xx), that he was not successful in the depiction of the alternating actions and reactions of the individual and the spirit of the age. In Meyer's opinion, he showed his naivety as a historian in portraying most readily and in greatest detail what struck him forcibly or repelled him, and did not truly realise the spirit of the epoch, or his own influence upon his contemporaries. To be sure, Goethe's first consideration was to make his own organic growth intelligible to his readers. He may well have been restrained from any more precise attempt to separate and specify what the environment and the spirit of the times respectively contributed to his making by a feeling that must be familiar to many who are trying to make clear to themselves the influence of the contemporary spirit upon their own mental development. A man is reluctant to attempt any more accurate analysis because he feels how precarious would be his efforts to tear apart the complicated web of experience, the actual workings of events, from his personal reactions to them. He is too close to them and knows too much about them. But for someone else, one can stand back and with an easier conscience attempt to sketch the story of his development. In his outline of Winckelmann and his century, Goethe made a closer study of the mutual interaction between the individual and the spirit of the age. As far as his own life was concerned, Goethe followed for the most part the easy path of the simple narrative historian. He might well have appealed to the fact that it was just such a simple narrative of the past that had not long before given him the most vivid and striking view of an individual life that was closely interwoven with its own time and environment, and that such a narrative had also given him the best impressions of the century as a whole. This narrative was the *Autobiography of Benvenuto Cellini*, the study of which had filled Goethe with such joy. As he wrote to H. Meyer in 1796: 'All the pragmatic characteristics of biography are no match at all for the naive detail of an important life.'

This impression, however, forced Goethe to go more deeply into Benvenuto's environment and origins and to apply to them the questions of primal forms and subsequent metamorphoses. For this is the question that tacitly underlies the 'rapid sketch of conditions in Florence' added as an appendix. The greatness as well as the limitations of Goethe's historical writing are both of them apparent enough in this splendid outline.

Goethe read Machiavelli's Florentine stories by way of background, and they gave him the impression of a wild chaos of civic struggles without any ultimate meaning. 'These are the defects characteristic of a badly ruled and ineffectively policed State.' Goethe's sense of order, and his dislike for war and power struggle, did not incline him to pursue his studies at a deeper level. But he now posed the fruitful historical question, how such a chaos could have given birth to so great and splendid an art and culture. At this point his own personal acquaintance with Florence, that which he had seen with his own eyes, came to his help. Just as he had earlier been able to formulate a definite conception from the topographical position of Rome and Venice of the 'primal form' of their history, so now he proceeded to do likewise with Florence. 'Such a spot, once it had been taken possession of by a society of men, could never again be abandoned.' Thus Goethe pictures vividly to himself, starting from the necessities lying close at hand, how handicrafts had arisen and developed, and how specifically in Florence handicrafts had given birth to the arts in connection with religion—an example of a typical development beginning to take on individual features. Out of all this had come the further development of a wealthy citizen community, with strong mercantile interests and a great love of splendour and display. This steady growth of a structure that corresponded to Goethe's idea of a positive historical development was now continually threatened by what he felt to be the negative pole of history—the internal civic strife which Goethe here characterises in classic terms as 'the inborn human inability to rule, or to let oneself be ruled'.

At this point there comes in a factor destined to lead on to a higher level of existence, a new primal form that has developed from the old but with new metamorphoses—the history of the Medici family, 'the highest example of what can be achieved in the community as a whole by good civic sense based upon efficiency and solid utilitarian values.' Goethe then follows up this development, from the simpler or lower stages up to the higher but more hazardous ones, until he reaches the brilliant climax of Lorenzo. After Lorenzo's death, however, collapse ensues with the introduction of a new factor of disaster in the 'monstrous and grotesque figure of Savonarola'.

A good deal remains in the background, or only very slightly suggested, in this picture. The modern historian would need to work in considerably more in order to make it quite intelligible. He could tell us much more about the dynamic of the social struggles, the economic background, the problems of the city states, the foreign policy situation, the peculiar psychological qualities of Renaissance humanity, and so on. Yet Goethe's way of looking at things does provide the prototype for what has later been developed through all the metamorphoses of modern research into the Renaissance, namely the slow emergence of a historical structure under the impulse of inner forces, the evolution of the individual from the typical, and the interference with this growth brought about by the incalculable forces of fate.

The upshot was, then, that Goethe remained aware of the general current of history, but only selected from it those phenomena he could master directly by means of his own principles of knowledge—because he loved them. This shows us, in fact, what Goethe's principles of historical selection really were. They are accurately stated in his regretful epilogue to his Florentine sketch.

If Lorenzo could have lived longer, and if there could have been a steady step-by-step progress in the conditions for which he had laid the foundations, then the history of Florence would have been one of the finest phenomena of all time; *but it would seem that in the course of this earthly life we are seldom allowed to experience the fulfilment of the fairest possibilities.*

The fulfilment of the fairest possibilities: this was what Goethe sought in history, and found now and again; but its rarity often put him out of temper with history in general. Once again, we are reminded of the eighteenth-century outlook, of Voltaire's selective principles, and his picture of the few fertile valleys in the midst of the deserts of history. Goethe's choice, indeed, went incomparably deeper, and was always aware of the mighty and all-inclusive dynamic of the world as a whole. Yet he seized upon the phenomena of culture that were so dear to him at the points where they were most directly rooted in the totality of the divine nature. To use some words that Goethe applied to the *Knaben Wunderhorn*,[1] 'he raised the single object, in spite of its limitations, to the stature of the all-embracing whole, so that even in a small space we behold as it were the entire world.' Thus what Goethe liked to find in history was individuals who were full of spirit and life, surrounded and sustained by the atmosphere of their own particular place and time, but using it for the spontaneous development of their own peculiar talents, and so becoming 'effective' (for this, too, was something he required of them (*Dicht. und Wahrh.*, II, 7) towards the realisation of the highest and finest possibilities of life. From Cellini onwards we can follow the succession of such figures through the historical writings of Goethe's old age. There was the brilliant collection of portraits in his *Theory of Colours*, his friends and acquaintances of youth in his autobiography, the Eastern poets in the notes on the *Divan*, and finally the strange figure of Philip Neri, whom Goethe was still studying in his last years. We could apply to most of them what Goethe said of Cellini (with a tendency to use the individual also as a type) that he 'might well serve as the representative of his century, and perhaps even of mankind as a whole'. They were the 'spiritual makers of history'. Goethe's whole interpretation of history might be called a kind of universal individualism. But it included, between the universal and the particular individual of the moment, the whole chain of human life and activity in all its primal and natural forms, from the simplest relationships of the family and the craft onwards, sympathetically viewed and expressed with all the freshness of Möser. The result was that even the greatest and the most unusual events were always pre-

---

[1] The first collection of German folksongs, 3 vols, 1806–8, ed. A. V. Arnim and Cl. Brentano, and reviewed by Goethe.

sented as a development from their natural setting in life and against the world background as a whole. The least credit was given (as we have already seen) to the primal and natural forms of political life and all their manifold metamorphoses. To anticipate for a moment, there was, therefore, in Goethe's historical pictures a consequent and very obvious lack of the universal viewpoints and illuminations which are produced by linking up the destinies of the great States and nations, as Ranke succeeded later on in doing. But as far as the universal history of Western thought is concerned, there could have been no more splendid flash of light upon them than what Goethe says in his *Theory of Colours*, where he maintains that the Bible and the works of Plato and Aristotle are the three chief monumental works whose effects have been the most decisive and sometimes also the most exclusive in history.

Thus Goethe was deeply struck not only by the sight of the single bright stars in history, but also by the universal connection between them, and their reactions upon one another. This put an end to his dissatisfaction. A key sentence in his *Theory of Colours*, giving his interpretation of history, runs as follows: 'This alone can rejoice us in history—that the real men of all ages herald one another in advance, point to one another, and prepare the way for one another.' If there is still discernible at this point some faint cloud of dissatisfaction, he could on other occasions see the clear skies of the divine nature shining down upon all history.

The human song of praise, which God so delights to hear, is nowhere silent; and we ourselves can feel a divine joy when we hear, running through all times and regions, the strains of harmony that reach us, now in single voices and choirs, now in fugal fashion, and now in the splendour of a full chorus (*Theory of Colours*, and in similar language to Jacobi, 1808).

This divine joy was exactly what Goethe in one of his most famous passages praised as the highest gain we all derive from history. It is the enthusiasm which history arouses in us.

One might perhaps misunderstand Goethe's principle of historical selection—the search for the fulfilment of the fairest possibilities, and the rejection of the rest as chaff. It might be objected that this represents an exclusively subjective interest, and that it made Goethe unfair to what he left on one side as chaff. And it must be granted that this was often the case. He himself, in one of his very last letters, said that he had always been attentive to those points in the history of the world, including the history of art and culture, from which it was possible to obtain a lofty, true and human education. But as far as

Goethe was concerned, this was directed fundamentally and deliberately not to his own particular subject in isolation, but to its connections with all the objective life of the world. Thus his selective principle had a very objective significance. He only selected in order to let the whole world resound within him; and the thing selected was intended to represent this whole, and with it everything else that had been left out of the selection. This is where Goethe's doctrine of symbolism comes in. He calls 'symbolic' that which points to something different and higher, and to the ultimate primal form. 'The true symbolism is where the particular represents the more general, not as a dream or shadow, but as a living momentary revelation of the unfathomable' (*Max. und Refl.*). The most characteristic part of his thinking (the thinking in pictures) shows at this point its effectiveness and fruitfulness. By virtue of this symbolism he saw all separate events as linked together with one another and with the world as a whole in a timeless and eternal interaction, no matter to what time they belonged. And yet the single event did not thereby lose any of its individuality. 'Everything that happens is symbolic, and in completely representing itself, it also points to all the rest' (to Schuberth, 1818). In other words, to put the point somewhat baldly, everything depends upon everything else. Goethe gave this trite saying an infinity of meaning. 'Relationships are everywhere, and relationships are life' (to Zelter, 1830). Behind his principle of historical selection, we can thus see the shadow of his universal philosophy based upon Neo-Platonism, in which everything is interwoven with the whole, interacts together and shares in a common life.

It also projects into all the remaining ideas of Goethe's historical outlook, which we have not yet dealt with in detail, though we have in fact already heard inevitable echoes of them, since they are all as logically interconnected and inseparable as were in Goethe's opinion all the phenomena of the universe.

This is particularly true of the notion of individuality. The idea had been grasped by Goethe in his early days, then blended in Italy with the doctrine of types and metamorphoses, and so was never in danger after that of being over-valued or treated in isolation. If anything, it was at times in danger of being under-valued. In the historical work of Goethe's old age, this thought was so greatly expanded that it became perceptible in almost every single utterance. In 1812, he confessed to Reinhard: 'Deep down, I am really only interested in the individual in its clearest definitions.' Again, as he wrote in 1826 (*Der junge Feldjäger*): 'However much we concern ourselves with history from youth upwards, we discover in the end that the particular, the specific and the individual give us the best information about men and affairs.' Goethe's need to start from the individual and work up to the general, and to seek the latter first and foremost in the specific character of the individual, became a basic requirement for historism. It was precisely along these lines that Ranke's work developed. With the subsequent historism, it has sometimes been not unfairly objected that its fondness for the restricted monograph often brought it to a halt at the first stage of the journey. Goethe was never tempted to stop at this point, though he had a great liking for such detailed work. As he wrote to Lappenberg in 1828: 'It is my peculiar delight to occupy myself with a monograph and so from this particular point survey the world around me as though from a watchtower.'

Goethe was successful in reducing his ideas about the primal form and its metamorphoses, as a piece of research in natural history, into formal and theoretical shape. But it never occurred to him, interestingly enough, to attempt any theoretical clarification of the *ineffabile* of human individuality. Characteristic form that develops as part of a living process was a *coincidentia oppositorum* eluding ordinary logic, but immediately evident to the intuition. And no thinker had ever taught men how to feel this as deeply as Goethe. Goethe completely transcended what Simmel calls the 'quantitative' individualism of the Enlightenment, the conception of an essential individuality composed ultimately of the same invariable elements, though from time to time the relative proportions of their mixture might alter. Goethe replaced this by a 'qualitative' individualism, which assumed a particular and unique kernel of individuality, persisting, yet capable of development. The basis on which this doctrine was founded is thoroughly characteristic of Goethe. It was not arrived at by any speculative deification of the mental powers in general, but practically, for it is only through man's actions that man, in Goethe's view, comes to know himself. As he says in *Wilhelm Meisters Lehrjahre*: 'Everything outside us is purely elemental; I would even go so far as to say everything with which we are connected; but deep down within us lies the creative power that is able to bring into being that which is to be' (cf. Schneiderreit, *Der individualistische Grundzug in Goethes Weltanschauung*, Goethejahrbuch, 33).

In spite of occasional turns of phrase reminiscent of the quantitative view of individualism, such as 'underneath the human clothing all are alike' (*Shakespeare und kein Ende*) (*Shakespeare and no End*), there can be no doubt about this point (in disagreement with Simmel's reservations, pp. 144, 150). For this similarity was only one of type, the type from which the individual developed, in Goethe's view, according to the primal form and its subsequent metamorphoses. There is no doubt that in his later years Goethe saw the typical element within the individual more strongly than in his youth. But he even saw the type as a higher kind of individuality, with the same permanent yet flexible characteristics, and the same qualitative specificity, as the individuals that evolved from it. It was only by means of such successive stages (each stage having its own peculiar laws, uniqueness and creative powers, both typical and individual) that Goethe could hope to ascend to the divine nature which was the creator of all things. In the process, there had been both a gain and a loss of freedom in Goethe's conception of individuality as compared with that of the Enlightenment. Goethe's man was less free inasmuch as he was much more narrowly bound up with the heart of the divine nature, and much more intensively fused with the universal creative process than the individual of the Enlightenment, put into the world by providence with the privilege of using his nature, with its chance and random make-up, in freely controlling a random environment. Goethe, on the other hand, endowed man with a freedom lent him in trust by the divine nature, which required him to live 'from within outwards'. Through the recognition of this truth, Goethe in his old age believed that he had been the 'liberator' of the German people (*Noch ein Wort für junge Dichter*). For Goethe, however, this freedom from within denoted an inner necessity. 'There must you be: you cannot flee from your true self.' But this inner necessity, which he portrayed so strikingly in the *Wahlverwandtschaften*, was no mechanical necessity, but was mysteriously conceived as one of the symbols of the divine nature and its purposeful creation. The conclusion of the primal Orphic expressions leaves us in no doubt that Goethe was dimly groping for some such way out of the dilemma of a lack of freedom, or an apparent but unreal freedom.

The persons of his poetry testify to this interpretation of individuality, with its mixture of inner and outer necessity, even more profoundly than his pronouncements upon historical personalities. As we look at the latter, we may well at times get the impression that Goethe had fixed his attention more upon the outward necessity, and given more consideration to the effects of the environment in respect of time and place than to the counteracting influence of the inner kernel of individuality. In his commentary on Cellini, for example: 'By looking at a remarkable man as a part of a whole, as a product of his age, place of birth and habitat, many peculiarities can be explained which would otherwise remain a mystery.' Like Herder (cf. p. 358 above), Goethe also considered the dependence of a man upon the sum-total of his inheritance, and used the well-known words of lighthearted irony in explanation of his own heritage ('Vom Vater hab' ich die Statur . . .' etc). In the same way he regarded Voltaire as the Frenchman *par excellence*, who united in himself the highest degree of his nation's virtues. Likewise a family stretching out over a long line could sometimes produce an individual who comprised within himself the characteristics of all his ancestors (*Note on Rameau's Nephew*).

Nevertheless, there can be no question of Goethe having formulated any positive theory of environment or inheritance. As his eye ranged to and fro, one or other of the poles in the relationship between individual and environment might come into sharper focus for the time being. Yet in the ultimate analysis, Goethe perceived an eternal alternative between the individual and the spirit of the age— the influence of world history, balanced by the counteraction of the individual (on Varnhagen and Solger, 1827). When you read the opening to *Dichtung und Wahrheit*, you hear a powerful deterministic strain stemming from Goethe's own experience, to the effect that the century 'carries along with it, shapes and determines not only the willing, but also the unwilling'. Yet he never forgets the individual, 'insofar as it remains the same under all circumstances'. Who could effect an accurate separation between these two elements? Goethe declared that this was an almost unattainable aim, and was quite content to place himself under the universal law decreeing that any man, if he had been born ten years earlier or later, would have been a different person. His universal sympathy, with its dynamic power to trace life everywhere and see its endless intertwinings, did not need to make any laborious division between the individual and the century.

At the end of the nineteenth century, a controversy arose between the individualist and the collectivist interpretation of history, to some extent as an attempt to control its division into scientific and artistic lines of thought. Goethe would probably have greeted it with inner poise, and with something of a smile, as a matter that did not concern him. He looked at the passing currents of history as they might appear to a detached observer—neither solely determined by the forces of number and time, nor by the predominance of great individuals. As far as he was concerned, now one and now the other might be in the ascendant. A great personality can at times merely wear himself out in fruitless struggle against numbers and the spirit of the age. At other times, he may well draw them under his own spell; but in order to become effective, he himself must then fall under their spell, as happened with Mahomet. At other times again, he may go on to complete his mission as the great enlightener, regulator and builder for the needs that are widespread, scattered and quietly growing among the generality of mankind. At other times the great personality may indeed have an effect, but it will soon be forgotten as the waves of error once more close in behind him. Or again, the influence of such great people may continue to be valid and effective for many centuries.[1]

Because Goethe could discern life everywhere, even in the smallest star, the collective powers did not appear to him in the guise of merely blind and mechanical forces. He particularly loved the collective life of primitive times—like Herder and the primitivists of the eighteenth century, only more in tune with all the other objects of his love. In this primitive life, Goethe saw that unknown men were already producing truly creative work. This is a point to which we shall later return. But the further these collective powers rose on the ladder of civilisation, the more uncongenial became 'the tyranny of whole masses'. Goethe fully recognised the importance of the masses as a power in modern life, albeit often with a sigh. The causes at work in history only interested him insofar as they are a legitimate interest of the more sensitive historian working at a deeper level—namely insofar as they have an encouraging or discouraging effect on the production of human cultural values. Here, Goethe could see himself too in the light of cause and effect, and could even call himself a great collective product, nourished by the lives of countless individuals (to Soret, 1832). And because ultimately it was great and small individuals who were the source of all creative life, and whose effect Goethe could trace in these collective powers, the masses and the more important individuals only appeared to him in the end as the warp and the woof on the great loom of history. The masses were the sphere where necessity operated; the important individuals were the sphere of freedom (*Max. und Refl.*).

Ranke then took up this interpretation, and the later historism, after ridding itself of the positivist fetters, also returned to it. It cannot be reduced to a single system with any final sharpness or clarity of focus. As soon as you clear away the logical difficulties, you find that a part of real life has been omitted. Necessity and freedom are so interwoven in all the life of history that they can only be approximately, and never radically, separated; and their interpenetration can only be described in as it were hovering terms. With Herder, who felt this interpenetration with a profound touch of genius, the terms used tended to dissolve into the infinite. Goethe, with his objective thinking, was the first, even before Ranke, to give this view a certain clarity, which as far as the historian is concerned fully replaces the false definiteness of merely conceptual thinking. Through the form Goethe imparted to his ideas of the individual and its environment in his poetic and dramatic work, he managed to convey it with full

[1] For further testimony, see Hissbach's useful work, *Die geschichtliche Bedeutung von Massenarbeit und Heroentum im Lichte Goethescher Gedanken* (*Jahresbericht des Eisenacher Realgymnasiums*), 1907.

success. His sense of form and his impulse to seek appropriate forms were able to win a lighthearted victory over the danger (inherent in his dynamic universal philosophy) of dissolving the outline of things in the general stream of life. Romanticism largely succumbed to this danger, but Goethe set himself deliberately to guard against it. As he wrote to Zelter on this point in 1808: 'No one will understand that the highest and one and only operation of nature and art is to find appropriate form, and within the form a particular specification, so that everything shall acquire and possess and retain its own specific importance.' We know well enough that with this idea of form, which (as he wrote to Humboldt in 1795) was his starting-point, there was always blended the concept of changing form. 'One can only conceive of a spring insofar as it flows' (*Dicht. und Wahrh.*, II, 6).

'Within the form a particular specification': that meant both that Goethe could see the individual in history layered one above the other; and that he could recognise, over and above the particular individual, the individuality of the supra-individual. The single individual appeared to him, by a free extension of Leibniz's doctrine, as a complex of several monads (to Falk, 1813). It was thus not difficult for him to consider the complexes arising from the co-operation of individuals as also possessed of individuality. In his *Theory of Colours*, Goethe could depict the London Royal Society of the seventeenth century as a human being with a warm personal life. The greatest supra-individual individuality within humanity as a whole, which again has its individual aspect, was the nation—discovered to be such by Herder in particular. It is almost unnecessary to add that Goethe never forgot the nation, its own specific life and influence on the lives of the individuals, even if he did not feel it as ardently as in the early Strassburg period, or look at it with as universal an interest as in his later days. For him, as for Herder, nations were like great plants, whose higher ranks and cultures could be compared to blossom and fruit (to Riemer, 1806). The hard and fast divisions between material cultures did not indeed satisfy Goethe's deepest longings. He sensed the danger that they might overpower and oppress the specific and characteristic nature of the individual (*Max. und Refl.*). His eyes were directed to more distant objects, to the higher training and advancement of all life. This was to him the essence of the divine nature; yet he had to admit that it did not always appear to act in accordance with this expectation. So he was led to the following notable thought: 'Nature sometimes hits upon a specification that turns out to be a blind alley; she can go no further, but does not want to retrace her steps. Hence the tough problem of national development' (*Max. und Refl.*).

Goethe's heart was in the cultural rather than the political products of the nations. And yet, as we have already seen, he realised what a powerful and dynamic political life could mean to a poet—and first and foremost to a Shakespeare. At the very time when Germany was going downhill in her national life, during the period of the Treaty of Basle, Goethe put forward the question: When and where does a classical national author arise? He then proceeded to answer it in almost sorrowful terms:

> When he can discover in the history of his nation great events and weave them and their results into a happy and significant unity . . . when he himself, penetrated by the national spirit, feels capable, by virtue of an indwelling genius, of sympathising alike with the past and with the present . . . (*Literar. Sansculottismus*).

These words about the national spirit make us prick up our ears. But this is not yet the Romantic *Volksgeist* of Grimm and Savigny, which produces from its obscure depths all that is particular about a nation. It is, rather, a preliminary stage of this doctrine, which began in Germany under the influence of Montesquieu with Möser's short study of the German national spirit, and in particular with the teaching of Herder. Goethe again and again stressed the power of a nation to stamp its individual members with a particular character, and took as a symbol of it the Englishman who took his tea-kettle to the summit of Mount Etna. Yet his views showed themselves in the end superior to the Romantic *Volksgeist* doctrine. For the latter isolated the single people and ignored the effects upon its intellectual and spiritual existence arising from the common political and cultural life of the nations. This was a blind spot which was destined to persist well on into the nineteenth century. But Goethe always looked at peoples, especially the more modern peoples, in the same way as he viewed the individual, within the atmosphere surrounding him, and in a reciprocal give-and-take relationship with all the environment. In relation to the Greeks, Goethe assumed somewhat erroneously, on the basis of his humanistic classicism, that they became what they were entirely without outside influence (*Gesch. der Farbenl.*). But, as he declared most unromantically in 1808 (*Plan eines lyr. Volksbuchs*, 1808), no latter-day nation could lay claim to absolute originality. As he remarked later on in his *Urteilsworte französ. Kritiken* (1817–20): 'The nation, like the single individual, is often based more upon that which existed of old, and on foreign influences, than on its own gifts, its own heritage or its own achievements.' All the same, Goethe was in thorough agreement with the heart of the *Volksgeist* doctrine when it sought to go back behind the externals of national idiosyncracies to the creative inner sources of them. These inner springs, as

461

he observed more soberly and profoundly than many of the Romantics, 'are not known or recognised; not by foreigners, and often not by the nation itself; but the inner nature of a whole nation, like that of an individual man, is often unconscious in its operation' (*Ferneres über Weltliteratur*, 1829). And for Goethe, who knew that he himself had taken in and assimilated so much intellectual material from outside sources, it was an accepted matter that the German need not be ashamed of receiving his culture from outside. 'After all, the foreign accessions have been made our own' (*Plan eines lyr. Volksbuchs*). He saw, incidentally, that the reception of cultural material from abroad can be an entirely organic and individual action, and a sign of vitality rather than weakness in the receiving nation.

Let us glance back now at Voltaire and Montesquieu. They too, in summary fashion, had sensed that the spirit of a people and the spirit of an age are individual creations. But their mechanistic thought-forms had not allowed them to discover the sphere of the unconscious and involuntarily creative forces from which these spirits arise —or, in the case of Montesquieu, only approximately. Voltaire had paid more attention to the spirit of the age than to the spirit of peoples, but had won great renown for the way in which he portrayed the former in his *Siècle de Louis XIV*. He succeeded in arousing a feeling for the inner coherence of a period, and the unity of style that belonged to all its activities. The intellectual revolution that burst the bonds of the Enlightenment in Germany was destined to give further warmth and depth to this movement, as we saw in Möser and Herder. Möser's ideas on the stylistic unity of an epoch had been taken up by Herder and Goethe in their joint youthful work *Von deutscher Art und Kunst* (*Of German Custom and Art*). It need hardly be said that Goethe, without ever saying so explicitly, always steadily kept in mind the inner unity and coherence of the epochs that he passed in review. Speaking of his own experience, he wrote in *Dichtung und Wahrheit* (book 13):

> Because in every period there is a certain coherence, with all the
> predominant opinions and attitudes intertwined in many ways,
> it has now gradually become the practice in jurisprudence to
> follow all the maxims that were applied in religion and morality.

Each period, then, presented its own coherent individual appearance. Goethe, with his constant eye for forms, did not look equally intently at every period. His selective principle of the fulfilment of the fairest possibilities prevented him from doing so. But it is most instructive to see how Goethe viewed the sequence of the various epochs of universal history.

The epoch in the world's history having perhaps the strongest claims to be treated by Goethe as an individual unified structure was the Grecian period. Here, the spirit of the time and the *Volksgeist* could be viewed in conjunction. The affinity of the pupil for the master attracted him to the 'form-loving' Greeks. From his youth onwards he was attracted to them, and the influence of Winckelmann and later on his Italian journey gave him fuller access. But as he himself admitted subsequently (*Parodie bei den Alten*, 1824), he had had gradually to tone down his Nordic nature and outlook in order to come on to really friendly terms with the Greeks.

He was disturbed for a long time by the unaccountable rift in Greek culture, with its juxtaposition of high tragic art and buffoonish farcical comedy and travesties following in its wake. In the end it became clear to him that nevertheless there was still a deep and vital connection between the two. 'No, among the Greeks everything is of a piece; everything is in the grand manner. It is the same marble and the same bronze that make possible a Zeus or a faun; and it is always the self-same spirit that gives to everything its appropriate dignity.' In his old age Goethe saw perfectly clearly that the Greek period was precisely the time when the most varied elements including political history (in spite of its dissensions that were so unwelcome to Goethe), art and literature, were all intimately interwoven. Yet there was indeed a touch of classical exaggeration about his judgement that this ensemble had 'in the course of history been only once achieved in all the fullness of vital interaction' (a notice of Schlosser's *Universalhist.*, reviewed in 1826).

Thus Goethe remained in a dual relationship to the Greek world. He could see it as a source of normative principle, and understand it with psychological insight, following here in the footsteps of Winckelmann, along a line which Herder had never quite abandoned either. But he was not only attracted by the belief that the Greeks had produced the highest works of art in conformity with nature. There was also another and deeper trait in him which gave him, like Winckelmann, a sense of affinity with them, namely the pagan naivety of their way of life. In his *Shakespeare und kein Ende*, he drew a famous contrast between the men of antiquity, naive, pagan, heroic, practical, compounded of necessity and duty, and modern man, sentimental, Christian, romantically inclined towards ideals, freedom and will-power. Goethe himself, however, as he gently hinted, was both ancient and modern at one and the same time. As a 'divinely-led being', he was naive and dutiful; as the Faust-nature, handed over by God to its own volition, he was sensitive and strong in will-power. In actual fact, his own development led him more from the modern side of his character (the original unbounded will of a Faust) in the direction of the ancient side (the naive and limited sense of duty), rather

S 463

than in the reverse direction, although both aspects remained alive in him. We are not concerned here to plumb all the depths of Goethe's character; we have only touched on this point in order to clarify his historical relationship to Greek civilisation.

Rome, 'with its confusion of forms', could never offer Goethe what he found in Hellas, however powerfully he had felt drawn to it in Italy. Yet he confessed in old age (on the subject of H. J. Collins's *Regulus*, 1802) that 'the monstrous and specific unity of this structure' confronted him in all its impressiveness. The powerful effect of Niebuhr's critical researches, with their balancing positive and genetic contribution, enabled him once more, as he admitted, to enjoy Roman history (to Niebuhr, 1812); and with the swing of the pendulum that belonged to his character, he could even say on one occasion (to Boisserée, 1815), that the Roman inheritance, with all its great intellectual power and order, attracted him more than the Greek. But the spirit of pure power politics repelled him even more than Roman realism attracted him; for as he remarks in his *Theory of Colours*, 'Roman power was only really interested in man insofar as it could win something from him by force or gain something by persuasion'. 'Roman history', he said to Eckermann in 1824, 'is really no longer relevant to us'.

In his youth, the Middle Ages never won his respect as a whole. He found them worthy of veneration only in singular remarkable revelations. And he became more estranged from them during the period of Classicism.

> Frozen, the rigid centuries went by,
> Reason and human feeling crept hidden o'er the earth.

Even the picture that Goethe formed of the Middle Ages in riper years lacked the impulse of love, which was necessary in his opinion for the fullest understanding. After he had ascended from Classicism to a universal outlook, he had been able to find in the Nordic *attrait* something that chimed in with his youthful attitude to the Middle Ages and to the moods that had been reflected in Faust and in his reactions to the cathedral at Strassburg, and was now stirred up again by the contemporary current of Romanticism. 'There is an attraction', he wrote, 'in vividly reconstructing for ourselves the valiant, but somewhat murky, conditions of the past, and enveloping ourselves in its twilight, allowing ourselves to be deliberately constrained by a certain foreboding and awe' (*Annalen*, 1805, on the occasion of a visit to the cathedral of Halberstadt). He was indeed quite willing to admit the validity of the return to the Middle Ages, but wished personally to keep at a respectful distance from them (letter to Reinhard, 1810). But the main personal question he still wished to ask of the

Middle Ages was this: what did they do towards fostering the great body of human culture, which Goethe saw as rooted in the Greek inheritance? Then there was apt to be an alternation between bitter judgements, smacking of the Enlightenment, upon the sad hiatus between the olden days and present times, a degenerate priesthood, the corruption of the Latin language (to Blumenthal, 1819); and striking words of understanding for those who, 'in their obscure but profound and energetic activities had in those days kept the sacred flame burning'. The 'chorus of humanity' could be heard ringing out from the Middle Ages also, whenever Goethe lent an attentive ear to it (to Jacobi, 1808).

As he wrote his *Theory of Colours*, he began to understand a large part of the intellectual and spiritual contribution made by the Middle Ages. And from this standpoint he again quickly sensed something that always refreshed his spirit when contemplating the works of the divine nature, namely the dovetailing of the parts into a well-rounded whole, and the vital thread of life that ran through all creation. One of Goethe's most splendid historical portraits is that of the monk Roger Bacon in his *Theory of Colours*, in which for once he allowed the political and the intellectual to blend. Goethe reckoned that Roger Bacon must have been in his prime about the year 1215, when Magna Carta was signed and became the foundation-stone of a new English freedom.

> Although Roger was only a monk and would have had to confine himself to the district of his own monastery, the atmosphere of this environment must have penetrated through every wall; and he must assuredly have been indebted to a certain thoughtful and rational disposition for his ability to rise above the sorry prejudices of his age and take a stride into the future.

As a young man, Goethe had glimpsed in connection with the greatest German architectural structure of the Middle Ages that something splendid could emanate from these dark times. He was not particularly concerned at that period to know exactly how this could happen. The starting- and ending-points of his historical thought can be seen by comparing the words of that period with what he wrote in the *Annalen* of 1822 about ancient German architecture. One must not make a comparison between their respective tones, for then one would miss in the words of his old age something of the bright and joyful freshness inherent in his youthful utterance. But they show an uncommon degree of growth in historical insight, in the capacity to see the single individual as a member of a supra-individual whole, and of an age in which everything was bound together by an inner coherence. He now expressed the opinion that in order to understand ancient German architecture, it was necessary to view the period, religion, manners and morals, the succession of styles, the needs of the time, the mood of the century—everything together as 'a great living unity'; and to consider along with the Church the world of chivalry which served somewhat different needs, but tended in the same direction.

Goethe was not able to see the periods of more recent history in the same light as great individual structures, for here he lacked the key to political understanding. The origins and development of the modern State could have provided him with the material for constructing large political entities. But his inclination did not lie that way. He saw clearly enough that in the sixteenth century it was precisely the 'outward world-events' that had 'unceasingly shaken together and confused' the cultural values that were so dear to him. But he did not think he could discern any inner relationship between the two—only an external and mechanical one (to S. Boisserée, 1826). The side of the sixteenth century illustrating the history of thought, however, attracted Goethe powerfully as a borderland where the older and the newer periods met one another in an atmosphere of strife and contention. This was the atmosphere of mingled light and darkness that entered into *Faust*. It was a century of emergent individuals, each possessing his own peculiar power;[1] with its mysterious and lively intricacies of human nature (as in Neri), and above all the heroic personality of Luther. But even towards Luther's work Goethe was not able to take up an unequivocal attitude. He was less disturbed by the element of superstition that he found in him, for he was above the shallow criticisms often levelled by the Enlightenment. It was rather the mixture of superstition and creative power that attracted him. He displayed towards Luther the same freedom of outlook that he had so often shown in examining the great dominating figures in the intellectual life of the nations. He expressed the opinion to Blumenthal in 1819 that it was through Luther and the language of his Bible that the Germans had first become a nation. But was the religious liberation accomplished by Luther in every respect a blessing—measured against Goethe's own attitude, which was inclined towards the purest humaneness? He was certainly ready to greet it

---

[1] Menke-Glückert, *Goethe als Geschichtsphilosoph*, p. 100, calls Goethe the first to interpret more recent history as a gradual freeing of the individual, because Goethe speaks in his *Theory of Colours* of 'the striving of individuals for freedom' in the sixteenth century. It must not be forgotten that the thinkers of the Enlightenment had preceded him in the thesis that the human spirit at that time was shaking off the fetters of authority, and (as Robertson puts it) were winning 'the power of enquiring and of thinking for themselves' (*History of Charles V and History of Scotland*). The difference between the Enlightenment and Goethe lies naturally in their different interpretation of the individual.

with heartfelt sympathy, because he could interpret it in a highly symbolical sense and transpose it into his own universal framework of thought (to Zelter, 1816). But when the anniversary celebrations for the Reformation drew near in 1817, he did his best to dissuade the authorities from fixing them for 31 October, and suggested holding them with the anniversary celebrations of the battle of Leipzig on 18 October. For a man of Goethe's mental integrity could scarcely feel unmixed pleasures over a special ecclesiastical celebration recalling the dissensions and disturbances and vast misfortunes of the past centuries, since they seemed to emphasise the divisions between Protestants and their Catholic compatriots. In spite of the fact that he often sharply criticised the operations of the Catholic priesthood, he could identify himself in surprising sympathy with the atmosphere and symbolism of the Catholic religion (cf. especially his description of the seven sacraments in *Dichtung und Wahrheit*, book 7). This was only because he knew the importance of religion as the soil in which the arts flourished; because the primal human values could also reveal themselves to him in the various religious confessions, and because all the symbolism of his own mind could find an echo there. For Goethe's profound religious tolerance the sixteenth century especially, intolerant as it was and creative at the same time, remained a discordant phenomenon. For this reason, too, he could see it as a great individual unity.

This was less possible, however, for the seventeenth century. The chief impression made upon Goethe by his studies for the history of Duke Bernard of Weimar was the 'confusion' of this century (*Annalen*, up to 1780). He was always more gripped by characters than by events; and so in his *Theory of Colours* he was able to give penetrating character-sketches of the later seventeenth-century scholars and the peculiar atmosphere of their times, in which 'the fashion of using mechanical and machine-like imagery' came to the fore. He saw clearly enough that the later seventeenth century formed a bridge to the eighteenth century from the point of view of the history of thought—the century in which he himself was rooted, and out of which he had himself developed.

And so, in the evening of his life, he saw this eighteenth century as an individual phenomenon in which he too had played a part, as we read in Varnhagen's *Biographische Denkmale*, 1824; 'for this is one of the great advantages of old age, in spite of all its failings, that it can pass a whole century in review and see it as something almost personal and present'. We have already noted his criticism of this 'self-satisfied century' with its 'culture of the intellect'. Here, we have only to recall what Goethe nevertheless owed to it, how he was able to transcend it, and yet to a large extent 'preserve' it in himself.

The element above all others that Goethe considered to be worth preserving and full of promise in the Enlightenment was its insistence on all that was supra-temporal and universal. There was also another feature of this century which Goethe recognised as significant because it was continued in a specific trait of his own character. In his biography of Philipp Hakkert, he praised the 'main trend of the century against all inactivity and everything that keeps men inactive, and the attraction towards all that is active and progressive'. But the rather limited purposefulness of this activity in the eyes of the Enlightenment was fused in Goethe with an active cast of mind and spirit that drew its strength from far deeper sources: 'The true festival to a genuine man is the deed' (*Pandora*).

The nineteenth century, to which Goethe was himself the most precious legacy from the eighteenth, could only be seen as an individuality in process of formation and not as a finished whole. Yet it was clear enough to Goethe that it would have an individual character, sharply divided from that of all previous centuries. Odyniec relates how in 1829 Goethe expressed an opinion that our nineteenth century would not be simply a continuation of the earlier centuries, but would definitely be the beginning of a new era. He even sketched out with a touch of genius the course it was likely to follow. Here, he was helped by his own experience of the painful political upheavals at the turn of the century; whereas in interpreting the earlier centuries he had not possessed the political understanding that binds everything into a whole. In Goethe's view, great events as experienced by us cannot fail to have correspondingly great consequences, although these may only grow and ripen gradually like the crops from the seed. He therefore saw the seed only ripening in the second half, and perhaps even in the last quarter of the century—just as it actually turned out. His attitude to the new century was therefore bound to be somewhat divided, or rather, ambivalent.

In the *Wanderjahre* (*Wilhelm Meister's Years as Journeyman*) Goethe contrasted with the educative individualism of the *Lehrjahre* (*Wilhelm Meister's Apprenticeship*) the ideal of 'renunciation', the life of practical and useful work for the common good. Through this contrast, Goethe was expressing his confidence that the inner regenerative powers of men could also win the mastery over the destructive tendencies of the new machine age. His universal faith sustained this hope. But there would seem to be more personal feeling in various gloomy utterances belonging to his last years about the threat of a general decline towards a shallow way of life—words which still ring in our ears today. As he remarked to Eckermann in 1828: 'I see a time coming when God will have no more joy in humanity, and will have to bring everything once again to an end and start a new and rejuvenated creation'. But his universal faith could prevail even against this prospect, and he was able to trace in the downward and upward tendencies of the coming century the heart-beat of an eternal divine nature.

We have deliberately refrained hitherto from mentioning the times of the Bible and early oriental history, those historical periods and worlds which ought by rights to belong to the beginning of our study in accordance with their position in universal history and their reflection in Goethe's mind. For with regard to these, Goethe for the most part used a notably different method of approach. This suggests that his inner relationship to them was different. He retained his love of the early times of the Bible from childhood up to advanced old age. 'The culture that has come to me through the Bible penetrates the whole of my life as a cultural gain' (to Rochlitz, 1812). In this love for the Bible there was a deep intertwining of Goethe's religious need for a pure and original conception of God, and the need to see humanity in its pure and original shape, which also attracted him to Homer.

We know that this need was connected with the Pre-Romantic currents of the eighteenth century, with the tendency to see primitive times as a prototype of humanity and study them in that light. Hamann had exhorted his hearers to recall to life 'the vanished language of nature' by a pilgrimage to the East. Goethe as a young man had sought to make contact with the Orient, and had never quite abandoned this intention. Herder's inclinations lay in the same direction; he too felt the attraction of Biblical times and the Orient. His later ardent enthusiasm for the poetry and culture of the Arabs no doubt also left its mark upon Goethe. Then the Romantics proceeded to throw new light upon the Orient. Thus the spirit of the age and Goethe's own needs combined to make him flee from the political storms of the time and seek refuge in the purity of the East. He composed his poem, *Der Westöstliche Divan*, and wrote the notes for it. As he himself recognised, his basic motive was to savour the atmosphere of the Patriarchs and to enter into the deepest origins of the various families of mankind. Here, as in the Bible, he found the world of primal human forms supremely attractive. There were no disturbing factors here as there were in the ages of classical antiquity or the later European developments; no divisive tendencies and no unwelcome interferences by power politics; in short, no confused interaction of forces that needed to be reshaped along the lines of individuality and development. It was rather the individual, especially as portrayed by Goethe in his splendid frescoes of the patriarchal period in the Bible (*Dicht. und Wahrh.*, I, 4), that was also at the same time the typical primitive human figure, as fresh and untouched as the morning dew. Goethe loved 'those quiet obscure ages in which man was still ignorant of himself, but was active under the impulse of a certain inner urge'. He considered the finest part of the whole historical tradition to be the point where history and legend came together (*Theory of Colours*). In such 'natural conditions of ideal delight' Goethe felt that, for some moments at least, he could shed the fearful burden cast upon us by the traditions of several thousand years (*Max. und Refl.*). Here, as in Herder, there was plainly something in this attraction of the old dreams of a Golden Age. But Goethe was able to convert such traditional thought-forms from a static to a dynamic pattern, and breathe into primitive man something of his own active ideals.

There is another feature in his picture of Biblical and other primitive ages in general which shows this same transformation. Goethe could not shut his eyes to the fact that the religion and life of the patriarchs was not only attractive and happy, but was also marked by a certain savagery and cruelty—a state 'from which mankind can emerge, or into which it can easily relapse'. This approach towards a naturalistic history of human development after the manner of Vico or Hume did not, however, fit into the rest of the picture, painted as it was in the colours of a Golden Age. Nevertheless, when Goethe returned to this theme later on, in 1830, with his *Ornamente aus Pompeji*, he did feel the two elements to be incongruous, but reflected upon them at length in some of his most genial and characteristic thinking.

> If people take us amiss when we say that the nations work their way up out of barbarism into a state of high culture, and then later on sink back into barbarism, then we would rather put it as follows: They grow up out of childhood with great energy into their middle years, then finally they long once more for the ease and indolence of their early days.

It was Goethe's own particular idea to conceive of humanity as a kind of magnified man, and to watch it grow from the typical stage of childhood onwards. In this way he saw that 'rawness and childhood' went together; but he preferred to linger on the attractive side of childhood, as Herder and the humanitarians of the eighteenth century had delighted to do.

Goethe could both idealise and typify at this point because he was concerned to discover primal forms in the age of the patriarchs and in the East. It is precisely this typification that distinguishes his pictures of this world from the sharper and more individual pictures of the ancient world and the later periods in the West. This by no means excludes an element of extreme individuality and genetic treatment in the wonderful notes for the *Westöstliche Divan*, which can still furnish food for thought in modern Oriental research. In dealing with Persian national development, Goethe showed with a few masterly touches, with reference to the Romantic doctrines of the *Volksgeist*, how marked traditional forms remained true to themselves and yet underwent living development. This led him on to the important historical insight that there was a fundamental contrast between the Indo-Germanic culture of Persia and the Semitic-Arabic invasion (pointed out by Burdach, *Goethe–Jahrbuch*, 17). The greatest individualising achievement, however, was the new valuation of Oriental poetry. Goethe continued and raised to a new level the work which Herder had begun. In his Classicist period, Goethe himself had yielded to the old inclination towards normative standards of judgement. But now, in sharp contradiction to the judgements previously expressed by him, he was prepared to allow Oriental poetry its own individual standards. 'It is to be compared only with itself, and honoured in its own circle; in appreciating it we must forget that the Romans and Greeks ever existed.'

Western rationalism had hitherto taken exception to the despotism and the intellectual and physical servility of the Oriental world. Goethe contradicted this assumption, and so unconsciously linked on to one of the most fruitful ideas in Herder's philosophy of history proclaimed in 1774. It was precisely in these Oriental deficiencies that Herder had discovered 'a vehicle of good'. Goethe asked himself the historical question, how culture and in particular poetry had ever been possible in the East. While not in any way concealing the other side of Oriental despotism, Goethe nevertheless showed that this element of submissiveness was an integral component of Oriental culture as a whole, and not in any way intrinsically contemptible. He believed that the Eastern virtues could not be separated from their defects, but were in sober reality the fruit of these same defects. The demand that all phenomena should be viewed and understood in the totality of their connections was something that had an extensive effect upon the historical outlook of the future.

But to Goethe 'the unchanging East' was above all the field in which great examples of primal forms and types, and their subsequent metamorphoses, were to be found. Examples of this were the 'primal elements' of the Arabic language and poetry, such as camel, horse, sheep, mountain, desert, and the firmament with its myriad stars. Rationalistic poetic criticism had designated these as metaphors, but for Goethe they were 'vital features'. Incidentally, he was inclined here, as in the early Bible period, to slip into a false idealisation. He carried over the conception of 'a pure and noble natural religion' of primitive times to the Persians of Zoroaster's day, and probably also over-estimated the cultural level of the Arabs before Mahomet.

We can clearly see the limitations of Goethe's ideas of development. For all these digressions turned him aside from the way he already saw ahead of him for following out in full logical sequence the true development of the human race from the lowest levels of crude barbarism. Is it possible that in natural science as well, Goethe's conception of development suffered from the same limitations? Korff has made a comment that goes to the heart of the matter. He says that Goethe was not interested in the development of the species in actual fact, but rather in their development from the hand of God (*Geist der Goethezeit*, vol. 2, p. 61). His realistic search for the ultimate causative forces stopped at the point where he thought he had discovered one of his favourite primal forms of divine origin. This was because his research did not arise from pure realism, but was strangely and completely fused with the loftiest idealism and spirituality. What Schiller remarked to Goethe (that his 'primal plant' was not an experience, but an idea) made Goethe himself, rather to his astonishment, aware of the difference.

Within these limitations, however, his ideas of development were of untold vitality and depth. They were clearer and more lucid than Herder's, more human and heartfelt, and closer to the actual phenomena, than those of Hegel. Not many further remarks are needed to complete the picture we have already pieced together out of a whole variety of testimony. We have already seen the first approaches to what might be called the dialectic of development in Möser and Herder, which later received their logical completion in Hegel's philosophy of history—and perhaps even some violent distortion. Here, in Goethe, they found the completion that can be supplied by contemplation and sympathy. As he observed to Falk with reference to nature, but no doubt also to history: 'There is something there that brings about a mutual seeking and penetration; and when it has become one, it again gives rise to a third element'. This was the peaceful and amicable side of the dialectic movement—the production of something new from two existing elements; to some extent one might call it the *eros* aspect. The other, the combative side, the wrestling between opposing forces, the more recent of which is nevertheless only born from the depths of the older; the development of new forces from this struggle, while the old ones still continue to exercise an after-effect—all this was set down by Goethe in the account of the intellectual and literary pilgrimage of his youth in the pages of *Dichtung und Wahrheit*. The grandiose sketch entitled *Geistesepochen* (*Spiritual Epochs*) (1817) shows how each stage of development produces elements which in turn lead to their own supersession by others. Thus to Goethe's mind there was no perfect and final state in which development could come to a static condition of rest. 'Everything perfect and complete after its own kind must transcend its own kind and become something else, something unique' (Ottilie in the *Wahlverwandtschaften*).

We have already noted how Goethe preferred to see the whole stream of development as running not in thunderous cataracts, but in steady currents where the movement lay deep down. It is very characteristic of Goethe that he once admitted always having had a liking for the genetic way of looking at objects, and only to have risen along this line to the dynamic standpoint (to Jacobi, 1800). But both these ways, he observed at the same time, come together (Diary, 6 December 1799). Among the many pictures of development that Goethe used, the most successful were those which showed how 'the progress through the centuries is marked by a quiet and to some extent secret advance' (*Cours de littérature grecque moderne*, 1827). He was at pains to show how 'great world events only develop when certain tendencies, concepts and purposes, sown singly and at random, stir into activity and grow in silence, until sooner or later a general interaction between them takes place' (Notes for the *Divan*). This particular stress upon the slow maturing of forces enabled him to apply his idea of development equally to nature and to mankind. He had no conception as yet of the modern distinctions between the various kinds of development. Although Goethe was always sensitive to the polarity between nature and mind, they nevertheless formed a single unity in the oneness of the divine nature.

This polarity of the forces that at times exerted a pull in opposite directions, and at other times worked in concert, this rhythm of systole and diastole, constituted to Goethe's mind the way in which slow growth actually came about. It was this which he always saw as the cause of metamorphosis. As he once observed (Diary, 17 May 1808), it is from metamorphosis that specific characters come into being; and from the systole and diastole of the world-mind comes the endless progress of life. It was the peculiar quality of his own mind, with a richer, stronger and more fruitful sense of polarity than perhaps any other man in history, together with his intimate inner experience, that led him to the concept of development. 'What a wonderful intricacy there is in human nature', he wrote during his Italian journey, on the subject of Philip Neri, 'it can unite the strongest of opposites—the material and the spiritual, the usual and the impossible, the repulsive and the attractive, the limited and the infinite'. This language, or something very like it, could have been used by a psychologist of the age of Natural Law, such as Montaigne or La Rochefoucauld. But they could only understand it as the mysterious mechanism governing the species of man, whereas for Goethe it was always ultimately the heartbeat of the ever-moving universal whole. As Goethe observed to Riemer in 1807: 'Nature does not proceed by leaps; so the single thing is always there for the sake of the whole, and the whole for the sake of the single; just because the one is also the whole'.

By this interweaving of all individual elements into the lifestream of the whole, Goethe's concept of development escaped the danger of becoming narrowed down to a mere evolutionary idea. 'Evolution' suggests an isolated procedure, through which all the possibilities previously implanted in the germ-cell gradually emerge, and so assume an explicit instead of an implicit existence. As we have already remarked, the Romantic doctrine of the *Volksgeist* had a considerably narrowing effect, for it represented the products of national spirits as mere evolution. It is true that Goethe did not distinguish strictly in terminology between development and evolution. He could say quite happily, for example (in *Paralipomena zu den Annalen*): 'Mine was the method of development or evolution'; yet he never thought of things as merely evolving out of themselves. On one occasion he used the word 'development' in the sense of simple evolution, but immediately launched into a polemic against this sense. 'The growth [of a child] is not mere development; the various organic systems that constitute a man arise from each other, follow one another, are transformed into one another, press upon one another and even devour one another' (*Dicht. und Wahrh.*, I, 2). But this struggle between the various systems within man was never viewed as a merely interior process. Even in the metamorphosis taking place in plants the environment always played its due part in bringing about modifications in the developmental process. True, in this as in the life of history, Goethe never saw development as something causal or mechanical operating from without, but always in close association with a spontaneous counter-development from within. On this point, he and Herder were very near to one another in thought. Where this intertwining of the outward and inward was not duly recognised in historical writing, Goethe always felt that something was missing. He criticised Johannes von Müller's autobiography (in the 1806 recension) for being too much of an isolated portrait. 'We do not find sufficient expression of the effects of great world events upon such a sensitive personality . . . contact with these external things must have produced great developments from within.'

With the sure touch of genius, Goethe succeeded in steering between two reefs. On the one side, there was the danger of narrowing down his thought to a mere concept of evolution; on the other side, there was the danger of fatalism and quietism—comfortable refuge in the notion that development reaches its fulfilment 'of its own accord'.

This consolation was not only dangerous in practice, but also false in theory. Much as Goethe loved to discern in history the quiet process of growth, as it could be observed in the plant world, he was under no illusions that it should be understood as automatic and independent of any outside co-operation. Even in the plants, he saw specific formative and active drives at work on an unconscious level. All the more so must man, once he has awoken to consciousness of the spirit within, do his part to set the process of historical development in motion:

> Always you miss the proper time for action,
> And say: 'But things must take their course.'
> Tell me, has ever anything developed
> Without your action when the time was ripe?

To use the words that Schiller wrote to Goethe in 1794: 'You ascend from the simplest organism, step by step, up to the more complicated, until you finally build up man in genetic fashion as the most complicated of all, using the materials found in the whole fabric of nature'. Schiller was here putting into somewhat rationalistic though very precise language the kernel of Goethe's developmental thought, and expressing the inner power of its universal scope. He realised how Goethe saw in every single life the whole divine nature at work, bringing new creations to birth. Goethe did not in fact proceed quite as consciously and schematically from the lowest to the highest stage as Schiller supposed. His method was rather that of Möser's 'total impression'. He was accustomed to perceive through the innumerable individual observations, to see in every single thing the universe in its constant change, the ἕν καὶ πᾶν and the πάντα ῥεῖ.

From this study of his developmental thought two further questions emerge. Did he use it in comparative fashion, and so usher in the triumphs of the comparative method in the arts and humanities? And how did he use it in the realm of universal history in order to link the epochs together into large unities?

Without steady comparison of historical phenomena, the universal viewpoint of Voltaire, Montesquieu and Hume would not have been possible. But they were bound down by a mechanical idea of causation, and content to state that like causes always produce like effects. We are reminded of Montesquieu's methods when Goethe, at the suggestion of Charles Augustus, once compared the Scots and the Serbs, and derived from their habitat in precipitous mountain country their superiority in defence and war over the plainsmen, as well as the power of their poetry (to Charles Augustus, 1826).

But Goethe's search for primal forms and metamorphoses in history too was destined to lead to a still deeper kind of compassion.

In the course of this, not only the working of universal laws, but also individual autonomy in specific phenomena, was brought to light. Herder had already achieved this by his own comparative method. But whereas Herder had proceeded with the intuition of a genius, Goethe was able to add more accurate observation. Even when he made no specific mention of the fact, Goethe would quietly carry out such comparisons in order to recognise both the common elements in what appeared to be distinct, and the individual elements in a common type. But at times he also spoke very distinctly of the necessity for comparison, and the fruitful results obtained from it. He called for a comparative description of Gothic architecture alongside the Greek and Roman, and the Oriental and Egyptian (*Dicht. und Wahrh.*, II, 9). Then in *Kultur und Altertum* (*Culture and Antiquity*), he himself produced an enlightening comparison between Hellenic and Christian art, and Byzantine art in particular as a special form of Christian art. 'Thus Hellenic art began to emerge from the general type and became lost at quite a late stage in the particular; whereas Christian art had the advantage of being able to start from innumerable individual forms, and then gradually ascend to the general.' In Byzantine art, these individualities then prevented 'an ancient, rigid and mummified style from losing all significance'. Goethe put forward one of the most fruitful problems in the comparative history of thought, which has not been worked upon until recent times. In connection with the autobiographical confessions of Cardano, he expressed an opinion that 'a comparison between the so-called confessions of all periods . . . would certainly produce splendid results'. With Cardano as with Montaigne, Goethe noted a new departure, in that 'what had hitherto been confided to the priest as an anxious secret in the confessional was now laid before the world with a kind of brazen confidence.' He read this to some extent as an indication of Protestantism (*Theory of Colours*). Always, however, Goethe was intent upon preserving in all comparisons respect for the individuality of each specific phenomenon.

> So let us leave separate what nature has separated, but join together what happens to be separate only by reason of the great distances that divide one thing from another upon this earth; and let us do so in a spirit of love, without in any way weakening the character of the individual (*Whit Monday*, 1820–1).

The inner structure of Goethe's idea of development, with its genius for keeping in mind both the individual and the typical, was now to decide how far it would be suitable for the formation of larger chains of development in the field of universal history, more

inclusive links between the different ages, and ultimately a meaningful plan of the whole course of the world's history. We are confronted
at this point with a problem of the very highest importance. For the
way in which Goethe answered this question raises him in solitary
pre-eminence above all the attempts at universal history made by
his contemporaries, and above a large part of his successors. No doubt,
the greatness of his achievement is associated with features which
appear from our standpoint to be defects. We have already called
attention to the most obvious of these—Goethe's indifference, if not
revulsion, in the face of all the links between one period and another
furnished by the destinies of the nations in politics and in warfare.
All the same, there is a direct connection in this respect between
Goethe and Ranke's liberating achievements. In a word, Goethe
preceded Ranke in breaking down the barriers imposed upon
historical thought by the interpretation of universal history in
strictly teleological terms.

This interpretation maintained the existence of progress, though
often restricted and hesitant in detail, but on the whole clearly
recognisable towards a meaningful universal goal in the development
of mankind. Its origin was the Christian philosophy of history, of
which Bossuet was the latest exponent; and it secularised the idea of
a divine scheme of salvation for weak and erring humanity. As we
have already noted, the Enlightenment did not at once begin this
process of secularisation. As long as it was still permeated by the
sense of reality belonging to the seventeenth century, it would seem
to have hoped for human progress in the sphere of reason, though it
had no certain belief that reason would finally triumph. But when
it reached its climax, the Enlightenment lost this scepticism. Yet even
the great German thinkers, who transformed the spirit of the
Enlightenment into idealism, paid their tribute to the Enlightenment
on this point, in that they, too, secularised the scheme of salvation
to suit their loftier purposes and goals for the human race. We have
already noted how Herder struggled to free himself from a teleological outlook, yet remained bound by it to the end and so produced
a mixture of secular and Christian motivation. Lessing and Schiller,
Kant and Fichte were even more strictly teleological in their account
of human development; and Hegel brought these attempts to a
powerful climax, from which a variety of successors made a gradual
descent to more secular levels. These secularised schemes of salvation
were no less fruitful for a deeper understanding of history than the
Christian philosophy of history had originally been. They produced
important heuristic insights, and helped to make intelligible the
unfolding of new stages of historical development from older ones
of a different kind, and to throw light upon the emergence of un-

expected results from causes of a different nature. In this way they contributed to an understanding of the heterogeneous character of causality. But they were rather like the artificial methods of regulating the course of a river by correcting its natural windings in the interests of greater practical efficiency. They were a powerful means of reducing the medley of rational and irrational forces in history to the common denominator of universal reason and satisfactory general achievements.

Goethe had no need of any such common denominator. His universal religion gave him an assurance that God would not be fully vindicated simply at the end of history, but that this was a universal and present process, and that the imperfections of life might well exist for human reason, but not for the wisdom that was divine. As we have already seen, life's purpose was to be found in life as it actually is; however full of movement it might be, it rested upon its own foundations. Thus every separate event in history that interested Goethe had its direct connection with the divine nature, and did not need to be given its sole status and value by being recognised as a necessary stage towards a higher perfection and thus at the same time being reduced to the rank of mere instrumentality, as it was displaced from being an end in itself and became a means towards an ultimate end. This immediate relationship between history and the divine plan, which Ranke was to express later on in the saying that every epoch stands in a direct relationship to God, had already been splendidly grasped by Herder in 1774, though he had not quite been able to divorce it from the limiting notion of a divine scheme of salvation. But Goethe expressed the idea in complete detachment when he said to Eckermann in 1823: 'Every condition, nay every moment, is of infinite value, for it is the representative of a whole eternity'.

We saw earlier on how Goethe in Italy was attached to the present, in the deepest sense of the word, and so opposed the belief in progress; and how in his old age he foresaw the coming of a time when God would no longer be able to take delight in His world. Nevertheless, he did recognise an element of permanent human progress, but in a different sense from that required by the secularised scheme of salvation. Goethe saw it as something unresting, often no doubt delayed by daemonic forces, but never standing still—a movement that was for ever striving to advance. To the question whether the movement was in an upward direction, he appeared at times to answer with a rather hesitant yes; but for the most part, his answer was doubtful. For as he saw things, every human gain was accompanied by a loss. In 1798, when Jean Paul sought to pin him down to the theme of 'world progress', he replied: 'Not progress, but circum-gress, should be the word. *A priori*, it would seem to follow from the idea of providence; but *a posteriori*, you cannot see progress in every change that has come about'. It will be observed that here Goethe separates the sphere of belief from that of knowledge. As a man of prophetic faith, Ranke also spoke subsequently of a divine providence; but for both men, history had a meaning apart from any idea of recognisable progress.

The circle or the spiral seemed to Goethe to give the right picture of the movements of historical mankind. In his *Theory of Colours*, Goethe depicted the circle of error and truth in science. As he observed a succession of works of art, Goethe thought he could discern something of a satisfying law of nature in the circular course pursued by art in its waxing and waning. 'Deviations, return to the right path, the dominance of a main epoch, the effects of individualities', —all these were noted in the *Annalen* of 1805. To Goethe, art was ζῷον, with its growth and decline, 'like every other organic being, only represented in a number of individuals' (Winckelmann).

Thus Goethe revived in his own mind the cyclic theory which was first put forward by Polybius in reference to the life of constitutions, but had often since been distorted into a purely mechanical interpretation of the course of human affairs. He once touched on the Polybian cyclic theory of political constitutions (monarchy, aristocracy and democracy) with certain variations in one of his famed *Xenien* (*Epigrams*) (IV, The government of the world—'on night', etc.). But he applied this cyclical theory very elastically to nations, to whom it could most easily be applied in a mechanical manner. This is shown by his verdict that nations are imperishable, so that it therefore depends upon them whether they will constantly renew their life from childhood to old age (*Ornamente usw. aus Pompeji*, 1830).[1] He thus recognised what modern cyclical theories can also take as their accepted doctrine, the regenerative power at work within a great collective individuality like the nation.

Thus for Goethe, there was nothing mechanical, shallow or depressing about the cyclical concept. The cycle, in his view, was the exterior form of historical life, within which all the valuable inner primal forms, with their rich metamorphoses, could have free play and development. Further, it was seen by him as a guarantee of a palingenesis for all living forms, a pledge that death can never have the last word. In the 'Song of the Spirits upon the Waters' he combined this thought in his early days with the Neo-Platonic image of the eternal regress of all things towards God. The picture of the

[1] There may perhaps be a trace here of a reminiscence from Vico, who meanwhile, since Goethe had become acquainted with him in Italy (see p. 399 above), had become better known through a German translation by Weber in 1821.

spiral, however, served to widen the scope of historical possibilities, and to suggest the thought that repetition at a higher level could signify a real advance. This image thus contributed to the macroscopic calm of Goethe's old age.

> Unconditional acceptance of the unfathomable will of God, a joyful outlook ranging over all the activities of this earth, with their constant cyclic and spiral recurrence; love and an attraction that hovers between two worlds; all reality becoming transparent and resolved in symbolism—what could a grandfather ask more than this? (to Zelter, 1820).

Unless we are mistaken, however, the idea of cyclic development, which Goethe conceived in his early days, was only the prelude to another idea also belonging to the early days, but increasing in importance with the years. This was the concept we have already met with, which seemed to be as it were the lever to his ideas of development—the idea of polarity, the systole and diastole, the συγκρίνειν and διακρίνειν, recomposition and decomposition, in nature and history. The ups and downs in the cyclic course of human affairs, their constant degeneration and rejuvenation, thus became a further kind of polarity. This rhythmic element in the life of the universe was one of Goethe's deepest concerns, for (as we have seen) he felt through it all the pulse of the divine nature. This rhythm, however (the ups and downs, life and death, day and night), did not fit in with the idea of a straight-line advance, which was the prevailing picture among the champions of universal progress, at any rate in its broader aspects. This is perhaps the deepest reason for Goethe's scorning of the consolatory view of the world espoused by so many of his great contemporaries. As the poet of the original *Faust*, Goethe had pictured the garment of God in terms of 'wechselnd Weben und glühend Leben', of alternating between weaving and living; and this was a more powerful, cosmic and eternal conception than any notion of an arrangement confined to this little planet of ours, whereby the world reason would gradually lead humanity out of error and incompleteness to a state of ultimate perfection.

As is well known, Goethe's latest and loftiest thoughts ranged beyond this planet, and so were a continuation of the many kinds of cosmological speculation of his eighteenth-century contemporaries, though he gave them a new and original content. With his mystical Neo-Platonic universal sensitivity, Goethe could not accept, like the rationalists, the idea that man was creation's final word. 'We all walk in a world of mystery', he remarked to Eckermann in 1827. 'We are surrounded by an atmosphere of which we are very ignorant. We do not as yet know what life is stirring in it, nor how it is connected with the life of our minds.' If there was such a thing as a forward movement which flowed from the essence of the divine nature, it could surely not be confined to the small empirically discernible sphere of humanity, but must largely operate in the realm of mystery. Even the deeper observation of the primal forms and their metamorphoses led Goethe to surmise that there was a higher idea hidden behind each organic being because none of them corresponded exactly to the idea that lay at their root (to von Müller, 1830). As he said in one of his famous conversations with Falk in 1809, nature stands as it were at the gaming-table, and cries out unceasingly: '*Au double!*' Who knows but what man as a whole is not simply a throw of the dice that is aiming at a higher goal? The processes of nature are unceasing on every side. Even the sun has probably not yet managed to complete the creation of its own planetary system. In the same way, the last moments of Faust are directed towards a renewal of life and activity in higher spheres, beyond the horizon of death.

Again, Goethe had links with Herder as regards those transmundane and cosmic religious speculations. We shall recall those moments when he studied Herder's philosophy of history (see p. 350 f. above). But the two men were very different in the use they made of all these conceptions and hopes in the rest of their thought, though the actual content was fairly similar. Herder, who was then moving in a theological atmosphere, insisted on some firm foothold, and maintained that these hopes for the future were based upon all the laws of nature. Goethe may also have believed that in the quiet of his own heart; but in what he said, he would not go beyond tentative surmise. He made a clear separation between beautiful aspirations about the beyond, and sober realism about life here and now. In spite of constantly recurring scepticism about life here and now, Herder could not suppress his expectations of finding some teleological interpretation. He was full of passionate longings, while Goethe could calmly weigh up all the evidence, renounce a final verdict, and yet continue to hope.

It will now be possible, against the background of these transmundane conceptions, to appreciate at its proper value Goethe's dislike of the usual teleological schemes of thought. This present world was proof enough to him of a 'moral world order'. All the more so did he find the progress that he surmised and hoped for beyond the empirical world a more satisfying substitute for a goal that could be reached in this world here and now. He conceived this progress as not to a more perfect final state, but towards a more perfect further advance. A final state to be reached here and now would only lead once more, in Goethe's view, down from the higher dynamic levels of life to a limited and static standpoint.

Instead of the equivocal word 'progress', Goethe in his later years used to prefer to express his cosmic hopes in the more apposite word *Steigerung* (meaning a gradual rise in intensity, elaboration and excellence) (to von Müller, 1828). For in his view, the apparently endless process of creation produced a higher elaboration of forms in which the life of the divine nature was ceaselessly expressed. Thus he recognised along with the polarity of a 'continuous attraction and repulsion' a 'constant upward striving'. This idea was, however, conceived on such a large scale *sub specie aeterni* that there was really no contradiction in Goethe's scepticism about the actual attainment of progress within the very small field represented by even several millennia of human history. As we have suggested, the image of the spiral hints at Goethe's recognition that within historical times an 'elaboration' of forms had quite possibly taken place; but to his mind, the predominant picture was one of a pendulum swinging between the polarities of history.

This point comes out most strongly in the famous verdict, expressed in his notes on the *Divan*, that in reality the one and only profound theme of universal human history, to which all else is subordinate, is the conflict between belief and unbelief. This saying may very well suggest, as it has to some (e.g. Burdach, *Faust und Moses*, vol. 3, p. 742), an echo of the religious stirrings which lay behind the renaissance of German intellectual life in the eighteenth century. But Goethe's freely developing universal religion could now only conceive of faith and disbelief in the widest sense, not as confined to a particular content, but as positive or negative forces, with fruitful or unfruitful results, leading up into the higher world of spirit, or down into the world of selfishness and materialism. According to whether one or other of these was dominant, so the particular age would be inclined to one or other of these polarities. A related distinction made by Goethe was that between the periods given over to retrogression and dissolution, which he called subjective epochs, and those with a progressive outlook, which he called objective (to Eckermann, 1826); and likewise between the ages of reason, *inward* acting, freely and peacefully developing, and the outward-directed, acquisitive, warlike, technical and scientific ages of intelligence.

Goethe, though influenced perhaps by Hegel's terminology, looked at these two driving-forces of reason and intellect in the light of his own experience of life as a young man and in old age. He saw them as not only successive, but sometimes also simultaneous; at times separate, at other times intertwined, affecting not only particular nations, but particular individuals (*Theory of Colours*). Thus he was satisfied with a general recognition of these truths, and felt no need to arrange the whole of world history according to this pattern. He did indeed make a few ingenious attempts to distinguish the various stages of developments in the historical life that specially interested him. But apart from the already mentioned *Spiritual Epochs* of 1817, the *Epochs of Social Civilisation* of 1831, and the distinctions made in the *Theory of Colours* between important, striking and historical ages, the classification remained very much in the realm of ideal types, and only gave a hint or two of the actual history that lay behind them. Here again, we may recall the apposite saying of Korff that Goethe was more interested in the development of the species from the hand of God than in their actual growth in the real world, that is to say, in time. In such an outlook, real historical time and the whole vast significance of the millennia were apt to be obscured, though they did not altogether disappear, for Goethe needed them to illustrate his principle of development. Yet something was lacking in the general coverage of historical time to contain the richness of phenomena, which Goethe's profounder perception revealed in greater abundance than any of his contemporaries. It could not be said for Goethe, as it was for Ranke later on, that the history of the world became an individual phenomenal whole. He could not say of history, as he could of the world of reason, that it was to be looked upon in its totality as a great immortal individual. No doubt he lived with an awareness of the millennia, but for his inner needs he compressed them into a timeless eternity.

> No more you count, or reckon time to be,
> For every step is now infinity.

In the ultimate analysis, history was to Goethe a part of an eternal drama in which the course of time is a means towards an eternal renewal of creation.

It is in this sense that we must interpret the striking words spoken by Goethe in the last year of his life to his friend Wilhelm von Humboldt, entrusting him as it were with a noble confession of faith: 'Let me freely admit to you, dear friend, in the confidence of an old relationship, that at my advanced age everything seems to become more and more historical to me . . . yes, even I myself seem to myself to be more and more a product of history.' Then in between comes this sentence, which characteristically transcends the merely temporal and historical: 'It is *all one to me* whether something in past time takes place in distant empires, or quite close at hand at this present time.' There was a combination of the mystical sense of the oneness of all things and a sublime irony about himself, for the passage continues: 'And as my kind daughter reads Plutarch aloud to me of an evening, I often see how ridiculous

I should look if I were to tell my own life story after this manner and purport.'

We are approaching the end of our study, and as we do so it would seem fitting (like Goethe, as he gathered the threads together in his old age) to link up our concluding remarks with our point of departure. The world in which Goethe grew up was a blend of past and present all in one; but the really original factor was that mysterious feeling that came over him for the first time in 1774, when he stood before the cathedral at Cologne. We interpreted it as a feeling of exaltation above the past and the present as perceived by the senses into a supra-temporal sphere. It was an experience that might bring either joy or terror. We have heard this note sounding more or less clearly again and again in the course of Goethe's subsequent development, in which it took on a variety of forms and applications— various metamorphoses, in fact, of the primal form. It shows us Goethe's basic relationship to the world of history.

On this point, only a few further observations are needed to complete the picture.

In his book on Goethe (p. 190) Simmel speaks of Goethe's fortunate instinct for transcending the past by actualising it in the present. When we apply this to past history, we can find a number of verdicts of Goethe confirming the fact that he was fond of making historical phenomena his own by an almost sensuous visualisation of them. He spoke of a 'delight in making the past vividly present' (*Annalen*, 1811), and he praised the philologist Wolf's 'almost magical skill in giving present reality to the past in the highest degree' (*Annalen*, 1805). 'The turning of the past into a picture' was to play a part in the continuation of *Pandora*. This was the prime requirement which Goethe's senses, with their passionate thirst for vividness, made upon the past. They demanded their full share in transcending and re-creating it.

That was only the first stage, however, in his feeling of oneness between the past and the present. The second and higher stage was to surmount both past and present in his own person, and experience them both simultaneously as symbols of the ever-creative divine nature. In this way Goethe's capacity for sympathetic historical identification served as a means of understanding human life as a whole in this symbolic sense, no matter whether it was past or present.

The intelligent man, not content with what is put before his eyes, sees everything the senses present to him as a mask behind which a higher intellectual and spiritual life is craftily and waywardly concealed, in order to attract us and lead us on to nobler regions (*Noten zum Divan*).

'What a life there is', exclaims Wilhelm Meister in the *Lehrjahre* (VIII, 5), 'in this hall of the past! It could equally well be called the hall of the present and the future. Thus all things were, and thus they shall continue to be! Nothing is perishable but the one who looks upon them and enjoys them'.

A detailed application of this outlook is to be seen in the way Goethe enjoyed great works of art from the past. He considered it indispensable, after the first passing stage of unreflecting admiration, to assess them historically, against their basic background and context of development, and to 'actualise' them afresh as creations that had once been in the present. Thus in *Dichtung und Wahrheit* (III, 12), he relates how through the work of Wood (cf. p. 209 above) he and his companions saw Homer in an entirely new light. 'We no longer saw a strained and inflated world of heroes, but truth as it had been enacted in a far-off present, and we sought to make this as much as we possibly could our own.' All the more so did he learn to understand works of art in Italy in the first place against their background of place and time. Then he would go on to examine them with a new enthusiasm, carried away beyond time and place, as we have already seen; they would impress him as 'the highest natural products of man, based upon true and natural laws', and he would cry out with rapture: 'There is necessity, there is God!'

In the same way, Winckelmann had already first learnt to see things with a critical eye, and subsequently to feel them with something of the Platonic *eros*. We shall recall that Goethe in Italy consciously followed in his footsteps. From the point of view of the history of thought, the difference between Winckelmann's and Goethe's outlook at that time may well not have been very great. But in his maturity, Goethe learnt to see things not only more universally, but also more historically, than Winckelmann.

In one particular point, he was already in Italy deviating from Winckelmann's reactions. The latter, as we saw, looked back at Greek art with what can only be called a romantic yearning. The peculiar structure of Goethe's feeling for oneness between present and past ensured, however, that there was never any risk of his succumbing, either in youth or old age, to a romantic longing for the revival of an idealised past. Even for the particular pasts towards which he had a specially deep love, the world of Ancient Greece and the early Biblical period, his feelings were quite unsentimental, and devoid of any selfish desire. 'If I love you, what is that to you?' was true of this love also. On the higher levels where past and present were one, Goethe already possessed as a living treasure all the beauty the past had to offer. And since his contemplation was never mere contemplation, and the sight of eternal creativeness was always fused with an impulse to be creative himself, he emphatically refused to take refuge in the past. This is a point on which he was radically different from the Romantics. 'There is no such thing as a past simply to be looked back upon; there is only an eternally new, built up from elements of the past used in a widened context; and genuine longing must always show a desire to be productive and create something new and better' (to von Müller, 1823).

The feeling of oneness between past and present has also evolved for itself a particular manner of description and a particular historical style. The mere narrator of past events who sees the past as past and nothing more is satisfied simply to tell the story and to connect up these events more or less vividly and in a fairly coherent pattern. The historian, on the other hand, who wants to draw the past towards the present, make it available for the present, or even fuse it with the present on a higher plane, can hardly do other than offer a reflective accompaniment to the course of events, and seek to interpret them, sometimes with vigour, sometimes in a more tentative fashion. This had been the case with Polybius, and often with Machiavelli and Guicciardini. Starting out from the timeless similarity of all things human, and their cyclic course of development, they felt compelled to comment upon them and draw didactic inferences. This tendency increased in the time of the Enlightenment, which had a more conscious sense of the unity and similarity of all things human, whether in the past or the present. Voltaire accompanies his narrative with the monotonously recurring principles of his basic enlightened philosophy of history, which he used as a yardstick for assessing events. When it mastered the field of history, the 'Sturm und Drang' movement, with its new sense of life and vitality, was all the more bent upon letting a breath of fresh air into it. With Herder (as far as he goes in for any historical narrative) the facts often entirely evaporate in a general idealised view of things. Goethe, however, having reached maturity and begun to write history, reestablished the balance between facts and ideas. Attention has often been called to his manner of combining, in *Dichtung und Wahrheit*, clear narrative of individual events with general upward and inward reflections of a didactic kind. But this needs to be linked up with the development of historical style; and it will then become clear that here at last the form of description had been found which the future historism required.

It provided a pendulum swinging between reality and the ideal, as can at once be appreciated when you think of Ranke. But the same pulse was first audible in Goethe, not only in *Dichtung und Wahrheit* but in his commentary on Cellini, in his *Theory of Colours*, and in his notes on the *Divan*. He did not, like Voltaire, produce rigid principles taken from a different system of reference and apply them indiscriminately, but allowed ideas to grow spontaneously out of the free living reality, and make unhindered contact, move, and change with it. 'To seek out the idea in experience'—this was the demand that Goethe made for all scientific research into nature as well as for the study of man. He was convinced that 'man is following out an idea in everything he undertakes' (*Zur Morphologie, Aphoristisches*). That was the 'delicate kind of empiricism which identifies itself with the object at the deepest level and so becomes a genuine theory' (to Zelter, 1828). One could call it a realism of ideals, or again the past and the present in one, because both of them (the reality as it was and its observer) meet on a common higher level.

We will venture to glance at a higher achievement than Goethe's specifically historical works and verdicts, because here too there are analogous observations to be made. What is the relationship between the past and the present in *Faust*? A small book could be written on the subject, but we shall be content with a single suggestion that has emerged from the reading of some recent research on *Faust*. For several decades the historical sources of the various motifs in *Faust* have been examined with a vast display of erudition and ingenuity. But since the turn of the century there has been a notable change in method and viewpoint. To earlier research, with its rather positivist tendencies, the innumerable echoes in *Faust* of very ancient themes in world literature and of certain definite ideas coming from ancient thought often looked like borrowings, to be dealt with on the same level as the examination by source-criticism of the use made of ancient material by an author, and the value ascribed to it. Since then, the idea of borrowings and simple reshaping of the borrowed material has been more and more replaced (especially since Burdach's incisive researches) by the more vital idea of fertilisation. For the mirror of Goethe's mind, which reflected these masses of historical reminiscence, was always a 'creative mirror'. The power with which these traditions and the cultural values of these millennia were taken up and given new life was far superior to the more traditional and restricted way in which the poets and humanists since the Renaissance have used them—with the one exception of Shakespeare. Dante, Shakespeare and Goethe were thus universal poets. They succeeded in raising the life all round them, and such of the world's history and literature as was accessible to them, and blending them with a new world by the breath of their spirit—a world which, in spite of its subjective origins, could nevertheless claim a high degree of objectivity. On this higher level, past and present, no less than subjective and objective, were fused into one. Dante and Shakespeare achieved this with an unconscious naivety. Goethe, too, was naive in his creative approach, allowing the seeds of the past to re-sow themselves, as it were, in his own garden. But in so doing, he was highly conscious of the relationship between the past and the present as interpreted by the new feeling for history. It was for this reason that he called himself a great collective being who drew his sustenance from thousands of individuals, past and present.

Goethe's relationship to those historical phenomena, with which he had an affinity that enabled him to take them into himself, was always both naive and self-conscious, both historical and supra-historical. And this relationship was only possible where the connection between a historical and a universal outlook, an inductive reverence for the small and a grandiose awareness of the great encompassing whole, were as deeply implanted as in Goethe. This connection became looser during the subsequent course of the nineteenth century. It allowed the intellectual threads that had been gathered together during Goethe's period to fall apart again, under the influence of the daemon of a division of labour and other evil spirits. Positivism required that wherever possible, science and universal philosophy should have nothing to do with one another. And even though the very nature of man prevented this outlook from penetrating universally, it had a very far-reaching influence upon the practice of historical research. The result was that other motives than those of history and nature as the inspiration of a universal philosophy were bound to become the basis of research-work, such as aesthetic delight in the colourful aspects of the past, and satisfaction with precise research into the facts, in the belief that this would serve the interests of strictly causal knowledge; or political and practical considerations; or in most cases an admixture of the ever-present antiquarian urge. In our day, however, when these motives began to wear thin or become suspect, the wider consequence was a rising malaise and confusion about the results produced by such intensive specialisation. To be sure, there was never an entire lack of positive counter-movements and achievements based upon more positive outlooks, with roots in a deeper universal philosophy. But in spite of these, the complaint waxed louder and louder that historism was leading into the bottomless pit of relativism, which understood all philosophies, but had none of its own.

Relativism existed, as we have more than once noted, before the rise of historism. There was the political relativism of statesmen and political theorists. The spirit of scepticism and the idea of tolerance, both of them bound up with the early stages of the Enlightenment, could likewise have a relativist tendency, and so could the discovery of new historical fields and complicated chains of causality. This remains true in spite of the simultaneous persistence of belief in the timeless truths of reason. But relativism received a deeper foundation with the newly awakened sense of the individual and its endless variety. Thus relativism and historism certainly belong together. This is clear enough in Goethe too, although he was only the greatest pioneer of the nascent historism, without himself fully entering into possession of it. In his early days as a protagonist of 'Sturm und Drang', he had pronounced a verdict suggestive of a relative outlook, namely that good and evil were as necessary to one another as a torrid zone and the freezing wastes of Lapland were necessary to produce a temperate zone (on Shakespeare's birthday, 1771). Later on, as a mature thinker, he often recognised that there were bound to be many possible ways of thinking and opposite poles of conviction, and that these were based upon the immense variety of human beings.

> I avert my eyes from what is repugnant to me. Yet there is much I do not exactly approve of, but am quite ready to recognise in its own particularity; and it mostly turns out that the others have as much right to exist in their own specific forms as I have in mine (*Kampagne*).

Goethe was of the opinion that one is born with a propensity for this or that philosophical inclination (to Falk, no date), thus anticipating a conclusion reached by modern thinkers since Dilthey, when they began to examine the innate thought-forms of philosophers. Goethe's inmost character predestined him to a certain relativism, for the Faust in him was balanced by the opposing tendency towards Mephistopheles, and the Tasso by a tendency towards Antonio. As he admitted to Jacobi in 1813:

> I for my part, with the manifold directions taken by my character, cannot be satisfied with a single thought-form . . . the things in heaven and earth constitute such an extensive kingdom that the organs of all living creatures combined would be needed to embrace them.

It was from Goethe's basic nature as a whole that the relativistic ideas of individuality, polarity, systole and diastole, took their origin, as well as the thought that only the sum-total of all men constitutes humanity.

The intellectual revolution consummated by 'Sturm und Drang' and by Goethe was bound, however, to work in a relativist direction. By releasing a deeper subjectivity, it shattered every kind of dogmatic belief in absolute standards, Christian beliefs no less than those bound up with a secular and naturalistic outlook. Goethe was largely right when in his old age he characterised his own time to Ecker- mann in 1826 as a subjective period. Whether it was therefore a re- gressive age, and on the way to dissolution, as he also stated, is less easy to decide. It all depended on whether the new individualism, subjectivism and relativism could be channelled into fresh courses. This could certainly not be done through a dogmatic faith of the old kind, which had now become impossible, but only through a new kind of faith in ultimate and absolute connecting-links that would show factual results, arising from the new outlook upon the world as a whole. Subjectivity, once it had been set free, needed, however, to revert to an objective understanding of the world, without losing the springs of individual experience and effort in the process. Goethe's own example showed that this was perfectly possible. This was the path he followed ever since the time that he turned towards Classi- cism. However relatively his objective understanding of the world might proceed in details, because it had passed through the medium of subjectivity, his objective outlook led, as far as the world as a whole was concerned, to this new kind of faith in 'him who creates himself from all eternity in the task of a creative vocation'.

Thus Goethe's relativism, like Möser's, was a much more deeply based and positive relativism, uninfected by any weakening doubts about the worth of the individual will, or by vagueness or shifty opportunism about the basic forces in history. Relativism can either lead to the profoundest depths or to the dreariest of plains, according to whether it is or is not backed in the last resort by a strong creative faith; according to whether humility and reverence in the face of the unsearchable are the result of a relativist outlook on the world, or are absent because of the prevailing view that human insight can discern nothing but an anarchy of values. Goethe possessed the necessary humility, and could therefore feel the antinomies of life and history not as lawlessness, but as necessary dissonances within the total harmony of the universe. Thence he drew the vigorous determination to maintain his own individuality (limited, one-sided and only rela- tively valid as he recognised it to be) in defiance of all invading forces, in order that he might remain true to the divine methods of action. He could well have said of himself, as he makes Tamerlane-Napoleon say: 'If Allah had meant me to be a worm, he would have created me as a worm.'

Thus a possible solution of the problem, for us as for Goethe, is to see one's own individual human and relative task as a divine ap- pointment. 'Spirit and matter, soul and body, thought and extension, will and movement', he wrote to Knebel in 1812, 'were, are, and al- ways will be the necessary dual ingredients of the universe, and both together may be looked upon as God's representatives. We men are one-sided in our actions, and always must be; but we must act so that our onesidedness may penetrate through to the other side, and where possible pierce it, so that we come out again the right way up at our antipodes'. This recipe for arriving at the antipodes was something that Goethe handed on to the developing historism. For it, too, has laid upon it the task of understanding the world in relative terms, while still recognising its own conditioned status, and yet not allowing this recognition to sunder it from the mysterious springs of power which flow from a belief in absolute values and an ultimate and primal origin of all life. This is an absolute that can neither be demonstrated nor defined, for, as Goethe says, 'its essence is to remain for ever unknown'. Like Plotinus before him, he transferred it to higher and more distant regions than either Natural Law or Christianity, regions that were quite unattainable by thought. Yet in so doing he preserved a permanent kernel of both Christianity and Natural Law. Thus Goethe arrived at what was perhaps the only possible synthesis between a relativistic and an absolute, an idealising and an individualising way of thought. One may point out logical gaps in this synthesis. But when it comes to deciding what are the ultimate connecting-links between our thought and our will, the intellect loses its competence over the soul, which refuses to let itself be robbed of its share, as a particular limited individuality, in the significance of life in all its immeasurable fullness.

IV *Summary and Conclusion*

It is now time to glance back over the course our study has followed. The task we set ourselves was to show how the historical world was set free from the rigidity into which it had fallen through Natural Law, pragmatism and the intellectualism of the Enlightenment. Thought-patterns of a pragmatic and intellectualistic type based upon Natural Law had existed from ancient time, either in conjunction or in opposition with the Christian revelation; and they had largely determined the interpretation of history. This change therefore represents one of the deepest and most incisive revolutions in the history of Western thought in general, whereby the Western genius worked out its own individuality in distinction from that of the ancient world without, however, losing the thread of continuity that bound them together. This Western process of individualisation had been preceded successively by the distinctive spirit of the Middle Ages, the Renaissance, the Reformation and the Enlightenment. Historism represented not only a new vision for the historian, but also for the whole of human life. It enabled the process of individualisation to become aware of itself by teaching men how to understand all history as the development of something individual, though always conditioned by typical successions of events and regularities.

We have only followed the rise of historism to the decisive point where its fundamental ideas broke through, but not as far as its full evolution. Its course has been European, though the movement matured in Germany and reached its climax in the work of Goethe. We saw that, especially during Goethe's Classicist period, this outlook was still permeated by some after-effects of the traditional normative thinking. But all the main threads that contributed to the rise of the historical outlook met and became more firmly joined together in Goethe. First there was the widespread Pre-Romantic need, which turned its attention to primitive and early times in human history and the life of the nations. Admittedly, it idealised them; but it did oppose to its own frigid civilisation contrasting pictures of a fuller and purer humanity, and so show men how to appreciate the past as a whole with a greater warmth of feeling. Then there was the pietist movement in Protestant Germany, nourished by mysticism, which penetrated human psychology in greater depth. It aroused the subjective consciousness as it passed from person to person, but at the same time it pointed the way to metaphysical and religious links with other experience, in such a manner that the mind became more receptive to new thoughts in general, even of a non-pietistic kind. And, thirdly, there was the new psychological relationship to the art of antiquity, in which Winckelmann led the way. In spite of the one-sided canonisation art incidentally received, the new relationship did nevertheless increase the inner readiness for new truth. Lastly, and the strongest formative power of all, there was the old Platonic–Neo-Platonic world of ideas, resuscitated in Leibniz's theory of monads and Shaftesbury's doctrine of the 'inward form'. This certainly pointed in the direction of individuality, and suggested a deeply-rooted basis in a living source that was related to God.

Each of these four elements represents one and the same basic process within the Western, and more particularly the German, development, namely a pendulum-swing from the exaggerated heights of Natural Law during the Enlightenment to the depths of the soul, which still remained unsatisfied; and to the new individualism already prepared for by the Protestant relationship between man and God with its sense of a spiritual affinity towards a higher entity. And the new German poetry, springing from the same source as historism, incidentally gave it an immense stimulus.

In Möser we saw the especially powerful action of the first of these four elements. The third and the fourth were at least clearly glimpsed, though his achievement as a whole was marked by an eminently practical openness towards the particular forms of actual life. Möser's openness was of the kind that could learn the new poetic language by a give-and-take intercourse with all the spirits of the age.

Herder was the first to bring all four elements into a synthesis. Great and creative as this was, it was not yet complete, for it was marked by hesitations and certain gaps; yet in its positive features it was clearly the work of a pioneer genius.

The fact remains that it was Goethe, Herder's pupil, who brought the synthesis of these four elements to completion under the primacy of the last one, the Platonic and Neo-Platonic outlook. His great idea was that of a creative divine nature, combining eternal being and eternal becoming, 'self-sufficient, living, creating from the highest to the lowest according to regular law', disclosing itself in productive primal forms, types and individuals. This new universal feeling, drawing upon all the food of past centuries, which also contained within itself a new feeling for history, provided Goethe with the powerful solvent that was able to free it from its state of torpidity.

It has been widely recognised that Goethe was the strongest and most active force in this revolution of the intellectual outlook. But this has not been made as clear as it should be with regard to the rise of historism. Goethe's achievement in this sphere has sometimes gone unrecognised because of his own ambivalent attitude. Under the strong impulsion of his fundamental nature, there was a certain cleavage in his attitude to the world of history. He could not help feeling it to be both a dead and a living world; and he therefore only applied his newly discovered principles of knowledge to a part of the historical world. The life of the State and warfare, not to mention economics, were altogether ignored, apart from a few flashes of thought which showed him to be perfectly capable of bringing his new light to bear upon them—much more capable, at any rate, than Herder. Goethe often showed a deep understanding of the importance of the masses, and the creations of what has been called the objective mind—the sphere of institutions and cultural works in the widest sense; but for the most part he only paid attention to them insofar as they provided the surrounding and conditioning atmosphere of active individuals. Creative man remained the principal interest for Goethe. He affirmed the Platonic thought that the actor was more significant than the action. But in order to penetrate the whole historical world with a new spirit, it was first of all necessary to take a new look at man himself in full depth, and the interplay of Daemon and Tyche, his spirit and his fate. Furthermore, instead of man being simply an atom among other atoms, as he was for the

Enlightenment, he needed to be blended with the general current of life and growth, from which standpoint he would be seen in a new and profounder light. Goethe's individualism had to become, as we pointed out, a universal individualism before it could act as a ferment of historism. When this sway of supra-personal forces, this interweaving of all separate elements into one universal process of becoming, was as penetratingly felt as by Goethe, it was easy to go a stage further. The things of which he had an inner grasp, as well as the sphere of history that he had left on one side, could be reshaped into lively historical pictures and incorporated into the general current of developing life. The method used by him in his researches into nature was also valid for the world of history; for nature 'must not be portrayed as a separate thing apart, but living and active, and striving to express the life of the whole in the parts' (*Paralipomena zu Annalen*). History had nothing to fear from Goethe's scientific methods, because they had already been freed from any trace of the mechanistic, and become essentially historical.

Goethe had reproached the Enlightenment with mechanising intellectualism, and had taken as his own watchword the term 'reason', though it was a word that had also been freely used by the Enlightenment. This very fact shows the degree of external continuity with the Enlightenment, in spite of the revolution Goethe had brought about. The fundamental impulses of his nature, which made him conscious of divided feelings towards the world of history, brought him into contact with certain effects of the Enlightenment. We have seen in our earlier chapters how the Enlightenment was already transcending its own limitations, and putting questions that it was itself unable to answer. Two factors particularly were impelling it towards new solutions. On the one hand, the embarrassment with which it confronted its analysis of the soul, the mysterious mixture that constituted human nature, the 'I know not what', as Hume called it. Then, on the other hand, the great attempts made by the Enlightenment to raise everything that wore a human look to the level of a single unity, and to comprehend it, by means of its mechanistic methods of knowledge and categories of Natural Law, as a supra-temporal unity of past and present. What the Enlightenment attempted to do for the psyche and for humanity as a whole from outside, Goethe completed from within.

Working outwards from his most individual experience and its close genetic connection with the divine nature, he too found that past and present became fused into one. This gave him the most exalted position above the world of history—perhaps the highest possible, superior in its inmost content to even the lofty position of Hegel, because it did not seek to control history according to a preconceived scheme of salvation. Goethe as a historical thinker stands not only between the Enlightenment and the later historism, but to some extent above them both. For only the highest representatives of the later historism succeeded in seeing history at every moment not only as temporal and individual, but also as supra-temporal, *sub specie aeterni*. No doubt it was an inevitable part of development, and essential to the constantly deepening inductive methods of research, that the temporal and individual aspects of history should somewhat eclipse the supra-temporal. Yet for Goethe, in the last analysis, especially in his maturest period, immutability throughout change, the mystical fulfilment of old age, would be eternally more important than the vision of change itself. The particular path towards these heights followed by Goethe is not immediately accessible to his successors, burdened as they are with the empiricism of the nineteenth century and the problems of the twentieth. Nevertheless, it is Goethe who still points the way towards these lofty regions.

Supplement

Leopold von Ranke

Memorial address given on 23 January 1936 in the Preussische Akademie der Wissenschaften

Leopold von Ranke died on 23 May 1886 at the age of ninety. He had been a member of our Academy for fifty-four years. It was in solemn mood that the young Berlin historians of those days followed the coffin from his house to the church. We knew even then, though not to the full, that we were accompanying one of the immortals on his last journey. Ranke called it the earthly immortality of the spirit, if one generation could leave behind to its successors, in a form that would preserve its effectiveness for all time, the sum of its experiences, which were then able to keep their significance beyond the fleeting present moment. It is perhaps possible to add something to help us grasp his own undying fame. When Ranke died, his effect on us could not be altogether separated from the dust of our schooldays. He was then reckoned by us first and foremost as the great teacher of a particular branch of knowledge. Today we can see him as standing in the succession of a line of great human achievements, and as one of its towering figures. We can appreciate his work as one of the greatest attempts to find a solution to an age-long problem with which humanity has wrestled ever since the ancient world. We must look at him in this succession if we are to understand him to the full. First of all, however, there must be some examination of his historical writings in respect of their inner content—insofar as our temporal limitations will allow us to apprehend it.

I should like to begin with the immediate impressions that he might make upon a receptive reader of today, not all at once, but as a result of repeated perusals. I suppose it is one of the pleasantest kinds of reading to return after a fairly long interval to some great and well-loved author. Because we ourselves have developed in the meanwhile, and are no longer quite the same reader, and yet essentially still the same person, our author as we read him also seems to unfold himself to us afresh and at a new depth, while still retaining our confidence. And so our ears now become more receptive to the music of Ranke's language. He was not content with juxtaposed sentences, but had an art of balancing them against one another; there was a floating rhythm in the way that finely woven narrative would suddenly be succeeded by lofty reflections arising from its texture. There is a similarity here between Ranke and Goethe. Using apparently only the simplest language, with only an occasional rare word setting off the whole like a jewel upon an elegant dress, it could express the profoundest of ideas. If one were to try and put them into the modern, conceptual language, a breath of the spirit, an inimitable something, would be lacking. The content might even sometimes, though perhaps not often, appear a little ordinary, and not particularly original. But at this point we must not forget Ranke's own pronouncement: 'We are often moved by a word that would have no special value in itself because of the man who utters it, the human being who stands behind it and gives it vitality'. To come back for a moment to the subject of rhythm, to the alternation between strictly objective narration and the sudden upward look which sublimates it, it soon becomes clear that a certain change took place in this respect during the course of his life. In his youthful work of 1824 on the Romano-Germanic peoples, there is a decided preponderance of colourful, picturesque and somewhat turbulent narrative. There is no over-indulgence in metaphor, but a delight in being able to summon up gay and lively pictures fresh from the living source. Alongside this, however, the need was developing to progress from the particular to the general, as can be seen preponderantly in his contemporary letters, and in the famous introduction on the unity of the Romance and Germanic peoples. Then in the masterpieces of his maturity, the History of the Popes and of the Reformation, we find narrative, the great upward glances and the wide perspectives all closely and organically interwoven with one another. Like great waves in a rough sea, which are always crowned by foaming crests, events in Ranke's narrative are always followed by an exalted reflection upon them. In the great works of his latter years, his *History of England* and his *Universal History*, the rhythm is different still. The sea appears calmer, the waves have a longer and more poised movement, and the narrative itself is charged with reflectiveness. In the wisdom of his old age, Ranke was able, even where mighty and stirring events were being narrated, to give his periods a certain comfortable roundness.

Not only in Ranke's ability to look up and to take a wide view but also in the actual narrative, the reader often feels exalted into another world. Men and things seem to be composed of finer material than usual. If one reads him rapidly, things sometimes seem to lose their ordinary clarity, and appear to become blurred, as they quickly melt into one another and their colours run together. The reader has to plunge more keenly and deeply into his author to recognise that these delicate allusions, these intertwinings and separatings of the various strands of narrative, are controlled by an extremely acute observation and a high degree of precise craftsmanship. Paradoxically enough, history now seems to grow both clearer and more mysterious. But we then become aware not only of a singularly high degree of art, but first and foremost of a steadfast purpose bent upon reproducing the reality of history with all the scientific and scholarly tools at its disposal. Ranke was always anxious to show 'what things had really been like'. In order to let the centuries come through with all their mighty power, he would have liked as it were to efface his own personality. This, as has often been rightly pointed out, was a wish that could not be fulfilled. And yet, however paradoxical this may sound, he needed this desire to inspire him to produce the highest of which he was capable. A serious and priestly approach lay concealed in this desire, and Ranke was indeed filled with something of the priest's exaltation. For him, the higher and finer world into which he raised things was also the real and essential world, because he was able to see it with profounder, as well as clearer, insight. At every turn, criticism and intuition worked together in intimate connection.

Ranke's critical work made a stronger impact on professional historians than his intuitive capacity, which was of a much more individual nature. It has been rightly noted that Ranke's methods of source-criticism, which were worked out for the first time in the supplement to his study of the Romano-Germanic peoples, entitled *Zur Kritik neuerer Geschichtsschreiber*, owed a good deal in its essentials to Niebuhr. But however generally accepted and inevitable this critical approach might be, there was something of Ranke's own individual character behind it. Even as a young research student, Ranke gave evidence of an innate sense of the need for strict veracity in the face of all the testimonies of human life, an unconditional demand for the most genuine and original sources, and a distaste for all that was dubious or distorted. On such occasions, his eye would flash, and this otherwise mild man would burst out into a tone of sharp contempt when he lighted upon any such elements in tradition. How much more would he wax indignant over a great deal offered us over a good many years now that passes itself off as history, in a world of readers whose critical standards have slackened. And was this quite specific demand for truth to be confined solely to the criticism and use of sources? May there not be pointers from this towards an understanding of what we have felt to be mysterious in his interpretation of history? We shall try to unravel a few of them (for our time will not allow of more) by selecting some of the more important problems that arise out of the abundance that Ranke handled in his books.

I will take my starting-point in a single straightforward observation. We come across (it may be in his history of the Reformation) descriptions of political struggles and complicated relationships between two German princes' courts. They make quite a different impression on us from his predecessors in the eighteenth century, well informed though they were, or from his successors in the late nineteenth century, who were often much more strongly armed with the latest material from the archives. No more of the prosaic pragmatism of the eighteenth century, which delineated in clear juristic terms the respective interests of the opposing princes, and recognised or criticised (as the case might be) the intelligent or unintelligent manner in which the statesmen perceived these interests. But neither is there anything of what I may perhaps venture to call the snobbism of practical politics; nothing of what often comes out in the later historians who reckoned they had learnt from Bismarck how a politician really handles things. In Ranke, however clearly the practical basis of these interests may be depicted, they immediately become endowed with a certain spirituality, and the men representing them act with a certain distinguished assurance, as though sustained by an invisible power still at work in and behind these interests. The practical and the spiritual are seen to be inseparably interwoven. This reminds us of one of the greatest sentences ever written by Ranke. It comes in the *Political Discourse* of 1836, where he is demonstrating that politics according to abstract principles, whether liberal or legitimist, are, as it were, so much empty air, but is maintaining at the same time that mere brutal power politics are equally invalid: 'The spiritual reality which suddenly rises up before you in all its unsuspected originality cannot be deduced from any higher principle.' The unseen spiritual power working itself out in practical interests and sustaining those who are led by it, is thus (according to Ranke) none other than the particular State involved, understood as a peculiar kind of individual.

As such, and in spite of all points of comparison and all points of connection with a higher level, this State is inwardly marked off from all other States, because a particular spiritual principle is at work in it, expressing itself outwardly in its constitution and politics.

'By the principle of a State', he says, 'we must understand not some abstraction, but its very inner life.' Here again, as so often, we are directed by him to something not definable in terms of ordinary logic. Yet he indicates a way in which we can have access to it. 'Only extensive historical research and combination will raise us to an intuitive recognition of the spiritual laws prevailing in the depth of life.' 'An intuitive recognition'—what an all-inclusive expression! It does not mean the forecast of results that are likely to accrue, such as even an accurate research-worker in natural fields can expect to make from the provisional half-way house he has reached along his projected line of enquiry. Even the latest knowledge acquired in this way is still a definite and conscious piece of knowledge and not merely an intuitive recognition. In Ranke, however, the way of knowledge, beginning quite empirically and on strictly critical lines, culminates in an inner fusing of intuition and knowledge. It is intuitive surmise when he looks upon the States as 'living individuals' and at the same time calls them 'thoughts of God'; likewise when he says of the interior formative principles or 'highest ideas': 'The idea is of divine origin.' This doctrine of States as individual living entities with their own specific laws of life, although Ranke did not at once press it home, was destined to prove epoch-making, in the political field no less than in the world of scholarship. But the metaphysical colouring that this doctrine finally acquires in Ranke will be sought in vain in the biological and morphological perspectives of Rudolf Kjellén, though he represents a revival of the essential idea. We shall bear him in mind as we now descend once again to the more matter-of-fact levels of Ranke's historical thought.

Ranke always liked to ascribe to the actions of statesmen, especially at decisive moments, a certain element of dignity, and to derive them from high motives, rather than petty and personal ones, as moralistic pragmatism was fond of doing. The high motives were those flowing from the inner vital principle of a State, interwoven with all its internal and external affairs, and constantly merging with the whole conjunction of motives on a world scale. There was no doubt a tendency to stress and even sometimes overstress these motives; and no doubt this led here and there to an excessive toning down of harsh historical contrasts, and a mitigation of the part played by elemental passions. This was the reverse side of Ranke's splendid pronouncement that it was right and proper for a historian to be kind and merciful in judgement. In his old age, this tendency even increased. This can be seen in the changes that took place in his portrait of Napoleon. There are earlier judgements which present Napoleon as an insatiable conqueror whose aim was to rule the whole world. In a later picture, however, he sharply criticised those who took him to be a 'conquering wild beast', instead of appreciating the world circumstances controlling his actions and drawing France into the decisive struggle against England. But the need for these large supra-personal motives was as much a part of his spiritual make-up as his demand for genuineness in his sources. This was already at work in him as a young man of twenty-one, when he wrote down for his own satisfaction, in 1817, some fragments on the subject of Luther—the germ of what was later to become his *History of the Reformation*. In the course of this, he discusses Charles V's plans after the war of the Schmalkaldic League for a federal reform of the Empire, and for measures to procure greater unity, and exclaims: 'How could a historian take it upon himself to ascribe to self-interest a great conception that was vital to the well-being of the nation!'

This observation will throw some light upon a hotly-debated question of the early nineteenth century—a question that was in truth wrongly framed: Ought the historian to interpret history in individual or in collective terms? Should he construe the great events and achievements as the work of creative personalities, or as the work of needs and tendencies residing in human communities? This collectivism could then easily descend to the level of a crude theory of economic class-struggle as exemplified in Marxism.

But in Ranke, there seems to be a much more refined kind of collectivism, exemplified by his fondness for deducing the actions of statesmen from the large-scale vital necessities of States. He would not have subscribed without demur to Treitschke's proud dictum that men make history, but he would have recognised a certain weight of truth in it. As far as he was concerned, there was no opposition here between different principles of interpretation. The same principle of interpretation enabled him to discern an ever-active polarity between creative personality on the one hand, and collective spirit and general tendencies on the other. Although there was a constant to-and-fro movement, with an astonishing variety of new combinations, one of these poles was not conceivable without the other. And so his way of cognition blended with his personal, ethical philosophy and its ideals. As Ranke writes in his *History of England*: 'The greatest thing that can happen to men is to find themselves defending a universal cause in defending their own interests. Personal existence then becomes broadened into a world historical moment.' One may perhaps gather from this and other utterances that Ranke accorded a primacy to the general cause and the supra-personal idea for which the heroes of history must live their lives. Yet he never interpreted this primacy in a one-sided or mechanical way. In another famous passage in his *History of the Papacy*, he affirms with deep feeling the creative part played by 'strong personalities of great inner power' in the genesis of ideas 'from the unfathomable depths of the human spirit'. And again in his *Universal History* we read: 'General tendencies are not the decisive factor in historical progress; there is always the need of great personalities to bring them to fruition.'

We can none of us forget the wealth of profound insights into the most individual and personal lives of historical characters scattered throughout his works, but always at well-considered points in the narrative. They are often hints of a hidden and intimate kind, which are then (especially in his earlier works) quickly transformed into the most colourful portrayal of a personality so vividly presented that you could almost touch the person with your hand—almost, for a certain delicate protective medium prevents the reader from coming too close. In the busy days of his youth, when he was working with superabundant enthusiasm on his first book, he exclaimed with a mixture of hope and despair: 'Every day knowledge and perspectives widen as I study the history of the world. But who can reveal the inner essence, the nature, and the pulsing life of the individual?' As far as it is possible for sympathetic insight into the souls of men to reveal this inner essence, Ranke was successful beyond any of his predecessors.

But there is another element in his character-sketches. He would have regarded it as a real lack of taste to take them as excerpts from his books and offer them as a portrait gallery to the reader. This was clean against Ranke's inmost intuitions. For it was his ambition, and a part of his innate demands, that personalities should be portrayed in all their full individuality, and yet wholly blended with the broad course of events. The delicate protective medium screening them from too close contact also surrounds and permeates the whole of his historical writing. 'The world-shaking events of the epoch', the general tendencies or ideas and the active individuals, appear in their context as one single and powerful process which, by virtue of the wealth of individual motives that compose it, eludes all abstract conceptual forms, yet makes itself known to us as an unendingly rich stream of life that still possesses an individual unity. For there is individuality in the tendencies or ideas, and still more in each single event; and more particularly so in what Ranke calls the 'moment' when all the single threads come crowding together and determine in a broad way the shape of things to come.

This brings us to the principal thesis in his interpretation of history as a whole, formulated by him for the *History of England*, but valid also for all that claimed his attention. It runs as follows: 'Everything, both general and individual, is an expression of spiritual life.'

This sentence must first be amplified with reference to what we have already said. With Ranke, everything spiritual is closely allied to reality; *real-geistig*, to use the expression of 1836. This was the real watchword that also holds good of the works he produced in his old age, when his outlook was more strongly spiritualised. Then we must explain what he really means here by the word 'general' [*allgemein*]. He uses the word, indeed, in two quite different senses. One of them is rarely used by him, and generally avoided for his own specific purposes. The other, which was increasingly used in his advancing years, expresses his own highest goal for knowledge. 'The formal is the general [*das Allgemeine*], the real is the particular [*das Besondere*], the living,' he says in his *Political Discourse* of 1836. This formal and generally abstract procedure in considering the State he left to others, without great confidence that they would be able to make much of it. He himself was disposed to be on his guard against subjecting history to such excessively abstract ideas as progress, decline, liberalism, absolutism and so on, for he was only prepared to admit the validity of 'living forces' which 'wrestle with one another for the mastery'. And yet he constantly demanded that 'the historian should keep his eyes open for the general'. This 'general' element, however, is first and foremost simply the course of events on a large scale, more or less the peaks and ridges of the historical mountain profile. When Ranke is dealing with world history, the contacts of one people with another and the destinies of those who have had pre-eminent influence upon others are brought into the foreground, and become part of the 'general' picture. When it is a question of the history of nations and national states or of the Papacy, the Western community of peoples, whom he so fervently admired, and once designated as the Romano-Germanic nation, becomes the sphere of the 'general'. We can now define this 'general' rather more exactly as the highest of the historical individualities in evidence at any particular time, which embrace and include all the rest. And as all the rest depend on it, while at the same time contributing to its formation, we are now for the first time in a position to understand the full content of Ranke's sentence quoted above: 'Everything, both general and individual, is an expression of spiritual life.' This deeply and fervently German spirit felt that its individuality and its very individual people were part and parcel of a higher community with which, for weal or for woe, they were closely entwined. In spite of all the conflicts that had taken place among them, Ranke saw in this process more of weal than of woe, for he knew that struggle and opposition are often a sign of life and a higher degree of life, and realised that the binding forces in this community were stronger than the divisive. He believed in the future of this Western genius.

Certain defects in Ranke's historical writing, which have come in for criticism, are undoubtedly connected with the greatness of this conception. It has been said that Ranke, following an out-of-date tradition of history, has too much about the actions of important people and States. True, there are splendid chapters by the way on the great figures in world literature, but the lives of the peoples are not described in any depth. In spite of many important digressions on these subjects, there is too little about social and economic forces and substructures. But it was Ranke's purpose to keep to this high line of generality through all the separate events, conditions, cultures, popular and spiritual movements included in the story. And he could only do this by highlighting the large-scale destinies of peoples and States, on which everything else was dependent. The tendency in this direction was increasing even early on in his career. H. Oncken has instructively proved that the original plan for Ranke's *Fürsten und Völker Südeuropas* (*Princes and Peoples of South Europe*) was, as he calls it, more static, more concerned with the separate and internal lives of these peoples. But the dynamic qualities of Western development as a whole, which began to fascinate Ranke more and more strongly, disrupted this original plan. The parts of the work corresponding with the original plan, 'the Osman and Spanish Monarchies', are to my way of thinking not at all static. Rather do they give a lively picture of the internal life of what was admittedly a limited individual community, and the forces of development within it are vividly brought before our eyes at each stage. Thus, it is really a question of a shifting of the accent from the individual to the general development; yet Ranke still treats the individual from the start as something that also undergoes development. And, as we have already seen, the general development is also interpreted as an individual phenomenon—in fact the biggest individual phenomenon of all.

Individuality and individual development are, however, the two basic ideas which, linked together, characterise the approach to history that is called historism in the best sense. It reaches its climax in Ranke's achievement. Individual historical development is no mere evolution of tendencies already present in the germ-cell. Rather does it possess a large measure of plasticity, of capacity to change and be regenerated as it is worked upon by the ever-changing forces of time. That is why the individual and the general are so inextricably interwoven, and why the current of historical development is a unity. Otherwise we should have a countless number of different evolutionary processes. As Ranke remarks in his *History of the Papacy*:

No doubt the particular life develops according to innate laws upon its specific spiritual foundations; and it progresses through the years according to its own pattern. But it is also unceasingly

504

subject to influences which have a powerful effect on the course
of its development.

The results of this development are therefore incalculable, and there
are an endless variety of phenomena produced by it. 'The form of
human nature is inexhaustible.' Does this mean that the life of history
is simply dissolved in a boundless ocean? Is the higher way of looking
at history left with no other alternative but an aesthetic luxuriating in
the richness of the centuries, which Ranke did, indeed, in his youth
consider to afford a high degree of pleasure? This danger did certainly exist, yet only for a later historism with a weaker world view,
but not for Ranke. He had too strong a sense of the 'general', of the
total individuality of world history which binds it all together, too
great an appreciation of the value and the future prospects of his
beloved 'Romano-Germanic nation', to miss the sense of the whole,
the spiritual bond that links it all into one. But he did not seek it in
the same way as his great senior contemporary Hegel, or many of his
younger contemporaries who tried so hard to be 'with it'. He could
not be bound down, like the latter, by an inexorable Natural Law,
nor, like the former, by an inexorable law of the spirit. For these, in
one way or another, like the eighteenth-century Enlightenment,
thought they could point along these lines to a definite human progress, an ascent of man to higher stages. To be sure, Ranke himself
also assumed as the ideal centre of human history a certain upward
movement towards ever higher powers. But for him, these were of an
entirely individual kind, and therefore shaped the general development in constantly new and individual ways, and could not be
brought into any straight and calculable line of progressive ascent.
In this, he was very close to Goethe's view, that there was no world
progress, but only a 'circum-gress'. Ranke was thus of the opinion
that on critical grounds, no less than from sympathetic universal
insight, he could not subscribe to any belief in a steady upward trend
of human progress (apart from in material matters) if one was to
allow the moral and spiritual values produced by each epoch to have
their own proper and distinctive weight. Otherwise one would have
to mediatise each of the earlier epochs and reduce its importance to
that of a mere stepping-stone to higher things. 'But I maintain',
Ranke wrote, 'that every epoch is directly before God; and its value
is not dependent on what it produces, but on its intrinsic existence
and its own distinctive identity.'

This is the second of those great general aphorisms into which his
historical thought was compressed. The first stands for the oneness of
general and individual as an essential mark of historical life; the
latter for its value and meaning. It contains both a philosophy and a

religion, more especially a religion, a religion of liberation. For it frees the mind from the feelings of inferiority latent in all history based upon the doctrine of perpetual progress, and more still upon the doctrine of the decline of the Western world. It gives not only to each epoch, but also to each action with any spiritual or moral significance, and to all moral energy, a direct relation to God (if we may borrow a phrase from Ranke himself) independent of any rise or decline in its life. 'Before God,' says Ranke, 'all generations of mankind are equal; and this is the light in which the historian must look at them.'

We must now go on to ask how this point of view, which appears to dissolve all historical life once more into single individual values, is to be reconciled with the grandiose conception of the 'general', the corporate individuality of the historical human race, and with the unceasing dynamics of its corporate development. One can sense that there are further religious ideas lying behind Ranke's words about the Divinity. It will be remembered that he called States the thoughts of God, and the idea embodied in them of divine origin. We are here drawing closer to the ultimate hidden source of light that shines through all his works and words, surrounding men and things with that delicate medium to which we have already called attention. There can be no question here of pantheism. He decisively rejected Hegel's doctrine of pantheism in the shape of humanity as an evolving God. Nor can one ascribe to him the dogmatic Christianity of Lutheranism, although it had contributed a great deal to his inner character, and he had felt himself to be a good evangelical Christian. He drew a veil over these intimate matters, through which we can only catch glimpses of a quite positive panentheism. God is above the world, the world was made by Him, and it is also inspired by His spirit. It is therefore related to God, yet at the same time earthly and imperfect. This clear separation between the creator and his creation, which was an echo of his Lutheranism, made it possible for him to allow his need for critical and empirical truth very free play over against the practical world of matter and spirit. This high degree of freedom was possible, though he did not keep God and the world completely asunder, but in order to make the world secure in God's control, held fast to the basic conceptions of Christian philosophy, the providence of God and His guidance in the whole human drama of history. This did indeed provide a way out of some difficult problems. He did not, however, altogether overcome them, but rather (in true Rankean manner) toned them down by resisting the temptation to trace the finger of God in each movement of history— as much from a sense of reverence for the divine mysteries, as from a feeling of critical responsibility. Now and again, in the great moments of history, Ranke thought he could discern the hand of God at work, but this was faith rather than knowledge. There are also some slightly teleological motives at work in the construction of his universal history, as he unfolds the meaning of its development from the world of the ancient peoples, through the Roman Empire and Christianity, to the Romano-Germanic community of nations. In so doing, he left the prehistory, which has now become so important, to other hands, though he did not in the least ignore its value. This was partly out of a reluctance to leave the ground of written tradition; partly from a certain religious and critical unwillingness to attempt to examine any scientific basis for the original monotheism of the human race, which was something he wanted to believe in. In order to secure a self-contained structure for his history of the world and give it a corporate individuality, he had to leave on one side the peoples and cultures of the Far East. He considered them to be more lacking in development than was actually the case. But it was this specific corporate individuality in which he felt the divine breath directly at work, infusing into it the power of vital historical development; and this was why he selected it from among all the other happenings of the human race and called it a movement of the 'general' or world history. This 'general' force was also the power of destiny for his own individual world, the world in which he lived. That was the second reason why he could call the section of world events he depicted 'world history'. For him, the 'general' was not only itself individual, but also filled with individualities, and everything originated in a life which was indeed of the earth, earthy, and yet related to God. This explains why Ranke did not, like Hegel, deify the world process of the 'general' but was prepared, with a combination of pride and modesty, to ascribe to all historical events a direct relationship to God.

There was thus in Ranke a combination of transcendental reverence for history and its background, and a keen-eyed empirical and critical examination and artistic appreciation of the course of history. There was also a close combination of religion, not only gnosis or speculation, with a realism of outlook. Such a blend was entirely individual and quite inimitable. It is thus not possible, in spite of the way that Ranke's achievements tower above all that came before and after him, simply to treat them as an example to others and without more ado to canonise his work. It also has its peculiar weaknesses, to which I have already alluded, and which are mostly connected with the source of his peculiar strength, his belief (too serene, perhaps) in the divine breath that inspires all earthly creation. It may therefore well be asked whether Ranke had really come to terms deep down with the mighty problems of a theodicy (the existence of evil in the world), however profoundly he was moved by them. We may also go on to ask whether he was able to feel the full and mysterious strength of chance in history, which could prevent Goethe from giving himself over completely to historical study. Further, there is his peculiarly weak relationship to the historically formative powers of the nineteenth century, especially to the movements in his own nation pressing towards nationalism and political unity. He was only able to follow them with some hesitation because his own political anchorage was in the aristocratic period of the Restoration, and the internal nationalisation of the separate German States was enough to satisfy his own requirements. And so over the whole field Ranke left room enough for other methods of handling history, equally scholarly, and with an equally powerful and original philosophical outlook, yet for all time owing him an incalculable debt.

It is not by imitation, but by their fruitful influence upon lives akin to them yet always fresh and with their own peculiar character, that great intellectual achievements influence the subsequent ages; and it is through such influence that they themselves have arisen. I shall forbear to survey the further prospect, or trace the line of historical writing that leads from Ranke to ourselves. Nor shall I go on to ask how far his heritage is still at work among us in the midst of the vast historical and intellectual transformations in which we are involved. Our hearts may be full of this question, and we may well feel that each of us in our inmost selves could find a definite answer. Yet it is right and proper on this occasion to avoid all controversy, and to let our thoughts rest in the peace of pure contemplation. I will simply attempt to indicate in a few strokes the context in the history of thought to which Ranke's achievement belongs.

Ranke belonged to the third of the specially creative periods and generations covered by the great German movement. The first was the 'Sturm und Drang' period; the second the decade from 1795 to 1805, characterised by the early Romantics and the rise of the Idealist School; the third began with the year 1815. Immediately after the experience of the Wars of Liberation, and deeply affected by that experience and by the ideas of the two previous generations, the new generation now sought out their own appropriate tasks, which were no longer first and foremost poetry and philosophy, but politics and scholarship. The German spirit now launched out into the world of concrete reality, whether to shape it or to acquire knowledge about it.

We now have some information about the thoughts of Ranke's youth through the posthumous material that has been published. A native of the Electorate of Saxony, he did not indeed see the Wars of Liberation at close quarters, but he experienced them deeply, so to speak, in retrospect. Although he did not belong to the *Burschen-*

schaft movement of German nationalist students, he certainly sympathised more warmly with certain of its ideals, such as the longing for a vigorous national State, than was formerly thought to be the case.

We can now trace the path that led from this point to the thoughts contained in the *Political Discourse* (*Politisches Gespräch*) of 1836. But more was needed than the frustrated political longings of young people at that time to call forth the basic ideas contained in this Discourse. More than this went to the making of all his historical writings about the material and spiritual, individual character of the States and their fundamental relationship to God, and their capacity to produce living individual structures. First of all we see Idealism and Romanticism confronting one another as the spiritual powers to which the youthful Ranke opened his soul. Fichte and Friedrich Schlegel had a powerful influence upon him. In Fichte, he took particular note of the aphorism: 'The divine idea is fundamental to all the phenomena of life.' But Fichte was scarcely able to satisfy his need for a sterner empiricism, and a blending of the empirical with the ideal. Friedrich Schlegel's *The Language and Wisdom of the Indians* offered him something more in this direction. A spiritualised realism applied to the writing of history was already represented by the examples of Thucydides and Niebuhr. But perhaps up till now insufficient attention has been paid to the contribution to Ranke made by his greatest contemporary, Goethe. In his fragment on Luther in 1817, Ranke wrote: 'O that your spirit might visit me, in its seventy-year-old wisdom! O that the ideal might be truly built up upon the firm foundations of history, and that from the forms which appear there might spring forth that which does not appear!' And in another essay of this period, something that is even more convincing proof of the example set him by Goethe in combining the practical and the spiritual outlook:

Yes, our so often misrepresented and misunderstood Goethe surely achieved his greatness only by means of his faithful and steady reliance upon nature. Simple, clear, harmonious, regular —so the idea arises in him in all its branches and all its forms, just as he shaped its form out of his own mind after the primal image of nature that dwells in every man.

Goethe, however, represents the climax of the great spiritual and intellectual revolution in Germany which must have preceded in order to make a Ranke possible. For here we touch again upon the great mysterious fact underlying all history, that one and the same phenomenon can be altogether individual and inimitable, and yet part and parcel of a universal context. We shall not diminish Ranke's individual achievements if we suggest that the very principles that make his historical writings so lively and fruitful were won by the efforts of the German spirit in the eighteenth century. I mean such principles as a sense of the individual, a feeling for the forces that shape men and things from within, an awareness of particular individual developments, and of the common basis in life which knits everything together. Europe, too, contributed its influence, and everywhere among the great Romano-Germanic nations there are approaches in this direction to be observed. Shaftesbury gave the German movement important material for thought in his doctrine of the inner form, at the same time that Leibniz was kindling a new flame in Germany with his theory of the monads and his σύμπνοια πάντα. This flame, which had long been smouldering, broke out again in the youthful Herder, when he once again exultantly took up these words of Leibniz and discovered the individuality of the various peoples, rooted in a common vital relationship to God. Then Goethe, again in quite an individual manner, took up these words and gave them a new inner depth and clarity. His aversion to history, which has frequently been noted, must not blind us to the fact that, as Ranke's youthful words recognised, Goethe showed new ways of understanding history and giving it a richer content. Yet in both Herder's and Goethe's youth there was as yet a lack of the powerful impetus required to reveal in history the blend of the ideal and the real, particularly in the State and in the forces of nationality on which the State is based. This impetus was given to Ranke by the experience of the Wars of Liberation, and the national and political movements to which they gave rise.

The task of effecting a marriage between the ideal and the real takes us back still further to the Ancient World and to earlier pioneers in thought who worked upon it in one way or another. We are taken back to Plato and Plotinus and the whole platonising line of thought which stretches from them to Shaftesbury, Leibniz and Goethe, and, we must now add, to Ranke. The verdict passed by Ranke upon Milton, that all the centuries had had a hand in shaping his view of the world, is also true of Ranke himself. We may legitimately speak of historism as born from the continuous working of the Platonic spirit. Fertilised by the interiorising principles of German Protestantism, it gave new meaning to the individual and its development, and laid a foundation on which all our work today is based. This was the highest stage so far reached in the fusing of the ideal with the real.

This lofty link, this golden chain, is both universal and yet at every moment individual. And there are yet more links in it to be forged in this our day and age.

Supplement

Σύμπνοια πάντα! (Translated by Leibniz as 'Tout est conspirant' as the Greeks understood it. 'In one cosmic, animated breath harmony is given to all.' See E. Boutroux (ed.), *Leibniz, La Monadologie* (Paris 1881), p. 177).

Index